PURE

CORBA

Fintan Bolton

SAMS

Pure CORBA

Copyright © 2002 by Sams Publishing

International Standard Book Number: 0-672-321812-1

Library of Congress Catalog Card Number: 99-66025

Printed in the United States of America

First Printing: July 2001

08 05 06 4 3 2

Trademarks

All terms mentioned in this book that are known to be trademarks or service marks have been appropriately capitalized. Sams Publishing cannot attest to the accuracy of this information. Use of a term in this book should not be regarded as affecting the validity of any trademark or service mark.

Warning and Disclaimer

Every effort has been made to make this book as complete and as accurate as possible, but no warranty or fitness is implied. The information provided is on an "as is" basis. The authors and the publisher shall have neither liability nor responsibility to any person or entity with respect to any loss or damages arising from the information contained in this book or from the use of the CD or programs accompanying it.

Executive Editor
Michael Stephens

Acquisitions Editor
Carol Ackerman

Development Editor
Heather Goodell

Managing Editor
Matt Purcell

Project Editor
George E. Nedeff

Copy Editors
Gene Redding
Michael Henry
Michael Dietsch

Indexer
Sandra Henselmeier

Proofreader
Benjamin Berg

Technical Editors
Jeremy L. Rosenberger
Ajay M.R.

Team Coordinator
Pamalee Nelson
Lynne Williams

Media Developer
Dan Scherf

Interior Designer
Karen Ruggles

Cover Designer
Aren Howell

Overview

Contents

4 Memory Management 151

About the Author

Fintan Bolton is a software consultant, trainer, and technical writer for IONA Technologies, the world's leading developer of CORBA tools and software. Mr. Bolton has trained developers in the use of CORBA-based software such as Orbix, OrbixWeb, and OrbixOTM. He has also written technical documentation for many CORBA-based products, including Orbix 2000 and OrbixOTM. He can be reached at `fbolton@pure-corba.com` or at the accompanying Web site for this book, `http://www.pure-corba.com`.

About the Contributing Authors

Jeremy L. Rosenberger is a cofounder of and principal consultant with Ivy Design Group LLC (also known as *ivy*Design™), a consulting firm specializing in enterprise application architecture using Java, CORBA, EJB, and J2EE technologies. Mr. Rosenberger is also the author of *Sams Teach Yourself CORBA in 14 Days* (Sams Publishing, 1998). He can be reached at `jeremy@ivydesign.com`.

Mark Shacklette is a principal with Leverett & Pierce, Inc. in Chicago, where he specializes in the design and implementation of distributed object e-Commerce solutions for clients which include the American Bar Association, Siemens, A. C. Nielsen, The Options Clearing Corporation, The Chicago Board of Trade, Kemper Insurance, CNA Insurance, and The Northern Trust Bank. He holds degrees from Furman and Harvard Universities, and is on the faculty of computer science at the University of Chicago, where he teaches courses on operating systems, distributed object technology, and object-oriented architecture, design, and methodology.

Lichun Wang, Ph.D., is a research scientist in applied computing and bioinformatics at EBI (the European Bioinformatics Institute), currently working on using CORBA and XML for accessing and distributing biological data.

Dedication

To Sylvia, for your love and support.

—Fintan

Acknowledgments

I owe thanks to many people who helped create this book: the editors, Carol Ackerman, Heather Goodell, and Gene Redding, for their dedication and the encouragement they gave me throughout the book's long gestation; the technical reviewers, Ajay M.R. and Jeremy Rosenberger, for their careful reading of the manuscript and constructive comments; the members of the Orbix code generation team, Ciaran McHale, Alan Conway, Adrian Skehill, and Anne Kinsella, who inadvertently provided me with the starting point for many of the code examples; and finally, to all of my colleagues in IONA Technologies who have patiently answered my questions over the years and shared their expertise in postings to internal newsgroups. This book could not have been written without them. *-Fintan*

Tell Us What You Think!

As the reader of this book, *you* are our most important critic and commentator. We value your opinion and want to know what we're doing right, what we could do better, what areas you'd like to see us publish in, and any other words of wisdom you're willing to pass our way.

As an executive editor for Sams Publishing, I welcome your comments. You can e-mail or write me directly to let me know what you did or didn't like about this book—as well as what we can do to make our books stronger.

Please note that I cannot help you with technical problems related to the topic of this book, and that due to the high volume of mail I receive, I might not be able to reply to every message.

When you write, please be sure to include this book's title and author as well as your name and phone or fax number. I will carefully review your comments and share them with the author and editors who worked on the book.

E-mail: `feedback@samspublishing.com`

Mail: Associate Publisher
Sams Publishing
800 East 96th Street
Indianapolis, IN 46240 USA

Introduction

This book is a practical guide to writing CORBA-compliant applications in C++ and Java. Rather than describing how to program using one particular ORB (or ORBs), this book focuses on the CORBA standard itself. Of course, examples have to be tested and for this purpose Orbix 2000 from IONA Technologies is used. In cases where there is any divergence from the standard, however, examples are written to be CORBA-compliant.

Equal priority for C++ and Java is ensured by presenting code fragments and examples in both languages throughout. A side effect of this is that a detailed comparison of the IDL-to-C++ and IDL-to-Java mappings can be made by comparing the code examples that appear throughout the book. Comments are liberally distributed throughout the code examples to aid legibility and to ensure that the examples can stand on their own.

At the time of writing, the eagerly-awaited CORBA 3 specification has yet to be released. Some aspects of the CORBA 3 specification are still being worked on but the most important element, the CORBA Component Model (CCM), is already available as an informal specification. Chapter 13, "CORBA Components," previews the CCM based on that specification. No commercial implementations of the CCM are yet available, however, so the code examples in that chapter are by necessity untested.

This book is intended for experienced C++ and Java developers who want to learn the rudiments of CORBA programming quickly and, thereafter, use the book mainly as a reference guide. From a CORBA perspective, the book is self-contained and requires no previous knowledge of distributed systems or of CORBA application development.

How This Book Is Organized

Chapters 1 and 2 provide a fast-track introduction to CORBA programming, as well as detailed descriptions of basic programming techniques. All of the chapters up to and including Chapter 8 cover the core topics that you need to understand to become an effective CORBA programmer. Chapters 9–14 discuss standalone topics that you can dip into as the need arises. The last part of the book, which spans Chapters 15–21, is a syntax reference that provides more than just syntax. Examples are provided and semantics are discussed, as necessary, to ensure that you can quickly make effective use of the various CORBA programming interfaces.

PART I

CONCEPTUAL REFERENCE

CHAPTER 1

CORBA Architecture

This chapter explains the basic concepts of the Common Object Request Broker Architecture (CORBA) that form a foundation for the rest of the book. An overview of the CORBA architecture is also provided, and the work of the Object Management Group, the CORBA standards body, is described.

The Rise of Middleware

Middleware thrives on the diversity of computer platforms found in a typical company's IT infrastructure. There are many factors at work that fuel the inhomogeneity of large computer systems:

- Legacy systems
  A company might aspire to replace old technology with new. However, it often proves too expensive and risky to replace an old system completely, so a mixture of old and new technology is used instead.
- Technology niches
  Some hardware platforms and software packages that deviate from the corporate norm might have to be used because their special features are needed.
- Legislation
  Legislation aimed at deregulating industry can have an impact on the computer infrastructure of affected companies. In general, deregulation places a requirement on computer systems to be more flexible and open.
- Mergers and acquisitions
  When a merger or acquisition takes place, the companies involved face the considerable technical challenge of successfully integrating their respective computer networks.

Often, an organization finds it can muddle along by letting diverse computer systems operate in parallel. An occasional manual intervention and batch transfer of files from one system to another can keep the whole edifice going. This approach, however, is becoming unsustainable with the growing importance of the World Wide Web. Web applications require seamless integration of an IT infrastructure so that transactions can be automated. Many organizations have found that the Web gives them a powerful motive to address integration problems and unify different systems across their organization. This goes some way toward explaining the increasing interest in middleware technology.

The Object Management Group

The Object Management Group (OMG) is the organization that steers the development of the CORBA standard. It was founded in 1989 by a group of companies with the aim of marrying two emerging strands of technology: remote procedure calls and object orientation. The OMG set itself the goal of producing a complete infrastructure for distributed computing, the *object management architecture (OMA)*. The CORBA standard, which is popularly used as a synonym for the whole of the OMA, is a core part of the OMA that describes the basic infrastructure needed to support distributed objects.

The OMG has put in place a formal procedure, the *technology process*, that describes how new elements of the CORBA standard are proposed and adopted. The technology process driving the CORBA standard has proved quite effective at ensuring that new specifications can be implemented and used in practice. The development of each part of the standard is coordinated by a task force, consisting of experts drawn from the OMG membership. Members have the right to submit proposals for new standards or for modifications to existing standards. Once a proposal is being considered for adoption, members vote to accept or reject the proposal. An architecture board has responsibility for overseeing the development of the CORBA standard and ensuring its overall consistency. In practice, Object Request Broker (ORB) implementors usually base a proposal on an existing implementation or partial implementation. Consequently, the proposed CORBA specifications tend to be realistic and implementable.

The CORBA standard is an open standard, and all of the specifications are freely downloadable from the OMG public Web site at `http://www.omg.org`. The documents can be divided into *formal specifications* that have been voted on and formally adopted, *adopted specifications* that have been adopted but are subject to minor changes, and *work in progress* documents. It is a good idea to take a look at the adopted specifications and work in progress documents, which can be found under the technology process pages at the OMG Web site, since many of the more recent specifications are only available there.

The Common Object Request Broker Architecture

The CORBA specification, which is the core part of the OMA, describes the basic infrastructure for making object-oriented remote procedure calls. This section presents a conceptual overview of CORBA, covering the following topics:

- Remote procedure calls
- CORBA requirements
- The OMG interface definition language
- The Internet inter-ORB protocol
- Basic CORBA concepts
- Locating and activating servers
- Finding CORBA objects
- Dynamic CORBA

Remote Procedure Calls

Throughout the 1980s, remote procedure call (RPC) technology was developed and began to be used widely. The two most popular kinds of RPC are SUN RPC and distributed computing environment (DCE) RPC.

To the application that calls it, a remote procedure call looks like a local function call but, instead of executing locally, the procedure's parameters are sent across the network to a remote application that evaluates the procedure. The procedure's return values, if any, are then sent back across the network to the calling application. The RPC infrastructure provides the rudiments of a distributed system. The calling application is a *client* and the called application is a *server*.

Figure 1.1 shows an outline of a basic remote procedure call. When a client makes a remote procedure call, the parameters of the call are marshaled into a *request* packet and sent across the network to the server, typically using either the user datagram protocol (UDP) or transmission control protocol (TCP) for the transport layer. *Marshaling* refers to the copying of parameters into a buffer in a format suitable for transmission over the network. A request is an RPC message, transported inside a UDP or TCP packet, that contains the name of the remote procedure and a list of its parameters.

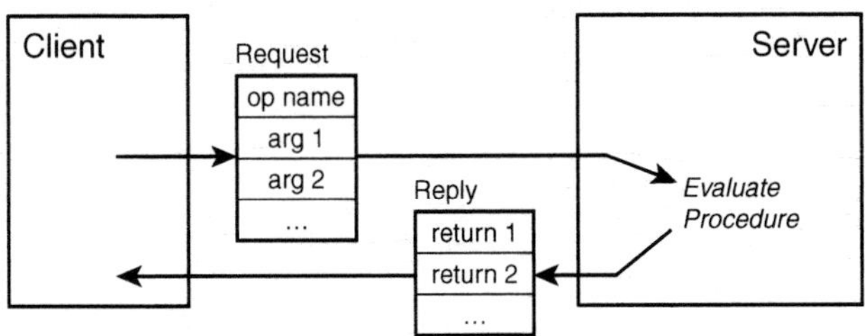

Figure 1.1

A basic remote procedure call.

When the request arrives at the server, the parameters are unmarshaled and the server evaluates the procedure. After evaluation, the procedure's return values are marshaled into a reply packet that is sent back to the waiting client. A *reply* is an RPC message containing either a collection of return values or an error status.

An interesting feature of this example is that the call is *synchronous*. That is, when the client makes a call, it is blocked until the matching reply is received from the server. Synchronous calling is the usual mode of operation for remote CORBA invocations as well.

CORBA Requirements

Because distributedsystems can potentially operate across different hardware platforms and use different operating systems and programming languages, it is desirable to abstract away platform and implementation details. Another aim is to ensure that remote procedure calls are almost as easy to use as native programming constructs. Therefore, CORBA is designed with the following goals in mind:

- Object orientation
- Location transparency
- Programming language neutrality
- Support for bridges

Object Orientation

One of the main improvements that CORBA offers over earlier RPC technology is object orientation. Remote operations are grouped into interfaces, in the same way that functions in C++ and Java are grouped into classes. An instance of an interface is known as a *CORBA object*. It should be born in mind, however, that a CORBA object is an abstract idea and, therefore, is not always directly identifiable with a C++ or Java object.

An invocation of an operation on a CORBA object is shown in Figure 1.2. The CORBA object lives in the server and an invocation (effectively a remote procedure call) is made by the client. To make a remote invocation, the client must obtain the identity of the CORBA object, represented by a CORBA *object reference*. An object reference encapsulates all the information (including location) that is needed to use the CORBA object.

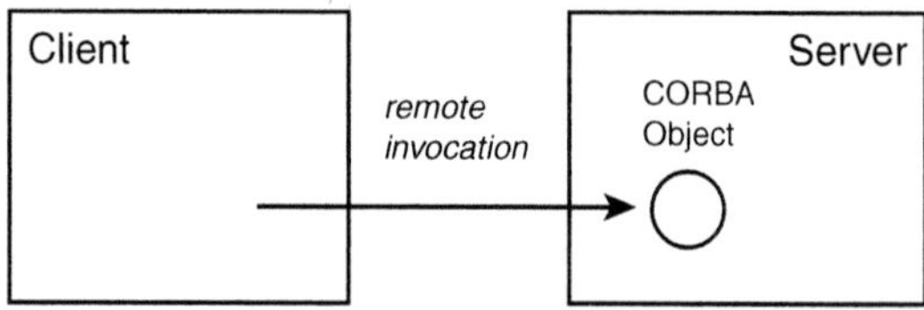

Figure 1.2

A CORBA invocation (remote procedure call).

Note that a particular object reference in CORBA refers to a unique CORBA object. If you use the same object reference at different times, invocations are routed to the same unique CORBA object.

Location Transparency

To make CORBA easier to use, *location transparency* of CORBA objects is supported. Location transparency means that it does not matter where the CORBA object is (local or remote). You always invoke operations on it using the same syntax.

This is illustrated by Figure 1.3, which shows applications A and B running on host platform X and application C running on host platform Y. Consider the code in application A that invokes on a CORBA object. It does not matter whether the CORBA object is in the same address space as application A, in another process on the same host (application B on host X), or even another process on a different host (application C on host Y). In every case, the invocation is made using the same syntax.

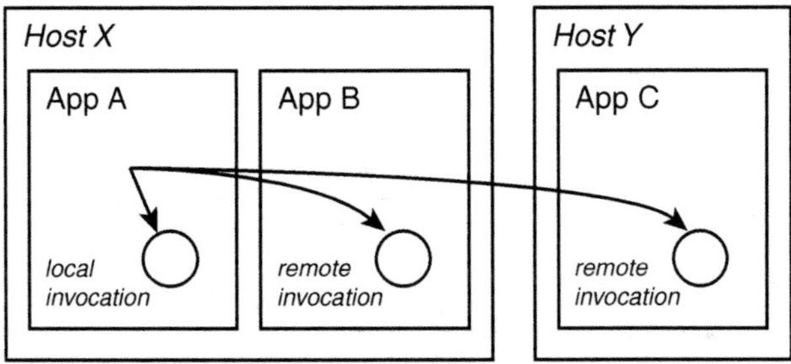

Figure 1.3

Location transparency of CORBA objects.

Programming Language Neutrality

CORBA is designed to work with multiple programming languages. Both invocation syntax (client-side code) and implementation of CORBA objects (server-side code) can be written in the programming language of your choice. Some programming languages for which language mappings currently exist are C, C++, Java, COBOL, Ada, Smalltalk, and Lisp.

Figure 1.4 shows a Java client invoking on a C++ CORBA object that, in turn, invokes operations on a COBOL CORBA object. You may wonder how it can make sense to talk about objects implemented in a language like COBOL, which is not even object oriented. It is possible because clients view a server through an object-oriented IDL interface. One of the strengths of CORBA is that it allows you to introduce object-oriented concepts to languages that are not inherently object oriented.

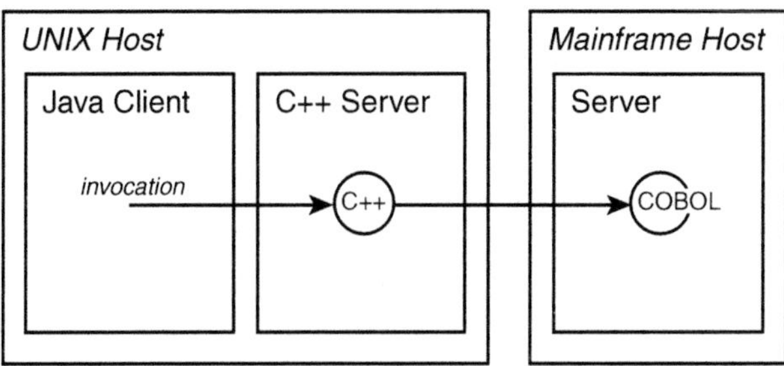

Figure 1.4

Using multiple programming languages.

Support for Bridges

CORBA is not the only technology to provide a distributed computing platform. Older specifications, such as distributed computing environment (DCE) RPC, and newer specifications, such as Microsoft's DCOM, also are widely used. The OMG anticipated that there would be a need to operate in conjunction with alternative technologies, and therefore it provides an interworking architecture as part of the core specification.

In practice, CORBA, DCOM, and DCE occupy slightly different niches in the realm of distributed technology, and ORB vendors have regarded bridges as an opportunity to promote acceptance of CORBA technology. Consequently, there are many commercially available CORBA/DCOM bridges.

OMG Interface Definition Language

The interface to a CORBA object is defined using OMG interface definition language (IDL). The OMG IDL is a language in its own right and is not derived from an existing programming language. Unlike regular programming languages, however, the OMG IDL is a purely declarative language—there are no syntactical constructs for evaluating expressions or describing algorithms.

There are many advantages to basing CORBA on IDL. The IDL is optimized to be adaptable to different programming languages, and the syntax can be expanded as necessary to deal with the demands of distributed systems. The only drawback is that developers have to learn a new language. However, the OMG IDL is relatively simple, and programmers familiar with C++ or Java will grasp the rudiments of IDL syntax in a very short time.

Listing 1.1 shows an example of an IDL interface, `CustomerAccount`, that might be used to represent a customer account in a bank.

Listing 1.1 IDL Interface Example

```
//IDL
interface CustomerAccount {
    string get_name();
    long   get_account_no();
```

Listing 1.1 continued

```
    boolean deposit_money(in float amount);
    boolean transfer_money(
        in float amount,
        in long  destination_account_no,
        out long confirmation_no
    );
};
```

An IDL interface is analogous to a class declaration for CORBA objects. The only surprise for a C++ or Java programmer in Listing 1.1 is the appearance of the `in` and `out` direction indicators. An `in` parameter is a parameter passed from the client to the server (pass by value), and an `out` parameter is a parameter passed from the server back to the client (an extra return value). The OMG IDL is discussed further in Chapter 2, "Programming with CORBA."

Internet Inter-ORB Protocol

The main innovation at the time of release of the CORBA 2.0 specification was the specification of the Internet inter-ORB protocol (IIOP). The IIOP defines a standard protocol for the mediation of CORBA invocations over the TCP/IP transport layer. In fact, IIOP is a specialization of the general inter-ORB protocol (GIOP), which defines the protocol independently of the transport layer.

One of the benefits of IIOP is that it facilitates interoperability between different vendor's ORBs. This means that a client written using one brand of ORB can communicate with a server implemented using a completely different brand of ORB. Prior to the introduction of IIOP, ORB vendors implemented proprietary protocols for the transmission of CORBA invocations, and interoperability was not possible.

Basic CORBA Concepts

This section describes the basic elements of the core CORBA specification. The following concepts are discussed:

- IDL compilers
- Language mappings
- Stub and skeleton code
- Object references
- Object adapters
- The object request broker

IDL Compilers

Defining the IDL for your system is the first step in the development of a CORBA application. It allows you to define interfaces to your CORBA objects in a manner that is platform independent, language neutral, and independent of implementation details. After you have written the application IDL, you can decide which platforms and programming languages you are going to use for the client and server.

An *IDL compiler* is used to map the IDL to a specific language. Consider, for example, a system where the client is implemented in Java and the server in C++. Figure 1.5 shows an outline of the steps involved.

- On the client side, the IDL file is passed through an IDL compiler for Java. The IDL compiler maps the IDL definitions to Java, producing Java *stub code* as output. The stub code provides a client with the code it needs to make Java invocations on the interfaces defined in the IDL file.
- On the server side, the IDL file is passed through an IDL compiler for C++. The IDL compiler produces C++ *skeleton code* as output. The skeleton code provides a server with the code needed to define CORBA object implementations.

Of course, the choice of languages could easily be reversed so that the client is implemented in C++ and the server in Java.

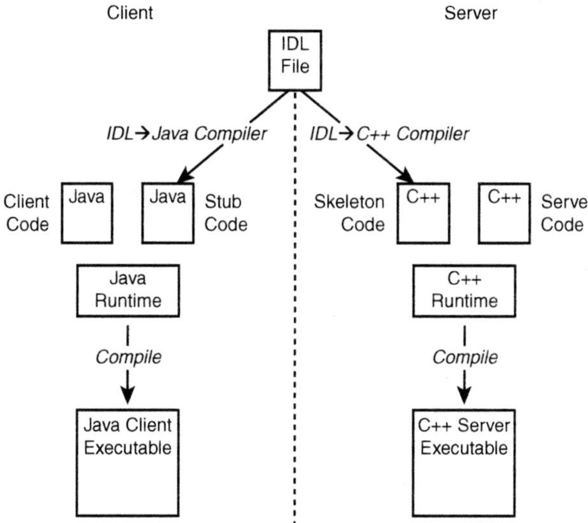

Figure 1.5

An example of a Java client and a C++ server.

An IDL compiler is typically provided as a command-line utility that reads an IDL file and produces files in the target language, either stub or skeleton code. IDL compilers are usually language specific: You would use one command-line utility for mapping IDL to Java and another utility for mapping IDL to C++.

Language Mappings

CORBA supplements the core specification with a number of language-mapping documents that specify how to translate IDL definitions into equivalent constructs in the target language. For example, if your target language is C++ or Java, the language mapping

- Defines how IDL data types map to equivalent C++ or Java data types.

- Defines how IDL interfaces map to classes, and how IDL operations map to member functions (C++) or methods (Java).
- Describes how to go about implementing CORBA objects on the server side.

To find the latest supported language mappings, look at the OMG Web site at `http://www.omg.org` and follow the link to the formal documentation pages. The formal specifications are freely available for download.

Stub and Skeleton Code

The stub and skeleton code generated by IDL compilers is used to make clients and servers, respectively, aware of the definitions appearing in the IDL file. The stub code is used on the client side, and it allows clients to invoke operations on remote CORBA objects using the same syntax as if they were local objects. For example, the Java stub code in Figure 1.5 contains the following Java definitions:

- Each IDL data type is represented by a corresponding Java data type.
- Each IDL interface is represented by a corresponding Java interface.
- Each IDL operation is represented by a corresponding Java method.

The skeleton code (a superset of the stub code) is used on the server side and enables servers to implement CORBA objects. For example, the C++ skeleton code in Figure 1.5 is used to associate IDL interfaces with C++ classes implemented by the developer. When a client invokes a particular IDL operation on an interface, the corresponding C++ member function of a C++ class is then invoked.

Object References

Figure 1.6 shows how the application code, stub, and ORB library fit together on the client side and how the application code, skeleton, and ORB library fit together on the server side. On the client side, the CORBA application programming interface (API) consists of the runtime library API, giving access to the ORB object and other standard objects, and the stub code API, giving access to user-defined IDL interfaces.

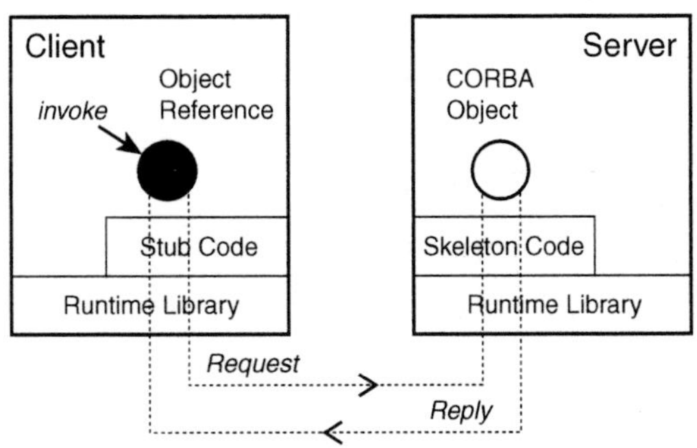

Figure 1.6

Using an object reference to make a remote invocation.

A client must have an object reference to make invocations on a CORBA object because the object reference encapsulates the location details of the CORBA object. In C++ and Java, the object reference is itself an object having member functions mapped from the operations of the corresponding IDL interface. When a client makes an invocation, it calls the appropriate member function on the object reference. As far as the client is concerned, the object reference might as well be the CORBA object. The object reference acts as a stand-in, or *proxy object*, for the CORBA object on the client side.

However, the object reference does not actually implement the invoked operation. Figure 1.6 shows what happens after the object reference's member function is called: A remote procedure call is initiated, with a request being sent to the remote server containing the parameters of the operation. On the server side, the invocation is routed to the appropriate CORBA object with the help of the ORB library and the skeleton code. The server executes the operation and then sends back a reply containing the return value and `out` parameters. Back on the client side, the object reference passes back the return value and `out` parameters to the application code.

Object Adapter

The language mappings for C++ and Java take advantage of the fact that C++ and Java are object oriented by letting you implement classes for CORBA objects in the same way as you would for ordinary C++ or Java objects.

After implementing a CORBA class, you need to indicate to the ORB that the class represents a particular IDL interface. You also need a way of telling the ORB how to make instances of this class, the CORBA objects, accessible to client applications. The part of the ORB responsible for these tasks is the *object adapter*.

The essential responsibilities of an object adapter are

- To provide a mechanism for associating a C++ or Java class with a particular IDL interface.
- To manage the lifecycle of CORBA objects. In particular, the object adapter must provide a way of *activating* CORBA objects (making them accessible to clients), and a way of *deactivating* CORBA objects (making them inaccessible to clients).

Two different kinds of object adapter are commonly used: the basic object adapter (BOA) and the portable object adapter (POA).

The BOA dates from earlier versions of the CORBA specification (pre-CORBA 2.2). Because the BOA is loosely specified, individual ORB vendors have been forced to introduce proprietary extensions to implement it. Consequently, code written using the BOA is not portable between ORB implementations.

The POA was added to the CORBA specification for CORBA 2.2 and is intended to replace the BOA. The POA specification is very detailed, allowing a good degree of portability between ORB implementations and adding many enhancements. The POA is described in detail in Chapter 7, "The Portable Object Adapter."

The Object Request Broker

At this stage, it would be nice if we could point at some entity and say "this is the ORB." However, there is no such entity because the ORB is an abstraction. An ORB is the sum total of the infrastructure that enables you to make remote invocations. A typical ORB has the following main elements:

- The stub and skeleton code that is obtained from your IDL and linked with your applications.
- A runtime library to link with your applications.
- A mechanism for locating and activating remote servers. Typically, a daemon process (or processes) fulfills this role.

Deployment of CORBA Applications

The basic deployment issues for a CORBA system are the configuration, the mechanism for locating CORBA objects, and the mechanism for activating server processes on demand. Different ORB implementations take varying approaches to these deployment issues. Differences also necessarily arise because of the demands of particular platforms.

The CORBA specification is deliberately open ended when it comes to deployment. However, there are some broad features that are common to most ORB implementations, and these are described in the following two sections.

Finding CORBA Objects

The basic entity used to encapsulate the location of a CORBA object is an object reference. An ORB using TCP/IP as the transport layer typically puts the following key pieces of information into an object reference:

- The IP hostname of the host where the server runs
- The IP port number that the server listens on
- A unique object identity

This information is sufficient to locate a remote server and identify a particular CORBA object that lives in that server. Object references contain all the information needed to find and use a CORBA object.

In C++ or Java ORBs, object references are represented as objects at runtime. However, object references can also be passed from place to place. A standard format, the *interoperable object reference (IOR)*, is defined for this purpose. An IOR can be passed in a request or a reply as part of a remote procedure call, or it can be converted into a string format, the *stringified IOR*.

Object references originate in servers. If a client needs to obtain an object reference, a server must create the object reference and pass it back to the client. This creates a Catch-22 situation, however, whereby the client cannot establish contact with a server until it gets an object reference that must be obtained from that server. The solution is to use an intermediary for passing object references.

Three common solutions for obtaining object references are

- To write stringified IORs to files.
  A server can stringify an IOR and write it to a file that is known to the client. This is a primitive approach that is useful for testing but does not scale to realistic distributed systems.
- To use the CORBA naming service.
  The naming service associates names with object references and stores these (name to object reference) bindings in a central location. A client needs only to know the location of the naming service and the names of some objects to bootstrap connections to servers. The naming service is described in Chapter 6, "Interoperable Naming Service."
- To use the CORBA trading object service.
  The trading service resembles the naming service in that it is a central repository of object references, but it is more flexible. The features offered by the trading service include the capability to search for object references by querying their properties. The trading service is not covered here.

Locating and Activating Servers

For a client to make a network connection to a server, the ORB has to provide a mechanism for locating the server. In addition, if the server is dormant, the ORB must be capable of activating the server on demand. Both of these mechanisms, locating and activating servers, are highly ORB-specific, and you will find that no two ORBs go about it in the same way.

Nevertheless, there are some features of locating and activating servers common to most ORBs. This section describes a generic model of an ORB implementation that illustrates some common features. Two important entities are used in this generic model:

- An ORB Daemon Process
  A daemon process is a concept that has its origins in the UNIX operating system (on Windows NT, the equivalent concept is a Windows NT service). It refers to a process that starts up automatically as a machine is booted up and remains running permanently in the background. The role of a daemon is to listen for service requests and activate server processes, when needed, to deal with the requests. For example, `ftpd` and `httpd` are UNIX daemons that service FTP and HTTP connection attempts, respectively.
  The purpose of an ORB daemon process is to listen for CORBA client connection attempts and to assist the client in connecting to the appropriate server. In fact, a particular ORB implementation might use several daemons. For example, the tasks of locating, activating, and licensing a server might be assigned to three separate daemons. In the generic model discussed here, however, it is assumed that all tasks are assigned to a single daemon.

- The Implementation Repository
  This repository stores details about each server process. At its most basic level, the implementation repository stores details about how to launch each server process, an *activation record*. It is also an appropriate place to record the permissions associated with each server process. Because this is precisely the information needed by the ORB daemon, the implementation repository is effectively a database used by the ORB daemon.

The following subsections describe basic scenarios, using the generic model for purposes of illustration.

Invoking on a Dormant Server

This scenario shows a CORBA client about to connect to a remote CORBA server. On the server machine (a UNIX host), there is an ORB daemon process running in the background. The CORBA server is dormant, but the information needed to activate it is stored in the implementation repository.

Figure 1.7 shows the steps that occur automatically to establish a connection between the client and the server.

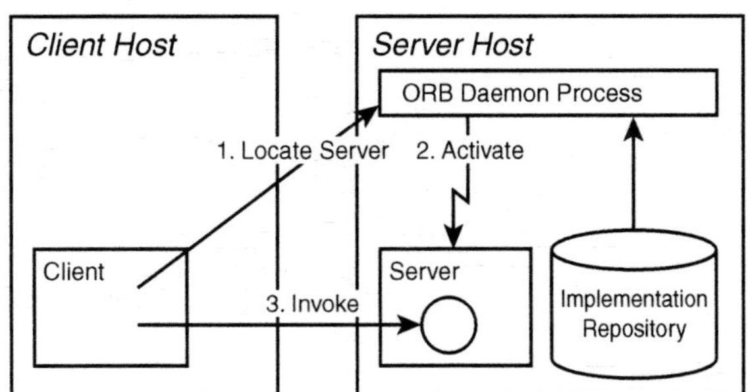

Figure 1.7

Invoking on a dormant server.

The steps are as follows:

1. Get the server location.
   The client opens a network connection to the remote ORB daemon and asks it for the server location details.
   This step presupposes that the client is able to find the ORB daemon in the first place. If the ORB implementation adheres strictly to the CORBA standard, the client gets this information from a cached object reference. On the other hand, many ORBs perform this step using a proprietary approach. For example, the client might assume that the ORB daemon is listening on a standard Internet protocol (IP) port number, or the client might use a UDP multicast message to find the ORB daemon.

2. Activate the server.
   Because the server is dormant, the ORB daemon retrieves the server's activation record from the implementation repository and uses this information to activate the server (that is, spawn a new server process). Each activation record in the implementation repository is associated with at most one server process. Older versions of the CORBA specification used to allow multiple server processes to be associated with a single activation record, depending on the *activation mode* that was chosen. Activation modes are now obsolete—they substituted for multithreading at a time when threads were still an exotic novelty.
3. Make CORBA invocations.
   Using the location information retrieved in step 1, the client can now open a network connection to the server and begin sending invocation requests.

Invoking on an Active Server

In this scenario the CORBA server is already running. The server has possibly already been activated in response to a client or manually started by an administrator.

Figure 1.8 shows the steps that occur automatically to establish a connection between the client and the server.

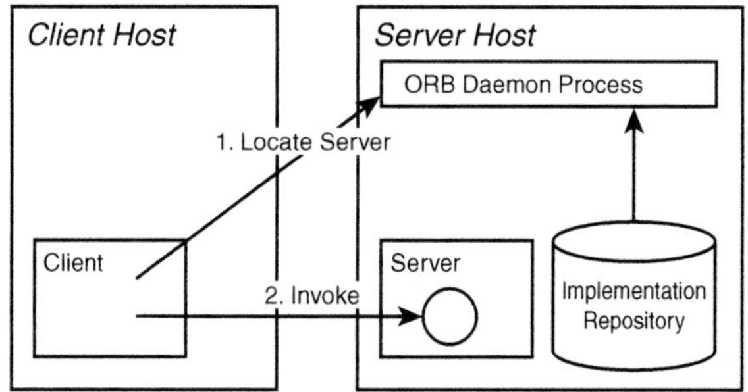

Figure 1.8

Invoking on an active server.

The steps are as follows:

1. Get the server location.
   It is assumed that the ORB daemon has some way of tracking the CORBA server processes activated within its domain and therefore knows the server's location.
2. Make CORBA invocations.
   It is possible that other clients are already connected to the server. A CORBA server can support as many clients as the operating system will allow. Typically, the first resource limit reached by a server is the maximum number of open connections allowed by the operating system.

Invoking on a Transient CORBA Object

A transient CORBA object is a short-lived object that survives at most as long as the server process that created it. The object reference for a transient CORBA object typically contains the server's IP port instead of the daemon's IP port. This enables the transient object to bypass the daemon when a server connection is being established.

Figure 1.9 shows the steps that occur automatically to establish a connection between the client and the server.

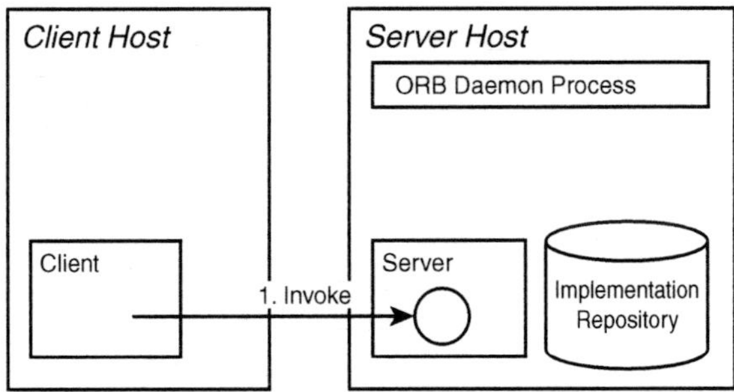

Figure 1.9

Invoking on a transient CORBA object.

The steps are as follows:

1. Make CORBA invocations.
   When an invocation is made on a transient object, the request message bypasses the ORB daemon and goes directly to the active server. The client opens the connection to the server and begins making invocations right away. This scenario assumes that the server is active. If it is not, the client invocation fails.

The Object Management Architecture

In addition to the CORBA core specification, the OMG defines the *CORBA Services* and the *CORBA Facilities*. Collectively, the components of the specification make up the object management architecture.

CORBA Services

The CORBA Services group together basic services that are commonly needed in a wide variety of applications, including security and support for transactions. Table 1.1 shows the complete list of services that have been adopted by the OMG at the time this book is being written.

Table 1.1 Adopted CORBA Services

CORBA Service	Description
Collection	A service for managing and moving groups of CORBA objects.
Concurrency	A service that enables you to perform distributed locking. Used by the Object Transaction Service.
Event	A simple messaging service.
Externalization	A service that enables CORBA data types to be stored in an external location.
Interoperable Naming	A basic directory service that stores name to object reference bindings in a central repository.
Licensing	A service to manage the licensing of a distributed application.
Life Cycle	A service to describe a pattern for remotely creating and destroying CORBA objects.
Notification	A flexible messaging service that supports message filtering and configurable qualities of service.
Persistent Object	(Obsolete) Superseded by the Persistent State Service.
Persistent State	A CORBA-friendly persistence mechanism.
Property	A simple service for associating names with properties.
Query	A service that is used to manipulate collections of CORBA objects.
Relationship	A service that can be used to define relationships between pairs of CORBA objects.
Security	A service to describe how an ORB provides secure communications and defines the different levels of security that can be provided.
Time	A basic service that provides the current time and other time-related services.
Trading Object	A flexible directory service that facilitates object discovery by querying the properties of an object.
Transaction	A service that allows safe simultaneous updates of databases by providing support for distributed transactions.

The Rest of the Object Management Architecture

The OMG has established a number of working groups to develop specifications that are useful in a broad range of industries. These specifications are divided up into a number of categories:

- CORBA Common Facilities
  The common facilities are similar to the CORBA services in that they are useful for a wide variety of applications, but they are not as fundamental as the CORBA services.

At the time this book is being written, there are two formally ratified specifications: the Internationalization and Time specification and the Mobile Agent Facility specification.

- Domain-Specific Specifications
  A number of OMG working groups, *domain task forces*, are entrusted with developing services for particular industry domains. Currently, there exist domain task forces for CORBA Business, CORBA Finance, CORBA Manufacturing, CORBA Medical, CORBA Telecoms, CORBA Transportation, CORBA E-Commerce, and CORBA Life Science.

The specifications developed by the various OMG task forces are available from the OMG Web site at `http://www.omg.org`.

Summary

This chapter discussed the motivations for using middleware technology and took a brief look at the work of the OMG, which develops and promotes the CORBA standard. Important characteristics that distinguish CORBA from most other distributed platforms are object-orientation, programming language neutrality, and the fact that CORBA is based on an open standard.

Some basic CORBA concepts are explained in this chapter. A special declarative language, OMG IDL, is introduced to declare interfaces for CORBA objects. Interfaces defined in IDL can be mapped to particular programming languages, such as C++ or Java, according to the rules of the CORBA language mapping specifications. This enables a developer to access and implement CORBA objects using a syntax that is similar to the native syntax for objects in the target language.

The roles of the IDL compiler, stub and skeleton code, and daemon process were briefly discussed. These aspects of an ORB tend to be highly ORB-specific and non-standard—consequently, IDL compilers and daemon processes are not discussed any further.

The rest of the book focuses on writing application code for CORBA clients and servers. The next chapter takes a relatively simple example of a client/server application and, building on the example as it goes along, introduces most of the fundamental concepts needed for CORBA programming.

CHAPTER 2

Programming with CORBA

This chapter provides a basic introduction to programming with CORBA in C++ and Java. A sample application, Book Repository, is developed in five stages, and various aspects of CORBA programming are discussed at each stage. The topics covered include how to write a basic client/server application using complex data types, exception handling, multiple IDL inheritance, and the CORBA Naming Service.

A Basic Client-Server Application—Example 1

This section introduces a book repository application that tracks and administers various book collections. The application might be used as a prototype for software that manages a book library. A central CORBA server is connected to a database backend that stores details of the books in each collection. Clients connect to the server to search for books and perform actions such as borrowing and returning books. This application is built up in stages throughout this chapter as the necessary CORBA features are introduced.

The first step in writing the CORBA application is to define the interface between client and server in terms of OMG IDL. Listing 2.1 shows the first draft of an IDL module, `BookRepository`, which defines a single IDL interface, `Collection`.

Listing 2.1 IDL `BookRepository` *Module for Example 1*

```
//IDL

module BookRepository {
    typedef long ISBN;
    enum FuzzyBoolean {NO, YES, UNKNOWN};

    interface Collection {
        // IDL attributes
        readonly attribute long    number_of_books;
        attribute          string  name_of_collection;

        // IDL operations
        FuzzyBoolean       is_in_collection(in ISBN book_id);
    };
};
```

The OMG IDL has a syntax that is similar to C++ and Java. The example in Listing 2.1 introduces the following IDL constructs:

- IDL comments, just like C++ and Java, are introduced by two forward slashes and continue until the end of the line.
- An IDL module—for example, module `BookRepository`—is simply a device for grouping related definitions together, like C++ namespaces and Java packages. A type defined within the `BookRepository` module gains `BookRepository::` as a prefix to its name, such as `BookRepository::FuzzyBoolean` and `BookRepository::Collection`.
- An IDL `typedef` defines a synonym for a type. This is often called *aliasing*. For example, in Listing 2.1 the type `ISBN` is defined to be an alias for `long` (a 32-bit integer).
- An enum type, `FuzzyBoolean`, is declared to have the allowed values `NO`, `YES`, and `UNKNOWN`. The IDL enum construct is similar to an enum in C or C++ (no native equivalent exists in the Java language, however).
- An IDL interface—for example, `Collection`—is analogous to an abstract class in C++ or an interface in Java. It is the most fundamental construct in IDL because it is used to define interfaces to CORBA objects.
- The `Collection` interface supports two attributes: `number_of_books` and `name_of_collection`. There are two possible kinds of attribute:
    - A read-only attribute is mapped to a single accessor function in the target language, which allows the attribute value to be read.
    - A plain attribute is mapped to an accessor and a modifier function in the target language, which allows the attribute value to be read and modified.
- The `Collection` interface defines a single IDL operation: `is_in_collection()`. The syntax of IDL operations is similar to regular functions in C++ or methods in Java. However, one significant difference is that operation parameters must be declared with a parameter passing mode—one of `in`, `inout`, or `out`. An `in` parameter—for example, `book_id` in Listing 2.1—is passed from the client to the server only.

The IDL effectively defines a contract between the client and server and forms the basis for communication between them. The following sections show you how to implement a client and a server, in both C++ and Java, using the IDL from Listing 2.1.

Client Code

Listing 2.2 and Listing 2.3 give the complete code for a client of the `BookRepository::Collection` interface in C++ and Java, respectively. The client connects to the Book Repository server and remotely invokes a couple of attributes and an operation to retrieve information about a `Collection` CORBA object.

Listing 2.2 C++ Client of the `Collection` Interface

```
//C++
//File: 'bk_collection.cxx'
#include <iostream.h>
#include <fstream.h>
#include <stdlib.h>
#include <sstream>
#include "BookRepository.hh"

CORBA::ORB_var
global_orb = CORBA::ORB::_nil();

// read_reference() -- read an object reference from file.
static
CORBA::Object_ptr
read_reference(
    const char*      file
)
{
    ifstream ifs(file);
    CORBA::String_var strV;
    ifs >> strV;
    if (!ifs) {
        cerr << "Error reading object reference from " << file << endl;
        return CORBA::Object::_nil();
    }
    return global_orb->string_to_object(strV);
}


int
main(int argc, char **argv)
{
    try
    {
```

Listing 2.2 continued

```
        // Step 1 - Initialize the ORB.
        global_orb = CORBA::ORB_init(argc, argv);

        // Parse command line arguments:
        if (argc != 1) {
            cout << "Usage: bk_collection " << endl;
            exit(0);
        }

        // Step 2 - Obtain 'BookRepository::Collection' object reference.
        CORBA::Object_var objV;
        objV = read_reference("BookRepository_Collection.ref");
        BookRepository::Collection_var collectionV
            = BookRepository::Collection::_narrow(objV);
        if (CORBA::is_nil(collectionV.in() ))
        {
            cerr << "error: failed to narrow to Collection." << endl;
            exit(1);
        }

        // Step 3 - Invoke on 'BookRepository::Collection' object.
        cout << "Details of book collection:" << endl;
        CORBA::String_var name_strV;
        name_strV = collectionV->name_of_collection();
        cout << "\tName of collection = \"" << name_strV.in() << "\"" << endl;
        CORBA::Long n_books;
        n_books = collectionV->number_of_books();
        cout << "\tNumber of books = " << n_books << endl;

        // Try changing the name of the book collection.
        cout << "Changing name of book collection..." << endl;
        collectionV->name_of_collection("Brand new collection!");
        cout << "checking name of collection..." << endl;
        name_strV = collectionV->name_of_collection();
        cout << "\tName of collection = \"" << name_strV.in() << "\"" << endl;
    }
    catch(CORBA::Exception &ex)
    {
        cerr << "Unexpected CORBA exception:  " << ex << endl;
    }

    // Step 4 - Shut down the ORB.
    try
    {
        global_orb->shutdown(1);
        global_orb->destroy();
    }
```

Listing 2.2 continued

```
    catch (...)
    {
        // Do nothing.
    }
    return 0;
}
```

Listing 2.3 Java Client of the `Collection` *Interface*

```
//Java
package Pure.BookRepository;

import org.omg.CORBA.*;
import org.omg.PortableServer.*;
import java.io.*;
import Pure.BookRepository.*;

public class bk_collection
{

   // global_orb -- make ORB public
   public static org.omg.CORBA.ORB global_orb = null;


   // read_reference() -- read an object reference from file.
   static org.omg.CORBA.Object read_reference(String file)
   {
      System.out.println("Reading stringified object reference from " + file);
      String ref = null;
      try
      {
         FileReader retrieve=new FileReader(file);
         BufferedReader in=new BufferedReader(retrieve);
         ref = in.readLine();
      } catch (IOException ex)
      {
         System.out.println("Error reading object reference from "
             + file + " : " + ex.toString()
         );
         return null;
      }
      org.omg.CORBA.Object obj = global_orb.string_to_object(ref);
      return obj;
   }


   public static void main  (String args[])
   {
```

Listing 2.3 continued

```
try
{
   // Step 1 - Initialize the ORB.
   global_orb = ORB.init(args, null);

   String app_args[] = remove_ORB_args(args);

  // Parse command line arguments:
  if (app_args.length != 0) {
      System.out.println("Usage: bk_collection ");
      System.exit(1);
  }

  // Step 2 - Obtain 'BookRepository::Collection' object reference.
  org.omg.CORBA.Object obj;
  obj = read_reference("BookRepository_Collection.ref");
  Collection theCollection = CollectionHelper.narrow(obj);

  // Step 3 - Invoke 'BookRepository::Collection' object.
  System.out.println("Details of book collection:");
  String name_str;
  name_str = theCollection.name_of_collection();
  System.out.println("\tName of collection = \"" + name_str + "\"");
  int n_books;
  n_books = theCollection.number_of_books();
  System.out.println("\tNumber of books = " + n_books);

  // Try changing the name of the book collection.
  System.out.println("Changing name of book collection...");
  theCollection.name_of_collection("Brand new collection!");
  System.out.println("checking name of collection...");
  name_str = theCollection.name_of_collection();
  System.out.println("\tName of collection = \"" + name_str + "\"");
}
catch(Exception ex)
{
   System.out.println("Unexpected CORBA exception: " + ex);
}

// Step 4 - Shut down the ORB.
try
{
   global_orb.shutdown(true);
   global_orb.destroy();
}
catch (Exception ex)
{
```

Listing 2.3 continued

```
            // Do nothing.
        }
        return;
    }
}
```

The bk_collection client performs the following steps:

1. **Initialize the ORB**—The first thing the client must do is create an ORB object, global_orb, calling CORBA::ORB_init() in C++ and org.omg.CORBA.ORB.init() in Java. The array of command-line arguments, argv in C++ and args in Java, is passed to the initialization function, giving the user an opportunity to pass parameters to the ORB. In Java, the ORB options must be explicitly removed, using remove_ORB_args(), before processing the rest of the command-line arguments. See the section "ORB Initialization," later in this chapter.
2. **Obtain an object reference**—To locate a remote CORBA object, the client has to obtain an object reference. The object reference contains complete location details for the object. For example, on a TCP/IP network the object reference contains the server host and IP port.
   In this example, the client reads the object reference, which is in stringified form, from a well-known file. A more sophisticated way of passing the object reference from server to client is to use the CORBA Naming Service, which is demonstrated in Example 5.
   The read_reference() function reads the stringified object reference from a file and converts the string to an object reference using string_to_object(). The return type of string_to_object() is CORBA::Object in C++ and org.omg.CORBA.Object in Java, which is the base class for all object reference types.
   The object reference returned by read_reference() is cast to the correct type using Collection::_narrow() in C++ and CollectionHelper.narrow() in Java. The narrow function makes a down cast, similar to dynamic_cast<Collection> in C++ and (Collection) in Java. Narrowing does more than that, however—it also checks that the down cast is legal with respect to the IDL inheritance hierarchy.
   In C++, a failed narrow returns a nil object reference that must be checked for using the CORBA::is_nil() function. In Java, a failed narrow raises the CORBA::BAD_PARAM system exception.
3. **Make remote invocations**—Use the remote object reference, collectionV in C++ and theCollection in Java, to begin making remote invocations. You can invoke any of the operations or attributes declared in the Collection IDL interface.

In C++, the `Collection` object reference is declared as a smart pointer type, `BookRepository::Collection_var`. The purpose of the `_var` types is to help you avoid memory leaks: The destructor of the `_var` type deletes the memory it is pointing at. The `Collection_var` type is designed to mimic the syntax of the `Collection*` pointer type—for example, the members of `collectionV` can be accessed using the `->` member access operator.

4. **Shut down the ORB**—The ORB must shut down correctly so that it can close connections in an orderly manner and release any other resources it is using. Two calls, `CORBA::ORB::shutdown()` and `CORBA::ORB::destroy()`,complete the shutdown.

NOTE

The `CORBA::ORB::destroy()` operation is a relatively recent addition to the CORBA specification and currently is not supported by all ORBs.

Server Code

The main programming task on the server side is to provide implementations for each of the IDL interfaces appearing in the IDL. This is the code that is executed in response to remote invocations by clients—it provides the meat of the user application. Listing 2.4 shows the declaration of the C++ `BookRepository_CollectionImpl` class, which provides an implementation of the `BookRepository::Collection` interface.

Listing 2.4 C++ `BookRepository_CollectionImpl` *Class Declaration*

```
//C++
//File: 'BookRepository_CollectionImpl.h'
#ifndef BOOKREPOSITORY_COLLECTIONIMPL_H_
#define BOOKREPOSITORY_COLLECTIONIMPL_H_

//Include the header for the server Skeleton code.
#include "BookRepositoryS.hh"

class BookRepository_CollectionImpl :
    public virtual PortableServer::RefCountServantBase,
    public virtual POA_BookRepository::Collection
{
public:
    // Constructor and Destructor
    BookRepository_CollectionImpl(PortableServer::POA_ptr);
    virtual ~BookRepository_CollectionImpl();

    // Override '_default_POA()' - inherited from 'ServantBase'
    virtual PortableServer::POA_ptr
    _default_POA();

    //----------
    // IDL operations
```

Listing 2.4 continued

```
    //----------
    virtual BookRepository::FuzzyBoolean
    is_in_collection(BookRepository::ISBN  book_id)
    throw (CORBA::SystemException);

    //----------
    // IDL attributes
    //----------
    virtual CORBA::Long number_of_books()
    throw (CORBA::SystemException);

    virtual char* name_of_collection()
    throw (CORBA::SystemException);

    virtual void name_of_collection(const char*  _new_value)
    throw (CORBA::SystemException);

private:
    // Instance variables for attributes.
    CORBA::Long                     m_number_of_books;
    CORBA::String_var               m_name_of_collectionV;

    // Private member variables
    PortableServer::POA_var         m_poaV;

    // The following are not implemented
    BookRepository_CollectionImpl(
        const BookRepository_CollectionImpl &
    );
    BookRepository_CollectionImpl& operator=(
        const BookRepository_CollectionImpl &
    );
};

#endif
```

The name of the implementation class, `BookRepository_CollectionImpl`, is arbitrary. No naming conventions are enforced by the ORB, but it is a good idea to follow a consistent convention. Common naming schemes add a suffix, such as `Impl` or `_i`, or a prefix, such as `I` (a common naming convention in Microsoft's DCOM).

In the context of the Portable Object Adapter (POA), the implementation class is known as a *servant* class. A servant class provides the code that implements CORBA objects.

The servant class inherits from `POA_BookRepository::Collection`, which indicates that the servant implements the `BookRepository::Collection` interface. The

POA_BookRepository::Collection class is declared in the skeleton code and has pure virtual member functions that must be overridden to implement each of the IDL attributes and operations.

The C++ inheritance hierarchy for the BookRepository_CollectionImpl servant class is shown in Figure 2.1.

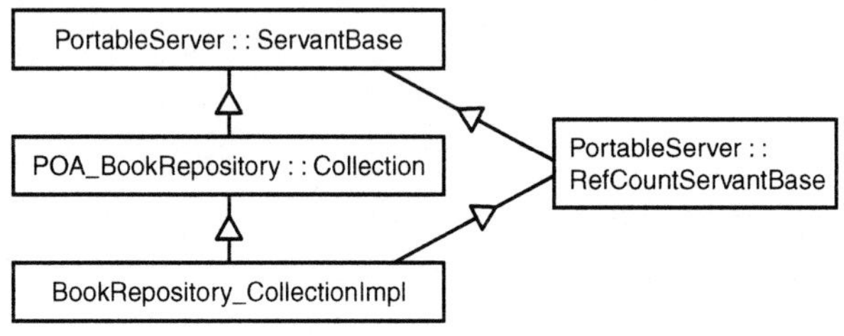

Figure 2.1

C++ servant inheritance hierarchy.

At the root of the hierarchy is PortableServer::ServantBase, which is the base of all C++ servant classes. An additional class, PortableServer::RefCountServantBase, is inherited into BookRepository_CollectionImpl. The RefCountServantBase class provides an implementation of the _add_ref() and _remove_ref() member functions to implement reference counting for servants.

TIP

Inheriting from RefCountServantBase is optional for servant classes but highly recommended. Including the inheritance allows you to use the PortableServer::ServantBase_var smart pointer class and diminishes the likelihood that servant instances are leaked.

The body of the BookRepository_CollectionImpl class declares functions that correspond to an IDL operation, is_in_collection(), and two IDL attributes, number_of_books and name_of_collection. The C++ function signatures are derived from IDL by following the rules of the IDL-to-C++ mapping. Generally, ORBs provide a tool that generates these signatures for you.

In Java, an outline of the servant class declaration is given by the following code fragment:

```
//Java
package Pure.BookRepository;

public class CollectionImpl
    extends Pure.BookRepository.CollectionPOA
{
    // Implementation not shown...
}
```

The Java inheritance hierarchy for the BookRepository.CollectionImpl servant class is shown in Figure 2.2.

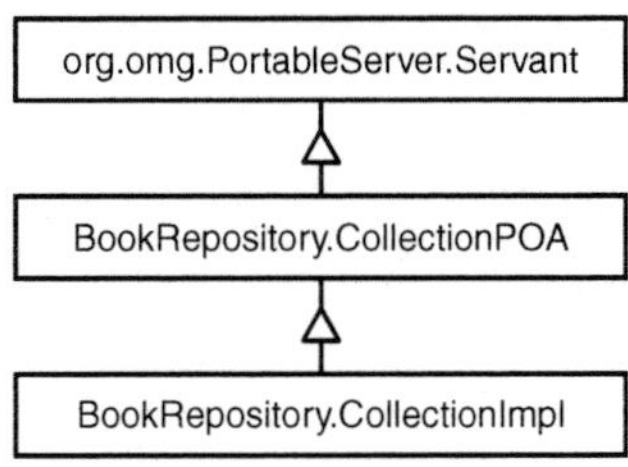

Figure 2.2

Java servant inheritance hierarchy.

At the root of the hierarchy is org.omg.PortableServer.Servant, which is the base of all Java servant classes.

The CollectionImpl servant class inherits from BookRepository.CollectionPOA, which indicates that the servant implements the BookRepository::Collection IDL interface. The BookRepository.CollectionPOA class is an abstract class, declared in the skeleton code, and its methods must be overridden to implement each of the IDL attributes and operations.

Listing 2.5 and Listing 2.6 show the implementation of the servant methods for C++ and Java, respectively.

Listing 2.5 C++ Implementation of BookRepository::Collection

```
//C++

#include <stdlib.h>
#include <iostream.h>
#include "BookRepository_CollectionImpl.h"


// Constructor
BookRepository_CollectionImpl::BookRepository_CollectionImpl(
    PortableServer::POA_ptr the_poa
) :
    m_poaV(PortableServer::POA::_duplicate(the_poa)),
    m_number_of_books(1000),
    m_name_of_collectionV(CORBA::string_dup("AssortedBooks"))
{ }

// ~BookRepository_CollectionImpl destructor.
BookRepository_CollectionImpl::~BookRepository_CollectionImpl()
{ }
```

Listing 2.5 continued

```
PortableServer::POA_ptr
BookRepository_CollectionImpl::_default_POA()
{
    return PortableServer::POA::_duplicate(m_poaV);
}

//----------------
// IDL Operations
//----------------

// is_in_collection()
BookRepository::FuzzyBoolean
BookRepository_CollectionImpl::is_in_collection(
    BookRepository::ISBN            book_id
) throw (
    CORBA::SystemException
)
{
    return BookRepository::UNKNOWN;
}

//----------------
// IDL Attributes
//----------------

// number_of_books -- Accessor
CORBA::Long
BookRepository_CollectionImpl::number_of_books()
throw (CORBA::SystemException)
{
    return m_number_of_books;
}

// name_of_collection -- Accessor
char*
BookRepository_CollectionImpl::name_of_collection()
throw (CORBA::SystemException)

{
    return CORBA::string_dup(m_name_of_collectionV);
}

// name_of_collection -- Modifier
void
BookRepository_CollectionImpl::name_of_collection(
    const char*  _new_value
```

Listing 2.5 continued

```
) throw (CORBA::SystemException)
{
    m_name_of_collectionV = CORBA::string_dup(_new_value);
}
```

Listing 2.6 Java Implementation of `BookRepository::Collection`

```
//Java
package Pure.BookRepository;

import org.omg.CORBA.ORB;
import Pure.BookRepository.*;


public class CollectionImpl
    extends CollectionPOA
{
    // Private member variables
    private int                                 m_number_of_books;
    private java.lang.String                    m_name_of_collection;
    private org.omg.PortableServer.POA          m_poa = null;

    // Constructor
    public CollectionImpl(org.omg.PortableServer.POA poa)
    {
        m_poa = poa;
        m_number_of_books    = 1000;
        m_name_of_collection = "AssortedBooks";
    }

    //-----------------
    // IDL Operations
    //-----------------

    public Pure.BookRepository.FuzzyBoolean is_in_collection(
        int                                 book_id
    )
    throws org.omg.CORBA.SystemException
    {
        return FuzzyBoolean.UNKNOWN;
    }

    //-----------------
    // IDL Attributes
    //-----------------

    public int number_of_books()
    {
```

Listing 2.6 continued

```
        return m_number_of_books;
    }

    public java.lang.String name_of_collection()
    {
        return m_name_of_collection;
    }

    public void name_of_collection(
            java.lang.String                _new_value
    )
    {
        m_name_of_collection = _new_value;
    }

    public org.omg.PortableServer.POA _default_POA()
    {
        return m_poa;
    }
}
```

The implementation of the IDL operation, `is_in_collection()`, is a simple placeholder that returns the value, `BookRepository::UNKNOWN` in C++ and `BookRepository.FuzzyBoolean.UNKNOWN` in Java. A proper implementation would consult a database backend to check if there is a valid record for the given `book_id`.

The implementation of the IDL attributes, `number_of_books` and `name_of_collection`, is simply a matter of reading or setting the corresponding private member variables, `m_number_of_books` and `m_name_of_collection`. It is *not* obligatory to define member variables for attributes, however—you can implement the accessor and modifier functions however you like. The IDL attributes are mapped to accessor and modifier functions, not to member variables.

In addition to providing implementations for the IDL operations and attributes, the servant overrides the `_default_POA()` function, which is inherited from the servant base class. The `_default_POA()` function can be called at any time to discover which POA object a servant is associated with. It is the developer's responsibility to implement `_default_POA()`. In this example, the servant simply returns a cached reference to a POA object—`m_poaV` in C++ or `m_poa` in Java—that is set by the servant's constructor.

CAUTION

> It is recommended that you always override `_default_POA()`in your servant classes. Otherwise, there is a serious risk that your servant objects could be accidentally activated by the *wrong* POA object. See the section "Implicit Activation and `_this()`," later in this chapter, for details of how this can happen.

The code to initialize a server is shown in Listing 2.7 for C++ and Listing 2.8 for C++ for Java. Most of this code appears in the server's `main()` function.

Listing 2.7 C++ Server Initialization

```
//C++
//File: 'server.cxx'
#include <iostream.h>
#include <fstream.h>
#include <string.h>
#include <stdlib.h>
#include <omg/PortableServer.hh>
#include "BookRepository_CollectionImpl.h"

CORBA::ORB_var
global_orb = CORBA::ORB::_nil();

// write_reference() -- export object reference to file.
void
write_reference(
    CORBA::Object_ptr                refP,
    const char*                      objref_file
)
{
    CORBA::String_var stringified_ref = global_orb->object_to_string(refP);
    cout << "Writing stringified object reference to " << objref_file << endl;

    ofstream os(objref_file);
    os << stringified_ref;
    if (!os.good())
    {
        cerr << "Failed to write to " << objref_file << endl;
    }
}


int
main(int argc, char **argv)
{
    // Step 1 - Declare variables to hold servant references.
    PortableServer::ServantBase_var the_BookRepository_Collection = 0;

    try
    {
        CORBA::Object_var objV;  // For temporary object references.

        // Step 2 - Initialise the ORB and Root POA.
        cout << "Initializing the ORB" << endl;
        global_orb = CORBA::ORB_init(argc, argv);
```

Listing 2.7 continued

```
        objV = global_orb->resolve_initial_references("RootPOA");
        PortableServer::POA_var root_poaV
            = PortableServer::POA::_narrow(objV);
        if (CORBA::is_nil(root_poaV.in()) ) {
            cerr << "error: failed to narrow root POA." << endl;
            exit(1);
        }
        PortableServer::POAManager_var root_poa_managerV
            = root_poaV->the_POAManager();
        if (CORBA::is_nil(root_poa_managerV.in()) ) {
            cerr << "error: failed to narrow root POA manager." << endl;
            exit(1);
        }

        PortableServer::ObjectId_var oid;

        // Step 3 - Create and activate a 'Collection' servant.
        the_BookRepository_Collection
            = new BookRepository_CollectionImpl(root_poaV);
        oid = root_poaV->activate_object(the_BookRepository_Collection.in() );
        objV = root_poaV->id_to_reference(oid);

        // Step 4 - Export a 'Collection' object reference
        write_reference(objV, "BookRepository_Collection.ref");

        // Step 5 - Activate the POA Manager.
        root_poa_managerV->activate();
        cout << "Waiting for requests..." << endl;

        // Step 6 - Let the ORB process requests.
        global_orb->run();
    }
    catch (CORBA::Exception& e)
    {
        cout << "Unexpected CORBA exception: " << e << endl;
    }

    // Servants are automatically deleted by '_var' types.

    try
    {
        global_orb->destroy();
    }
    catch (...)
    {
        // Do nothing.
    }
    return 0;
}
```

Listing 2.8 Java Server Initialization

```
//Java
package Pure.BookRepository;

import org.omg.CORBA.*;
import org.omg.PortableServer.*;
import java.io.*;

import java.text.DateFormat;

public class server {
   public static ORB global_orb = null;

   // write_reference() -- export object reference to file.
   static void write_reference(
      org.omg.CORBA.Object              ref,
      String                            objref_file
   )
   {
      String stringified_ref = global_orb.object_to_string(ref);
      System.out.println(
          "Writing stringified object reference to " + objref_file
      );

      try
      {
         FileWriter store = new FileWriter(objref_file);
         store.write(stringified_ref);
         store.flush();
         store.close();
      }
      catch (IOException ex)
      {
         System.out.println("error: failed to create " + objref_file);
      }
   }

    public static void main(String args[])
    {
       // Step 1 - Declare variables to hold servant references.
       Servant the_BookRepository_Collection = null;

       try
       {
           org.omg.CORBA.Object obj = null;

           // Step 2 - Initialise the ORB and Root POA.
           System.out.println( "Initializing the ORB" );
```

Listing 2.8 continued

```
    try
    {
        global_orb = ORB.init(args, null);
        obj = global_orb.resolve_initial_references("RootPOA");
    }
    catch (org.omg.CORBA.ORBPackage.InvalidName ex)
    {
        System.out.println(
            "error: unexpected exception while resolving"
            + "the root POA : " + ex
        );
        System.exit(1);
    }
    POA root_poa = POAHelper.narrow(obj);
    POAManager root_poa_manager = root_poa.the_POAManager();

    byte[] oid;

    try{
        // Step 3 - Create and activate the 'Collection' servant.
        the_BookRepository_Collection
            = new Pure.BookRepository.CollectionImpl(root_poa);
        oid = root_poa.activate_object(the_BookRepository_Collection);
        obj = root_poa.id_to_reference(oid);

        // Step 4 - Export a 'Collection' object reference
        write_reference(obj,"BookRepository_Collection.ref");
    }
    catch (Exception ex)
    {
        System.out.println(ex);
        ex.printStackTrace();
        System.exit(1);
    }

    // Step 5 - Activate the POA Manager.
    try
    {
        root_poa_manager.activate();
    }
    catch (org.omg.PortableServer.POAManagerPackage.AdapterInactive ex)
    {
        System.out.println("error: could not activate POA manager"+ex);
        System.exit(1);
    }

    // Step 6 - Let the ORB process requests.
    System.out.println("Waiting for requests..." );
```

Listing 2.8 continued

```
            global_orb.run();
        }
        catch (Exception ex)
        {
            System.out.println("error: unexpected exception: " + ex);
        }

        try
        {
            global_orb.destroy();
        }
        catch (Exception e)
        {
            // Do nothing.
        }
        return;
    }
}
```

The server `main()` function performs the following steps:

1. **Declare variables to hold servant references**—A variable, `the_BookRepository_CollectionV` in C++ and `the_BookRepository_Collection` in Java, is declared to hold a servant reference.
   In C++, the servant reference is declared as `PortableServer::ServantBase_var`, which is a smart pointer that mimics the `PortableServer::ServantBase*` type. The `ServantBase_var` type helps you avoid a memory leak because its destructor deletes the servant automatically for you. To use the `ServantBase_var` type with a particular servant, you *must* declare the servant class to inherit from `PortableServer::RefCountServantBase`.
   In Java, the servant reference is declared as `org.omg.PortableServer.Servant`, which is a reference to the servant base class. Alternatively, you could declare it as a `BookRepository.CollectionImpl` reference.
2. **Initialize the ORB and root POA**—To initialize a servant, you need to obtain references to both an ORB and a POA object. An ORB object provides a level of service that is typically sufficient for a client application. A POA object provides the extra functionality needed by server applications.
   The ORB instance, `global_orb`, is initialized in the same way as a client ORB. To obtain a reference to the root POA, you use the `CORBA::ORB::resolve_initial_references()` operation object, passing the string `RootPOA` as its argument. The `resolve_initial_references()` operation provides the bootstrap mechanism for obtaining basic CORBA objects.

Because the return value of `resolve_initial_references()` is a base class type, `CORBA::Object_ptr` in C++ and `org.omg.CORBA.Object` in Java, it is necessary to down cast the return value to the correct type, using `PortableServer::POA::_narrow()` in C++ and `org.omg.PortableServer.POAHelper.narrow()` in Java.

CAUTION

Always use a `narrow` function, instead of a native cast, to down cast an object reference. In addition to performing the down-cast, a `narrow` function checks that the cast is typesafe with respect to IDL inheritance.

A reference to the root POA Manager object is obtained by invoking `the_POAManager()` on the POA object. The root POA Manager is implicitly created at the same time as the root POA, and it is used in step 5.

3. **Create and activate servants**—A single servant, of type `BookRepository_CollectionImpl` in C++ and `BookRepository.CollectionImpl` in Java, is created. The constructor is passed a reference to the root POA, which is cached in the servant instance and returned by the `_default_POA()` member function.
   A servant has to be *activated* before it can be used by a client. Activation associates the servant with a particular POA object and a particular object ID. The object ID returned by the `CORBA::POA::activate_object()` operation, `oid`, is automatically generated by the root POA.
4. **Export object references**—An object reference encapsulates the location of a CORBA object. A server makes CORBA objects accessible to clients by publishing object references to a well-known location.
   In this example, the `write_reference()` function publishes a stringified object reference to the `BookRepository_Collection.ref` file. This presupposes that the client has access to the file, possibly through a networked file system (NFS). A more realistic and scalable approach is to use the CORBA Naming Service, which is discussed in the section "Adding CORBA Naming Service Support—Example 5," later in this chapter.
5. **Activate the POA Manager**—A POA Manager is a kind of valve that controls the flow of invocation requests into a POA object. It must be in the *active* state to allow invocations to reach the POA. The `PortableServer::POAManager::activate()` operation activates the POA Manager.
   A POA Manager can also be in a *holding*, *discarding*, or *inactive* state. See Chapter 7, "The Portable Object Adapter," for more information.
6. **Let the ORB process requests**—At this point, the server initialization is complete. You are ready to hand over control of the application to the ORB by calling the `CORBA::ORB::run()` operation.
   When `CORBA::ORB::run()` is called, the server begins listening on an IP port (assuming the Transport layer is TCP/IP). The server can now respond to client connection attempts and process invocations received from clients.

The `CORBA::ORB::run()` operation blocks. It returns when one of the following events occurs:

- The `CORBA::ORB::shutdown()` operation is called with a FALSE argument: `0` in C++ and `false` in Java. Because `CORBA::ORB::run()` grabs the main thread, the only opportunities for calling `shutdown()` occur in the course of an operation invocation or from a subthread.
- A signal is sent to the server. In this case, you should install a signal handler that catches the signal and calls `CORBA::ORB::shutdown()` with a false argument, `0` in C++ and `false` in Java.

Basic IDL Mapping (Example 1)

The IDL features introduced in Example 1 are discussed further in the following subsections:

- IDL identifiers
- IDL mapping for basic types
- Modules and interfaces
- C++ `_var` and `_ptr` types

IDL Identifiers

An IDL identifier is a sequence of ASCII alphabetic, numeric, and underscore (_) characters of any length. All characters are significant. The first character of an identifier must be an ASCII alphabetic character unless it is an *escaped identifier*. Escaped identifiers begin with an underscore character followed by an ASCII alphabetic character.

Case Sensitivity

The following rules apply:

- Every occurrence of a particular identifier must be spelled with the same case.
- Two identifiers differing only by case collide if they occur in the same scope.

Colliding identifiers usually give rise to a compilation error. These rules ensure that IDL identifiers can be mapped consistently to either case-sensitive or non–case-sensitive programming languages.

Escaped Identifiers

At the time CORBA 2.3 was defined, it was realized that introducing new keywords to IDL was problematic because a new keyword might collide with an existing user-defined identifier. Unless such collisions can be prevented, it might prove impossible to compile legacy IDL using a CORBA 2.3 (or later) IDL compiler.

An example occurs in the CORBA Lifecycle Service IDL, which defines an IDL interface called `Factory`. The `Factory` identifier collides with the `factory` keyword introduced in CORBA 2.3.

To solve this problem, the CORBA 2.3 specification introduced the underscore (_) as an IDL escape character (also valid in later versions of CORBA). If an identifier begins with an underscore, an IDL compiler skips the step of checking for keyword collisions, strips the _ prefix from the identifier, and otherwise treats the stripped identifier as a normal identifier.

For example, to compile the CORBA Lifecycle Service IDL using a CORBA 2.3 (or later) IDL compiler, change the name of the `Factory` interface to `_Factory`. The code generated by the IDL compiler is then exactly the same as if the interface had been called `Factory`, except that no collision with the `factory` keyword occurs.

IDL Mapping for Basic Types

The mapping from IDL to C++ and Java for the basic types is shown in Table 2.1.

Table 2.1 Mapping for Basic Types

OMG IDL	C++	Java
`short`	`CORBA::Short`	`short`
`unsigned short`	`CORBA::UShort`	`short`
`long`	`CORBA::Long`	`int`
`unsigned long`	`CORBA::ULong`	`int`
`long long`	`CORBA::LongLong`	`long`
`unsigned long long`	`CORBA::ULongLong`	`long`
`float`	`CORBA::Float`	`float`
`double`	`CORBA::Double`	`double`
`long double`	`CORBA::LongDouble`	*not yet available*
`octet`	`CORBA::Octet`	`byte`
`char`	`CORBA::Char`	`char`
`wchar`	`CORBA::WChar`	`char`
`boolean`	`CORBA::Boolean`	`boolean`
`string`	`char*`	`java.lang.String`
`wstring`	`CORBA::WChar*`	`java.lang.String`
`fixed`	`CORBA::Fixed`	`java.lang.BigDecimal`
`any`	`CORBA::Any`	`org.omg.CORBA.Any`

These basic IDL types can mostly be represented using built-in types in both C++ and Java. The C++ types appearing in Table 2.1 are simply `typedef`s of C++ types.

The Integer Types

An IDL `short` has 16 bits, a `long` 32 bits, and a `long long` 64 bits of precision. The mapping of integer IDL types to C++ is straightforward because C++ has native support for both signed and unsigned integer types.

The mapping of integer IDL types to Java is complicated by the fact that Java has no support for unsigned integers. For example, the IDL `short` and `unsigned short` types both map to a Java `short`. It is your responsibility to ensure that large unsigned integers are not treated as negative integers in your Java code.

The Floating Point Types

The IDL floating point types, `float`, `double`, and `long double`, are based on Institute of Electrical and Electronics Engineers (IEEE) standards. See Chapter 17, "IDL Data Types." The extended floating point type, `long double`, is not widely supported yet.

The `octet` and `char` Types

The IDL `octet` and `char` types are both transmitted in the form of an 8-bit byte.

- An `octet` is intended to hold binary data and is guaranteed not to undergo conversion when it is transmitted.
- A `char` is intended to hold character data and might undergo conversion if the transmitting and receiving platforms have different native character sets.

In C++, the `CORBA::Octet` type is typically a `typedef` of `unsigned char`, and the `CORBA::Char` type is typically a `typedef` of `char`.

The `wchar` Type

The IDL `wchar` type represents an international (wide) character. In standard C++, the `CORBA::WChar` type can be a `typedef` of the `wchar_t` type; with older C++ compilers, it might be represented by an integer type instead.

In Java, the IDL `wchar` type maps naturally to the Java `char` type, which already supports international characters in Unicode format.

The `boolean` Type

In standard C++, the `CORBA::Boolean` type can be a `typedef` of `bool`; with older C++ compilers, `CORBA::Boolean` might be a `typedef` of `char` or `unsigned char` instead.

The true and false Boolean values should be represented in C++ by `1` and `0`, respectively, to ensure portability between the various representations.

In Java, the IDL `boolean` type maps to the Java `boolean` type.

The `string` and `wstring` Types

The IDL `string` and `wstring` types hold strings of narrow characters and strings of wide characters, respectively.

In C++, an IDL `string` type maps to `char*`. The IDL `wstring` type maps to `CORBA::WChar*`. Both narrow and wide strings must be null terminated, like regular C++ strings. The terminating null is not counted as part of the length of the string.

But there is a bit more to it than that. The C++ mapping also defines smart pointer types for manipulating strings and wide strings. Table 2.2 shows the mapping, including smart pointers.

A *smart pointer* is a type that has syntax similar to an ordinary pointer but does something extra as a side-effect of its use.

Table 2.2 C++ Mapping for `string` *and* `wstring` *Types*

OMG IDL	C++ Dumb Pointer	C++ Smart Pointer
`string`	`char*`	`CORBA::String_var`
`wstring`	`CORBA::WChar*`	`CORBA::WString_var`

The reason for introducing smart pointers, `_var` types, is to aid in memory management. See the section "C++ `_var` and `_ptr` Types," later in this chapter, for a brief discussion of `_var` types. See Chapter 4, "Memory Management," for a detailed discussion.

In C++, both strings and wide strings must be allocated on the free store. However, you must *not* use `new` and `delete` to allocate and deallocate memory for strings. Instead, use the functions shown in Table 2.3.

Table 2.3 String Allocation and Deallocation Functions

C++ Function	Description
`char * CORBA::string_alloc( CORBA::ULong len )`	Allocate `len` bytes on the free store to hold a string. The allocated memory can hold up to `len-1` characters.
`char * CORBA::string_dup(char *p)`	Make a duplicate of the `p` string and return a pointer to the new copy.
`void CORBA::string_free(char *p)`	Deallocate the memory associated with the `p` string.
`char * CORBA::wstring_alloc( CORBA::ULong len )`	Allocate `len` bytes on the free store to hold a wide string. The allocated memory can hold up to `len-1` characters.
`char * CORBA::wstring_dup(char *p)`	Make a duplicate of the `p` wide string and return a pointer to the new copy.
`void CORBA::wstring_free(char *p)`	Deallocate the memory associated with the `p` wide string.

In Java, the IDL `string` and `wstring` types both map to `java.lang.String`, which natively supports both narrow and wide strings.

The `fixed` and `any` Types

The IDL `fixed` type represents fixed-precision decimal numbers and is useful for representing money amounts. See Chapter 17 for a detailed description of the `fixed` type.

The IDL any type, technically a basic type because it has simple syntax in IDL, is a self-describing data type that can hold any valid IDL type. See Chapter 8, "The any Type," for a detailed discussion.

Modules and Interfaces

An overview of the mapping from IDL to C++ and Java for modules and the client-side mapping for interfaces is shown in Table 2.4.

Table 2.4 Mapping for Modules and Interfaces

OMG IDL	C++	Java
`module Foo { }`	`namespace Foo { }`	`package Foo;`
	`(standard C++)`	
	`class Foo { }`	
	`(older C++)`	
`interface Bar { }`	`class Bar`	`interface Bar`
	`class Bar_ptr`	`class BarHelper`
	`class Bar_var`	`class BarHolder`

Modules

An IDL module provides a convenient way of grouping collections of IDL definitions into a common scope. For example, consider the following IDL:

```
//IDL
module M1 {
    typedef short AliasShort;
    interface Foo {
        AliasShort getShort();
    };
};

module M2 {
    typedef M1::AliasShort DoublyAliasShort;
};
```

The fully scoped names of the `AliasShort` and `Foo` entities appearing in module `M1` are `M1::AliasShort` and `M1::Foo`, respectively. The basic effect of a module is that the name of the module, `M1`, is prefixed to the entities defined within its scope. Modules are useful because they help you to avoid polluting the global namespace.

Definitions at the `M1` scope are also visible within nested scopes. For example, the `AliasShort` type is visible within the scope of interface `Foo`.

Outside the scope of `M1`, it is necessary to refer to `AliasShort` using its fully scoped name. For example, within module `M2`, the `M1::AliasShort` scoped name must be used to refer to `AliasShort`.

The following IDL sample illustrates two further properties of modules:

```
//IDL
module M1 {
    module M2 {
        // definitions
    };
};

module M1 {
    // more definitions for 'M1'
};
```

The properties are

- Modules can be nested. A module `M2` can be declared within the scope of module `M1`.
- Modules can be reopened (in theory, at least). In the preceding fragment, module `M1` is opened twice.
  However, there is a problem with reopening modules. Depending on the particular language and platform the IDL is mapped to, it may prove impossible for an ORB vendor to implement module reopening.

In standard C++, an IDL module maps to a C++ namespace. The namespace construction is a relatively new addition to the C++ standard; its properties are similar to those of an IDL module. For example, a namespace can be reopened just like an IDL module.

With older C++ compilers that lack support for C++ namespaces, an IDL module is mapped to a C++ class instead. This has the disadvantage that class declarations cannot be reopened and, consequently, module reopening is also not supported.

In Java, an IDL module maps naturally to a Java package.

Interfaces—Client-Side Mapping

An interface is the fundamental unit of IDL. It defines a class of objects and the actions that can be performed on those objects, represented by operations and attributes. Additionally, it is possible to declare data types within the scope of an IDL interface—a convenient way of grouping type declarations.

In C++, an IDL interface maps to three C++ classes on the client side. For example, an interface—`Bar`—maps to the C++ classes `Bar`, `Bar_ptr`, and `Bar_var`:

- The *signature class*, `Bar`, represents the client's view of a CORBA object. Its member functions are mapped from the operations and attributes of the original IDL interface.
  Signature class pointers are used to point at object references (proxy objects). Clients invoke member functions on an object reference to access local or remote CORBA objects.

The `signature` class also exposes miscellaneous static functions needed by the client. The names of the static functions are prefixed by an underscore character (_) to avoid clashing with operation and attribute names.

- The `Bar_ptr` type represents a simple pointer to a `Bar` object reference. It is often just a `typedef` of `Bar*`, but you should not rely on this assumption. Always use `Bar_ptr` to ensure portability for your code.
- The `Bar_var` type represents a smart pointer to a `Bar` object reference. See the following section, "C++ `_var` and `_ptr` Types," and Chapter 5, "Object References."

In Java, an IDL interface maps to a Java interface and auxiliary `Helper` and `Holder` classes. For example, an IDL interface `Bar` maps to the Java interface `Bar` and the `BarHelper` and `BarHolder` classes:

- The *signature Java interface*, `Bar`, represents the client's view of a CORBA object. Its methods are mapped from the operations and attributes of the original IDL interface.
  Signature Java interfaces are used to reference object references (proxy objects). Clients invoke methods on object references to access local or remote CORBA objects.
- The `BarHelper` class exposes miscellaneous static methods needed by the client. These static methods are deliberately defined in a separate class to accommodate the CORBA Java-to-IDL reverse mapping specification.
- The `BarHolder` class is needed to facilitate pass-by-reference semantics when passing `Bar` instances as parameters, because pass-by-reference is not natively supported by the Java language. See the section "Java Holder and Helper Types," later in this chapter.

C++ _var and _ptr Types

Because the parameters and return values of IDL operations are often dynamically allocated, you need to take care to avoid memory leaks. To lessen the risk of memory leaks, the IDL-to-C++ mapping provides smart pointers, `_var` types, for most IDL types. In the case of `_var` types, the `_var` destructor deallocates the memory it is pointing at.

For example, consider the following (from Listing 2.2), which uses a `CORBA::String_var` type to point to a string.

```
//C++
        //...
        // Invoke on 'BookRepository::Collection' object.
        CORBA::String_var name_strV;
        name_strV = collectionV->name_of_collection();
        cout << "\tName of collection = \"" << name_strV.in() << "\"" << endl;
        //...
    } // End of current scope --> 'name_strV' auto-deallocates string.
```

The name_strV variable is declared to be of CORBA::String_var type and is intended to be used in exactly the same way as if it was a char* type. The crucial difference from char* becomes apparent at the end of the current scope. A char* instance would have to be deleted explicitly to avoid a memory leak. However, because name_strV is of the type CORBA::String_var, it automatically deallocates the string in its destructor.

In general, _var types are generated for all types that can be allocated on the heap. In most cases, if T is the C++ name of a type, T_var is the name of the corresponding _var type.

An object reference is a special case. In addition to the smart pointer, _var type, object references also have an associated dumb pointer, _ptr type. A given T_ptr dumb pointer behaves just like a T* pointer (in some ORB implementations it may even be just a typedef of a T*). You are required to use the T_ptr type for object references instead of T* to be CORBA compliant.

Initializing a CORBA Application

The CORBA standard defines a complete API for bootstrapping an application. Standard initialization usually takes place in three stages:

1. A reference to an ORB object is obtained. CORBA allows you to create multiple ORB objects, but most applications use just one.
2. References to a number of fundamental objects are obtained by invoking resolve_initial_references() on the ORB object. Typical initial references include a naming service object and a root POA instance.
3. Further object references can be obtained from the naming service by resolving a given set of names.

Each stage of initialization is discussed in detail in the following sections.

ORB Initialization

An ORB object the basic bootstrap mechanism for a CORBA application. Basic object references are obtained via the ORB object.

The configuration of a CORBA application is aligned closely with ORB initialization. An ORB instance is intended to encapsulate the basic properties of a CORBA application. These might include the type of transport used, the qualities of service, the location of basic services, and many other properties.

CORBA allows you to instantiate more than one ORB object per application, each ORB being uniquely identified by its *ORB ID*. An ORB ID is significant in two respects:

- An ORB ID is a string that uniquely identifies a particular ORB object and can be used to obtain a reference to that ORB object from anywhere within the application.

- An ORB ID is also significant from an administrative viewpoint because it can be used to associate an ORB with a set of externally defined properties. Depending on the ORB implementation you are using, some of the ORB properties might be read automatically from a file or imported from an external database.
  This is an area that can differ greatly between ORBs because the standard does not dictate exactly how a CORBA system should be administered.

When an ORB object is initialized, its properties are obtained from the following sources:

- **Administrative files or database** A typical ORB implementation provides a way for administrators to configure CORBA applications by editing files or updating a database.
  Some implementations associate a set of properties with a particular ORB ID. This is an *administrative domain*. Applications that use the same ORB ID share the same basic properties—that is, they belong to the same administrative domain.
- **Command-line parameters** The properties of an ORB can be overridden by supplying command-line arguments as the application starts up. Given an application executable called `app`, an ORB property can be specified using command-line arguments. One of the following three syntaxes can be used:
  ```
  % app -ORBOption Value%
  app "-ORBOption Value"
  % app -ORBOptionValue
  ```
  This sets the `Option` property equal to `Value`. The first syntax specifies the option name and value as separate, consecutive command-line parameters. The second syntax puts the option name and value into a single parameter, using white space as a separator. The third syntax puts the option name and value into a single parameter, without any white space. This last syntax, although legal, is not recommended because it makes the command-line arguments difficult to parse.
  For example, the following sets the ORB ID of an application that has an executable called `app_executable`:
  ```
  app_executable -ORBid MyOrbId
  ```
  The `-ORBid` flag is used to specify the ORB ID.
- **Java system properties** A natural way of passing parameters to a Java application is to use the system properties, and this approach is supported. For an applet, it is usually the only convenient way of passing properties.

The following basic properties are always initialized:

- **The ORB id** If an ORB ID is not set explicitly when the ORB is created, a reference to the default ORB is returned. The default ORB has an ORB ID equal to `""` (empty string).

- **Initial references** Every ORB needs to know where to find its basic services. At a minimum, this includes references to the naming service and the Interface Repository. See the section "Resolving Initial References," later in this chapter.

The following sections describe the syntax for creating ORB objects in C++ and Java.

C++ ORB Creation

The static `CORBA::ORB_init()` function is used to get a reference to an ORB object:

```
//C++
namespace CORBA {
    typedef char* ORBid;
    static ORB_ptr ORB_init(
        int& argc,
        char** argv,
        const char* orb_identifier = ""
    );
}
```

The conventional `argc` and `argv` parameters of the C++ `main()` function should be passed directly to `ORB_init()`. The `ORB_init()` function searches the `argv` string array for one of the following argument combinations:

- A `-ORB`*`Option`* argument followed by a *`Value`* argument.
- A single argument of the form `-ORB`*`Option Value`*, where *`Option`* and *`Value`* are separated by arbitrary white space.
- A single argument of the form `-ORB`*`OptionValue`*.

If *`Option`* is recognized, it is set equal to *`Value`*. If *`Option`* is not recognized, a `CORBA::BAD_PARAM` system exception is raised instead. The `-ORB`*`Option Value`* arguments are removed from the `argv` list before `ORB_init()` returns.

The `orb_identifier` parameter optionally specifies the ORB ID. If the `orb_identifier` parameter is omitted (or set equal to `""`), the command-line parameters are searched instead, to find an `-ORBid` option. Failing that, `ORB_init()` returns a reference to the default ORB object.

The first time `ORB_init()` is called with a particular ORB ID, a new `CORBA::ORB` object is created. Subsequent calls to `ORB_init()` with the same ORB ID return a reference to the same ORB object each time.

Java Application ORB Creation

The first form of the `org.omg.CORBA.ORB.init()` method is meant to be used with standalone Java applications. It has the following Java signature:

```
//Java
public static org.omg.CORBA.ORB
org.omg.CORBA.ORB.init(String[] args, java.util.Properties props);
```

The conventional args parameter of the Java main() method should be passed directly to org.omg.CORBA.ORB.init(). The ORB.init() method searches the args string array for one of the following argument combinations:

- A -ORB*Option* argument followed by a *Value* argument.
- A single argument of the form -ORB*Option Value*, where *Option* and *Value* are separated by arbitrary white space.
- A single argument of the form -ORB*OptionValue*.

If *Option* is recognized, it is set equal to *Value*. If *Option* is not recognized, an org.omg.CORBA.BAD_PARAM system exception is raised instead.

CAUTION

In Java, the -ORB*Option Value* arguments are not removed from the args list by ORB.init(). Therefore, the developer must provide code to remove (or skip) these parameters when parsing the other command-line arguments. See "Java Removing ORB Options," later in this chapter.

The props argument allows you to set the properties shown in Table 2.5.

***Table 2.5 Properties Recognized by* ORB.init()**

Property	Description
org.omg.CORBA.ORBClass	The name of the class that implements the newly created ORB object.
org.omg.CORBA.ORBSingletonClass	The name of the class that implements the ORB singleton object.

The properties in Table 2.5 are currently the *only* ones recognized by ORB.init(). They are discussed further in the section "The orb.properties File," later in this chapter. Other properties in props are ignored.

The first time ORB.init() is called with a particular ORB ID, a new org.omg.CORBA.ORB object is created. Subsequent calls to ORB.init() with the same ORB ID return a reference to the same ORB object each time.

Java Removing ORB Options

The syntax of the Java ORB.init() method does not allow ORB options to be removed from the list of command-line arguments (the formal parameter type, String[], cannot be modified by the called code). Because of this, you are obliged to remove the ORB parameters yourself. The following helper method, remove_ORB_args(), can be used for this purpose:

```
//Java
public static String[] remove_ORB_args(String args[])
{
```

```
    String temp[] = new String[args.length];
    int i         = 0;
    int arg_count = 0;
    while (i < args.length)
    {
        java.util.StringTokenizer st
            = new java.util.StringTokenizer(args[i]);
        int n_skip = 0;
        if (st.countTokens() > 0)
        {
            if (st.nextToken().startsWith("-ORB") ) {
                n_skip++;
                if (st.countTokens() == 0) { n_skip++; }
            }
        }

        if (n_skip==0) {
            temp[arg_count++] = args[i++];
        }
        else {
            i += n_skip;
        }
    }

    String result[] = new String[arg_count];
    for (i=0; i<arg_count; i++) {  result[i] = temp[i]; }

    return result;
}
```

The return value of `remove_ORB_args()` is an argument list from which all ORB options have been removed. The method removes ORB options supplied either as separate arguments, `-ORB`*`Option Value`*, or as single arguments, `"-ORB`*`Option Value`*`"`.

Java Applet ORB Creation

The second form of the `org.omg.CORBA.ORB.init()` method is meant to be used with Java applets. It has the following Java signature:

```
//Java
public static org.omg.CORBA.ORB
org.omg.CORBA.ORB.init(java.applet.Applet app, java.util.Properties props);
```

The `app` argument is a reference to the `Applet` object that is using the ORB.

The `props` argument allows you to set the properties shown in Table 2.5, as described in the preceding section.

Java Singleton ORB Creation

The third form of the `org.omg.CORBA.ORB.init()` method returns a slightly different type of ORB object, known as a *singleton ORB*. It has the following Java signature:

```
//Java
public static org.omg.CORBA.ORB
org.omg.CORBA.ORB.init();
```

The singleton `ORB.init()` method takes no arguments and returns a reference to the same static ORB object each time it is called.

The role of the singleton ORB is to provide quick and easy access to certain static methods needed for using `Any` and `TypeCode` types. The singleton ORB is very restricted—only the methods shown in Table 2.6 are supported.

Table 2.6 Methods Supported by the Singleton ORB

Method Name	Description
`create_`*`type`*`_tc()`	A method to create type codes dynamically for a non-trivial *type*. For example, `create_struct_tc()` creates a type code for an IDL `struct`.
`get_primitive_tc()`	A method that returns references to basic type codes.
`create_any()`	A method to create an `org.omg.CORBA.Any` object.

The `orb.properties` File

If you are using Sun's Java Development Kit (JDK) to build your CORBA application, it is necessary to create or modify the `orb.properties` file to get it to work with your chosen ORB. The reason for this is that Sun's JDK already contains an ORB runtime, which it uses by default. The `orb.properties` file can be used to override this default ORB runtime.

In fact, there are two ways of specifying the ORB runtime used by the JDK:

- **In the `orb.properties` file** In the *`JDKHome`*`/jre/lib` directory, create an `orb.properties` file containing the following two lines:
  ```
  org.omg.CORBA.ORBClass=ORBClassName
  org.omg.CORBA.ORBSingletonClass=ORBSingletonClassName
  ```
  `ORBClassName` and *`ORBSingletonClassName`*, specifying the `ORBClass` and `ORBSingletonClass`, respectively, can be found in your ORB's documentation.
- **As arguments to the Java interpreter** The ORB properties can also be specified as command-line arguments to the `java` interpreter. For example, an application called `foo.Client` might be run using the following command:
  ```
  java -Dorg.omg.CORBA.ORBClass=ORBClassName
       -Dorg.omg.CORBA.ORBSingletonClass=ORBSingletonClassName  foo.Client
  ```

Both of these approaches are clumsy and inconvenient. A proposed modification to the CORBA specification, however, would require a Java interpreter to search the user's home directory (given by the `user.home` system property) for an `orb.properties` file. Unfortunately, this is not possible at present (JDK1.2.x or JDK1.3).

Resolving Initial References

References to basic CORBA services can be obtained from the ORB object by invoking the `resolve_initial_references()` operation, which has the following signature in C++ and Java:

```
//C++
CORBA::Object CORBA::ORB::resolve_initial_references(const char *identifier)

//Java
org.omg.CORBA.Object org.omg.CORBA.ORB.resolve_initial_references(
    String identifier
)
```

The `identifier` parameter is used to select the particular service for which an object reference is returned. Common `identifier` values are `"RootPOA"`, `"NameService"`, and `"InterfaceRepository"`.

The `resolve_initial_references()` operation is discussed in detail in the section "The Initialization Service" in Chapter 6, "Interoperable Naming Service."

Locating CORBA Objects

The location of a CORBA object is encapsulated in an object reference. The process of locating a CORBA object therefore is reduced to obtaining an object reference.

An object reference is generated by the server process containing the CORBA object. The object reference must then be passed somehow from the server to a client. Two simple alternatives are available to solve this bootstrap problem:

- **Use stringified object references** An object reference can be converted to a standard string format (*stringified object reference*), which easily can be written to a file or passed around in other ways.
  Two functions, `object_to_string()` and `string_to_object()`, are defined to enable conversion to and from the stringified object reference format. These functions have the following signatures:

  ```
  //C++
  static char * CORBA::ORB::object_to_string(const CORBA::Object_ptr)
  static CORBA::Object_ptr CORBA::ORB::string_to_object(const char *)

  //Java
  public static String
  ➥org.omg.CORBA.ORB.object_to_string(org.omg.CORBA.Object)
  public static org.omg.CORBA.Object
  ➥org.omg.CORBA.ORB.string_to_object(String)
  ```

  For example, a server that wants to make a CORBA object known to clients could convert an object reference to a string using `object_to_string()` and write the stringified object reference to a file. Assuming a client also has access to the file, the client can read the stringified object reference and convert it back to an object reference. This approach is useful for simple demonstrations and testing, but it is not scalable.

- **Use the CORBA naming service** The naming service is a central repository for storing object references that associates an object reference with a specific name.

  To use the naming service, a server stores a (name, object reference) binding in the naming service. Clients can then look up the object reference by supplying its name. A naming service therefore provides a convenient way of publicizing object references.

  See the section "Adding CORBA Naming Service Support—Example 5," later in this chapter, and Chapter 6 for more details about the naming service.

Adding an IDL Interface for Searching—Example 2

The second example adds the `SearchableCollection` IDL interface. This interface supports a single operation, `find_by_title()`, to let you search for a particular book. The structure and sequence IDL types are introduced as well.

Listing 2.9 shows the second draft of the `BookRepository` IDL module, with these additions.

Listing 2.9 IDL `BookRepository` *Module for Example 2*

```
//IDL

module BookRepository {
    typedef long ISBN;

    struct PersonName {
        string first_name;
        string second_name;
    };

    struct Date {
        short day;
        short month;
        short year;
    };

    struct BookDetails {
        PersonName   author;
        string       title;
        ISBN         book_id;
```

Listing 2.9 continued

```
        Date          publication_date;
    };
    typedef sequence<BookDetails> BookDetailsSeq;

    enum FuzzyBoolean {NO, YES, UNKNOWN};

    interface Collection {
        readonly attribute long    number_of_books;
        attribute          string  name_of_collection;

        FuzzyBoolean is_in_collection(in ISBN book_id);
    };

    interface SearchableCollection : Collection {
        boolean find_by_title(
                    in string          title,
                    out BookDetailsSeq books_found
                );
    };
};
```

The following IDL constructs are introduced in Listing 2.9:

- Three IDL structures are declared: `PersonName`, `Date`, and `BookDetails`. An IDL structure is a convenient way of grouping related data items. For example, the declaration beginning `struct PersonName` defines a new IDL type, `PersonName`, which has two string fields, `first_name` and `second_name`.
  The syntax for declaring an IDL struct is similar to the syntax in C and C++, but it is more restricted. For example, inheritance is not supported, and only data members can be declared.
- An IDL sequence, `BookDetailsSeq`, is declared. A construction of the form `sequence<`*`ElementType`*`>` declares an unbounded sequence of *`ElementType`* elements. A sequence is like a one-dimensional array, except that the number of elements in the sequence is arbitrary.
- The `SearchableCollection` IDL interface is defined to inherit from `Collection`. This implies that `SearchableCollection` supports the attributes and operations defined in `Collection`, in addition to the explicitly declared `find_by_title()` operation.
  The second parameter of `find_by_title()`, `books_found`, is specified as an `out` parameter. An `out` parameter is similar to a return value—it is passed from the server back to the client.

The following sections show you how to implement a client and a server, in both C++ and Java, using the IDL from Listing 2.9.

Client Code

Listing 2.10 and Listing 2.11 give the complete code for a client of the `BookRepository::SearchableCollection` interface in C++ and Java, respectively. The `bk_search` client prints details of the books that match a given title, which is supplied as a command-line argument. The client code connects to the Book Repository server and invokes `find_by_title()` to obtain the `BookDetailsSeq` sequence containing details of the matching books.

Listing 2.10 C++ Client of the `SearchableCollection` *Interface*

```
//C++

#include <iostream.h>
#include <fstream.h>
#include <stdlib.h>

#include "BookRepository.hh"

CORBA::ORB_var
global_orb = CORBA::ORB::_nil();

// read_reference() -- read an object reference from file.
// ...same definition as Example 1...

int
main(int argc, char **argv)
{
    try
    {
        CORBA::Object_var objV;  // For temporary object references.

        // Initialize the ORB.
        global_orb = CORBA::ORB_init(argc, argv);

        // Parse command line arguments:
        if (argc != 2) {
            cout << "Usage: bk_search " << " <book_title>" << endl;
            exit(0);
        }
        const char * book_title = argv[1];

        // Obtain 'BookRepository::SearchableCollection' object reference.
        objV = read_reference("BookRepository_SearchableCollection.ref");
        BookRepository::SearchableCollection_var searchableCollectionV
            = BookRepository::SearchableCollection::_narrow(objV);
        if (CORBA::is_nil(searchableCollectionV.in() ))
        {
```

Listing 2.10 continued

```
            cerr << "error: failed to narrow to SearchableCollection." << endl;
            exit(1);
        }

        // Invoke on BookRepository::SearchableCollection object.
        BookRepository::BookDetailsSeq_var detailsSeqV;
        CORBA::Boolean wasFound;
        wasFound = searchableCollectionV->find_by_title(
                                          book_title,
                                          detailsSeqV.out()
                                      );
        if (wasFound) {
            cout << "Found the following matching titles:" << endl;
        }
        else {
            cout << "No matching titles."  << endl;
        }

        // Print out the list of books (if any)
        for (CORBA::ULong i=0; i < detailsSeqV->length(); i++) {
            cout << "Book[" << i << "]" << endl;
            cout << "\tAuthor: " << detailsSeqV[i].author.second_name
                 << ", "         << detailsSeqV[i].author.first_name << endl;
            cout << "\tTitle:  " << detailsSeqV[i].title << endl;
            cout << "\tISBN:   " << detailsSeqV[i].book_id << endl;
            cout << "\tPublication Date: "
                 << detailsSeqV[i].publication_date.day   << "/"
                 << detailsSeqV[i].publication_date.month << "/"
                 << detailsSeqV[i].publication_date.year  << endl;
        }
    }
    catch(CORBA::Exception &ex)
    {
        cerr << "Unexpected CORBA exception: " << ex << endl;
    }

    // Shut down the ORB.
    try
    {
        global_orb->shutdown(1);
        global_orb->destroy();
    }
    catch (...)
    {
        // Do nothing.
    }
    return 0;
}
```

Listing 2.11 Java Client of the `SearchableCollection` *Interface*

```
//Java
package Pure.BookRepository;

import org.omg.CORBA.*;
import org.omg.PortableServer.*;
import java.io.*;
import Pure.BookRepository.*;

public class bk_search
{

   // global_orb -- make ORB public
   public static org.omg.CORBA.ORB global_orb = null;


   // read_reference() -- read an object reference from file.
   // ...same definition as Example 1...

   public static void main (String args[])
   {
      try
      {
         // Initialise the ORB.
         global_orb = ORB.init(args, null);

         String app_args[] = remove_ORB_args(args);

        // Parse command line arguments:
        if (app_args.length != 1) {
            System.out.println("Usage: bk_search " + " <book_title>");
            System.exit(1);
        }
        String book_title = app_args[0];

        // Obtain 'BookRepository:: SearchableCollection' object reference.
        org.omg.CORBA.Object obj;
        obj = read_reference("BookRepository_SearchableCollection.ref");
        SearchableCollection theSearchableCollection
             = SearchableCollectionHelper.narrow(obj);

        // Invoke on BookRepository::SearchableCollection object.
        BookDetailsSeqHolder detailsSeqH
            = new BookDetailsSeqHolder();
        boolean wasFound;
        wasFound = theSearchableCollection.find_by_title(
                                              book_title,
                                              detailsSeqH
                                          );.
```

Listing 2.11 continued

```
        if (wasFound) {
            System.out.println("Found the following matching titles:");
        }
        else {
            System.out.println("No matching titles.");
        }

        // Print out the list of books (if any)
        for (int i=0; i < detailsSeqH.value.length; i++) {
            System.out.println("Book[" + i + "]");
            System.out.println("\tAuthor: "
                 + detailsSeqH.value[i].author.second_name + ", "
                 + detailsSeqH.value[i].author.first_name);
            System.out.println("\tTitle:  " + detailsSeqH.value[i].title);
            System.out.println("\tISBN:   " + detailsSeqH.value[i].book_id);
            System.out.println("\tPublication Date: "
                 + detailsSeqH.value[i].publication_date.day   + "/"
                 + detailsSeqH.value[i].publication_date.month + "/"
                 + detailsSeqH.value[i].publication_date.year);
        }
      }
      catch(Exception ex)
      {
         System.out.println("Unexpected CORBA exception: " + ex);
      }

      try
      {
         global_orb.shutdown(true);
         global_orb.destroy();
      }
      catch (Exception ex)
      {
         // Do nothing.
      }
      return;
   }
}
```

The `bk_search` client performs the following steps:

1. **Initialize the ORB** A new ORB object is created and assigned to `global_orb`.
2. **Obtain an object reference** A `BookRepository::SearchableCollection` object reference is obtained by reading a stringified object reference from the `BookRepository_SearchableCollection.ref` file.
3. **Invoke the `find_by_title()` operation** The `find_by_title()` remote operation is invoked to find the books that match the specified `title`.

In C++, a smart pointer, `detailsSeqV`, is used to access the result of the search. Because it is an `out` parameter, the `detailsSeqV` smart pointer is declared but not initialized. After the invocation, `detailsSeqV` points to the result. The `out()` method (for example, `detailsSeqV.out()`) converts `detailsSeqV` explicitly to the correct formal parameter type. If your ORB does not support the `out()` method, you can pass the parameter as `detailsSeqV` instead and rely on implicit type conversion.

In Java, a `BookDetailsSeqHolder` object, `detailsSeqH`, is used to hold the result of the search. Holder types are generated by the Java mapping for all user-defined types to facilitate the semantics of `out` parameters. The Holder types are needed to get around the fact that Java does not support pass-by-reference semantics for method parameters. See the sections "Java Holder and Helper Types" and "Returning Parameters," later in this chapter.

4. **Print out list of books** A `for` loop iterates over the elements of the `BookDetailsSeq` sequence—`detailsSeqV[i]` in C++ and `detailsSeqH.value[i]` in Java—to print details of the matching books. The `BookDetailsSeq` data is already stored locally on the client side. No remote invocations need to be made within the scope of this `for` loop.
5. **Shut down the ORB** Two calls `CORBA::ORB::shutdown()` and `CORBA::ORB::destroy()` are made to shut down the ORB.

Server Code

The interesting feature of the server code in Example 2 is that it demonstrates how to implement an inherited IDL interface. That is, it shows the implementation of the `SearchableCollection` interface, which inherits from the `Collection` interface.

Listing 2.12 shows the declaration of the C++ `BookRepository_SearchableCollectionImpl` class, which provides the implementation of the `BookRepository::SearchableCollection` interface.

Listing 2.12 C++ `BookRepository_SearchableCollectionImpl` *Servant Class Declaration*

```
//C++
#ifndef BOOKREPOSITORY_SEARCHABLECOLLECTIONIMPL_H_
#define BOOKREPOSITORY_SEARCHABLECOLLECTIONIMPL_H_

#include "BookRepositoryS.hh"
#include "BookRepository_CollectionImpl.h"

#include "Collection_DB.h"

class BookRepository_SearchableCollectionImpl :
    public virtual POA_BookRepository::SearchableCollection,
    public virtual BookRepository_CollectionImpl
{
```

Listing 2.12 continued

```
public:
    BookRepository_SearchableCollectionImpl(PortableServer::POA_ptr);

    virtual ~BookRepository_SearchableCollectionImpl();

    // Overriding inherited IDL operations
    virtual BookRepository::FuzzyBoolean
    is_in_collection(
        BookRepository::ISBN            book_id
    ) throw (CORBA::SystemException);

    //----------
    // IDL operations
    //----------
    virtual CORBA::Boolean
    find_by_title(
        const char*                     title,
        BookRepository::BookDetailsSeq_out books_found
    ) throw (CORBA::SystemException);

private:
    // Private member variables.
    Collection_DB    m_collection_db;

    // ...
};

#endif
```

The `BookRepository_SearchableCollectionImpl` servant class inherits from `POA_BookRepository::SearchableCollection`, which indicates that the servant implements the `BookRepository::SearchableCollection` interface. This inheritance relationship is necessary.

The `BookRepository_SearchableCollectionImpl` servant class also inherits from `BookRepository_CollectionImpl`. This inheritance relationship is *not* necessary, but it is very convenient. It implies that the IDL inheritance hierarchy is mirrored by the C++ hierarchy of implementation classes, allowing you to make the most of C++'s support for object orientation.

The `PortableServer::RefCountServantBase` class is also a base class of `BookRepository_SearchableCollectionImpl` (inherited indirectly via `BookRepository_CollectionImpl`). This ensures support for servant reference counting.

The `is_in_collection()` member function demonstrates how to implement a polymorphic IDL operation in C++. Because the `is_in_collection()` function is overridden in the derived class, `BookRepository_SearchableCollectionImpl`, two implementations are available: `Collection` CORBA objects use the `BookRepository_CollectionImpl` version, and `SearchableCollection` CORBA objects use the `BookRepository_SearchableCollectionImpl` version of the function. Effectively, you are using a standard C++ mechanism—overriding virtual member functions—to implement polymorphic IDL operations.

In Java, an outline of the `SearchableCollectionImpl` servant class declaration is given by the following code fragment:

```
//Java
package Pure.BookRepository;

public class SearchableCollectionImpl
    extends Pure.BookRepository.SearchableCollectionPOA
{
    // Implementation not shown...
}
```

The `SearchableCollectionImpl` servant class extends `BookRepository.SearchableCollectionPOA`, which indicates that the servant implements the `BookRepository::SearchableCollection` interface. This inheritance relationship is necessary.

It would be convenient if `SearchableCollectionImpl` could also extend `CollectionImpl`. Unfortunately, this is not possible, because Java is limited to single inheritance. You are forced to re-implement all of the attributes and operations already implemented in the `CollectionImpl` class. However, there is a way around this problem—see "Adding a Multiply-Inheriting IDL Interface—Example 4."

To implement a polymorphic IDL operation using Java, simply provide a different implementation for the operation in the servant class that implements the derived IDL interface. For example, the `SearchableCollectionImpl` version of `is_in_collection()` is different from the `CollectionImpl` version.

Listing 2.13 and Listing 2.14 show the implementation of the servant methods for C++ and Java, respectively.

Listing 2.13 C++ Implementation of **`BookRepository::SearchableCollection`** *Interface*

```
//C++

#include <stdlib.h>
#include <iostream.h>
#include "BookRepository_SearchableCollectionImpl.h"

// Constructor
BookRepository_SearchableCollectionImpl::\
```

Listing 2.13 continued

```
BookRepository_SearchableCollectionImpl(
    PortableServer::POA_ptr the_poa
) :
    BookRepository_CollectionImpl(the_poa)
{
}

// Destructor.
BookRepository_SearchableCollectionImpl::\
~BookRepository_SearchableCollectionImpl()
{
}

// is_in_collection() -- inherited from 'BookRepository::Collection' interface
BookRepository::FuzzyBoolean
BookRepository_SearchableCollectionImpl::is_in_collection(
    BookRepository::ISBN            book_id
) throw (CORBA::SystemException)
{
    if (m_collection_db.is_in_collection(book_id) ) {
        return BookRepository::YES;
    }
    else {
        return BookRepository::NO;
    }
}

// find_by_title()
CORBA::Boolean
BookRepository_SearchableCollectionImpl::find_by_title(
    const char*                     title,
    BookRepository::BookDetailsSeq_out books_found
) throw (CORBA::SystemException)
{
    books_found = m_collection_db.getByTitle(title);
    return (books_found->length() > 0);
}
```

Listing 2.14 Java Implementation of **BookRepository::SearchableCollection** *Interface*

```
//Java
package Pure.BookRepository;

import org.omg.CORBA.ORB;
import Pure.BookRepository.Collection_DB;
```

Listing 2.14 continued

```
public class SearchableCollectionImpl
    extends Pure.BookRepository.SearchableCollectionPOA
{
    // Private member variables.
    private int                                m_number_of_books;
    private java.lang.String                   m_name_of_collection;
    private Collection_DB                      m_collection_db;
    private org.omg.PortableServer.POA         m_poa = null;

   public SearchableCollectionImpl(org.omg.PortableServer.POA poa)
    {
        m_poa = poa;
        m_number_of_books    = 1000;
        m_name_of_collection = "AssortedBooks";
        m_collection_db      = new Collection_DB();
   }

    public Pure.BookRepository.FuzzyBoolean is_in_collection(
        int                            book_id
    )
    throws org.omg.CORBA.SystemException
    {
        if (m_collection_db.is_in_collection(book_id) ) {
            return FuzzyBoolean.YES;
        }
        else {
            return FuzzyBoolean.NO;
        }
    }

    public boolean find_by_title(
        java.lang.String               title,
        BookDetailsSeqHolder books_found
    )
    throws org.omg.CORBA.SystemException
    {
        System.out.println("find_by_title(): called.");

        books_found.value = m_collection_db.getByTitle(title);
        return (books_found.value.length > 0);
    }

    public int number_of_books()
    {
        return m_number_of_books;
    }
```

Listing 2.14 continued

```
    public java.lang.String name_of_collection()
    {
        return m_name_of_collection;
    }

    public void name_of_collection(
           java.lang.String                _new_value)
    {
        m_name_of_collection = _new_value;
    }

    public org.omg.PortableServer.POA _default_POA()
    {
        return m_poa;
    }
}
```

The implementation of the servant, `BookRepository_SearchableCollectionImpl` in C++ and `BookRepository.SearchableCollectionImpl` in Java, is fairly straightforward. In C++, an implementation of `is_in_collection()` is provided to override the inherited implementation. In Java, every attribute and operation from both the `Collection` and `SearchableCollection` IDL interfaces has to be implemented.

Both the C++ and Java servants delegate most of their functionality to a database class, `Collection_DB`. The `Collection_DB` class is a wrapper class that accesses the database table where the book details are stored. Listing 2.15 and Listing 2.16 show the declarations of the `Collection_DB` class.

Listing 2.15 C++ Declaration of the `Collection_DB` Class

```
// C++
#ifndef _COLLECTION_DB_
#define _COLLECTION_DB_

// ...

// Include definitions from the stub code.
#include "BookRepository.hh"

class Collection_DB {
public:
    Collection_DB();

    CORBA::Boolean
    is_in_collection(CORBA::Long book_id);
```

Listing 2.15 continued

```
    BookRepository::BookDetails*
    get(CORBA::Long book_id);

    BookRepository::BookDetailsSeq*
    getByTitle(const char * title);

    //...
};
#endif
```

Listing 2.16 Java Declaration of the `Collection_DB` Class

```
// Java
package Pure.BookRepository;

public class Collection_DB
{
    // Private member variables
    //...

    // Public methods
    public Collection_DB()
    { ... }

    public boolean is_in_collection(int book_id)
    { ... }

    public BookDetails get(int book_id)
    { ... }

    public BookDetails[] getByTitle(String title)
    { ... }
}
```

The `Collection_DB` class can be implemented using the database adapter of your choice. The implementation details are not shown here.

IDL Mapping for Some Complex Types (Example 2)

The IDL features introduced in Example 2 are discussed further in the following subsections:

- The `struct` type
- The unbounded `sequence` type
- Java Holder and Helper types

The struct Type

The mapping of an IDL `struct` to C++ and Java is shown in Table 2.7.

Table 2.7 Mapping for the `struct` Type

OMG IDL	C++	Java
`struct Foo {...};`	`struct Foo {...};`	`class Foo {...}`
	`class Foo_var`	`class FooHelper`
		`class FooHolder`

An IDL struct has a very similar syntax to a struct in the C programming language. For example

```
//IDL
module BookRepository {
    struct Date {
        short day;
        short month;
        short year;
    };
};
```

defines a `BookRepository::Date` struct having three members: `day`, `month`, and `year`. The `Date` type can be used as a parameter or return value of an IDL operation.

In C++, an IDL struct maps directly to a C++ struct. For example

```
//C++
namespace BookRepository {
    //...
    struct Date {
        CORBA::Short day;
        CORBA::Short month;
        CORBA::Short year;
    };
};
```

As well as the `Date` struct, the C++ mapping also defines a `Date_var` type to assist with memory management of heap-allocated `Date` structs.

In Java, an IDL struct maps to a Java class (there is no `struct` type in Java). For example

```
//Java
package BookRepository;
    //...
    final public class Date
      implements org.omg.CORBA.portable.IDLEntity
    {
        public short day;
```

```
        public short month;
        public short year;

        // 'Date' Constructors
        public Date() {}
        public Date(short day, short month, short year) { ... }
    };
};
```

Each member of the IDL `Date` struct maps to a public field of the Java `Date` class. The `Date` class provides a constructor that allows you to set all the fields in one go.

In Java, two auxiliary classes—`DateHelper` and `DateHolder`—are defined. See the section "Java Holder and Helper Types," later in this chapter, for an explanation of these classes.

Initializing a Struct

In C++, a struct can be allocated on the stack or on the heap. For example

```
//C++
// Allocate 'Date' on the stack.
BookRepository::Date stackDate;

// Allocate 'Date' on the heap.
BookRepository::Date_var heapDateV = new BookRepository::Date();
```

The `BookRepository::Date_var` smart pointer is used here instead of a `BookRepository::Date*` dumb pointer to take advantage of the memory management features of `_var` types.

A mapped C++ struct must be initialized member by member. For example

```
//C++
heapDateV->day   = 7;
heapDateV->month = 7;
heapDateV->year  = 1999;
```

In Java, a struct can be allocated and initialized in a single step. For example

```
//Java
BookRepository.Date theDate = new BookRepository(
                                      7,    //day
                                      7,    //month
                                      1999  //year
                              );
```

The order of the arguments in the constructor is the same as the order of the corresponding members.

Copying a Struct

In C++, a deep copy of a struct can be made by copying a reference to a struct. For example

```
//C++
BookRepository::Date_var origDate = new BookRepository::Date();
BookRepository::Date_var copiedDate = new BookRepository::Date();

// Initialize 'origDate' (not shown)
...

// Make a deep copy of 'origDate'
*copiedDate = *origDate;
```

Assignment of structs is performed using member-wise copying. If a member of a struct is a constructed type (for example, the `publication_date` member of the `BookRepository::BookDetails` struct in Listing 2.9), the constructed type member is also deep copied. See Chapter 4 for further details.

In Java, performing a deep copy of a `struct` type is relatively difficult—the standard IDL-to-Java mapping does not define a `clone()` method for the mapped Java class. The only alternatives are

- To copy the struct explicitly, member by member.
- To use some advanced CORBA features. For example, you could use the dynamic `any` module to make a copy of a struct (see Chapter 19).

Deallocating a Struct

In C++, heap-allocated structs are deallocated using `delete`. However, if you are using a `_var` type, the deallocation is done for you automatically. For example

```
//C++
{
    BookRepository::Date* heapDateP = new BookRepository::Date();
    // Initialize, etc...
    ...
    // Deallocate 'heapDateP' explicitly.
    delete heapDateP;
}
{
    BookRepository::Date_var heapDateV = new BookRepository::Date();
    // Initialize, etc...
    ...
    // No 'delete' necessary
    // 'heapDateV' implicitly deallocates the struct.
}
```

In Java, the garbage collector automatically takes care of deallocating the struct for you.

The Unbounded sequence Type

The mapping of an IDL unbounded sequence to C++ and Java is shown in Table 2.8.

Table 2.8 Mapping for the `struct` *Type*

OMG IDL	C++	Java
typedef	class FooSeq	Foo[]
sequence<Foo>		
FooSeq;	class FooSeq_var	class FooSeqHelper
		class FooSeqHolder

Only unbounded sequences are described here because the bounded `sequence` type is not used very often. For details of bounded sequences, see Chapter 17.

IDL sequences are almost always defined using a `typedef` statement (but there are exceptions to this rule—see the section "Recursive IDL Types," later in this chapter). For example, the following IDL defines a sequence of octets:

```
//IDL
typedef sequence<octet> OctetSeq;
```

The `OctetSeq` type can be used as a parameter or return value of an IDL operation and is a natural type to use for sending binary data.

In C++, an IDL sequence maps to a C++ class of the same name. For example, the IDL `OctetSeq` alias maps to the C++ `OctetSeq` class.

The main functions and operations supported by a C++ sequence object are as follows:

- An `operator[]` that accesses the sequence elements.
- A `length()` accessor function that returns the number of accessible sequence elements.
- A `length()` modifier function that sets the number of accessible sequence elements.
- A `maximum()` accessor function that returns the total number of allocated sequence elements. For an unbounded sequence, the `maximum()` is automatically increased as the `length()` is increased.

A corresponding `_var` type is defined to aid memory management. For example, the `OctetSeq_var` class is generated for `OctetSeq`.

NOTE

A sequence `_var` class has one special property not shared by other `_var` classes: The `operator[]` is overloaded to provide convenient access to the sequence elements. For example, if `v` is a sequence `_var` type, you can access the sequence elements either as `v[j]` or as `(*v)[j]`.

In Java, an IDL sequence type maps directly to a one-dimensional array. For example, `OctetSeq` maps directly to the Java `byte[]` array.

The Holder and Helper classes, `OctetSeqHolder` and `OctetSeqHelper`, are defined. See the section "Java Holder and Helper Types" for details.

Initializing a Sequence

In C++, the `OctetSeq` can be initialized to contain three bytes of data, as follows:

```
//C++
OctetSeq_var theSeq = new OctetSeq(3);  // maximum = 3, length = 0
theSeq->length(3);                       // set length = 3
theSeq[0] = 0x20;    // Use 'operator[]' defined on the _var
theSeq[1] = 0x33;
theSeq[2] = 0x44;
```

You must *always* set the length of a C++ sequence before you use it, because initially the length equals zero. If you already have a block of memory containing some binary data, it would be highly inefficient to copy it into the sequence, octet by octet, in this way. Instead, a special form of the `OctetSeq` constructor can be used, for example

```
//C++
// Given 'buf', which points to binary data

OctetSeq_var theSeq = new OctetSeq(
    1000,     // maximum
    1000,     // length
    buf,      // buffer pointer 'CORBA::Octet*'
    0         // release flag = FALSE
);
```

In this example, `buf` is a pointer to a contiguous buffer containing 1000 bytes of binary data. The release flag is zero, which indicates that the `OctetSeq` destructor should not call `delete buf` as the sequence is destroyed.

In Java, the `OctetSeq` can be initialized to contain three bytes of data, as follows:

```
//Java
byte[] = new byte[3];
byte[0] = 0x20;
byte[1] = 0x33;
byte[2] = 0x44;
```

Because the IDL `octet` type maps to the Java `byte` type, the sequence is a simple `byte[]` array.

Accessing Sequence Elements

In C++, individual elements of a sequence are accessed using the `operator[]`, as for an array. The elements can also be accessed using the `operator[]` defined on the sequence `_var` type.

If an `OctetSeq` contains a large block of binary data, however, it is more efficient to retrieve the data in the form of a single contiguous buffer. The `OctetSeq::get_buffer()` function is supplied for this purpose:

```
//C++
...
CORBA::Octet* buf;
buf = theSeq->get_buffer(
                 0    // orphan flag
              );
```

The orphan flag is `0`, specifying that the sequence retains ownership of the buffer. If the orphan flag is equal to `1`, the sequence either yields ownership if it owns the buffer or returns a `NULL` pointer if it does not.

In Java, the elements of a sequence are accessed as a normal array.

Copying a Sequence

In C++, a sequence is copied using the overloaded `operator=` assignment operator. For example, an `OctetSeq` is copied as follows:

```
//C++
// Allocate the sequence on the stack.
OctetSeq origSeq(1000);     // maximum = 1000, length = 0
// Initialize 'origSeq' (not shown)
...

OctetSeq copiedSeq(0);     // maximum = 0, length = 0
copiedSeq = origSeq;
```

Assignment between two `_var` types also makes a copy of a sequence:

```
//C++
// Allocate the sequence on the heap.
OctetSeq_var origSeqV = new OctetSeq(1000);  // maximum = 1000, length = 0
// Initialize 'origSeq' (not shown)
...

OctetSeq_var copiedSeqV = new OctetSeq(0);    // maximum = 0, length = 0
copiedSeqV = origSeqV;
```

In this respect, `_var` type semantics differ from pointer type semantics because the whole sequence is copied, instead of just a pointer to the sequence. See Chapter 4 for more details.

In Java, a sequence is copied by iterating over the sequence and copying every element, like a normal array:

```
//Java
byte[] origSeq = new byte[1000];
// Initialize 'origSeq' (not shown)
...

byte[] copiedSeq = new byte[origSeq.length];
for (int i; i < origSeq.length; i++) {
    copiedSeq[i]  = origSeq[i];
}
```

Deallocating a Sequence

In C++, heap-allocated sequences are deallocated using `delete`. If you are using a `_var` type, the deallocation is made in the `_var` destructor. See Chapter 4 for details.

In Java, the garbage collector automatically takes care of deallocating the sequence.

Java Holder and Helper Types

In Java, every IDL type, *`IDLType`*, maps to one or more Java types, as follows:

- *`JavaType`* (not defined for type aliases)
  The *`JavaType`* class (or, in some cases, interface) represents an *`IDLType`* instance in Java.
  Type aliases (that is, IDL types defined using a `typedef` declaration) are a special case. There is no mapped *`JavaType`* for a type alias because Java does not support the `typedef` construction. The *`IDLType`* maps to the original (unaliased) Java type instead.
- *`JavaType`*`Holder`
  The *`JavaType`*`Holder` class is needed to enable the passing of `inout` and `out` parameters in an operation invocation.
  Holder classes are defined for all built-in types and all named user-defined types.
- *`JavaType`*`Helper` (not defined for built-in types)
  The *`JavaType`*`Helper` class provides an assortment of standard methods that are useful for manipulating *`JavaType`* instances.
  No Helper class is provided for the built-in types. The equivalent functionality for built-in types is available directly from the ORB runtime library.

Table 2.9 shows how various IDL types map to the corresponding Java Holder and Helper types.

Table 2.9 Java Mapping to Holder and Helper Types

OMG IDL	Java Holder Type	Java Helper Type
`short`	`org.omg.CORBA.ShortHolder`	*none*
`unsigned short`	`org.omg.CORBA.ShortHolder`	*none*
`long`	`org.omg.CORBA.IntHolder`	*none*
`unsigned long`	`org.omg.CORBA.IntHolder`	*none*
`long long`	`org.omg.CORBA.LongHolder`	*none*
`unsigned long long`	`org.omg.CORBA.LongHolder`	*none*
`float`	`org.omg.CORBA.FloatHolder`	*none*
`double`	`org.omg.CORBA.DoubleHolder`	*none*
`long double`	*not yet available*	*none*
`octet`	`org.omg.CORBA.ByteHolder`	*none*
`char`	`org.omg.CORBA.CharHolder`	*none*
`wchar`	`org.omg.CORBA.CharHolder`	*none*
`boolean`	`org.omg.CORBA.BooleanHolder`	*none*
`string`	`org.omg.CORBA.StringHolder`	*none*
`wstring`	`org.omg.CORBA.StringHolder`	*none*
`fixed`	`org.omg.CORBA.FixedHolder`	*none*
`any`	`org.omg.CORBA.AnyHolder`	*none*
`UserType`	*`UserType`*`Holder`	*`UserType`*`Helper`
`typedef` *`OriginalType`* *`AliasType`*`;`	*`AliasType`*`Holder`	*`AliasType`*`Helper`
`Object`	`org.omg.CORBA.ObjectHolder`	*none*
`CORBA::TypeCode`	`org.omg.CORBA.TypeCodeHolder`	*none*

Generally, the naming scheme for Holder types is based on the *mapped* name of the IDL type. For example, the IDL `long long` type has the `org.omg.CORBA.LongHolder` Holder type because the IDL `long long` type maps to the Java `long` type. An IDL user-defined type, `FooScope::Foo`, has the `FooScope.FooHolder` Holder type because the IDL `FooScope::Foo` type maps to the Java `FooScope.Foo` type.

CAUTION

There is one exception to the general rule that a Holder type is named after its mapped Java type. The Holder type for the fixed IDL type is called `FixedHolder`, not `BigDecimalHolder`.

Holder Types

The Holder types are necessary to compensate for the fact that Java's parameter-passing semantics support only pass-by-value, not pass-by-reference. Using `inout` and `out` parameters requires pass-by-reference semantics so that changes made to parameters in the called code are also visible in the calling code.

For example, consider the following IDL:

```
//IDL
interface Test {
    void get_values(inout long inOutVal, out long outVal);
};
```

You might try to map this to the following Java method:

```
//Java
//WRONG! This is not the way 'get_values()' maps to Java.
public void Test.get_values(int inOutVal, int outVal);
```

This naïve attempt at defining an IDL-to-Java mapping for `get_values()` is a failure. When the `get_values()` method is invoked, the `inOutVal` and `outVal` parameters are copied and, in the called code, only the local copies of the parameters can be changed. When `get_values()` returns, the `inOutVal` and `outVal` parameters remain unchanged.

Instead of mapping the `inout` and `out` parameters to a plain `int` type, the parameters map to the `org.omg.CORBA.IntHolder` type. The correct mapping of the `get_values()` operation is

```
//Java
import org.omg.CORBA.*;
public void Test.get_values(IntHolder inOutVal, IntHolder outVal);
```

The `org.omg.CORBA.IntHolder` class is defined in outline as follows:

```
//Java
package org.omg.CORBA;

final public class IntHolder
    implements org.omg.CORBA.portable.Streamable
{
    public int value;

    public IntHolder() {}
    public IntHolder(int initial_value) {...}
    //...
};
```

The public value member is used to hold a Java int value (corresponding to an IDL long). The IntHolder.value member is the actual value of the inout or out parameter. For example, the get_values() operation can be invoked from Java as follows:

```
//Java
import org.omg.CORBA.*;
IntHolder inOutValH = new IntHolder(23);
IntHolder outValH   = new IntHolder();

testObj.get_values(inOutValH, outValH);

System.out.println("Parameters: inOutVal = " + inOutValH.value);
System.out.println("            outVal   = " + outValH.value);
```

The IntHolders must be created before get_values() is invoked. The IntHolder.value field provides access to the inout and out parameters after the invocation returns. Further examples of using Holder types are provided in the section "Returning Parameters," which follows.

Helper Types

The Java Helper classes provide standard methods for manipulating types. Helper types are defined for all user-defined IDL types, including IDL type aliases defined using typedef. No Helper types are defined for built-in types. Refer to Table 2.9.

Given an *IDLType* user-defined type, a partial outline of the corresponding *JavaType*Helper class is as follows:

```
//Java
abstract public class JavaTypeHelper
{
    public static void insert(org.omg.CORBA.Any a, JavaType t) {...}
    public static JavaType extract(org.omg.CORBA.Any a) {...}
    public static org.omg.CORBA.TypeCode type() {...}
    public static string id() {...}
    // only helpers for non-abstract interface with
    // no abstract base interface
    public static JavaType narrow(org.omg.CORBA.Object obj) {...}
    //...
};
```

The methods shown in the preceding example are the most commonly used methods of *JavaType*Helper. A full definition of the Helper class is provided in Chapter 17.

Returning Parameters

In addition to a single return value, CORBA operations also permit you to define out parameters that are effectively like extra return values passed from server to client. The following sections outline how to call and how to implement an operation with out parameters.

Using out Parameters on the Client Side

In C++, out parameters are handled in a number of ways, depending on the type of parameter passed. Details of how to use out parameters in C++ are presented in Chapter 4.

In Java, out parameters are handled using Holder types. A Holder type has to be used for an out parameter because Java does not natively support pass-by-reference semantics. For example, the invocation of the `SearchableCollection::find_by_title()` operation, which has an out parameter of type `BookRepository::DetailsSeq`, is shown in Listing 2.17.

Listing 2.17 Java Invocation of the `SearchableCollection::find_by_title()` *Operation*

```
//Java
//-----------------------------------------------------
// Given the following variables are already initialized:
//    theSearchableCollection - an object reference

// Step 1: Prepare the parameters.
String book_        title = "Of Mice and Men";
BookDetailsSeqHolder detailsSeqH = new BookDetailsSeqHolder();
boolean wasFound;
// Step 2: Invoke 'find_by_title()'.
wasFound = theSearchableCollection.find_by_title(
                              book_title,    // 'in' parameter
                              detailsSeqH    // 'out' parameter
                         );
// Step 3: Use the returned sequence, 'detailsSeqH.value'
//...(not shown)...
```

The second parameter of the `find_by_title()` operation, `detailsSeqH`, is an out parameter. It is used as follows:

1. **Prepare the parameters** A Holder object of `BookRepository.BookDetailsSeqHolder` type, `detailsSeqH`, is allocated but not initialized.
2. **Invoke `find_by_title()`** The `detailsSeqH` Holder object is passed as a placeholder to receive the out parameter from the server.
3. **Use the returned sequence** After the invocation, the returned sequence is accessible as `detailsSeqH.value`.

Using out Parameters on the Server Side

In C++, the server side also handles out parameters in different ways according to the parameter type. This is beyond the scope of this chapter—details are presented in Chapter 4.

In Java, the server code has to initialize the value of a Holder object for each `out` parameter. Listing 2.18 shows how this is done in the implementation of `find_by_title()`.

Listing 2.18 Java Implementation of the `SearchableCollection::find_by_title()` *Operation*

```
//Java
// Defined in class 'SearchableCollectionImpl'
public boolean find_by_title(
    java.lang.String              title,
    BookDetailsSeqHolder books_found
)
throws org.omg.CORBA.SystemException
{
    books_found.value = m_collection_db.getByTitle(title);
    return (books_found.value.length > 0);
}
```

The second parameter, `books_found`, is an `out` parameter. It is initialized by assigning a `BookDetailsSeq` object to `books_found.value`.

Adding Exception Handling—Example 3

The third example adds the `BorrowableCollection` IDL interface, which supports a single operation, `borrow_book()`, to let you record the borrowing of a book.

Listing 2.19 shows the `BookRepository` IDL module with these additions.

Listing 2.19 IDL `BookRepository` *Module for Example 3*

```
//IDL

module BookRepository {
    typedef long ISBN;

    struct PersonName {
        string first_name;
        string second_name;
    };

    struct Date {
        short day;
        short month;
        short year;
    };

    struct BookDetails {
        PersonName   author;
        string       title;
```

Listing 2.19 continued

```
        ISBN         book_id;
        Date         publication_date;
    };
    typedef sequence<BookDetails> BookDetailsSeq;

    enum FuzzyBoolean {NO, YES, UNKNOWN};

    interface Collection {
        readonly attribute long    number_of_books;
        attribute          string  name_of_collection;

        FuzzyBoolean is_in_collection(in ISBN book_id);
    };

    interface SearchableCollection : Collection {
        boolean find_by_title(
                    in string          title,
                    out BookDetailsSeq books_found
                );
    };

    interface BorrowableCollection : Collection {
        exception Unavailable {
            Date when_available;
        };

        void borrow_book(
                in ISBN       book_id,
                in PersonName borrower,
                out Date      return_date
            )
            raises (Unavailable);
    };
    //...
};
```

The following IDL constructs are introduced in Listing 2.19:

- A CORBA user exception, `Unavailable`, is defined within the scope of the `BorrowableCollection` interface. The exception definition is introduced by the `exception` keyword, and syntactically it resembles a struct definition. An exception has member fields, like a struct, that enable you to pass useful information about the exception condition back to the client.
- A `raises()` clause is added to the `borrow_book()` operation declaration to indicate that `borrow_book()` can raise the `Unavailable` user exception. A user exception is not supported unless it is declared in the `raises()` clause of an operation.

The following sections show you how to implement a client and a server in both C++ and Java, using the IDL from Listing 2.19.

Client Code

Listing 2.20 and Listing 2.21 give the code for a client of the `BookRepository::BorrowableCollection` interface in C++ and Java, respectively. The `bk_borrow` client invokes the `borrow_book()` operation to record the borrowing of a book. If the book is already on loan, the `BookRepository::BorrowableCollection::Unavailable` user exception is caught by the client.

Listing 2.20 C++ Client of the `BorrowableCollection` *Interface*

```
//C++
#include <iostream.h>
#include <fstream.h>
#include <stdlib.h>
#include <sstream>

#include "BookRepository.hh"

CORBA::ORB_var
global_orb = CORBA::ORB::_nil();

// read_reference() -- read an object reference from file.
// ...same definition as Example 1...

int
main(int argc, char **argv)
{
    try
    {
        CORBA::Object_var objV;  // For temporary object references.

        // Initialize the ORB.
        global_orb = CORBA::ORB_init(argc, argv);

        // Parse command line arguments:
        if (argc != 4) {
            cout << "Usage: bk_borrow "
                 << "<your_first_name> <your_second_name> <book_id>" << endl;
            exit(0);
        }
        const char * borrower_first_name  = argv[1];
        const char * borrower_second_name = argv[2];
        const char * isbn_string          = argv[3];

        // Obtain 'BookRepository::BorrowableCollection' object reference.
        objV = read_reference("BookRepository_BorrowableCollection.ref");
```

Listing 2.20 continued

```
        BookRepository::BorrowableCollection_var borrowableCollectionV =
            BookRepository::BorrowableCollection::_narrow(objV);
        if (CORBA::is_nil(borrowableCollectionV ))
        {
            cerr << "error: failed to narrow BorrowableCollection." << endl;
            exit(1);
        }

        // Invoke 'borrow_book()' operation.
        CORBA::Long book_id;
        std::string s = isbn_string;
        std::istringstream ist(s);
        ist >> book_id;
        BookRepository::PersonName borrower;
        borrower.first_name  = CORBA::string_dup(borrower_first_name);
        borrower.second_name = CORBA::string_dup(borrower_second_name);
        BookRepository::Date_var return_dateV;
        try {
            borrowableCollectionV->borrow_book(
                                       book_id,
                                       borrower,
                                       return_dateV.out()
                                   );
            cout << "Book [ISBN=" << book_id << "] has been borrowed." << endl;
            cout << "Please return by: "
                 << return_dateV->day   << "/"
                 << return_dateV->month << "/"
                 << return_dateV->year  << endl;
        }
        catch (BookRepository::BorrowableCollection::Unavailable& bk_ex) {
            cout << "Sorry, book [ISBN=" << book_id
                 << "] is unavailable until "
                 << bk_ex.when_available.day   << "/"
                 << bk_ex.when_available.month << "/"
                 << bk_ex.when_available.year  << endl;
        }
    }
    catch(CORBA::Exception &ex)
    {
        cerr << "Unexpected CORBA exception: " << ex << endl;
    }

    try
    {
        global_orb->shutdown(1);
        global_orb->destroy();
    }
```

Listing 2.20 continued

```
    catch (...)
    {
        // Do nothing.
    }
    return 0;
}
```

Listing 2.21 Java Client of the `BorrowableCollection` *Interface*

```
//Java
package Pure.BookRepository;

import org.omg.CORBA.*;
import org.omg.PortableServer.*;
import java.io.*;
import Pure.BookRepository.BorrowableCollectionPackage.*;

public class bk_borrow
{

   // global_orb -- make ORB public
   public static org.omg.CORBA.ORB global_orb = null;


   // read_reference() -- read an object reference from file.
   // ...same definition as Example 1...

   public static void main (String args[])
   {
      try
      {
         // Initialize the ORB.
         global_orb = ORB.init(args, null);

         String app_args[] = remove_ORB_args(args);

        // Parse command line arguments:
        if (app_args.length != 3) {
            System.out.println("Usage: bk_borrow "
                 + "<your_first_name> <your_second_name> <book_id>");
            System.exit(1);
        }
        String borrower_first_name  = app_args[0];
        String borrower_second_name = app_args[1];
        String isbn_string          = app_args[2];

        // Obtain 'BookRepository::BorrowableCollection' object reference.
        org.omg.CORBA.Object obj;
```

Listing 2.21 continued

```
        obj = read_reference("BookRepository_BorrowableCollection.ref");
        BorrowableCollection theBorrowableCollection
            = BorrowableCollectionHelper.narrow(obj);

        // Invoke 'borrow_book()' operation.
        int book_id;
        book_id = Integer.parseInt(isbn_string);
        PersonName borrower  = new PersonName();
        borrower.first_name  = borrower_first_name;
        borrower.second_name = borrower_second_name;
        DateHolder return_dateH  = new DateHolder();
        try {
            theBorrowableCollection.borrow_book(
                                       book_id,
                                       borrower,
                                       return_dateH
                                   );
            System.out.println("Book [ISBN="
                + book_id + "] has been borrowed.");
            System.out.println("Please return by: "
                 + return_dateH.value.day   + "/"
                 + return_dateH.value.month + "/"
                 + return_dateH.value.year);
        }
        catch (Unavailable bk_ex) {
            System.out.println("Sorry, book [ISBN="
                 + book_id + "] is unavailable until "
                 + bk_ex.when_available.day   + "/"
                 + bk_ex.when_available.month + "/"
                 + bk_ex.when_available.year);
        }
      }
      catch(Exception ex)
      {
         System.out.println("Unexpected CORBA exception: " + ex);
      }

      try
      {
         global_orb.shutdown(true);
         global_orb.destroy();
      }
      catch (Exception ex)
      {
         // Do nothing.
      }
      return;
   }
}
```

The bk_search client performs the following steps:

1. **Initialize the ORB** A new ORB object is created and assigned to global_orb.
2. **Obtain an object reference** A BookRepository::BorrowableCollection object reference is obtained by reading a stringified object reference from the BookRepository_BorrowableCollection.ref file.
3. **Invoke the borrow_book() operation** The borrow_book() operation is invoked to record the borrowing of a book.
   In C++, after a successful invocation, the return_dateV variable holds the date when the borrower is expected to return the book. Because return_dateV is an out parameter, it is not initialized prior to the invocation. See the section "Returning Parameters," earlier in this chapter.
   In Java, after a successful invocation, the return_dateH variable holds the date when the borrower is expected to return the book. Because return_dateH is an out parameter, it is declared as a DateHolder type. After the invocation, the return date is given by return_dateH.value. See the sections "Java Holder and Helper Types" and "Returning Parameters," earlier in this chapter.
4. **Catch the Unavailable user exception** If the book is already on loan, the server raises the Unavailable user exception. This exception, bk_ex, is caught explicitly by the client code.
   The client examines the body of the Unavailable exception (refer to Listing 2.19) to find out when the book is expected to become available again. The when_available field of bk_ex contains the expected availability date, which is in the form of a BookRepository::Date struct.
5. **Shut down the ORB** Two calls, CORBA::ORB::shutdown() and CORBA::ORB::destroy(), are made to shut down the ORB.

Server Code

The server code for Example 3 implements the BorrowableCollection IDL interface and illustrates how CORBA user exceptions are thrown.

Listing 2.22 shows the declaration of the C++ BookRepository_BorrowableCollectionImpl class, which provides the implementation of the BookRepository::BorrowableCollection interface.

Listing 2.22 C++ BookRepository_BorrowableCollectionImpl Class Declaration

```
//C++
#ifndef BOOKREPOSITORY_BORROWABLECOLLECTIONIMPL_H_
#define BOOKREPOSITORY_BORROWABLECOLLECTIONIMPL_H_

#include "BookRepositoryS.hh"
#include "BookRepository_CollectionImpl.h"
```

Listing 2.22 continued

```
#include "Borrower_DB.h"


class BookRepository_BorrowableCollectionImpl :
    public virtual POA_BookRepository::BorrowableCollection,
    public virtual BookRepository_CollectionImpl
{
public:
    BookRepository_BorrowableCollectionImpl(PortableServer::POA_ptr);

    virtual ~BookRepository_BorrowableCollectionImpl();

    //----------
    // IDL operations
    //----------
    virtual void
    borrow_book(
        BookRepository::ISBN            book_id,
        const BookRepository::PersonName& borrower,
        BookRepository::Date_out        return_date
    ) throw (
        CORBA::SystemException,
        BookRepository::BorrowableCollection::Unavailable
    );

private:
    // Private member variables.
    Borrower_DB                 m_borrower_db;

    // Private member functions
    BookRepository::Date&
    current_date();

    void
    increment_date(BookRepository::Date& given_date, int days);

    // ...
};

#endif
```

The declaration of the `BookRepository_BorrowableCollectionImpl` class follows the same pattern as the `BookRepository_SearchableCollectionImpl` class of Example 2. One new IDL operation, `borrow_book()`, is declared.

Two private functions, `current_date()` and `increment_date()`, are declared to facilitate working with dates.

The Borrower_DB database wrapper class accesses a database table that records every book that has been borrowed but not yet returned. An instance of the Borrower_DB class, m_borrower_db, is created to provide the necessary access to the database.

Listing 2.23 and Listing 2.24 show the implementation of the servant methods for C++ and Java, respectively.

Listing 2.23 C++ Implementation of **BookRepository::BorrowableCollection**

```
//C++

#include <stdlib.h>
#include <iostream.h>
#include "BookRepository_BorrowableCollectionImpl.h"

#include <time.h>

// Constructor
BookRepository_BorrowableCollectionImpl::\
BookRepository_BorrowableCollectionImpl(
    PortableServer::POA_ptr the_poa
) :
    BookRepository_CollectionImpl(the_poa)
{
}

// Destructor.
BookRepository_BorrowableCollectionImpl::\
~BookRepository_BorrowableCollectionImpl()
{
}

BookRepository::Date&
BookRepository_BorrowableCollectionImpl::current_date()
{
    time_t utc_time = time(0);
    tm *   time_details = gmtime(&utc_time);

    BookRepository::Date* todayP = new BookRepository::Date();
    todayP->day   = (CORBA::Short) time_details->tm_mday;
    todayP->month = (CORBA::Short) time_details->tm_mon + 1;
    todayP->year  = (CORBA::Short) time_details->tm_year + 1900;
    return *todayP;
}

void
```

Listing 2.23 continued

```
BookRepository_BorrowableCollectionImpl::increment_date(
    BookRepository::Date& given_date,
    int days
)
{
    static const int seconds_per_day = 24*60*60;

    tm time_details;
    time_details.tm_sec   = 0;
    time_details.tm_min   = 0;
    time_details.tm_hour  = 2;
    time_details.tm_mday  = given_date.day;
    time_details.tm_mon   = given_date.month - 1;
    time_details.tm_year  = given_date.year - 1900;
    time_details.tm_isdst = -1;
    time_t utc_time = mktime(&time_details);

    utc_time += days*seconds_per_day;

    tm *   new_details = gmtime(&utc_time);
    given_date.day   = (CORBA::Short) new_details->tm_mday;
    given_date.month = (CORBA::Short) new_details->tm_mon + 1;
    given_date.year  = (CORBA::Short) new_details->tm_year + 1900;
}

// borrow_book()
void
BookRepository_BorrowableCollectionImpl::borrow_book(
    BookRepository::ISBN            book_id,
    const BookRepository::PersonName& borrower,
    BookRepository::Date_out        return_date
) throw (
    CORBA::SystemException,
    BookRepository::BorrowableCollection::Unavailable
)
{
    Borrower_DB::LoanRecord loan;

    // Check availability of book:
    if ( m_borrower_db.get(book_id, loan) ) {
        // Throw CORBA user exception
        throw BookRepository::BorrowableCollection::Unavailable(
                  loan.return_date
              );
    }
```

Listing 2.23 continued

```
    // Calculate the return date (today + two weeks)
    return_date = current_date();
    increment_date(return_date, 14);

    // Create a record of the loan in the Borrower_DB database.
    loan.borrower = borrower;
    loan.return_date = return_date;
    m_borrower_db.put(book_id, loan);
}
```

Listing 2.24 Java Implementation of **BookRepository::BorrowableCollection**

```
//Java
package Pure.BookRepository;

import org.omg.CORBA.ORB;
import Pure.BookRepository.Borrower_DB;
import Pure.BookRepository.BorrowableCollectionPackage.*;


public class BorrowableCollectionImpl
    extends Pure.BookRepository.BorrowableCollectionPOA
{
    // Private member variables
    private int                         m_number_of_books;
    private java.lang.String            m_name_of_collection;
    private Borrower_DB                 m_borrower_db;
    private org.omg.PortableServer.POA  m_poa = null;

    public BorrowableCollectionImpl(org.omg.PortableServer.POA poa)
    {
        m_poa = poa;
        m_number_of_books    = 1000;
        m_name_of_collection = "AssortedBooks";
        m_borrower_db        = new Borrower_DB();
    }

    public FuzzyBoolean
    is_in_collection(
            int                             book_id
    )
    throws org.omg.CORBA.SystemException
    {
```

Listing 2.24 continued

```
        return FuzzyBoolean.UNKNOWN;
    }

    public Pure.BookRepository.Date
    current_date()
    {
        Pure.BookRepository.Date today
            = new Pure.BookRepository.Date();

        java.util.Calendar c = java.util.Calendar.getInstance();
        today.day   = (short) c.get(java.util.Calendar.DATE);
        today.month = (short) (c.get(java.util.Calendar.MONTH) + 1);
        today.year  = (short) c.get(java.util.Calendar.YEAR);

        return today;
    }

    public Pure.BookRepository.Date
    increment_date(
        Pure.BookRepository.Date given_date,
        int days
    )
    {
        Pure.BookRepository.Date new_date
            = new Pure.BookRepository.Date();

        java.util.Calendar c = java.util.Calendar.getInstance();
        c.set((int) given_date.year,
              (int) given_date.month - 1,
              (int) given_date.day
        );
        c.add(java.util.Calendar.DATE, days);

        new_date.day   = (short) c.get(java.util.Calendar.DATE);
        new_date.month = (short) (c.get(java.util.Calendar.MONTH) + 1);
        new_date.year  = (short) c.get(java.util.Calendar.YEAR);
        return new_date;
    }

    public void borrow_book(
            int                            book_id,
            Pure.BookRepository.PersonName borrower,
            Pure.BookRepository.DateHolder return_date
    )
    throws org.omg.CORBA.SystemException,
           Pure.BookRepository.BorrowableCollectionPackage.Unavailable
    {
```

Listing 2.24 continued

```
        // Check availability of book:
        Borrower_DB.LoanRecord loan = m_borrower_db.get(book_id);
        if ( loan != null ) {
            // Throw CORBA user exception.
            throw new Unavailable(loan.return_date);
        }

        // Calculate the return date (today + two weeks).
        return_date.value = increment_date(current_date(), 14);

        // Create a record of the loan in the Borrower_DB database.
        loan = new Borrower_DB.LoanRecord();
        loan.borrower = borrower;
        loan.return_date = return_date.value;
        m_borrower_db.put(book_id, loan);
    }

    public int number_of_books()
    {
        return m_number_of_books;
    }

    public java.lang.String name_of_collection()
    {
        return m_name_of_collection;
    }

    public
    void name_of_collection(
           java.lang.String                _new_value)
    {
       m_name_of_collection = _new_value;
    }

    public org.omg.PortableServer.POA _default_POA()
    {
      return m_poa;
    }
}
```

The date functions, `current_date()` and `increment_date()`, are implemented using the standard POSIX time functions in C++ (declared in the `time.h` header file) and are implemented using the `java.util.Calendar` class in Java. The `current_date()` function returns today's date in the form of a `BookRepository::Date`, and the `increment_date()` function adds the specified number of days to the given date.

The implementation of the `borrow_book()` function illustrates how CORBA user exceptions are thrown in a server. The `borrow_book()` function signature lists `Unavailable` as one of the exceptions that might be thrown. The availability of the book identified by `book_id` is checked by invoking `Borrower_DB::get()` in C++ and `Borrower_DB.get()` in Java (see the declaration of the `Borrower_DB` class in Listing 2.25 and Listing 2.26). There are two possible outcomes, depending on the result of the `get()` call:

- If a `book_id` loan record does *not* exist, the book is available. A new loan record is created that stores the borrower's name and the calculated return date (two weeks from today) along with the `book_id`, which is used as a database key. The return date, `return_date`, is returned as an `out` parameter.
- If a `book_id` loan record *does* exist, the book is already on loan and is therefore unavailable. The server throws an `Unavailable` CORBA user exception to indicate to the client that the book cannot be borrowed at this time. The expected return date, `loan.return_date`, is passed to the `Unavailable` constructor and initializes the `when_available` field of the exception.

Both the C++ and Java servants delegate some functionality to a database class, `Borrower_DB`. The `Borrower_DB` class is a wrapper class that records every book that has been borrowed but not yet returned. Listing 2.25 and Listing 2.26 show the declarations of the `Borrower_DB` methods.

Listing 2.25 C++ Declaration of the `Borrower_DB` *Class*

```
// C++
#ifndef _BORROWER_DB_
#define _BORROWER_DB_

...

// Inlude definitions from the stub code.
#include "BookRepository.hh"

class Borrower_DB {
public:
    struct LoanRecord {
        BookRepository::PersonName borrower;
        BookRepository::Date       return_date;
    };

    Borrower_DB();

    CORBA::Boolean
    get(CORBA::Long book_id, LoanRecord&);

    CORBA::Boolean
    put(CORBA::Long book_id, const LoanRecord&);
```

Listing 2.25 continued

```
private:
    ...
};
#endif
```

Listing 2.26 Java Declaration of the `Borrower_DB` *Class*

```
// Java
package Pure.BookRepository;

public class Borrower_DB {

    // Public static inner class
    public static class LoanRecord {
        public PersonName                borrower;
        public Pure.BookRepository.Date return_date;
    };

    // Private member variables
    //...

    public Borrower_DB()
    { ... }

    public LoanRecord get(int book_id)
    { ... }

    public boolean put(int book_id, LoanRecord new_loan)
    { ... }
}
```

The `LoanRecord` type, declared in the `Borrower_DB` scope, is used to hold a record of the `borrower` name (of `BookRepository::PersonName` type) and the `return_date` (of `BookRepository::Date` type).

There are two public methods declared in the `Borrower_DB` class:

- The `put()` function creates a new database record containing the `book_id` (database key) and the `new_loan` record.
- The `get()` function searches for a database record using `book_id` as a key.

The `Borrower_DB` class can be implemented using the database adapter of your choice. The implementation details are not shown here.

IDL Mapping (3)

CORBA has a well-developed exception-handling capability that integrates with languages such as C++ and Java that support native exception handling. There are two categories of CORBA exceptions:

- **CORBA user exceptions** These are open-ended exceptions that can be defined in IDL by the application developer. User exceptions reflect application-level semantics. See the section "CORBA User Exceptions".
- **CORBA system exceptions** These are a closed set of exceptions, pre-defined by the CORBA specification. System exceptions are reserved for ORB-level exceptions and are usually thrown by the ORB runtime, not by the application developer See the section "CORBA System Exceptions," which follows.

All exceptions thrown by a CORBA invocation, whether local or remote, must fall into one of these two categories. A CORBA invocation that throws an exception that is not a user or system exception might be a symptom of a bug in the ORB runtime.

Figure 2.3 shows the overall hierarchy of CORBA exception classes in C++.

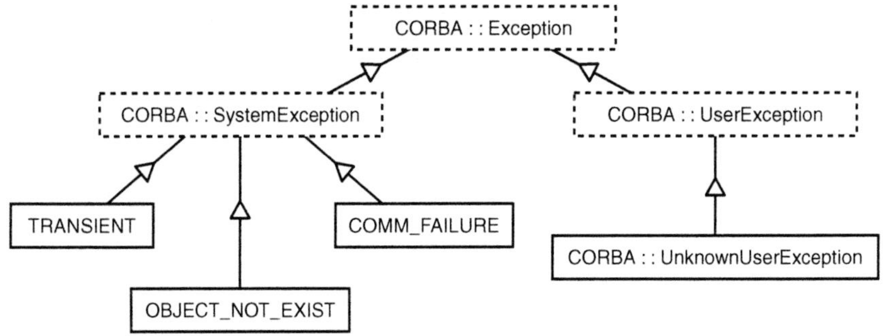

Figure 2.3

The C++ exception class hierarchy.

The `CORBA::Exception` class is the abstract base class for all CORBA exceptions in C++ (no direct instances can be created). The two main categories of exception, `CORBA::UserException` and `CORBA::SystemException`, are derived from `CORBA::Exception` and serve as base classes for the different types of user and system exceptions, respectively.

The `CORBA::UnknownUserException` class is a special type of user exception that is used in conjunction with the dynamic invocation interface (DII). See Chapter 20, "Dynamic Invocation Interface," for details.

Figure 2.4 shows the overall hierarchy of CORBA exception classes in Java.

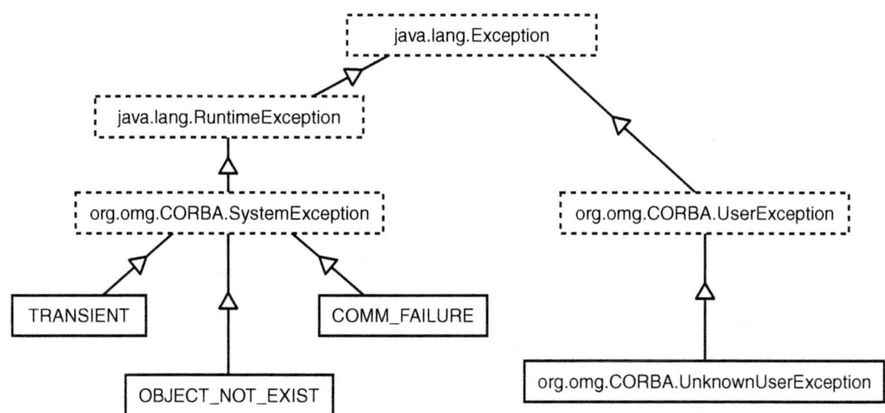

Figure 2.4

The Java exception class hierarchy.

The `java.lang.Exception` class is the abstract base class for all CORBA exceptions in Java (no direct instances can be created). The two main categories of exception are `org.omg.CORBA.UserException` and `org.omg.CORBA.SystemException`. The `UserException` and `SystemException` classes derive from `java.lang.Exception` in different ways, affecting the way the exceptions are treated:

- **Checked exceptions** Because `UserException` extends `java.lang.Exception` directly, it is treated as a *checked exception*. Java forces you to handle checked exceptions by refusing to compile your code unless you either catch the exception or insert a `throws` clause in the method signature.
- **Unchecked exceptions** Because `SystemException` extends `java.lang.RuntimeException` directly, it is treated as an *unchecked exception*. Java does not require you to handle unchecked exceptions. However, it is good practice to catch `SystemExceptions` anyway.

The `org.omg.CORBA.UnknownUserException` class is a special type of user exception that is used in conjunction with the dynamic invocation interface (DII). See Chapter 20 for details.

The following subsections provide a basic introduction to CORBA user and system exceptions. The first subsection explains why the Java mapping of the `Unavailable` user exception in Example 3 appears in the scope of the `BookRepository.BorrowableCollectionPackage` Java package.

Java Mapping for Types Declared in IDL Interfaces

In most cases, a scoped IDL type name maps directly to an equivalent scoped Java type name. For example, the `A::B::C` IDL type usually maps to the `A.B.C` Java type (making allowance for the special cases that arise when there is a risk of clashing identifiers—see the section "IDL Identifiers," earlier in this chapter). However, when a type is defined within the scope of an IDL interface, the Java mapping treats it as a special case.

Consider the following IDL:

```
//IDL
exception FooAtGlobalScope { };
module M {
    exception FooAtModuleScope { };
    interface I {
        exception FooAtInterfaceScope { };
    };
};
```

The exception types defined in the preceding IDL are mapped to Java, as shown in Table 2.10.

Table 2.10 Java Mapping of Exception Types Defined at Different Scopes

IDL Scoped Name	Java Scoped Name
`::FooAtGlobalScope`	`FooAtGlobalScope`
`::M::FooAtModuleScope`	`M.FooAtModuleScope`
`::M::I::FooAtInterfaceScope`	`M.IPackage.FooAtInterfaceScope`

The `FooAtInterfaceScope` exception class is put into the `M.IPackage` Java package instead of appearing at the `M.I` scope. The exception class cannot be defined at the `M.I` scope because `M.I` is a Java interface, and Java interfaces do not support inner classes.

TIP

The general rule is: If applying the default Java mapping rules would put a class into the scope of a Java interface, `I`, the class is put into the `IPackage` scope instead.

This rule affects all IDL types defined in the scope of an interface. It also affects related Java Helper and Holder classes.

CORBA User Exceptions

User exceptions are thrown by server developers to signal application-level exceptions that occur while processing IDL operations. Client developers can then catch and process the user exception. User exceptions offer the following advantages:

- **Informative exceptions** User exceptions can contain data that provides details about the exception condition.
- **Integration with native exception handling** You can raise and handle user exceptions using the familiar `throw`/`catch` native syntax in both C++ and Java.

- **Propagation across the network** When a user exception is thrown in the body of an operation, the exception propagates back to the code that invoked the operation. If the invocation is remote, the ORB sends exception data back across the network and re-creates the exception on the client side.

The following subsections explain how user exceptions work in practice.

IDL Syntax of User Exceptions

A user exception must be declared in IDL before it can be used by either a client or a server. There are two aspects of IDL syntax relating to user exceptions:

- **Exception type declaration** The declaration of an exception type is similar to a struct, except that the exception declaration is introduced by the `exception` keyword instead of the `struct` keyword.
- **Raises clause** A `raises` clause, `raises(`*exc1*`,`*exc2*`,...)`, containing a comma separated list of user exceptions must be appended to the declaration of exception-raising operations. The absence of a `raises()` clause implies that *no* user exceptions can be raised.

For example, the following IDL declares an `OutOfRange` exception that is used within a graphics package to indicate when a line extends beyond the limits of the screen:

```
//IDL
module Graphics {
    interface Screen {
        exception OutOfRange {
            long maxHeight;
            long maxWidth;
        };

        void draw(x1, y1, x2, y2) raises (OutOfRange);
    };
};
```

The `OutOfRange` exception has two fields, `maxHeight` and `maxWidth`, that can be set to the current screen limits when the exception is raised. The `draw()` operation specifies a `raises()` clause to enable it to throw the `OutOfRange` exception.

Throwing User Exceptions

In both C++ and Java, a constructor that initializes the exception fields is provided. For example, the `OutOfRange` exception can be thrown as shown in the following C++ and Java code:

```
//C++
throw Graphics::Screen::OutOfRange(1000, 2000);

//Java
throw new Graphics.ScreenPackage.OutOfRange(1000, 2000);
```

The constructor arguments initialize the exception fields according to the order declared in IDL (in this case, `maxHeight` is initialized to `1000` and `maxWidth` to `2000`).

In C++, note the contrast between a mapped exception, which supports a multi-argument constructor, and a mapped struct, which does not.

In Java, because `OutOfRange` is declared inside the scope of an IDL interface, `Screen`, the Java `OutOfRange` class is placed in an *`InterfaceName`*`Package` scope.

Catching User Exceptions

User exceptions can be caught individually if desired using standard C++ and Java syntax:

```
//C++
// Given 'screenObj' is initialized as a 'Graphics::Screen' object
try {
    screenObj->draw(x1, y1, x2, y2);
}
catch (Graphics::Screen::OutOfRange& oor) {
    cerr << "error: exceeded range: "
         << "maxHeight = " << oor.maxHeight
         << "maxWidth = "  << oor.maxWidth << endl;
}

//Java
// Given 'screenObj' is initialized as a 'Graphics::Screen' object
try {
    screenObj.draw(x1, y1, x2, y2);
}
catch (Graphics.ScreenPackage.OutOfRange oor) {
    System.out.println("error: exceeded range: "
         + "maxHeight = " + oor.maxHeight
         + "maxWidth = "  + oor.maxWidth  );
}
```

Alternatively, you can catch the user exception generically as a `CORBA::UserException` in C++ and an `org.omg.CORBA.UserException` in Java.

CORBA System Exceptions

System exceptions are thrown by the ORB runtime to warn users of low-level errors in the ORB or incorrect use of the ORB programming interface. System exceptions are not usually thrown by the application developer, but it is legal (and occasionally useful) to do so.

Table 2.11 lists a sample of commonly encountered system exceptions, with an explanation of the most common cause of each exception:

Table 2.11 Commonly Encountered System Exceptions

System Exception	Most Common Cause
CORBA::TRANSIENT	The client failed to open a network connection to a server.
CORBA::COMM_FAILURE	The client has already established a network connection, but a network problem subsequently arises.
CORBA::OBJECT_NOT_EXIST	The server cannot find the particular CORBA object you are trying to use.
CORBA::UNKNOWN	The operation implementation raised a non-CORBA exception.

Chapter 21, "CORBA System Exceptions," contains definitions of these and other system exceptions. The following subsections explain how system exceptions work in practice.

Throwing System Exceptions

It is occasionally useful for an application developer to throw system exceptions. You might find it useful to raise a system exception when

- A particular system exception provides a good match for an exception condition that occurs in your application code.
- Constraints on the design of your IDL interfaces prevent you from adding new user exceptions where they are needed. System exceptions might be used as approximate substitutes in some cases.

One advantage of system exceptions is that they do not have to be declared in the `raises()` clause of an operation—system exceptions are always available. To throw a system exception, *SysExc*, use one of the following constructors in C++ and Java:

```
//C++
CORBA::SysExc(CORBA::ULong minor, CORBA::CompletionStatus status);
CORBA::SysExc();

//Java
org.omg.CORBA.SysExc(int minor, org.omg.CORBA.CompletionStatus status);
org.omg.CORBA.SysExc();
```

The first system exception constructor takes two arguments. The minor code number, `minor`, specifies the system exception more precisely. The completion status, `status`, indicates whether or not the invocation had finished before the exception was raised. See Chapter 23 for details.

The default system exception constructor sets the minor code to `0` and the completion status to `COMPLETED_MAYBE`.

Consider for example the `CORBA::PERSIST_STORE` system exception, which can be raised when there is a problem with persistent storage on the server side. `CORBA::PERSIST_STORE` is thrown as follows in C++ and Java:

```
//C++
throw CORBA::PERSIST_STORE(0, CORBA::COMPLETED_NO);

//Java
throw new org.omg.CORBA.PERSIST_STORE(
    0, org.omg.CORBA.completion_status.COMPLETED_NO
);
```

Catching System Exceptions

System exceptions can be caught individually using standard C++ and Java syntax:

```
//C++
// Given 'screenObj' is initialized as a 'Graphics::Screen' object
try {
    screenObj->draw(x1, y1, x2, y2);
}
catch (CORBA::TRANSIENT& sysEx) {
    cerr << "error: failed to connect to server: " << sysEx << endl;
}

//Java
// Given 'screenObj' is initialized as a 'Graphics::Screen' object
try {
    screenObj.draw(x1, y1, x2, y2);
}
catch (org.omg.CORBA.TRANSIENT sysEx) {
    System.out.println("error: failed to connect to server: " + sysEx);
}
```

Alternatively, you can catch the system exception generically as a `CORBA::SystemException` in C++ and an `org.omg.CORBA.SystemException` in Java.

Adding a Multiply-Inheriting IDL Interface—Example 4

The fourth example adds the `FlexibleCollection` IDL interface, which inherits from both the `SearchableCollection` and `BorrowableCollection` interfaces. The `FlexibleCollection` interface enables the server application to define a book collection that supports both book-searching operations and book-borrowing operations.

Listing 2.27 shows the `BookRepository` IDL module with this addition.

Listing 2.27 IDL `BookRepository` *Module for Example 4*

```
//IDL

module BookRepository {
    //...
    interface Collection {
```

Listing 2.27 continued

```
        //...
    };

    interface SearchableCollection : Collection {
        //...
    };

    interface BorrowableCollection : Collection {
        //...
    };

    interface FlexibleCollection
      : BorrowableCollection, SearchableCollection { };
};
```

No new operations or attributes are defined in `FlexibleCollection`. The `FlexibleCollection` interface illustrates the syntax for declaring multiple inheritance in IDL—a colon (`:`) followed by a comma-separated list of interface names.

The next section shows you how to implement the `FlexibleCollection` interface in both C++ and Java.

Server Code

The server code for Example 4 implements the `FlexibleCollection` IDL interface and illustrates how to implement a multiply inheriting IDL interface.

Listing 2.28 shows the declaration of the C++ `BookRepository_FlexibleCollectionImpl` class, which provides the implementation of the `BookRepository::FlexibleCollection` interface.

Listing 2.28 C++ `BookRepository_FlexibleCollectionImpl` Class Declaration

```
//C++
#ifndef BOOKREPOSITORY_FLEXIBLECOLLECTIONIMPL_H_
#define BOOKREPOSITORY_FLEXIBLECOLLECTIONIMPL_H_

#include "BookRepositoryS.hh"
#include "BookRepository_BorrowableCollectionImpl.h"
#include "BookRepository_SearchableCollectionImpl.h"

class BookRepository_FlexibleCollectionImpl :
    public virtual POA_BookRepository::FlexibleCollection,
    public virtual BookRepository_BorrowableCollectionImpl,
    public virtual BookRepository_SearchableCollectionImpl
{
public:
```

Listing 2.28 continued

```
    BookRepository_FlexibleCollectionImpl(PortableServer::POA_ptr);
    virtual ~BookRepository_FlexibleCollectionImpl();

private:
    //...
};

#endif
```

The C++ `BookRepository_FlexibleCollectionImpl` class inherits from `BookRepository_BorrowableCollectionImpl` and `BookRepository_SearchableCollectionImpl`, from which it gets the definitions of all its operations and attributes. The C++ implementation inheritance tree is thus a mirror of the IDL inheritance tree.

The C++ `BookRepository_FlexibleCollectionImpl` class also inherits from `POA_BookRepository::FlexibleCollection`, which indicates to the ORB that it is an implementation of the `FlexibleCollection` IDL interface.

Listing 2.29 shows the implementation of the servant methods for C++.

Listing 2.29 C++ Implementation of `BookRepository::FlexibleCollection`

```
//C++
#include <stdlib.h>
#include <iostream.h>
#include "BookRepository_FlexibleCollectionImpl.h"

// Constructor
BookRepository_FlexibleCollectionImpl::BookRepository_FlexibleCollectionImpl(
    PortableServer::POA_ptr the_poa
) :
    BookRepository_CollectionImpl(the_poa),
    BookRepository_BorrowableCollectionImpl(the_poa),
    BookRepository_SearchableCollectionImpl(the_poa)
{
}

// Destructor.
BookRepository_FlexibleCollectionImpl::~BookRepository_FlexibleCollectionImpl()
{
}
```

The C++ implementation of `FlexibleCollection` is trivial, consisting of just a constructor and a destructor. The definitions for the operations and attributes are inherited.

Listing 2.30 shows the declaration of the Java `BookRepository.FlexibleCollectionImpl` class, which provides the implementation of the `BookRepository::FlexibleCollection` interface.

Listing 2.30 Java Implementation of **BookRepository::FlexibleCollection**

```
//Java
package Pure.BookRepository;

import org.omg.CORBA.ORB;

public class FlexibleCollectionImpl
    extends Pure.BookRepository.FlexibleCollectionPOA
{
    // Private member variables
    private org.omg.PortableServer.POA      m_poa = null;

    public BorrowableCollectionImpl(org.omg.PortableServer.POA poa)
    {
        m_poa = poa;
    }

    public org.omg.PortableServer.POA _default_POA()
    {
      return m_poa;
    }

    // IDL Operations and Attributes
    // (implement all IDL ops and attributes inherited from
    // 'SearchableCollection' and 'BorrowableCollection')
    // ...not shown...
}
```

The Java `FlexibleCollectionImpl` class cannot inherit from `BorrowableCollectionImpl` or `SearchableCollectionImpl` because the single inheritance slot is used up by inheriting from `BookRepository.FlexibleCollectionPOA`. The Java implementation inheritance tree is therefore *not* a mirror of the IDL inheritance tree.

As a consequence of this limitation of Java inheritance, it is necessary to repeat the definitions of the inherited operations and attributes within the scope of the `FlexibleCollectionImpl` class. The method definitions can be cut and pasted from the `BorrowableCollectionImpl` and `SearchableCollectionImpl` classes—however, this is fairly inconvenient. The section "Java Inheritance and Delegation (Tie) Approach" discusses an alternative approach to implementing IDL interfaces that partly circumvents this difficulty.

Multiple Inheritance and the Delegation (Tie) Approach (Example 4)

Example 4 introduces multiple IDL inheritance and shows you how to implement multiply inheriting interfaces in C++ and Java. The following sections discuss multiple inheritance issues in greater detail, paying particular attention to dealing with the limitations of Java.

Multiple Inheritance of Interfaces

In C++, the servant inheritance hierarchy is generally arranged in parallel to the IDL interface inheritance hierarchy. For example, Figure 2.5 illustrates the servant inheritance hierarchy for the `BookRepository_FlexibleCollectionImpl` class.

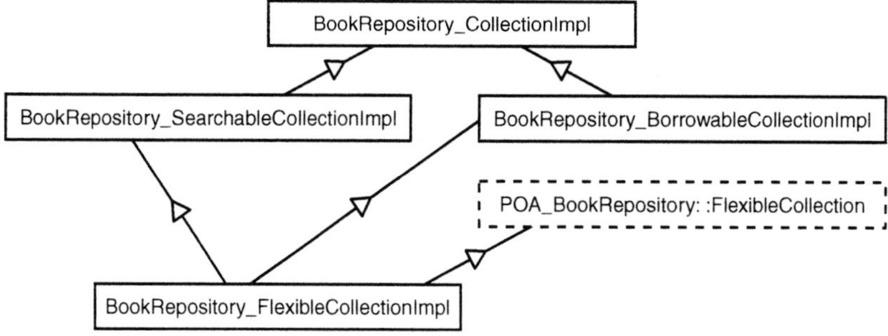

Figure 2.5

The C++ servant inheritance hierarchy for the `BookRepository_FlexibleCollectionImpl` *class.*

When an IDL interface multiply inherits from other IDL interfaces, the servant class also multiply inherits from other servant classes. This approach makes the most of the C++ support for multiple inheritance. It is worth bearing in mind, however, that you could implement a different inheritance relationship (or none) between servant classes if you prefer.

In Java, the servant inheritance hierarchy *cannot* be arranged in parallel to the IDL interface inheritance hierarchy, because Java is limited to single inheritance only. For example, Figure 2.6 illustrates the servant inheritance hierarchy for the `BookRepository.FlexibleCollectionImpl` class.

In Figure 2.6, the Java `FlexibleCollectionImpl` class inherits from `FlexibleCollectionPOA`, and this uses up the single available inheritance slot. The operations and attributes inherited from the `BorrowableCollection` and `SearchableCollection` IDL interfaces must therefore be defined again within the scope of the `FlexibleCollectionImpl` class.

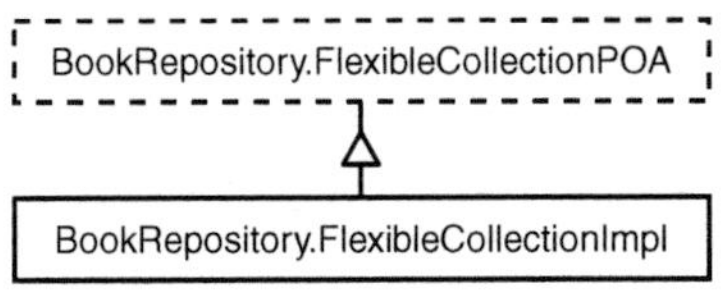

Figure 2.6

Java servant inheritance hierarchy for the `BookRepository.FlexibleCollectionImpl` *class.*

Java Inheritance and Delegation (Tie) Approach

CORBA supports two approaches to implementing IDL interfaces in Java:

- *The inheritance approach* is characterized by the fact that the connection between a `Foo` IDL interface and a `FooImpl` implementation class is established by *inheritance*. The `FooImpl` class inherits from a `FooPOA` Java base class. This is the approach used in this chapter up to this point.
- *The delegation (tie) approach* is characterized by the fact that the connection between a `Foo` IDL interface and a `FooImpl` implementation class is established by *delegation*. For every `FooImpl` object that is created, an auxiliary `FooPOATie` object is created that holds a reference pointing at the `FooImpl` object. Operation invocations made on the `FooPOATie` object are delegated to the `FooImpl` object.

NOTE

The tie approach is also available in C++, where the tie class implementation is usually based on templates. However, the tie approach is of much less importance in C++.

The tie approach is illustrated in Figure 2.7.

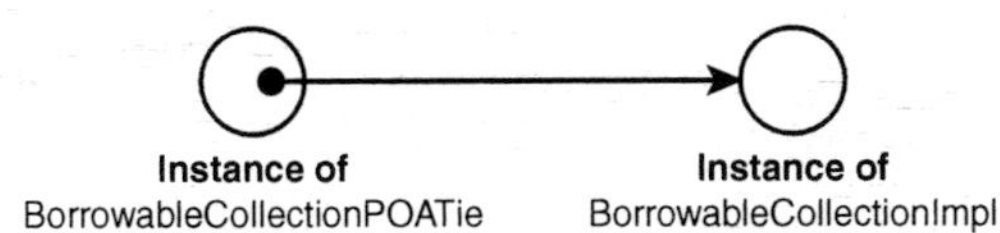

Figure 2.7

Java implementation of `BookRepository::BorrowableCollection` *using the tie approach.*

Whenever a single servant is created using the tie approach in Java, it is necessary to create two Java objects: an implementation object, for example `BorrowableCollectionImpl`, and a tie object, for example `BorrowableCollectionPOATie`. A pointer to the implementation object is passed to the constructor of the tie object to establish a connection between the two objects. In the tie approach, two Java objects represent one servant.

The payoff in the tie approach is that it frees up the single inheritance slot. For example, Figure 2.8 shows the Java inheritance hierarchy when the tie approach is applied to the `CollectionImpl` and `BorrowableCollectionImpl` classes.

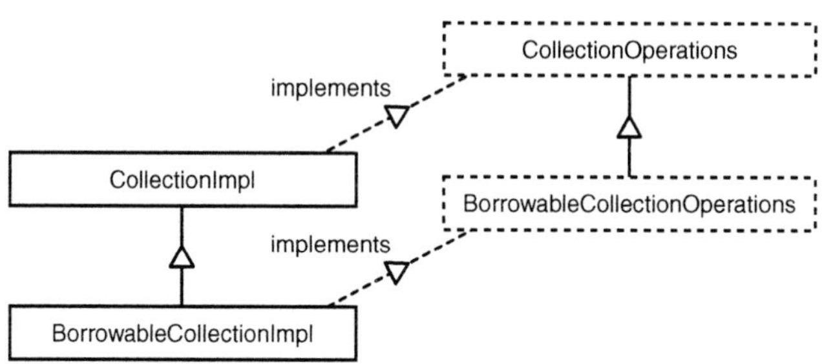

Figure 2.8

Java inheritance hierarchy when using the tie approach.

Using the tie approach, it is now possible for `BorrowableCollectionImpl` to inherit directly from `CollectionImpl`. Consequently, it is not necessary for the `CollectionImpl` methods to be repeated in `BorrowableCollectionImpl`.

Listing 2.31 shows how to define the Java `BorrowableCollectionImpl` class using the tie approach.

Listing 2.31 Java Implementation of `BookRepository::BorrowableCollection` *(Delegation Approach)*

```
//Java
package Pure.BookRepository;

import org.omg.CORBA.ORB;
import Pure.BookRepository.Borrower_DB;
import Pure.BookRepository.BorrowableCollectionPackage.*;

public class BorrowableCollectionImpl
    extends    CollectionImpl
    implements BorrowableCollectionOperations
{
    // Private member variables
    //...

    public static Pure.BookRepository.BorrowableCollectionPOATie
    _create(org.omg.PortableServer.POA the_poa)
    throws org.omg.CORBA.SystemException
    {
      BorrowableCollectionImpl tied_object = new BorrowableCollectionImpl();
      Pure.BookRepository.BorrowableCollectionPOATie the_tie
          = new Pure.BookRepository.BorrowableCollectionPOATie(
```

Listing 2.31 continued

```
                tied_object, the_poa
            );
        return the_tie;
    }

    public BorrowableCollectionImpl()
    {
        //...
    }

    // IDL Operations and Attributes
    // (implement extra IDL ops and attributes
    // defined in 'BorrowableCollection')
    // ...not shown...
}
```

The single inheritance slot is now occupied by `CollectionImpl`. The `BorrowableCollectionImpl` class also `implements` the `BorrowableCollectionOperations` Java interface. In general, an *`InterfaceName`*`Operations` Java interface contains just the signatures of the operations and attributes associated with the *`InterfaceName`* IDL interface.

The `BorrowableCollectionImpl::_create()` method is a convenient method defined in order to simplify the creation of a servant under the tie approach. Recall that the tie approach requires two Java objects for every servant: the implementation object and the tie object. Both are created when you call `_create()`.

The `BorrowableCollectionPOATie()` constructor takes two arguments. The first argument, `tied_object`, is cached by the tie object and used to delegate invocations to the implementation object. The second argument, `the_poa`, sets the POA that is returned if `_default_POA()` is invoked on the tie object.

Because `BorrowableCollectionImpl` inherits from `CollectionImpl`, it is only necessary to define the extra operations and attributes defined in the `BorrowableCollection` IDL interface. Alternatively, you can override the inherited methods if you require different behavior for `BorrowableCollection` objects.

Adding CORBA Naming Service Support—Example 5

The fifth example adds support for the CORBA Naming Service to the application. Instead of the server passing object references to the client by writing to a file, the code is modified so that the server publishes object references to the naming service. The client can then retrieve object references from the naming service by resolving names.

No changes are made to the example IDL.

Client Code

Listing 2.32 and Listing 2.33 give the code for a client of the `BookRepository::Collection` interface in C++ and Java, respectively. This client obtains the `Collection` object reference using the CORBA Naming Service.

Listing 2.32 C++ `Collection` Client Using the CORBA Naming Service

```
//C++
#include <iostream.h>
#include <fstream.h>
#include <stdlib.h>
#include <sstream>
#include <omg/CosNaming.hh>
#include "BookRepository.hh"

CORBA::ORB_var
global_orb = CORBA::ORB::_nil();

int
main(int argc, char **argv)
{
    try
    {
        CORBA::Object_var objV;  // For temporary object references.

        // Initialise the ORB.
        global_orb = CORBA::ORB_init(argc, argv);

        // Parse command line arguments:
        if (argc != 1) {
            cout << "Usage: bk_collection " << endl;
            exit(0);
        }

        // Obtain Naming Service reference.
        CosNaming::NamingContext_var rootContextV;
        objV = global_orb->resolve_initial_references("NameService");
        rootContextV = CosNaming::NamingContext::_narrow(objV);
        if (CORBA::is_nil(rootContextV.in()) ) {
            cerr << "error: failed to narrow root naming context." << endl;
            exit(1);
        }

        // Obtain 'BookRepository::Collection' object reference.
        CosNaming::Name objectName(2);
        objectName.length(2);
        objectName[0].id   = CORBA::string_dup("BookRepository");
        objectName[0].kind = CORBA::string_dup("");
```

Listing 2.32 continued

```
        objectName[1].id   = CORBA::string_dup("PlainCollection");
        objectName[1].kind = CORBA::string_dup("");
        objV = rootContextV->resolve(objectName);
        BookRepository::Collection_var collectionV =
            BookRepository::Collection::_narrow(objV);
        if (CORBA::is_nil(collectionV.in() ))
        {
            cerr << "error: failed to narrow to Collection." << endl;
            exit(1);
        }

        // Invoke 'BookRepository::Collection' object.
        cout << "Details of book collection:" << endl;
        CORBA::String_var name_strV;
        name_strV = collectionV->name_of_collection();
        cout << "\tName of collection = \"" << name_strV.in() << "\"" << endl;
        CORBA::Long n_books;
        n_books = collectionV->number_of_books();
        cout << "\tNumber of books = " << n_books << endl;

        // Try changing the name of the book collection.
        cout << "Changing name of book collection..." << endl;
        collectionV->name_of_collection("Brand new collection!");
        cout << "checking name of collection..." << endl;
        name_strV = collectionV->name_of_collection();
        cout << "\tName of collection = \"" << name_strV.in() << "\"" << endl;
    }
    catch(CORBA::Exception &ex)
    {
        cerr << "Unexpected CORBA exception: " << ex << endl;
    }

    // Shut down the ORB.
    try
    {
        global_orb->shutdown(1);
        global_orb->destroy();
    }
    catch (...)
    {
        // Do nothing.
    }
    return 0;
}
```

Listing 2.33 Java `Collection` *Client Using the CORBA Naming Service*

```
//Java
package Pure.BookRepository;

import org.omg.CORBA.*;
import org.omg.PortableServer.*;
import java.io.*;
import Pure.BookRepository.*;

public class bk_collection
{

   // global_orb -- make ORB public
   public static org.omg.CORBA.ORB global_orb = null;

   public static void main (String args[])
   {
      try
      {
         org.omg.CORBA.Object obj;

         // Initialise the ORB.
         global_orb = ORB.init(args, null);

         String app_args[] = remove_ORB_args(args);

        // Parse command line arguments:
        if (app_args.length != 0) {
            System.out.println("Usage: bk_collection ");
            System.exit(1);
        }

        // Obtain Naming Service reference.
        org.omg.CosNaming.NamingContext rootContext = null;
        obj = global_orb.resolve_initial_references("NameService");
        rootContext = org.omg.CosNaming.NamingContextHelper.narrow(obj);

        // Obtain 'BookRepository::Collection' object reference.
        org.omg.CosNaming.NameComponent[] objectName
            = new org.omg.CosNaming.NameComponent[2];
        objectName[0]
            = new org.omg.CosNaming.NameComponent("BookRepository", "");
        objectName[1]
            = new org.omg.CosNaming.NameComponent("PlainCollection", "");
        obj = rootContext.resolve(objectName);
        Collection theCollection
            = CollectionHelper.narrow(obj);

        // Invoke 'BookRepository::Collection' object.
        System.out.println("Details of book collection:");
```

Listing 2.33 continued

```
            String name_str;
            name_str = theCollection.name_of_collection();
            System.out.println("\tName of collection = \"" + name_str + "\"");
            int n_books;
            n_books = theCollection.number_of_books();
            System.out.println("\tNumber of books = " + n_books);

            // Try changing the name of the book collection.
            System.out.println("Changing name of book collection...");
            theCollection.name_of_collection("Brand new collection!");
            System.out.println("checking name of collection...");
            name_str = theCollection.name_of_collection();
            System.out.println("\tName of collection = \"" + name_str + "\"");
        }
        catch(Exception ex)
        {
            System.out.println("Unexpected CORBA exception: " + ex);
        }

        // Shut down the ORB.
        try
        {
            global_orb.shutdown(true);
            global_orb.destroy();
        }
        catch (Exception ex)
        {
            // Do nothing.
        }
        return;
    }
}
```

The `bk_collection` client performs almost the same sequence of steps as the client in Example 1 (Listing 2.2 and Listing 2.3). The only difference is that the client in this example uses the CORBA Naming Service instead of the `read_reference()` function to obtain the `Collection` object reference:

1. **Obtain a naming service reference** An initial reference to the naming service is obtained by invoking `CORBA::ORB::resolve_initial_references()` with the string `NameService` as its argument.
   The object reference returned by `resolve_initial_references()` is normally obtained from an ORB-specific configuration mechanism. For some ORBs, the naming service location can be specified in a configuration file. Other ORBs let you specify the location using command-line parameters (which would then be extracted from the `args` parameter passed to `ORB_init()` in C++ and `ORB.init()` in Java).

The naming service initial reference is an object of `CosNaming::NamingContext` type (or `CosNaming::NamingContextExt` type, if you are using the extended functionality of the CORBA Interoperable Naming Service). The `NamingContext` IDL interface provides most of the operations that you need when you are using the naming service.

2. **Obtain the `Collection` object reference** The `Collection` object reference is obtained by resolving the name `BookRepository/PlainCollection`, for which a server has already created a binding in the naming service.

   The `CosNaming::NamingContext::resolve()` operation has the following IDL signature:

```
//IDL
#pragma prefix "omg.org"

module CosNaming {
    typedef string Istring;
    struct NameComponent {
        Istring id;
        Istring kind;
    };
    typedef sequence<NameComponent> Name;
    ...
    interface NamingContext {
        ...
        Object resolve (in Name n)
               raises(NotFound, CannotProceed, InvalidName);
        ...
    };
    ...
};
```

   The `resolve()` operation takes an argument of `CosNaming::Name` type, which is a sequence of `NameComponent` structs. In this example, the `objectName` has two name components: The first component is `BookRepository`, and the second component is `PlainCollection`.

   The return type of `resolve()` is the base type, `Object`, which maps to `CORBA::Object` in C++ and `org.omg.CORBA.Object` in Java. The return value, therefore, must be cast to the correct type using `Collection::_narrow()` in C++ and `CollectionHelper.narrow()` in Java.

   The naming service is described in detail in Chapter 6.

Server Code

The server shown in Listing 2.34 for C++ and Listing 2.35 for Java uses the CORBA Naming Service to publish its object references.

Listing 2.34 C++ Server Initialization Using the CORBA Naming Service

```
//C++
#include <iostream.h>
#include <fstream.h>
#include <string.h>
#include <stdlib.h>
#include <omg/PortableServer.hh>
#include <omg/CosNaming.hh>
#include "BookRepository_CollectionImpl.h"
#include "BookRepository_SearchableCollectionImpl.h"
#include "BookRepository_BorrowableCollectionImpl.h"
#include "BookRepository_FlexibleCollectionImpl.h"


CORBA::ORB_var
global_orb = CORBA::ORB::_nil();

int
main(
    int argc,
    char **argv
)
{
    // Variables to hold servants.
    PortableServer::ServantBase_var the_BookRepository_Collection = 0;
    PortableServer::ServantBase_var
        the_BookRepository_SearchableCollection = 0;
    PortableServer::ServantBase_var
        the_BookRepository_BorrowableCollection = 0;
    PortableServer::ServantBase_var the_BookRepository_FlexibleCollection = 0;

    try
    {
        CORBA::Object_var objV;  // For temporary object references.

        // Initialize the ORB and Root POA.
        cout << "Initializing the ORB" << endl;
        global_orb = CORBA::ORB_init(argc, argv);
        objV = global_orb->resolve_initial_references("RootPOA");
        PortableServer::POA_var root_poaV
            = PortableServer::POA::_narrow(objV);
        if (CORBA::is_nil(root_poaV.in()) ) {
            cerr << "error: failed to narrow root POA." << endl;
            exit(1);
        }
        PortableServer::POAManager_var root_poa_managerV
            = root_poaV->the_POAManager();
        if (CORBA::is_nil(root_poa_managerV.in()) ) {
```

Listing 2.34 continued

```
        cerr << "error: failed to narrow root POA manager." << endl;
        exit(1);
    }

    // Obtain Naming Service reference.
    CosNaming::NamingContext_var rootContextV;
    objV = global_orb->resolve_initial_references("NameService");
    rootContextV = CosNaming::NamingContext::_narrow(objV);
    if (CORBA::is_nil(rootContextV.in()) ) {
        cerr << "error: failed to narrow root naming context." << endl;
        exit(1);
    }

    // Make sure that a 'BookRepository' naming context exists.
    CosNaming::Name objectName(2);
    objectName.length(1);
    objectName[0].id   = CORBA::string_dup("BookRepository");
    objectName[0].kind = CORBA::string_dup("");
    try {
        rootContextV->bind_new_context(objectName);
    }
    catch (CosNaming::NamingContext::AlreadyBound& ) {  }

    // Create servants and export object references.
    PortableServer::ObjectId_var oid;

    // Create and activate a 'Collection' servant.
    the_BookRepository_Collection
        = new BookRepository_CollectionImpl(root_poaV);
    oid = root_poaV->activate_object(the_BookRepository_Collection.in() );
    objV = root_poaV->id_to_reference(oid);

    // Create an object binding in the CORBA Naming Service.
    objectName.length(2);
    objectName[0].id   = CORBA::string_dup("BookRepository");
    objectName[0].kind = CORBA::string_dup("");
    objectName[1].id   = CORBA::string_dup("PlainCollection");
    objectName[1].kind = CORBA::string_dup("");
    rootContextV->rebind(objectName, objV);

    // Similarly, create other servants and create object bindings.
    // ...(not shown)...

    // Activate the POA Manager and let the ORB process requests.
    root_poa_managerV->activate();
    cout << "Waiting for requests..." << endl;
    global_orb->run();
}
```

Listing 2.34 continued

```
    catch (CORBA::Exception& e)
    {
        cout << "Unexpected CORBA exception: " << e << endl;
    }

    // Servants are automatically deleted by '_var' types.

    // Shut down the ORB.
    try
    {
        global_orb->destroy();
    }
    catch (...)
    {
        // Do nothing.
    }
    return 0;
}
```

Listing 2.35 Java Server Initialization Using the CORBA Naming Service

```
//Java
package Pure.BookRepository;

import org.omg.CORBA.*;
import org.omg.PortableServer.*;
import java.io.*;

public class server {

    public static ORB global_orb = null;

    public static void main(String args[])
    {
        // Variables to hold the servants.
        Servant the_BookRepository_Collection = null;
        Servant the_BookRepository_SearchableCollection = null;
        Servant the_BookRepository_BorrowableCollection = null;
        Servant the_BookRepository_FlexibleCollection = null;

        try
        {
            org.omg.CORBA.Object obj = null;

            // Initialize the ORB and Root POA.
            System.out.println("Initializing the ORB");
            global_orb = ORB.init(args, null);
```

Listing 2.35 continued

```
obj = global_orb.resolve_initial_references("RootPOA");
POA root_poa = POAHelper.narrow(obj);
POAManager root_poa_manager = root_poa.the_POAManager();

// Obtain Naming Service reference.
org.omg.CosNaming.NamingContext rootContext = null;
obj = global_orb.resolve_initial_references("NameService");
rootContext = org.omg.CosNaming.NamingContextHelper.narrow(obj);

// Make sure that a 'BookRepository' naming context exists.
org.omg.CosNaming.NameComponent[] objectName
    = new org.omg.CosNaming.NameComponent[1];
objectName[0]
    = new org.omg.CosNaming.NameComponent("BookRepository", "");
try {
    rootContext.bind_new_context (objectName);
}
catch (org.omg.CosNaming.NamingContextPackage.AlreadyBound e) {  }

// Create servants and export object references.
byte [] oid;

try{
    // Create and activate the 'Collection' servant.
    the_BookRepository_Collection
        = new Pure.BookRepository.CollectionImpl(root_poa);
    oid = root_poa.activate_object(the_BookRepository_Collection);
    obj = root_poa.id_to_reference(oid);

    // Create a object binding in the CORBA Naming Service.
    objectName = new org.omg.CosNaming.NameComponent[2];
    objectName[0]
      = new org.omg.CosNaming.NameComponent("BookRepository", "");
    objectName[1]
      = new org.omg.CosNaming.NameComponent("PlainCollection", "");
    rootContext.rebind(objectName, obj);

    // Similarly, create other servants and create object bindings.
    // ...(not shown)...
}
catch (Exception ex)
{
    System.out.println(ex);
    ex.printStackTrace();
    System.exit(1);
}

// Activate the POA Manager.
try {
```

Listing 2.35 continued

```
                root_poa_manager.activate();
            }
            catch (POAManagerPackage.AdapterInactive ex) {
                System.out.println( "error: could activate POA manager" + ex);
                System.exit(1);
            }

            //Let the ORB process requests.
            System.out.println("Waiting for requests..." );
            global_orb.run();
        }
        catch (Exception ex)
        {
            System.out.println("error: unexpected exception: " + ex);
        }

        try
        {
            global_orb.destroy();
        }
        catch (Exception e)
        {
            // Do nothing.
        }
        return;
    }
}
```

The server initialization performs almost the same sequence of steps as the server initialization in Example 1 (Listing 2.7 and Listing 2.8). The only difference is that the CORBA Naming Service is used to distribute object references to clients instead of the `write_reference()` function:

1. **Obtain a naming service reference** An initial reference to the naming service is obtained by invoking `CORBA::ORB::resolve_initial_references()` with the string `NameService` as its argument.
2. **Make sure that a `BookRepository` naming context exists** The server creates a *context binding* named `BookRepository` if it does not already exist. A context binding associates an object name with a `NamingContext` object.
   The `BookRepository` naming context defines a scope within the naming context hierarchy. Subsequently, object bindings can be created within this scope—for example, `BookRepository/PlainCollection`, `BookRepository/SearchableCollection` and so on (see step 3).
   The `CosNaming::NamingContext::bind_new_context()` operation creates new context bindings. It has the following IDL signature:

```
//IDL
#pragma prefix "omg.org"

module CosNaming {
    typedef string Istring;
    struct NameComponent {
        Istring id;
        Istring kind;
    };
    typedef sequence<NameComponent> Name;
    ...
    interface NamingContext {
        ...
        NamingContext bind_new_context(in Name n)
            raises(NotFound, AlreadyBound, CannotProceed, InvalidName);
        ...
    };
    ...
};
```

The `bind_new_context()` operation creates a binding that associates the name `n` with a newly created `NamingContext` object. The new `NamingContext` object is a CORBA object that lives in the naming service. A naming service implementation normally provides some kind of persistent storage to preserve the state of these `NamingContext` objects.

If the `BookRepository` naming context already exists, the naming service notifies the server by throwing the `CosNaming::NamingContext::AlreadyBound` user exception. This is not a serious error: The server simply proceeds to use the existing naming context. In Listing 2.34 and Listing 2.35, the `AlreadyBound` exception is caught to enable the server to continue uninterrupted.

The full details of `bind_new_context()` are described in Chapter 6.

3. **Create object bindings in the CORBA Naming Service** An object reference is published to the naming service by creating an *object binding* that associates an object name with an object reference.

The `CosNaming::NamingContext::rebind()` operation creates object bindings. It has the following IDL signature:

```
//IDL
#pragma prefix "omg.org"

module CosNaming {
    typedef string Istring;
    struct NameComponent {
        Istring id;
        Istring kind;
    };
    typedef sequence<NameComponent> Name;
    ...
```

```
    interface NamingContext {
        ...
          void rebind(in Name n, in Object obj)
               raises(NotFound, CannotProceed, InvalidName);
        ...
    };
    ...
};
```

The `rebind()` operation creates a binding that associates the name `n` with the object reference `obj`. Clients can later retrieve the object reference by resolving its associated name.

The `rebind()` operation works in *clobber mode* (to borrow the Unix term). It can either create a new binding with name `n` or, if a binding with that name already exists, overwrite the existing binding. This is convenient if, as is usually the case, you want to refresh the object bindings each time the server starts up.

The full details of `rebind()` are described in Chapter 6.

More IDL Syntax and Rules for Mapping Identifiers

Miscellaneous IDL features are discussed in the following subsections:

- IDL constants
- Recursive IDL types
- Unique type identifiers—`RepositoryIds`
- C++ mapped identifiers and keywords
- Java mapped identifiers and keywords
- Contexts

IDL Constants

The IDL syntax allows constants to be defined for basic types, enumerations, and aliases (`typedefs`) of basic types and enumerations. Listing 2.36 gives some examples of IDL constant definitions.

Listing 2.36 Sample IDL Constant Definitions

```
//IDL
// Characters constants
const char A_LETTER = 'p';
const char A_NEWLINE = '\n';
const char A_SINGLE_QUOTE = '\'';

// Wide character constants
const wchar A_WIDE_LETTER = L'q';
const wchar A_UNICODE_LETTER = L'\u039b';  // capital Lambda
```

Listing 2.36 continued

```
// String constants
const string SALUTATION = "Hello!\n";
const string CONCATENATED = "Put" " me" " together" " again.";
const string<8> BOUNDED = "Not long";

// Wide string constant
const wstring GREEK_LETTERS  = L"\u039b=2\u0393";  // Lambda = 2 Gamma

// Octet constant
const octet BIGGEST_OCTET = 0xff;

// Integer constants
const long A_DECIMAL_INT = 365;
const long AN_OCTAL_INT = 0555;
const long A_HEX_INT = 0x16d;
const long A_BIGGER_INT = A_DECIMAL_INT + 100;

// Floating point constants
const float A_FLOAT_EXPR = 2.0/3.0;
const float A_SMALL_FLOAT = 1.2e-10;

// Enumeration constant
enum Shade { black, grey, white };
const Shade CAVE_INTERIOR = black;

// Fixed point constant
const fixed MONEY_AMOUNT = 23.45D;
```

The syntax of IDL literals is similar to the syntax of C++ and Java literals. The examples in Listing 2.36 illustrate the following points:

- Character literals follow the ISO Latin-1 standard. Non-graphic characters can be specified using `\` (backslash) escape sequences, familiar from C++ and Java. See Chapter 18 for details.
- Wide character literals consist of a character literal preceded by the `L` (capital L) character. International characters can be specified using a Unicode escape sequence, `'\uXXXX'` where `XXXX` is a hexadecimal number.
- String literals have a similar format to C++ and Java. Consecutive string literals, separated only by whitespace, are concatenated before being assigned to a string constant. For example, the `CONCATENATED` string constant of Listing 2.36 is set equal to `"Put me together again."`.
- Wide string literals consist of a string preceded by the `L` (capital L) character. In addition, Unicode escape sequences, of the form `\uXXXX`, are allowed to appear in wide string literals.
- Octets can be specified in decimal, octal, or hexadecimal format.

- Integers can be specified in decimal, octal, or hexadecimal format. It is also possible to assign integer expressions to an integer constant.
- Floating point constants can be set equal to a floating point expression. All floating point literals appearing in a floating point expression must contain a decimal point (mixed integer and floating point arithmetic is not allowed).
- Enumeration constants can be defined.
- Fixed-point constants can be defined. A fixed-point literal is always terminated by the letter `d` (small d) or `D` (capital D). See Chapter 17 and Chapter 18 for details.

The IDL syntax allows numerical types to be specified as arithmetical expressions. The supported arithmetical operations are shown in Table 2.12.

Table 2.12 Operations Allowed in Constant Expressions

IDL Types	Unary Operations	Binary Operations
float	+	*
double	-	/
long double		+
fixed		-
short	+	*
unsigned short	-	/
long	~	%
unsigned long		+
long long		-
unsigned long long		<<
		>>
		&
		^

The additional integer operations are described in Chapter 18. These include ~ (two's complement), % (remainder), << (shift bits left), >> (shift bits right), & (bitwise AND), | (bitwise OR), and ^ (bitwise exclusive OR).

Constants at Different Scopes

IDL constants can be defined at different scopes, as shown in Listing 2.37.

Listing 2.37 IDL Constants Defined at Different Scopes

```
//IDL
const string GLOBAL_SCOPE = "global";

module MyModule {
    const string MODULE_SCOPE = "in MyModule";
    //...
```

Listing 2.37 continued

```
    interface MyInterface {
        const string INTERFACE_SCOPE = "in MyInterface";
        //...
    };
};
```

Listing 2.37 defines three string constants: `GLOBAL_SCOPE`, `MODULE_SCOPE`, and `INTERFACE_SCOPE`. The mapping of these string constants to C++ and Java is described in the following sections.

C++ Mapping

The IDL constants from Listing 2.37 are mapped to C++ as shown in Listing 2.38.

Listing 2.38 C++ Mapping of Constants Defined at Different Scopes

```
//C++
const char * const GLOBAL_SCOPE = "global";

namespace MyModule {
    const char * const MODULE_SCOPE = "in MyModule";
    //...
    class MyInterface {
        static const char * const INTERFACE_SCOPE;
        //...
    };
};
...
// Initialisation of 'INTERFACE_SCOPE'
MyModule::MyInterface::INTERFACE_SCOPE = "in MyInterface";
...
```

To refer to the mapped string constants, you can use the fully scoped names: `GLOBAL_SCOPE`, `MyModule::MODULE_SCOPE`, and `MyModule::MyInterface::INTERFACE_SCOPE`. The mapping in Listing 2.38 assumes that you are using standard ANSI C++. Hence, the IDL `module MyModule` is mapped to a C++ namespace.

Java Mapping

The IDL constants from Listing 2.37 are mapped to Java as shown in Listing 2.39 and Listing 2.40.

Listing 2.39 Java Mapping of Global Constants

```
//Java
// File containing global constants:
interface GLOBAL_SCOPE {
    String value = "global";
};
...
```

Listing 2.40 Java Mapping of Constants at Module and Interface Scopes

```
//Java
package MyModule;

interface MODULE_SCOPE {
    String value = "in MyModule";
};

interface MyInterface
{
    String INTERFACE_SCOPE = "in MyInterface";
    //...
};
```

To refer to the mapped string constants, you can use the fully scoped names: `GLOBAL_SCOPE.value`, `MyModule.MODULE_SCOPE.value`, and `MyModule.MyInterface.INTERFACE_SCOPE`.

NOTE

In Java mapping, a distinction is made between constants declared in the scope of an IDL interface and other constants. Constants in the scope of an IDL interface map intuitively to a scoped identifier—for example, `MyModule.MyInterface.INTERFACE_SCOPE`. Constants declared outside an IDL interface, however, map to a Java interface with a single `value` member—for example, `GLOBAL_SCOPE.value`.

Recursive IDL Types

In general, sequences must be given an alias, using the IDL `typedef` construction, before they can be used. The following IDL fragment, for example, contains an error:

```
//IDL
typedef sequence<long> LongSeq;

interface TestSequence {
    void set_sequence(in LongSeq numbers);  // OK. Uses 'LongSeq' alias.
    sequence<long> get_sequence();          //WRONG! Will not compile.
};
```

The anonymous sequence type, `sequence<long>`, cannot be used as the return value or parameter of an IDL operation. You must use the `LongSeq` alias instead.

However, there are two contexts in IDL where it is legal to use an anonymous sequence type (apart from a `typedef`):

- As a struct member (a recursive struct)
- As a union member (a recursive union)

The following IDL fragment shows an example of a recursive struct definition:

```
//IDL
struct Node {
    string info;
    sequence<Node> recur;
};
```

The Node struct is recursive because the sequence<Node> sequence is defined in terms of the Node struct itself.

In C++, the sequence<Node> sequence is mapped in a special way. Because the sequence has no name in IDL, it is mapped to the Node::_recur_seq class. In general, when a *MemberName* member of a *StructName* struct is declared as an anonymous sequence, it is mapped to the *StructName*::_*MemberName*_seq class.

In Java, the sequence<Node> sequence is mapped to Node[].

Unique Type Identifiers—Repository IDs

Every named IDL type is associated with a unique identifier string, known as a *repository ID*. Repository IDs are used by the Interface Repository, a type repository for IDL, to keep track of IDL data types—hence the name. However, repository IDs are used in many other contexts as unique type identifiers.

For example, consider the IDL fragment in Listing 2.41, which defines a number of new named IDL types.

Listing 2.41 A Sample IDL Illustrating Repository IDs

```
//IDL
module MyModule {
    struct MyStruct {
        string FirstMember;
        long   SecondMember;
    ;
    typedef sequence<MyStruct> MyStructSeq;

    interface MyInterface {
        MyStructSeq getSequence();
    };
};
```

The IDL types defined in Listing 2.41 are associated with the repository IDs shown in Table 2.13.

Table 2.13 Sample Repository IDs in OMG IDL Format

IDL Scoped Name	Repository ID
`::MyModule`	`IDL:MyModule:1.0`
`::MyModule::MyStruct`	`IDL:MyModule/MyStruct:1.0`
`::MyModule::MyStructSeq`	`IDL:MyModule/MyStructSeq:1.0`
`::MyModule::MyInterface`	`IDL:MyModule/MyInterface:1.0`

By default, each named IDL type is associated with a repository ID in OMG IDL format. In general, the OMG IDL repository ID format has the following form:

```
IDL:ModifiedScopedName:major.minor
```

The *`ModifiedScopedName`* is equal to the scoped name of the IDL type with `/` (forward slash) used in place of `::` to separate components of the name. A version number, of the form *`major.minor`*, appears at the end of the repository ID, where the *`major`* and *`minor`* version numbers are decimal unsigned short integers. The default version number is 1.0.

Repository IDs are generated by the IDL compiler as it generates the stub code for the target language of your CORBA application.

In C++, you can access the `MyModule::MyInterface` repository ID as follows:

```
//C++
CORBA::String_var rep_idV = MyModule::_tc_MyInterface->id();
cout << "The MyModule::MyInterface repository id is: " << rep_idV << endl;
```

The `MyModule::_tc_MyInterface` object is an example of a CORBA type code, which is generated by the IDL compiler. CORBA type codes are discussed further in Chapter 8, "The `any` Type."

In Java, you can access the `MyModule::MyInterface` repository ID as follows:

```
//C++
String rep_id = MyModule.MyInterfaceHelper.id();
System.out.println("The MyModule::MyInterface repository id is: " + rep_id);
```

Java provides a short cut to access the repository ID via the `id()` method of the `MyInterfaceHelper` class. (You can also access the repository ID using the type code for `MyInterface`.)

The generation of repository IDs by the IDL compiler can be influenced by inserting `#pragma` preprocessor directives into the IDL code. This enables repository IDs to be modified in three ways:

- Using the `#pragma prefix` preprocessor directive
- Using the `#pragma version` preprocessor directive
- Using the `#pragma ID` preprocessor directive

The #pragma prefix Preprocessor Directive

To avoid polluting the global namespace of IDL repository IDs, it is often useful to apply a prefix to all of the repository IDs defined in a particular IDL file. The #pragma prefix preprocessor directive is used for this purpose.

Consider, for example, that a #pragma prefix directive is inserted at the start of the IDL shown in Listing 2.41. This gives the following IDL fragment:

```
//IDL
#pragma prefix "pure-corba-3.com"

module MyModule {
    //... As before.
};
```

The quotation marks around the "pure-corba-3.com" prefix string are compulsory, and the #pragma prefix directive should appear at the beginning of the IDL file. The IDL types defined by the preceding fragment are associated with the following repository ID strings:

```
"IDL:pure-corba-3.com/MyModule:1.0"
"IDL:pure-corba-3.com/MyModule/MyStruct:1.0"
"IDL:pure-corba-3.com/MyModule/MyStructSeq:1.0"
"IDL:pure-corba-3.com/MyModule/MyInterface:1.0"
```

The prefix is intended to be a unique identifier for a particular organization that produces IDLs. Because the authors of the OMG specification believe that a Web domain name is a particularly appropriate form of prefix, the repository ID format allows the use of the hyphen (-) and period (.) characters in its components. This makes it possible to use Internet addresses (for example, pure-corba-3.com) as IDL prefixes.

The #pragma version Preprocessor Directive

You can use the #pragma version directive to associate a version number with any IDL definition. The effect of the #pragma version directive is to modify the version field of a repository ID.

Consider, for example, that you produce a new version of the IDL from Listing 2.41, adding a new field to MyModule::MyStruct and a new operation to MyModule::MyInterface. This gives rise to the following IDL fragment:

```
//IDL
#pragma prefix "pure-corba-3.com"

module MyModule {
#pragma version MyModule 1.1
    struct MyStruct {
#pragma version MyStruct 1.1
        string FirstMember;
        long   SecondMember;
```

```
        short  ExtraMember;
    ;
    typedef sequence<MyStruct> MyStructSeq;

    interface MyInterface {
#pragma version MyInterface 1.1
        MyStructSeq getSequence();
        void putSequence(in MyStructSeq seq);
    };
};
```

The repository IDs defined by the preceding IDL fragment are modified as follows:

```
"IDL:pure-corba-3.com/MyModule:1.1"
"IDL:pure-corba-3.com/MyModule/MyStruct:1.1"
"IDL:pure-corba-3.com/MyModule/MyStructSeq:1.0"
"IDL:pure-corba-3.com/MyModule/MyInterface:1.1"
```

Use of the `#pragma version` directive is compatible with the `#pragma prefix` directive, as this example shows.

The #pragma ID Preprocessor Directive

For specialized applications, it is sometimes useful to override the standard IDL format for a repository ID and define a more or less arbitrary repository ID instead. The `#pragma ID` directive allows you to do this.

The following IDL fragment shows you how to assign a new repository ID to `MyModule`:

```
//IDL
#pragma prefix "pure-corba-3.com"

module MyModule {
#pragma ID MyModule "FORMAT: Any string at all"
    //... As before.
};
```

The preceding `#pragma ID` directive replaces the `IDL:pure-corba-3.com/MyModule:1.0` repository ID with the `FORMAT: Any string at all` repository ID. The most general allowed form of a repository ID is

```
format:string
```

Here, *`format`* is a short name for the repository ID format, which must not contain a colon (`:`) character, and *`string`* is a string that conforms to the given format.

C++ Mapped Identifiers and Keywords

In general, IDL identifiers map to C++ identifiers with the same capitalization. For example, the `rANdOm_CaSE` IDL identifier maps to the `rANdOm_CaSE` C++ identifier.

However, two kinds of clashes can occur that are treated as special cases. These are discussed in the following two sections.

Clash with C++ Keywords

If an IDL identifier clashes with a C++ keyword, the identifier is prefixed by `_cxx_` when it is mapped to C++. For example, consider the following IDL:

```
//IDL
interface New {
    void continue();
    void friend();
};
```

The IDL identifiers `New`, `continue`, and `friend` are mapped to the C++ identifiers `_cxx_New`, `_cxx_continue`, and `_cxx_friend`, respectively. The `_cxx_` prefix is added to avoid a clash with C++ keywords.

Clash with Suffixes and Prefixes

C++ mapping forms additional C++ types from a given IDL type by adding suffixes to the IDL identifier. For example, a `Foo` interface has associated `Foo_var` and `Foo_ptr` types, formed by adding the `_var` and `_ptr` suffixes, respectively.

The use of suffixes can lead to an identifier clash, as shown by the following IDL:

```
//IDL
struct foo {...};

struct foo_var {...};  //WARNING! Bad for C++.
```

The `foo` IDL struct maps to a `foo` class and a `foo_var` smart pointer class. The `foo_var` IDL struct maps to a `foo_var` class (conflicting with the previous `foo_var` smart pointer class) and a `foo_var_var` smart pointer class. The conflict between the `foo_var` classes cannot be resolved. The only solution is to avoid these kinds of identifiers in your IDL files.

A similar problem can occur with C++ identifiers formed by adding a prefix to an IDL identifier—for example, the `POA_` prefix that is used to form the name of a servant's base class. Avoid defining an IDL interface or module whose name begins with `POA_`.

Java Mapped Identifiers and Keywords

In general, IDL identifiers also map to identical Java identifiers with the same capitalization. For example, the `rANdOm_CaSE` IDL identifier maps to the `rANdOm_CaSE` Java identifier. However, two kinds of clashes can occur that must be treated as special cases. These are discussed in the following two sections.

Clash with Java Keywords

An IDL identifier that clashes with a Java keyword is prefixed by an underscore (_) when it is mapped to Java. For example, consider the following IDL:

```
//IDL
interface New {
    void break();
    void final();
};
```

The IDL identifiers `New`, `break`, and `final` are mapped to the Java identifiers `_New`, `_break`, and `_final`, respectively. The underscore (_) prefix is added to avoid a clash with Java keywords.

Clash with Suffixes

Java mapping forms additional Java types from an IDL type by adding suffixes to the IDL identifier. For example, a `Foo` interface has associated `FooHelper`, `FooHolder`, `FooOperations`, `FooPOA`, and `FooPOATie` types.

The use of suffixes can lead to an identifier clash, as shown by the following IDL:

```
//IDL
struct foo {...};

struct fooHelper {...};
```

The `foo` IDL struct maps to a `foo` class and a `fooHelper` Helper class (and other types). The `fooHelper` IDL struct maps to a `_fooHelper` class and a `_fooHelperHelper` Helper class. The conflict between class names is avoided by adding the underscore (_) prefix to the `fooHelper` identifier when it is mapped to Java. The mapping is summarized in Table 2.14.

Table 2.14 Mapping of IDL Types to Java

IDL Identifier	Java Identifier	Java Helper Class
foo	foo	fooHelper
fooHelper	_fooHelper	_fooHelperHelper

In general, multiple clashing suffixes are resolved by prefixing more than one underscore (_) character, with the number of underscores equal to the number of suffixes that appear in the IDL identifier. For example, the `fooHelperPOA` IDL identifier maps to the `__fooHelperPOA` Java identifier.

Contexts

A *context* expression is a syntax associated with an operation definition that enables you to send a group of variables (with string values) from a client to a server. For example, when searching for books, using the `find_by_title()` operation, you might want to vary the size of the returned list depending on the client hardware. Context variables could be used to send this type of information:

```
//IDL
module BookRepository {
    ...
    interface SearchableCollection : Collection {
        boolean find_by_title(
                    in string          title,
                    out BookDetailsSeq books_found
                ) context (TERMINAL_TYPE, SCREEN_SIZE_*);
    };
};
```

The context expression picks out the `TERMINAL_TYPE`, `SCREEN_SIZE_WID`, and `SCREEN_SIZE_HGT` variables to send to the server (the `*` character is a wildcard).

Contexts are not covered in this book for the following reasons:

- **Obsolescence** The role of contexts in providing auxiliary data for an operation has been largely superseded by the use of service contexts and interceptors. Service contexts provide a more elegant solution because they do not need to be declared for each operation in IDL.
- **Poor ease of use** To use contexts, you have to learn new IDL syntax (which, unlike the rest of IDL's syntax, is not intuitive) and more mapping rules. However, there is nothing you can do with contexts that cannot also be done using plain operation parameters.
- **Poor Type Safety** Context variables are weakly typed (all context values are passed as strings).
- **Lack of support** In the author's experience, use of contexts in real-life projects is rare. Therefore, commercial ORB vendors receive few bug reports on contexts, and potential problems might remain undiscovered.
  Additionally, some leading ORB vendors have already dropped support for IDL contexts altogether.

More About Servers

For the sake of simplicity, this chapter focuses throughout on using the root POA. In realistic applications, however, you generally create your own POA instances and use these instead. Chapter 7 explains in detail how to create POA instances and what you can do with a POA.

The following sections highlight some basic POA features that are important to know about when you start to develop CORBA applications.

Transient and Persistent CORBA Objects

When using the POA, CORBA objects can be divided into two fundamental categories:

- **Transient CORBA Object** A short-lived object whose lifetime is bounded by the lifetime of the server process in which it is created.
- **Persistent CORBA Object** A long-lived object whose lifetime is unbounded. For example, an object whose state is permanently stored in a database should be managed as a persistent CORBA object.

CORBA objects associated with the root POA instance are always transient. Chapter 7 explains how to create a POA instance that has the PERSISTENT lifetime policy, enabling you to manage persistent CORBA objects as well.

Implicit Activation and _this()

The root POA supports *implicit activation*, which is a feature that allows CORBA objects to be activated using an abbreviated syntax. Compare the long syntax for creating and activating a CORBA object, shown in Listing 2.42 for C++ and Listing 2.43 for C++ for Java, with the abbreviated syntax using the _this() method, shown in Listing 2.44 for C++ and Listing 2.45 for Java.

Listing 2.42 C++ Activating a Collection *Object—Long Syntax*

```
//C++
//-------------------------------------------------------
// Given the following variables already initialized:
// root_poaV - a reference to the root POA instance

PortableServer::ObjectId_var oid;
CORBA::Object_var            objV;

// Create and activate a 'Collection' servant.
the_BookRepository_Collection
            = new BookRepository_CollectionImpl(root_poaV);
oid = root_poaV->activate_object(the_BookRepository_Collection.in() );
objV = root_poaV->id_to_reference(oid);
```

Listing 2.43 Java Activating a Collection *Object—Long Syntax*

```
//Java
//-------------------------------------------------------
// Given the following variables already initialized:
// root_poa - a reference to the root POA instance

byte[]                oid;
org.omg.CORBA.Object  obj;

try{
    // Create and activate the 'Collection' servant.
    the_BookRepository_Collection
        = new Pure.BookRepository.CollectionImpl(root_poa);
    oid = root_poa.activate_object(the_BookRepository_Collection);
    obj = root_poa.id_to_reference(oid);
}
catch (Exception ex) { ... }
```

Listing 2.44 C++ Activating a `Collection` Object—Using `_this()`

```
//C++
//-----------------------------------------------------
// Given the following variables already initialized:
// root_poaV - a reference to the root POA instance

CORBA::Object_var           objV;

// Create and activate a 'Collection' servant.
the_BookRepository_Collection
            = new BookRepository_CollectionImpl(root_poaV);
objV = the_BookRepository_Collection->_this();
```

Listing 2.45 Java Activating a `Collection` Object—Using `_this()`

```
//Java
//-----------------------------------------------------
// Given the following variables already initialized:
// root_poa - a reference to the root POA instance

byte[]                oid;
org.omg.CORBA.Object  obj;

try{
    // Create and activate the 'Collection' servant.
    the_BookRepository_Collection
        = new Pure.BookRepository.CollectionImpl(root_poa);
    obj = the_BookRepository_Collection._this();
}
catch (Exception ex) { ... }
```

The `_this()` method activates the CORBA object as a side-effect of returning an object reference. Using `_this()` has the benefit of simplifying object activation. However, implicit activation is more of a liability than a benefit for the following reasons:

- Using `_this()` hides too many details. In particular, you cannot see explicitly which POA instance is used to activate the CORBA object.
- Sometimes `_this()` activates a CORBA object using the *wrong* POA instance. This can easily happen because of the way `_this()` determines the POA instance. The `_this()` method implicitly calls `_default_POA()` on the servant class to get a reference to a POA instance. Unless you have explicitly overridden `_default_POA()` in the servant implementation, `_default_POA()` returns a reference to the root POA. In general, this is not what you want to happen at all. The root POA is rarely used in real applications.

For these reasons, it is preferable to avoid using implicit activation altogether.

Summary

This chapter introduces the main CORBA features that you need to write basic client and server applications. A typical CORBA application begins with the definition of an interface specification written in OMG IDL. The IDL definitions are then compiled into your chosen target language using an IDL compiler. The resulting stub code enables you to access the data types, IDL interfaces, operations, and attributes using your chosen development language, for example C++ or Java.

As a CORBA application starts up, the first thing it does is initialize an ORB object (or objects) and obtain references to basic objects using `resolve_initial_references()`. Clients can then obtain references to objects in CORBA servers by reading stringified object references from files or using the naming service.

CORBA supports a range of data types that can be passed as parameters to IDL operations or used as return values. In addition to basic types, such as strings, integer types, and floating point types, CORBA also supports complex types, such as structs and sequences. A special difficulty for C++ programmers is the fact that IDL data types are often allocated dynamically (on the heap). Special `_var` pointer types are defined for most IDL data types to help C++ programmers avoid memory leaks when dealing with dynamically allocated data.

Exception handling is extremely important in distributed applications because of the complex interactions between components and the potential for network failures. CORBA has a well-developed exception-handling capability that integrates with C++ and Java native exception handling.

Multiple inheritance of IDL interfaces is supported. In C++, the IDL inheritance hierarchy maps naturally to a parallel inheritance hierarchy of implementation classes. In Java, which does not support multiple inheritance, implementing multiple inheritance is less convenient. However, the situation in Java is better if you adopt the tie approach to implementing interfaces.

The last section introduces the CORBA Naming Service as a standard way for clients to locate services and retrieve named object references. This rounds out the basic CORBA programming introduction.

PART II

TECHNIQUES

CHAPTER 3

A Sample CORBA System

This chapter introduces the Recycle Broker application, which is used as the basis for many of the code examples throughout this book. This example is also intended to illustrate some basic principles of IDL design. The Recycle Broker IDL module contains several interfaces and is long enough to demonstrate how IDL interfaces typically are used together.

Complete source code for the Recycle Broker application is available for download, as detailed in the introduction.

Recycle Broker Architecture

The Recycle Broker application is devised as an e-business infrastructure for an imaginary waste management company, ACME Recycling Ltd. ACME Recycling is an established recycling business that has one large head office and a couple dozen small branch offices spread throughout the country. Attached to each branch office is a depot where customers who sell waste can deposit their waste material. The waste material is stored at the depot until it can be collected by specialist recycling companies. ACME Recycling thus acts as a middleman, collecting and storing waste until it can be sold in large quantities to recycling factories or to other customers.

The senior management of ACME Recycling have heard about the Internet and are beginning to think about how it could be used to improve their business model. They have had problems in the past with depots running out of space to store waste. It occurs to the managers that, in the case of customers who produce a large amount of waste, it would make more sense to transport the waste directly to the recipient, bypassing the waste depot. The Internet is an ideal way to broker this kind of arrangement. It is also apparent to the management that offering a service on the Internet could broaden the customer base and increase the volume of business.

An e-business consulting company is engaged to devise an Internet strategy. The consultants draw up a plan for a CORBA-based system, the Recycle Broker application. The Recycle Broker architecture is shown in Figure 3.1. The application is a distributed system with servers running at each of the company sites. There is a single head office server and branch office servers at each of the regional branches.

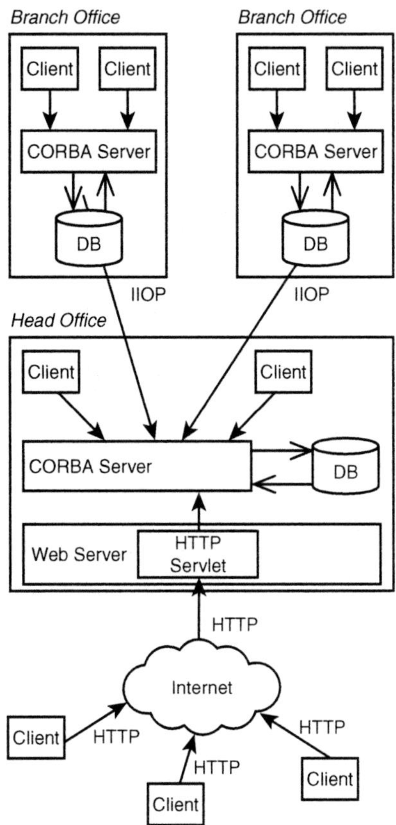

Figure 3.1

Architecture for the Recycle Broker system.

A three-tier system is put into each branch office, consisting of clients (tier 1), a branch office server (tier 2), and a local database (tier 3). Each branch office keeps track of local customers and the waste items in its depot, using its own database. It is important to store these details locally, because connectivity with the head office is not reliable, and IT staff are not readily available to fix problems at each of the branch offices.

The head office server acts as a central repository for all of the information in the company. Details stored in each of the branch office databases are regularly copied over to the head office database. The company Web server is also located in the head office.

To automate the process of buying and selling waste items, the Web server must access the head office server directly.

The bridge between the head office server and the Internet is provided by Java Servlet technology combined with CORBA. An HTTP Servlet, which runs on the Web server, acts as a CORBA client with respect to the head office server. This internal link uses the Internet inter-ORB protocol (IIOP), as shown in Figure 3.1. The HTTP Servlet processes HTML forms and generates Web pages in response to clients using ordinary Web browsers. This external link uses the HTTP protocol.

NOTE

Another solution would be to use JavaServer Pages (JSP) in combination with an HTTP Servlet. JSP enables generated Web pages to be updated more easily.

The Recycle Broker CORBA servers at branch offices and at the head office provide access to customer data and record details of transactions to buy and sell waste items. The purpose of the Internet service is to automate the buying and selling of waste items online.

Recycle Broker IDL

Listing 3.1 shows the complete IDL for the `RecycleBroker` IDL module. This IDL is supported by both the head office and the branch office CORBA servers.

Listing 3.1 `RecycleBroker` *IDL Module*

```
//IDL
module RecycleBroker {
    typedef string      NameType;
    typedef string      AddressType;
    typedef long        KeyType;
    typedef float       PriceType;

    enum WasteType {
        BROWN_GLASS, GREEN_GLASS, CLEAR_GLASS, SCRAP_STEEL,
        ALUMINIUM_CANS, PLASTIC_BOTTLES, WASTE_PAPER
    };

    // User Exceptions
    exception NoPermission { };
    exception NotLoggedOn  { };
    exception NotFound     { };
    exception InsufficientQuantity { };
    exception NetworkError {
        string reason;
```

Listing 3.1 continued

```
        string telephone;
    };

    // struct RecycleBroker::CustomerDetails
    struct CustomerDetails {
        NameType          name;
        AddressType       address;
        string            email_address;
        string            password;
    };

    struct CustomerDetailsFull {
        CustomerDetails  public_details;
        KeyType           branch_id;
        KeyType           customer_id;
    };

    // struct RecycleBroker::WasteItemDetails
    struct WasteItemDetails {
        WasteType         waste;
        long              quantity;
        PriceType         price_per_kilo;
    };

    struct WasteItemDetailsFull {
        WasteItemDetails public_details;
        KeyType           branch_id;
        KeyType           customer_id;
        KeyType           wasteitem_id;
    };

    // struct RecycleBroker::BranchDetails
    struct BranchDetails {
        AddressType       address;
        string            telephone;
    };

    struct BranchDetailsFull {
        BranchDetails     public_details;
        KeyType           branch_id;
    };

    interface Office;

    interface Customer {
        // attributes
        attribute NameType          name;
```

Listing 3.1 continued

```
        attribute AddressType      address;
        attribute string           email_address;
        attribute string           password;
        readonly attribute KeyType branch_id;
        readonly attribute KeyType customer_id;

        // operations
        CustomerDetails  get_details();
    };

    interface WasteItem {
        // attributes
        attribute WasteType        waste;
        attribute long             quantity;
        attribute PriceType        price_per_kilo;
        readonly attribute KeyType branch_id;
        readonly attribute KeyType customer_id;
        readonly attribute KeyType wasteitem_id;

        // operations
        WasteItemDetails get_details();
    };

    typedef sequence<KeyType> CustomerIdSeq;
    typedef sequence<CustomerDetails> CustomerDetailsSeq;

    interface CustomerAdmin {
        Customer create(
             in  CustomerDetails initialData,
             out KeyType         customer_id
        )
        raises (NoPermission);

        Customer find(in KeyType customer_id)
        raises (NoPermission, NotFound);

        CustomerIdSeq find_by_name(in NameType name)
        raises (NoPermission, NotFound);
    };

    typedef sequence<KeyType>   WasteItemIdSeq;
    typedef sequence<WasteItem> WasteItemSeq;
    typedef sequence<WasteItemDetails> WasteItemDetailsSeq;

    interface WasteItemAdmin {
        WasteItem create(
             in  WasteItemDetails initialData,
```

Listing 3.1 continued

```
            out KeyType          wasteitem_id
        )
        raises (NoPermission);

        WasteItem find(in KeyType wasteitem_id)
        raises (NotFound);
        WasteItemIdSeq find_by_waste(in WasteType waste)
        raises (NotFound);
        WasteItemIdSeq find_by_branch(in KeyType branch_id)
        raises (NotFound);
        WasteItemIdSeq find_all();

        WasteItemDetailsSeq get_details(in WasteItemIdSeq id_seq)
        raises (NotFound);
    };

    typedef sequence<BranchDetails> BranchDetailsSeq;

    interface OfficeAdmin {
        BranchDetailsSeq get_all_details();
    };

    interface Browsing {
        WasteItemAdmin get_waste_item_admin();
    };

    interface Selling {
        enum Status {INITIAL,
                     LOGGED_ON,
                     LOGGED_OFF };

        readonly attribute Status current_status;

        Customer      create_customer(
                          in CustomerDetails initialData,
                          out KeyType        customer_id
                      );

        Customer      log_on(in NameType name, in string password)
                      raises (NoPermission);

        WasteItem     create_waste_item(
                           in WasteItemDetails  initialData,
                           out KeyType          wasteitem_id
                      )
                      raises (NotLoggedOn);
```

Listing 3.1 continued

```
        void            log_off()  raises (NotLoggedOn);
    };

    interface Buying {
        enum Status {INITIAL,
                    LOGGED_ON,
                    LOGGED_OFF };

        readonly attribute Status current_status;

        Customer        create_customer(
                            in CustomerDetails initialData,
                            out KeyType        customer_id
                        );

        Customer        log_on(in NameType name, in string password)
                        raises (NoPermission);

        void            buy_item(
                            in KeyType wasteitem_id,
                            in long    quantity
                        )
                        raises (NotFound,
                                InsufficientQuantity,
                                NetworkError,
                                NotLoggedOn
                        );

        void            log_off()  raises (NotLoggedOn);
    };

    interface Office {
        // attributes
        readonly attribute string address;
        readonly attribute long   branch_id;

        // Customer operations
        Browsing        get_browsing();
        Selling         get_selling();
        Buying          get_buying();

        // Agent operations
        CustomerAdmin  get_customer_admin();
        WasteItemAdmin get_waste_item_admin();
    };
```

Listing 3.1 continued

```
    typedef sequence<WasteItemDetailsFull> WasteItemDetailsFullSeq;
    typedef sequence<CustomerDetailsFull>  CustomerDetailsFullSeq;

    interface HeadOffice : Office {
        void replicate_waste_item_details(
             in WasteItemDetailsFullSeq detailsSeq
        );

        void replicate_customer_details(
            in CustomerDetailsFullSeq detailsSeq
        );
    };

    interface BranchOffice : Office { };
};
```

The starting point for any client is to obtain a reference to an `Office` object. There are two sub-types of the `Office` interface: the `HeadOffice` interface, used by clients of the head office server, and the `BranchOffice` interface, used by clients of a branch office server. The initial reference to an `Office` object can either be cached on the client side or be obtained using the CORBA Naming Service.

Once a client has a reference to an `Office` object, the client can navigate to all of the other objects in the server. The operations in the `Office` interface are grouped into the categories *customer operations* and *agent operations*, depending on the type of client using the server:

- A customer client is an application that accesses the `RecycleBroker` server directly on behalf of a customer. This category covers customers accessing Recycle Broker via the Internet. For security reasons, customer clients are granted limited access to the server. If a customer client attempts to perform a forbidden action, the `RecycleBroker::NoPermission` user exception is raised.
- An agent client is an application that accesses the `RecycleBroker` server on behalf of an ACME Recycling employee. For this category of client, security is more relaxed because employees must be able to update customer records and waste item records directly.

The activities available to customer clients are to browse the list of available waste items by calling `get_browsing()`, offer waste items for sale by calling `get_selling()`, or purchase waste items by calling `get_buying()`. Each of these operations returns references to CORBA objects that organize the tasks of browsing, selling, and buying and limit the degree of access to the server.

Agent clients have the option of calling `get_customer_admin()` and `get_waste_item_admin()`. The `CustomerAdmin` and `WasteItemAdmin` object references returned by these operations allow the agent to make arbitrary updates to the database records.

The interfaces appearing in the RecycleBroker module can be grouped into the following categories:

- *Data interfaces* represent objects that consist primarily of persistent data. These are typically objects whose state is stored in a backend data base attached to the server. The Customer and WasteItem interfaces fall into this category.
- *Control interfaces* represent objects that encapsulate the steps needed to perform certain tasks. The Browsing, Selling, and Buying interfaces fall into this category.
- *Factory interfaces* represent objects that create, find, and manage instances of other objects. The CustomerAdmin, WasteItemAdmin, HeadOffice, and BranchOffice interfaces fall into this category.
- *Base interfaces* appear in the inheritance hierarchy solely so that other interfaces can derive from them. No instances of a base interface are created. The Office interface falls into this category.

The preceding categories are not part of the standard CORBA terminology, nor is there any IDL syntax available to make a distinction between them. However, you will often see these interface categories reflected in the design of CORBA applications. For example, many modules designed by the OMG, such as the interface repository IDL in Chapter 23, "CORBA System Exceptions," exhibit this kind of pattern. The following subsections discuss data, control, and factory interfaces in more detail.

Data Interfaces

Instances of Customer and WasteItem represent database records, making the data available to clients through the Customer and WasteItem IDL interfaces. Both the Customer and WasteItem interfaces consist mainly of attributes that allow clients to access individual data fields.

Consider the Customer interface. It supports a single operation, get_details(), that returns a CustomerDetails struct. The CustomerDetails struct contains most of the fields that appear as attributes in the corresponding Customer object. Additionally, a CustomerDetailsFull struct is defined to contain all of the attributes of the Customer object (including the readonly attribute).

This association between an interface, Customer, and a struct, CustomerDetails, is a common pattern in IDL design. If a client needs to access multiple fields of the Customer object, it is very inefficient to invoke each attribute and incur the overhead of several remote invocations. It is better for these clients to obtain a CustomerDetails struct using a single remote invocation.

Control Interfaces

The Browsing, Selling, and Buying interfaces are examples of control interfaces because they encapsulate the steps needed to perform certain tasks. These kinds of objects have very little state associated with them. Both the Selling and Buying objects behave as state machines, moving through the three states: INITIAL, LOGGED_ON, and LOGGED_OFF.

It is debatable as to whether you would really want to define all the steps for buying and selling items in the server application—it is often more convenient to put this logic on the client side. However, it is useful to put in place some steps to regulate logging in and logging out. This provides the server with some protection against buggy client code and unauthorized users.

Factory Interfaces

The use of factory interfaces is a fundamental pattern in IDL design. Factory objects are used to create, find, and manage instances of other CORBA objects.

The `HeadOffice` and `BranchOffice` interfaces are typical of factories that create only short-lived CORBA objects. The `Office` interface provides an operation to create each object—for example, `get_browsing()` for a new `Browsing` object—but provides no operations to find or otherwise manage the objects it creates. Servers typically clean up short-lived objects automatically, clearing them out of memory if they have been dormant for too long.

The `ConsumerAdmin` and `WasteItemAdmin` factory interfaces manage long-lived CORBA objects—`Customer` and `WasteItem`, respectively.

Recycle Broker Implementation

On the server side of a CORBA application, some common patterns for the implementation and management of CORBA objects can be identified. CORBA objects can therefore be divided into categories as follows:

- *Entity objects* are long-lived CORBA objects whose state is stored persistently so that they can be re-created after the server is stopped and restarted.
  For example, `Customer` and `WasteItem` objects are entity objects because they represent records in a database. Entity objects require a well-defined identity to facilitate later retrieval. They also tend to have an associated factory object, which manages the entity object's lifecycle and provides search operations.
  Scalability is a major issue for entity objects. Because these objects often represent records in a database, there might be many millions of them. It is generally impossible, or at least highly inefficient, for a server to keep all of these objects in memory at the same time. It is therefore essential for a server to have the capability to load entity objects dynamically into memory only as they are needed. The POA provides just this sort of functionality—full details are discussed in Chapter 7, "The Portable Object Adapter."
- *Session objects* are short-lived CORBA objects created to do some work on behalf of a client. When the client finishes its interaction with the server, the associated session objects typically are no longer needed and can be discarded.
  For example, `Browsing`, `Selling`, and `Buying` objects are session objects because they each manage particular tasks on behalf of a client. Session objects do not usually require a well-defined identity, because they are used once and then discarded.

Some form of garbage collection has to be implemented for session objects. When a server is active for a long time, more and more clients connect to the server, which causes the number of session objects to grow without limit. Determining when it is safe to discard a session object is difficult, in general. However, a common approach is to discard session objects that remain unused for a certain length of time. The POA supports this kind of session management—see Chapter 7 for details.

- *Process objects* are long-lived objects that are closely associated with the server process. There is only a single instance of each type of process object.
  For example, `HeadOffice` and `BranchOffice` objects are process objects. They are intended to be the first point of contact for clients and provide access, directly or indirectly, to all of the other CORBA objects in the server.
  Process objects are given a precise meaning in the context of the CORBA Components model, which is discussed in Chapter 15, "CORBA Components."

Many of the issues that server programmers have to deal with are related to managing the lifecycle of CORBA objects. These kinds of issues are dealt with in Chapter 7.

Summary

This chapter presented a basic outline of the Recycle Broker application, which is used as the basis for a number of examples throughout the book. The interfaces in the `RecycleBroker` IDL module follow common patterns and are described here as data, control, and factory style interfaces.

The implementation of the `RecycleBroker` interfaces is discussed in terms of common patterns such as entity objects, session objects, and process objects. These object categories are revisited in Chapter 7, which covers how to create and configure the POA to manage each type of object effectively. In Chapter 15, the object categories are discussed in the context of the CORBA Components framework.

CHAPTER 4

Memory Management

CORBA provides a rich variety of data types, including a number of compound types such as structs, sequences, unions, and arrays. These complex data types tend to be of variable size, so it is often appropriate to allocate them on the free store (heap allocation) using `new`. The CORBA programmer has to understand where to allocate memory for the CORBA data and, more importantly, where to deallocate the memory. In other words, the programmer needs to have an understanding of CORBA memory management.

The issue of memory management is one that specifically affects C++ programmers. The flexibility of allocating memory on the free store brings with it the responsibility of freeing the memory at the appropriate time. Java solves this problem conveniently with the garbage collector, which does the deallocation for you. The C++ language does not offer such a convenient solution, and programmers must learn the principles of memory management when programming with CORBA and C++.

It is particularly important to adopt good practices in memory management when programming with CORBA in C++. Certain programming practices that you might get away with in a standalone application simply will not work in a distributed application. A server providing for thousands of clients will rapidly be brought to its knees by any memory leaks, for example.

To program effectively with CORBA in C++ you need to have a grasp of the following fundamentals:

- Allocating and initializing CORBA data types
- Deallocating CORBA data types

- Assigning and copying CORBA data types
- Passing CORBA data type parameters
- Using smart pointers to manage memory effectively

This chapter covers each of these topics, enabling you to manage the complete lifecycle of CORBA data. The difficult part, however, is to know when to carry out the basic steps in the lifecycle of a parameter. This chapter explains what happens as parameters are passed in a CORBA invocation so that you can understand the logic underlying the CORBA memory management rules.

The good news for C++ programmers is that they are not entirely on their own when it comes to memory management. CORBA provides help in the form of smart pointer types (also known as `_var` types) that are designed to ease the burden.

C++ Smart Pointer Types _var

This section introduces the idea of `_var` types in the C++ mapping. For almost all CORBA types, apart from some of the basic types, the C++ mapping defines a corresponding `_var` type. For each IDL type `T`, a class `T_var` is generated by the C++ mapping.

The main purpose of the `_var` types is to assist the C++ programmer with memory management, and in particular to help avoid memory leaks. The `_var` types also have some additional features, including helper methods that can simplify parameter passing in CORBA operations.

This section begins with an explanation for the concept of a smart pointer. The `_var` type for managing CORBA strings, `CORBA::String_var`, is then presented before discussing the general properties of `_var` types.

What Is a Smart Pointer?

A *smart pointer* is a C++ class that is designed to imitate the syntax of an ordinary pointer. For example, the dereferencing operator `operator*()` and the member referencing operator `operator->()` are frequently overloaded in a smart pointer class:

```
class SmartPtr {
     T* m_ptr;
public:
     T& operator*();
     T* operator->();
     // Definitions of constructors etc.
     ...
};
```

An instance of the class `SmartPtr` is intended to be used as a pointer to the type `T`. In other words, `SmartPtr` is a replacement for the dumb pointer `T*` and holds a pointer to a `T` instance. The `operator*()` is used to dereference the smart pointer, returning the value of the corresponding `T` instance. The `operator->()` is used to access the members of the corresponding `T` instance (needed in cases where `T` is a `class`, `struct`, or `union` type).

More overloaded operators can be defined for the class `SmartPtr` as required (in particular, the subscripting operator `operator[]()` is frequently overloaded as well). With a little effort, a class `SmartPtr` can be defined that imitates the built-in pointer `T*` in almost every respect.

The power of a smart pointer lies in the fact that every time it is accessed via an overloaded operator, some special behavior can be programmed to occur. This allows a smart pointer to behave in a more intelligent manner than an ordinary pointer. For example, an attempt to dereference a null pointer in C++ usually has grave consequences. A smart pointer instance, however, can be designed to generate a warning message and avoid the program crashing.

In the context of the CORBA C++ mapping, smart pointer classes are used to aid memory management and avoid memory leaks.

The `CORBA::String_var` Type

An example of a smart pointer is the type `CORBA::String_var`. CORBA specifies that the IDL type `string` maps to either of the C++ types given in Table 4.1.

Table 4.1 Dumb and Smart Pointers for CORBA Strings

Pointer Type	Description
`char *`	Dumb pointer type—A CORBA string has the same layout as a standard C++ string and can be referenced via a simple `char *` pointer.
`CORBA::String_var`	Smart pointer type—A CORBA string can also be referenced using this smart pointer type. The smart pointer automatically manages the memory associated with the string, deleting it as necessary.

Consider a simple code fragment that dynamically allocates a string:

```
// C++
{  // Begin local scope
    // Allocate and Initialize the string 's'
    char * s = CORBA::string_dup("Hello Earth");

    // Print out various bits of the string
    cout << s << endl;
    cout << s[0] << s[1] << s[2] << s[3] << s[4] << endl;

    // Deallocate the string 's'
    CORBA::string_free(s);
}  // End local scope
```

As usual in C++ you must take particular care to deallocate the string before exiting the current scope. If you forget to call `CORBA::string_free()` on the pointer `s`, the memory associated with the string (12 bytes worth) will be leaked.

The above code fragment can be rewritten with the help of the smart pointer type `CORBA::String_var` as follows:

```
// C++
{
    // Allocate and Initialize the string 's'
    CORBA::String_var s = CORBA::string_dup("Hello Earth");

    // Print out various bits of the string
    cout << s.in() << endl;
    cout << s[0] << s[1] << s[2] << s[3] << s[4] << endl;
} // String 's' is automatically Deallocated
```

The key difference here is that the `_var` type relieves you of the burden of calling `CORBA::string_free()` at the end of the function. The destructor of the `CORBA::String_var` class makes a call to `CORBA::string_free()`, and this destructor is called automatically as soon as `s` goes out of scope.

When the `CORBA::String_var` is streamed to `cout`, it is converted to an ordinary `char*` by calling `s.in()`. With ANSI-compliant C++ compilers, you can print out the string directly, as in `cout << s << endl`. However, automatic type conversion is not properly supported by some C++ compilers, and for these compilers the `CORBA::String_var::in()` function might need to be called.

NOTE

> You can use array subscripting on `CORBA::String_var`, for example `s[0]`, just like an ordinary string. This is because the `operator[]()` is also overloaded for the `CORBA::String_var` class.

General Form of a _var Class

The CORBA C++ language mapping specifies that smart pointer classes representing structured IDL types should have the following general form (from section 1.9.1, p. 1–22 of "C++ Language Mapping Specification," June 1999):

```
// C++
class T_var
{
public:
    T_var();
    T_var(T *);
```

```
    T_var(const T_var &);
    ~T_var();

    T_var &operator=(T *);
    T_var &operator=(const T_var &);

    T* operator->();
    const T* operator->() const;

    /* in parameter type */ in() const;
    /* inout parameter type */ inout();
    /* out parameter type */ out();
    /* return type */ _retn();

    // other conversion operators to support
    // parameter passing
};
```

The T_var class for structured types invariably overloads the assignment operator operator=() as well as the member access operator operator->(). The methods in(), inout(), and out() were introduced in CORBA 2.3. They allow you to convert T_var explicitly to the appropriate type for passing as an in, inout, or out parameter. Some C++ compilers require you to use these functions—with ANSI-compliant compilers their use is optional.

The key feature of the T_var class is that its destructor ~T_var() always frees the memory referenced by the T_var. However, there are a number of other important features. Assignment semantics are affected and parameter passing of T_var types is aided by the in(), inout(), and out() methods. These features are discussed in the following sections.

Assignment Semantics

CORBA _var types always overload the assignment operator=(). This is done in order to make assignment to _var a more intelligent operation that reduces the danger of leaking memory. A key concept here is that of ownership. A _var type owns the memory it references and so long as it keeps ownership of this memory there is no danger of that memory being leaked. The _var type is designed so that this remains true irrespective of the operations carried out on it and, in particular, irrespective of the assignment operations carried out on it.

Assignment semantics are discussed in detail in the section "Assignment and Copying," later in this chapter.

Use of in(), inout(), out(), and _retn()

The methods T_var::in(), T_var::inout(), T_var::out(), and T_var::_retn() were introduced in the CORBA 2.3 specification to facilitate conversion of T_vars to the appropriate type when used as parameters or return values in CORBA invocations. Table 4.2 summarizes the use of the methods:

Table 4.2 Conversion of `_var` Type to Parameter Type

Conversion Method	Description
`T_var::in()`	Convert `T_var` to the type that should be used when passing the referenced data as an `in` parameter.
`T_var::inout()`	Convert `T_var` to the type that should be used when passing the referenced data as an `inout` parameter.
`T_var::out()`	Convert `T_var` to the type that should be used when passing the referenced data as an `out` parameter.
`T_var::_retn()`	Yield ownership of the referenced data and return a pointer of the appropriate type for use as a return value.

In the case of `in()`, `inout()`, and `out()`, `T_var` retains ownership of the memory it references. The effect of the methods is to convert `T_var` cleanly to the appropriate type for each parameter-passing mode.

The method `_retn()` is a special case. A call on `_retn()` forces `T_var` to give up ownership of its referenced data. After the call, `T_var` is effectively null and ceases to reference the data. The method can be a useful aid to avoid memory leaks associated with return values. The use of `_retn()` is discussed in the section "Return Values and `_retn()`," later in this chapter.

In previous versions of the CORBA specification the `_var` types relied on implicit conversion when passed as parameters. For backward compatibility, ORBs still support implicit conversion. However, some C++ compilers do not implement implicit conversion correctly. For these compilers, it is necessary to perform conversion explicitly using `in()`, `inout()`, and `out()`.

Sample IDL

The following IDL is used as a source of examples throughout the rest of the chapter. The module `SampleTypes` defines a selection of user-defined types and an interface `Foo` that passes some of these types back and forth.

Listing 4.1 IDL for Sample Data Types (`04Listing01.idl`)

```
// IDL
// Sample Data Types

#pragma prefix "pure-corba-3.com"

module SampleTypes {
    enum Shape { Square, Circle, Triangle };

    typedef string< 64 >   BoundedString;
    typedef wstring< 128 > BoundedWString;

    struct FixLen {
        short theShort;
```

Listing 4.1 continued

```
        float theFloat;
    };
    struct VarLen {
        string theString;
        long theLong;
    };

    typedef sequence< FixLen > SeqOfFixLen;
    typedef sequence< VarLen > SeqOfVarLen;
    typedef sequence< VarLen, 5 > BSeqOfVarLen;

    typedef fixed<6,2> Money;

    union Poly switch(short) {
        case 1: short theShort;
        case 2: string theString;
    };

    typedef FixLen ArrOfFixLen[10];
    typedef VarLen ArrOfVarLen[10];

    exception GenericExc {
        string reason;
    };

    interface Foo {
        void passIn(in FixLen fl);
        void passInout(inout FixLen fl);
        void passInout2(inout VarLen vl);
        void receiveOut(out FixLen fl);
        void receiveOut2(out VarLen vl);
        VarLen getResult(out VarLen vl) raises (GenericExc);
    }; // interface Foo

}; // module SampleTypes
```

The IDL defines some basic types: an `enum`, a bounded string, and a bounded wide string. Two different sorts of struct are defined: `FixLen` and `VarLen`. These two structs are useful samples for highlighting the difference between a fixed-length type and a variable-length type, respectively. This distinction is discussed in the section "Parameter Passing," later in this chapter.

Some sequences both unbounded (`SeqOfFixLen`, `SeqOfVarLen`) and unbounded (`BSeqOfBarLen`) are defined. A miscellany of other data types are also defined, including a `fixed` type, a `union`, `arrays`, and an `exception` type.

The interface Foo comes in useful in the section "Parameter Passing," where it is used to illustrate how parameters are passed for each of the parameter-passing modes in, inout, and out.

Allocating and Initializing

There is a variety of ways of allocating memory for CORBA data types. Most of these data types, apart from very simple types such as CORBA::Short, may be allocated either on the stack or on the heap (free store).

It is a general principle that CORBA data types are always initialized before being passed in an invocation. For example, a blank string should always be initialized as "" (empty string) and never as NULL.

The following sections give examples of how to allocate and initialize a wide variety of CORBA data types. Basic data types such as short, unsigned short, long, unsigned long, float, double, long long, unsigned long long, and the enum type are not covered, because they are trivial.

String Types

CORBA strings can only be allocated on the heap. This is done with the help of the CORBA::string_alloc() function. The following code illustrates string allocation using a smart pointer CORBA::String_var.

```
// C++
#include <string.h>

// Allocation using smart pointer
CORBA::String_var strV = CORBA::string_alloc(5+1);

// Initialization
strncpy((char*) strV, "Hello", 5);
```

The following code illustrates string allocation using a dumb pointer char*.

```
// C++
#include <string.h>

// Allocation using dumb pointer
char * strP = CORBA::string_alloc(5+1);

// Initialization
strncpy((char*) strP, "Hello", 5);

// Beware! Remember to Deallocate strP
CORBA::string_free(strP);
```

CORBA strings are null terminated, just like ordinary C++ strings. That is why the number of bytes allocated by CORBA::string_alloc() is 1 greater than the length of the string.

Allocation and initialization of a string can be compressed into a single step with the help of the function `CORBA::string_dup()`. This is illustrated by the following code fragment:

```
// C++
//Allocation and Initialization using smart pointer
CORBA::String_var strV = CORBA::string_dup("Hello");
```

Bounded String Types

The following is an example of a bounded string declared in IDL:

```
// IDL
typedef string<64> BoundedString;
```

The integer value between angle brackets declares the maximum allowed length of the string `BoundedString`.

Bounded strings are allocated and initialized in exactly the same way as unbounded strings. Bounds checking occurs when an attempt is made to pass the string as a parameter or return value that was declared bounded. A compliant ORB will raise an exception at this point if the bound is exceeded.

WString Types

Wide strings consist of an array of wide characters `CORBA::WChar` (typically unicode characters). Wide strings are discussed further in Chapter 17, "IDL Data Types." Allocation and initialization follow a pattern similar to that of ordinary strings.

The following code illustrates allocation using a smart pointer `CORBA::WString_var`.

```
// C++
//Allocation using smart pointer
CORBA::WString_var wstrV = CORBA::wstring_alloc(5+1);

// Initialization
wstrV[0] = L'H';
wstrV[1] = L'e';
wstrV[2] = L'l';
wstrV[3] = L'l';
wstrV[4] = L'o';
wstrV[5] = L'\0';
```

The following code illustrates allocation using a dumb pointer `CORBA::WChar*`.

```
// C++
// Allocation using dumb pointer
CORBA::WChar* wstrP = CORBA::wstring_alloc(5+1);

// Initialization
wstrP[0] = L'H';
```

```
wstrP[1] = L'e';
wstrP[2] = L'l';
wstrP[3] = L'l';
wstrP[4] = L'o';
wstrP[5] = L'\0';

// Beware! Remember to Deallocate wstrP
CORBA::wstring_free(wstrP);
```

Allocation and initialization of a wide string can be compressed into a single step with the help of the function `CORBA::wstring_dup()`. This is illustrated by the following code fragment:

```
// C++
// Allocation and Initialization using smart pointer
CORBA::WString_var wstrV = CORBA::wstring_dup(L"Hello");
```

Bounded `wstring` Types

The following is an example of a bounded wide string declared in IDL:

```
// IDL
typedef wstring<128> BoundedWString;
```

The integer value between angle brackets declares the maximum allowed length of the wide string `BoundedWString`.

Bounded wide strings are allocated and initialized in exactly the same way as unbounded wide strings. Bounds checking for wide strings occurs when an attempt is made to pass the wide string as a parameter or return value that was declared bounded. A compliant ORB will raise an exception at this point if the bound is exceeded.

Struct Types

A user-defined struct can be allocated either on the stack or on the heap. Consider the struct `VarLen`, defined in the IDL of Listing 4.1.

```
// IDL
module SampleTypes {
     ...
     struct VarLen {
          string theString;
          long theLong;
     };
     ...
};
```

The following code illustrates allocation on the stack.

```
// C++
// Allocation and Initialization on the stack
SampleTypes::VarLen aVarLen;

// Initialization
aVarLen.theString = CORBA::string_dup("Initial string");
aVarLen.theLong   = (CORBA::Long) 32;
```

The following code illustrates allocation on the heap using a smart pointer.

```
// C++
// Allocation using smart pointer
SampleTypes::VarLen_var aVarLenV = new SampleTypes::VarLen();

// Initialization
aVarLenV->theString = CORBA::string_dup("Initial string");
aVarLenV->theLong   = (CORBA::Long) 32;
```

The following code illustrates allocation on the heap using a dumb pointer.

```
// C++
// Allocation using dumb pointer
SampleTypes::VarLen * aVarLenP = new SampleTypes::VarLen();

// Initialization
aVarLenP->theString = CORBA::string_dup("Initial string");
aVarLenP->theLong   = (CORBA::Long) 32;

// Beware! Remember to Deallocate 'aVarLenP'
delete aVarLenP;
```

A struct owns the memory associated with its members. Therefore, when a struct is deleted, it recursively deletes each of its members.

Unbounded Sequence Types

A sequence can be allocated either on the stack or on the heap. Three different constructors are provided for sequences (see Chapter 18, "IDL Grammar"), but the most commonly used is the constructor that sets the `maximum()` of the sequence. Consider an instance of `SampleTypes::SeqOfVarLen`, declared in the IDL of Listing 4.1.

```
// IDL
module SampleTypes {
      ...
      typedef sequence< VarLen > SeqOfVarLen;
      ...
};
```

The following code illustrates allocation on the stack.

```
// C++
// Allocation on the stack
SampleTypes::SeqOfVarLen aSeqOfVarLen(2);      // maximum = 2
                                               // length = 0
// Set the length to a sensible value
aSeqOfVarLen.length(2);

// Initialize the sequence
CORBA::ULong i=0;
aSeqOfVarLen[i].theString = CORBA::string_dup("First");
aSeqOfVarLen[i].theLong   = (CORBA::Long) 64;
++i;
aSeqOfVarLen[i].theString = CORBA::string_dup("Second");
aSeqOfVarLen[i].theLong   = (CORBA::Long) 128;
```

Note that the sequence index is of type `CORBA::ULong`. It is not satisfactory to use simple integer arguments here, such as `aSeqOfVarLen[0]` or `aSeqOfVarLen[1]`. Such code would not always compile, because the `operator[]()` is overloaded on an argument of type `CORBA::ULong` and not `int`.

NOTE

> It is not necessary to explicitly allocate memory for the `VarLen` structs in the preceding code fragment. Sequence types are constructed in a way that is analogous to C++ arrays: When the length of a sequence is set, the sequence elements are initialized by calling the default constructor for the element type.

The following code illustrates allocation on the heap using a smart pointer:

```
// C++
// Allocation on the heap
SampleTypes::SeqOfVarLen_var aSeqOfVarLenV =
            new SampleTypes::SeqOfVarLen(2);  // maximum = 2
                                              // length = 0
// Set the length to a sensible value
aSeqOfVarLenV->length(2);

// Initialize the sequence
CORBA::ULong i=0;
aSeqOfVarLenV[i].theString = CORBA::string_dup("First");
aSeqOfVarLenV[i].theLong   = (CORBA::Long) 64;
++i;
aSeqOfVarLenV[i].theString = CORBA::string_dup("Second");
aSeqOfVarLenV[i].theLong   = (CORBA::Long) 128;
```

The syntax used for accessing sequence elements in the last example, `aSeqOfVarLenV[i]`, is apparently inconsistent. You would expect to write `(*aSeqOfVarLenV)[i]` instead, assuming `aSeqOfVarLenV` is interpreted as a pointer. In fact, both forms of syntax are supported, because the `operator[]()` is overloaded.

The following code illustrates allocation on the heap using a dumb pointer.

```
// C++
// Allocation on the heap
SampleTypes::SeqOfVarLen * aSeqOfVarLenP =
            new SampleTypes::SeqOfVarLen(2);  // maximum = 2
                                              // length = 0
// Set the length to a sensible value
aSeqOfVarLenP->length(2);

// Initialize the sequence
CORBA::ULong i=0;
(*aSeqOfVarLenP)[i].theString = CORBA::string_dup("First");
(*aSeqOfVarLenP)[i].theLong   = (CORBA::Long) 64;
++i;
(*aSeqOfVarLenP)[i].theString = CORBA::string_dup("Second");
(*aSeqOfVarLenP)[i].theLong   = (CORBA::Long) 128;

// Beware! Remember to deallocate 'aSeqOfVarLenP'
delete aSeqOfVarLenP;
```

Bounded Sequence Types

Bounded sequences are rarely used, because they defeat the primary advantage of a sequence, which is the capability to extend the sequence to hold an arbitrary number of elements. Consider an instance of a bounded sequence, `SampleTypes::BseqOfVarLen`, declared in the IDL of Listing 4.1.

```
// IDL
module SampleTypes {
     ...
     typedef sequence< VarLen, 5 > BSeqOfVarLen;
     ...
};
```

The following code illustrates allocation on the stack.

```
// C++
// Allocation on the stack
SampleTypes::BSeqOfVarLen aBSeqOfVarLen;     // maximum = 5
                                             // length  = 0
// The maximum is implicitly, and irrevocably, set equal to the bound
// that was declared in the IDL.
```

```
// Set the length to a sensible value
aBSeqOfVarLen.length(2);

// Initialize the sequence
CORBA::ULong i=0;
aBSeqOfVarLen[i].theString = CORBA::string_dup("First");
aBSeqOfVarLen[i].theLong   = (CORBA::Long) 64;
++i;
aBSeqOfVarLen[i].theString = CORBA::string_dup("Second");
aBSeqOfVarLen[i].theLong   = (CORBA::Long) 128;
```

The default constructor is used, and the maximum is implicitly set equal to the bound declared in the IDL. Otherwise the syntax is the same as in the case of an unbounded string.

The length of a bounded sequence cannot be set greater than its maximum. The consequences of trying to do so are undefined and may result in a core dump.

Fixed Types

Fixed types are passed by reference as operation parameters and by value as return values. In other words, although fixed types are objects, they are treated more like basic types.

A number of constructors are provided that enable a fixed type to be initialized from any CORBA integer type, floating-point type, or string. You should be wary of initializing fixed data from a floating point number—it could lead to undesirable rounding errors.

Consider the following definition of a fixed type `Money`:

```
// IDL
module SampleTypes {
    ...
    typedef fixed< 6, 2> Money;
    ...
};
```

This defines a six-digit precision number that has two decimal places. The most convenient and accurate way to initialize a fixed type is by assigning numbers in string format. This method of initialization is illustrated by the following code fragment.

```
// C++
// Allocation on the stack
SampleTypes::Money f1 = "1234.56";     // Use the maximum number of digits
SampleTypes::Money f2 = "-9999.99";    // The most negative number
SampleTypes::Money f3 = "0.04";
```

Union Types

Unions can be allocated on the stack or on the heap. A union is allocated using its default constructor, and it does not contain any valid value until it has been initialized. Consider the union type `SampleTypes::Poly`, declared in the IDL of Listing 4.1.

```
// IDL
module SampleTypes {
     ...
     union Poly switch(short) {
          case 1: short theShort;
          case 2: string theString;
     };
     ...
};
```

The following code illustrates allocation on the stack.

```
// C++
// Allocation of union on the stack
SampleTypes::Poly aPoly;

// Initialization to type short
aPoly.theShort(2);                    //Discriminant = 1

// Change to type string
aPoly.theString("A new identity.");  // Discriminant = 2
```

Note how the discriminant is automatically set to the value of the appropriate case label.

The following code illustrates allocation on the heap using a smart pointer.

```
// C++
// Allocation of union on the heap
SampleTypes::Poly_var aPolyV = new SampleTypes::Poly();

// Initialization
aPolyV->_default();  // Discriminant = some value not equal to 1 or 2
```

The use of method `_default()` is a special case of initialization of the union. Whenever a union is declared in IDL without a `default` case label, the method `_default()` is generated by the IDL compiler. By initializing via `_default()`, the union is left empty and the discriminant set to a value that does not appear in the case labels (the value selected isimplementation dependent).

NOTE

Effectively, this enables you to initialize an empty union. It is legal to marshal this empty union as a parameter in a CORBA invocation.

Array Types

Arrays can be allocated either on the stack or on the heap. Because arrays map to a C++ built-in type, in certain respects they are a special case. In particular, the use of array slice pointers is needed to reference dynamically allocated arrays. Consider the type `SampleTypes::ArrOfVarLen`, defined in the IDL of Listing 4.1.

```
// IDL
module SampleTypes {
     ...
     typedef VarLen ArrOfVarLen[10];
     ...
};
```

The following code illustrates allocation on the stack.

```
// C++
// Allocate an instance of a 10-element array
SampleTypes::ArrOfVarLen anArrOfVarLen;

// Initialize the first element explicitly
anArrOfVarLen[0].theString = CORBA::string_dup("First Element");
anArrOfVarLen[0].theLong   = (CORBA::Long) 256;
// Accept default initial values for other elements
```

Note that as `anArrOfVarLen` is initialized it calls the default constructor of `VarLen` for each of its 10 elements.

The following code illustrates allocation on the heap using a smart pointer.

```
// C++
// Allocate an instance of a 10-element array
SampleTypes::ArrOfVarLen_var anArrOfVarLenV = SampleTypes::ArrOfVarLen_alloc();

// Initialize the first element explicitly
anArrOfVarLenV[0].theString = CORBA::string_dup("First Element");
anArrOfVarLenV[0].theLong   = (CORBA::Long) 256;
// Accept default initial values for other elements
```

This example uses `SampleTypes::ArrOfVarLen_alloc()` to allocate the array on the heap. It is not possible to use `new` to perform the allocation.

The following code illustrates allocation on the heap using a dumb pointer.

```
// C++
// Allocate an instance of a 10-element array
SampleTypes::ArrOfVarLen_slice * anArrOfVarLenSl =
➥SampleTypes::ArrOfVarLen_alloc();

// Initialize the first element explicitly
anArrOfVarLenSl[0].theString = CORBA::string_dup("First Element");
```

```
anArrOfVarLenSl[0].theLong   = (CORBA::Long) 256;
// Accept default initial values for other elements

// Beware! Remember to Deallocate 'anArrOfVarLenSl'
SampleTypes::ArrOfVarLen_free(anArrOfVarLenSl);
```

This example uses `SampleTypes::ArrOfVarLen_slice*` as the dumb pointer type. In this case, with a one-dimensional array, the slice pointer is equivalent to the type `SampleTypes::VarLen *`. However, in the general case there is no natural representation of a dumb pointer. The type *`arrayType`*`_slice*` is generated to fit this role—see Chapter 18 for more details.

any Type

The `any` type can be allocated either on the stack or on the heap. The `any` is covered separately in Chapter 8, "The `any` Type." A simple example of initializing an `any` is where a basic type such as a `CORBA::Long` is inserted into the `any`.

The following code illustrates allocation on the stack.

```
// C++
// Allocate an instance of an 'any'
CORBA::Any anAny;

// Initialization by inserting a 'long'
anAny <<= (CORBA::Long) 123;
```

The left-shift assignment operator (<<=) is used to insert data into an `any`. In this case, the inserted data is a `CORBA::Long`, but in general it could be any user-defined CORBA type.

The following code illustrates allocation on the heap using a smart pointer.

```
// C++
// Allocate an instance of an 'any' on the heap
CORBA::Any_var anAnyV = new CORBA::Any();

// Initialization by inserting a 'long'
(*anAnyV) <<=  (CORBA::Long) 123;
```

Object References

Object references are never instantiated directly by the user. All object references originate in the ORB. They are obtained either directly from the ORB (for example, via the Initialization Service) or as return values from a CORBA invocation.

Nevertheless, the user is still responsible for deleting the object reference. To assist with the memory management of object references, a smart pointer class *`interfaceName`*`_var` is defined. Details about object references can be found in Chapter 5, "Object References."

Deallocating

If you follow the recommended style of CORBA programming and use _var types as much as possible, you will find that explicit deallocation of CORBA data types is rarely necessary.

Most CORBA data types can be deallocated using the delete operator. The complete list of deallocating methods is shown in Table 4.3.

Table 4.3 CORBA Methods for Deallocation of Memory

Deallocation Method	Description
`void CORBA::string_free(char *)`	This function must always be used to deallocate a CORBA string. If you do not use this method, your C++ code will not be portable across all platforms.
`void CORBA::wstring_free(CORBA::WChar*)`	This function must always be used to deallocate a CORBA wide string. If you do not use this method, your C++ code will not be portable across all platforms.
`void <arrayName>_free(<arrayName>_slice*)`	For every array of type *arrayName*, a corresponding function of this kind is generated by the IDL compiler. This function is convenient because it enables multi-dimensional arrays to be deleted in a single step.
`void CORBA::release(CORBA::Object_ptr)`	This function is used to free object references of any type. It is discussed in Chapter 5.
`delete`	All other heap-allocated CORBA types are deallocated using the delete operator.

There are specific methods made available to deallocate strings, wide strings, and arrays that have been allocated on the heap. Object references are a special case, being released (but not necessarily deallocated straightaway) by the function CORBA::release.

In all other cases, a simple delete suffices to deallocate CORBA data that has been allocated on the heap.

Recursive Deletion

It is a general principle that an instance of a nested CORBA type can be deleted simply by calling delete on the outermost containing instance. All of the members and subelements of the nested type are recursively deleted.

Take as an example the struct VarLen, whose nested members include a string and a long. The following code fragment shows the allocation, initialization, and deletion of an instance of VarLen.

```
// C++
// Allocation using dumb pointer
SampleTypes::VarLen * aVarLenP = new SampleTypes::VarLen();

// Initialization
aVarLenP->theString = CORBA::string_dup("Initial string");
aVarLenP->theLong   = (CORBA::Long) 32;

// Beware! Remember to Deallocate 'aVarLenP'
delete aVarLenP;
```

When the struct instance aVarLenP is deleted, it automatically deletes the nested instance of the string pointed at by aVarLenP->theString. This is not what would happen with an ordinary struct—this requires some trickery in the implementation. In fact, a string occurring as a member of a struct behaves just like the _var type CORBA::String_var. See Chapter 17 for details.

A common variation is where some of the nested members are already assigned to a _var type before being assigned to the nested structure. For example

```
// C++
// Allocation using dumb pointer
SampleTypes::VarLen * aVarLenP = new SampleTypes::VarLen();

// Initialize and assign string to a _var
CORBA::String_var sV = CORBA::string_dup("Initial string");

// Initialization of struct
aVarLenP->theString = sV;
aVarLenP->theLong   = (CORBA::Long) 32;

// Beware! Remember to Deallocate 'aVarLenP'
delete aVarLenP;
```

The question then arises: Who is responsible for deallocating the string member? Is it the smart pointer sV or the member aVarLenP->theString (which also behaves like a _var)? In fact, both smart pointers perform deallocation, because there are two strings to deallocate. The assignment aVarLenP->theString = sV results in a deep copy of the original string. The assignment operator=() is overloaded to perform a deep copy whenever both sides of the assignment statement are smart pointers. This is consistent with the semantics of assignment and copying, as discussed in the next section of this chapter, "Assignment and Copying."

The principle of recursive deletion applies to all CORBA data types and to arbitrary degrees of nesting. For example, a sequence of structs containing a `union`, an `any`, and an `array` of structs, each of which contains `strings`, `anys`, and `unions`, could be deallocated simply by calling `delete` on the pointer to the parent `sequence` (assuming it was allocated on heap).

You have a choice of whether to use a smart or a dumb pointer for the topmost parent data type (`sequence` in this case). However, you have no such choice for the data types nested within the parent. All elements of a sequence are automatically deleted along with the parent sequence. Likewise, all members of a struct are deleted along with the parent struct. Any pointer members of a struct recursively delete the memory they reference. This is because they are smart pointers. And so it continues down the chain. CORBA uses smart pointers by default wherever one data type is nested inside another. This is what makes recursive deletion of CORBA data possible.

There are just two exceptions to the principle of recursive deletion. The `sequence` types and the `any` type both provide a special form of constructor that allows you to switch off smart memory-management behavior. In other words, they would cease to own the memory they use. This is an option that should be used with considerable caution because of the danger of introducing memory leaks. See Chapters 8 and 18.

Assignment and Copying

This section takes a look at the copying of CORBA data types in C++. This is a trivial exercise for simple data types such as `short` or `float`, but for compound types the operation of copying is complicated by a couple of factors.

First of all, you have to decide if you want to make a physical copy of the data or if you just want to copy a pointer to the original data. The concept of deep and shallow copy is introduced to clarify copying semantics.

You also have to contend with the fact that there are different ways of referring to CORBA data in C++ (by value, by pointer, or by smart pointer). Mixed assignments between these different representations are possible. Some of the resulting assignment permutations are discussed below.

Deep and Shallow Copy

The CORBA data types have been designed to simplify copying as far as possible, particularly when it comes to compound and nested types. There are generally two kinds of copy operation that are useful:

- Shallow copy
- Deep copy

In a *shallow copy*, only a pointer to the data is copied. The data itself is not copied. The following code fragment shows an example of a shallow copy:

```
//C++
SampleTypes::VarLen * p;
SampleTypes::VarLen * q;

// Allocate and Initialize original 'VarLen' struct
p = new SampleTypes::VarLen();
p->theString = CORBA::string_dup("Nested String");
p->theLong   = (CORBA::Long) 36;

// Shallow copy from pointer 'p' to pointer 'q'
q = p;

// Beware! Remember to deallocate the 'VarLen' struct
delete p;
```

This example uses the struct type `VarLen`, defined in Listing 4.1. The situation after performing the shallow copy `p=q` is illustrated by Figure 4.1. After the assignment, there is just one copy of the `VarLen` struct, and both `p` and `q` reference the same data.

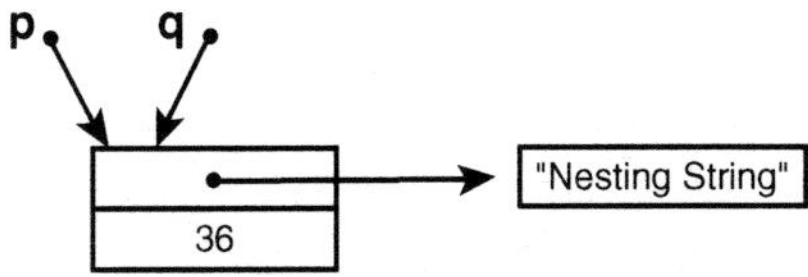

Figure 4.1

Shallow copy.

The other useful copy operation is a *deep copy*. In this case, a complete copy of the `VarLen` struct is made, including all of its nested elements (and, recursively, all the nested data). The following code fragment illustrates how a deep copy of the `VarLen` struct is made:

```
//C++
SampleTypes::VarLen * p;
SampleTypes::VarLen * q;

// Allocate and Initialize original 'VarLen' struct
p = new SampleTypes::VarLen();
p->theString = CORBA::string_dup("Nested String");
p->theLong   = (CORBA::Long) 36;

// Allocate second 'VarLen' struct
q = new SampleTypes::VarLen();

// Deep copy from '*p' to '*q'
*q = *p;
```

```
// Beware! Remember to deallocate both of the 'VarLen' structs
delete p;
delete q;
```

The situation after the struct assignment `*q = *p` is illustrated in Figure 4.2. If you are familiar with the semantics of struct assignment in C++, you might guess that there is some trickery going on behind the scenes. Figure 4.2 shows that `q` references a completely new copy of the data, including a newly allocated copy of the nested string. However, the standard semantic for struct assignment in C++ is memberwise assignment. In other words, the following are equivalent:

```
// C++
// This assignment...
*q = *p;

//...is equivalent to this memberwise assignment...
q->theString = p->theString;
q->theLong   = p->theLong;
```

Therefore, if the `theString` member were an ordinary pointer, the nested string would not be duplicated at all, because the above assignment copies just the pointer to the string. However, the `theString` member is not an ordinary pointer. It is a smart pointer with properties identical to the type `CORBA::String_var`—see Chapter 18 for details.

You do not need to worry about the mechanism underlying the deep copy. That is an implementation detail for the ORB vendor. You only need to know that when a CORBA compound type is copied, it is designed so that all of its nested data is recursively copied. You end up with a completely new copy of the data. There is no overlap between the original and the new copy. This is true no matter how complex and nested the data type may be.

In summary, a CORBA data type can be copied either as a shallow copy (pointers only) or as a deep copy (a complete new copy). There is nothing between these two extremes.

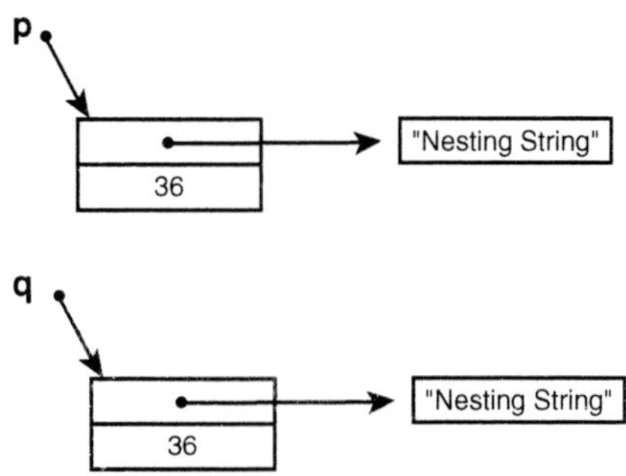

Figure 4.2

Deep copy.

Mixed Assignment

Each data type can be referenced either by a smart or a dumb pointer. As a result, there is a variety of mixed assignments that can occur.

The mixed assignments are summarized in Table 4.4:

Table 4.4 Summary of Mixed Pointer Assignments

Type of Assignment	Description
`T *= T *`	Shallow copy. Pointer value only is copied.
`T_var = T *`	Shallow copy. Old data referenced by `T_var` is deallocated. After assignment, `T_var` references the same data as `T *` and assumes ownership of this data.
`T_var = T_var`	Deep copy. Old data referenced by `T_var` is deallocated. After assignment, `T_var` on the left side references a new copy of the data from the right side.
`T * = T_var`	Shallow copy. Pointer value of `T_var` is assigned to `T *`. Old data referenced by dumb pointer `T *` ought to be deallocated before reaching this step. `T_var` retains ownership of its data.

The following sections look at the different kinds of mixed assignments for each CORBA data type.

String Types (Unbounded and Bounded)

The following code fragment shows examples of mixed pointer assignments between dumb pointers and `_var` pointers for strings:

```
// C++
char *              origStringP = CORBA::string_dup("Dumb");
CORBA::String_var origStringV = CORBA::string_dup("Smart");
char *              copiedStringP;
CORBA::String_var copiedStringV;
...
// dumb_pointer = dumb_pointer
delete copiedStringP;
copiedStringP = origStringP;     //Shallow copy.
...
// dumb_pointer = duplicate(dumb_pointer)
delete copiedStringP;
copiedStringP = CORBA::string_dup(origStringP);     // Deep copy.
...
//_var = dumb_pointer
copiedStringV = origStringP;     // Shallow copy.
                                 // the 'copiedStringV' assumes ownership of
memory
...
```

```
//_var = _var
copiedStringV = origStringV      // Deep copy.
                                 // each _var manages its own copy
...
// dumb_pointer = _var
delete copiedStringP;
copiedStringP = origStringV      // Shallow copy
                                 // the 'origStringV' retains ownership of
memory
```

The semantics of assignment and copying are identical for both unbounded and bounded strings.

WString Types (Unbounded and Bounded)

The copying of wide strings works in a manner that is analogous to the copying of ordinary strings. The following fragment shows examples of mixed pointer assignments between dumb pointers and _var pointers for wide strings:

```
// C++
CORBA::WChar *     origWStringP = CORBA::wstring_dup(L"Dumb");
CORBA::WString_var origWStringV = CORBA::wstring_dup(L"Smart");
CORBA::WChar *     copiedWStringP;
CORBA::WString_var copiedWStringV;
...
// dumb_pointer = dumb_pointer
delete copiedWStringP;
copiedWStringP = origWStringP;     // Shallow copy.
...
// dumb_pointer = duplicate(dumb_pointer)
delete copiedWStringP;
copiedWStringP = CORBA::wstring_dup(origWStringP);     // Deep copy.
...
//_var = dumb_pointer
copiedWStringV = origWStringP;     // Shallow copy.
                               // the 'copiedWStringV' assumes ownership of memory
...
//_var = _var
copiedWStringV = origWStringV     // Deep copy.
                                  // each _var manages its own copy
...
// dumb_pointer = _var
delete copiedWStringP;
copiedWStringP = origWStringV     // Shallow copy
                                 // the 'origWStringV' retains ownership of memory
```

The semantics of assignment and copying are identical for both unbounded and bounded wide strings.

Struct Types

The following fragment shows examples of mixed pointer assignments between dumb pointers and _var pointers for the struct type VarLen:

```
// C++
SampleTypes::VarLen *   origStructP = new SampleTypes::VarLen();
origStructP->theString = CORBA::string_dup("Dumb");
origStructP->theLong   = (CORBA::Long) 32;

SampleTypes::VarLen_var origStructV = new SampleTypes::VarLen();
origStructV->theString = CORBA::string_dup("Smart");
origStructV->theLong   = (CORBA::Long) 64;

SampleTypes::VarLen *   copiedStructP;
SampleTypes::VarLen_var copiedStructV;
...
// dumb_pointer = dumb_pointer
copiedStructP = origStructP;     // Shallow copy.
...
//_var = dumb_pointer
copiedStructV = origStructP;     // Shallow copy.
                                 // the 'copiedStructV' assumes ownership
                                 // of memory
...
//_var = _var
copiedStructV = origStructV;    // Deep copy.
                                // each _var manages its own copy
...
// dumb_pointer = _var
copiedStructP = origStructV._retn();    // Shallow copy
copiedStructP = origStructV;    // Shallow copy
                               // the 'origStructV' retains ownership of memory
```

Making a deep copy of a CORBA struct is particularly easy because of the way this type has been designed. All you need to do is assign a value of a struct to a value of a struct—for example, `*copiedStructP = *origStructP`. This results in recursive copying of all struct members and all of the nested data referenced by these members. Consider the following examples using the struct type VarLen:

```
// C++
SampleTypes::VarLen *   copiedStructP;
SampleTypes::VarLen_var copiedStructV;
...
// *(dumb_pointer) = *(dumb_pointer)
copiedStructP = new SampleTypes::VarLen();
*copiedStructP = *origStructP;     // Deep copy.
...
```

```
// *(_var) = *(dumb_pointer)
copiedStructV = new SampleTypes::VarLen();
*copiedStructV = *origStructP;     // Deep copy.
...
// *(_var) = *(_var)
*copiedStructV = *origStructV;    // Deep copy.
// (same effect as 'copiedStructV = origStructV')
...
// *(dumb_pointer) = *(_var)
*copiedStructP = *origStructV;    // Deep copy
...
delete origStructP;
delete copiedStructP;
```

As usual, it is safest to delete dumb pointers before assigning to them. This will not do any harm if the pointers are already NULL.

Sequence and Union Types

The types sequence and union can be grouped together because they are represented by C++ classes and therefore have identical syntax for assignment and copying. The sequence type is taken as a representative example and discussed in detail.

The following fragment shows examples of mixed pointer assignments between dumb pointers and _var pointers for the sequence SeqOfVarLen:

```
// C++
SampleTypes::SeqOfVarLen *   origSeqP =
            new SampleTypes::SeqOfVarLen(2);  // maximum = 2
     // Initialize the sequence 'origSeqP' (not shown)

SampleTypes::SeqOfVarLen_var origSeqV =
            new SampleTypes::SeqOfVarLen(2);  // maximum = 2
     // Initialize the sequence 'origSeqV' (not shown)

SampleTypes::SeqOfVarLen *   copiedSeqP;
SampleTypes::SeqOfVarLen_var copiedSeqV;

// dumb_pointer = dumb_pointer
copiedSeqP = origSeqP;     // Shallow copy.

//_var = dumb_pointer
copiedSeqV = origSeqP;     // Shallow copy.
                           // the 'copiedSeqV' assumes ownership of memory

//_var = _var
copiedSeqV = origSeqV;    // Deep copy.
                          // each _var manages its own copy
```

```
                            // Beware! 'origSeqP' and 'copiedSeqP' are now
                            // both dangling pointers.

// dumb_pointer = _var
copiedSeqP = origSeqV._retn();    // Shallow copy
delete copiedSeqP;

copiedSeqP = origSeqV;      // Shallow copy
                            // the 'origSeqV' retains ownership of memory
```

Making a deep copy of a sequence type is easy because the assignment operator `operator=()` is overloaded for values of the sequence. For example, the assignment `*copiedSeqP = *origSeqP` results in all of the elements of the sequence being deep copied. Consider the following examples:

```
// C++
SampleTypes::SeqOfVarLen *   copiedSeqP;
SampleTypes::SeqOfVarLen_var copiedSeqV;

// *(dumb_pointer) = *(dumb_pointer)
copiedSeqP = new SampleTypes::SeqOfVarLen(2);
*copiedSeqP = *origSeqP;     // Deep copy.

// *(_var) = *(dumb_pointer)
copiedSeqV = new SampleTypes::SeqOfVarLen(2);
*copiedSeqV = *origSeqP;     // Deep copy.

// *(_var) = *(_var)
*copiedSeqV = *origSeqV;    // Deep copy.
// (same effect as 'copiedSeqV = origSeqV')

// *(dumb_pointer) = *(_var)
*copiedSeqP = *origSeqV;    // Deep copy

delete origSeqP;
delete copiedSeqP;
```

The above examples of copying sequences are similar to the examples involving structs. Likewise, the `union` type is assigned and copied in a manner similar to that of the sequence type.

Array Types

Array types are exceptional because they are mapped directly to a native C++ pointer type instead of a specialized class. Operator overloading cannot be used to the same extent as with other compound types and some helper functions are needed.

The following fragment shows examples of mixed pointer assignments between dumb pointers and _var pointers for sample arrays of type ArrOfVarLen:

```
// C++
SampleTypes::ArrOfVarLen_slice * origArrP = SampleTypes::ArrOfVarLen_alloc();
     // Initialize the array 'origArrP' (not shown)

SampleTypes::ArrOfVarLen_var     origArrV = SampleTypes::ArrOfVarLen_alloc();
     // Initialize the array 'origArrV' (not shown)

SampleTypes::ArrOfVarLen_slice * copiedArrP;
SampleTypes::ArrOfVarLen_var     copiedArrV;

// dumb_pointer = dumb_pointer
copiedArrP = origArrP;     // Shallow copy.

//_var = dumb_pointer
copiedArrV = origArrP;     // Shallow copy.
                           // the 'copiedArrV' assumes ownership of memory

//_var = _var
copiedArrV = origArrV;    // Deep copy.
                          // each _var manages its own copy
                          // Beware! 'origArrP' and 'copiedArrP' are now
                          // both dangling pointers.

// dumb_pointer = _var
copiedArrP = origArrV._retn();    // Shallow copy
// copiedArrP = origArrV;     // Shallow copy
                          // the 'origArrV' retains ownership of memory
```

When copying arrays, it is not possible to implement an appropriate overloaded assignment operator, so a helper function *arrayName*_dup(const *arrayName*_slice*) is supplied. For example

```
// C++
// dumb_pointer = dup(dumb_pointer)
SampleTypes::ArrOfVarLen_free(copiedArrP);
copiedArrP = SampleTypes::ArrOfVarLen_dup(origArrP);     // Deep copy.
```

The effect of the *arrayName*_dup() function is to allocate space for a new array on the heap and then make a deep copy of every element in the original array to the new array. In other words, a deep copy is made.

Note that using *arrayName*_dup() is an inefficient way of copying large arrays of basic types. Consider the following IDL array type:

```
// IDL
typedef long LongArr[100000];
```

Copying a `LongArr` along the lines of this example would involve reallocating the array assigned to. This is unnecessary and inefficient. Reallocation can be avoided by using the *arrayName*`_copy()` helper function. Consider the following example:

```
// C++
LongArr_slice * longArrP = LongArr_alloc();
...     // Initialize the array 'longArrP' (not shown)
LongArr_slice * copiedLongArrP = LongArr_alloc();
...     // Initialize the array 'copiedLongArrP' (not shown)
...
// dumb_pointer = dup(dumb_pointer)  [The INEFFICIENT method]
LongArr_free(copiedLongArrP);
copiedLongArrP = LongArr_dup(longArrP);     // Deep copy.

// copy(dumb_pointer, dumb pointer)  [The EFFICIENT method]
// (assume 'copiedLongArrp' already points at a valid array)
LongArr_copy(copiedLongArrP, longArrP);     // Deep copy.
```

When *arrayName*`_copy()` is used to copy `longArrP` to `copiedLongArrP`, the array `copiedLongArrP` of 10,000 `longs` is modifed in place. The unnecessary reallocation of the array is avoided.

Parameter Passing

One of the key concepts that needs to be understood to program with CORBA in C++ is the semantics of parameter passing. With each distributed invocation, the ORB copies parameters from the client and makes them temporarily available to the server. Return values from the server are subsequently copied back to the client address space. A lot of allocation, copying, and deletion is going on in the background. It is essential that you understand how responsibility for memory management is divided up between client, server, and ORB so that you can avoid leaking any of this memory.

This section takes you step-by-step through the semantics of parameter passing. It considers each of the following cases:

- `in` parameters
- `inout` parameters
- `out` parameters (fixed-length types)
- `out` parameters (variable-length types)
- Return values

In each case, it is explained where to allocate, initialize, and deallocate the data that is passed.

Fixed- and Variable-Length Types

The IDL to C++ mapping divides CORBA data types into two categories: fixed and variable length. It is important to distinguish between these two categories because they are treated differently with respect to parameter passing and memory management.

A *fixed-length* type is any CORBA data type whose size is known at compile time.

Conversely, a *variable-length* type is any CORBA data type whose size is not known at compile time.

For example, simple types such as `char`, `short`, `unsigned short`, `long`, `unsigned long`, `long long`, `unsigned long long`, `enum`, `float`, and `double` are all of fixed length. A `string` or `wstring` is of variable length, however, because it can contain an arbitrary number of characters.

Compound types can be of either fixed or variable length, depending on what they contain. A struct is fixed length if all its members are of fixed length. Otherwise it is variable length. For example, the struct `SampleTypes::FixLen` defined in Listing 4.1 is fixed length because it contains a `short` and a `float`, both fixed-length types. The struct `SampleTypes::VarLen` is variable length because it has a `string` member, a variable length type.

Sequences are always variable length because the number of elements is arbitrary. Bounded sequences are also treated as variable length. For example, the sample types defined in Listing 4.1 (`SampleTypes::SeqOfFixLen`, `SampleTypes::SeqOfVarLen`, and `SampleTypes::BseqOfVarLen`) are all variable length.

Arrays can be either fixed or variable length, depending on the type of the array elements. For example, considering the array types defined in Listing 4.1, `SampleTypes::ArrOfFixLen` is fixed length, and `SampleTypes::ArrOfVarLen` is variable length.

Unions can be either fixed or variable. A union is fixed length if all members are fixed length and variable length otherwise.

An instance of type `fixed` is fixed length (this is true, in spite of the fact that the `fixed` type can occupy anything from 1 to 16 bytes when transmitted). An `any`, an object reference, and a `valuetype` are all variable length.

The distinction between fixed- and variable-length types is not part of IDL syntax. However, the distinction between them is sufficiently important to the C++ programmer that it is helpful to think of them as distinct types in the context of C++.

Parameter Lifecycle

There are three significant steps that occur during the lifecycle of any CORBA parameter:

- *Allocation*—Allocate memory for the CORBA data, either on the stack or on the heap.
- *Initialization*—Fill the CORBA data item with initial data. This must always be done before a CORBA data item can be used as an operation parameter.
- *Deallocation*—Delete the memory associated with a CORBA data type.

Of these three, the most important is deallocation, because if you forget deallocation you have a program that leaks.

There are two roles, or participants, involved in a CORBA invocation—the *caller* and the *callee*. You can think of caller and callee as corresponding loosely to client and server. However, since a CORBA object is allowed to make invocations on any other CORBA object, it is common for caller and callee to inhabit the same address space. In this case, the invocation is a *collocated* invocation.

TIP

In the following subsections, a number of rules are outlined for managing memory in connection with parameter passing. The most important rule, which holds in every case, is this:

The caller is *always* responsible for deallocating parameters and return values.

The following examples are based on the `SampleTypes` module defined in Listing 4.1.

Passing `in` Parameters—Collocated Case

This example illustrates passing a fixed-length struct `SampleTypes::FixLen` as an `in` parameter when caller and callee are collocated. Figure 4.3 shows what happens when the operation `passIn()` is invoked on an instance of `SampleTypes::Foo`. The steps involved in the process are

1. Caller allocates memory for the fixed-length struct `fl`.
2. Caller initializes the fixed-length struct `fl`.
3. Caller invokes the operation `passIn()`, implemented by the callee, passing `fl` as an `in` parameter.
4. Callee gets read-only access to parameter `fl`.
5. If callee requires access to `fl` after the function returns, it should make a private copy of `fl`.
6. Callee returns.
7. Caller deallocates the parameter `fl` (at some later stage).

A key point here is that the allocation, initialization, and deallocation lifecycle of the parameter `fl` is managed entirely by the caller. The callee gets just read-only access to the parameter for the duration of the invocation.

Here is some C++ sample code for the caller:

```
// C++
//-----------------------------------------
// This code assumes that the object reference
// 'objV' is already initialized to point at an
// instance of 'SampleTypes::Foo'.
//-----------------------------------------
{
```

```
    // Allocate 'fl' on the stack
    SampleTypes::FixLen fl;

    // Initialize 'fl'
    fl.theShort = (CORBA::Short)15;
    fl.theFloat = (CORBA::Float)3.14;

    // Invoke 'passIn()'
    objV->passIn(fl);
} //'fl' is automatically deallocated
```

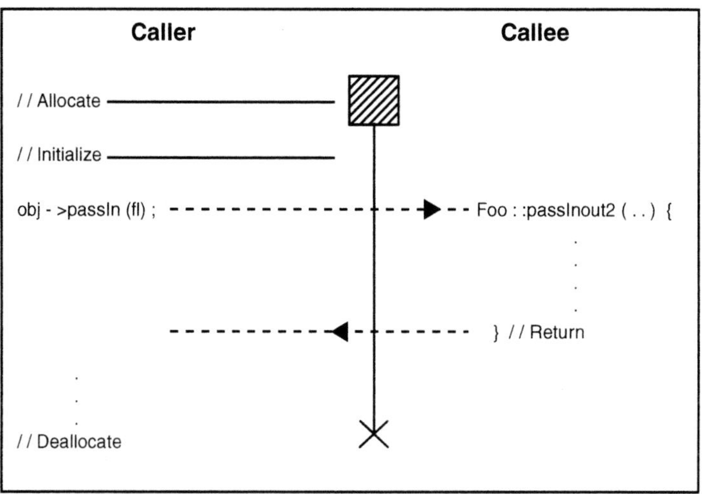

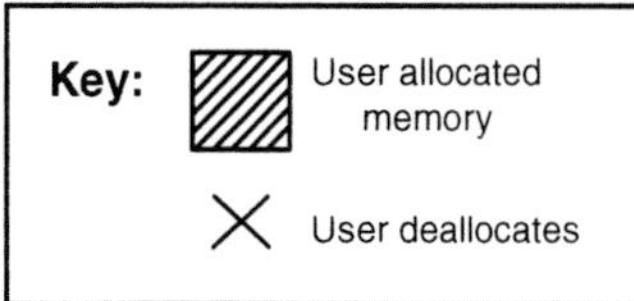

Figure 4.3

Passing an `in` *parameter—collocated case.*

The code can be rewritten to allocate the parameter on the heap instead:

```
// C++
{
    // Allocate 'fl' on the heap
    SampleTypes::FixLen_var fl = new SampleTypes::FixLen();
```

```
    // Initialize 'fl'
    fl->theShort = (CORBA::Short)15;
    fl->theFloat = (CORBA::Float)3.14;

    // Invoke 'passIn()'
    objV->passIn(fl.in());
} //'fl' is automatically deallocated by the _var
```

The invocation `passIn()` uses the `in()` method of `_var` to convert it to the appropriate parameter type such that it is maximally portable.

Sample code for the callee is given by the implementation of the method `passIn()`:

```
// C++
void SampleTypes_FooImpl::passIn( const SampleTypes::FixLen&     fl)
    throw (CORBA::SystemException)
{
    // Use readonly access - Do not modify 'fl'!
    cout << "fl.theShort = " << fl.theShort << endl;
    cout << "fl.theFloat = " << fl.theFloat << endl;
    // If access to 'fl' is needed after this function returns,
    // then make a private copy now!
}
```

The reason you need to make a private copy of `fl`, if you want to access it after `passIn()` returns, is discussed in the next section.

Passing in Parameters

This example illustrates passing the fixed-length struct `SampleTypes::FixLen` as an `in` parameter when the invocation is made remotely. Figure 4.4 shows what happens when the operation `passIn()` is invoked in this case. The steps involved in the process are

1. Caller allocates memory for the fixed-length struct `fl`.
2. Caller initializes the fixed-length struct `fl`.
3. Caller invokes the operation `passIn()`, implemented by the callee, passing `fl` as an `in` parameter.
4. ORB copies `fl` to callee's address space and makes it temporarily available.
5. Callee gets read-only access to local copy of `fl`.
6. If callee requires access to `fl` after the function returns, it should make a private copy of `fl`.
7. Callee returns.
8. ORB deallocates the callee's copy of `fl`.
9. Caller deallocates the parameter `fl` (at some later stage).

The basic difference between this and the collocated case is that the ORB has to copy the parameter `fl` across to the callee's address space. A key point is that the lifecycle of the callee's temporary copy is always shorter (sometimes much shorter) than the original instance in the caller's address space. As soon as the method `passIn()` returns, the parameter `fl` is deallocated by the ORB.

This reveals a subtle semantic difference between collocated and remote invocations. In the collocated case a parameter instance may remain valid long after the invocation has finished, whereas in the remote case the parameter is guaranteed to be deleted straightaway (the ORB takes care of this for you). Since the callee code must work in both cases, you are forced to assume that the parameter will cease to be available as soon as the method returns. If the callee wants to have access to the parameter for a longer time, it must make a private copy.

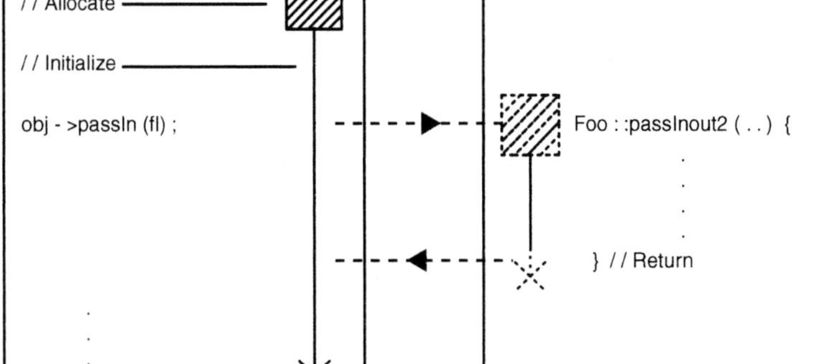

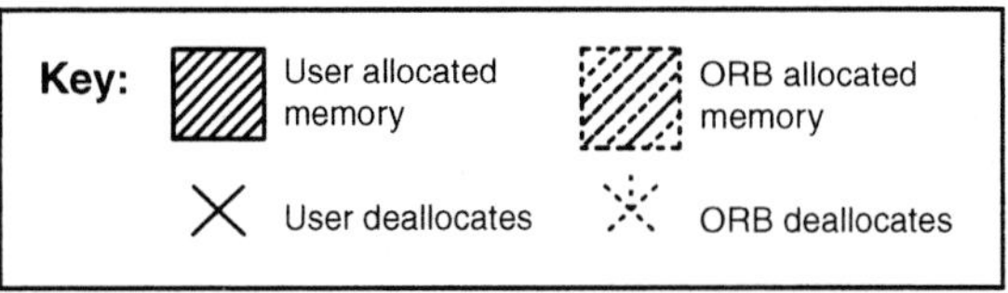

Figure 4.4

Passing an `in` parameter—remote invocation.

The sample code for this case is identical to the previous section.

Passing `inout` Parameters—No Reallocation

This example illustrates passing the fixed-length struct `SampleTypes::FixLen` as an `inout` parameter when the invocation is made remotely and the parameter is modified in place. In the case of a fixed-length parameter, no reallocation of the parameter is needed when it is modified. Figure 4.5 shows what happens when the operation `passInout()` is invoked. The steps involved in the process are

1. Caller allocates memory for the fixed length struct `fl`.
2. Caller initializes the fixed-length struct `fl`.
3. Caller invokes the operation `passInout()`, implemented by the callee, passing `fl` as an `inout` parameter.
4. ORB copies `fl` to callee's address space and makes it temporarily available.
5. Callee (optionally) modifies local copy of `fl`. Since `fl` is fixed length, it can be modified in place. No reallocation is required.
6. If callee requires access to `fl` after the function returns, it should make a private copy of `fl`.
7. Callee returns.
8. ORB sends the (possibly modified) callee's copy of `fl` back to the caller address space and modifies the original instance of `fl` in place.
9. ORB deallocates the callee's copy of `fl`.
10. Caller deallocates `fl` (at some later stage).

In this case, the callee code has read and write access to the parameter `fl` so it has the option of modifying it. There is no need to reallocate `fl` if the callee modifies it, because it is a fixed-length type.

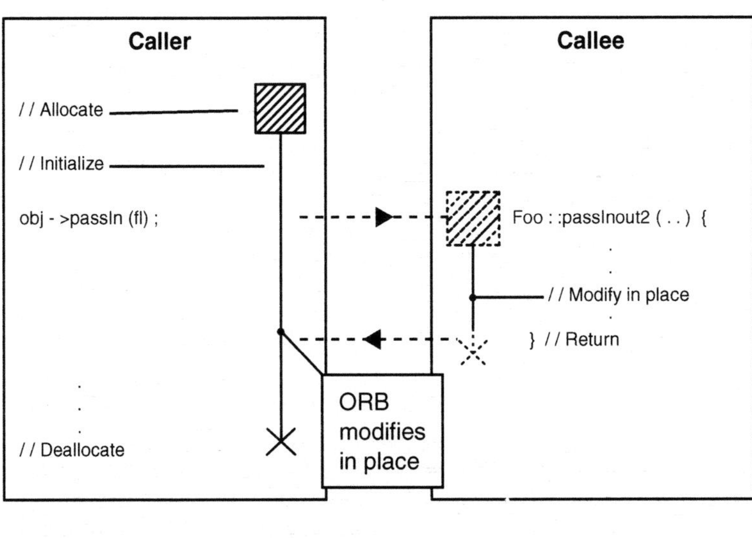

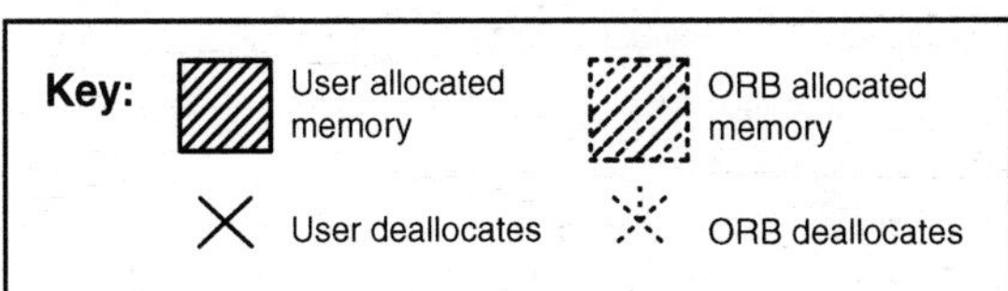

Figure 4.5

Passing an `inout` parameter—no reallocation.

Here is some C++ sample code for the caller:

```
// C++
//-------------------------------------------
// This code assumes that the object reference
// 'objV' is already initialized to point at an
// instance of 'SampleTypes::Foo'.
//-------------------------------------------
{
    // Allocate 'fl' on the stack
    SampleTypes::FixLen fl;

    // Initialize 'fl'
    fl.theShort = (CORBA::Short)15;
    fl.theFloat = (CORBA::Float)3.14;

    // Invoke 'passInout()'
    objV->passInout(fl);

    cout << "fl.theShort = " << fl.theShort << endl;
    cout << "fl.theFloat = " << fl.theFloat << endl;
} //'fl' is automatically deallocated
```

The code can be rewritten to allocate the parameter on the heap instead:

```
// C++
{
    // Allocate 'fl' on the heap
    SampleTypes::FixLen_var fl = new SampleTypes::FixLen();

    // Initialize 'fl'
    fl->theShort = (CORBA::Short)15;
    fl->theFloat = (CORBA::Float)3.14;

    // Invoke 'passInout()'
    objV->passInout(fl.inout());

    cout << "fl->theShort = " << fl->theShort << endl;
    cout << "fl->theFloat = " << fl->theFloat << endl;
} //'fl' is automatically deallocated by the _var
```

The invocation `passInout()` uses the `inout()` method of the `_var` to convert it to the appropriate parameter type in such a way that it is maximally portable.

Sample code for the callee is given by the implementation of the method `passInout()`:

```
// C++
void SampleTypes_FooImpl::passInout(SampleTypes::FixLen& fl)
    throw (CORBA::SystemException)
{
```

```
    // Callee has read and write access to 'fl'
    cout << "fl.theShort = " << fl.theShort << endl;
    cout << "fl.theFloat = " << fl.theFloat << endl;

    // Modify 'fl' in place
    fl.theShort = (CORBA::Short)100;
    fl.theFloat = (CORBA::Float)3.14;

    // If access to 'fl' is needed after this function returns,
    // then make a private copy now!
}
```

Passing `inout` Parameters—Reallocating

This example illustrates passing the variable-length struct `SampleTypes::VarLen` as an `inout` parameter when the invocation is made remotely and the parameter is reallocated by the callee. In the case of a variable-length parameter, this reallocation is sometimes necessary. For example, if the callee wants to replace a string with a longer string, reallocation is necessary. But if the callee wants to replace the string with a shorter string, reallocation is not needed. Figure 4.6 shows what happens when the operation `passInout2()` is invoked and the callee reallocates the `inout` parameter. The steps involved in the process are

1. Caller allocates memory for the variable-length struct `vl`.
2. Caller initializes the variable-length struct `vl`.
3. Caller invokes the operation `passInout2()`, implemented by the callee, passing `vl` as an `inout` parameter.
4. ORB copies `vl` to callee's address space and makes it temporarily available.
5. Callee (optionally) modifies local copy of `vl`. If modifications call for a different size struct `vl`, then the existing copy of `vl` must be deallocated and a new struct `vl` of the appropriate size allocated.
6. If callee requires access to `vl` after the function returns, it should make a private copy of `vl`.
7. Callee returns.
8. ORB sends the (possibly modified) callee's copy of `vl` back to the caller address space. ORB modifies the original instance of `vl` by reallocating `vl` and initializing it with the value received from the callee.
9. ORB deallocates the callee's copy of `vl`.
10. Caller deallocates `vl` (at some later stage).

Note that it is not always strictly necessary to reallocate an `inout` parameter in the callee if the new data can fit inside the old instance. However, reallocation is usually needed when a variable-length type is modified.

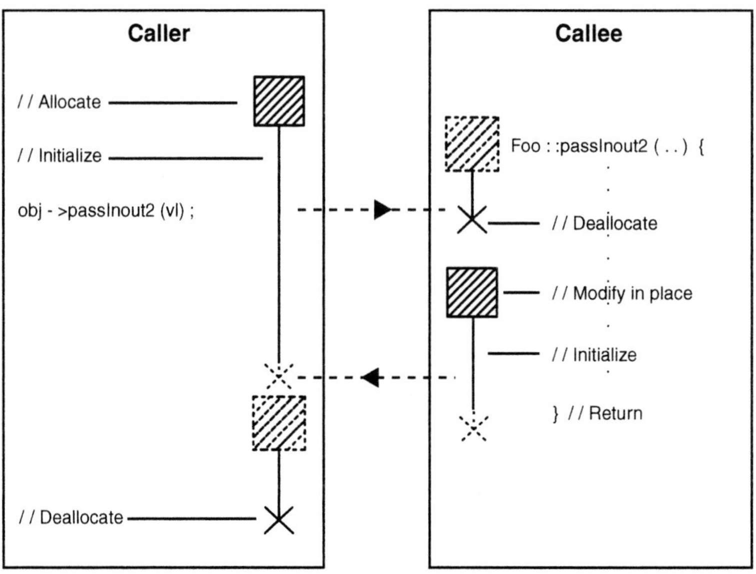

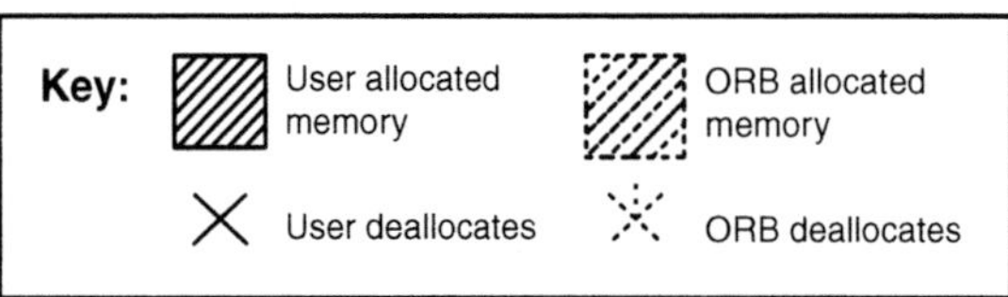

Figure 4.6

Passing an `inout` *parameter—reallocating.*

Here is some C++ sample code for the caller:

```
// C++
//-----------------------------------------
// This code assumes that the object reference
// 'objV' is already initialized to point at an
// instance of 'SampleTypes::Foo'.
//-----------------------------------------
{
    // Allocate 'vl' on the stack
    SampleTypes::VarLen vl;

    // Initialize 'vl'
    vl.theString = CORBA::string_dup("Doomed string");
    vl.theLong   = (CORBA::Long)10000;
```

```
    // Invoke 'passInout2()'
    objV->passInout2(vl);

    cout << "vl.theString = " << vl.theString << endl;
    cout << "vl.theLong   = " << vl.theLong   << endl;
} //'vl' is automatically deallocated
```

The code can be rewritten to allocate the parameter on the heap instead:

```
// C++
{
    // Allocate 'vl' on the heap
    SampleTypes::VarLen_var vl = new SampleTypes::VarLen();

    // Initialize 'vl'
    vl->theString = CORBA::string_dup("Doomed string");
    vl->theLong   = (CORBA::Long)10000;

    // Invoke 'passInout2()'
    objV->passInout2(vl.inout());

    cout << "vl->theString = " << vl->theString << endl;
    cout << "vl->theLong   = " << vl->theLong   << endl;
} //'vl' is automatically deallocated by the _var
```

The invocation `passInout2()` uses the `inout()` method of `_var` to convert it to the appropriate parameter type in such a way that it is maximally portable.

Sample code for the callee is given by the implementation of the method `passInout2()`:

```
// C++
void SampleTypes_FooImpl::passInout2(SampleTypes::VarLen& vl)
throw (CORBA::SystemException)
{
    // Callee has read and write access to 'vl'
    cout << "vl.theString = " << vl.theString << endl;
    cout << "vl.theLong   = " << vl.theLong   << endl;

    // Modify 'vl' - Reallocation
    // The assignment to 'vl.theString' has the following effect:
    //     Deallocates old value of 'vl.theString' (implicit)
    //     Allocates new value of string (via 'string_dup()' )
    vl.theString = CORBA::string_dup("New string of greater length");
    vl.theLong   = (CORBA::Long)10000000;

    // If access to 'vl' is needed after this function returns,
    // then make a private copy now!
}
```

Receiving out Parameters—Fixed-Length Types

This example illustrates receiving the fixed-length struct `SampleTypes::FixLen` as an `out` parameter when the invocation is made remotely. Figure 4.7 shows what happens when the operation `receiveOut()` is invoked. The steps involved in the process are

1. Caller allocates memory for the fixed-length struct `fl` (but `fl` is *not* initialized).
2. Caller invokes the operation `receiveOut()`, implemented by the callee, specifying `fl` as a placeholder for the `out` parameter.
3. ORB allocates an uninitialized placeholder for `fl` in the callee's address space.
4. Callee initializes the placeholder `fl`.
5. If callee requires access to `fl` after the function returns, it should make a private copy of `fl`.
6. Callee returns.
7. ORB sends the newly initialized `fl` back to the caller address space and uses this data to initialize the caller's instance of `fl`.
8. ORB deallocates the callee's `fl`.
9. Caller deallocates `fl` (at some later stage).

This case is unusual because it is the only time the caller allocates the parameter but does not initialize it. Of course, it would not make sense for a caller to initialize the `out` parameter, because the parameter is never passed from caller to callee. The instance of `fl` given to `receiveOut()` is just a placeholder for the reception of the `out` parameter.

Here is some C++ sample code for the caller:

```
// C++
//-----------------------------------------
// This code assumes that the object reference
// 'objV' is already initialized to point at an
// instance of 'SampleTypes::Foo'.
//-----------------------------------------
{
    // Allocate 'fl' on the stack
    SampleTypes::FixLen fl;

    // Invoke 'receiveOut()'
    objV->receiveOut(fl);

    // Do something with 'fl'...
    cout << "fl.theShort = " << fl.theShort << endl;
    cout << "fl.theFloat = " << fl.theFloat << endl;
} //'fl' is automatically deallocated
```

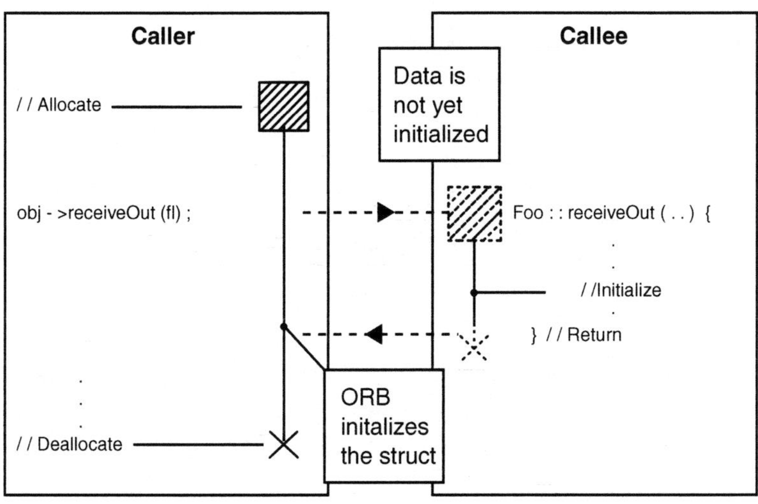

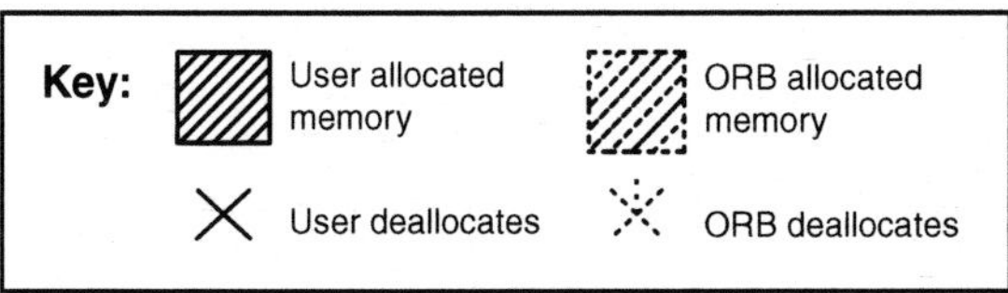

Figure 4.7

Passing an `out` *parameter—fixed-length type.*

The code can be rewritten to allocate the parameter on the heap instead:

```
// C++
{
    // Allocate 'fl' on the heap
    SampleTypes::FixLen_var fl = new SampleTypes::FixLen();

    // Invoke 'receiveOut()'
    objV->receiveOut(fl.out());

    // Do something with 'fl'...
    cout << "fl->theShort = " << fl->theShort << endl;
    cout << "fl->theFloat = " << fl->theFloat << endl;
} //'fl' is automatically deallocated by the _var
```

The invocation `receiveOut()` uses the `out()` method of the `_var` to convert it to the appropriate parameter type in such a way that it is maximally portable.

Sample code for the callee is given by the implementation of the method `receiveOut()`:

```
// C++
void SampleTypes_FooImpl::receiveOut(SampleTypes::FixLen& fl)
     throw (CORBA::SystemException)
{
     // Initialize 'fl'
     fl.theShort = (CORBA::Short)100;
     fl.theFloat = (CORBA::Float)3.14;

     // If access to 'fl' is needed after this function returns,
     // then make a private copy now!
}
```

Receiving out Parameters—Variable Length Types

This example illustrates receiving the variable-length struct `SampleTypes::VarLen` as an `out` parameter when the invocation is made remotely. Figure 4.8 shows what happens when the operation `receiveOut2()` is invoked. The steps involved in the process are

1. The caller invokes the operation `receiveOut2()`, implemented by the callee, specifying `vl` as a placeholder for the `out` parameter (the parameter `vl` is passed as an uninitialized pointer).
2. The callee allocates `vl` in the callee's address space.
3. The callee initializes `vl`.
4. If the callee requires access to `vl` after the function returns, it should make a private copy of `vl`.
5. The callee returns.
6. ORB copies `vl` back to the caller, allocating and initializing an instance of `vl` in the caller's address space.
7. ORB deallocates the callee's `vl`.
8. The caller deallocates `vl` (at some later stage).

In contrast to the previous section (fixed-length struct as `out` parameter), the caller does not allocate the parameter at all. Instead, the caller passes an uninitialized pointer (or else a `_var`) as a placeholder for the `out` parameter.

Here is some C++ sample code for the caller. The caller must specify the parameter as either a plain pointer or a `_var` type.

```
// C++
//-----------------------------------------
// This code assumes that the object reference
// 'objV' is already initialized to point at an
// instance of 'SampleTypes::Foo'.
//-----------------------------------------
```

```
{
    SampleTypes::VarLen_var vl;

    // Invoke 'receiveOut2()'
    objV->receiveOut2(vl.out());

    // Do something with 'vl'...
    cout << "vl->theString = " << vl->theString << endl;
    cout << "vl->theLong   = " << vl->theLong   << endl;
} //'vl' is automatically deallocated
```

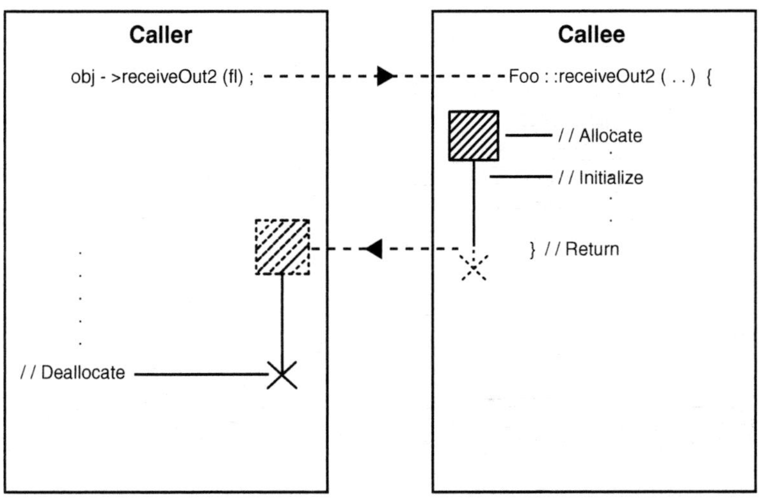

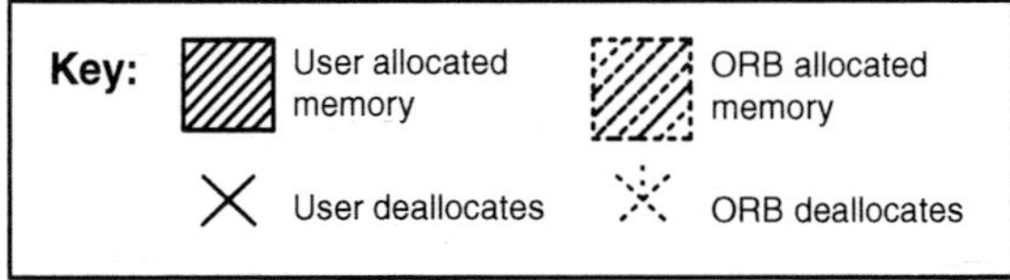

Figure 4.8

Passing an `out` *parameter—variable-length type.*

The invocation `receiveOut2()` uses the `out()` method of the `_var` to convert it to the appropriate parameter type in such a way that it is maximally portable.

Sample code for the callee is given by the implementation of the method `receiveOut2()`:

```
// C++
void SampleTypes_FooImpl::receiveOut2(SampleTypes::VarLen*& vl)
throw (CORBA::SystemException)
{
     // Allocate 'vl' on the heap
     vl = new SampleTypes::VarLen();

     // Initialize 'vl'
     vl->theString = CORBA::string_dup("New string");
     vl->theLong   = (CORBA::Long)10000000;

     // If access to 'vl' is needed after this function returns,
     // then make a private copy now!
}
```

Return Values and `_retn()`

The rules for memory management of return values are almost identical to the rules for variable length `out` parameters. The steps for allocation, initialization, and deallocation of return values are similar to those of `out` parameters.

As is the case with `out` parameters, variable-length and fixed-length data types are treated differently.

A danger with both `out` parameters and return values is that they are susceptible to memory leaks when an exception is thrown. The example presented in this section illustrates how the `_retn()` method used in conjunction with a `_var` type can help you avoid this sort of memory leak.

Consider the IDL operation `getResult()`, defined in Listing 4.1:

```
// IDL
module SampleTypes {
     ...
     interface Foo {
          ...
          VarLen getResult(out VarLen vl) raises (GenericExc);
          ...
     };

};
```

The following sections show caller and callee code for this invocation. Exception handling is explicitly shown in these examples.

Caller Code

Here is some sample C++ code for the caller:

```
// C++
//--------------------------------------------
// This code assumes that the object reference
// 'objV' is already initialized to point at an
// instance of 'SampleTypes::Foo'.
//--------------------------------------------
{
     SampleTypes::VarLen_var vlParamV;
     SampleTypes::VarLen_var vlReturnV;
     CORBA::Boolean excRaised = 0;

     try {
          // Invoke 'getResult()'
          vlReturnV = objV->getResult(vlParamV.out());
     }
     catch (CORBA::UserException& ) {
          excRaised = 1;
     }
     catch (CORBA::SystemException& ) {
          excRaised = 1;
     }

     if (!excRaised) {
          // Case 1: Operation succeeded, proceed normally.
     }
     else {
          // Case 2: Exception was raised.
          //         'vlReturnV' and 'vlParamV' are undefined.
     }

} //'vlParamV' is automatically deallocated
```

Consider what happens if an exception is raised during the invocation of `getResult()`. Both the `out` parameter `vlParamV` and the return value `vlReturnV` will be undefined. You will have to proceed along different logical paths, depending on whether or not an exception was thrown.

Callee Code

Sample code for the callee is given by the implementation of the method `getResult()`.

```
// C++
SampleTypes::VarLen*
SampleTypes_FooImpl::getResult(SampleTypes::VarLen*& vl)
    throw (CORBA::SystemException, SampleTypes::GenericExc)
{
```

```
    // Declare temporary 'out' variable as a '_var'
    SampleTypes::VarLen_var tmpOutV;

    // Allocate 'tmpOutV' on the heap
    tmpOutV = new SampleTypes::VarLen();

    // Initialize 'tmpOutV'
    tmpOutV->theString = CORBA::string_dup("New string");
    tmpOutV->theLong   = (CORBA::Long)10000000;

    // Declare temporary result variable as a '_var'
    SampleTypes::VarLen_var resultV;

    // Allocate '_resultV' on the heap
    resultV = new SampleTypes::VarLen();

    // Initialize '_resultV'
    resultV->theString = CORBA::string_dup("The result.");
    resultV->theLong   = (CORBA::Long) 123;

    // Beware! Risk of an exception throw!
    funcThatMightThrowAnException();

    // Force '_var's to yield ownership
    vl = tmpOutV._retn();
    return resultV._retn();
}
```

After allocating and initializing the out parameter tmpOutV and return value resultV, the callee calls the function funcThatMightThrowAnException(), which throws an exception from time to time. This function is potentially dangerous. If an out parameter or a return value has been allocated, the thrown exception could prevent a pointer to this memory being passed back to the calling code. The calling code would therefore never get a chance to delete the memory. How can this memory leak be avoided?

The trick is to use a _var type to hold the temporary result value and temporary out value. This ensures that, whenever execution of getResult() is interrupted by an exception, these return values are automatically freed as the stack unwinds.

At first sight this solution appears to have a flaw—the _var normally deallocates its data at the end of the function call. If the function returns normally, the return values will be deleted before the callee gets a chance to use them. This difficulty is solved, however, with the help of the _retn() method, which forces the _var to yield ownership of the referenced data. After _retn() is called on a _var, the _var no longer references the data and will not attempt to deallocate it. In this way, ownership of the data passes from _var to the calling code. The calling code can then delete the data at some later time.

Table of Parameter-Passing Types

Table 4.5 summarizes the parameter types that are used in the various parameter-passing modes. These parameter types are used in the signatures of C++ methods that implement IDL operations.

Table 4.5 Parameter Types Used for Passing CORBA Data

Data Type	in	inout	out	return
basic	*Basic*	*Basic&*	*Basic&*	*Basic*
fixed	const fixed&	fixed&	fixed&	fixed
string	const char*	char*&	char*&	char*
wstring	const WChar*	WChar*&	WChar*&	WChar*
object reference	objref_ptr	objref_ptr&	objref_ptr&	objref_ptr
fixed-length struct	const struct&	struct&	struct&	struct
variable-length struct	const struct&	struct&	struct*&	struct*
sequence	const sequence&	sequence&	sequence*&	sequence*
fixed-length union	const union&	union&	union&	union
variable-length union	const union&	union&	union*&	union*
fixed-length array	const array	array	array	array_slice*
variable-length array	const array	array	array_slice*&	array_slice*
any	const any&	any&	any*&	any*

The *basic* types refer to the simple IDL types short, unsigned short, long, unsigned long, long long, unsigned long long, float, double, long double, boolean, char, wchar, octet, and enum.

A distinction is made between fixed-length and variable-length data types. This distinction is important in the case of out parameters and return values.

It would be impractical to memorize the above table in its entirety. Fortunately, that is not necessary. If you use a _var type as a parameter, the parameter automatically converts itself to the correct type. Alternatively, the methods in(), inout(), and out() explicitly convert a _var type to the appropriate parameter type. These methods effectively memorize the table on your behalf, saving you the bother of doing so.

Table of Memory Management Rules

Table 4.6 summarizes the memory management rules for parameter passing in C++. The column headings enumerate the parameter passing modes, and the rows of the table show the responsibilities of the caller and callee in each case.

Table 4.6 Summary of C++ Memory Management Rules

Parameter Passing Mode	Caller Responsibilities	Callee Responsibilities
`in`	Allocate Initialize Deallocate	Copy
`inout`	Allocate Initialize Deallocate	Copy
`out` (fixed length)	Allocate Deallocate Copy	Initialize
`out` (variable length)	Deallocate Initialize Copy	Allocate
return value	Deallocate Initialize Copy	Allocate

The copying refers to the fact that the callee might want to have access to the parameter/return value after the invocation has returned. In that case, it is necessary for the callee to make an explicit copy of the data in order for the data to be available at a later time.

Summary

Once you begin using the more complicated structured types that CORBA has to offer, you inevitably have to deal with dynamically allocated memory. The CORBA C++ mapping gives you a hand with this by providing the `_var` types. `_var` types implement smart pointer functionality that helps you to avoid memory leaks. Even so, the issues surrounding memory management in a distributed system can be bewildering.

Most of the rules in this chapter could be described as nothing more than good practice in C++ programming. What is unusual about distributed programming, however, is that you are forced to work with heap-allocated data practically all of the time (with the consequent danger of memory leaks). By contrast, a typical standalone application uses stack-allocated data more often.

If you are just beginning to learn CORBA memory management rules, there is one rule of thumb that is useful to bear in mind: The caller always owns the memory associated with parameters and return values. In other words, it is the caller's responsibility to delete parameters and return values.

CHAPTER 5

Object References

Object references in CORBA provide a key abstraction, encapsulating the location details of a remote CORBA object and abstracting away the network protocol layer. In a CORBA system augmented by CORBA services, object references do even more work, being responsible for encapsulating security details and propagating transaction context.

From the perspective of the developer, however, object references appear to be quite simple. They are objects much the same as regular C++ or Java objects. You invoke the methods of an object reference like any normal object. It is then up to the ORB to take care of locating the CORBA object, establishing a connection, negotiating secure connections, sending and receiving messages, and whatever else is needed to complete a remote procedure call. If you scratch the surface of an object reference, you will find a lot of hidden details.

CORBA Objects and Object References

There is a complementary relationship between CORBA objects and object references. A CORBA object is the entity that provides the implementation of the object and does the work. An object reference is the entity that knows where to find a CORBA object and delegates work to the CORBA object. Object references effectively provide a window to a CORBA object.

Because CORBA objects do the real work of an invocation, you might be inclined to think of them as more concrete than object references. In fact, the reverse is the case. The portable object adapter (POA) does not even define entities that correspond to CORBA objects (see Chapter 7, "The Portable Object Adapter").

The OMG recognized that there is no need to represent CORBA objects as concrete objects and, moreover, that it would be a disadvantage to do so. A group of cooperating entities constitutes a CORBA object instead. In the world of the POA, a CORBA object is an abstraction.

Figure 5.1(a) shows a naive view of a CORBA object.

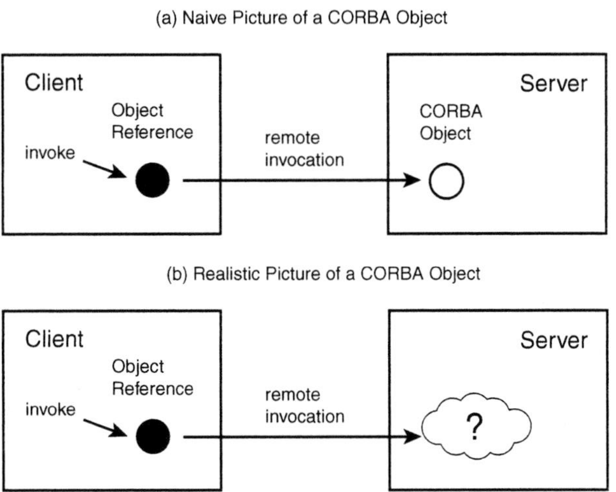

Figure 5.1

Naive and realistic views of a CORBA object.

A given IDL interface is implemented by a concrete C++ or Java object—the CORBA object. To support remote invocations on this CORBA object, client programs create an object reference to act as a proxy. The object reference supports the same set of IDL operations as the CORBA object and delegates invocations to it by exchanging messages over the network. The object reference acts like a remote control for the CORBA object.

The naive picture is often a useful model when discussing CORBA concepts. However, it should not be taken too literally. To insist that a CORBA object is represented literally as a language-specific object is unnecessarily restrictive. The lifecycle of a CORBA object, for example, is independent of the lifecycle of the C++ or Java object that represents it. It is also worth recalling that CORBA supports languages such as C and COBOL that are not even object-oriented.

Figure 5.1(b) shows a more realistic picture of a CORBA object. Here, the CORBA object is represented by an indeterminate mechanism on the server side. If the server uses a POA, the operations are ultimately executed by a servant object.

The client has the same view of the CORBA object as before; it uses the object reference to invoke operations. As far as the client is concerned, the server is a black box that processes remote invocations. The CORBA object need not exist at all; it is an abstraction.

What Is an Object Reference?

An object reference encapsulates the following kind of information:

- *The type of the CORBA object* An object reference knows the interface type of the CORBA object that it refers to. It follows that the supported operations and attributes are known (either statically via the stubs or dynamically via the Interface Repository).
- *The location of the CORBA object* An object reference encapsulates the location of its corresponding CORBA object. This typically includes the host and port of the relevant server and an object key that the server uses to identify an object instance uniquely.
- *Additional information* In some cases, a CORBA object is used in conjunction with one or more CORBA services. Some of these services (for example, the security service) need to supply the client with extra information. The most convenient way to provide this information is to supply it as part of the object reference.

The detailed definition of an object reference changes continuously as the CORBA specification is updated and expanded. However, these detailed changes normally do not matter to a developer, because they are hidden. The object reference is exposed to the developer in an opaque form.

Representation of an Object Reference

Although an ORB has to perform a number of steps to locate the CORBA object and establish a network connection to the server, all of this remains hidden from the developer. To use the CORBA object, all that is needed is an object reference.

The main representations of an object reference are

- *An object reference instance* This is the form of object reference that a developer usually encounters. Invocations of the object reference cause the corresponding operations (or attributes) to be invoked on the CORBA object.
- *An interoperable object reference (IOR)* An IOR is the form an object reference is converted to when it is sent across the wire as a parameter or return value of an operation. Details are given in the section "Interoperable Object Reference," later in this chapter.
- *A stringified object reference* A stringified object reference is one that has been converted to a text string using the operation `CORBA::ORB::object_to_string()`. It is derived from the format of an IOR. A stringified object reference encapsulates the state of the object reference. If written to persistent storage, it is possible to restore the object reference at a later stage by reading the string and invoking

CORBA::ORB::string_to_object(). As long as the corresponding CORBA object continues to exist, the object reference can be used to make invocations.

Aspects of a CORBA Object

When you read about the POA (see Chapter 7), you will see that a number of entities, in addition to an object reference, are defined to support the notion of a CORBA object. They are

- Object key
- POA name
- Object ID
- Servant

The relationship between these entities can be clarified by taking a closer look at an IOR. Figure 5.2 shows a schematic picture of an IOR that focuses on the location information for the CORBA object.

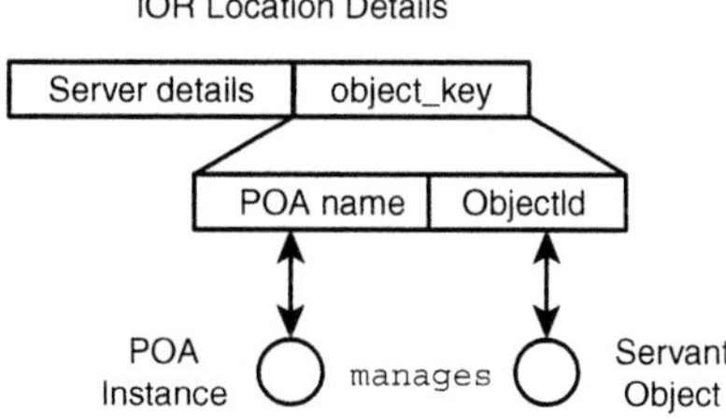

Figure 5.2

Part of an IOR focusing on location information.

The server details give the host and port of the server process. This information is used by the client to locate the server process.

The `object_key` is an opaque sequence of octets (a stream of bytes) used by the server process to uniquely identify a CORBA object in its address space. The client might not understand the format of the `object_key`, but this does not matter, because the `object_key` is used exclusively by the server.

The contents of an `object_key` are not specified by the OMG. It is left as an implementation detail for the ORB vendor. The details of an `object_key` depend on the type of object adapter used. For example, the `object_key` format will be different for a basic object adapter (BOA), a portable object adapter (POA), a COBOL object adapter (COA), or a PL/I object adapter (POD).

The POA is the only object adapter considered here. Although the format of the `object_key` is implementation dependent, in the case of the POA you can be sure it encompasses two pieces of information: the CORBA object's POA name and object ID.

The POA name identifies the POA instance that manages the CORBA object in question. The object ID is a unique identifier for the CORBA object and is defined relative to a particular POA instance.

These two pieces of information, POA name and object ID, enable the server to uniquely identify the CORBA object. You should not assume, however, that there is a one-to-one correspondence between an object ID and a servant. The POA supports many models for mapping object IDs to servants, as discussed in Chapter 7.

Conversion Methods

Given the variety of entities associated with a CORBA object, it is often useful to navigate between them. In addition to the `CORBA::ORB::string_to_object()` and `CORBA::ORB::object_to_string()` methods already introduced, the provides a number of other conversion methods. They are summarized here:

```
// IDL
#pragma prefix "omg.org"

module PortableServer {
     ...
     native Servant;
     typedef sequence<octet> ObjectId;
     ...
     interface POA {
          ...
          exception ObjectNotActive {};
          exception ServantNotActive {};
          exception WrongAdapter {};
          exception WrongPolicy {};
          ...
          // Identity mapping operations
          ObjectId servant_to_id(in Servant p_servant)
                   raises (ServantNotActive, WrongPolicy);

          Object servant_to_reference(in Servant p_servant)
                   raises (ServantNotActive, WrongPolicy);

          Servant reference_to_servant(in Object reference)
                   raises (ObjectNotActive, WrongPolicy);

          ObjectId reference_to_id(in Object reference)
                   raises (WrongAdapter, WrongPolicy);

          Servant id_to_servant(in ObjectId oid)
                   raises (ObjectNotActive, WrongPolicy);

          Object id_to_reference(in ObjectId id)
                   raises (ObjectNotActive, WrongPolicy);
```

```
    };
    ...
};
```

It is not always legal to call these operations. To understand how to use the conversion operations properly and to know when it makes sense to use them, you need an understanding of the POA.

Lifecycle of Object References

One of the features of the POA is the way it completely separates the lifecycle of object references from the lifecycle of implementation objects (servants). For anyone familiar with the old basic object adapter (prior to CORBA 2.2), this is a striking difference between the two types of object adapter.

In fact, using the POA, it is possible to create object references in the server without instantiating any servant objects. The operations that do this are `create_reference()` and `create_reference_with_id()`, as declared in the following IDL code fragment:

```
// IDL
#pragma prefix "omg.org"

module PortableServer {
    ...
    typedef sequence<octet> ObjectId;
    ...
    interface POA {
        ...
        exception WrongPolicy {};
        ...
        // Reference creation operations
        Object create_reference(in CORBA::RepositoryId intf)
               raises (WrongPolicy);

        Object create_reference_with_id(
                    in ObjectId oid,
                    in CORBA::RepositoryId intf
               ) raises (WrongPolicy);
        ...
    };
    ...
};
```

While it is possible to create the object references independently of the servant object, you should make sure that the server also has a mechanism in place to instantiate the corresponding servant on demand. The mechanisms for instantiating servants on demand are described in Chapter 7.

Both of the operations for creating references take an argument of type `CORBA::RepositoryId`. This is a string that identifies the type of the corresponding interface. For example, an interface called `Bar` might have a repository ID `IDL:Bar:1.0`. See Chapter 6, "Interoperable Naming Service," for details.

- The operation `create_reference()` can be used when the POA `IdAssignmentPolicy` of `SYSTEM_ID` is in force. In this case a unique object ID is assigned automatically to the object reference (and embedded within the object reference).

  This approach is appropriate for short-lived CORBA objects that will not be needed again after the server process shuts down.
- The operation `create_reference_with_id()` is intended to be used when the POA `IdAssignmentPolicy` of `USER_ID` is in force. In this case the user can choose the object ID.

  This approach is appropriate for long-lived CORBA objects such as those that are stored in a database. Remember that the object ID, in combination with the POA name, uniquely identifies a CORBA object. Therefore, you should take care that you use a consistent scheme for assigning object IDs and that different CORBA objects are assigned unique IDs. A typical approach is to use a database key as the object ID.

Object Reference from `_this()`

Another way of getting an object reference is by invoking the `_this()` method on a servant object. You can use this method when you already have an instance of a servant.

For example, given an interface `Foo` and a servant instance `myFooServant`, you can get an object reference by invoking `myFooServant._this()` (C++ or Java). You should be aware of the fact that invoking `_this()` actually does two things:

- It returns an object reference of type `Foo_ptr` (C++) or `Foo` (Java) that is associated with the given servant.
- As a side effect, `_this()` activates the servant if it is not already active.

A limitation of `_this()` is that it makes sense only if you have a one-to-one mapping between servants and object references. This is not always the case—it depends on the particular POA policies that you have chosen. See Chapter 7 for details.

Longevity of Object References

After an object reference is created, it is usually exported to other processes as a parameter or return value of an IDL operation.

Once the object reference goes outside the server address space, the server has no control over what happens to it. The object reference can be passed from application to application, stored in a naming service or trader service, or written to a file in the form of a stringified object reference. It can easily happen that an object reference outlives the CORBA object to which it refers. If an application attempts to make an invocation on a stale object reference, the invocation is relayed to the server, but the server responds with a `CORBA::OBJECT_NOT_EXIST` system exception. This indicates that the corresponding CORBA object has been permanently deleted.

Location Transparency

An important feature of CORBA is that it does not matter whether a CORBA object is implemented in the same process as the code that calls it or is implemented in a separate process. The same calling code can be used to make local or remote invocations. This is known as *location transparency*.

There are many benefits to location transparency:

- Sections of code that work in a local application will work just as well in a remote application.
- Developers use a consistent style of coding whether they are using remote or local CORBA objects.
- Interceptors are called for both local and remote invocations.
- Local invocations are subject to the same security checks as remote invocations.
- When using the CORBA Transaction Service, both local and remote objects can take part in a transaction.

An ORB is allowed to make optimizations in the way it handles local invocations, as long as the optimizations do not affect location transparency. For example, an ORB is allowed to optimize the network layer so that marshaling and transmission steps are omitted for local invocations.

There are two aspects to location transparency: *syntax* and *semantics*. The basic object adapter (BOA) requires the syntax to be the same for local and remote invocations but is rather vague about semantics. In many BOA implementations, local invocations would bypass some or all of the dispatching mechanisms. For example, interceptors, persistence mechanisms, and security mechanisms might all be bypassed in a local invocation.

The situation is much better with the POA, which explicitly requires the semantics of local invocations to be the same as remote invocations. That is, local invocations are required to pass through the usual ORB dispatching mechanisms, including interceptors, the POA manager, and mechanisms that implement services such as security and transactions. Invocations on an object reference always pass through POA dispatching mechanisms before reaching a servant.

IDL Syntax of Interfaces

An interface is the fundamental building block of OMG IDL. There are two basic flavors described here: ordinary interfaces that can be implemented by anyone and pseudo-interfaces that can be implemented only by ORB vendors.

Interfaces

Interfaces contain the declarations of operations and attributes. That is their most important feature. They can also contain other kinds of declarations. The entities that can be contained in an interface are

- Attribute declarations
- Operation declarations
- Exception declarations
- Type declarations
- Constant declarations

For example, the following interface illustrates these kinds of declarations:

```
// IDL
interface SquareGrid {
     // Constant declarations
     const long MAX_HEIGHT = 1000;
     const long MAX_WIDTH  = 500;

     // Type declarations
     typedef double GridType[MAX_HEIGHT][MAX_WIDTH];

     // Exception declaration
     exception OutOfBounds {
          long heightBound;
          long widthBound;
     };

     // Operations
     void setValue(in long x, in long y, in double d)
          raises (OutOfBounds);
     double getValue(in long x, in long y)
          raises (OutOfBounds);

     // Attributes
     attribute long currentHeight;
     attribute long currentWidth;
};
```

Entities declared in the interface are also scoped within the interface. For example, the fully scoped name of the constant `MAX_HEIGHT` is `SquareGrid::MAX_HEIGHT`, and the fully scoped name of the exception `OutOfBounds` is `SquareGrid::OutOfBounds`. If you need to refer to these entities outside the scope of `SquareGrid`, you must use the fully scoped names.

Forward Declarations

Forward declarations of IDL interfaces are allowed. This allows interfaces to be mutually referential. For example

```
// IDL

// Forward declaration of 'Foo'
interface Foo;
```

```
interface Bar {
    Foo getAssociatedFoo();
};

// Actual declaration of 'Foo'
interface Foo {
    Bar getAssociatedBar();
};
```

The syntax for a forward declaration is `interface IntfName;` where the braces ({ and }) are omitted. In this IDL fragment, `interface Foo;` is an example of a forward declaration.

It is not legal to inherit from an interface before it has been fully declared. For example, the following IDL is illegal and will not compile:

```
// IDL

// Forward declaration of 'Foo'
interface Foo;

interface Bar : Foo {     // ILLEGAL! Will not compile
    Foo getAssociatedFoo();
};
...
```

However, this example can easily be corrected, as shown in the following IDL:

```
// IDL

// Forward declaration of 'Bar'
interface Bar;

interface Foo {
    Bar getAssociatedBar();
};

// Actual declaration of 'Bar'
interface Bar : Foo {
    Foo getAssociatedFoo();
};
```

The order of declaration has been reversed so that a forward reference is declared for `Bar` instead of `Foo`.

No Overloading of Operations

Unlike C++ and Java, which allow you to overload methods, IDL does not support overloading of operations. CORBA identifies an operation based on its fully scoped name. It is not possible to distinguish operations based on the number or types of their arguments.

For example, the following interface is illegal:

```
// IDL
interface TooMuchLikeCPlusPlus {
     void contactDetails(in string name, in fixed<20,0> telephone);
     void contactDetails(in string name, in string emailAddress);  // ILLEGAL!
};
```

This fragment of IDL will not compile, because of the ambiguous declaration of `contactDetails()`.

Inheritance

Inheritance in IDL implies that all of the entities declared in the base interface become available to the derived interface. In other words, all of the operations, attributes, type definitions, exceptions, and constants are inherited by the derived interface.

Multiple inheritance of interfaces is supported in IDL. It is therefore possible to define a diamond-shaped inheritance graph as follows:

```
// IDL
interface A {};

interface B1 : A {};

interface B2 : A {};

interface C : B1, B2 {};
```

This kind of inheritance graph does not give rise to ambiguities in IDL, because there is no state associated with interfaces. Contrast this with the situation in C++, where a similar kind of inheritance graph involving classes can be interpreted in various ways, depending on whether virtual or non-virtual inheritance is used.

No Ambiguous Operations or Attributes

The use of inheritance can give rise to name clashes between entities declared in different interfaces. For operations and attributes, the rule is that no ambiguity arising from interface inheritance is allowed.

The basic inheritance cases, illustrated by Figure 5.3, are

- In Figure 5.3(a), if an operation `A::op()` is declared in the scope of interface `A`, the operation cannot be redeclared in interface `B`. If you are accustomed to virtual functions in C++ or method overriding in Java, you might find this prohibition surprising. See the section "No Redeclaration of Operations," later in this chapter, for more details.
- In Figure 5.3(b), if an operation `A1::op()` is declared in `A1` and an operation `A2::op()` is declared in `A2`, the amalgamation of the two interfaces via multiple inheritance into `B` gives rise to a name clash. A name clash is illegal in IDL, and you must rewrite the IDL to avoid it.

These restrictions generalize to arbitrarily complex inheritance graphs. Any example where two identically named operation or attribute declarations are inherited into the same scope is illegal.

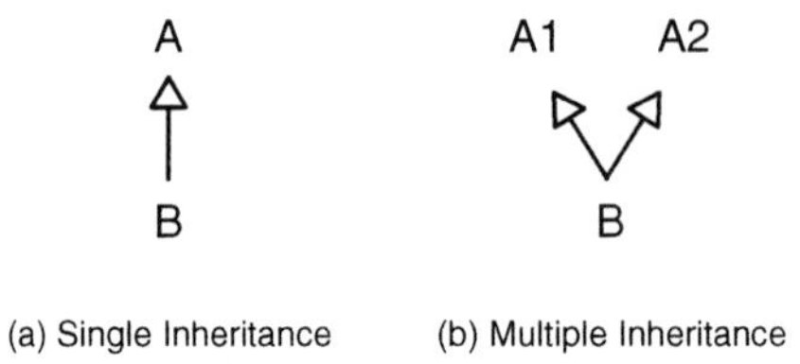

Figure 5.3

Inheritance and clashing identifiers.

Ambiguous Types, Exceptions and Constants

For all other declarations—that is, for type definitions, exceptions, and constant declarations—name clashes arising from interface inheritance are allowed in IDL. The ambiguity is resolved by using fully scoped names.

CAUTION

Avoid using ambiguous declarations of types, exceptions, and constants in your IDL. There is a great danger of causing confusion and introducing bugs if you try to use this mis-feature of IDL.

The basic inheritance cases illustrated by Figure 5.3 are

- In Figure 5.3(a), consider that type `A::T` is declared in the scope of interface `A` and type `T` is redeclared in the derived interface `B`. This can be illustrated by the following IDL fragment:

```
// IDL
interface A {
     // Declare 'A::T'
     typedef string T;
};

interface B : A {
     // Redeclaration of 'T'
     typedef long T;

     T    getLong();     // Ok - refers to 'B::T'
     A::T getString();   // Ok - refers to 'A::T'
};
```

  The ambiguity is resolved by using `T` to refer to `B::T` and using the fully scoped name `A::T` to refer to the `T` declared in the base class.

- In Figure 5.3(b), consider that type `A1::T` is declared in the scope of `A1` and the type `A2::T` is declared in the scope of `A2`. A name clash occurs when `A1` and `A2` are inherited into interface `B`. The ambiguity is resolved by using fully scoped names to refer to `A1::T` and `A2::T` whenever they appear in `B`.

Pseudo-IDL

The CORBA specification has to specify an API for a number of objects that make up the nuts and bolts of the ORB. For example, ORB objects and POA objects belong to this basic API. Typically, code for these objects is supplied as a library (C++ ORBs) or a class package (Java ORBs). However, CORBA faces a unique difficulty in that it must simultaneously define its basic API for a whole range of languages.

Rather than painstakingly rewrite the core CORBA document for every language that CORBA supports, the architects of CORBA took advantage of IDL to help them specify the API in a language-neutral format.

Consequently, the declaration of objects such as the ORB and the POA is written in a form that closely resembles IDL. However, it is not really IDL but Pseudo-IDL (PIDL). There are many significant differences between IDL and PIDL:

- PIDL interfaces do not represent CORBA objects, and invocations of PIDL objects are treated differently (typically as normal function calls).
- PIDL objects are normally local objects, not remote.
- PIDL operations and attributes do not have to follow the regular rules for a particular language mapping.
- PIDL can use constructs that are not a part of regular IDL. For example, the `native` keyword is used to declare types that are language specific.

The main thing to bear in mind is that PIDL is just a guideline for the OMG committees that specify language mappings. Parts of the PIDL can be mapped in an *ad hoc* manner to suit the requirements of a particular language mapping.

C++ Memory Management

Object references in C++ are dynamically allocated and, consequently, care has to be taken to avoid leaking the associated memory. As with other heap-allocated CORBA data (see Chapter 4, "Memory Management"), object references can be by either dumb or smart pointers. The C++ language mapping specifies that two C++ classes are generated for each IDL interface, as given in Table 5.1:

Table 5.1 C++ Mapping of Interfaces

C++ Mapped Type	Description
`IntfName``_ptr`	A dumb pointer representation of the object reference for *`IntfName`*. This pointer has the semantics of *`IntfName`* `*`. However, for standards compliance and portability you must always use *`IntfName`*`_ptr` as the type of the dumb pointer.

Table 5.1 C++ Mapping of Interfaces Continued

C++ Mapped Type	Description
*IntfName*_var	A smart pointer representation of the object reference. This pointer follows the semantics of a _var type (see Chapter 4). The _var type guards against memory leaks by automatically deleting its referenced memory when necessary.

The next two section discuss the semantics of the _ptr and _var types. The memory management rules are explained for each type of pointer.

Using _ptr Types

The dumb _ptr types do not give you any help at managing the memory of the associated object reference. The lifecycle of an object reference must therefore be managed explicitly. The basic steps in the object reference lifecycle are given in Table 5.2.

Table 5.2 Object Reference Lifecycle Operations

Lifecycle Operation	Method	Description
Creation	Various	An object reference can be created in various ways: via the Initialization Service, via the Naming Service, or via operations defined in the POA.
Copying	*IntfName*::_duplicate()	Duplication of dumb pointers *IntfName*_ptr must be performed explicitly using the _duplicate() method.
Destruction	CORBA::release()	This is the only safe way to destroy object references. It must be called explicitly when dumb pointers *IntfName*_ptr are used. Never use delete to destroy an I object reference.

These stages in the lifecycle of an object reference can be illustrated by a simple example. Consider an IDL interface Foo that maps to the dumb pointer class Foo_ptr. It does not matter what operations Foo supports—we are only interested in looking at the creation, copying, and destruction of Foo object references. The following code fragment illustrates the object reference lifecycle:

```
// C++
...
{   // begin first local scope
    Foo_ptr firstP = /* Initialize 'Foo' reference */;
    ...
```

```
    {    // begin second local scope
         Foo_ptr secondP = Foo::_duplicate(firstP);
         ...
         // must 'release' reference before end of scope
         CORBA::release(secondP);
    }
    ...
    // must 'release' reference before end of scope
    CORBA::release(firstP);
}
```

In this example, both `firstP` and `secondP` are defined as automatic variables. They remain valid over their respective scopes: the reference `firstP` over the outer scope and the reference `secondP` over the inner scope. Both `firstP` and `secondP` point to their own copies of an object reference. It is therefore necessary to call `CORBA::release()` on each of them. The call to `CORBA::release()` is made before the pointers reach the end of their respective scopes. If this is not done, a memory leak would result.

In practice, the duplication and deletion of object references is simulated using reference counting. The effect of calling `IntfName::_duplicate()` is to increment the reference count by 1; the effect of calling `CORBA::release()` is to decrement the reference count by 1.

The practice of simulating the lifecycle of object references via reference counting is illustrated in Figure 5.4. The figure shows how the preceding code fragment might actually be implemented by an ORB that uses reference counting.

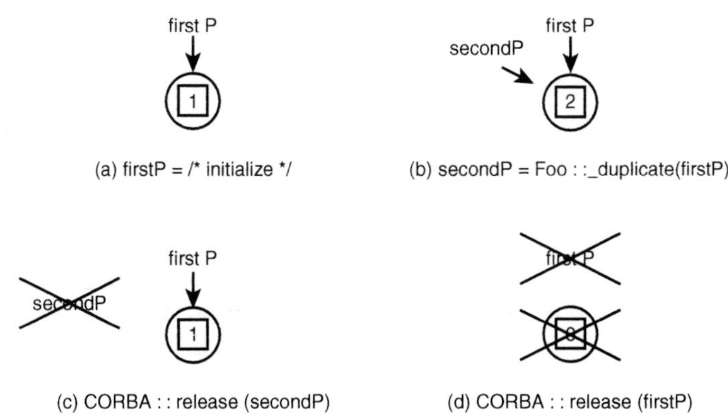

Figure 5.4

Reference counting with dumb pointers.

Figure 5.4(a) shows an object reference pointed at by a single dumb pointer `firstP`. Figure 5.4(b) shows the object reference after it has been duplicated. The reference count is increased to 2, and it is pointed at by two pointers. Figure 5.4(c) shows the object reference after secondP is released. The reference count drops back to 1. Figure 5.4(d) shows the object reference after firstP is released. The reference count falls to 0, resulting in the destruction of the object reference.

Though you might think of CORBA::release() as a method that destroys an object reference, this is not how it behaves in a reference-counting implementation. In Figure 5.4, it is only the last invocation of CORBA::release() that destroys the object reference. This is why it is such a serious error to call delete directly on an object reference. It would play havoc with the semantics of reference counting.

CAUTION

Never call delete on an object reference. In a reference-counting implementation, this gives rise to dangling pointers. Your program will crash as soon as an attempt is made to dereference one of these dangling pointers.

Using _var Types

The IDL interface Foo also maps to a smart pointer type Foo_var. This _var type is designed to help avoid memory leaks. Its semantics are similar to the semantics of the _var types for dynamically allocated CORBA data types, as described in Chapter 4.

A Foo object reference that is referenced by Foo_var is *owned* by Foo_var. This means that Foo_var is responsible for releasing the object reference. The destructor of Foo_var will call CORBA::release() on its associated object reference. Assignment to a Foo_var will also cause CORBA::release() to be called on the old value of the object reference. Consider the following code fragment, which illustrates the use of Foo_var:

```
// C++
...
{    // begin first local scope
     Foo_var firstV = /* Initialize 'Foo' reference */;
     ...
     {    // begin second local scope
          // duplicate the object reference
          Foo_var secondV = firstV;
          ...
          // reference automatically released at end of scope
     }
     ...
     // reference automatically released at end of scope
}
```

When firstV is initialized, it assumes ownership of the corresponding object reference. The assignment statement secondV = firstV results in duplication of the object reference. In other words, the first object reference is implicitly duplicated using Foo::_duplicate(), and the result of this duplication is assigned to secondV. As each of the smart pointers secondV and firstV goes out of scope, there is no need to worry about calling `CORBA::release()`. The `_var` destructor takes care of calling `CORBA::release()` automatically.

The preceding code fragment is illustrated in more detail by Figure 5.5. This figure shows what happens behind the scenes in an ORB that implements reference counting of object references.

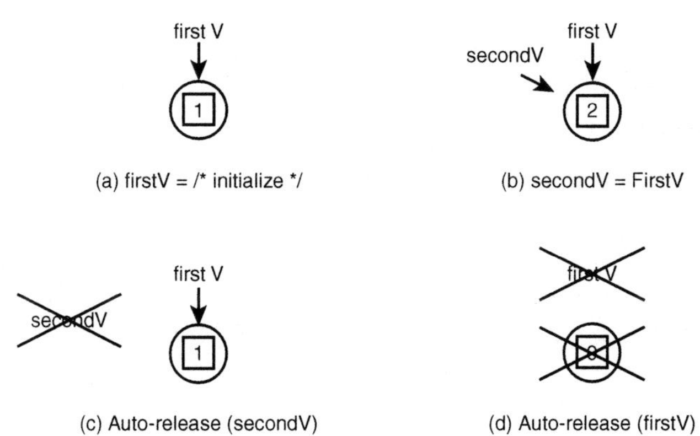

Figure 5.5

Reference counting with smart pointers.

In Figure 5.5(a), the object reference is referenced by a single smart pointer `firstV`, and its reference count is `1`. The arrow connecting `firstV` to the object reference is drawn with a heavy line to indicate that `firstV` owns the object reference.

Figure 5.5(b) shows the object reference after the assignment statement `secondV = firstV`. The object reference is incremented to `2` because of implicit duplication. The `_var` pointers `firstV` and `secondV` each own one unit of the reference count.

Figure 5.5(c) shows the situation after `secondV` goes out of scope. The destructor of `secondV` calls `CORBA::release()`, and the reference count decreases to `1`.

Figure 5.5(d) shows the situation after `firstV` goes out of scope. The destructor of `firstV` calls `CORBA::release()`, reducing the reference count to `0`. The object reference self-destructs as soon as its reference count reaches `0`.

Another important feature of the `_var` type is that it guards against memory leaks in assignment statements. Consider the following code fragment:

```
// C++
...
{     // begin local scope
      Foo_var firstV  = /* Initialize 'Foo' reference to 'obj1' */;
      Foo_var secondV = /* Initialize 'Foo' reference to 'obj2' */;
      ...
```

```
    // Perform assignment between '_var's
    secondV = firstV;
    ...
    // reference automatically released at end of scope
}
```

The _var's firstV and secondV are initialized to refer to two distinct object references, obj1 and obj2. When the assignment secondV = firstV is made, it looks as if the memory associated with obj2 might be leaked. However, the leak does not occur because secondV is smart enough to release obj2 before completing the assignment operation. This behavior is illustrated in Figure 5.6 (for a reference-counting implementation).

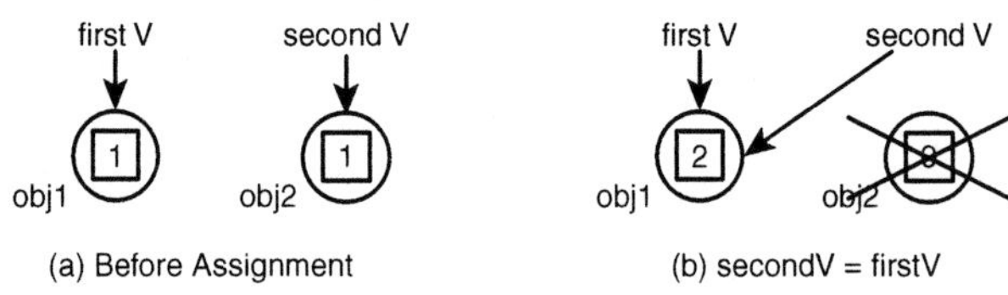

Figure 5.6

Assignment behavior with smart pointers.

Figure 5.6(a) shows the initial situation. firstV and secondV reference distinct object references obj1 and obj2, respectively.

Figure 5.6(b) shows the situation after assignment. The smart pointer secondV automatically calls CORBA::release() on its old object reference. This reduces the reference count of obj2 to 0, resulting in its destruction. After assignment, the reference count on obj1 is increased to 2.

Ultimately, _var types for object references are used in the same way as _var types for dynamically allocated CORBA data. It is just the implementation, substituting reference counting for deep copying, which is different. Moreover, the conversion methods, such as Foo_var::in(), Foo_var::inout(), Foo_var::out(), and Foo_var::_retn(), are also defined on object reference _var types.

Mixed Assignments Between _ptr and _var Types

The _ptr and _var types are frequently mixed together in the same section of code. Therefore, you need to understand the semantics of mixed assignment between these types. Two types of assignment are considered here:

- Assignments of type _var = _ptr
- Assignments of type _ptr = _var

The semantics of these mixed assignments are similar to mixed assignments as described in Chapter 4. It is helpful to see how these assignments are implemented using reference counting.

Assignment of Type _var = _ptr

The following code fragment shows the assignment of a dumb pointer to a smart pointer:

```
// C++
{     // begin local scope
      Foo_var dumbP  = /* Initialize 'Foo' reference to 'obj1' */;
      Foo_ptr smartV   = /* Initialize 'Foo' reference to 'obj2' */;

      // Assignment '_var = _ptr'
      smartV = dumbP;
}
```

After assignment, the smart pointer smartV assumes ownership of the object reference and is responsible for releasing it. This assignment is illustrated in Figure 5.7.

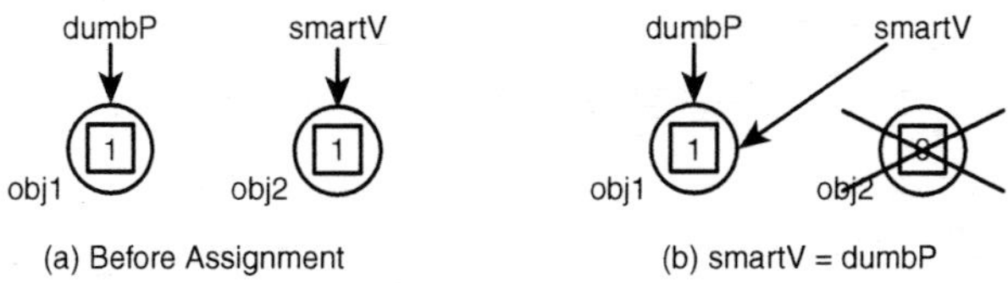

Figure 5.7

Assignment _var = _ptr.

Figure 5.7(a) shows that before assignment dumbP and smartV refer to the object references obj1 and obj2, respectively. Figure 5.7(b) shows the situation after assignment. smartV automatically calls CORBA::release() on obj2. This reduces its reference count to 0, causing obj2 to self-destruct. The reference count of obj1 is not incremented.

Assignment of Type _ptr = _var

The following code fragment shows the assignment of a smart pointer to a dumb pointer:

```
// C++
{     // begin local scope
      Foo_var dumbP  = /* Initialize 'Foo' reference to 'obj1' */;
      Foo_ptr smartV   = /* Initialize 'Foo' reference to 'obj2' */;

      // Assignment '_ptr = _var'
      CORBA::release(dumbP);     // Beware! Remember to release old value.
      dumbP = smartV;
}
```

Before making an assignment to dumbP, it is essential to call CORBA::release(). Otherwise, the memory associated with obj2 is leaked. This assignment is illustrated in Figure 5.8.

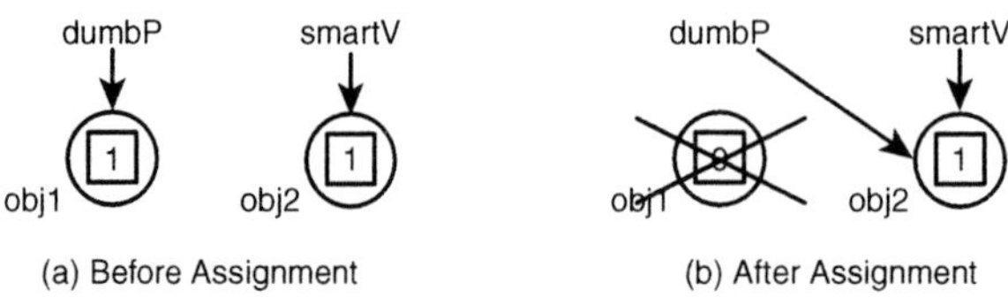

Figure 5.8

Assignment `_ptr = _var`.

Figure 5.8(a) shows that before assignment dumbP and smartV refer to separate object references, obj1 and obj2. Figure 5.8(b) shows the situation after assignment. The object reference obj1 is released by the explicit call CORBA::release(dumbP). After assignment, both smartV and dumbP refer to obj2. The reference count for obj2 is not incremented.

Nil Object Reference

In general, it is illegal for null pointers (C++) or null references (Java) to be passed as arguments to CORBA operations when concrete values are expected. For example, if an empty string is to be passed as an in parameter, it must be represented as the string "" rather than a null value.

Object references are a special case, however. It is permissible to pass an empty value for an object reference—these are known as *nil object references*. The representation of nil object references depends on the language mapping.

The reason nil object references are permitted is that it is often useful to supply one as a default value. For example, a finder operation might return a nil value to indicate that an object reference was not found. This offers alternative semantics to raising an exception.

The syntax of nil object references for C++ and Java is described in the next two sections.

C++ Nil Object References

Nil object references in C++ are created using the _nil() static method that is defined on every object reference class:

```
// C++
InterfaceName_ptr  InterfaceName::_nil()
```

This `_nil()` method is used to create a nil object reference of type *InterfaceName*. If you want to test whether a given object reference is nil, use the standard function `CORBA::is_nil()`, defined in the CORBA module:

```
// C++
CORBA::Boolean  CORBA::is_nil(CORBA::Object_ptr obj)
```

The following code fragment shows nil objects in use for an interface type `Foo`:

```
// C++
{    // Open a local scope

     // Create 'nil' object reference
     Foo_var foo1V = Foo::_nil();

     if (CORBA::is_nil(foo1V)) {
          cout << "Yes, it's nil." << endl;
     }

     // Duplicate a 'nil' object reference
     Foo_ptr foo2P = Foo::_duplicate(foo1V);
     ...
     // Release a 'nil' object reference
     CORBA::release(foo2P);      // Call release to be on the safe side
     // 'foo1V' auto-releases memory
}
```

These object references can legally be duplicated and released, just like ordinary object references. However, these functions effectively are no-ops, since reference counting is not done for nil object references.

Attempting to invoke a nil object reference is a serious error. In some ORB implementations where nil is represented as a null pointer, an attempted invocation would lead to a core dump.

Java Nil Object References

There is no special representation of a nil object reference in Java. A nil object reference is represented as an ordinary null reference.

Likewise, there is no special method for testing for nilness. A simple test for equality to null does the trick.

The following code fragment shows nil objects in use for an interface type `Foo`:

```
// Java
{    // Open a local scope

     // Create 'nil' object reference
     Foo foo1=null;
```

```
    if (foo1==null) {
        cout << "Yes, it's nil." << endl;
    }

    // Copy the 'nil' object reference
    Foo foo2 = foo1;
    ...
}
```

Attempting to invoke a nil object reference in Java is a serious error that results in a runtime exception.

Factory Objects

In distributed systems, clients are often required to create objects on remote servers. For example, a customer at a bank needs to create an `Account` object when opening a new account. Something like a remote constructor is what is needed. Java and C++ both support constructor methods, but the constructors are not remotely accessible.

The solution to the problem of creating remote objects is to use a *factory* design pattern. This involves defining a factory interface in IDL that can create and manage object references of a particular type. No new features are introduced to help define factory objects. It is simply a design pattern that uses standard IDL syntax.

Consider, for example, a client in a financial application needs to create new `Account` objects. The IDL given in Listing 5.1 introduces a corresponding `AccountFactory` interface:

Listing 5.1 Interfaces for `Account` *and* `AccountFactory`

```
// IDL

#pragma prefix "pure-corba-3.com"

typedef fixed<10, 2> MoneyAmount;

interface Account {
    ...
};

interface AccountFactory {
    Account create(
                in string name,
                in MoneyAmount initialBalance
            );

    Account find(in string name);

    // No operation supplied to destroy Accounts
};
```

Interface `AccountFactory` is introduced to manage `Account` objects. The interface defines two operations: `create()` and `find()`.

- The `create()` operation is used to make new `Account` objects and is analogous to a remote constructor method. The characteristic feature of `create()` is that its return value is the name of an interface `Account`.
- The `find()` operation is used to locate existing `Account` objects, given the name of the account. It is common to declare finder methods in a factory interface. Sometimes an interface consists solely of finder operations, in which case it can be referred to as a *finder interface*.

The `AccountFactory` interface does not provide an operation to destroy `Account` objects. In this example a `destroy` operation would be inappropriate, because the application intends to keep a permanent record of all accounts that have been opened. An operation to deactivate accounts could probably be provided instead.

In some cases it is appropriate to provide a `destroy` operation in the factory interface. In other cases, for example when the objects created are short lived, it may be more appropriate for the server to implement a form of garbage collection.

Polymorphism

From the outset, CORBA was intended to provide strong support for object-oriented programming concepts. Polymorphism is, therefore, one of the fundamental features of CORBA. The following are some of the object-oriented features supported:

- Inheritance of interfaces, including multiple inheritance
- Polymorphism

The IDL module `Zoo`, given in Listing 5.2, is used here to illustrate the features of inheritance and polymorphism.

Listing 5.2 The IDL for Module `Zoo`

```
// IDL

#pragma prefix "pure-corba-3.com"

module Zoo {
    interface Animal;
    typedef sequence<Animal> AnimalSeq;
    typedef sequence<string> StringSeq;

    interface ZooManager {
        AnimalSeq getAllAnimals();
        ...
    };

    // Base Interfaces
    interface Animal {
        readonly attribute string species;
```

Listing 5.2 The IDL for Module Zoo Continued

```
        readonly attribute short numberOfLegs;
    };

    interface Poisonous : Animal { };
    interface Spider : Animal { };

    // Concrete Interfaces
    interface Giraffe : Animal { };
    interface Elephant : Animal { };
    interface Kangaroo : Animal { };
    interface Lion : Animal { };
    interface Centipede : Animal { };
    interface Tarantula : Spider, Poisonous { };
};
```

An interface `Animal` is defined that serves as the base class for a number of `Animal` types, `Giraffe`, `Elephant`, and so on. Two other base classes, `Spider` and `Poisonous`, are defined. They are used in the discussion of multiple inheritance.

Widening Object References

The *widening* of object references refers to an assignment where a derived type is assigned to a base type.

C++ Widening Object References

Because each interface maps to both a `_ptr` and a `_var` type, there are a number of permutations possible when widening in C++. Consider widening type `Giraffe` to type `Animal`. Four permutations of assignment are possible:

- `_ptr` to `_ptr`
- `_ptr` to `_var`
- `_var` to `_ptr`
- `_var` to `_var`

Most of these assignments work as expected and have semantics similar to that described in the section "Mixed Assignments Between `_ptr` and `_var` Types." There is one nasty surprise, however: Widening a `_var` to a `_var` does not work.

The following code fragment illustrates the widening of type `Giraffe` to `Animal`:

```
// C++
{
    // Assignment of _ptr = _ptr
    Zoo::Giraffe_ptr giraffeP = /* Initialize object reference */;
    Zoo::Animal_ptr animalP;

    animalP = giraffeP;  // Ok - shallow copy

    CORBA::release(animalP);  // Cleanup
```

```
}
{
    // Assignment of _ptr = _var
    Zoo::Giraffe_var giraffeV = /* Initialize object reference */;
    Zoo::Animal_ptr  animalP;

    animalP = giraffeV;  // Ok - shallow copy

    // No cleanup necessary - 'giraffeV' owns the memory
}
{
    // Assignment of _var = _ptr
    Zoo::Giraffe_ptr giraffeP = /* Initialize object reference */;
    Zoo::Animal_var animalV;

    animalV = giraffeP;  // Ok - shallow copy
                         // 'animalV' assumes ownership of object reference

    // No cleanup necessary - 'animalV' owns the memory
}
{
    // Assignment of _var = _var
    // Beware! Direct assignment is not possible.
    Zoo::Giraffe_var giraffeV = /* Initialize object reference */;
    Zoo::Animal_var animalV;

    // Use _duplicate to help assignment
    animalV = Zoo::Animal::_duplicate(giraffeV);  // Ok - duplicate copy

    // No cleanup necessary - '_vars do auto-cleanup
}
```

The first three cases work as expected and are similar to normal mixed pointer assignments. The exception is the assignment of `_var` to `_var`. In fact, a direct assignment between the `_vars`, such as `animalV = giraffeV`, is not possible and will not compile. The two `_var` types are not related by inheritance, and the number of conversions required to make the assignment exceeds the limit of an ANSI C++ compiler. You need to give the C++ compiler a little help at converting `Zoo::Giraffe_var` to `Zoo::Animal_var`. This is done by making the explicit call to `Zoo::Animal::_duplicate()`. At the end of this assignment statement the reference count on the `Giraffe` object is `2`.

TIP

Widening of object references works as you would expect (similarly to assignment between object references of the same type) except for widening a *derived*`_var` to a *base*`_var`. In that case, use *base*`::_duplicate()` (or *derived*`::_duplicate()`) to help perform the assignment.

Keep a lookout for occasions when widening a _var to a _var is required. For example, consider a struct AnimalFamily, defined in IDL:

```
// IDL
module Zoo {
     ...
     struct AnimalFamily {
          Animal mother;
          Animal father;
          AnimalSeq children;
     };
};
```

Here is a fragment of code to initialize the struct for a family of Giraffes:

```
// C++
Zoo::AnimalFamily family;
Zoo::Giraffe_var giraffeV;
...
giraffeV = /* Initialize to object reference for Giraffe mother */;
family.mother = Zoo::Animal::_duplicate(giraffeV);

giraffeV = /* Initialize to object reference for Giraffe father */;
family.father = Zoo::Animal::_duplicate(giraffeV);

// No children in this 'AnimalFamily'
family.children.length(0);
...
```

The use of _duplicate() is required in assignments to the struct members mother and father because the assignments implicitly widen Giraffe to Animal. You may recall that struct members referencing heap-allocated memory are smart pointers. The semantics of assignment are therefore the same as widening a _var to a _var. The call to _duplicate() is necessary to aid the type conversion.

Java Widening Object References

The widening of object references in Java is straightforward. There is just one case to consider:

```
// Java
{
     // Assignment of 'Animal = Giraffe'
     Zoo.Giraffe theGiraffe = /* Initialize object reference */;
     Zoo.Animal theAnimal;

     theAnimal = theGiraffe;  // Ok
}
```

The assignment `theAnimal = theGiraffe` corresponds to ordinary widening of a reference in Java.

Narrowing Object References

Narrowing consists of taking a base type object reference and converting it to a derived type. Narrowing is generally more complicated than widening. For example, consider the relationship between the types `Giraffe` and `Animal`. While it is clear that a `Giraffe` is always an `Animal` (widening), it is not so clear whether a given `Animal` is actually a `Giraffe` (narrowing). To perform a narrowing cast, the compiler has to know that the most derived type of the object is `Giraffe` and that `Giraffe` inherits from `Animal`.

There are two distinct kinds of difficulty with performing narrowing casts:

- Limitations of the particular mapped language may make it difficult to perform narrowing. For example, pre-ANSI C++ compilers do not provide a general mechanism for making narrowing casts.
- Implicit knowledge of the IDL inheritance hierarchy is needed by the ORB. For example, to perform a cast from `Animal` to `Giraffe`, the ORB needs to know that `Giraffe` inherits from `Animal`. This information is normally obtained from the stub code that is linked with your application.

Because of the special requirements associated with narrowing, a narrow function (`_narrow()` in C++, `narrow()` in Java) is provided to help perform these casts. This narrow function must always be used to make a cast down the IDL object hierarchy.

The first reason for using the narrow function is that it works around any language or compiler specific limitations to make the narrowing cast possible.

The second and more important reason for using narrow is that it automatically checks IDL inheritance relationships for you. The narrow succeeds only if the type you narrow from really is an IDL base of the type you narrow to. In other words, the use of the narrow function guarantees type safety with respect to IDL interfaces.

C++ Narrowing Object References

Narrowing from a base type *`base`* to a derived type *`derived`* is performed using the static `_narrow()` function that has the following signature:

```
// C++
derived_ptr derived::_narrow(CORBA::Object_ptr theBaseReference)
```

The method takes an object reference of type `CORBA::Object`, in this case of type *`base`*, and returns an object reference of type *`derived`*. The object reference is implicitly duplicated when `_narrow()` is invoked. The `_narrow()` works for all permutations of assignment between `_ptrs` and `_vars`.

If the type *`derived`* is not derived from type *`base`*, the narrowing fails and returns a nil object reference. You can test for nilness of the returned object reference using the `CORBA::is_nil()` function.

TIP

You should *always* test the return value of a narrow function for nilness in C++ using `CORBA::is_nil()`. This may seem pedantic at first, but it is important when debugging your application.

The following code fragment illustrates the narrowing of type `Animal` to `Giraffe` for a variety of mixed assignments between `_ptr`s and `_var`s:

```
// C++
{
    // Assignment of _ptr = _ptr
    Zoo::Giraffe_ptr giraffeP;
    Zoo::Animal_ptr animalP = /* Initialize as a Giraffe */;

    giraffeP = Zoo::Giraffe::_narrow(animalP);  // Implicit duplication
    if (CORBA::is_nil(giraffeP)) {
        cerr << "Narrow to Giraffe failed!" << endl;
    }

    CORBA::release(animalP);   // Cleanup
    CORBA::release(giraffeP);  // Cleanup
}
{
    // Assignment of _ptr = _var
    Zoo::Giraffe_ptr giraffeP;
    Zoo::Animal_var  animalV = /* Initialize as a Giraffe */;

    giraffeP = Zoo::Giraffe::_narrow(animalV);   // Implicit duplication
    if (CORBA::is_nil(giraffeP)) {
        cerr << "Narrow to Giraffe failed!" << endl;
    }

    CORBA::release(giraffeP);  // Cleanup
    // 'animalV' calls release automatically
}
{
    // Assignment of _var = _ptr
    Zoo::Giraffe_var giraffeV;
    Zoo::Animal_ptr  animalP = /* Initialize as a Giraffe */;

    giraffeV = Zoo::Giraffe::_narrow(animalP);  // Implicit duplication
    if (CORBA::is_nil(giraffeV)) {
        cerr << "Narrow to Giraffe failed!" << endl;
    }

    CORBA::release(animalP);  // Cleanup
    // 'giraffeV' calls release automatically
```

```
}
{
     // Assignment of _var = _var
     Zoo::Giraffe_var giraffeV;
     Zoo::Animal_var  animalV = /* Initialize as a Giraffe */;

     giraffeV = Zoo::Giraffe::_narrow(animalV);  // Implicit duplication
     if (CORBA::is_nil(giraffeV)) {
          cerr << "Narrow to Giraffe failed!" << endl;
     }

     // No cleanup necessary - '_vars do auto-cleanup
}
```

All of these examples are regular, and the `_narrow()` method is used the same way throughout.

CAUTION

An important point to bear in mind is that `_narrow()` duplicates the object reference. Therefore, you must ensure that `CORBA::release()` eventually gets called both on the original object reference and on the narrowed copy.

Java Narrowing Object References

Narrowing from a base type *base* to a derived type *derived* is performed using the static `narrow()` method, which is defined in the *derived*`Helper` class:

```
// Java
derived  derivedHelper.narrow(org.omg.CORBA.Object theBaseReference)
```

The method takes an object reference of type `CORBA.Object` and returns an object reference of type *derived*.

If the type *derived* is not derived from type *base*, the narrowing fails and raises the system exception `CORBA::BAD_PARAM`.

The following code fragment illustrates the narrowing of type `Animal` to `Giraffe` in Java:

```
// Java
try {
     // Assignment of 'Giraffe = Animal'
     Zoo.Giraffe theGiraffe;
     Zoo.Animal  theAnimal = /* Initialize as a Giraffe */;

     theGiraffe = Zoo.GiraffeHelper.narrow(theAnimal);  // Ok
}
catch (org.omg.CORBA.BAD_PARAM ex) {
     System.err.println("Attempted to narrow to wrong type: " + ex);
```

```
}
catch (org.omg.CORBA.SystemException sysex) {
    System.err.println(sysex);
}
```

The method `Zoo.GiraffeHelper.narrow()` is invoked to perform the down-cast. Optionally, you can catch the `CORBA::BAD_PARAM` exception explicitly, as shown above. This enables you to print out an informative error message if the `narrow()` fails.

The `Object` Base Type

CORBA defines the special type `Object` that is the base type for all IDL interfaces. Effectively, it is as if every IDL interface is inherited from type `Object`. However, inheritance from `Object` is implicit, so there is no need to declare inheritance from it. In fact, explicit inheritance from `Object` is illegal.

The `Object` type is useful for defining general-purpose finder operations that have to return a wide variety of object references. For example, the `Object` type is used by the CORBA Naming Service for the return value of the `resolve_str()` operation:

```
// IDL
...
module CosNaming {
    ...
    interface NamingContextExt : NamingContext {
        typedef string StringName;
        ...
        Object resolve_str(in StringName n);
        ...
    };
};
```

The `resolve_str()` operation provides a simple lookup service. Given the name of an object in a string format, it returns the corresponding object reference. Since the naming service needs to be able to store object references of any type, the only feasible return type that can be used here is `Object`.

C++ `CORBA::Object` Type

The IDL type `Object` maps to the C++ type `CORBA::Object`. All object reference types in C++ inherit from the class `CORBA::Object`.

There are a number of methods defined on the base class `CORBA::Object`, and all of these method names are preceded by an underscore to avoid clashing with operation names. For example, you have already encountered the methods `CORBA::Object::_duplicate()`, `CORBA::Object::_nil()`, and `CORBA::Object::_is_a()` in this chapter. The complete set of methods for `CORBA::Object` is given in Chapter 17, "IDL Data Types."

As an example of how to use the `CORBA::Object` type in C++, imagine that a `Giraffe` object reference is registered in the naming service under the name `"Animals/Giraffe1"`. The `Giraffe` object reference can be looked up using the `resolve_str()` operation:

```
// C++
...
CosNaming::NamingContextExt_var  rootContextV;
CORBA::Object_var                objV;
Zoo::Giraffe_var                 giraffeV;

//-------------------------
// Initialize 'rootContextV' (not shown)
...
// Resolve the name "Animals/Giraffe1"
objV = rootContextV->resolve_str("Animals/Giraffe1");
giraffeV = Zoo::Giraffe::_narrow(objV);
if (CORBA::is_nil(giraffeV)) {
     cerr << "Narrow to Giraffe failed." << endl;
     return;
}

// Now you are ready to use 'giraffeV'...
```

This example is typical of the way clients find object references. First an object reference `objV` of `CORBA::Object` type is returned from `resolve_str()`. This object reference is not directly useful, because `CORBA::Object` does not declare any methods for `Giraffe`s. The object reference must be narrowed to type `Zoo::Giraffe` before it can be used.

Java `org.omg.CORBA.Object` Type

The IDL type `Object` maps to the Java classes `org.omg.CORBA.Object` and `org.omg.CORBA.ObjectHelper`. All object reference types in Java extend the class `org.omg.CORBA.Object`.

There are a number of methods defined in the base class `org.omg.CORBA.Object`. All of these method names are preceded by an underscore to avoid clashing with operation names. The complete set of methods for `org.omg.CORBA.Object` is given in Chapter 18.

As an example of how to use the `org.omg.CORBA.Object` type in Java, imagine that a `Giraffe` object reference is registered in the naming service under the name `"Animals/Giraffe1"`. The `Giraffe` object reference can be looked up using the `resolve_str()` operation:

```
// Java
...
CosNaming.NamingContextExt  rootContext;
org.omg.CORBA.Object        obj;
```

```
Zoo.Giraffe                   giraffe;

//---------------------------
// Initialize 'rootContext' (not shown)
//---------------------------
...
try {
     // Resolve the name "Animals/Giraffe1"
     obj = rootContext.resolve_str("Animals/Giraffe1");
     giraffe = Zoo.GiraffeHelper.narrow(obj);

     // Now you are ready to use 'giraffe'...
}
catch (org.omg.CORBA.BAD_PARAM ex) {
     System.err.println("Attempted to narrow to wrong type: " + ex);
}
catch (org.omg.CORBA.SystemException sysex) {
     System.err.println(sysex);
}
```

This example is typical of the way clients find object references. First an object reference `obj` of `org.omg.CORBA.Object` type is returned from `resolve_str()`. This object reference is not directly useful, because `org.omg.CORBA.Object` does not declare any methods for `Giraffes`. The object reference must be narrowed to type `Zoo.Giraffe` before it can be used.

Polymorphism and IDL Operations

All IDL operations support dynamic binding (that is, they behave similarly to virtual member functions in C++ and methods in Java). This can be illustrated by a short example. Consider the interface `ZooManager` that was declared in Listing 5.2:

```
module Zoo {
     interface Animal;
     typedef sequence<Animal> AnimalSeq;

     interface ZooManager {
          AnimalSeq getAllAnimals();
          ...
     };
     ...
};
```

The operation `ZooManager::getAllAnimals()` returns a sequence containing various animal types. It is therefore convenient to declare the elements of the returned sequence to be of type `Animal`. Because IDL operations support dynamic binding, it is possible to get sensible results by invoking methods directly in the base class `Animal`. Narrowing is not required if the operations you need are already declared in the base class. For example

```
// C++
Zoo::ZooManager_var zooManagerV;
Zoo::AnimalSeq_var animalSeqV;

// Initialize zooManager (not shown)
...
animalSeqV = zooManagerV->getAllAnimals();

for (CORBA::ULong i=0; i < animalSeqV->length(); i++) {
     // Assign to 'String_var' to avoid a memory leak
     CORBA::String_var strV = animalSeqV[i]->species();
     cout << "The "  << strV
          << " has " << animalSeqV[i]->numberOfLegs() << " legs." << endl;
}

// Java
Zoo.ZooManager zooManager = null;
Zoo.Animal[]  animalSeq = null;

// Initialize zooManager (not shown)
...
animalSeq = zooManager.getAllAnimals();

for (int i=0; i < animalSeq.length; i++) {
     System.out.println("The " + animalSeq[i].species()
          + " has " + animalSeq[i].numberOfLegs() + " legs.");
}
```

If the returned sequence contains the three elements `Giraffe`, `Centipede`, and `Tarantula`, you would get output that looks like the following:

```
The Giraffe has 4 legs.
The Centipede has 60 legs.
The Tarantula has 8 legs.
```

The polymorphism of CORBA objects ensures that the correct implementations of the attributes `species` and `numberOfLegs` are invoked even though the invocation is made on the base class `Animal`. The implementation of an operation is selected on the basis of the underlying type of the object reference.

No Redeclaration of Operations

If you are familiar with virtual methods (C++) or method overriding (Java), you might be tempted to write the IDL for `Zoo` in the following way:

```
// IDL

#pragma prefix "pure-corba-3.com"

module Zoo {
```

```
    ...
    // Base Interfaces
    interface Animal {
        readonly attribute string species;
        readonly attribute short numberOfLegs;
    };
    ...
    // Concrete Interfaces
    interface Giraffe : Animal {
        // Redeclaration of Animal attributes/operations
        readonly attribute string species;      // ILLEGAL!
        readonly attribute short numberOfLegs;  // ILLEGAL!

        // Declare operations specific to Giraffe
        ...
    };
};
```

However, the redeclaration of attributes `species` and `numberOfLegs` is illegal IDL syntax. The author of such an IDL module is presumably trying to indicate that the attributes `species` and `numberOfLegs` should be implemented differently in interface `Giraffe`. There is no need to redeclare them, however. You are already free to provide different implementations of these attributes for interface `Animal` and interface `Giraffe` without redeclaration.

Polymorphic Implementation of Operations

When it comes to implementing operations in the mapped language, you can use whatever mechanism the mapped language provides to help you implement them.

Take the C++ language for example: If you want operations declared in interface `Animal` to be implemented differently by `Giraffe` objects, you can use virtual member functions to achieve this. In the implementation class for `Giraffe`, you would redeclare the virtual member functions and provide implementations specific to the `Giraffe` class. This is the standard approach to implementing virtual functions in C++.

In Java, you would use method overriding to achieve the same result.

Pitfalls of Narrowing

The operation of narrowing, as described in the previous section, sounds straightforward. However, when you use narrowing in a realistic application, you may experience some surprises. The surprises arise from the fact that there are two distinct kinds of narrowing operation:

- *Narrowing using stubs* In this case, knowledge of the IDL inheritance hierarchy is derived from the stub code linked with your application. The narrowing is straightforward and executes locally.

- *Narrowing using dynamic CORBA* This arises when knowledge of the IDL inheritance hierarchy is missing from the stub code. A remote invocation must be made in the course of narrowing to determine whether the given cast is type safe.

The choice of narrowing algorithm is made automatically by the ORB. If the ORB encounters an object reference of unknown type, it defaults to the dynamic narrowing algorithm and makes a remote invocation to decide if a cast is legal.

Unfortunately, if you have not anticipated the possibility of dynamic narrowing, the side effects can be unpleasant. At the very least, the application is slowed by the overhead of an extra remote call. In some cases, an unexpected remote call can lead to deadlock (see Chapter 10, "Threading").

The next two sections discuss how dynamic narrowing can arise in practice and how you might avoid it.

Hiding Interfaces

A common feature of object-oriented design is the definition of a public and a private part of an interface. This approach is often desirable in commercial packages that expose a public API for the user of the package, while hiding a private API that is used internally.

For example, the public methods of an IDL interface could be made available to both client and server while the private methods are available only to the server application. The IDL for such an application might be split across two files.

The first file (`public.idl`, given in Listing 5.3) contains the public part of the interface and is meant to be used by all clients of the application.

Listing 5.3 Public IDL for Clients

```
// IDL
// File: 'public.idl'

#pragma prefix "example-company.com"

interface PublicInterface {
     void publicOp();
};
```

The second file (`non-public.idl`, given in Listing 5.4) contains both the public and hidden parts of the interface. The interfaces in this file are implemented by the server.

Listing 5.4 Hidden IDL for Servers Only

```
// IDL
// File: 'non-public.idl'

#pragma prefix "example-company.com"
```

Listing 5.4 continued

```
interface PublicInterface {
     void publicOp();
};

interface HiddenInterface : PublicInterface {
     void hiddenOp();
};
```

This IDL features a typical object-oriented approach: The hidden operations are defined in the class `HiddenInterface`, which derives from `PublicInterface`. This achieves a clean separation of the public and private parts of the interface. The server instantiates objects of type `HiddenInterface` that support both `HiddenInterface` and `PublicInterface`. From the server's perspective, `PublicInterface` is a base interface.

Elegant though this approach is, it suffers from one drawback: It forces clients to use dynamic narrowing. This occurs because the server knows about an interface, `HiddenInterface`, of which clients know nothing. Knowledge of this interface is missing from the client stub code.

Consider what happens when the server publishes an object of type `HiddenInterface` to the naming service under the name `"Example/Public"`. A client wanting to narrow this interface to the type `PublicInterface` uses the following code:

```
// C++
...
CosNaming::NamingContextExt_var  rootContextV;
CORBA::Object_var                objV;
PublicInterface_var              publicInterfaceV;
...
// Initialize 'rootContextV' (not shown)
...
// Resolve the name "Example/Public"
objV = rootContextV->resolve_str("Example/Public");
publicInterfaceV = PublicInterface::_narrow(objV);  // Dynamic narrowing!

if (CORBA::is_nil(publicInterfaceV)) {
     cerr << "Narrow to Giraffe failed." << endl;
     return;
}

// Java
...
CosNaming.NamingContextExt  rootContext;
org.omg.CORBA.Object        obj;
PublicInterface             pub;
...
// Initialize 'rootContext' (not shown)
...
try {
```

```
        // Resolve the name "Example/Public"
        obj = rootContext.resolve_str("Example/Public");
        pub = PublicInterfaceHelper.narrow(obj);  // Dynamic narrowing!
}
catch (org.omg.CORBA.SystemException sysex) { ... }
```

The narrow from the IDL type `Object` to the type `PublicInterface` can succeed only if the object is really of type `PublicInterface`. By examining the state of the object, the ORB can determine that the real type of the object is `HiddenInterface`. The IDL in Listing 5.3 makes no mention of `HiddenInterface`. Therefore, based on stub code alone, the ORB is unable to determine if the object inherits from `PublicInterface`. The ORB is forced to discover the inheritance dynamically. Two different approaches are commonly employed in response to this situation:

- The ORB can invoke `CORBA::Object::is_a()` on the remote `HiddenInterface` object, passing the repository ID `"IDL:example-company.com/PublicInterface:1.0"`. Since the server has access to the stub code for the full IDL in Listing 5.4, it knows that `HiddenInterface` inherits from `PublicInterface`. The `is_a()` operation therefore returns the value `TRUE`, indicating that the narrow should succeed.
  The main drawback of this approach, apart from the overhead of an extra remote call, is the fact that it can lead to deadlock in certain circumstances. Note that although the operation `CORBA::Object::is_a()` is defined in pseudo-IDL, it results in a remote invocation. This is a rare example of a remote invocation defined by pseudo-IDL.
- The ORB might elect to consult the Interface Repository instead of invoking `CORBA::Object::is_a()`. The Interface Repository would have to be populated with the complete IDL in Listing 5.4 for this to work. The advantage of this approach is that there is no possibility of deadlock occurring.

Each of these approaches has its drawbacks. On the whole, it is probably better to avoid dynamic narrowing altogether if you can. One way of avoiding it is to try hiding operations instead of hiding interfaces.

Hiding Operations

The problem with hiding interfaces from CORBA clients is that the clients subsequently have difficulty figuring out the inheritance relationships between interfaces. A compromise solution is possible. The IDL exposed to clients can include all private interfaces in the form of placeholders that declare no operations. Inheritance relationships are declared, and this gives clients all the information they need to perform narrowing. For example, the public IDL in Listing 5.3 would be replaced by that in Listing 5.5.

Listing 5.5 Modified Public IDL for Clients

```
// IDL
// File: 'modified-public.idl'
```

Listing 5.5 continued

```
#pragma prefix "example-company.com"

interface PublicInterface {
    void publicOp();
};

// Dummy declaration of 'HiddenInterface'
interface HiddenInterface :  PublicInterface {};
```

In this example, every interface is available to clients, but the operations of `HiddenInterface` remain hidden. Clients can now obtain complete information about inheritance relationships from the stub code. Dynamic narrowing is no longer necessary.

It might seem odd to declare the interface `HiddenInterface` one way for clients (Listing 5.5) and another way for servers (Listing 5.4). The effect of this is benign. Clients can invoke only operations that they know about, so the set of operations clients can use is restricted to those inherited from `PublicInterface`.

CAUTION

> You should not get carried away with declaring distinct IDL for clients and servers, however. For example, it is imperative that clients and servers use identical declarations of IDL data types. Otherwise the ORB would not be able to marshal parameters correctly.

Interoperable Object Reference

When developing a CORBA application, you usually encounter object references in the form of an object instance (a C++ object or a Java object). There are occasions, however, when object references have to be converted to a stream of bytes:

- When marshalling an object reference for transmission as a parameter or return value in an IIOP message (see Chapter 16, "Internet Inter-ORB Protocol").
- When `CORBA::ORB::object_to_string()` is called to stringify a given reference.

The use of `object_to_string()` is of particular interest in this chapter. It is easy to dump the state of an object reference into a string by calling `object_to_string()`. The information that can be extracted from the resulting string is often very helpful when it comes to debugging your distributed application.

The following sections outline the structure of an interoperable object reference (IOR).

Structure of an IOR

A schematic outline of the structure of an IOR is shown in Figure 5.9.

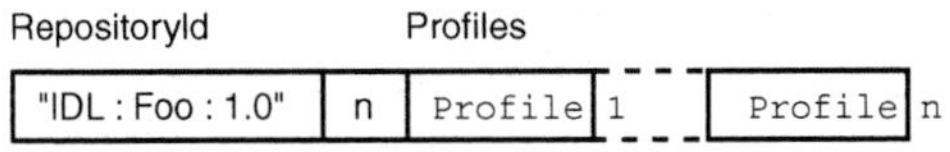

Figure 5.9

The overall structure of an IOR.

Figure 5.9 shows that an IOR consists of a repository ID followed by an arbitrary number of profiles.

The repository ID identifies the type of object. For example, a CORBA object of type `Giraffe` (as defined in Listing 5.2) would have a repository ID `"IDL:pure-corba-3.com/Zoo/Giraffe:1.0"`. The number at the end of the repository ID refers to the version of the IDL interface and is usually just `1.0`. The type given in the repository ID should always be the *most derived type* of the CORBA object. For example, if the CORBA object is of type `Giraffe`, it would be incorrect to put the `Animal` repository ID `"IDL:pure-corba-3.com/Zoo/Animal:1.0"` into the object reference. However, since object references are created by the ORB, this is not something you usually have to worry about.

A series of profiles is given after the repository ID. Each profile is specific to a particular transport protocol and contains complete details about the location of an object and how to open a connection to the object. A client uses the information in a single IOR profile to locate a CORBA object.

You may therefore be wondering: If a single profile contains all the necessary information, why include multiple profiles in the IOR? In many cases the IOR does indeed contain just one profile. However, there are a couple of reasons multiple profiles are potentially useful:

- An ORB that supports multiple transport protocols can make the same object accessible via a number of different protocols. The ORB would include an IOR profile for each supported transport protocol. For example, an ORB might support shared memory transport or multicast transport (these are not yet standardized by the OMG, however).
- Multiple profiles can be used as a way of implementing fault tolerance. The same CORBA object could be made available on a number of different servers and an IOR profile included for each server.

Currently there is only one standard profile type of interest here: the IIOP profile. This profile specifies the location details of a CORBA object reachable via the TCP/IP transport. It is described in the next section.

Structure of an IIOP Profile

The schematic structure of an IIOP profile is shown in Figure 5.10.

Tag	IIOP Version				
0	1.2	host	port	object_key	optional components

Figure 5.10

The structure of an IIOP profile.

The profile begins with a tag that identifies it as an IIOP profile. The tag is called `TAG_INTERNET_IOP` and has the value `0`. It is followed by the CDR encapsulation of the profile body. The main pieces of information in the profile body are as follows:

1. It begins by giving the version of IIOP supported by this particular object. At the time of this writing, the IIOP version could be 1.0, 1.1, or 1.2.
2. The endpoint details, host and port, are given for a listening point on the server where the CORBA object lives. The host is a string that can contain either the server hostname or an IP address in dotted decimal notation.
3. An `object_key` is given in the form of a sequence of octets. The `object_key` is binary data that uniquely identifies the CORBA object in the address space of the server. The format of the `object_key` might not be understood by the client, but this does not matter, because the `object_key` is only interpreted by the server.
4. If the version of this IIOP profile is 1.1 or 1.2, the profile may include a series of *IOR components*. The purpose of these components is to give miscellaneous information that may be needed to use the CORBA object. For example, the CORBA Security Service defines several types of component to facilitate secure connections to a CORBA object.

The formal CDR encoding of an IIOP profile is defined in Chapter 16. With the details given here, it is possible to understand the contents of a typical stringified object reference.

Stringified Object References

A stringified object reference is derived from the standard format of an IOR. An ORB creates a stringified object reference using the following algorithm:

1. The IOR is marshalled into a buffer as a CDR encapsulation. (The details of CDR encapsulation are described in Chapter 16.) An important feature of an encapsulation is that it begins with a flag to indicate whether the rest of the data is big-endian or little-endian. A value of `0` indicates big-endian, and `1` indicates little-endian.
2. Each byte of the IOR is converted to a pair of hexadecimal characters (either upper- or lowercase). The resulting series of hexadecimal characters is concatenated into a string.
3. The string `"IOR:"` is prefixed to the string of hexadecimal numbers.

Consider the following example of a stringified object reference:

```
IOR:010000000e00000049444c3a48656c6c6f3a312e300000000001000000000000004e000000010
10200100000003139332e3132302e3232312e3130320048050000 1b0000003a3e0231310c010000
007100000023480000080000000000000000000001000000060000000600000001000000 1100
```

This object reference was generated by an IONA Orbix 2000 server. Table 5.3 shows how this object reference can be parsed to extract location details and other details of the CORBA object.

Table 5.3 An Example of a Parsed Stringified Object Reference

Bytes of IOR	Description
`+0 [01]`	Byte order of IOR: (1) little-endian
`+1 [00][00][00]`	(Padding)
`+4 [0e][00][00][00]`	`TypeId` length: 14 bytes (including null)
`+8`	`TypeId` value:
`[49][44][4c][3a][48][65][6c]`	`'IDL:Hello:1.0.'`
`[6c][6f][3a][31][2e][30][00]`	
`+22 [00][00]`	(Padding)
`+24 [01][00][00][00]`	Number of tagged profiles: 1
`+28 [00][00][00][00]`	Tag: (0) `TAG_INTERNET_IOP`
`+32 [4e][00][00][00]`	Profile length: 78 bytes
`+36 [01]`	Byte order: (1) little-endian
`+37 [01][02]`	Version: `1.2`
`+40 [10][00][00][00]`	Host length: 16 bytes (including null)
`+44`	Host string:
`[31][39][33][2e][31][32][30]`	`'193.120.221.102.'`
`[2e][32][32][31][2e][31][30]`	
`[32][00]`	
`+60 [48][05]`	Port: `1352`
`+62 [00][00]`	(Padding)
`+64 [1b][00][00][00]`	Object key length: 27 bytes (including any trailing null)
`+68`	Object key data: (opaque binary data)
`[3a][3e][02][31][31][0c][01]`	
`[00][00][00][71][00][00][00]`	
`[23][48][00][00][08][00][00]`	
`[00][00][00][00][00][00]`	
`+95 [00]`	(Padding)
`+96 [01][00][00][00]`	Number of tagged components: 1
`+100 [06][00][00][00]`	Tag: (6) `ENDPOINT_ID_POSITION`
`+104 [06][00][00][00]`	Component length: 6 bytes
`+108 [01]`	Component byte order: (1) little-endian
`+109 [00]`	(padding)
`+110 [00][00]`	`EndpointId` begin (index): 0
`+112 [11][00]`	`EndpointId` end (index): 17

Because the stringified object reference is encoded as a CDR encapsulation, it begins with a byte to indicate whether the following data is big or little-endian. Note that the first integer that appears, the `TypeId` length, is indeed little-endian.

From the `TypeId` you can see that the object implements an interface called `Hello`. The object reference holds a single profile. The server is located on host `193.120.221.102` and listens on the IP port 1352. The `object_key` is not legible, consisting of binary data that is interpreted by the server to identify the object.

At a number of points in the IOR, some null bytes are inserted as padding. This is to satisfy the requirement that CDR encoding align data on its natural boundaries. For example, any CORBA `longs` (4-byte integers) occurring in the IOR begin at a position that is divisible by four. For details of CDR encoding and its alignment requirements, consult Chapter 16.

There are a couple of points at which encapsulation is used again within the stringified IOR (effectively, encapsulation within an encapsulation). Both the profile and the tagged component are encapsulated. The telltale sign of an encapsulation is a 4-byte integer giving the size of the data block, followed by a byte order flag and then the encapsulated data.

At the end of the IOR there is a single tagged component. This component is used to impart additional information about the object. These components are discussed in more detail in the following section.

IOR Components

As explained in the section "Structure of an IIOP Profile," an IIOP profile might include a set of components (for IIOP versions 1.1 or later). The components provide extra information about how the object reference is meant to be used.

Each component begins with a tag to indicate what kind of component it is. The following tags are allowed in an IIOP profile that conforms to IIOP 1.1:

- `TAG_ORB_TYPE = 0`
  This tag is followed by an unsigned long (4-byte integer) that gives the unique ID of the ORB that generated the object references. An ORB manufacturer can apply to the OMG to obtain a unique ID to identify its ORB.
- `TAG_CODE_SETS = 1`
  A server can use this component to indicate the character formats that it understands for both ordinary characters and wide characters. It indicates its native code set and any additional code sets that it understands.
  The process of code set negotiation is required primarily for wide characters, because there are many standards for extended character sets. Unicode is a popular choice on many computing platforms.
- `TAG_SEC_NAME = 14`
  This tag is a sequence of octets that gives the secure identity of the target object. It is used by the CORBA Security Service specification.

- `TAG_ASSOCIATION_OPTIONS = 13`
  This tag describes the degree of security supported by and required by the server. It is used by the CORBA Security Service specification.
- `TAG_GENERIC_SEC_MECH = 22`
  This tag is used by the CORBA Security Service.
- `TAG_SSL_SEC_TRANS = 20`
  This tag is used by the CORBA Security Service.
- `TAG_SPKM_1_SEC_MECH = 15`
  This tag is used by the CORBA Security Service.
- `TAG_SPKM_2_SEC_MECH = 16`
  This tag is used by the CORBA Security Service.
- `TAG_KerberosV5_SEC_MECH = 17`
  This tag is used by the CORBA Security Service.
- `TAG_CSI_ECMA_Secret_SEC_MECH = 18`
  This tag is used by the CORBA Security Service.
- `TAG_CSI_ECMA_Hybrid_SEC_MECH = 19`
  This tagis used by the CORBA Security Service.
- `TAG_CSI_ECMA_Public_SEC_MECH = 21`
  This tag is used by the CORBA Security Service.
- `TAG_JAVA_CODEBASE = 25`
  This tag is used by Java-to-IDL mapping. It contains a space-separated list of URL strings that specify directories (or JAR files) from which Java classes can be loaded.

The following tags are allowed in an IIOP profile that conforms to IIOP 1.2.

- `TAG_ALTERNATE_IIOP_ADDRESS = 3`
  This component allows an alternative endpoint (or endpoints) to be specified for the object. The body of this tag contains the following struct encoded as a CDR encapsulation:
  ```
  //PIDL
  struct {
      string HostID;
      short Port;
  };
  ```
  This component can be used by an ORB to implement fault-tolerant behavior. If a client fails to contact the server at the endpoint given in the main part of the profile, it can try this alternative endpoint instead.
- `TAG_POLICIES = 2`
  This tag is used by the asynchronous messaging specification. It contains a list of policies that specify the qualities of service supported by the target object.
- `TAG_DCE_STRING_BINDING = 100`
  This tag contains a DCE string binding. It provides all the information required to establish communication with a DCE server.
- `TAG_DCE_BINDING_NAME = 101`

This tag contains a name that can be looked up in a DCE naming service to obtain a binding handle for a DCE connection.

- `TAG_DCE_NO_PIPES = 102`
  This is a hint to an ORB that the server does not support the `dce_ciop_pipe` DCE-RPC interface.
- `TAG_DCE_SEC_MECH = 103`
  This tag is used by the CORBA Security Service.
- `TAG_COMPLETE_OBJECT_KEY = 5`
  In the context of DCE, this tag may be specified as part of a `TAG_MULTIPLE_COMPONENTS` profile to specify the `object_key` for the object. This tag never appears as part of a `TAG_INTERNET_IOP` profile.
- `TAG_ENDPOINT_ID_POSITION = 6`
  This component is used to specify a range of bytes within the profile's `object_key` that uniquely identifies the endpoint associated with this object. The component holds the following struct:

  ```
  //PIDL
  struct EndpointIdPositionComponent {
      unsigned short begin;
      unsigned short end;
  };
  ```

  If many IORs have the same endpoint ID, this gives a hint to the ORB that it can re-use the same connection to communicate with all of those objects. Because of the elaborate location semantics in CORBA, this is a more reliable way of determining if a connection can be reused.
- `TAG_LOCATION_POLICY = 12`
  This tag contains a flag that customizes the location semantics of DCE (or other protocols). The flag is used to indicate how often the client attempts to locate the remote object.

More IOR components may periodically be added to this list as the CORBA standard is expanded.

Summary

This chapter has presented the basic essentials you need to program using object references. The details of memory management were presented for the C++ language. The essential concepts of polymorphism and how to widen and narrow object references were discussed. For most of the CORBA programming you do, this level of knowledge is sufficient. You can treat object references as black boxes that give you access to the CORBA object.

If you want to uncover the detailed state of an object reference, you can stringify the object reference and parse it. Most ORBs provide some sort of utility for parsing stringified object references. The amount of information that can be stored in the object reference is open ended. An IOR can contain any number of tagged components. As the CORBA services are extended, many more of these tagged components may be defined. You may need to consult the CORBA service specifications from time to time to analyze all of the information in an IOR.

CHAPTER 6

Interoperable Naming Service

The CORBA naming service is used by clients to locate CORBA objects and by servers to advertise specific CORBA objects. It plays the role of a bootstrap service, enabling clients to find other services and facilitating initial connections between clients and servers.

The basic function of the naming service is the association of names with object references. A server creates associations between names and object references for those CORBA objects that are intended to serve as initial points of contact. A client that knows the name of an object can then retrieve its object reference by querying the naming service.

The naming service is available in two major versions:

- The original CORBA Naming Service.
- The CORBA Interoperable Naming Service. This is a more recent extension and revision of the original naming service. The semantics of certain operations are specified more precisely. A string format and a URL format are defined for names. New operations are declared in the `CosNaming::NamingContextExt` interface.

This chapter describes the newer Interoperable Naming Service. If you want to use the original CORBA Naming Service, you must restrict yourself to the subset of IDL that excludes the interface `NamingContextExt`.

Overview

The naming service is a simple locating service that allows clients to look up an object location using a name as a key.

The name can be specified in a human-readable stringified name format or in a raw name format.

Before a client can look up an object, the association between the object location and its name must be created. This association is known as an *object binding*, and it is normally made by a CORBA server.

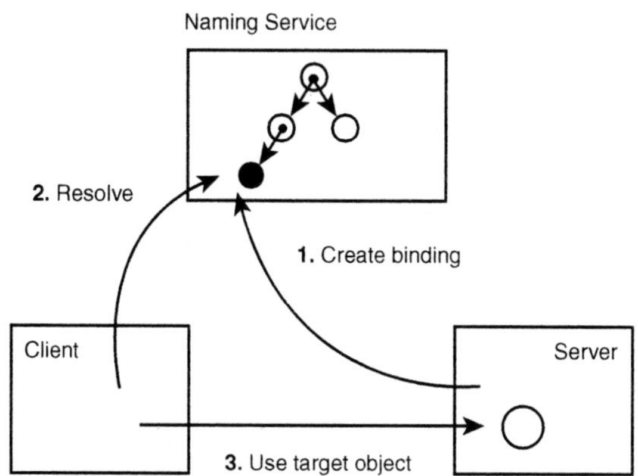

Figure 6.1

Basic use of the CORBA naming service.

Figure 6.1 illustrates the steps in using the naming service. It is typically implemented as a standalone process that runs independently of the client and server. These steps are followed:

1. Create an object binding. As a server is starting up, it creates a number of CORBA objects that will serve as points of initial contact for clients. These objects are advertised to clients by creating object bindings in the naming service. The bindings consist of a series of name/object reference associations.
2. Resolve a name. A client can access each of the objects advertised in the previous step by *resolving* a name. This consists of looking up an object reference using its name as a key.
3. Use the target object. Since an object reference is all the client needs to access an object, the client can now go ahead and use the object.

This is the main functionality provided by the naming service, which is, essentially, a database of object bindings. The collection of object bindings is usually—but not always—arranged in a hierarchy. There are two kinds of bindings in the hierarchy:

- Context binding—An association between a name and a naming context.
- Object binding—An association between a name and an object reference.

The hierarchy is illustrated in Figure 6.2. In many ways it resembles the directory structure of a file system. Open circles represent *naming contexts*, which play a role analogous to directories in a file system. Closed circles represent object references, which play a role analogous to files in a file system. They are the leaves of the hierarchical tree.

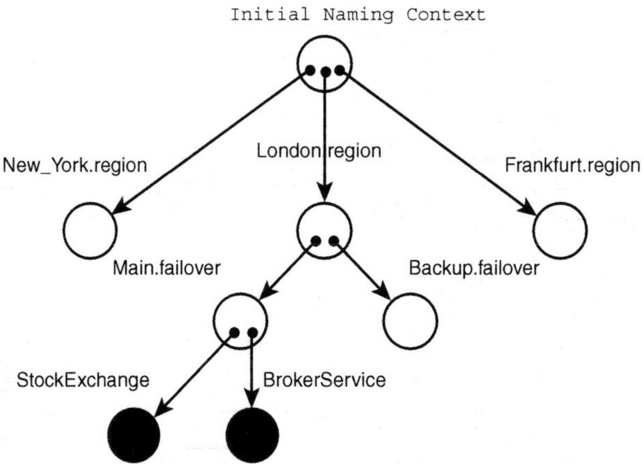

Figure 6.2

A sample naming service hierarchy.

At the top of the sample hierarchy is the initial context. Immediately below the initial context are three naming contexts: `London.region`, `New_York.region`, and `Frankfurt.region`. At a lower level of nesting are the naming contexts `London.region/Main.failover` and `London.region/Backup.failover`. At a lower level again are some object references, for example `London.region/Main.failover/StockExchange`.

Names

Two types of name format are specified in the CORBA Interoperable Naming Service:

- Stringified name format—Stringified names have an intuitive format that is easy to read and pass from place to place.
- Raw name format—Raw names are defined in terms of IDL complex types and can be used only within a CORBA program.

The following sections describe both of these name formats in detail.

Stringified Names

Consider the fully qualified name of the object `StockExchange`. Its structure is shown in Figure 6.3.

The name is divided into three components by the component separator character `/` (forward slash). The individual components consist of an `id` field and a `kind` field, joined by the `kind` separator character `.` (dot). When the `kind` field is omitted, as in the third component, it is implicitly empty.

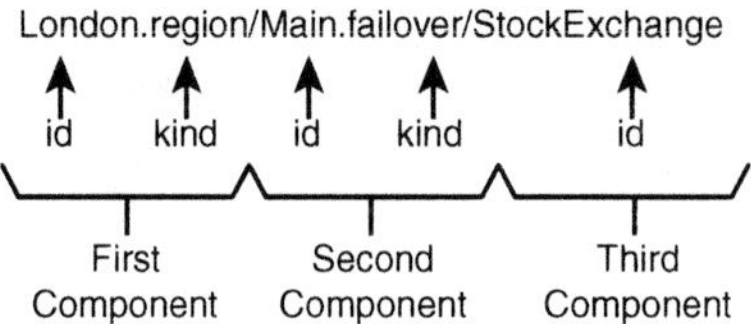

Figure 6.3

The structure of a sample stringified name.

Each component of a name maps to an entity in the naming service (either a naming context or an object reference). For example, the components shown imply the existence of three context bindings and one object binding, as given in Table 6.1.

Table 6.1 Components of a Stringified Name

Stringified Name	Binds To
empty string	Initial naming context
`London.region`	Naming context
`London.region/Main.failover`	Naming context
`London.region/Main.failover/StockExchange`	Object reference

The initial naming context is always present and serves as the entry point to the naming service.

The `kind` field is intended to describe how a name component is used. For example, we have used the `.region` suffix above to indicate that a naming context refers to a particular geographical location. This resembles the way in which suffixes are used by a file system. For example `client.cxx`, `client.obj`, and `client.exe` would represent three related, but distinct, files under Windows NT.

The naming service specification does not specify how the `kind` field should be used, nor does it reserve any specific values for it. The only specific direction given is that the `kind` field is part of the unique identity of a name. That is, the names `London.region` and `London` are distinct and refer to two different entities in the naming service.

Escape Character

An escape character \ (backslash) is reserved for use in stringified names. The escape sequences are defined in Table 6.2.

Table 6.2 Escape Sequences in Stringified Names

Escape Sequence	Value
`\/`	Literal /
`\.`	Literal .
`\\`	Literal \

Other escape sequences (that is, \ followed by any other character) are reserved by the OMG for future use. The existing escape sequences allow you to embed any of the characters /, ., and \ in an id field or a kind field. For example, the name component

```
"www\.omg\.org\/index\.html.hierarchy\\of\\kinds"
```

is interpreted as

```
id = "www.omg.org/index.html", kind = "hierarchy\of\kinds"
```

when parsed by the naming service. This allows the id and kind fields to be arbitrary strings.

Special Cases

Spaces are legal in both id fields and kind fields.

There are some special constructions for representing empty fields.

- An empty kind field is indicated by omitting the kind field and kind separator . (dot), for example, London/Main. It is not correct to append a trailing . character to either of the name components. Thus, London./Main. is illegal.
- An empty id field is indicated by starting the name component directly with a kind separator . (dot), such as .region/.failover. However, some implementations of the naming service might forbid the use of empty id fields.
- An empty id field and an empty kind field are denoted by a single . (dot). For example, a sequence of three empty name components ././. is the only legal representation of a name component with empty id and kind fields. Some implementations of the naming service might forbid the use of empty name components.

Raw Names—CosNaming::Name

Stringified names are a convenient way of representing names in a readable format, but that is not how they are represented internally by the naming service. The raw format of a name is defined by the following IDL extract:

```
//IDL

#pragma prefix "omg.org"

module CosNaming {
     typedef string Istring;

     struct NameComponent {
          Istring id;
          Istring kind;
     };
     typedef sequence<NameComponent> Name;
     ...
};
```

This defines the data type CosNaming::Name, which is the canonical form of a name. It consists of a sequence of NameComponents. Each NameComponent is broken down into an id field and a kind field.

The definition of Istring is a historical artifact and is simply an alias for the type string. Originally, it was defined as a placeholder for an internationalized string (subsequently introduced into IDL as the type wstring). The definition of Istring has not been changed because of backward-compatibility issues.

A raw name is basically a sequence of structs and can be manipulated using the rules for IDL compound types. Consider, for example, how to represent the stringified name London.region/Backup.failover in raw form:

```
//C++
CosNaming::Name exName(2);      //maximum = 2
                                //length = 0
exName.length(2);

exName[(CORBA::ULong) 0].id = CORBA::string_dup("London");
exName[(CORBA::ULong) 0].kind = CORBA::string_dup("region");

exName[(CORBA::ULong) 1].id = CORBA::string_dup("Backup");
exName[(CORBA::ULong) 1].kind = CORBA::string_dup("failover");

//Java
org.omg.CosNaming.NameComponent exName[]
        = new org.omg.CosNaming.NameComponent[2];

exName[0] = new org.omg.CosNaming.NameComponent();
exName[0].id = "London";
exName[0].kind = "region";

exName[1] = new org.omg.CosNaming.NameComponent();
exName[1].id = "Backup";
exName[1].kind = "failover";
```

The Initialization Service

When a CORBA application starts up, it must get references to a basic set of initial objects, for example the ORB, the object adapter, and the naming service. The CORBA standard defines the CORBA initialization service to take care of this task.

At the beginning of every CORBA application, you will see the initialization service being used to initialize the ORB. It is a simple service that declares just a few associated operations, given in Table 6.3.

Table 6.3 Initialization Service Operations

Operation Name	Description
`CORBA::ORB_init()`	Return an object reference to the `CORBA::ORB` object.
`CORBA::ORB::resolve_initial_references()`	Return an object reference to the named service.
`CORBA::ORB::list_initial_services()`	Return a list of services available from this ORB instance.

The signatures of these operations depend on the details of the language mapping. The pseudo-IDL for these operations is given at the end of this chapter.

The operations are illustrated by example in the rest of this chapter.

A common use of the initialization service is to get hold of a reference to an initial naming context. Once an application has a reference to the initial naming context, it can resolve references to numerous other CORBA and application-specific services.

Typical steps followed by a CORBA application during its initialization phase are

1. Get a reference to an ORB object using `CORBA::ORB_init()`.
2. Get a reference to a POA object using `CORBA::ORB::resolve_initial_references()` (server only).
3. Get a reference to a `NamingContext` object (or a `NamingContextExt` object) using the operation `CORBA::ORB::resolve_initial_references()`.

These initialization steps are demonstrated in Listing 6.1 and Listing 6.2 for C++ and Java.

Listing 6.1 C++ Obtaining Initial Reference to the Naming Service

```
//C++
int
main (int argc, char *argv[])
{
    CORBA::ORB_var orbV;

    try
    {
        cout << "Initializing the ORB" << endl;

        //--------------------------------------------------------
        // Step 1. Get reference to ORB
        //--------------------------------------------------------
        orbV = CORBA::ORB_init(argc, argv);
        if (CORBA::is_nil(orbV.in() ))
        {
            cerr << "Nil ORB object reference" << endl;
            return 1;
        }
```

Listing 6.1 continued

```
        //------------------------------------------------------------
        // Step 2. (Server only) Get reference to POA
        //------------------------------------------------------------
        CORBA::Object_var objV;
        PortableServer::POA_var poaV;

        objV = orbV->resolve_initial_references("RootPOA");
        poaV = PortableServer::POA::_narrow(objV.in() );
        if (CORBA::is_nil(poaV.in() )) {
            cerr << "Nil POA object reference" << endl;
            return 1;
        }

        //------------------------------------------------------------
        // Step 3. Get reference to CosNaming::NamingContextExt
        //------------------------------------------------------------
        CosNaming::NamingContextExt_var rootContextExtV; // INS Root ContextExt

        try {
            objV = orbV->resolve_initial_references("NameService");
            rootContextExtV = CosNaming::NamingContextExt:: _narrow(objV.in()
➥);
        }
        catch (CORBA::SystemException &sysEx) {
            cerr << sysEx << endl;
            return 1;
        }
        if (CORBA::is_nil(rootContextExtV.in() )) {
            cerr << "Nil root naming context" << endl;
            return 1;
        }

        // Now make use of 'rootContextExtV'...
        ...
}
```

Listing 6.2 Java Obtaining Initial Reference to the Naming Service

```
//Java

import org.omg.CORBA.*;
import org.omg.CosNaming.*;
import org.omg.CosNaming.NamingContextPackage.*;
import org.omg.PortableServer.POAManagerPackage.*;

public class Server
{
    private static ORB m_orb;
```

Listing 6.2 continued

```
    public static void main(String args[])
    {
        //-------------------------------------------------------------
        // Step 1. Get reference to ORB
        //-------------------------------------------------------------
        m_orb = ORB.init(args,null);

        //-------------------------------------------------------------
        // Step 2. (Server only) Get reference to POA
        //-------------------------------------------------------------
        org.omg.CORBA.Object obj = null;
        org.omg.PortableServer.POA poa = null;

        try {
            obj = m_orb.resolve_initial_references("RootPOA");
            poa = org.omg.PortableServer.POAHelper.narrow(obj);
        }
        catch (org.omg.CORBA.SystemException ex) {
            System.err.println("error: failed to get reference to POA" + ex);
            System.exit(1);
        }
        catch (org.omg.CORBA.UserException ux) {
            System.err.println("error: failed to get reference to POA" + ux);
            System.exit(1);
        }

        //-------------------------------------------------------------
        // Step 3. Get reference to CosNaming::NamingContextExt
        //-------------------------------------------------------------
        NamingContextExt rootContextExt=null;

        try {
           obj = m_orb.resolve_initial_references("NameService");
           rootContextExt = NamingContextExtHelper.narrow(obj);
        }
        catch (org.omg.CORBA.SystemException ex) {
            System.err.println(ex);
            System.exit(1);
        }
        catch (org.omg.CORBA.UserException ux) {
            System.err.println(ux);
            System. exit(1);
        }
    }
}
```

The function `resolve_initial_references()` is used twice. The first time it is invoked with the argument `RootPOA`. The second time it is invoked with the argument `NameService`. In each case, the returned object reference has to be cast to the correct type using a narrow function (`_narrow()` in C++ and `narrow()` in Java).

TIP

In C++, always test an object reference for nilness with the `CORBA::is_nil()` function after it has been returned from a `_narrow()` method.

The argument passed to `resolve_initial_references()` is known as an `ObjectId` (this choice of name is unfortunate—it has nothing to do with object IDs in the context of the POA). The `ObjectId` string is used to select a particular service type and determines the type of object reference returned by `resolve_initial_references()`. Allowable values for `ObjectId` are specified by the OMG. Some of these values are given in Table 6.4.

Table 6.4 Some OMG-Defined Values for **`ObjectId`**

`ObjectId` String	Type of Reference Returned
`RootPOA`	`PortableServer::POA`
`POACurrent`	`PortableServer::Current`
`NameService`	`CosNaming::NamingContextExt` or `CosNaming::NamingContext`
`TradingService`	`CosTrading::Lookup`
`InterfaceRepository`	`CORBA::Repository`
`SecurityCurrent`	`SecurityLevel1::Current` or `SecurityLevel2::Current`
`TransactionCurrent`	`CosTransactions::Current`
`DynAnyFactory`	`DynamicAny::DynAnyFactory`

The list in Table 6.4 may be extended from time to time as the OMG adds new services to the CORBA specification.

The naming service is a special case, since the type of object returned depends on the naming service version. If it conforms to the CORBA Interoperable Naming Service specification, you will obtain a reference to a `CosNaming::NamingContextExt` object. Alternatively, if it conforms to the older naming service specification you will obtain a reference to a `CosNaming::NamingContext` object instead.

Basic Operations

The basic operations of the naming service are defined either in the interface `CosNaming::NamingContext` (the subset of operations in the old naming service specification) or the interface `CosNaming::NamingContextExt` (the extensions introduced in the CORBA Interoperable Naming Service specification). Some of the basic tasks you need to perform on the naming service are to

- Create object bindings
- Create context bindings

- Resolve names
- Convert name formats

The following IDL fragment highlights some of the operations you can use for these tasks:

```
//IDL
#pragma prefix "omg.org"

module CosNaming {
     ...
     interface NamingContext {
          ...
          void rebind(in Name n, in Object obj)
               raises(NotFound, CannotProceed, InvalidName);

          void bind(in Name n, in Object obj)
               raises(NotFound, CannotProceed, InvalidName, AlreadyBound);

          Object resolve (in Name n)
               raises(NotFound, CannotProceed, InvalidName);

          NamingContext bind_new_context(in Name n)
               raises(NotFound, AlreadyBound, CannotProceed, InvalidName);
          ...
     };
     ...
     interface NamingContextExt: NamingContext {
          ...
          typedef string StringName;

          Object resolve_str(in StringName n)
               raises(NotFound, CannotProceed, InvalidName, AlreadyBound);

          StringName to_string(in Name n) raises(InvalidName);
          Name       to_name(in StringName sn)
                         raises(InvalidName);
          URLString  to_url(in Address addr, in StringName sn)
               raises(InvalidAddress, InvalidName);
          ...
     };
};
```

Parts of the module `CosNaming` have been omitted from this listing (including the declaration of user exceptions). For a full listing of the IDL, see the section "Naming Service IDL," later in this chapter.

The following sections give the semantics for each of these basic operations.

Create Object Bindings—rebind() and bind()

To create an object binding, you can use either rebind() or bind(). Both operations create an object binding that associates the name n (in raw format) with the naming context nc. The semantics, however, are different:

- rebind()—the operation creates a new object binding for the given name n or, if a binding already exists with that name, overwrites the existing binding.
- bind()—the operation creates a new object binding for the given name n as long as there is no existing binding with that name. If a binding already exists, an AlreadyBound exception is thrown.

The semantics of rebind() are more convenient so you will probably use it instead of bind() most of the time.

Note that these operations create object bindings *relative* to the naming context on which they are invoked. For example, if you want to create an object binding with the name A/B/C/MyObj you can either invoke rebind() on the initial naming context, using the full name A/B/C/MyObj, or invoke rebind() on the naming context A/B/C, using the short name MyObj.

Create Context Bindings—bind_new_context()

To create a new context binding you can use the operation bind_new_context() to create the context in one step. It takes the name of the context you want to create as an argument (in raw format) and returns an object reference for the newly created naming context.

The immediate parent of the context binding you want to create must already exist, otherwise a NotFound exception is raised. For example, you can only create the context A/B/C if the context A/B already exists.

Resolve Names—resolve_str() and resolve()

To resolve a binding in the naming service you can use either resolve_str() or resolve(). The only difference between these two operations is that resolve_str() takes a stringified name as its argument while resolve() takes a raw name.

Note the following points:

- The return value is of type Object so the returned object reference always needs to be narrowed to the actual type before it can be used.
- The operation resolve_str() is available only on the interface NamingContextExt. You must narrow your naming context to NamingContextExt before you can access this operation.
- The resolve operations can be used to resolve either object or context bindings. For context bindings, narrow to NamingContext or NamingContextExt as appropriate.

Conversion Operations

Three conversion operations are provided in the interface NamingContextExt. These are to_string(), to_name(), and to_url().

The conversion operations to_string() and to_name() are used to convert back and forth between stringified name format and raw name format. The exception InvalidName is raised by either of these operations if the argument is malformed in some way.

Server Example

The main interaction a server has with the naming service is to create object bindings to advertise objects to clients. The operations most often used are rebind() or bind(), to create object bindings, and bind_new_context(), to create context bindings that hold the object bindings.

However, the operations provided directly by the naming service interface are fairly primitive. In most real-life projects you will find it helpful to build some kind of utility or wrapper around the naming service. In the examples that follow a class NameUtil is defined that provides a more convenient way of accessing the naming service.

One of the things missing from the naming IDL is a way to create multiple components in a single step. For example, if you want to create a naming context named A/B/C/D, and neither A, B, C, nor D exists yet, it will take at least four explicit invocations of bind_new_context() to create the naming context. To simplify this process, our name utility defines the following operations:

- NameUtility::createContextPath()—create a multi-component naming context. For example, if you want to create the naming context A/B/C/D, it fills in any context bindings missing between A and D.
- NameUtility::bindObjectPath()—create a multi-component object binding. For example, if you want to create the object binding A/B/C/D/MyObj it fills in any context bindings missing between A and MyObj.

The code for these two methods is given in the following sections.

Name Utility—createContextPath()

The method createContextPath() is used to create a name component, filling in any missing components along the way. The implementation of the method in C++ and Java is given in Listing 6.3 and Listing 6.4.

***Listing 6.3 C++ Implementation of* createContextPath()**

```
// C++
//---------------------------------------
// method: 'createContextPath()'
//
// purpose: For each 'NameComponent' in 'name',
//          create a corresponding 'NamingContext'.
//---------------------------------------
```

Listing 6.3 continued

```
void
NameUtil::createContextPath(
          const CosNaming::NamingContext_ptr nc,
          const CosNaming::Name&  name
          )
{
    int isNotFound = 0;
    CORBA::ULong lengthMissing = 0;

    CosNaming::NamingContext_var tmpCtxVar;
    try {
        tmpCtxVar = nc->bind_new_context(name);
    }
    catch (CosNaming::NamingContext::NotFound& nf) {
        isNotFound = 1;
        lengthMissing = nf.rest_of_name.length();
    }
    if (lengthMissing==name.length() ) {
        cerr << "This cannot happen!" << endl;
    }

    if (isNotFound) {
        for (CORBA::ULong l=name.length()-lengthMissing;
                          l <= name.length();
                          l++)
        {
             CosNaming::Name tmpName = name;
             tmpName.length(l);
             tmpCtxVar = nc->bind_new_context(tmpName);
        }
    }

}
```

Listing 6.4 Java Implementation of `createContextPath()`

```
// Java
package Pure.Util;

import org.omg.CORBA.*;
import org.omg.CosNaming.*;
import org.omg.CosNaming.NamingContextPackage.*;
import org.omg.PortableServer.POAManagerPackage.*;

public class NameUtil {

  //----------------------------------------
  // method: 'createContextPath()'
  //
  // purpose: For each 'NameComponent' in 'name',
```

Listing 6.4 continued

```
//          create a corresponding 'NamingContext'.
//-------------------------------------
public static void createContextPath(
        NamingContext nc,
        NameComponent[]  name
        )
        throws org.omg.CORBA.UserException
{
  boolean isNotFound = false;
  int lengthMissing = 0;

  NamingContext tmpCtx;
  try {
      tmpCtx = nc.bind_new_context(name);
  }
  catch (NotFound nf) {
      isNotFound = true;
      lengthMissing = nf.rest_of_name.length;
  }

  if (isNotFound && lengthMissing==name.length ) {
      System.err.println("This cannot happen!");
      return;
  }

  if (isNotFound) {
      for (int len = name.length-lengthMissing;
                     len <= name.length;
                     len++)
      {
          NameComponent[] tmpName = new NameComponent[len];
          for (int i=0; i < len; i++) { tmpName[i] = name[i]; }
          tmpCtx = nc.bind_new_context(tmpName);
      }
  }
}
...
}
```

The implementation makes interesting use of the `NotFound` exception. The `NotFound` exception is declared in IDL as follows:

```
// IDL
module CosNaming {
     ...
     interface NamingContext {
          ...
          enum NotFoundReason { missing_node, not_context, not_object };
```

```
            exception NotFound {
                NotFoundReason why;
                Name rest_of_name;
            };
        ...
        };
};
```

Consider, for example, what happens if you want to create the naming context `A/B/C/D` but only `A` exists initially. The `createContextPath()` method performs the following steps:

1. A call to `bind_new_context()` is made. This only works if the naming context `A/B/C` already exists. Since `B` and `C` are missing, the `NotFound` exception is thrown.
2. The `NotFound` exception is caught and the length of the missing part of the name is extracted. Since two components, `B` and `C`, are missing between `A` and `D`, the number of missing components is `2`. The value of `rest_of_name` is `B/C`.
3. A `for` loop creates all of the components needed to complete the path—`A/B`, `A/B/C`, and `A/B/C/D`

The `NotFound` exception allows you avoid using trial and error to identify the components that need to be created. The approach used here minimizes the number of remote calls that must be made.

Name Utility—`bindObjectPath()`

The method `bindObjectPath()` is used to create an object binding, filling in any missing components along the way. The implementations of the method in C++ and Java are given in Listing 6.5 and Listing 6.6.

***Listing 6.5** C++ Implementation of* **`bindObjectPath()`**

```
// C++
//----------------------------------------
// method: 'bindObjectPath()'
//
// purpose: For the first [0, length-2] NameComponents of
//          'name', create a corresponding 'NamingContext'.
//          For the length-1 NameComponent of 'name', bind it
//          to the object reference 'obj'.
//----------------------------------------
void
NameUtil::bindObjectPath(
            const CosNaming::NamingContext_ptr nc,
            const CosNaming::Name&  name,
            const CORBA::Object_ptr obj
            )
{
    try {
```

Listing 6.5 continued

```
        nc->rebind(name, obj);
    }
    catch (CosNaming::NamingContext::NotFound& ) {
        CosNaming::Name tmpName = name;
        tmpName.length(tmpName.length()-1);
        createContextPath(nc, tmpName);

        nc->bind(name, obj);
    }
}
```

Listing 6.6 Java Implementation of `bindObjectPath()`

```
// Java
package Pure.Util;

import org.omg.CORBA.*;
import org.omg.CosNaming.*;
import org.omg.CosNaming.NamingContextPackage.*;
import org.omg.PortableServer.POAManagerPackage.*;

public class NameUtil {

  //----------------------------------------
  // method: 'bindObjectPath()'
  //
  // purpose: For the first [0, length-2] NameComponents of
  //          'name', create a corresponding 'NamingContext'.
  //          For the length-1 NameComponent of 'name', bind it
  //          to the object reference 'obj'.
  //----------------------------------------
  public static void bindObjectPath(
         NamingContext nc,
         NameComponent[]  name,
         org.omg.CORBA.Object obj
         )
         throws org.omg.CORBA.UserException
  {
     try {
         nc.rebind(name, obj);
     }
     catch (NotFound nf) {
        NameComponent[] tmpName = new NameComponent[name.length-1];
        for (int i=0; i < name.length-1; i++) { tmpName[i] = name[i]; }
        createContextPath(nc, tmpName);

        nc.bind(name, obj);
     }
  }
}
```

This utility method delegates most of the work to the `createContextPath()` method. Consider, for example, that you are creating an object binding called `A/B/C/D/MyObj`. If the invocation of `rebind()` gives rise to a `NotFound` exception, a call to `createContextPath()` is used to complete the path `A/B/C/D` before invoking `bind()` to create the object binding `A/B/C/D/MyObj`.

Server Mainline

Consider a server that instantiates a single `StockExchange` object and publishes it to the naming service. For this example, the functionality of the object is not of interest, so a trivial placeholder can be used for the `StockExchange` interface:

```
// IDL
interface StockExchange { };
```

Assuming that the interface is implemented by a servant class called `StockExchange_i` (not shown), the server mainline is given by Listing 6.7 and Listing 6.8.

Listing 6.7 C++ Server Binding a Name

```
// C++
int
main(int argc, char* argv[])
{
    ...
    //----------------------------------------------------------------
    // The usual initialization boilerplate comes here (not shown).
    // The following variables are defined by the initialization code:
    //
    // 'orbV'                - a pointer to the ORB object
    //
    // 'poaV'                - a pointer to the root POA object
    //
    // 'namingContextExtV'   - a pointer to the root naming context
    //----------------------------------------------------------------

    StockExchange_i myStockServant;
    StockExchange_var myStockV = myStockServant._this();

    try
    {
        nameV = rootContextExtV->to_name(
                  "London.region/Main.failover/StockExchange"
                );

        NameUtil::bindObjectPath(
            rootContextExtV.in(),
            nameV.in(),
            myStockV.in() );
    }
    catch (CORBA::SystemException& se) {
```

```
        cerr << se << endl;
        return 1;
    }
    catch (CORBA::UserException& ue) {
        cerr << ue << endl;
        return 1;
    }


    try
    {
        cout << "Activating the POA manager." << endl;
        PortableServer::POAManager_var poa_manager= poaV->the_POAManager();
        poa_manager->activate();

        cout << "Invoking ORB::run()." << endl;
        orbV->run();
    }
    catch (CORBA::SystemException& se)
    {
        cerr << "ORB::run() failed: " << se << endl;
        return 1;
    }

    //Cleanup
    orbV->destroy();
    return 0;
}
```

Listing 6.8 Java Server Binding a Name

```
// Java

package Pure.NamesDemo;

import Pure.Util.*;

import org.omg.CORBA.*;
import org.omg.CosNaming.*;
import org.omg.CosNaming. NamingContextPackage.*;
import org.omg.PortableServer.POAManagerPackage.*;


public class Server
{
...
    //------------------------------------------------------------------------
    // The usual initialization boilerplate comes here (not shown).
    // The following variables are defined by the initialization code:
    //
    // 'm_orb'              - a reference to the ORB object
```

Listing 6.8 continued

```
    //
    // 'poa'                  - a reference to the root POA object
    //
    // 'namingContextExt'   - a reference to the root naming context
    //-------------------------------------------------------------------

    //
    // Instantiate a 'StockExchange' object
    //
    StockExchange_i myStockServant = new StockExchange_i();
    StockExchange myStock = myStockServant._this(m_orb);

    try
    {
        name = rootContextExt.to_name(
                  "London.region/Main.failover/StockExchange"
              );
        NameUtil.bindObjectPath(rootContextExt, name, myStock );

    }
    catch (org.omg.CORBA.SystemException ex) {
        System.err.println(ex);
        System.exit(1);
    }
    catch (org.omg.CORBA.UserException ux) {
        System.err.println(ux);
        System.exit(1);
    }


    try
    {
        System.out.println("Activating the POA manager.");
        org.omg.PortableServer.POAManager poa_manager = poa.the_POAManager();
        poa_manager.activate();

        System.out.println("Invoking ORB::run().");
        m_orb.run();
    }
    catch (org.omg.CORBA.SystemException ex) {
        System.err.println(ex);
        System.exit(1);
    }
    catch (org.omg.CORBA.UserException ux) {
        System.err.println(ux);
        System.exit(1);
    }
  }
}
```

An object reference for the `StockExchange` object is obtained by invoking `_this()` on the servant, which simultaneously activates the object. A stringified name is converted to a raw name using `to_name()`, and the object binding is then created with the help of the `bindObjectPath()` utility method.

Client Example

A client normally nteracts with the naming service in the following manner:

1. It obtains an object reference by resolving the given name (using either `resolve_str()` or `resolve()`).
2. It narrows the object reference returned by the previous step to cast it to the correct type.
3. It uses the object reference.

Listing 6.9 and Listing 6.10 show sample clients in C++ and Java that use the naming service to look up the `StockExchange` object.

Listing 6.9 C++ Client Resolving a Name

```
// C++
...
int
main (int argc, char *argv[])
{

    ...
    //-------------------------------------------------------------------
    // The usual initialization boilerplate comes here (not shown).
    // The following variables are defined by the initialization code:
    //
    // 'orbV'                - a pointer to the ORB object
    //
    // 'namingContextExtV'   - a pointer to the root naming context
    //-------------------------------------------------------------------

    try
    {
        CORBA::Object_var objV;
        StockExchange_var stockV;

        objV = rootContextExtV->resolve_str(
                        "London.region/Main.failover/StockExchange"
                        );
        stockV = StockExchange::_narrow(objV.in() );

        if (CORBA::is_nil(stockV.in() )) {
            cout << "Nil reference returned for StockExchange object." << endl;
            return 1;
        }
        CORBA::String_var strV = orbV->object_to_string(stockV);
```

Listing 6.9 continued

```
        cout << strV << endl;
        // Now make some invocations on the object reference 'StockV'
        //...
    }
    catch (CORBA::UserException& ue) {
        cerr << ue << endl;
        return 1;
    }

    return 0;
}
```

Listing 6.10 Java Client Resolving a Name

```
// Java
package Pure.NamesDemo;

import Pure.Util.*;

import org.omg.CORBA.*;
import org.omg.CosNaming.*;
import org.omg.CosNaming.NamingContextPackage.*;


public class Client
{
  private static ORB m_orb;

  public static void main(String args[])
  {
    ...
    //-----------------------------------------------------------------
    // The usual initialization boilerplate comes here (not shown).
    // The following variables are defined by the initialization code:
    //
    // 'm_orb'              - a reference to the ORB object
    //
    // 'namingContextExt'   - a reference to the root naming context
    //-----------------------------------------------------------------

    org.omg.CORBA.Object obj = null;

    try
    {
        //
        // Resolve the 'StockExchange' object reference
        //
        obj = rootContextExt.resolve_str(
                  "London.region/Main.failover/StockExchange"
```

Listing 6.10 continued

```
                );
        StockExchange Stock = StockExchangeHelper.narrow(obj);

        System.out.println("The 'StockExchange' object reference:");
        System.out.println(m_orb.object_to_string(obj) );
        // Now make some invocations on the object reference 'Stock'
        //...
    }
    catch (org.omg.CORBA.SystemException ex) {
        System.err.println(ex);
        System.exit(1);
    }
    catch (org.omg.CORBA.UserException ux) {
        System.err.println(ux);
        System.exit(1);
    }
  }
}
```

In this example, once the client has the object reference, it stringifies it and prints it to standard output. The client can make remote invocations once it has initialized the object reference.

Federated Naming Service

The naming service supports federation; that is, distinct naming servers can be linked together to create a single naming graph. A client can then navigate seamlessly throughout the naming graph without being aware that it is federated.

The key to federation support is the operation `bind_context()`, declared in the following IDL fragment:

```
//IDL
#pragma prefix "omg.org"

module CosNaming {
    ...
    interface NamingContext {
        ...
        void bind_context(in Name n, in NamingContext nc)
            raises(NotFound, CannotProceed, InvalidName, AlreadyBound);
        ...
    };
    ...
};
```

The `bind_context()` operation binds a given naming context `nc` to a name `n`, enabling arbitrary crosslinks to be created. It is conceptually similar to creating a symbolic link with the UNIX command `ln -s`.

Figure 6.4 shows an example of two distinct naming services that have been linked together using `bind_context()`. This link could be created by invoking `bind_context()` on the initial context of naming service *X*, giving the name `A/B/C` as the first argument and a reference to naming context `C` as the second argument.

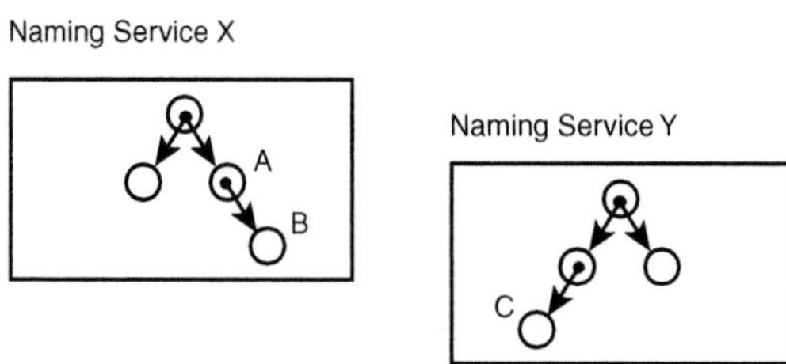

Figure 6.4

Making a crosslink between naming services.

The existence of crosslinks has an important impact on the architecture of the naming service. Simple invocations on a naming service can give rise to a chain of remote invocations across the federated graph.

For example, consider a client that resolves an object with the name `A/B/C/MyObject`. Figure 6.4 shows that the contexts `A/B` and `A/B/C` are located in two distinct naming services. When the client invokes `resolve()` on the naming service *X*, this naming service cannot complete the resolution on its own, so it makes a further invocation of `resolve()` on context `C` in naming service *Y*.

Graph or Hierarchy?

The topology of the naming service is typically a tree structure. However, there is nothing in the naming service specification that requires the topology to be a tree. In fact, the topology was deliberately left as flexible as possible to allow the CORBA naming service to be layered on top of a wide variety of naming services. The naming service can take the form of an arbitrary directed graph.

It is therefore possible to introduce cycles into the naming graph, as illustrated in Figure 6.5.

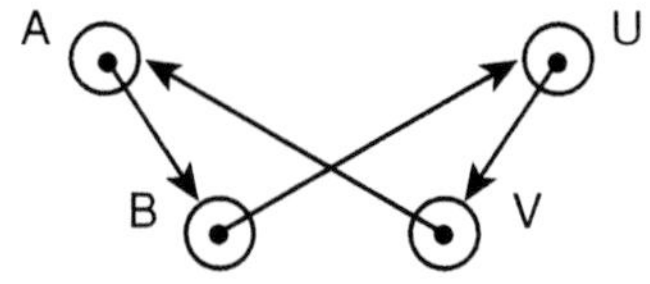

Figure 6.5

Creating a cycle in a naming graph.

By introducing a crosslink between B and U and a further crosslink between V and A, this graph assumes the shape of a bowtie. If you follow the directed links of the graph, it takes you in a complete circuit. For example, the context A can be accessed under any of the names A, A/B/U/V/A, or A/B/U/V/A/B/U/V/A.

If cycles are likely to occur in your naming service, you must avoid getting caught in an infinite loop when traversing the graph. The code examples shown in this chapter are not designed to be used in a naming graph that has cycles.

Binding Iterators and the `list()` Operation

Another basic operation on the naming service is the `list()` operation, which returns the contents of a naming context. In addition to the simple task of printing out the contents of a naming context, the `list()` operation is useful for any tasks that require traversal of the naming graph.

The IDL Interface for `list()` and `BindingIterator`

At first, it would appear that `list()` should be a simple operation: It is invoked on a naming context and returns a list of bindings contained by that naming context. But what if the naming context happens to contain one million objects? This might seem a little far-fetched for the particular project you are working on, but it is realistic for some applications. For example, if the naming service is used to wrap a database, it would not be unusual to find millions of objects in a naming context. In order to cope with this situation, the naming service defines a `BindingIterator` interface that sends over parts of the listing in manageable-size pieces.

The IDL relating to the `list()` operation is declared as follows:

```
// IDL
module CosNaming {
     enum BindingType { nobject, ncontext };

     struct Binding {
          Name binding_name;
          BindingType binding_type;
     };

     typedef sequence <Binding> BindingList;

     interface NamingContext {
          ...
          void list(
               in unsigned long how_many,
               out BindingList bl,
               out BindingIterator bi
               );
     };

     interface BindingIterator {
          boolean next_one(out Binding b);
```

```
        boolean next_n(in unsigned long how_many, out BindingList bl);
        void destroy();
    };
    ...
};
```

When the `list()` operation is invoked on a naming context, it returns `BindingList`, which holds a sequence of bindings belonging to that naming context. The `how_many` argument is used to specify the maximum number of bindings that can be returned in `BindingList`.

Two cases arise, according to whether or not the returned `BindingIterator bi` is null:

- If the `BindingIterator bi` is a null object reference, the `BindingList bl` returned by `list()` is complete.
- If the `BindingIterator bi` is not null, the `BindingList bl` returned by `list()` is incomplete. It is then necessary to invoke the `BindingIterator` object to retrieve the remaining bindings. You can retrieve the remaining values either one-by-one, using `next_one()`, or in larger chunks, using `next_n()`. The operations `next_one()` and `next_n()` return true if more bindings remain to be retrieved and false if the end of the list has been reached.

Semantics of `list()` and `BindingIterator`

The CORBA specification gives a good deal of latitude to the implementation of `list()` and `BindingIterator`. The following points are important:

- The argument `how_many` specifies a maximum for the number of returned bindings. There is no guarantee that you will get all of the bindings with an invocation of `list()`, even if the number of bindings in the naming context is fewer than `how_many`. The specification requires a minimum of only one binding to be returned from a non-empty naming context. Therefore, you must always check whether or not a returned `BindingIterator` is null.
- Likewise, in the operation `next_n()`, the argument `how_many` specifies a maximum for the number of returned bindings. The number of bindings returned may lie anywhere in the range `[1..how_many]`, irrespective of the number of bindings that remain to be listed.
- It is legal to pass a zero value of `how_many` to `list()`. This is taken to indicate that you want to use the binding iterator `bi` to retrieve the list of bindings. In this case, the returned binding list `bl` is always a zero-length sequence.
- It is illegal to pass a zero value of `how_many` to `next_n()`; this will give rise to a `CORBA::BAD_PARAM` exception.

Cleanup After Listing Is Finished

There are a few points to take care of once a listing is finished:

- The only way to tell if a listing is finished is by checking the return value of `next_one()` or `next_n()`. A value of `false` indicates that there are no more bindings to retrieve and that the current return value is empty. A further call to `next_one()` or `next_n()` after they have returned `false` has undefined behavior.

- The `BindingIterator` object in the server has to be deleted. The best approach is for the client to explicitly call `destroy()` on the `BindingIterator` object. Alternatively, the server may spontaneously delete the `BindingIterator` (garbage collection) in order to keep its memory usage under control. The client has to be prepared to deal with a `CORBA::OBJECT_NOT_EXIST` in that case.

The garbage collection of `BindingIterator` is a typical issue that crops up in a distributed system. In general, for any session object (such as `BindingIterator`), a server might need to implement garbage collection to clean out those objects that have been lying dormant for a relatively long time.

Name Utility—`listBindings()`

The combination of `list()` and `BindingIterator` to retrieve lists of bindings is flexible but awkward to use. It is easier to use a method that returns the listing in a single invocation. The `listBindings()` method of our name utility is such a method.

An implementation of `listBindings()` is shown for C++ and Java in Listing 6.11 and Listing 6.12:

Listing 6.11 C++ Implementation of `listBindings()`

```
// C++
//----------------------------------------
// method: 'listBindings()'
//
// purpose:
//----------------------------------------
CosNaming::BindingList *
NameUtil::listBindings(
          const CosNaming::NamingContext_ptr nc,
          const CosNaming::Name&  name,
          CORBA::ULong max_list_size
          )
{
     CosNaming::BindingList_var     basicListV;
     CosNaming::BindingIterator_var bIterV;

     CORBA::Object_var objV;
     CosNaming::NamingContext_var tmpContextV;

     if (name.length()==0) {
          tmpContextV = CosNaming::NamingContext::_duplicate(nc);
     }
     else {
          objV = nc->resolve(name);
          tmpContextV = CosNaming::NamingContext::_narrow(objV);
```

Listing 6.11 continued

```
    }
    if (CORBA::is_nil(tmpContextV)) {
        cerr << "listBindings: Nil context" << endl;
        return 0;
    }

    tmpContextV->list(max_list_size, basicListV.out(), bIterV.out());

    CORBA::Long     max_remaining = max_list_size - basicListV->length();
    CORBA::Boolean  moreBindings  = !CORBA::is_nil(bIterV);

    if (moreBindings) {
        while (moreBindings && (max_remaining > 0) ) {
            CosNaming::BindingList_var tmpListV;

            moreBindings = bIterV->next_n(max_remaining, tmpListV.out());

            //Append 'tmpListV' to 'basicListV'
            CORBA::ULong basicListLen = basicListV->length();
            basicListV->length(basicListLen+tmpListV->length());
            for (CORBA::ULong i=0; i < tmpListV->length(); i++) {
                (*basicListV)[i+basicListLen] = (*tmpListV)[i];
            }

            //Re-calculate 'max_remaining'
            max_remaining = max_list_size - basicListV->length();
        }
        bIterV->destroy();
    }

    return basicListV._ retn();
}
```

Listing 6.12 Java Implementation of `listBindings()`

```
// Java
  //----------------------------------------
  // method: 'listBindings()'
  //
  // purpose:
  //----------------------------------------
  public static Binding[] listBindings(
          NamingContext nc,
          NameComponent[]  name,
          int max_list_size
          )
          throws org.omg.CORBA.UserException
  {
```

Listing 6.12 continued

```
Binding[]     basicList;
BindingIterator bIter;

org.omg.CORBA.Object obj;
NamingContext tmpContext;

if (name.length==0) {
     tmpContext = nc;
}
else {
     obj = nc.resolve(name);
     tmpContext = NamingContextHelper.narrow(obj);
}

BindingListHolder basicList_out
     = new BindingListHolder();
BindingIteratorHolder bIter_out
     = new BindingIteratorHolder();
tmpContext.list(
     max_list_size,
     basicList_out,
     bIter_out
     );
basicList = basicList_out.value;
bIter     = bIter_out.value;

int      max_remaining = max_list_size - basicList.length;
boolean  moreBindings  = (bIter!=null);

if (moreBindings) {
     while (moreBindings && (max_remaining > 0) ) {
          Binding[] tmpList;
          Binding[] oldList;
          BindingListHolder tmpList_out
               = new BindingListHolder();

          moreBindings = bIter.next_n(
               max_list_size,
               tmpList_out
               );
          tmpList = tmpList_out.value;

          //Append 'tmpList' to 'basicList'
          oldList = basicList;
          basicList = new Binding[oldList.length+tmpList.length];
          for (int i=0; i < oldList.length; i++) {
              basicList[i] = oldList[i];
          }
```

Listing 6.12 continued

```
            for (int i=0; i < tmpList.length; i++) {
                basicList[i+oldList.length] = tmpList[i];
            }

            // Re-calculate 'max_remaining'
            max_remaining = max_list_size - basicList.length;
        }
        bIter.destroy();
    }

    return basicList;
}
```

The naming context that you want to obtain the listing for is specified by passing the initial naming context `nc` and the name of the context relative to the initial context. The argument `max_list_size` is used to specify the largest length of `BindingList` that you find acceptable. The implementation of `listBindings()` does not return until either it has retrieved all of the bindings or it reaches the limit `max_list_size`.

Name Utility—`recursiveUnbind()`

As an application of the utility function `listBindings()`, consider the common task of deleting a naming context and all its contents. In order to delete the naming context completely, it is necessary to recurse into all of the sub-contexts and delete their contents as well.

With the help of `listBindings()`, it is straightforward to implement `recursiveUnbind()`, as shown in Listing 6.13 and Listing 6.14 for C++ and Java:

***Listing 6.13 C++ Implementation of* `recursiveUnbind()`**

```
// C++
//-----------------------------------------
// method: 'recursiveUnbind()'
//
// purpose:
//-----------------------------------------
void
NameUtil::recursiveUnbind(
        const CosNaming::NamingContext_ptr nc,
        const CosNaming::Name&  name
    )
{
    CORBA::Object_var objV;
    CosNaming::NamingContext_var tmpContextV;

    objV = nc->resolve(name);
    tmpContextV = CosNaming::NamingContext::_narrow(objV);
    if (CORBA::is_nil(tmpContextV)) {
```

Listing 6.13 continued

```
        cerr << "recursiveUnbind: Nil context reference" << endl;
        return;
    }

    CosNaming::BindingList_var blV;
    CosNaming::Name tmpName;
    tmpName.length(0);

    blV = NameUtil::listBindings(tmpContextV.in(),
                tmpName,
                10000   // 'max_list_size'
            );

    for (CORBA::ULong i=0; i<blV->length(); i++)
    {
        tmpName = (*blV)[i].binding_name;

        if      ( (*blV)[i].binding_type==CosNaming::nobject)
        {
            tmpContextV->unbind(tmpName);
        }
        else if ( (*blV)[i].binding_type==CosNaming::ncontext)
        {
            NameUtil::recursiveUnbind(tmpContextV.in(), tmpName);
        }
    }
    nc->unbind(name);
    tmpContextV->destroy();
}
```

Listing 6.14 Java Implementation of `recursiveUnbind()`

```
// Java
//---------------------------------------
// method: 'recursiveUnbind()'
//
// purpose:
//---------------------------------------
public static void recursiveUnbind(
          NamingContext nc,
          NameComponent[]  name
      )
      throws org.omg.CORBA.UserException
{
    org.omg.CORBA.Object obj;
    NamingContext tmpContext;

    obj = nc.resolve(name);
    tmpContext = NamingContextHelper.narrow(obj);
```

Listing 6.14 continued

```
    Binding[] bl;
    NameComponent[] tmpName = new NameComponent[0];

    bl = NameUtil.listBindings(tmpContext,
                  tmpName,
                  10000    // max_list_size
              );

    for (int i=0; i < bl.length; i++)
    {
        tmpName = bl[i].binding_name;

        if      ( bl[i].binding_type==BindingType.nobject)
        {
             tmpContext.unbind(tmpName);
        }
        else if ( bl[i].binding_type==BindingType.ncontext)
        {
             NameUtil.recursiveUnbind(tmpContext, tmpName);
        }
      }
      nc.unbind(name);
      tmpContext.destroy();
}
```

The naming context that you want to delete is specified by passing the initial naming context `nc` and the name of the context relative to the initial context. Note there are a couple of limitations of `recursiveUnbind()` that make it less than industrial strength. The maximum list size cannot be specified, nor does it deal with a situation in which the maximum list size is exceeded. Also, this method makes the assumption that the naming service is arranged strictly in the form of a tree. It cannot deal with naming graphs containing cycles.

Object URLs

CORBA defines a number of uniform resource locator (URL) formats that can be used to specify the location of a CORBA object. The allowed URL formats are summarized in Table 6.5.

Table 6.5 Object URL Formats

Format	Description
`IOR:`	A stringified IOR. The prefix `IOR:` is followed by a string of hexadecimal numbers.
`corbaloc:rir:`	Specify an object reference that is implicitly resolved using `resolve_initial_references()`.
`corbaloc:iiop:` or `corbaloc::`	Specify the location of a CORBA object in a form that is appropriate for the IIOP protocol.

Table 6.5 continued

Format	Description
`corbaname:rir:`	Specify a name that is resolved relative to the initial naming context.
`corbaname:iiop:` or `corbaname::`	Specify a name that is resolved relative to the given naming context.
`file://`	Indicates a file that may contain a URL or a stringified IOR of a CORBA object.
`ftp://`	Indicates a file, retrieved using FTP, that may contain a URL or a stringified IOR for a CORBA object.
`http://`	An HTTP URL that can be used to retrieve a URL or a stringified IOR for a CORBA object.

The first five URL formats—`IOR:`, `corbaloc:rir:`, `corbaloc:iiop:`, `corbaname:rir:`, and `corbaname:iiop:`—must be supported by a CORBA 3 ORB. However, support for the URL formats `file://`, `ftp://`, and `http://` is currently optional.

Converting an Object URL to an Object Reference

Any of the above object URLs can be passed as an argument to the function `CORBA::ORB::string_to_object()`. You are not restricted to passing the format `IOR:...`, as was the case with versions of CORBA prior to CORBA 3. The way to convert an object URL to an object reference is

```
//C++
// Given:
//     'orbV'              -- a reference to a CORBA::ORB instance
//     'objectURLString'  -- an arbitrary object URL string
CORBA::Object_var objV;
objV = orbV->string_to_object(objectURLString);
...

//Java
// Given:
//     'orb'               -- a reference to a org.omg.CORBA.ORB instance
//     'objectURLString'  -- an arbitrary object URL string
org.omg.CORBA.Object obj;
obj = orb.string_to_object(objectURLString);
...
```

The object reference has to be narrowed to the correct type after it is returned by `string_to_object()`.

The ORB may need to carry out a number of steps internally to resolve the object URL passed to `string_to_object()`. This can include making one or more remote invocations.

URL Escape Mechanism for Strings

An escape mechanism is needed to encode data in a URL. There are two reasons the escape mechanism is needed:

- Object URLs frequently need to include binary data. The binary data must be mapped to printable characters before it can be included in a URL.
- Certain non-alphanumeric characters can become garbled when transmitted across the Internet.

For these reasons, an escape mechanism is defined by the Internet Engineering Task Force (IETF) RFC 2396 specifically for URLs. The escape mechanism ensures that arbitrary strings and binary data can be sent across the Internet without being corrupted. The URL escape mechanism is defined as follows:

- ASCII-encoded alphanumeric characters remain unchanged.
- The following printable ASCII characters remain unchanged:
  `;`, `/`, `:`, `?`, `@`, `&`, `=`, `+`, `$`, `,`, `-`, `_`, `.`, `!`, `~`, `*`, `'`, `(`, `)`
- All other characters are escaped. The escaped characters are represented as a `%` (percent sign) followed by a two-digit hexadecimal number.

`corbaloc:rir:` Object URL

The `corbaloc:rir:` URL has the following general form:

```
corbaloc:rir:[/ObjectId]
```

The protocol identifier `rir` stands for *resolve initial references*. It indicates that URLs of this form are resolved by making an implicit call to the method `resolve_initial_references()`. The optional part *`ObjectId`* is used to select one of the initial reference types, listed in Table 6.4. For example, *`ObjectId`* might be `NameService` or `RootPOA`. If *`ObjectId`* is omitted, it is assumed to be `NameService` by default.

Some examples of `corbaloc:rir:` URLs are given in Table 6.6.

Table 6.6 Examples of `corbaloc:rir:` Object URLs

Object URL	Description
`corbaloc:rir:/TradingService`	Resolves to an object reference of type `CosTrading::Lookup`.
`corbaloc:rir:/NameService`	Resolves to an object reference of type `CosNaming::NamingContext`.
`corbaloc:rir:`	Resolves to an object reference of type `CosNaming::NamingContext`.

For example, the following invocation of the `string_to_object()` method

```
//C++
// Given orbV initialized to an instance of CORBA::ORB
CORBA::Object_var objV = orbV->string_to_object("corbaloc:rir:");
```

```
//Java
// Given orb initialized to an instance of org.omg.CORBA.ORB
org.omg.CORBA.Object obj = orb.string_to_object("corbaloc:rir:");
```

is equivalent to an invocation of the `resolve_initial_references()` method:

```
//C++
// Given orbV initialized to an instance of CORBA::ORB
CORBA::Object_var objV = orbV->resolve_initial_references("NameService");

//Java
// Given orb initialized to an instance of org.omg.CORBA.ORB
org.omg.CORBA.Object obj = orb.resolve_initial_references("NameService");
```

The `corbaloc:rir:` URL can be used in any context where a stringified object reference is expected.

`corbaloc:iiop:` Object URL

The `corbaloc:iiop:` URL is used to specify the location of a CORBA object in a relatively readable form. It has the following general form:

```
corbaloc:[iiop]:[version@]host[:port][/URL_escaped_object_key]
```

The protocol identifier `iiop` is optional. A blank protocol identifier is taken to be `iiop` by default. The *`version`* refers to the IIOP version supported by the object. Currently, it can be 1.0, 1.1, or 1.2. The default is 1.0. The host and port of the server process can be specified. If *`port`* is omitted, it is set to `2089` by default. *`URL_escaped_object_key`* is derived from the `object_key` that is part of an IOR (see Chapter 5, "Object References"). The octets of the original `object_key` are converted to characters using the URL escape mechanism described previously.

Some examples of `corbaloc:iiop:` URLs are shown in Table 6.7.

Table 6.7 Examples of* `corbaloc:iiop:` *Object URLs

Object URL	Description
`corbaloc:iiop:1.2@myhost:1234/xyz`	A server that supports IIOP 1.2, located on host `myhost` and listening on port `1234`. The `object_key` is `xyz`.
`corbaloc::myhost:1234/xyz`	A server that supports IIOP 1.0, located on host `myhost` and listening on port `1234`. The `object_key` is `xyz`.
`corbaloc::myhost/xyz`	A server that supports IIOP 1.0, located on host `myhost` and listening on port `2089`. The `object_key` is `xyz`.

The `corbaloc:iiop:` URL can be used in place of a stringified IOR in calls to `string_to_object()`. The URL contains the same sort of location information that is found in an IIOP profile. However, unlike the IOR, the URL cannot encode IOR components, so it is not an exact replacement for the IOR.

Fault-Tolerant corbaloc:iiop: Object URL

It is possible to specify a comma-separated list of addresses in place of a single address in the corbaloc:iiop: URL. For example

```
corbaloc::1.2@myhost:1200,:1.2@mybackuphost:1200,iiop:1.2@myotherbackup:1240/xy
```

Note that the protocol specifier (iiop: or :) is considered to be part of an address. In this case, the ORB has three different servers to choose from, with each of them running on a different host. If the ORB fails to contact the first host, it can try the second or third one.

corbaname:rir: Object URL

The corbaname:rir: URL has the following general form:

```
corbaname:rir:[/NameService][#URL_escaped_string_name]
```

This URL is used to specify an object reference by giving a stringified name that is resolved relative to the initial naming context. The protocol identifier rir: indicates that the initial naming context is resolved by invoking resolve_initial_references("NameService"). The ObjectId, specified as /NameService, can be omitted from the URL. The *URL_escaped_string_name* is a stringified name that has been subjected to the URL escape mechanism.

Some examples of corbaname:rir: URLs are shown in Table 6.8.

Table 6.8 Examples of corbaname:rir: *Object URLs*

Object URL	Description
corbaname:rir:/NameService#Foo/Bar	Resolves the object with the stringified name Foo/Bar relative to the initial naming context.
corbaname:rir:#Foo/name%20with%20spaces	Resolves the object with the stringified name Foo/name with spaces relative to the initial naming context.
corbaname:rir:#Foo%5c%5cwith%20backslash	Resolves the object with the stringified name Foo\\with backslash relative to the initial naming context. Note that \\ is an escaped backslash that represents a single backslash.
corbaname:rir:	Resolves to the initial naming context.

A sample URL of the form corbaname:rir:#Foo/Bar and the following invocation of the string_to_object() method

```
//C++
// Given orbV initialized to an instance of CORBA::ORB
CORBA::Object_var objV = orbV->string_to_object("corbaname:rir:#Foo/Bar");
```

```
//Java
// Given orb initialized to an instance of org.omg.CORBA.ORB
org.omg.CORBA.Object obj = orb.string_to_object("corbaname:rir:#Foo/Bar");
```

yields a result similar to the following code fragment:

```
//C++
// Given orbV initialized to an instance of CORBA::ORB
CORBA::Object_var objV = orbV->resolve_initial_references("NameService");
CosNaming::NamingContextExt_var rootCtxV
    = CosNaming::NamingContextExt::_narrow(objV.in() );
if (CORBA::is_nil(rootCtxV.in()) ) {
    cerr << "Error: Failed to narrow to type NamingContextExt" << endl;
    exit(1);
}
objV = rootCtxV->resolve_str("Foo/Bar");

//Java
// Given orb initialized to an instance of org.omg.CORBA.ORB
org.omg.CosNaming.NamingContextExt rootCtx = null;
org.omg.CORBA.Object obj = orb.resolve_initial_references("NameService");
rootCtx = org.omg.CosNaming.NamingContextExtHelper.narrow(obj);
obj = rootCtx.resolve_str("Foo/Bar");
```

For simplicity, the error handling is not shown in the above example. The object reference obtained needs to be narrowed to the appropriate type before it can be used.

`corbaname:iiop:` Object URL

The `corbaname:iiop:` URL has the following general form:

```
corbaname:[iiop]:[version@]host[:port][/URL_escaped_object_key]
[#URL_escaped_string_name]
```

This URL format is closely related to the `corbaloc:iiop:` object URL. The address portion of the URL

`[iiop]:[`*`version@`*`]`*`host`*`[:`*`port`*`][/`*`URL_escaped_object_key`*`]`

is identical to the address used in a `corbaloc:iiop:` URL. In the context of a `corbaname:iiop:` URL, the address is taken to specify the location of a `CosNaming::NamingContext` object. The *`URL_escaped_string_name`* is a stringified name that has been subjected to the URL escape mechanism. The stringified name is resolved relative to the specified naming context to yield the object reference to which the URL refers.

Some examples of `corbaname:iiop:` URLs are shown in Table 6.9.

Table 6.9 Examples of `corbaname:iiop:` *Object URLs*

Object URL	Description
`corbaname::1.2@myhost:1234/xyz#Foo/Bar`	An object reference given by the stringified name `Foo/Bar`, resolved relative to the naming context given by `:1.2@myhost:1234/xyz`.
`corbaname::myhost/xyz#Foo/Bar`	An object reference given by the stringified name `Foo/Bar`, resolved relative to the naming context given by `:myhost/xyz`.

Fault-Tolerant `corbaname:iiop:` Object URL

In a manner similar to the `corbaloc:iiop:` URL, it is possible to specify a comma-separated list of addresses in place of a single address in the `corbaname:iiop:` URL. For example

```
corbaname::1.2@myhost:1200,:1.2@mybackuphost:1200,iiop:1.2@myotherbackup:1240
/xyzxyzxyz#Foo/Bar
```

If the ORB fails to contact the first host, it can try the second or third one. This is particularly valuable in the case of the naming service. If clients locate all application services using the naming service, it is potentially a single point of failure. Using multiple addresses in a URL provides a simple way of redirecting clients to a backup naming host.

Specifying Values for Initial References

The API associated with the initialization service tells you how an application can get hold of initial object references. It says nothing, however, about where these object references come from or how to specify their values to the ORB. This question is left as an implementation detail for the ORB vendor. Different ORBs will let you set initial references in different ways. Typically, the values are stored in a configuration file that is accessible to the application.

Irrespective of the approach used, the existence of a standard API for the initialization service means that application code remains independent of the ORB configuration mechanism.

In addition to an unspecified mechanism for setting default initial references, the initialization service also provides a mechanism for overriding defaults. You may specify initial references using one of the command-line arguments `-ORBInitRef` or `-ORBDefaultInitRef`. These command-line arguments are described in the following sections.

Command-Line Argument `-ORBInitRef`

The command-line argument `-ORBInitRef` allows you to override default values of initial references. For example, consider a C++ server that is initialized using the code given in Listing 6.1, and suppose the name of the server executable is `server`. If you want to force the server to use a naming service other than the one specified by the default ORB configuration mechanism, you could run the server as follows:

```
$ server -ORBInitRef NameService=IOR:010000001600000049444c3a53746f...
```

where `NameService` is the `ObjectId` for the naming service and `IOR:0100000016...` is the stringified object reference of a specific `CosNaming::NamingContext` or `CosNaming::NamingContextExt` object. The specified object reference will be returned in place of the default when the application invokes `resolve_initial_references("NameService")`.

In Listing 6.1 you can see that the command-line arguments held in the string array `argv[]` are passed to `CORBA::ORB_init()`. As the ORB initializes, it scans the supplied argument list looking for options of the form `-ORB`*`suffix`*. In this case it finds a single option `-ORBInitRef`. This option, along with its associated parameter `NameService=IOR:0100000016...`, is removed from the argument list `argv[]`, and the value is used as the initial reference for the naming service.

Command-Line Argument `-ORBDefaultInitRef`

The command-line argument `-ORBDefaultInitRef` allows you to usurp the initialization service completely by specifying a location from which all initial references are retrieved. The format for this option is

```
-ORBDefaultInitRef URLStem
```

`URLStem` can be given either as a `corbaloc:iiop:` or `corbaname:iiop:` URL. When `resolve_initial_references("`*`ObjectId`*`")` is subsequently invoked, the initial reference to *`ObjectId`* is resolved as follows:

1. An object URL is constructed from *`URLStem`* by appending a `/` (forward slash) to *`ObjectId`*. This gives a URL string of the general form *`URLStem/ObjectId`*.
2. The resulting URL *`URLStem/ObjectId`* is resolved in the standard way and passed back as the return value of `resolve_initial_references()`.

For example, if the following command-line argument is passed to `ORB_init()`

```
-ORBDefaultInitRef corbaname::1.2@myhost:1234/xyz#Foo/Bar
```

a call of the form `resolve_initial_references("TradingService")` will result in the construction of the URL `corbaname::1.2@myhost:1234/xyz#Foo/Bar/TradingService`. The ORB will then look for an object of type `CosTrading::Lookup` bound under the name `Foo/Bar/TradingService` in the naming service given by the address `:1.2@myhost:1234/xyz`.

Summary

The naming service is used to establish points of contact between clients and servers. Together with the initialization service, it provides the basic bootstrap service in CORBA. Because of this bootstrap role, the naming service is also, potentially, a single point of failure. If you are interested in developing fault-tolerant applications, you will need to pay a lot of attention to this component of your architecture.

Naming is a relatively basic service. The operations give you the functionality you need to associate names with object references and to maintain a graph of naming contexts. If you need more sophisticated features, for example a flexible search operation or utilities that can cope with cycles, you have to supply these yourself. In most development projects you will probably find it necessary to build a library layered on top of the naming service that provides the features you need.

Occasionally, you might want to go a step further and implement the whole naming service yourself. This is not as difficult as it sounds, and sometimes there are compelling reasons for doing so. If you already have a non-CORBA naming service that forms part of your architecture, it makes a lot of sense to re-use the old naming service. You could implement the CORBA naming service IDL as a wrapper around the old service. It is precisely this kind of flexibility that is the strength of the CORBA naming service.

Initialization Service Pseudo-IDL

Listing 6.15 shows the IDL for the Initialization Service, which is contained in the module `CORBA`.

Listing 6.15 IDL for the Initialization Service

```
//PIDL
module CORBA {
     ...
     typedef string ORBid;
     typedef sequence<string> arg_list;
     ORB ORB_init(inout arg_list argv, in ORBid orb_identifier);
     ...
     interface ORB {
          typedef string ObjectId;
          typedef sequence<ObjectId> ObjectIdList;
          ...
          ObjectIdList list_initial_services();
          ...
          Object resolve_initial_references(
                    in ObjectId identifier
               );
          ...
     };  // interface ORB
     ...
}; //module CORBA
```

Naming Service IDL

Listing 6.16 shows the IDL for the Interoperable Naming Service, which is contained in the module `CosNaming`.

Listing 6.16 IDL for the `CosNaming` *Module*

```
//IDL
// File: CosNaming.idl
#ifndef _COSNAMING_IDL_
#define _COSNAMING_IDL_

#pragma prefix "omg.org"

module CosNaming {

     typedef string Istring;

     struct NameComponent {
          Istring id;
          Istring kind;
     };

     typedef sequence<NameComponent> Name;

     enum BindingType { nobject, ncontext };

     struct Binding {
          Name binding_name;
          BindingType binding_type;
     };

     // Note: In struct Binding, binding_name is incorrectly defined
     // as a Name instead of a NameComponent. This definition is
     // unchanged for compatibility reasons.
     typedef sequence <Binding> BindingList;

     interface BindingIterator;

     interface NamingContext {
          enum NotFoundReason {
               missing_node, not_context, not_object
          };
          exception NotFound {
               NotFoundReason why;
               Name rest_of_name;
          };
          exception CannotProceed {
               NamingContext cxt;
               Name rest_of_name;
          };
          exception InvalidName{};
          exception AlreadyBound {};
          exception NotEmpty{};
```

Listing 6.16 continued

```
        void bind(in Name n, in Object obj)
            raises(
                NotFound, CannotProceed,
                InvalidName, AlreadyBound
            );
        void rebind(in Name n, in Object obj)
            raises(NotFound, CannotProceed, InvalidName);
        void bind_context(in Name n, in NamingContext nc)
            raises(
                NotFound, CannotProceed,
                InvalidName, AlreadyBound
            );
        void rebind_context(in Name n, in NamingContext nc)
            raises(NotFound, CannotProceed, InvalidName);
        Object resolve (in Name n)
            raises(NotFound, CannotProceed, InvalidName);
        void unbind(in Name n)
            raises(NotFound, CannotProceed, InvalidName);
        NamingContext new_context();
        NamingContext bind_new_context(in Name n)
            raises(
                NotFound, AlreadyBound,
                CannotProceed, InvalidName
            );
        void destroy() raises(NotEmpty);
        void list(
            in unsigned long how_many,
            out BindingList bl,
            out BindingIterator bi
            );
    };

    interface BindingIterator {
        boolean next_one(out Binding b);
        boolean next_n(in unsigned long how_many, out BindingList bl);
        void destroy();
    };

    interface NamingContextExt: NamingContext {
        typedef string StringName;
        typedef string Address;
        typedef string URLString;
        StringName to_string(in Name n) raises(InvalidName);
        Name to_name(in StringName sn)
            raises(InvalidName);
        exception InvalidAddress {};
        URLString to_url(in Address addr, in StringName sn)
            raises(InvalidAddress, InvalidName);
```

```
        Object resolve_str(in StringName n)
            raises(
                NotFound, CannotProceed,
                InvalidName, AlreadyBound
            );
    };
};
#endif // _COSNAMING_IDL_
```

CHAPTER 7

The Portable Object Adapter

The purpose of an object adapter is to make CORBA objects accessible to CORBA clients via the network. An object adapter is analogous to a socket into which you can plug your CORBA objects. By plugging your objects into an object adapter, you effectively plug them into the network.

The primary responsibility of the object adapter is to ensure that an invocation, whether local or remote, reaches the object for which it is intended. When an object adapter receives a request message, it identifies the appropriate target object and invokes the corresponding operation on behalf of the client.

The portable object adapter (POA) is a standard object adapter described in the CORBA specification, and its programming interface is fully specified. In principle, therefore, code written using the POA should be portable across different ORB implementations.

Understanding the POA

The POA is a powerful and flexible object adapter. In particular, it has been designed very much with scalability in mind—it is able to cope efficiently with applications that support millions of CORBA objects.

The downside of this flexibility is that the POA can appear bewilderingly complex when you approach it for the first time. It is helpful to keep in mind that the POA is not so much an object adapter as a whole family of object adapters. The designers of the POA could have specified a variety of object adapters, each with different characteristics and each suitable for different kinds of applications. Instead, they chose to define a single type of adapter, the POA, whose characteristics are defined at creation time by a set of *POA policies*.

Different combinations of POA policies can be used to create very different kinds of object adapters. Although an enormous number of POA policy combinations are theoretically possible, a few examples are sufficient to illustrate the typical and intended uses of POA policies. Most applications use no more than two or three different kinds of POA.

An Abstract View of an Invocation

Figure 7.1 shows a high-level view of a remote invocation. Two object references in the client, labelled `"Fred"` and `"Anna"`, are shown invoking operations on two corresponding CORBA objects that live in the server. The interesting entities in this view are

- `ObjectId` The identity of a CORBA object is represented by the type `PortableServer::ObjectId`. In Figure 7.1, the `ObjectIds` are represented by the labels `"Fred"` and `"Anna"`.
- Object Reference An object reference in the client encapsulates both the location and the identity of the corresponding CORBA object. The `ObjectId` for a CORBA object is therefore embedded in its object reference.
- CORBA Object A CORBA object has an identity, which is represented by its `ObjectId`. In Figure 7.1, the `ObjectIds` are `"Fred"` and `"Anna"`.

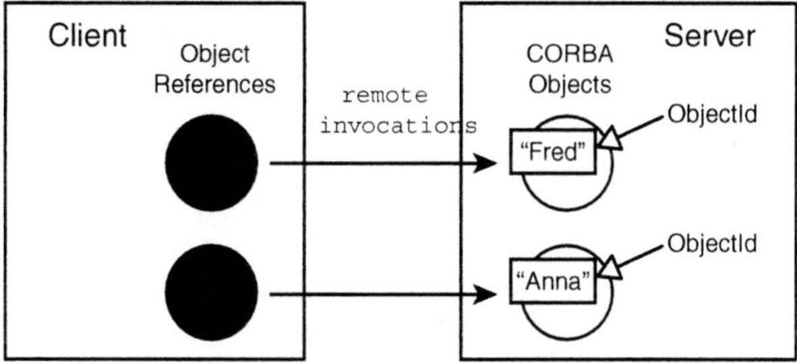

Figure 7.1

An abstract view of remote invocations.

An object reference in a client encapsulates the location and identity of the corresponding CORBA object. If an operation is invoked on, say, the `"Anna"` object reference, the invocation is forwarded to the remote CORBA object with `ObjectId` equal to `"Anna"`. A CORBA object, therefore, has an intrinsic identity, an `ObjectId`, according to which invocations are routed.

The Role of the POA

Figure 7.2 gives a more detailed view of invocation routing, assuming that the POA is used on the server side. Two entities are introduced in this figure:

- **Servant** A servant class is a class that provides the implementation of an IDL interface. Servant instances have no intrinsic identity; they are effectively anonymous.
- **Active Object Map** An active object map is a lookup table that is built into a POA. It associates `ObjectIds` with a corresponding pointer (C++) or reference (Java) to a servant object.

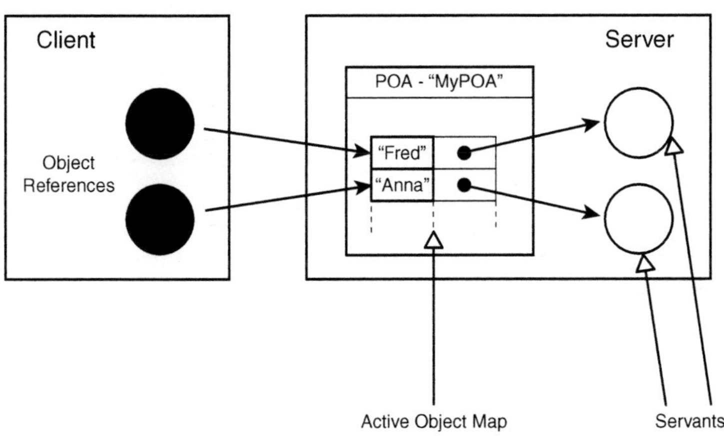

Figure 7.2

POA mapping `ObjectIds` *to servants.*

Invocations that arrive in the server are first routed to the appropriate POA object. The POA takes the `ObjectId` for the invocation and looks it up in the active object map to find the target servant object.

Note an important feature of the POA: The POA completely separates the notions of identity and implementation. A CORBA object is effectively decomposed into

- An identity, represented by `PortableServer::ObjectId`
- An implementation, provided by a servant instance

The decomposition of a CORBA object into an identity and an implementation is slightly counterintuitive. You might tend to identify a servant as a CORBA object. However, you cannot do so. A CORBA object has an identity; a servant does not.

TIP

A CORBA object is composed of an `ObjectId`, a servant instance, and the association that exists between them. A servant is not a CORBA object.

There is no object in the server that corresponds directly to a CORBA object. The CORBA object is effectively an abstraction.

The idea of separating identity from implementation is a powerful one. It provides the key to implementing highly scalable systems using the POA.

The POA has two major responsibilities within the server:

- Locating a servant object to service each incoming invocation request.
- Invoking the appropriate operation on the servant object as specified in the invocation request.

A servant is located based on the `ObjectId` contained in the invocation request. The POA can exercise considerable flexibility in the way it maps `ObjectIds` to servants. Figure 7.3 shows three different ways of mapping `ObjectIds` to servants.

In Figure 7.3(a), the POA implements a one-to-one mapping between `ObjectIds` and servants. This straightforward approach is used by default and is supported by the POA's built-in active object map.

In Figure 7.3(b), the POA maps many different `ObjectIds` to a single servant object. This approach might be appropriate for stateless servants. For example, it could be used for a servant that implements an interface for telling the time. This approach is supported by the POA's built-in active object map.

In Figure 7.3(c), the POA maintains a pool of servants. The mapping of `ObjectIds` to servants is carried out dynamically; as soon as an invocation request arrives, the POA attempts to locate the appropriate servant. This approach is not supported by the POA's active object map. Instead, you must take advantage of advanced POA features that allow you to customize `ObjectId` to servant mapping.

Once the servant is located, the POA automatically invokes the appropriate operation on it. However, if you want a greater degree of control over the POA, you can write code to select the operation yourself. This requires the use of the dynamic skeleton interface (DSI), described in Chapter 22, "Dynamic Skeleton Interface."

Servant Activation

In most cases, the association between an `ObjectId` and a servant is established when an entry is made in the POA's active object map. If the association is established in this way, it is called *activating the servant*. Removing an association from the active object map is called *deactivating the servant*.

Creating a CORBA object typically entails two steps:

1. Create a servant object.
2. Activate the servant object.

In addition, if you want to make this CORBA object available to clients, you create an object reference and export the object reference to a well-known location.

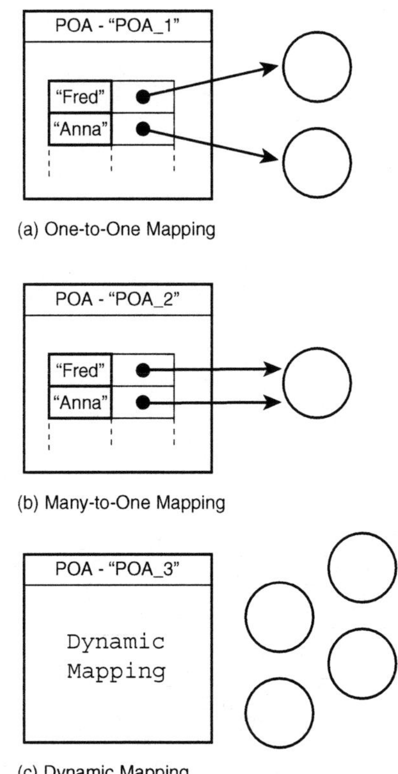

Figure 7.3

Different ways of mapping `ObjectIds` *to servants.*

The Role of the POA Manager

The picture of how invocation requests are routed to a servant object has been slightly simplified up to this point. Before an invocation request gets to the POA, it must first pass through a POA manager object. A POA manager is used to control the flow of requests into its associated POA (or POAs). This is illustrated in Figure 7.4.

A POA manager can be in one of four states: *holding*, *active*, *discarding,* and *inactive*. It acts as a kind of valve to control the flow of incoming requests. The POA manager must be put into the active state before its associated POA (or POAs) can begin processing requests.

The `RootPOA` Object and the POA Hierarchy

When a CORBA server boots up, there is initially just one POA object available, the `RootPOA`. The `RootPOA` is configured with a default set of POA policies and can be used right away to activate servant objects. Alternatively, the `RootPOA` can create new POA objects, *child POAs*, which can be configured to have a custom set of POA policies.

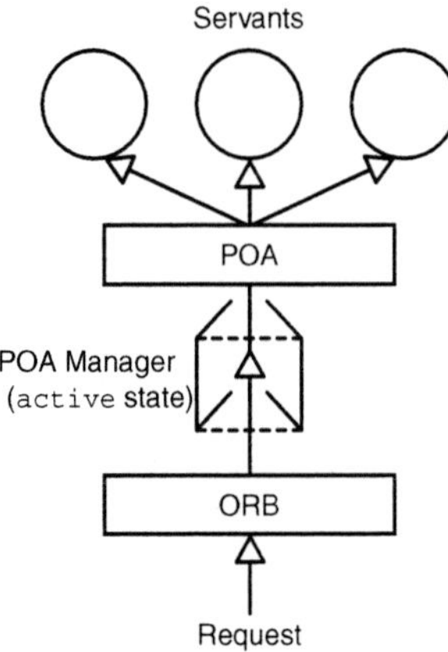

Figure 7.4

The POA manager controlling the flow of incoming requests.

The `PortableServer` module, however, enables you to create any number of POA objects using the `PortableServer::POA::create_POA( )` operation. A typical server would create a number of POA objects, with each of these POA objects configured to manage a group of CORBA objects in a particular way.

For example, if you have a server application that implements the `Customer` and `CustomerAdmin` IDL interfaces, you could create two separate POA objects:

- A POA object named `customer_POA` that manages `Customer` servant objects.
- A POA object named `customerAdmin_POA` that manages `CustomerAdmin` servant objects.

The resulting POA hierarchy is illustrated in Figure 7.5. At the top of the hierarchy is `RootPOA`. The two new POA objects are created as children of `RootPOA`.

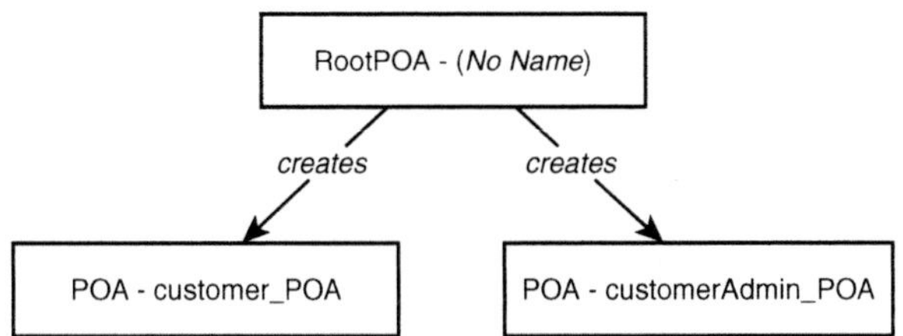

Figure 7.5

A sample POA hierarchy under the root POA.

Other arrangements of the hierarchy are possible. For example, the `customer_POA` POA could be created as a child of the `customerAdmin_POA` POA, which in turn could be created as a child of `RootPOA`. In this way you can create POA hierarchies that are nested to an arbitrary degree.

Obtaining a Reference to RootPOA

A reference to the RootPOA object is obtained using the initialization service, as shown in the following for C++ and Java:

```
//C++
CORBA::ORB_var global_orbV = CORBA::ORB::_nil();

int main(int argc, char * argv[])
{
    PortableServer::POA_var root_poaV;

    try {
        global_orbV = CORBA::ORB_init(argc, argv);
        CORBA::Object_var poa_objV =
            global_orbV->resolve_initial_references("RootPOA");
        root_poaV = PortableServer::POA::_narrow(poa_objV);
        if (CORBA::is_nil(poaV.in()) ) {
            cerr << "error: failed to narrow RootPOA object." << endl;
            return 1;
        }
    }
    catch (CORBA::SystemException&) {
        //Exception code not shown
    }
    ...
}

//Java
import org.omg.CORBA.*;

public class javaserver
{
  public static ORB global_orb;

  public static void main(String args[])
  {

    try
    {
        System.out.println("Initializing the ORB");

        global_orb = ORB.init(args, null);
        org.omg.CORBA.Object poa_obj
          = global_orb.resolve_initial_references("RootPOA");
        org.omg.PortableServer.POA root_poa
          = org.omg.PortableServer.POAHelper.narrow(poa_obj);
        //...
    }
```

```
    catch(org.omg.CORBA.SystemException ex)
    {
        //Exception code not shown
    }
  }
  //...
}
```

The `resolve_initial_references()` operation is invoked on the `CORBA::ORB` object with `"RootPOA"` as its argument.

Creating a Child POA

A child POA is created using the `PortableServer::POA::create_POA()` IDL operation. The definition of the `create_POA()` operation is given by the following IDL:

```
//IDL
module PortableServer {
    interface POA {
        POA create_POA(
            in string adapter_name,
            in POAManager a_POAManager,
            in CORBA::PolicyList policies
        )
        raises (AdapterAlreadyExists, InvalidPolicy);
        //...
    };
};
```

The `create_POA()` operation is invoked on an existing POA instance, the parent POA, and returns a reference to a new POA instance, the child POA. The `adapter_name` string identifies the new POA uniquely with respect to its parent POA.

The `a_POAManager` parameter is a reference to a `POAManager` object. If a `POAManager` object is specified for this parameter, it is used to control the flow of request messages into the child POA. Alternatively, if a nil object reference is specified, a new `POAManager` object is created for the child POA.

The `policies` parameter enables you to customize the configuration of the child POA. The `CORBA::PolicyList` type is a sequence of `CORBA::Policy` objects, as described in the next section.

POA Policies

Policies provide a generic mechanism for configuring a CORBA ORB. Each policy is represented by an object that inherits from the `CORBA::Policy` IDL interface. They are used extensively by the POA. Table 7.1 gives a list of standard POA policy types and the allowed values for each policy.

Table 7.1 POA Policy Types

POA Policy Type	Allowed Values
ThreadPolicy	ORB_CTRL_MODEL
	SINGLE_THREAD_MODEL
LifespanPolicy	TRANSIENT
	PERSISTENT
IdAssignmentPolicy	SYSTEM_ID
	USER_ID
IdUniquenessPolicy	UNIQUE_ID
	MULTIPLE_ID
RequestProcessingPolicy	USE_ACTIVE_OBJECT_MAP_ONLY
	USE_DEFAULT_SERVANT
	USE_SERVANT_MANAGER
ServantRetentionPolicy	RETAINNON_RETAIN
ImplicitActivationPolicy	NO_IMPLICIT_ACTIVATION
	IMPLICIT_ACTIVATION

When all of the POA policies are used in combination, theoretically there are a lot of ways of configuring a newly created POA. However, some policy combinations do not make sense and are not permitted.

Detailed explanations of each POA policy are presented later in this chapter in the context of code examples.

RootPOA Policies and Default POA Policies

POA policies are set at the time a POA object is created. They cannot subsequently be altered. Because the `RootPOA` object is implicitly created by the ORB, its POA policies are set automatically and are immutable. Table 7.2 shows the standard policy values used by the `RootPOA` object.

Table 7.2 Policy Values for **RootPOA**

POA Policy Type	RootPOA Policy Value
ThreadPolicy	ORB_CTRL_MODEL
LifespanPolicy	TRANSIENT
IdAssignmentPolicy	SYSTEM_ID
IdUniquenessPolicy	UNIQUE_ID
RequestProcessinPolicy	USE_ACTIVE_OBJECT_MAP_ONLY
ServantRetentionPolicy	RETAIN
ImplicitActivationPolicy	IMPLICIT_ACTIVATION

The POA policies for a child POA are set at creation time by the `CORBA::PolicyList` that is passed as one of the parameters to the `create_POA()` operation. Any policies not explicitly set in `CORBA::PolicyList` are implicitly set to a default value, as given in Table 7.3.

Table 7.3 Default Policy Values for Child POAs

POA Policy Type	Default Policy Value
ThreadPolicy	ORB_CTRL_MODEL
LifespanPolicy	TRANSIENT
IdAssignmentPolicy	SYSTEM_ID
IdUniquenessPolicy	UNIQUE_ID
RequestProcessinPolicy	USE_ACTIVE_OBJECT_MAP_ONLY
ServantRetentionPolicy	RETAIN
ImplicitActivationPolicy	NO_IMPLICIT_ACTIVATION

The ImplicitActivationPolicy default value, NO_IMPLICIT_ACTIVATION, is different from the RootPOA ImplicitActivationPolicy policy value, IMPLICIT_ACTIVATION.

CAUTION

The RootPOA policy values are distinct from the default policy values used by child POAs.

IDL for POA Policies

Listing 7.1 provides IDL extracts that show the interfaces and operations used for manipulating POA policies. Detailed code examples using POA policies are presented in the section "A POA for Session Objects" and in the sections following that.

Listing 7.1 IDL for POA Policies

```
//IDL

#pragma prefix "omg.org"

module CORBA {
    typedef unsigned long PolicyType;

    //Basic IDL definition
    interface Policy {
        readonly attribute PolicyType policy_type;
        Policy copy();
        void destroy();
    };

    typedef sequence<Policy> PolicyList;
};


module PortableServer {
    //...
    // Policy interfaces
    const CORBA::PolicyType THREAD_POLICY_ID = 16;
```

Listing 7.1 continued

```
const CORBA::PolicyType LIFESPAN_POLICY_ID = 17;
const CORBA::PolicyType ID_UNIQUENESS_POLICY_ID = 18;
const CORBA::PolicyType ID_ASSIGNMENT_POLICY_ID = 19;
const CORBA::PolicyType IMPLICIT_ACTIVATION_POLICY_ID = 20;
const CORBA::PolicyType SERVANT_RETENTION_POLICY_ID = 21;
const CORBA::PolicyType REQUEST_PROCESSING_POLICY_ID = 22;

enum ThreadPolicyValue {
    ORB_CTRL_MODEL,
    SINGLE_THREAD_MODEL
};
interface ThreadPolicy : CORBA::Policy {
    readonly attribute ThreadPolicyValue value;
};

enum LifespanPolicyValue {
    TRANSIENT,
    PERSISTENT
};
interface LifespanPolicy :  CORBA::Policy {
    readonly attribute LifespanPolicyValue value;
};

enum IdUniquenessPolicyValue {
    UNIQUE_ID,
    MULTIPLE_ID
};
interface IdUniquenessPolicy : CORBA::Policy {
    readonly attribute IdUniquenessPolicyValue value;
};

enum IdAssignmentPolicyValue {
    USER_ID,
    SYSTEM_ID
};
interface IdAssignmentPolicy : CORBA::Policy {
    readonly attribute IdAssignmentPolicyValue value;
};

enum ImplicitActivationPolicyValue {
    IMPLICIT_ACTIVATION,
    NO_IMPLICIT_ACTIVATION
};
interface ImplicitActivationPolicy : CORBA::Policy {
    readonly attribute ImplicitActivationPolicyValue value;
};
```

Listing 7.1 continued

```
    enum ServantRetentionPolicyValue {
        RETAIN,
        NON_RETAIN
    };
    interface ServantRetentionPolicy : CORBA::Policy {
        readonly attribute ServantRetentionPolicyValue value;
    };

    enum RequestProcessingPolicyValue {
        USE_ACTIVE_OBJECT_MAP_ONLY,
        USE_DEFAULT_SERVANT,
        USE_SERVANT_MANAGER
    };
    interface RequestProcessingPolicy : CORBA::Policy {
        readonly attribute RequestProcessingPolicyValue value;
    };

    // POA interface
    interface POA {
        //...
        // Factories for Policy objects
        ThreadPolicy create_thread_policy(
            in ThreadPolicyValue value
        );
        LifespanPolicy create_lifespan_policy(
            in LifespanPolicyValue value
        );
        IdUniquenessPolicy create_id_uniqueness_policy(
            in IdUniquenessPolicyValue value
        );
        IdAssignmentPolicy create_id_assignment_policy(
            in IdAssignmentPolicyValue value
        );
        ImplicitActivationPolicy create_implicit_activation_policy(
            in ImplicitActivationPolicyValue value
        );
        ServantRetentionPolicy create_servant_retention_policy(
            in ServantRetentionPolicyValue value
        );
        RequestProcessingPolicy create_request_processing_policy(
            in RequestProcessingPolicyValue value
        );
        //...
    };
    //...
};
```

Types of CORBA Objects

Before we present the different kinds of POAs that can be created using POA policies, it is helpful to divide CORBA objects into different categories. A number of common patterns can be identified. For example, some CORBA objects have their state stored in a database, and others do not. Some CORBA objects are short lived, others are long lived, some are transactional, and others are not transactional.

The basic categories discussed in this section are as follows:

- **Transient and Persistent Objects** These are categories specific to the POA and relate to the `TRANSIENT` and `PERSISTENT` lifespan policies.
- **Session and Entity Objects** These object categories are derived from component technologies, such as Sun's Enterprise JavaBeans (EJB) and the CORBA Components specification. They are used in this chapter in an informal way to motivate some of the POA policies.
- **Factory Objects** The concept of a factory object is derived from the CORBA Lifecycle Service and refers to objects that create other objects.

Transient and Persistent Objects

The POA distinguishes between the two following categories of CORBA object:

- **Transient Objects** Short-lived objects whose lifetime is bounded by the lifetime of the server process in which they are created.
- **Persistent Objects** Long-lived objects whose lifetime is unbounded. The server in which a persistent object is created can be started, stopped, and restarted multiple times. The persistent object remains valid throughout.

This concept is illustrated in Figure 7.6, which shows a server that is started and stopped three times in a row. The first time the server is started, it creates a transient object, `T1`, and a persistent object, `P`. At the end of the first run of the server, `T1` is destroyed and ceases to exist. The persistent object, `P`, remains valid but dormant.

When the server is started up for the second time, it creates a new transient object, `T2`. The old `T1` transient object is no longer accessible. If a client holds an object reference for the old `T1` session object and attempts to invoke an operation on it, it receives a `CORBA::OBJECT_NOT_EXIST` system exception from the server. In contrast to this, the persistent object, `P`, remains valid and can still have its operations invoked by a CORBA client.

The following two subsections summarize the basic properties of transient and persistent objects.

Transient Objects

Transient objects have the following basic properties:

- Transient objects typically represent short-lived objects that perform some work on behalf of clients.

For example, the RecycleBroker application from Chapter 3, "A Sample CORBA System," features the `Selling` and `Buying` interfaces that represent the action of a client selling or buying `WasteItem` objects. These interfaces can be implemented as transient objects.

- The lifetime of a transient object is bounded by the lifetime of the POA instance that is used to activate it.
- Once its associated POA has been destroyed, any attempt to use a transient object reference generates a `CORBA::OBJECT_NOT_EXIST` system exception.
- The fact that transient objects are guaranteed to be short lived enables an ORB implementation to make optimizations. In some ORBs, interoperable object references (IORs) are constructed in a special way for transient objects. For example, transient IORs typically hold location details for making a direct connection to the server, bypassing any ORB daemon process.

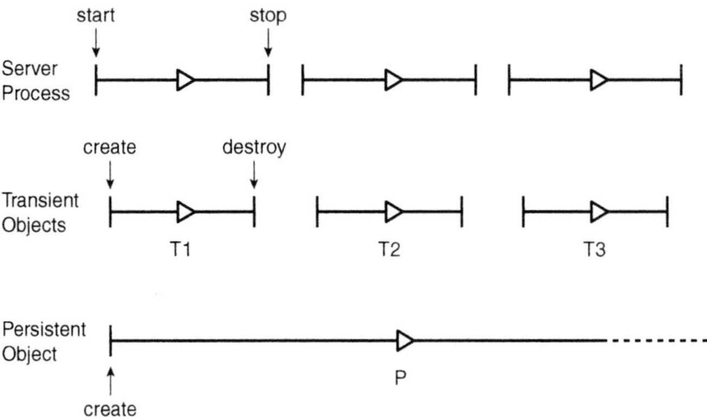

Figure 7.6

The lifecycles of transient and persistent objects.

Persistent Objects

Persistent objects have the following basic properties:

- Persistent objects typically represent objects with persistent state that is stored in a database.

  For example, the `RecycleBroker` application from Chapter 3 features the `RecycleBroker::Customer` and `RecycleBroker::WasteItem` interfaces. These interfaces represent `Customer` and `WasteItem` records, respectively, that are stored in a database. The interfaces can be implemented as persistent objects.
- The lifetime of a persistent object is unbounded.
- Once its associated POA has been destroyed, a persistent object becomes dormant. It can be reactivated, however, when the server is restarted and the POA reinstantiated.

- In some ORBs, IORs specify the details for making a connection to a form of locator daemon instead of specifying a direct connection to the server. This enables an ORB to automatically restart the server process if necessary. The client is redirected to the appropriate server process using the GIOP location-forwarding mechanism (see Chapter 16, "The Internet Inter-ORB Protocol").

Session and Entity Objects

In concept, session and entity objects are closely related to transient and persistent objects. The terminology of session and entity objects appears in both the Enterprise JavaBeans specification and the CORBA Components specification.

The terms *session object* and *entity object* are not used in the core CORBA specification. However, it is helpful to introduce the terms informally to motivate POA policies and use patterns. In this chapter, the terms are used in the following way:

- Session object—A transient object, augmented by its typical usage pattern.
- Entity object—A persistent object, augmented by its typical usage pattern.

Session Objects

A session object is typically

- **Short-lived** It is created with a transient lifespan.
- **Non-persistent** The state of a session object does not need to be stored in a database. However, a session object can provide access to a database.

These two characteristics of a session object influence how its lifecycle is managed. Figure 7.7 illustrates how a CORBA session object is created.

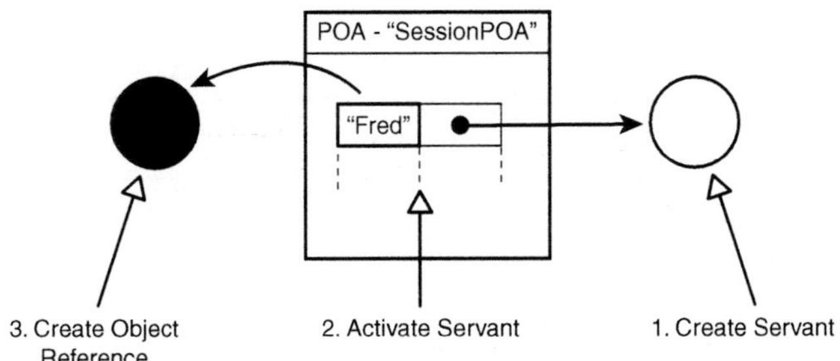

Figure 7.7

Creating a CORBA session object.

A session object is created in three steps:

1. **Create the servant object** The servant is initialized with state that depends on the context in which it is created.

2. **Activate the servant object** The servant is activated with a POA that has a lifespan policy equal to `TRANSIENT`.
3. **Create an object reference** The object reference is exported to advertise the session object to clients.

Entity Objects

An entity object is typically

- **Long-lived** It is created with a persistent lifespan.
- **Persistent** It usually has some state that must be stored in a database.

These two characteristics of an entity object influence how its lifecycle is managed. Figure 7.8 illustrates how a CORBA entity object is created.

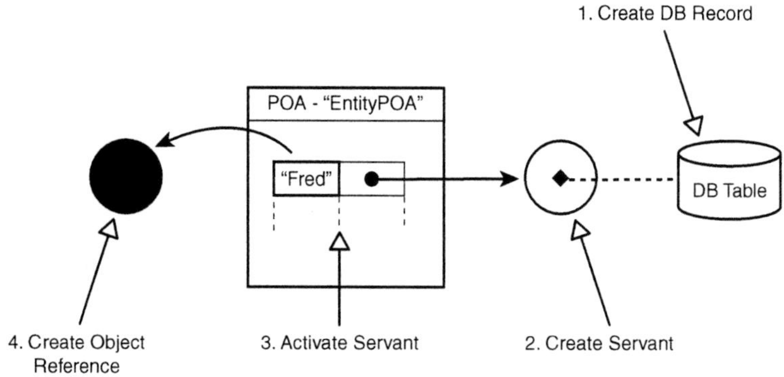

Figure 7.8

Creating a CORBA entity object.

An entity object is created in four steps:

1. **Create a database record** The database record holds the persistent state of the entity object.
2. **Create the servant object** The servant is initialized by reading its state from the database.
3. **Activate the servant object** The servant is activated with a POA that has a lifespan policy equal to `PERSISTENT`.
4. **Create an object reference** The object reference is exported to advertise the session object to clients.

Factory Objects

In the context of the POA, factory objects are important because they are concerned with lifecycle operations such as creating, finding, and destroying other objects.

For example, in the RecycleBroker application of Chapter 3, `WasteItem` objects are managed by the `WasteItemAdmin` interface. The `WasteItemAdmin` interface features operations for creating and finding `WasteItem` objects.

The implementation of the `create()` function depends heavily on the particular style of lifecycle management used for the `WasteItem` objects. It is affected by the fact that `WasteItem` objects are entity objects and by the exact choice of POA policies. There are two main sorts of factory objects:

- **Factory objects for session objects** The `create()` operation performs the three steps described in the previous section to create a session object.
- **Factory objects for entity objects** The `create()` operation performs the four steps listed previously to create an entity object.

The factory objects themselves may be either session or entity objects. A factory object that serves as the first point of contact between client and server is often treated as an entity object. For example, in the RecycleBroker application the `BranchOffice` and `HeadOffice` interfaces might be implemented as entity objects.

Sub-factories created by other factories are often treated as session objects. There is no need to make the sub-factories long lived, because they can easily be regenerated by invoking on the original factory. For example, in the RecycleBroker application, the `Browsing` factory interface might be implemented as a session object.

A POA for Session Objects

This section describes how to create and use a POA instance that is appropriate for activating and managing session objects. The sample IDL used to illustrate the POA for session objects is given in Listing 7.2.

Listing 7.2 A Sample IDL

```
//IDL

module RecycleBroker {
    //...

    // Interface for Session Objects
    interface Browsing {
        // operations and attributes not shown...
    };

    // Base Interface for Session Object Factory
    interface Office {
        Browsing get_browsing();
    };

    // Interface for Session Object Factory
    interface BranchOffice :  Office { };
};
```

This example is based on the RecycleBroker application described in Chapter 3.

`Browsing` objects are created for a short time to allow a particular user to browse the list of available `WasteItems`. A `Browsing` object has the characteristics of a session object.

The `BranchOffice::get_browsing()` operation (inherited from the `Office` interface) creates `Browsing` objects on demand. A `BranchOffice` object has the characteristics of a session object factory.

This section is divided into three parts that explain how to create and use a POA that is appropriate for activating and managing session objects.

Creating the POA

For convenience, a class `POAUtility` and a static function `POAUtility::create_basic_POA()` are defined here to encapsulate the basic steps needed to create a POA for session objects. The code for the static `create_basic_POA()` function is shown for C++ in Listing 7.3 and for Java in Listing 7.4. The `create_basic_POA()` function is basically a wrapper for the `PortableServer::POA::create_POA()` function:

Listing 7.3 C++ Creating a POA for Session Objects

```
//C++
#include "POAUtility.h"

PortableServer::POA_ptr
POAUtility::create_basic_POA(
    PortableServer::POA_ptr           parentPOAP,
    PortableServer::POAManager_ptr    POAManagerP,
    char *                            POAName,
    CORBA::Boolean                    isMultiThread,
    CORBA::Boolean                    isPersistent
)
{
    // Create a policy list.
    CORBA::PolicyList policies;
    policies.length(3);
    CORBA::ULong i = 0;

    // Thread Policy
    PortableServer::ThreadPolicyValue threadPolicy;

    if (isMultiThread) {
        threadPolicy = PortableServer::ORB_CTRL_MODEL;
    }
    else {
        threadPolicy = PortableServer::SINGLE_THREAD_MODEL;
    }
    policies[i] = parentPOAP->create_thread_policy(threadPolicy);

    // Lifespan and IdAssignment Policies
    PortableServer::LifespanPolicyValue     lifeSpanPolicy;
    PortableServer::IdAssignmentPolicyValue idAssignPolicy;

    if (isPersistent) {
        // Policies for 'Entity' objects
```

Listing 7.3 continued

```
        lifeSpanPolicy = PortableServer::PERSISTENT;
        idAssignPolicy = PortableServer::USER_ID;
    }
    else {
        // Policies for 'Session' objects
        lifeSpanPolicy = PortableServer::TRANSIENT;
        idAssignPolicy = PortableServer::SYSTEM_ID;
    }

    // Lifespan Policy
    i++;
    policies[i] = parentPOAP->create_lifespan_policy(lifeSpanPolicy);

    // IdAssignment Policy
    i++;
    policies[i] = parentPOAP->create_id_assignment_policy(idAssignPolicy);

    // IdUniqueness Policy         - Default = UNIQUE_ID

    // ImplicitActivation Policy   - Default = NO_IMPLICIT_ACTIVATION

    // RequestProcessing Policy    - Default = USE_ACTIVE_OBJECT_MAP_ONLY

    // ServantRetention Policy     - Default = RETAIN

    return parentPOAP->create_POA(POAName,  POAManagerP, policies);
}
```

Listing 7.4 Java Creating a POA for Session Objects

```
//Java
package Pure.Util;

import org.omg.PortableServer.*;

public class POAUtility {
  public static org.omg.PortableServer.POA
  create_basic_POA(
        org.omg.PortableServer.POA        parentPOA,
        org.omg.PortableServer.POAManager POAManager,
        String                            POAName,
        boolean                           isMultiThread,
        boolean                           isPersistent
  )
  throws org.omg.PortableServer.POAPackage.InvalidPolicy,
         org.omg.PortableServer.POAPackage.AdapterAlreadyExists
  {
    // Create a policy list.
    org.omg.CORBA.Policy policies[] = new org.omg.CORBA.Policy[3];
    int i = 0;
```

Listing 7.3 continued

```
    // Thread Policy
    org.omg.PortableServer.ThreadPolicyValue threadPolicy = null;

    if (isMultiThread) {
        threadPolicy = ThreadPolicyValue.ORB_CTRL_MODEL;
    }
    else {
        threadPolicy = ThreadPolicyValue.SINGLE_THREAD_MODEL;
    }
    policies[i] = parentPOA.create_thread_policy(threadPolicy);

    // Lifespan and IdAssignment Policies
    org.omg.PortableServer.LifespanPolicyValue     lifeSpanPolicy = null;
    org.omg.PortableServer.IdAssignmentPolicyValue idAssignPolicy = null;

    if (isPersistent) {
        // Policies for 'Entity' objects
        lifeSpanPolicy = LifespanPolicyValue.PERSISTENT;
        idAssignPolicy = IdAssignmentPolicyValue.USER_ID;
    }
    else {
        // Policies for 'Session' objects
        lifeSpanPolicy = LifespanPolicyValue.TRANSIENT;
        idAssignPolicy = IdAssignmentPolicyValue.SYSTEM_ID;
    }

    // Lifespan Policy
    i++;
    policies[i] = parentPOA.create_lifespan_policy(lifeSpanPolicy);

    // IdAssignment Policy
    i++;
    policies[i] = parentPOA.create_id_assignment_policy(idAssignPolicy);

    // IdUniqueness Policy        -  Default = UNIQUE_ID

    // ImplicitActivation Policy  -  Default = NO_IMPLICIT_ACTIVATION

    // RequestProcessing Policy   -  Default = USE_ACTIVE_OBJECT_MAP_ONLY

    // ServantRetention Policy    -  Default = RETAIN

    return parentPOA.create_POA(POAName,  POAManager, policies);
  }
  //...
}
```

The first parameter, `parentPOAP`, is a reference to the POA that serves as a parent to the POA returned by this function.

The second parameter, `POAManagerP`, specifies the `POAManager` object that is passed into `create_POA()` and controls the flow of messages into the newly created POA.

The third parameter, `POAName`, sets the name of the newly created POA (relative to the parent POA).

The fourth parameter, `isMultiThread`, determines whether or not you want this POA to be multithreaded. This is discussed in more detail in the next section.

The fifth parameter, `isPersistent`, determines whether objects activated by this POA will be short lived or long lived. Effectively, it determines whether you want to treat your objects as session objects or entity objects. In this example, it is always set equal to `FALSE` to indicate session objects.

The body of the `create_basic_POA()` function is taken up mostly with initializing the list of policies. `CORBA::PolicyList` is declared as `sequence<CORBA::Policy>` and contains a list of `CORBA::Policy` objects that are used to initialize the POA returned by `create_POA()`. Listing 7.1 shows the IDL used to create individual POA `CORBA::Policy` objects.

The three policies explicitly set here are discussed in the following sections.

Thread Policy

The thread policy, of `PortableServer::ThreadPolicy` type, specifies whether the newly created POA is single-threaded or multithreaded. There are two possible values for this policy:

- `SINGLE_THREAD_MODEL`
  This policy value makes the POA single-threaded. Invocation requests are dispatched to the POA's servants in a sequential manner. Only one request at a time is processed. This policy value is useful if you want to implement servants that are not thread aware.
  However, using a single-threaded POA does not necessarily isolate servants from threading issues. If the application as a whole is multithreaded, some servant methods might be invoked directly from multiple threads, or the servants might need to access synchronized resources. Servants managed by a single-threaded POA need to be thread aware under these circumstances.
- `ORB_CTRL_MODEL`
  This policy value makes the POA multithreaded. However, details of the multithreading model are not described in the CORBA standard. Typically, an ORB provides some kind of thread pool to process requests: As each request arrives at the POA, it is assigned to the next available thread. In this way, many requests can execute concurrently. This policy value requires servant code to be thread aware.

Lifespan Policy

The lifespan policy, of `PortableServer::LifespanPolicy`, is used to indicate whether the POA's objects are transient or persistent. There are two possible values for this policy:

- `TRANSIENT`
  This policy value specifies that the POA's objects are short lived. The lifetime of an object activated by a particular POA instance is bounded by the lifetime of the POA instance. Once the POA has been deactivated, its objects permanently cease to exist. This policy value is always used for session objects.
- `PERSISTENT`
  This policy value specifies that the POA's objects are long lived (entity objects). Objects activated by this POA can continue to exist after the POA has been deactivated and the server process shut down. This policy value is always used for entity objects.

ID Assignment Policy

The ID assignment policy, of `PortableServer::IdAssignmentPolicy` type, is used to indicate whether `ObjectIds` are assigned by the developer or automatically assigned by the POA:

- `SYSTEM_ID`
  This policy value specifies that the POA always automatically generates its own `ObjectIds`. For short-lived objects, this policy value is very convenient. It saves the administrative overhead of having to maintain some kind of counter to generate `ObjectIds` yourself.
- `USER_ID`
  This policy value specifies that the developer must always supply the `ObjectId` used to identify a servant. The `ObjectId` must be unique per POA.
  Typically, this policy value is needed for entity objects. For example, it allows a developer to embed a database key in an `ObjectId`.

The `IdAssignmentPolicy` value determines which operation you are allowed to call to activate a servant object. There are two IDL operations provided for activating servants:

```
//IDL
module PortableServer {
    //...
    // POA interface
    interface POA {
        exception ObjectAlreadyActive {};
        exception ServantAlreadyActive {};
        exception WrongPolicy {};

        // Compatible with 'SYSTEM_ID' policy value
        ObjectId activate_object(
            in Servant p_servant)
        raises (ServantAlreadyActive, WrongPolicy);
```

```
        // Compatible with 'USER_ID' policy value
        void activate_object_with_id(
            in ObjectId id,
            in Servant p_servant)
        raises ( ServantAlreadyActive, ObjectAlreadyActive, WrongPolicy);
    };
};
```

The `activate_object()` operation can be used only for a POA that has a `SYSTEM_ID` policy value. The `activate_object_with_id()` operation is mainly intended to be used for a POA that has a `USER_ID` policy value. The operation can also be used for a POA that has a `SYSTEM_ID` policy value, but only if the supplied object ID was previously generated by the system.

The use of the `activate_object()` and `activate_object_with_id()` operations is illustrated by example in this section and in the following sections.

Implementing a Session Object Factory

The way to create and activate a servant object is affected by the particular set of policies chosen for the POA. The implementation of the `RecycleBroker::BranchOffice::get_browsing()` operation, given in Listing 7.5 and Listing 7.6, illustrates how to create a session object of `Browsing` type.

Listing 7.5 C++ Implementation of the `RecycleBroker::BranchOffice::get_browsing()` *Operation*

```
//C++
//-----------------------------------------------------
// Given the following variables:
//    m_poa_for_childrenV - a cached pointer to a 'PortableServer::POA' object
//        used for activating and managing 'Browsing' objects.
//        It is a private member variable of 'RecycleBroker_BranchOffice_i'
//        and is initialized by the constructor.
//

RecycleBroker::Browsing_ptr

RecycleBroker_BranchOffice_i::get_browsing()
throw (CORBA::SystemException)
{
    PortableServer::ServantBase_var the_BrowsingV;
    PortableServer::ObjectId_var    oidV;
    CORBA::Object_var               objV;
    RecycleBroker::Browsing_var     refV;

    cout << "RecycleBroker_BranchOffice_i::get_browsing() called"
         << endl;

    // Case: Use Basic POA
```

Listing 7.5 continued

```
    // Step 1 - Create a 'Browsing_i' servant object
    // (constructor arguments not shown)
    the_BrowsingV = new RecycleBroker_Browsing_i();

    // Step 2 - Activate the CORBA object
    oidV = m_poa_for_childrenV->activate_object(the_BrowsingV.in());

    // Step 3 - Create an object reference
    objV = m_poa_for_childrenV->id_to_reference(oidV);
    refV = RecycleBroker::Browsing::_narrow(objV.in() );

    return refV. _retn();
}
```

Listing 7.6 Java Implementation of the `get_browsing()` Operation

```
//Java
//-------------------------------------------------------
// Given the following variables:
//    m_poa_for_children - a cached reference to a 'PortableServer.POA' object
//        used for activating and managing 'Browsing' objects.
//        It is a private member variable of 'RecycleBroker_BranchOffice_i'
//        and is initialized by the constructor.
//
package Pure.POADemo;

import Pure.POADemo.RecycleBroker.*;

public class RecycleBroker_BranchOffice_i
    extends  BranchOfficePOA
{
  // IDL operations
  public Browsing get_browsing()
  throws org.omg.CORBA.SystemException
  {
    org.omg.PortableServer.Servant the_Browsing;
    byte[]                         oid;
    org.omg.CORBA.Object           obj;
    Browsing                       ref;

    System.out.println("RecycleBroker_BranchOffice_i.get_browsing() called");

    // Case: Use Basic POA

    // Step 1 - Create a 'Browsing_i' servant object
    // (constructor arguments not shown)
    the_Browsing = new RecycleBroker_Browsing_i();
```

Listing 7.6 continued

```
        try {
            // Step 2 - Activate the CORBA object
            oid = m_poa_for_children.activate_object(the_Browsing);

            // Step 3 - Create an object reference
            obj = m_poa_for_children.id_to_reference(oid);
            ref = BrowsingHelper.narrow(obj);
        }
        catch (Exception ex) {
            // Error: details of exception handling not shown
            ref = null;
        }

        return ref;
    }
    //...
}
```

The `get_browsing()` operation creates and returns an object reference for a `RecycleBroker::Browsing` object. The `m_poa_for_childrenV` variable is a private member variable that caches a pointer to the POA used to activate new `Browsing` objects.

Because the `Browsing` interface fits the pattern of a session object, the three steps illustrated in Figure 7.7 are used to create the `Browsing` CORBA object.

1. **Create the servant object** Though not shown in this example, typically the servant constructor for a session object is initialized with some arguments.
2. **Activate the servant object** Because the POA has been created with an ID assignment policy of `SYSTEM_ID`, the developer must call `activate_object()` to activate the servant. The return value of `activate_object()` is an automatically generated `ObjectId` for the servant.
3. **Create an object reference** The `id_to_reference()` operation is used to convert the `ObjectId` to a `Browsing` object reference that can be returned from `get_browsing()`.

Creating the Factory

The `BranchOffice` factory object can create any number of `Browsing` objects on demand. Before this can happen, however, there must be at least one instance of a `BranchOffice` object to get things started. Listing 7.7 and Listing 7.8 show how the `BranchOffice` object is created and activated.

Listing 7.7 C++ Creating and Activating a `BranchOffice` Object

```
//C++
//-----------------------------------------------------
// Given the following variables:
//     root_poaV - a pointer to the root POA object.
//     root_poa_managerV - the root POAManager object that is
```

Listing 7.7 continued

```
//        obtained from the root POA object.
//
...
// Create a basic POA for 'Session' objects.
basic_session_poaV =
    POAUtility::create_basic_POA(
        root_poaV.in(),
        root_poa_managerV.in(),
        "basic_session_poa",
        0,                  // Single threaded
        0                   // for 'Session' objects
    );

//---------------------------------------
// Create Factories and export their object references.
//---------------------------------------
PortableServer::ObjectId_var oidV;
CORBA::Object_var refV;

// Step 1 - Create a servant for the 'BranchOffice' interface.
the_BranchOfficeV = new RecycleBroker_BranchOffice_i(
    basic_session_poaV.in(),        //POA for the Factory
    basic_session_poaV.in()         //POA for the children
);

// Step 2 - Activate the CORBA object
oidV = basic_session_poaV->activate_object(the_BranchOfficeV.in());

// Step 3 - Create an object reference
refV = basic_session_poaV->id_to_reference(oidV);

// Export the 'BranchOffice' object reference,  'refV', to the Naming Service
...
```

Listing 7.8 Java Creating and Activating a `BranchOffice` Object

```
//Java
//-----------------------------------------------------
// Given the following variables:
//    root_poa - a reference to the root POA object.
//    root_poa_manager - the root POAManager object that is
//        obtained from the root POA object.
//
...
// Create a basic POA for 'Session' objects.
POA basic_session_poa =
    Pure.Util.POAUtility.create_basic_POA(
        root_poa,
        root_poa_manager,
```

Listing 7.8 continued

```
        "basic_session_poa",
        false,                  // Single threaded
        false                   // for 'Session' objects
    );

//-----------------------------------------
// Create Factories and export their object references.
//-----------------------------------------
byte[] oid = null;
org.omg.CORBA.Object ref = null;

// Step 1 - Create a servant for the 'BranchOffice' interface.
Servant the_BranchOffice = new RecycleBroker_BranchOffice_i(
    basic_session_poa               //POA for the children
);

// Step 2 - Activate the CORBA object
oid = basic_session_poa.activate_object(the_BranchOffice);

// Step 3 - Create an object reference
ref = basic_session_poa.id_to_reference(oid);

// Export the 'BranchOffice' object reference, 'refV',  to the Naming Service
...
```

The basic_session_poaV object is created using the POAUtility::create_basic_POA() function. This is the POA used to activate session objects in this example.

Because the BranchOffice object itself is created as a session object, the steps to create and activate a BranchOffice object are essentially the same as the steps for Browsing objects in the previous section.

Note that the RecycleBroker_BranchOffice_i constructor takes two arguments. The first is the POA used to activate this BranchOffice object; the second is the POA that will be used to activate the Browsing objects created by the BranchOffice object. In this case, the same POA can be used for both purposes.

A POA for Entity Objects

This section describes how to create and use a POA that is appropriate for activating and managing entity objects. The sample IDL used to illustrate the POA for entity objects is given in Listing 7.9.

Listing 7.9 A Sample IDL

```
//IDL

module RecycleBroker {
    //...
```

Listing 7.9 continued

```
    typedef long        KeyType;
    typedef float       PriceType;
    enum WasteType {
        BROWN_GLASS, GREEN_GLASS, CLEAR_GLASS, SCRAP_STEEL,
        ALUMINIUM_CANS, PLASTIC_BOTTLES, WASTE_PAPER
    };

    // struct RecycleBroker::WasteItemDetails
    struct WasteItemDetails {
        WasteType       waste;
        long            quantity;
        PriceType       price_per_kilo;
    };

    // Interface for Entity Objects
    interface WasteItem {
        // operations and attributes not shown...
    };

    // Interface for Entity Object Factory
    interface WasteItemAdmin {
        WasteItem create(
             in  WasteItemDetails initialData,
             out KeyType          wasteitem_id
        );
        WasteItem find(in KeyType wasteitem_id);
    };
};
```

A `WasteItem` object represents a consignment of waste of a particular `WasteType`, for example `BROWN_GLASS` or `SCRAP_STEEL`. The `WasteItemDetails` struct encapsulates some of the properties of a `WasteItem` object. A `WasteItem` object has the characteristics of an entity object.

The `WasteItemAdmin` interface is effectively a factory for creating and managing `WasteItem` objects. Two operations are defined:

- The `create()` operation creates a new `WasteItem` object and returns an object reference for it. The first parameter, a `WasteItemDetails` struct, is used to initialize the new `WasteItem`. The second parameter, `wasteitem_id`, is an `out` parameter that returns the database key associated with the new `WasteItem` object.
- The `find()` operation finds an existing `WasteItem` object. It takes the `wasteitem_id` database key as its argument and returns the corresponding `WasteItem` object reference.

A `BranchOffice` object has the characteristics of an entity object factory.

This section is divided into five parts explaining how to create and use a POA that is appropriate for activating and managing entity objects.

Creating the POA

The `POAUtility::create_basic_POA()` function, presented in Listing 7.3 and Listing 7.4, can also be used to create a POA suitable for entity objects. The function is called with the `isPersistent` argument equal to `TRUE` and the `isMultiThread` argument equal to `FALSE` (see Listing 7.16 and Listing 7.17).

In this example, the set of POA policies used to manage entity objects is given in Table 7.4.

Table 7.4 POA Policies Used for Entity Objects

Policy Name	Policy Value
ThreadPolicy	SINGLE_THREAD_MODEL
LifespanPolicy	PERSISTENT
IdAssignmentPolicy	USER_ID
IdUniquenessPolicy	UNIQUE_ID
ImplicitActivationPolicy	NO_IMPLICIT_ACTIVATION
RequestProcessingPolicy	USE_ACTIVE_OBJECT_MAP_ONLY
ServantRetentionPolicy	RETAIN

Two of these policies relate specifically to the management of entity objects:

- The `PERSISTENT` lifespan policy value specifies that objects managed by this POA can outlive the server process in which they are created.
- The `USER_ID` ID assignment policy value specifies that `ObjectId`s are set explicitly instead of being automatically generated.

The last four policies are left at their default values. These policies are discussed as the need arises in the later sections of this chapter.

Mapping Database Keys to `ObjectId`s

Because the ID assignment policy for this POA is equal to `USER_ID`, the developer is responsible for choosing `ObjectId`s for its CORBA objects. Fundamentally, the ORB combines two pieces of information on the server side to uniquely identify a CORBA object:

- A POA name (or sequence of names, in the case of a nested POA hierarchy).
- An `ObjectId`, which is required to be unique per POA.

Given an `ObjectId`, you want to be able to find the corresponding persistent object. When an entity object's state is stored in a database, it makes sense to embed the object's database key in the `ObjectId`. The database key alone, however, is not enough. You also need to know which table to search to retrieve the object's state. Since objects of a particular type are usually stored in the same table, it is often enough to identify the type of the CORBA object in addition to its key.

NOTE

The ORB does not use the type of an object to track its identity. This makes sense in general. However, for this particular example it is convenient to have the type of the object form part of its identity.

The approach used here is to embed both the type of the CORBA object and its database key in the `ObjectId`. The type of the CORBA object is represented here by its local interface name (you could also use `CORBA::RepositoryId` or a more compact hash key) and the database key is assumed to be an integer. The format used for an `ObjectId` is *`interface_name db_key`*, where a single space serves as a separator. For example, a `WasteItem` object with the database key `1234` is mapped to the following `ObjectId`:

```
WasteItem 1234
```

An `ObjectId` is, in fact, not a string but a sequence of octets. In C++, the following functions are provided to convert between string and `ObjectId` types:

```
//C++
//Conversion between 'ObjectId' and narrow strings.
PortableServer::ObjectId *  PortableServer::string_to_ObjectId(const char * s);
char* PortableServer::ObjectId_to_string(const PortableServer::ObjectId& oid);

//Conversion between 'ObjectId' and wide strings.
PortableServer::ObjectId *
PortableServer::wstring_to_ObjectId(const CORBA::WChar * ws);
CORBA::WChar *
PortableServer::ObjectId_to_wstring(const PortableServer::ObjectId& oid);
```

In Java an `ObjectId` is represented as a byte array, `byte[]`, which can be converted to and from a string format using `java.lang.String.String(byte[])` and `java.lang.String.getBytes()`.

The sample application uses the helper class `ObjectIdMapper` to perform the mapping between `ObjectId`s and an interface name/database key combination. Listing 7.10 and Listing 7.11 give the implementation of this class in C++ and Java, respectively.

Listing 7.10 C++ Implementation of the `ObjectIdMapper` Class

```
//C++
//--------------------------------------------
// class 'ObjectIdMapper'
//--------------------------------------------

#include <sstream>
#include "ObjectIdMapper.h"

// Manipulation of 'ObjectId'
```

Listing 7.10 continued

```
PortableServer::ObjectId *
ObjectIdMapper::make_ObjectId(const char * type,  CORBA::Long key)
{
    std::ostringstream ost;

    ost << type << " " << (int) key;

    return PortableServer::string_to_ObjectId(ost.str().c_str());
}

CORBA::Long
ObjectIdMapper::extract_key_from_ObjectId(const PortableServer::ObjectId & oid)
{
    CORBA::String_var strV;
    std::string       type;
    CORBA::Long       key;

    strV = PortableServer::ObjectId_to_string(oid);
    std::string s = strV.in();
    std::istringstream ist(s);
    ist >> type >> key;

    return key;
}

char *
ObjectIdMapper::extract_type_from_ObjectId(
    const PortableServer::ObjectId & oid
)
{
    CORBA::String_var strV;
    std::string       type;
    CORBA::Long       key;

    strV = PortableServer::ObjectId_to_string(oid);
    std::string s = strV.in();
    std::istringstream ist(s);
    ist >> type >> key;

    return CORBA::string_dup(type.c_str());
}
```

Listing 7.11 Java Implementation of the `ObjectIdMapper` Class

```
//Java
//-----------------------------------------------
// class 'ObjectIdMapper'
//-----------------------------------------------
```

Listing 7.10 continued

```
package Pure.POADemo;

public class ObjectIdMapper {

  // Manipulation of 'ObjectId'
  public static byte[]
  make_ObjectId(String type, int key)
  {
    String out_str = type + " " + key;

    return out_str.getBytes();
  }

  public static int
  extract_key_from_ObjectId(byte[] oid)
  {
    String str = new String(oid);

    int indexOfDelimiter = str.indexOf(' ');
    int key  = Integer.parseInt(
                      str.substring(indexOfDelimiter+1, str.length())
               );

    return key;
  }

  public static String
  extract_type_from_ObjectId(byte[] oid)
  {
    String str = new String(oid);

    int indexOfDelimiter = str.indexOf(' ');
    String type = str.substring(0, indexOfDelimiter);

    return type;
  }
}
```

The `ObjectIdMapper` class is used throughout this chapter to manage the `ObjectIds` associated with entity objects.

Managing the Database Record

It is assumed that a `WasteItem` object has its state stored persistently, for example in a database. The mechanism for storing and retrieving the state of `WasteItem` objects is not presented here—see Chapter 13, "Persistent State Service," for a discussion of how to make CORBA objects persistent.

One aspect of persistent storage that does concern us in this chapter is how to create and find database records for `WasteItem` objects. This functionality is needed by the `WasteItemAdmin` factory object.

Two static functions are added to the `WasteItem` class to support creating and finding `WasteItem` database records, as shown in Listing 7.12 and Listing 7.13.

Listing 7.12 C++ Declaration of Functions to Create and Find Database Records

```
//C++
class RecycleBroker_WasteItem_i :
    public virtual ServantBaseOverrides,
    public virtual POA_RecycleBroker::WasteItem
{
public:
    static CORBA::Boolean
    _find_DB_record(CORBA::Long key);

    static CORBA::Long
    _create_DB_record(
        const RecycleBroker::WasteItemDetails& initialData
    );
    //...
};
```

Listing 7.13 Java Declaration of Functions to Create and Find Database Records

```
//Java
package Pure.POADemo;

import Pure.POADemo.RecycleBroker.*;

public class RecycleBroker_WasteItem_i extends WasteItemPOA
{
  public static boolean
  _find_DB_record(int key)
  {
    //...
  }

  public static int
  _create_DB_record(WasteItemDetails initialData)
  {
    //...
  }
  //...
};
```

The `_find_DB_record()` function is used to find an existing `WasteItem` database record in which the `key` argument is the primary key of the `WasteItem` database table. The function returns `TRUE` if a record is found and `FALSE` otherwise.

The `_create_DB_record()` function is used to create a new `WasteItem` database record. The `initialData` argument initializes the record, and the return value gives the record's primary key.

The implementation of the two functions is not shown here—it is primarily an exercise in database programming. Typically, the two functions would be implemented using embedded Structured Query Language (SQL) code to access and update the database.

Implementing an Entity Object Factory

The `create()` and `find()` operations of the `WasteItemAdmin` class are implemented in Listing 7.14 and Listing 7.15 for C++ and Java, respectively.

Listing 7.14 C++ Implementation of the `RecycleBroker::WasteItemAdmin::create()` *and* `find()` *Operations*

```
//C++
// create() - Implements IDL operation "RecycleBroker::WasteItemAdmin::create".
RecycleBroker::WasteItem_ptr
RecycleBroker_WasteItemAdmin_i::create(
    const RecycleBroker::WasteItemDetails& initialData,
    RecycleBroker::KeyType_out       wasteitem_id
) throw (
    CORBA::SystemException,
    RecycleBroker::NoPermission
)
{
    PortableServer::ObjectId_var    oidV;
    PortableServer::ServantBase_var servantV;
    CORBA::Object_var               objV;
    RecycleBroker::WasteItem_var    refV;

    // Case: Use Basic POA

    // Step 1 - Create a database record.
    wasteitem_id  = RecycleBroker_WasteItem_i::_create_DB_record(initialData);

    // Construct an 'ObjectId' from the database key, 'wasteitem_id'
    oidV = ObjectIdMapper::make_ObjectId("WasteItem", wasteitem_id);

    // Step 2 - Create the servant object.
    servantV = new RecycleBroker_WasteItem_i(
                   m_poa_for_childrenV.in(),
                   wasteitem_id
               );
```

Listing 7.14 continued

```
    // Step 3 - Activate the servant object.
    m_poa_for_childrenV->activate_object_with_id(
                oidV,
                servantV.in()
            );

    // Step 4 - Create an object reference.
    objV = m_poa_for_childrenV->id_to_reference(oidV.in() );
    refV = RecycleBroker::WasteItem::_narrow(objV.in() );

    return refV._retn();
}


// find() -- Implements IDL operation "RecycleBroker::WasteItemAdmin::find".

RecycleBroker::WasteItem_ptr
RecycleBroker_WasteItemAdmin_i::find(
    RecycleBroker::KeyType          wasteitem_id
) throw (
    CORBA::SystemException
)
{
    PortableServer::ObjectId_var    oidV;
    PortableServer::ServantBase_var servantV;
    CORBA::Object_var               objV;
    RecycleBroker::WasteItem_var    refV;

    // Case: Use Basic POA

    // Construct an 'ObjectId' from the database key, 'wasteitem_id'
    oidV = ObjectIdMapper::make_ObjectId("WasteItem", wasteitem_id);

    // Step 1 - Search the active object map.
    try {
        // Look up the 'oid' in the 'Active Object Map'
        objV = m_poa_for_childrenV->id_to_reference(oidV.in() );
    }
    catch (PortableServer::POA::ObjectNotActive& ) {
        objV = CORBA::Object::_nil();
    }

    if (CORBA::is_nil(objV.in()) ) {
        // Step 2 - Check for the existence of a database record.
        if (RecycleBroker_WasteItem_i::_find_DB_record(wasteitem_id) ) {
            // Step 3 - Create the servant object.
            servantV = new RecycleBroker_WasteItem_i(
```

Listing 7.14 continued

```
                            m_poa_for_childrenV.in(),
                            wasteitem_id
                        );

            // Step 4 - Activate the servant object.
            m_poa_for_childrenV->activate_object_with_id(
                        oidV,
                        servantV.in()
                    );
            // Step 5 - Create an object reference.
            objV = m_poa_for_childrenV->id_to_reference(oidV.in() );
        }
        else {
            objV = CORBA::Object::_nil();
        }
    }

    refV = RecycleBroker::WasteItem::_ narrow(objV.in() );
    return refV._retn();
}
```

Listing 7.15 Java Implementation of the `RecycleBroker::WasteItemAdmin::create()` and `find()` Operations

```
//Java
package Pure.POADemo;

import Pure.POADemo.RecycleBroker.*;

public class RecycleBroker_WasteItemAdmin_i
    extends  WasteItemAdminPOA
{
  //...

  // create() - Implements IDL operation "RecycleBroker.WasteItemAdmin.create".
  public WasteItem
  create(
    WasteItemDetails             initialData,
    org.omg.CORBA.IntHolder      wasteitem_id
  )
  throws org.omg.CORBA.SystemException, Pure.POADemo.RecycleBroker.NoPermission
  {
    byte[]                          oid;
    org.omg.PortableServer.Servant  servant;
    org.omg.CORBA.Object            obj;
    WasteItem    ref;

    // Case: Use Basic POA
```

Listing 7.14 continued

```
    // Step 1 - Create a database record.
    wasteitem_id.value
        = RecycleBroker_WasteItem_i._create_DB_record(initialData);

    // Construct an 'ObjectId' from the database key, 'wasteitem_id'
    oid = ObjectIdMapper.make_ObjectId("WasteItem", wasteitem_id.value);

    try {
        // Step 2 - Create the servant object.
        servant = new RecycleBroker_WasteItem_i(
                        wasteitem_id.value
                  );

        // Step 3 - Activate the servant object.
        m_poa_for_children.activate_object_with_id(
                    oid,
                    servant
                );

        // Step 4 - Create an object reference.
        obj = m_poa_for_children.id_to_reference(oid);
    }
    catch (Exception ex) {
        // Error: details of exception handling not shown
        obj = null;
    }

    ref = WasteItemHelper.narrow(obj);
    return ref;
  }


  // find() -- Implements IDL operation "RecycleBroker.WasteItemAdmin.find".
  public WasteItem
  find(
    int          wasteitem_id
  )
  throws org.omg.CORBA.SystemException
  {
    byte[]                           oid;
    org.omg.PortableServer.Servant  servant;
    org.omg.CORBA.Object            obj;
    WasteItem         ref;

    System.out.println(
        "RecycleBroker_WasteItemAdmin_i.find(" + wasteitem_id + ") called"
    );
```

Listing 7.14 continued

```
    // Case: Basic POA

    // Construct an 'ObjectId' from the database key, 'wasteitem_id'
    oid = ObjectIdMapper.make_ObjectId("WasteItem", wasteitem_id);

    try {
        // Step 1 - Search the active object map.
        try {
            obj = m_poa_for_children.id_to_reference(oid);
        }
        catch (org.omg.PortableServer.POAPackage.ObjectNotActive ona) {
            obj = null;
        }

        if (obj==null) {
            // Step 2 - Check for the existence of a database record.
            if (RecycleBroker_WasteItem_i._find_DB_record(wasteitem_id) ) {
                // Step 3 - Create the servant object.
                servant = new RecycleBroker_WasteItem_i(
                              wasteitem_id
                          );

                // Step 4 - Activate the servant object.
                m_poa_for_children.activate_object_with_id(
                          oid,
                          servant
                      );

                // Step 5 - Create an object reference.
                obj = m_poa_for_children.id_to_reference(oid);
            }
            else {
                obj = null;
            }
        }
    }
    catch (Exception ex) {
        // Error: details of exception handling not shown
        obj = null;
    }

    ref = WasteItemHelper.narrow(obj);
    return ref;
  }

  //---------------------------
  // Private member variables
  //---------------------------
  org.omg.PortableServer.POA  m_poa_for_children;
}
```

The `create()` and `find()` operations are described in the two following subsections.

The `RecycleBroker::WasteItemAdmin::create()` Operation

The `create()` operation takes some initial data, `WasteItemDetails`, as an argument to initialize a new database record and returns an object reference for the corresponding `WasteItem` object. The private member variable `m_poa_for_childrenV` (C++) or `m_poa_for_children` (Java) caches a POA pointer that is used to activate new `WasteItem` objects.

The algorithm for the `create()` operation consists of the following steps (see Figure 7.8):

1. **Create a database record** The `WasteItem` CORBA object exists from this point onward, though it is initially dormant.
2. **Create the servant object** The `WasteItem` object's state is retrieved from the database.
3. **Activate the servant object** The POA used to activate the `WasteItem` object is a POA suitable for entity objects.
4. **Create an object reference** The `WasteItem` object reference is used as the return value from `create()`. Note that it is not legal to return a pointer to the servant object.

The `RecycleBroker::WasteItemAdmin::find()` Operation

The `find()` operation takes the `wasteitem_id` database key as an argument and returns the object reference for an existing `WasteItem` object. If the object does not exist, `find()` returns a nil object reference.

The algorithm for the `find()` operation consists of the following steps:

1. Search the active object map.
   The `PortableServer::POA::id_to_reference()` operation searches the active object map for an object with the given `ObjectId`. If the object is in the active object map, its corresponding object reference is returned; otherwise the `ObjectNotActive` user exception is thrown.
2. Check for the existence of the database record.
   If the CORBA object is not found in the active object map, it is then necessary to create and activate the CORBA object in memory.
   The static `_find_DB_record()` function is called to determine whether the `wasteitem_id` key corresponds to an existing database record.
3. Create the servant object.
   If `wasteitem_id` is a valid key, the servant object is created.
4. Activate the servant object.
5. Create an object reference.

Creating the Factory

Listing 7.16 and Listing 7.17 show how the `WasteItemAdmin` object, a factory for `WasteItem` objects, is created and activated.

Listing 7.16 C++ Creating and Activating a `WasteItemAdmin` *Object*

```
//C++
...
// Create a basic POA for 'Session' objects.
basic_session_poaV =
    POAUtility::create_basic_POA(
        root_poaV.in(),
        root_poa_managerV.in(),
        "basic_session_poa",
        0,  // 'isMultiThread' = FALSE  =>  Single threaded
        0   // 'isPersistent'  = FALSE  =>  'Session' objects
    );

// Create a basic POA for 'Entity' objects.
basic_entity_poaV =
    POAUtility::create_basic_POA(
        root_poaV.in(),
        root_poa_managerV.in(),
        "basic_entity_poa",
        0,  // 'isMultiThread' = FALSE  =>  Single threaded
        1   // 'isPersistent'  = TRUE   =>  'Entity' objects
    );

//-----------------------------------------
// Create Factories and export their object references.
//-----------------------------------------
PortableServer::ObjectId_var oidV;
CORBA::Object_var refV;

// Create a servant for the 'Browsing' interface.
the_WasteItemAdminV = new RecycleBroker_WasteItemAdmin_i(
    basic_session_poaV.in(),        //POA for the Factory
    basic_entity_poaV.in()          //POA for the children
);
oidV = basic_session_poaV->activate_object(the_WasteItemAdminV.in());
refV = basic_session_poaV->id_to_reference(oidV);

// Export the 'WasteItemAdmin' object reference, 'refV', to the Naming Service
...
```

Listing 7.17 Java Creating and Activating a `WasteItemAdmin` *Object*

```
//Java
...
// Create a basic POA for 'Session' objects.
System.out.println("Creating basic session POA");
POA basic_session_poa =
    Pure.Util.POAUtility.create_basic_POA(
```

Listing 7.16 continued

```
        root_poa,
        root_poa_manager,
        "basic_session_poa",
        false,  // 'isMultiThread' = FALSE  =>  Single threaded
        false   // 'isPersistent'  = FALSE  =>  'Session' objects
    );

// Create a basic POA for 'Entity' objects.
System.out.println("Creating basic entity POA");
POA basic_entity_poa =
    Pure.Util.POAUtility.create_basic_POA(
        root_poa,
        root_poa_manager,
        "basic_entity_poa",
        false,  // 'isMultiThread' = FALSE  =>  Single threaded
        true    // 'isPersistent'  = TRUE   =>  'Entity' objects
    );

//------------------------------------------
// Create Factories and export their object references.
//------------------------------------------
byte[] oid = null;
org.omg.CORBA.Object ref = null;

// Create a servant for the 'Browsing' interface.
Servant the_WasteItemAdmin = new RecycleBroker_WasteItemAdmin_i(
    basic_entity_poa         //POA for the children
);
oid = basic_session_poa.activate_object(the_WasteItemAdmin);
ref = basic_session_poa.id_to_reference(oid);

// Export the 'WasteItemAdmin' object reference,  'ref', to the Naming Service
...
```

The `basic_entity_poaV` object (C++) or `basic_entity_poa` object (Java) is created using `create_basic_POA()`. The `isPersistent` flag is set to `TRUE`, indicating that the POA is used to manage entity objects.

The `WasteItemAdmin` object itself is created as a session object, in the manner described in the section "A POA for Session Objects."

The `RecycleBroker_WasteItemAdmin_i` constructor takes two arguments. The first, `basic_session_POA`, is the POA used to activate this `WasteItemAdmin` object; the second, `basic_entity_POA`, is the POA used to activate the `WasteItem` objects created by the `WasteItemAdmin` object.

A POA for Service Objects

A *service object* is a particularly simple kind of session object that has no associated state. Service objects have the following properties:

- They are short lived. Like session objects, they have a transient lifespan.
- A single service object can be used by several clients. This is because the service object does not store any client-specific state.
- Service objects are insensitive to the order in which their operations are invoked.

For example, a library of mathematical functions could be implemented as a service object.

The service objects described here correspond informally to service objects as defined in the CORBA Components specification or stateless session beans as defined in the Enterprise JavaBeans specification.

The sample IDL used in this section is given in Listing 7.2, earlier in this chapter. It is the same IDL as is used in the section "A POA for Session Objects."

The `Browsing` objects are implemented and managed as service objects in this section. The `BranchOffice` object, as implemented in this section, has the characteristics of a service object factory.

This section is divided into three parts that explain how to create and use a POA that is appropriate for activating and managing service objects.

Creating the POA

For convenience, basic steps needed to create a POA for session objects are encapsulated in the `POAUtility::create_service_POA()` function. The code for the static `create_service_POA()` function is shown in Listing 7.18 and Listing 7.19.

Listing 7.18 C++ Creating a POA for Service Objects

```
//C++
PortableServer::POA_ptr
POAUtility::create_service_POA(
    PortableServer::POA_ptr           parentPOAP,
    PortableServer::POAManager_ptr    POAManagerP,
    char *                            POAName,
    CORBA::Boolean                    isMultiThread
)
{
    // Create a policy list.
    CORBA::PolicyList policies;
    policies.length(2);
    CORBA::ULong i = 0;

    // Thread Policy
    PortableServer::ThreadPolicyValue threadPolicy;
```

Listing 7.18 continued

```
    if (isMultiThread) {
        threadPolicy = PortableServer::ORB_CTRL_MODEL;
    }
    else {
        threadPolicy = PortableServer::SINGLE_THREAD_MODEL;
    }
    policies[i] = parentPOAP->create_thread_policy(threadPolicy);

    // LifeSpan Policy              -  Default = TRANSIENT

    // IdAssignment Policy          -  Default = SYSTEM_ID

    // IdUniqueness Policy
    i++;
    policies[i] = parentPOAP->create_id_uniqueness_policy(
        PortableServer::MULTIPLE_ID
    );

    // ImplicitActivation Policy   -  Default = NO_IMPLICIT_ACTIVATION

    // RequestProcessing Policy    -  Default = USE_ACTIVE_OBJECT_MAP_ONLY

    // ServantRetention Policy     -  Default = RETAIN

    return parentPOAP->create_POA(POAName, POAManagerP, policies);
}
```

Listing 7.19 Java Creating a POA for Service Objects

```
//Java
package Pure.Util;

import org.omg.PortableServer.*;

public class POAUtility {
  public static org.omg.PortableServer.POA
  create_service_POA(
        org.omg.PortableServer.POA        parentPOA,
        org.omg.PortableServer.POAManager POAManager,
        String                            POAName,
    boolean                           isMultiThread
  )
  throws org.omg.PortableServer.POAPackage.InvalidPolicy,
         org.omg.PortableServer.POAPackage.AdapterAlreadyExists
  {
    // Create a policy list.
    org.omg.CORBA.Policy policies[] = new org.omg.CORBA.Policy[2];
    int i = 0;
```

Listing 7.18 continued

```
        // Thread Policy
        org.omg.PortableServer.ThreadPolicyValue threadPolicy = null;

        if (isMultiThread) {
            threadPolicy = ThreadPolicyValue.ORB_CTRL_MODEL;
        }
        else {
            threadPolicy = ThreadPolicyValue.SINGLE_THREAD_MODEL;
        }
        policies[i] = parentPOA.create_thread_policy(threadPolicy);

        // LifeSpan Policy              -  Default = TRANSIENT

        // IdAssignment Policy          -  Default = SYSTEM_ID

        // IdUniqueness Policy
        i++;
        policies[i] = parentPOA.create_id_uniqueness_policy(
            IdUniquenessPolicyValue.MULTIPLE_ID
        );

        // ImplicitActivation Policy   -  Default = NO_IMPLICIT_ACTIVATION

        // RequestProcessing Policy    -  Default = USE_ACTIVE_OBJECT_MAP_ONLY

        // ServantRetention Policy     -  Default = RETAIN

        return parentPOA.create_POA(POAName, POAManager, policies);
    }
}
```

The first parameter, `parentPOAP`, is a reference to the POA that serves as a parent to the POA returned by this function.

The second parameter, `POAManagerP`, specifies the `POAManager` object that is passed to `create_POA()` and that controls the flow of messages into the newly created POA.

The third parameter, `POAName`, sets the name of the newly created POA (relative to the parent POA).

The fourth parameter, `isMultiThread`, determines whether or not you want this POA to be multithreaded.

The body of the `create_service_POA()` function is taken up mostly with initializing the list of policies. The `CORBA::PolicyList` is declared as `sequence<CORBA::Policy>` and contains a list of `CORBA::Policy` objects that are used to initialize the POA returned by `create_POA()`. Listing 7.1, earlier in this chapter, shows the IDL used to create individual POA `CORBA::Policy` objects.

In this example, the set of POA policies used to manage service objects is given by Table 7.5.

Table 7.5 POA Policies Used for Service Objects

Policy Name	Policy Value
ThreadPolicy	SINGLE_THREAD_MODEL
LifespanPolicy	TRANSIENT
IdAssignmentPolicy	SYSTEM_ID
IdUniquenessPolicy	MULTIPLE_ID
ImplicitActivationPolicy	NO_IMPLICIT_ACTIVATION
RequestProcessingPolicy	USE_ACTIVE_OBJECT_MAP_ONLY
ServantRetentionPolicy	RETAIN

Three of these policies relate specifically to the management of service objects:

- The `TRANSIENT` lifespan policy value specifies that objects managed by this POA cease to exist after the POA is destroyed.
- The `SYSTEM_ID` ID assignment policy value specifies that `ObjectIds` are automatically generated by the POA.
- The `MULTIPLE_ID` ID uniqueness policy value is discussed in the following section, "ID Uniqueness Policy."

The last three policies are left at their default values. These policies are discussed in the later sections of this chapter as the need arises.

ID Uniqueness Policy

The POA's ID uniqueness policy, of `PortableServer::IdUniquessPolicy` type, determines whether servant references appearing in the active object map are forced to map to a unique `ObjectId`. Two alternatives are possible:

- `UNIQUE_ID`
  This policy value specifies that each servant is associated with a unique `ObjectId` in the active object map. If either `activate_object()` or `activate_object_with_id()` are called on a servant that is already activated, the POA throws a `PortableServer::POA::ServantAlreadyActive` user exception.
- `MULTIPLE_ID`
  This policy value specifies that each servant can be associated with many `ObjectIds` in the active object map. This allows a many-to-one association between `ObjectIds` and servants, as previously illustrated in Figure 7.3(b). The `MULTIPLE_ID` policy value puts implicit restrictions on the servant implementation, effectively requiring it to be a service object.

Implementing a Service Object Factory

The implementation of the `RecycleBroker::BranchOffice::get_browsing()` operation, given in Listing 7.20 and Listing 7.21, illustrates how to create a service object of `Browsing` type.

Listing 7.20 C++ Implementation of the **RecycleBroker::BranchOffice::get_browsing()** *Operation*

```
//C++
RecycleBroker::Browsing_ptr
RecycleBroker_BranchOffice_i::get_browsing()
throw (CORBA::SystemException)
{
    PortableServer::ServantBase_var the_BrowsingV;
    PortableServer::ObjectId_var    oidV;
    CORBA::Object_var               objV;
    RecycleBroker::Browsing_var     refV;

    // Case: Use Service POA

    // Step 1 - Retrieve a pointer to the cached servant object.
    // Check cached servant
    if (! m_browsing_servantV.in()) {
        // Create a 'Browsing' servant
        // (constructor arguments not shown)
        m_browsing_servantV = new RecycleBroker_Browsing_i();
    }

    // Step 2 - Activate the servant object.
    oidV = m_poa_for_childrenV->activate_object(m_browsing_servantV.in());

    // Step 3 - Create an object reference.
    objV = m_poa_for_childrenV->id_to_reference(oidV);
    refV = RecycleBroker::Browsing::_narrow(objV.in() );

    return refV._ retn();
}
```

Listing 7.21 Java Implementation of the **RecycleBroker::BranchOffice::get_browsing()** *Operation*

```
//Java
package Pure.POADemo;

import Pure.POADemo.RecycleBroker.*;

public class RecycleBroker_BranchOffice_i
    extends  BranchOfficePOA
{
  //...

  // IDL operations
  public Browsing get_browsing()
  throws org.omg.CORBA.SystemException
  {
```

Listing 7.21 continued

```
    byte[]                          oid;
    org.omg.CORBA.Object            obj;
    Browsing            ref;

    // Case: Use Service POA

    // Step 1 - Retrieve a pointer to the cached servant object.
    // Check cached servant
    if (m_browsing_servant==null) {
        // Create a 'Browsing' servant
        org.omg.PortableServer.POA poa_for_grandchildren
            = m_poa_for_children;
        m_browsing_servant = new RecycleBroker_Browsing_i(
                                poa_for_grandchildren
                            );
    }
    try {
        // Step 2 - Activate the servant object.
        oid = m_poa_for_children.activate_object(m_browsing_servant);

        // Step 3 - Create an object reference.
        obj = m_poa_for_children.id_to_reference(oid);
        ref = BrowsingHelper.narrow(obj);
    }
    catch (Exception ex) {
        // Error: details of exception handling not shown
        ref = null;
    }

    return ref;
  }
  //...

  //------------------------------
  // Private member variables
  //------------------------------
  private org.omg.PortableServer.POA     m_poa_for_children;
  private org.omg.PortableServer.Servant m_browsing_servant;

}
```

The `get_browsing()` operation creates and returns an object reference for a `RecycleBroker::Browsing` object.

The private member variable `m_poa_for_childrenV` (C++) or `m_poa_for_children` (Java) caches a pointer to a POA that is used to activate `Browsing` objects.

`m_browsing_servantV` (C++) or `m_browsing_servant` (Java) is a private member variable that caches a reference to a single `RecycleBroker_Browsing_i` servant object.

In this example, the `get_browsing()` operation is implemented in such a way that only a single cached servant object is ever created. Each time `get_browsing()` is called, the same servant object is activated.

The following steps are used to generate a `Browsing` object reference (service object):

1. Retrieve a pointer to the cached servant object.
   Only one `RecycleBroker_Browsing_i` servant object is ever created. The servant object is created and cached the first time `get_browsing()` is called.
2. Activate the servant object.
   Because the POA has been created with an ID assignment policy of `MULTIPLE_ID`, the developer is allowed to activate the same servant object many times (see Figure 7.3(b)). Each time `activate_object()` is called, the cached servant becomes associated with a new, automatically generated `ObjectId`.
3. Create an object reference.
   The `id_to_reference()` operation converts the newly-generated `ObjectId` to a `Browsing` object reference that can be returned from `get_browsing()`.

Creating the Factory

Listing 7.22 and Listing 7.23 show how the `BranchOffice` object is created and activated.

Listing 7.22 C++ Creating and Activating a `BranchOffice` *Object*

```
//C++
//-----------------------------------------------------
// Given the following variables:
//    root_poaV - a reference to the root POA object.
//    root_poa_managerV - the root POAManager object that is
//        obtained from the root POA object.
//
// Create a basic POA for 'Session' objects.
basic_session_poaV =
    POAUtility::create_basic_POA(
        root_poaV.in(),
        root_poa_managerV.in(),
        "basic_session_poa",
        0,                   // Single threaded
        0                    // for 'Session' objects
    );

// Create a POA for 'Service' objects.
service_poaV =
    POAUtility::create_service_POA(
        root_poaV.in(),
        root_poa_managerV.in(),
        "service_poa",
        0                    // Single threaded
    );
```

Listing 7.22 continued

```
//-------------------------------------------
// Create Factories and export their object references.
//-------------------------------------------
PortableServer::ObjectId_var oidV;
CORBA::Object_var refV;

// Step 1 - Create a servant for the 'BranchOffice' interface.
the_BranchOfficeV = new RecycleBroker_BranchOffice_i(
    basic_session_poaV.in(),       //POA for the Factory
    service_poaV.in()              //POA for the children
);

// Step 2 - Activate the CORBA object
oidV = basic_session_poaV->activate_object(the_BranchOfficeV.in());

// Step 3 - Create an object reference
refV = basic_session_poaV->id_to_reference(oidV);

// Export the 'BranchOffice' object reference,  'refV', to the Naming Service
...
```

Listing 7.23 Java Creating and Activating a `BranchOffice` Object

```
//Java
//-------------------------------------------------------
// Given the following variables:
//    root_poa - a reference to the root POA object.
//    root_poa_manager - the root POAManager object that is
//        obtained from the root POA object.
//
...
// Create a basic POA for 'Session' objects.
POA basic_session_poa =
    Pure.Util.POAUtility.create_basic_POA(
        root_poa,
        root_poa_manager,
        "basic_session_poa",
        false,                  // Single threaded
        false                   // for 'Session' objects
    );

// Create a POA for 'Service' objects.
System.out.println("Creating basic service POA");
POA service_poa =
    Pure.Util.POAUtility.create_service_POA(
        root_poa,
        root_poa_manager,
        "service_poa",
```

Listing 7.22 continued

```
        false                       // Single threaded
    );

//----------------------------------------
// Create Factories and export their object references.
//----------------------------------------
byte[] oid = null;
org.omg.CORBA.Object ref = null;

// Step 1 - Create a servant for the 'BranchOffice' interface.
Servant the_BranchOffice = new RecycleBroker_BranchOffice_i(
    service_poa                 //POA for the children
);

// Step 2 - Activate the CORBA object
oid = basic_session_poa.activate_object(the_BranchOffice);

// Step 3 - Create an object reference
ref = basic_session_poa.id_to_reference(oid);

// Export the 'BranchOffice' object reference,  'ref', to the Naming Service
...
```

The `service_poaV` (C++) or `service_poa` (Java) object is created using the `POAUtility::create_service_POA()` function. This is the POA used to activate session objects in this example.

The `BranchOffice` object itself is created as a session object. See the section "A POA for Session Objects."

Note that the `RecycleBroker_BranchOffice_i` constructor takes two arguments. The first is the POA used to activate that `BranchOffice` object; the second is the POA that will be used to activate the `Browsing` objects created by the `BranchOffice` object. The `service_poaV` (C++) or `service_poa` (Java) object is passed as the second argument and is used to initialize the `m_poa_for_childrenV` (C++) or `m_poa_for_children` (Java) member variable.

Servant Activator POA

This section describes the first of the advanced POA features designed to provide increased scalability for CORBA servers. If you are designing and developing a small-scale CORBA application—an application for which all of the CORBA objects can easily fit in memory—it is likely that the examples in the preceding sections have all the functionality that you need.

On the other hand, if you are implementing a large-scale system—one that manages thousands or even millions of CORBA objects—you will need to manage those objects in the most efficient manner possible. Using a `PortableServer::ServantManager` object in conjunction with a POA allows you much greater freedom to manage the life-cycle and activation of servant objects. There are two kinds of `ServantManager` objects:

- `PortableServer::ServantActivator`
  A servant activator is used with a POA that has an active object map. If an invocation arrives at the POA and the `ObjectId` cannot be found in the active object map, the POA asks the `ServantActivator` to *incarnate* (create and activate) the appropriate servant object.
- `PortableServer::ServantLocator`
  A servant locator is used with a POA that does *not* have an active object map. It is more flexible than a servant activator and is discussed in detail in the section "Servant Locator POA," later in this chapter.

The IDL for the `ServantManager` and `ServantActivator` interfaces is shown in Listing 7.24.

Listing 7.24 IDL for the `ServantActivator` *Interface*

```
//IDL
module PortableServer {
    //...
    interface ServantManager{ };

    local interface ServantActivator : ServantManager {
        Servant incarnate (
            in ObjectId oid,
            in POA adapter
        )
        raises (ForwardRequest);

        void etherealize (
            in ObjectId oid,
            in POA adapter,
            in Servant serv,
            in boolean cleanup_in_progress,
            in boolean remaining_activations
        );
    };

    // POA interface
    interface POA {
        //...
        exception WrongPolicy {};

        // Servant Manager registration:
        ServantManager get_servant_manager()
        raises (WrongPolicy);
```

Listing 7.24 continued

```
        void set_servant_manager(
            in ServantManager imgr
        )
        raises (WrongPolicy);
        //...
    };
};
```

The `ServantManager` interface has no operations. It is used as a base interface.

`ServantActivator` declares two operations, `incarnate()` and `etherealize()`, that are associated with the activation and deactivation of servants. This interface must be implemented by the developer to customize the behavior of the `ServantActivator`.

A `ServantActivator` becomes associated with a particular POA by registering it using the `PortableServer::POA::set_servant_manager()` operation.

This section describes how to write a server application that manages the lifecycle of entity objects to minimize the length of time that the objects spend in working memory. Two basic patterns are used in combination to manage the lifecycle of entity objects:

- **Lazy activation** When a client asks a factory object to create another object, the factory does not have to create and activate the servant right away. The server can wait, instead, until the first invocation is made on the new object.
- **The evictor pattern** When too many objects of a certain type occupy working memory, the server can *evict* some of the objects. To evict an object, the server deactivates and deletes the corresponding servant from memory.

Both of these principles are applied to the example described in the following sections.

Lazy Activation

One of the applications of the `ServantActivator` is to implement *lazy activation* of servants. Instead of activating a servant immediately when a factory operation is invoked, you can wait until the first invocation on the corresponding CORBA object is made. Lazy activation saves memory and resources on the server side. Often, clients obtain a large number of object references from a CORBA server, many of which they never use.

Consider, for example, the lazy activation of `WasteItem` entity objects—the IDL for this example is given in Listing 7.9. The steps involved in the lazy activation of an entity object are illustrated in Figure 7.9.

Figure 7.9(a) shows what happens when a CORBA object is created using lazy activation. For example, when a client invokes `WasteItemAdmin::create()`, the server creates a CORBA object without creating a corresponding servant object. The developer implements `WasteItemAdmin::create()` to perform the following steps:

1. Store the entity object's initial state in a database record.
2. Create an object reference from the entity object's `ObjectId`, using the `POA::create_reference_with_id()` operation. The `ObjectId` is based on the primary key of the database record.

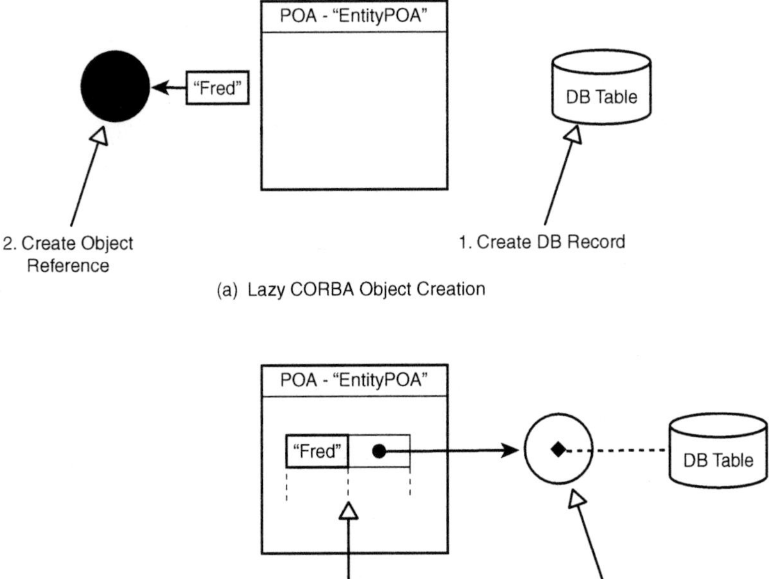

Figure 7.9

Lazy activation of an entity object.

Figure 7.9(b) shows what happens when the first invocation is made on the new entity object. The first invocation of an operation on the `WasteItem` object causes the POA to call `incarnate()` on its `ServantActivator` object (see Listing 7.24). The developer implements `incarnate()` to perform the following steps:

3. Create a servant object that provides an implementation of the entity object.
4. Activate the servant object, using the `ObjectId` supplied as a parameter to `incarnate()`.

The IDL operations shown in Listing 7.25 are of key importance to lazy activation.

Listing 7.25 IDL Operations to Create Object References

```
//IDL
module PortableServer {
    //...
    interface POA {
```

Listing 7.25 continued

```
        //...
        // reference creation operations
        Object create_reference (
            in CORBA::RepositoryId intf
        )
        raises (WrongPolicy);

        Object create_reference_with_id (
            in ObjectId oid,
            in CORBA::RepositoryId intf
        )
        raises (WrongPolicy);
        //...
    };
};
```

These operations allow you to create an object reference without having to create and activate a servant beforehand. The first operation, `create_reference()`, is used with POAs that have the `SYSTEM_ID` ID assignment policy value. The second operation, `create_reference_with_id()`, is used with POAs that have the `USER_ID` ID assignment policy value. The examples in the following sections show how these operations are used.

The Evictor Pattern

A common problem facing the designer of a CORBA server is how to prevent the number of CORBA objects in memory from running out of control. Typically, entity objects map to individual database records, and there may be millions of them. Fortunately, only a fraction of those objects need to be active in the server at any one time.

However, the difficulty is deciding when the server is finished with particular entity objects. A long-running server may gradually (or even rapidly) be brought to its knees unless it can clear dormant CORBA objects out of its working memory. Two basic approaches can be used to clean up the server's memory:

- **Client-driven** The client tells the server when it is finished using particular CORBA objects. For example, the client might invoke a `destroy()` operation on the objects.
- **Server-driven** The server decides, independently of the client, when a CORBA object should be deactivated and destroyed. For example, a server may impose a time limit on the lifetime of a particular type of CORBA object.

In practice, most applications use a combination of client-driven and server-driven memory management. Of the two approaches, server-driven memory management is the most important. You can never rely completely on clients to perform object cleanup. The server must always have the capability to keep its resource use within acceptable limits.

This section describes the *evictor pattern*, which is a simple pattern used to limit the number of CORBA objects that are active in the server at any one time. There are two basic elements of this pattern:

- **Object eviction** The server monitors the number of objects of a particular type that are active at any one time. If a maximum limit is exceeded, the excess CORBA objects must be *evicted*. A servant object is evicted by deactivating it and deleting it from memory.
- **Automatic object activation** It can happen that a CORBA object gets evicted just before a client tries to invoke on it. It would be unacceptable for the server to generate an `OBJECT_NOT_EXIST` system exception at this point. Instead, the server should be capable of automatically reactivating the object. This capability is provided by installing a `ServantActivator` in the POA, as described in the earlier section, "Lazy Activation."

Figure 7.10 illustrates how servant objects are managed using the evictor pattern. Typically, the evictor is applied to objects of a particular type. For example, in this section the evictor is applied to `WasteItem` objects.

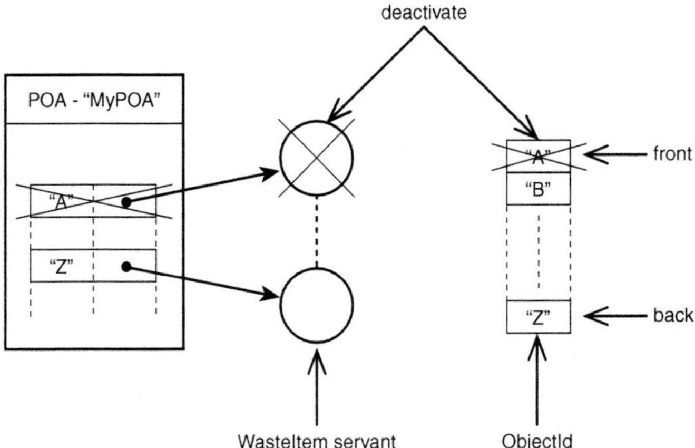

Figure 7.10

Implementation of an evictor pattern.

To implement the evictor, you need to maintain a list of active servant objects. Figure 7.10 shows a simple first-in, first-out queue containing a list of `ObjectIds`. Each time a `WasteItem` object is activated, its `ObjectId` is added to the back of the queue. Once the queue reaches a certain maximum size, it becomes necessary to start evicting older objects at the front of the queue.

Every time a new object is about to be activated, a check can be made to test if the queue is about to exceed its maximum allowed length. If the queue is at its maximum length, the `WasteItem` object at the front of the queue is evicted, as follows:

1. The `ObjectId` is removed from the front of the queue.
2. The servant object with the given `ObjectId` is deactivated and destroyed.

Servant deactivation is discussed in the following section.

Servant Deactivation

Servant deactivation is performed using the `deactivate_object()` operation, as defined by the IDL in Listing 7.26.

Listing 7.26 IDL Operation to Deactivate Objects

```
//IDL
module PortableServer {
    //...
    interface POA {
        exception ObjectNotActive {};
        exception WrongPolicy {};
        //...
        void deactivate_object(in ObjectId oid)
        raises (ObjectNotActive, WrongPolicy);
    };
};
```

The `deactivate_object()` operation looks up the POA's active object map and removes the entry for the `ObjectId` given by the `oid` argument.

The `ObjectNotActive` user exception is raised if `oid` is not found in the POA's active object map.

The `WrongPolicy` user exception is raised if the POA does not have an active object map. This is the case if the POA is created with a servant retention policy of `NON_RETAIN`. See the section "Servant Locator POA," later in this chapter.

The `deactivate_object()` operation is intended to work in cooperation with the `ServantActivator`'s `etherealize()` operation. Deactivation of a CORBA object is a more delicate operation than you might think. It can easily happen that `deactivate_object()` is called while the corresponding servant is in the middle of processing a request. Deactivation is performed using the following algorithm:

1. The developer calls `deactivate_object()`, passing the appropriate `ObjectId` as the argument. The corresponding active object map entry is marked and the `deactivate_object()` operation returns *immediately*. The object is still active at this point.
2. At the next opportunity, the POA checks whether the marked object is currently processing a request. If the marked object is busy processing, the POA does nothing, waiting until the next opportunity to check the object.
   If the marked object is not busy processing, the POA removes the marked entry from the active object map and calls `etherealize()` on its associated `ServantActivator` object.

3. The `etherealize()` operation is implemented by the developer. It is responsible for deleting the servant object and cleaning up other resources associated with the CORBA object.

Effectively, `deactivate_object()()` performs a gentle shutdown of a CORBA object. Even after `deactivate_object()`has been called, a CORBA object can remain active for some time while processing outstanding requests.

In theory, it is possible to call `deactivate_object()` without implementing a corresponding `etherealize()` operation. However, it would be impossible to delete deactivated servants in a thread-safe manner, so this approach is not recommended.

Creating the POA

The code to create a POA that uses a `ServantActivator` is conveniently encapsulated in the `create_servant_activator_POA()` function, shown in Listing 7.27 and Listing 7.28.

Listing 7.27 C++ Creating a POA That Uses a Servant Activator

```
//C++
PortableServer::POA_ptr
POAUtility::create_servant_activator_POA(
    PortableServer::POA_ptr          parentPOAP,
    PortableServer::POAManager_ptr   POAManagerP,
    char *                           POAName,
    CORBA::Boolean                   isMultiThread,
    CORBA::Boolean                   isPersistent
)
{
    // Create a policy list.
    CORBA::PolicyList policies;
    policies.length(4);
    CORBA::ULong i = 0;

    // Thread Policy
    PortableServer::ThreadPolicyValue threadPolicy;

    if (isMultiThread) {
        threadPolicy = PortableServer::ORB_CTRL_MODEL;
    }
    else {
        threadPolicy = PortableServer::SINGLE_THREAD_MODEL;
    }
    policies[i] = parentPOAP->create_thread_policy(threadPolicy);

    PortableServer::LifespanPolicyValue     lifeSpanPolicy;
    PortableServer::IdAssignmentPolicyValue idAssignPolicy;

    // Lifespan and IdAssignment Policies
    if (isPersistent) {
```

Listing 7.27 continued

```
        // Policies for 'Entity' objects
        lifeSpanPolicy = PortableServer::PERSISTENT;
        idAssignPolicy = PortableServer::USER_ID;
    }
    else {
        // Policies for 'Session' objects
        lifeSpanPolicy = PortableServer::TRANSIENT;
        idAssignPolicy = PortableServer::SYSTEM_ID;
    }

    // Lifespan Policy
    i++;
    policies[i] = parentPOAP->create_lifespan_policy(lifeSpanPolicy);

    // IdAssignment Policy
    i++;
    policies[i] = parentPOAP->create_id_assignment_policy(idAssignPolicy);

    // IdUniqueness Policy        -  Default = UNIQUE_ID

    // ImplicitActivation Policy  -  Default = NO_IMPLICIT_ACTIVATION

    // RequestProcessing Policy
    i++;
    policies[i] = parentPOAP->create_request_processing_policy(
        PortableServer::USE_SERVANT_MANAGER
    );

    // ServantRetention Policy    -  Default = RETAIN

    return parentPOAP->create_POA(POAName,  POAManagerP, policies);
}
```

Listing 7.28 Java Creating a POA That Uses a Servant Activator

```
//Java
package Pure.Util;
import org.omg.PortableServer.*;

public class POAUtility {
  //...
  public static org.omg.PortableServer.POA
  create_servant_activator_POA(
        org.omg.PortableServer.POA        parentPOA,
        org.omg.PortableServer.POAManager POAManager,
        String                            POAName,
        boolean                           isMultiThread,
        boolean                           isPersistent
  )
```

Listing 7.28 continued

```
throws org.omg.PortableServer.POAPackage.InvalidPolicy,
       org.omg.PortableServer.POAPackage.AdapterAlreadyExists
{
  // Create a policy list.
  org.omg.CORBA.Policy policies[] = new org.omg.CORBA.Policy[4];
  int i = 0;

  // Thread Policy
  org.omg.PortableServer.ThreadPolicyValue threadPolicy = null;

  if (isMultiThread) {
      threadPolicy = ThreadPolicyValue.ORB_CTRL_MODEL;
  }
  else {
      threadPolicy = ThreadPolicyValue.SINGLE_THREAD_MODEL;
  }
  policies[i] = parentPOA.create_thread_policy(threadPolicy);

  org.omg.PortableServer.LifespanPolicyValue     lifeSpanPolicy = null;
  org.omg.PortableServer.IdAssignmentPolicyValue idAssignPolicy = null;

  // Lifespan and IdAssignment Policies
  if (isPersistent) {
      // Policies for 'Entity' objects
      lifeSpanPolicy = LifespanPolicyValue.PERSISTENT;
      idAssignPolicy = IdAssignmentPolicyValue.USER_ID;
  }
  else {
      // Policies for 'Session' objects
      lifeSpanPolicy = LifespanPolicyValue.TRANSIENT;
      idAssignPolicy = IdAssignmentPolicyValue.SYSTEM_ID;
  }

  // Lifespan Policy
  i++;
  policies[i] = parentPOA.create_lifespan_policy(lifeSpanPolicy);

  // IdAssignment Policy
  i++;
  policies[i] = parentPOA.create_id_assignment_policy(idAssignPolicy);

  // IdUniqueness Policy        -  Default = UNIQUE_ID

  // ImplicitActivation Policy  -  Default = NO_IMPLICIT_ACTIVATION

  // RequestProcessing Policy
  i++;
```

Listing 7.28 continued

```
    policies[i] = parentPOA.create_request_processing_policy(
        RequestProcessingPolicyValue.USE_SERVANT_MANAGER
    );

    // ServantRetention Policy    -  Default = RETAIN

    return parentPOA.create_POA(POAName, POAManager, policies);
  }
}
```

Two policies are particularly relevant to the use of `ServantActivator`: the *servant retention policy* and the *request processing policy*. The values of these policies that must be used in combination with a `ServantActivator` are shown in Table 7.6.

Table 7.6 POA Policies Used with `ServantActivator`

Policy Name	Policy Value
`ServantRetentionPolicy`	`RETAIN`
`RequestProcessingPolicy`	`USE_SERVANT_MANAGER`

Servant Retention Policy

The servant retention policy, of `PortableServer::ServantRetentionPolicy` type, determines whether or not a POA uses an active object map.

- `RETAIN` This policy value specifies that the POA uses an active object map. It must be set if you want to use a `ServantActivator`.
- `NON_RETAIN` This policy value specifies that the POA does *not* use an active object map. This implies that the POA is configured to support some other way of locating servant objects. It must be set if you want to use a `ServantLocator`.

Either policy value is compatible with the use of a default servant. See the section "Default Servant POA."

Request Processing Policy

The request processing policy, of `PortableServer::RequestProcessingPolicy` type, influences how a POA locates a servant to process an incoming request.

- `USE_ACTIVE_OBJECT_MAP_ONLY` The POA extracts an `ObjectId` from the incoming request and uses the `ObjectId` to look up the active object map. If an entry is found, the POA assigns the request to the corresponding servant. Otherwise, an `OBJECT_NOT_EXIST` system exception is raised by the POA back to the client.
- `USE_DEFAULT_SERVANT` In this case, a default servant object must be registered with the POA. If the POA fails to find the request's `ObjectId` in the active object map, it will pass the request on to the POA's default servant for processing. See the section "Default Servant POA" for details.

- `USE_SERVANT_MANAGER` In this case, either a `ServantActivator` or `ServantLocator` object must be registered with the POA, depending on the value of the servant retention policy. A `ServantActivator` is used in conjunction with an active object map (`RETAIN` servant retention policy value). Use of a `ServantLocator` is discussed in the section "Servant Locator POA." A `ServantLocator` is used instead of an active object map (`NON_RETAIN` servant retention policy value).

Local Interfaces

There are certain IDL interfaces defined by the CORBA standard, *locality-constrained interfaces*, that are never called remotely. This category includes most of the pseudo-IDL interfaces, for example `CORBA::ORB` and `PortableServer::POA`. A regular CORBA developer does not normally have to worry about implementing pseudo-IDL interfaces—the pseudo-IDL implementations are supplied by an ORB vendor.

However, the CORBA developer does occasionally have to implement interfaces that are not intended to be accessed remotely—for example, the `PortableServer::ServantActivator` interface. It would be clumsy and inefficient to insist that a `ServantActivator` object should be activated using a POA. To avoid this, the `PortableServer::ServantActivator` interface is declared as a *local interface*, as shown in the following code fragment:

```
//IDL
module PortableServer {
    ...
    interface ServantManager{ };

    local interface ServantActivator : ServantManager {
        ...
    };
    ...
};
```

The IDL keyword `local` introduces the definition of a local IDL interface. A local interface has the following properties:

- A local interface cannot be accessed remotely. Attempting to marshal a local object reference or to convert a local object reference to a stringified IOR gives rise to a `CORBA::MARSHAL` system exception.
- A local interface can inherit from another local interface or from an *unconstrained interface* (ordinary interface). However, an unconstrained interface cannot inherit from a local interface.
- A local object does not need to be activated.

The following subsections describe how to implement a local interface in C++ and Java.

C++ Implementation of a Local Interface

In C++, a local interface is implemented by inheriting from the signature class (the class with the same name as the IDL interface) and the class `CORBA::LocalObject`. The IDL attributes and operations are implemented in the same way as a regular servant object. For example, an outline of a C++ implementation of the `ServantActivator` local interface is shown in the following code fragment:

```
//C++
...
class ServantActivatorImpl :
    public virtual PortableServer::ServantActivator,
    public virtual CORBA::LocalObject
{
    // Implement IDL attributes and operations.
    // (not shown)
    ...
};
```

See Listing 7.29 for the complete code. The principal difference between this implementation and the implementation of an unconstrained interface is the list of base classes.

To create a local `ServantActivator` object, call a `ServantActivatorImpl()` constructor. The `ServantActivatorImpl` instance can be referenced directly using the `PortableServer::ServantActivator_ptr` type or the `PortableServer::ServantActivator_var` type.

Reference counting must be implemented explicitly by overriding the `_add_ref()` and `_remove_ref()` functions, which are inherited from `CORBA::LocalObject`. Unfortunately, there is no equivalent to the convenient `PortableServer::RefCountServantBase` class when implementing local interfaces.

Java Implementation of a Local Interface

In Java, a local interface is implemented by extending the `org.omg.CORBA.LocalObject` class and implementing the signature Java interface (the Java interface with the same name as the IDL interface). The IDL attributes and operations are implemented in the same way as a regular servant object. For example, an outline of a Java implementation of the `ServantActivator` local interface is given in the following code fragment:

```
//Java
...
public class ServantActivatorImpl
    extends org.omg.CORBA.LocalObject
    implements org.omg.PortableServer.ServantActivator
{
    ...
}
```

See Listing 7.31 for the complete code. The principal difference between this implementation and the implementation of an unconstrained interface is the list of inherited classes.

To create a local `ServantActivator` object, simply call a `ServantActivatorImpl()` constructor. The `ServantActivatorImpl` instance can then be referenced directly using the `org.omg.PortableServer.ServantActivator` type (as if it were an object reference).

Implementing the Servant Activator

The class declaration for a C++ implementation of the `ServantActivator` is shown in Listing 7.29 (the Java implementation of `ServantActivator` is shown in Listing 7.31).

Listing 7.29 C++ Declaration of a Servant Activator Class

```
//C++
#include <omg/PortableServer.hh>

#include <queue>

// ServantActivatorImpl -- a local object implementation.
class ServantActivatorImpl :
    public virtual PortableServer::ServantActivator,
    public virtual CORBA::LocalObject
{
  public:
    ServantActivatorImpl(CORBA::Long queueSizeLimit);

    virtual
    ~ServantActivatorImpl();

    virtual PortableServer::Servant
    incarnate(
        const PortableServer::ObjectId & oid,
        PortableServer::POA_ptr          adapter
    ) throw (
        CORBA::SystemException,
        PortableServer::ForwardRequest
    );

    virtual void
    etherealize(
        const PortableServer::ObjectId & oid,
        PortableServer::POA_ptr          adapter,
        PortableServer::Servant          serv,
        CORBA::Boolean                   cleanup_in_progress,
        CORBA::Boolean                   remaining_activations
    ) throw (CORBA::SystemException);
```

Listing 7.29 continued

```
  private:
    typedef std::queue<PortableServer::ObjectId> QType;

    // Private Member Variables
    QType                                   m_queue;
    CORBA::Long                             m_queueSizeLimit;

    // Not implemented for this class
    ServantActivatorImpl(const ServantActivatorImpl&);
    ServantActivatorImpl& operator=(const ServantActivatorImpl&);
};
```

The `ServantActivatorImpl` class inherits from `PortableServer::ServantActivator` and overrides the `incarnate()` and `etherealize()` operations. The `ServantActivatorImpl` constructor takes a `queueSizeLimit` argument that specifies the maximum number of `WasteItem` objects that should be active at any time. This value is stored in the `m_queueSizeLimit` private member variable.

The list of active `WasteItem` objects is stored in a `std::queue<`*`element_type`*`>` template class. The `queue` container type is one of the container types supported by the C++ standard template library (STL). A comprehensive description of the template library can be found in *The C++ Programming Language* by Bjarne Stroustrup (ISBN 0201700735). For this example, we note that the `queue` template class supports three useful functions:

- `front()` Returns a copy of the element at the front of the queue.
- `push(`*`element_type`*` elem)` Inserts the `elem` element at the back of the queue.
- `pop()` Removes the element at the front of the queue.

Listing 7.30 and Listing 7.31 show the implementation of `ServantActivatorImpl` in C++ and Java, respectively.

Listing 7.30 C++ Implementation of a Servant Activator Class

```
//C++
//File: 'ServantActivatorImpl.cxx'
#include <stdlib.h>
#include <stdio.h>

#include "ServantActivatorImpl.h"
#include "RecycleBroker_WasteItem_i.h"

#include "ToyDB.h"
#include "ObjectIdMapper.h"


// Constructor.
ServantActivatorImpl::ServantActivatorImpl(
    CORBA::Long queueSizeLimit
```

Listing 7.30 continued

```
)
  : m_queueSizeLimit(queueSizeLimit)
{ }


// Destructor.
ServantActivatorImpl::~ServantActivatorImpl()
{ }


// incarnate()
PortableServer::Servant
ServantActivatorImpl::incarnate(
    const PortableServer::ObjectId & oid,
    PortableServer::POA_ptr          poa
) throw (
    CORBA::SystemException,
    PortableServer::ForwardRequest
)
{
    // Step 1 - Obtain the object's type
    CORBA::String_var typeV = ObjectIdMapper::extract_type_from_ObjectId(oid);

    if (strcmp(typeV.in(), "WasteItem")==0)
    {
        // Step 2 - Evict overflow servant
        if (m_queue.size() == m_queueSizeLimit)
        {
            PortableServer::ObjectId& _tmp = m_queue.front();
            poa->deactivate_object(_tmp);
            m_queue.pop();
        }

        // Step 3 - Incarnate this servant
        m_queue.push(oid);
        return RecycleBroker_WasteItem_i::_incarnate(oid, poa);
    }
    else
    {
        throw CORBA::OBJECT_NOT_EXIST();
    }
}


// etherealize()
void
ServantActivatorImpl::etherealize(
    const PortableServer::ObjectId & oid,
```

Listing 7.30 continued

```
    PortableServer::POA_ptr          poa,
    PortableServer::Servant          servant,
    CORBA::Boolean                   cleanup_in_progress,
    CORBA::Boolean                   remaining_activations
) throw (
    CORBA::SystemException
)
{
    if (!remaining_activations)
    {
        servant->_remove_ref();
    }
}
```

Listing 7.31 Java Implementation of a Servant Activator Class

```
//Java
package Pure.POADemo;

import Pure.POADemo.RecycleBroker.*;

public class ServantActivatorImpl
    extends org.omg.CORBA.LocalObject
    implements org.omg.PortableServer.ServantActivator
{
  public ServantActivatorImpl(int queueSizeLimit)
  {
    m_queueSizeLimit = queueSizeLimit;
    m_queue          = new java.util.Vector(queueSizeLimit);
  }

  public org.omg.PortableServer.Servant
  incarnate(byte[] oid, org.omg.PortableServer.POA poa)
  throws org.omg.PortableServer.ForwardRequest
  {

    // Step 1 - Obtain the object's type
    String id_string = new String(oid);
    String type      = ObjectIdMapper.extract_type_from_ObjectId(oid);

    System.out.println("Calling incarnate for id " + id_string);
    System.out.println("type = " + type);

    if (type.equals("WasteItem"))
    {
        // Step 2 - Evict overflow servant
        if (m_queue.size() == m_queueSizeLimit)
        {
            byte[] _tmp = (byte[]) m_queue.firstElement();
```

Listing 7.30 continued

```
            try {
                poa.deactivate_object(_tmp);
            }
            catch (org.omg.PortableServer.POAPackage.ObjectNotActive ona) { }
            catch (org.omg.PortableServer.POAPackage.WrongPolicy wp) { }
            m_queue.remove(0);
        }

        // Step 3 - Incarnate this servant
        m_queue.add(oid);
        return RecycleBroker_WasteItem_i._incarnate(oid, poa);
    }
    else
    {
        throw new org.omg.CORBA.OBJECT_NOT_EXIST();
    }
  }

  public void etherealize(
    byte[] oid,
    org.omg.PortableServer.POA poa,
    org.omg.PortableServer.Servant servant,
    boolean cleanup_in_progress,
    boolean remaining_activations
  )
  {
  }

  //-----------------------------
  // Private Member Variables
  //-----------------------------
  private  java.util.Vector      m_queue;
  private  int                   m_queueSizeLimit;
};
```

The `ServantActivator::incarnate()` Operation

The `ServantActivatorImpl::incarnate()` function is called whenever a servant needs to be created and activated. Because we are using lazy activation, this is the only place in the code where a `RecycleBroker_WasteItem_i` servant is created.

The POA invokes `incarnate()`, passing the `ObjectId` (`oid`) and the POA (`poa`) associated with this CORBA object. The `poa/oid` pair represents the fundamental identity of the CORBA object. Recall that the `ObjectId` format we are using for `WasteItem` objects is

`WasteItem` *`integerKeyValue`*

The `ServantActivatorImpl::incarnate()` function implements the following steps:

1. The `ObjectIdMapper::extract_type_from_ObjectId()` function is used to extract the `WasteItem` string from this object ID. The returned string is tested to confirm that the object we are dealing with really is a `WasteItem` object.
2. The code then checks whether the maximum queue size has been reached and evicts an object if necessary.
3. The final step is to go ahead and incarnate the `WasteItem` object. For convenience, this task is delegated to a static `RecycleBroker_WasteItem_i::_incarnate()` function. This `_incarnate()` function is not a standard CORBA function; it just provides a convenient way of organizing our sample code.

Listing 7.32 and Listing 7.33 show a sample implementation of `_incarnate()` in C++ and Java, respectively.

Listing 7.32 C++ `RecycleBroker__WasteItem_i::_incarnate()` *Function*

```
//C++
RecycleBroker_WasteItem_i*
RecycleBroker_WasteItem_i::_incarnate(
    const PortableServer::ObjectId & oid,
    PortableServer::POA_ptr      poa
) throw (
    CORBA::SystemException,
    PortableServer::ForwardRequest
)
{
    CORBA::Long       key;

    key = ObjectIdMapper::extract_key_from_ObjectId(oid);

    if (!ToyDB::DB_instance().is_valid_key(key) )
    {
        throw CORBA::OBJECT_NOT_EXIST();
    }

    return new RecycleBroker_WasteItem_i(poa, key);
}
```

Listing 7.33 Java `RecycleBroker__WasteItem_i._incarnate()` *Method*

```
//Java
package Pure.POADemo;
import Pure.POADemo.RecycleBroker.*;

public class RecycleBroker_WasteItem_i extends WasteItemPOA
{
  //...
  public static RecycleBroker_WasteItem_i
  _incarnate(
```

Listing 7.32 continued

```
    byte[]                          oid,
    org.omg.PortableServer.POA      poa
  )
  throws org.omg.CORBA.SystemException, org.omg.PortableServer.ForwardRequest
  {
    int key;

    key = ObjectIdMapper.extract_key_from_ObjectId(oid);
    System.out.println("Entity key = \"" + key + "\"");

    if (!ToyDB.DB_instance().is_valid_key(key) )
    {
        throw new org.omg.CORBA.OBJECT_NOT_EXIST();
    }

    return new RecycleBroker_WasteItem_i(key);
  }
  //...
}
```

The `_incarnate()` function calls the constructor for the servant object. However, because `WasteItem` is an entity type, it is first necessary to check that a corresponding database record exists for the given `key`.

The `ToyDB::DB_instance()` refers to a hypothetical database adapter class (implementation not shown) that has an associated `is_valid_key()` function to test whether a given key can be found in the database.

C++ `ServantActivator::etherealize()` Function

The responsibility of the `etherealize()` operation is to clean up the resources associated with the CORBA object identified by the `poa` and `oid` parameters. In practice, this usually means deleting the servant.

There are two ways of implementing the `etherealize()` operation. The first way is used with servant reference counting, as shown in Listing 7.34.

Listing 7.34 C++ `etherealize()` Implementation with Servant Reference Counting

```
//C++
// etherealize()
void
ServantActivatorImpl::etherealize(
    const PortableServer::ObjectId & oid,
    PortableServer::POA_ptr          poa,
    PortableServer::Servant          servant,
    CORBA::Boolean                   cleanup_in_progress,
    CORBA::Boolean                   remaining_activations
```

Listing 7.34 continued

```
) throw (
    CORBA::SystemException
)
{
    if (!remaining_activations)
    {
        servant->_remove_ref();
    }
}
```

The second way is used in the absence of servant reference counting, as shown in Listing 7.35.

Listing 7.35 C++ `etherealize()` Implementation Without Servant Reference Counting

```
//C++
// etherealize()
void
ServantActivatorImpl::etherealize(
    const PortableServer::ObjectId & oid,
    PortableServer::POA_ptr          poa,
    PortableServer::Servant          servant,
    CORBA::Boolean                   cleanup_in_progress,
    CORBA::Boolean                   remaining_activations
) throw (
    CORBA::SystemException
)
{
    if (!remaining_activations)
    {
        delete servant;
    }
}
```

In these examples, care is taken to ensure that the `etherealize()` function is compatible with the `MULTIPLE_ID` ID uniqueness policy value. You may recall from the section "A POA for Service Objects" that a POA with an `IdUniquenessPolicy` of `MULTIPLE_ID` might have many entries in its active object map that refer to the same servant object—see Figure 7.3(b). The `remaining_activations` flag is `TRUE` if there are further entries in the active object map that refer to `servant`. Therefore, in Listing 7.34 and Listing 7.35, the `remaining_activations` flag is checked to make sure it is `FALSE` before deleting the servant.

When the `MULTIPLE_ID` policy value is set, the servant reference counting approach (Listing 7.34) works as follows:

1. The servant object is created with a reference count equal to `1`.

2. After being returned by the `ServantActivator::incarnate()` function, the servant object is activated by the POA and has its reference count increased by one (the POA calls `_add_ref()` on the servant). After `N` incarnations of the servant object, the reference count becomes equal to `N+1`.
3. Each time the servant is deactivated, its reference count is automatically decreased by one (the POA calls `_remove_ref()` on the servant). The `etherealize()` function has no effect during the first `N-1` deactivations, because the `remaining_activations` flag is equal to `TRUE`.
4. At the last deactivation, both the POA and the `etherealize()` function call `_remove_ref()` on the servant object (the `remaining_activations` flag is equal to `FALSE`). This reduces the reference count from `2` to `0`, causing the servant object to be deleted.

The other flag passed to `etherealize()` is the `cleanup_in_progress` flag. This flag is equal to `TRUE` if `etherealize()` is called as a consequence of either `PortableServer::POA::deactivate()` or `PortableServer::POA::destroy()` being called with its `etherealize_objects` parameter set to `TRUE`.

Java `ServantActivator.etherealize()` Method

The Java implementation of `etherealize()` is usually trivial, as shown in Listing 7.36.

Listing 7.36 Java `etherealize()` Implementation

```
//Java
// ServantActivatorImpl -- a local object implementation.
package Pure.POADemo;
import Pure.POADemo.RecycleBroker.*;

public class ServantActivatorImpl
    extends org.omg.CORBA.LocalObject
    implements org.omg.PortableServer.ServantActivator
{
  //...
  public void etherealize(
    byte[] oid,
    org.omg.PortableServer.POA poa,
    org.omg.PortableServer.Servant servant,
    boolean cleanup_in_progress,
    boolean remaining_activations
  )
  {
    // Let the Java garbage collector take care of cleaning
    // up the servant.
  }
};
```

As soon as the last servant reference is removed from the active object map, the Java garbage collector takes care of servant cleanup. The `etherealize()` method is occasionally useful when other resources need to be cleaned up at the same time as the servant object.

Implementing a Lazy Factory

The `create()` and `find()` operations of the lazy `WasteItemAdmin` factory class are implemented in Listing 7.37 and Listing 7.38 for C++ and Java, respectively.

Listing 7.37 C++ Implementation of `RecycleBroker::WasteItemAdmin` *Servant with Lazy Activation*

```
//C++
#include <stdlib.h>
#include <iostream.h>

#include "RecycleBroker_WasteItem_i.h"
#include "RecycleBroker_WasteItemAdmin_i.h"
#include "ObjectIdMapper.h"


// RecycleBroker_WasteItemAdmin_i constructor
RecycleBroker_WasteItemAdmin_i::RecycleBroker_WasteItemAdmin_i(
    const PortableServer::POA_ptr poa,
    const PortableServer::POA_ptr poa_for_children
) :
    ServantBaseOverrides(poa),
    m_poa_for_childrenV(PortableServer::POA::_duplicate(poa_for_children))
{ }


// ~RecycleBroker_WasteItemAdmin_i destructor.
//
RecycleBroker_WasteItemAdmin_i::~RecycleBroker_WasteItemAdmin_i()
{ }


// create() - Implements IDL operation "RecycleBroker::WasteItemAdmin::create".
RecycleBroker::WasteItem_ptr
RecycleBroker_WasteItemAdmin_i::create(
    const RecycleBroker::WasteItemDetails& initialData,
    RecycleBroker::KeyType_out      wasteitem_id
) throw (
    CORBA::SystemException,
    RecycleBroker::NoPermission
)
{
    PortableServer::ObjectId_var    oidV;
    CORBA::RepositoryId_var         repIdV;
    CORBA::Object_var               objV;
    RecycleBroker::WasteItem_var    refV;

    cout << endl
         << "RecycleBroker_WasteItemAdmin_i::create() called" << endl;
```

Listing 7.37 continued

```
    // Case: Servant Activator POA

    // Create a DB record for the new CORBA object
    wasteitem_id  = RecycleBroker_WasteItem_i::_create_DB_record(initialData);

    // Construct an 'ObjectId' from the database key, 'wasteitem_id'
    oidV = ObjectIdMapper::make_ObjectId("WasteItem", wasteitem_id);

    // Create a 'WasteItem' object reference
    repIdV = RecycleBroker::_tc_WasteItem->id();
    objV = m_poa_for_childrenV->create_reference_with_id(
                oidV,
                repIdV
            );

    refV = RecycleBroker::WasteItem::_ narrow(objV.in() );
    return refV._retn();
}


// find() -- Implements IDL operation "RecycleBroker::WasteItemAdmin::find".
RecycleBroker::WasteItem_ptr
RecycleBroker_WasteItemAdmin_i::find(
    RecycleBroker::KeyType          wasteitem_id
) throw (
    CORBA::SystemException
)
{
    PortableServer::ObjectId_var    oidV;
    CORBA::RepositoryId_var         repIdV;
    CORBA::Object_var               objV;
    RecycleBroker::WasteItem_var    refV;

    // Case: Activator POA

    // Construct an 'ObjectId' from the database key, 'wasteitem_id'
    oidV = ObjectIdMapper::make_ObjectId("WasteItem", wasteitem_id);

    try {
        // Look up the 'oid' in the 'Active Object Map'
        objV = m_poa_for_childrenV->id_to_reference(oidV.in() );
    }
    catch (PortableServer::POA::ObjectNotActive& ) {
        objV = CORBA::Object::_nil();
    }

    if (CORBA::is_nil(objV.in()) ) {
        // Object not active --> check validity of 'wasteitem_id'
```

Listing 7.37 continued

```
        if (RecycleBroker_WasteItem_i::_find_DB_record(wasteitem_id) ) {
            // Create a 'WasteItem' object reference
            repIdV = RecycleBroker::_tc_WasteItem->id();
            objV = m_poa_for_childrenV->create_reference_with_id(
                        oidV,
                        repIdV
                    );
        }
        else {
            objV = CORBA::Object::_nil();
        }
    }

    refV = RecycleBroker::WasteItem::_ narrow(objV.in() );
    return refV._retn();
}
```

Listing 7.38 Java Implementation of `RecycleBroker::WasteItemAdmin` Servant with Lazy Activation

```
//Java
package Pure.POADemo;
import Pure.POADemo.RecycleBroker.*;

public class RecycleBroker_WasteItemAdmin_i
    extends  WasteItemAdminPOA
{

  // RecycleBroker_WasteItemAdmin_i constructor
  public RecycleBroker_WasteItemAdmin_i(
    org.omg.PortableServer.POA poa_for_children
  )
  {
    m_poa_for_children = poa_for_children;
  }


  // create() - Implements IDL operation "RecycleBroker.WasteItemAdmin.create".
  public WasteItem
  create(
    WasteItemDetails             initialData,
    org.omg.CORBA.IntHolder      wasteitem_id
  )
  throws org.omg.CORBA.SystemException, Pure.POADemo.RecycleBroker.NoPermission
  {
    byte[]                         oid;
    String                         repId;
    org.omg.CORBA.Object           obj;
    WasteItem                      ref;
```

Listing 7.37 continued

```
    // Case: Servant Activator POA

    // Create a DB record for the new CORBA object
    wasteitem_id.value
        = RecycleBroker_WasteItem_i._create_DB_record(initialData);

    // Construct an 'ObjectId' from the database key, 'wasteitem_id'
    oid = ObjectIdMapper.make_ObjectId("WasteItem", wasteitem_id.value);

    try {
        // Create a 'WasteItem' object reference
        repId = WasteItemHelper.type().id();
        obj   = m_poa_for_children.create_reference_with_id(
                    oid,
                    repId
                );
    }
    catch (Exception ex) {
        System.err.println(
            "error: WasteItemAdmin.create\n" + ex
        );
        obj = null;
    }

    ref = WasteItemHelper.narrow(obj);
    return ref;
}


// find() -- Implements IDL operation "RecycleBroker.WasteItemAdmin.find".
public WasteItem
find(
    int          wasteitem_id
)
throws org.omg.CORBA.SystemException
{
    byte[]                          oid;
    String                          repId;
    org.omg.CORBA.Object            obj;
    WasteItem          ref;

    // Case: Servant Activator POA

    // Construct an 'ObjectId' from the database key, 'wasteitem_id'
    oid = ObjectIdMapper.make_ObjectId("WasteItem", wasteitem_id);

    try {
        try {
```

Listing 7.37 continued

```
            // Look up the 'oid' in the 'Active Object Map'
            obj = m_poa_for_children.id_to_reference(oid);
        }
        catch (org.omg.PortableServer.POAPackage.ObjectNotActive ona) {
            obj = null;
        }

        if (obj==null) {
            // Object not active --> check validity of 'wasteitem_id'
            if (RecycleBroker_WasteItem_i._find_DB_record(wasteitem_id) ) {
                // Create a 'WasteItem' object reference
                repId = WasteItemHelper.type().id();
                obj   = m_poa_for_children.create_reference_with_id(
                            oid,
                            repId
                        );
            }
            else {
                obj = null;
            }
        }
    }
    catch (Exception ex) {
        // Error: details of exception handling not shown
        obj = null;
    }

    ref = WasteItemHelper.narrow(obj);
    return ref;
  }

  //---------------------------
  // Private member variables
  //---------------------------
  org.omg.PortableServer.POA  m_poa_for_children;
}
```

The lazy `create()` and `find()` operations are described in the following two subsections.

The `RecycleBroker::WasteItemAdmin::create()` Operation

The algorithm for the lazy `create()` operation consists of the following steps:

1. Create a database record.
2. Create an object reference.

The lazy `create()` operation does not create and activate a servant right away. It returns a plain object reference instead, using the `create_reference_with_id()` function, and lets the `ServantActivator` take care of activating the servant on demand.

The `RecycleBroker::WasteItemAdmin::find()` Operation

The lazy `find()` operation takes the `wasteitem_id` database key as an argument and returns the object reference for an existing `WasteItem` object. If the object does not exist, `find()` returns a nil object reference.

The algorithm for the lazy `find()` operation consists of the following steps:

1. Search the active object map.
   The `PortableServer::POA::id_to_reference()` operation searches the active object map for an object with the given `ObjectId`.
   Considering that we could create an object reference straight away using `create_reference_with_id()`, this step might appear unnecessary. However, remember that for an entity object we must verify that the `wasteitem_id` corresponds to a real database record. Searching for an existing entry in the active object map is the fastest way to confirm this.
2. Check for the existence of the database record.
   If the CORBA object is not found in the active object map, the static `_find_DB_record()` function must be called to determine whether the `wasteitem_id` key corresponds to an existing database record.
3. Create an object reference.
   Once the existence of the `WasteItem` object has been confirmed, we can create an object reference using the `create_reference_with_id()` function.

Creating the Factory

Listing 7.39 and Listing 7.40 show how the `WasteItemAdmin` object, a factory for `WasteItem` objects, is created and activated in C++ and Java, respectively. The listings also show how the `ServantActivator` object is constructed and registered with a POA.

Listing 7.39 C++ Creating and Activating a `RecycleBroker::WasteItemAdmin` *Object*

```
//C++
// Create a basic POA for 'Session' objects.
basic_session_poaV =
    POAUtility::create_basic_POA(
        root_poaV.in(),
        root_poa_managerV.in(),
        "basic_session_poa",
        0,                   // Single threaded
        0                    // for 'Session' objects
    );

// Create an activator POA for 'Entity' objects.
entity_activator_poaV =
    POAUtility::create_servant_activator_POA(
        root_poaV.in(),
        root_poa_managerV.in(),
        "entity_activator_poa",
```

Listing 7.39 continued

```
        0,                  // Single threaded
        1                   // for 'Entity' objects
    );

//----------------------------------------
// Create an 'Evictor' for the 'entity_activator_poa'
//----------------------------------------
entity_activatorV = new ServantActivatorImpl(
                        10      // Queue size limit
                    );
entity_activator_poaV->set_servant_manager(
        entity_activatorV.in()
);

//----------------------------------------
// Create Factories and export their object references.
//----------------------------------------
PortableServer::ObjectId_var oidV;
CORBA::Object_var refV;

// Create a servant for the 'Browsing' interface.
the_WasteItemAdminV = new RecycleBroker_WasteItemAdmin_i(
    basic_session_poaV.in(),           //POA for the Factory
    entity_activator_poaV.in()         //POA for the children
);
oidV = basic_session_poaV->activate_object(the_WasteItemAdminV.in());
refV = basic_session_poaV->id_to_reference(oidV);

// Export the 'WasteItemAdmin' object reference, 'refV', to the Naming Service
...
```

Listing 7.40 Java Creating and Activating a **RecycleBroker::WasteItemAdmin** Object

```
//Java
// Create a basic POA for 'Session' objects.
System.out.println("Creating basic session POA");
POA basic_session_poa =
    Pure.Util.POAUtility.create_basic_POA(
        root_poa,
        root_poa_manager,
        "basic_session_poa",
        false,                  // Single threaded
        false                   // for 'Session' objects
    );

// Create an activator POA for 'Entity' objects.
System.out.println("Creating activator POA");
POA entity_activator_poa =
```

Listing 7.39 continued

```
    Pure.Util.POAUtility.create_servant_activator_POA(
        root_poa,
        root_poa_manager,
        "entity_activator_poa",
        false,                  // Single threaded
        true                    // for 'Entity' objects
    );

//------------------------------------------
// Create an 'Evictor' for the 'entity_activator_poa'
//------------------------------------------
ServantActivatorImpl entity_activator = new ServantActivatorImpl(
                         10       // Queue size limit
                     );
entity_activator_poa.set_servant_manager(
        entity_activator
    );

//------------------------------------------
// Create Factories and export their object references.
//------------------------------------------
System.out.println("Creating WasteItemAdmin object");

byte[] oid = null;
org.omg.CORBA.Object ref = null;

// Create a servant for the 'Browsing' interface.
Servant the_WasteItemAdmin = new RecycleBroker_WasteItemAdmin_i(
    entity_activator_poa         //POA for the children
);
oid = basic_session_poa.activate_object(the_WasteItemAdmin);
ref = basic_session_poa.id_to_reference(oid);

// Export the 'WasteItemAdmin' object reference, 'refV', to the Naming Service
...
```

Servant Locator POA

The second kind of `ServantManager` object is a `ServantLocator`. A servant locator is used in conjunction with a POA that has no active object map. Instead of recording the association between `ObjectIds` and servants statically in an active object map, a servant locator is used to map dynamically between `ObjectIds` and servants—shown schematically in Figure 7.3(c).

Recall two major responsibilities of the POA, mentioned at the beginning of this chapter:

- Locating a servant object to service each incoming invocation request.
- Invoking the appropriate operation on the servant object as given in the invocation request.

When a servant locator is used, responsibility for locating a servant is delegated entirely to the ServantLocator object.

The IDL for the ServantManager and ServantLocator interfaces is shown in Listing 7.41.

Listing 7.41 IDL for the ServantLocator *Interface*

```
//IDL
module CORBA {
    //...
    typedef string Identifier;
};

module PortableServer {
    //...
    typedef sequence<octet> ObjectId;
    exception ForwardRequest {
        Object forward_reference;
    };

    interface ServantManager{ };

    interface ServantLocator : ServantManager {
        native Cookie;

        Servant preinvoke(
            in ObjectId oid,
            in POA adapter,
            in CORBA::Identifier operation,
            out Cookie the_cookie)
        raises (ForwardRequest);

        void postinvoke(
            in ObjectId oid,
            in POA adapter,
            in CORBA::Identifier operation,
            in Cookie the_cookie,
            in Servant the_servant
        );
    };
    //...
};
```

The ServantLocator interface defines two operations, preinvoke() and postinvoke(). These operations are called for every invocation processed by the POA. When using a servant locator, the POA processes an invocation as follows:

1. A request invocation arrives in the POA, triggering the invocation processing.
2. The POA calls preinvoke() to locate a servant.

The `preinvoke()` operation, which is implemented by the developer, returns a servant object and a `Cookie`.

3. The POA invokes the appropriate IDL operation on the servant object returned by `preinvoke()`.
4. The POA calls `postinvoke()`, passing back the `Cookie`, to let the servant locator know that this invocation is complete.
   The `Cookie` is used by the servant locator to match a `preinvoke()` call with a `postinvoke()` call. The servant locator is therefore able to determine when a particular invocation has finished and to clean up any resources associated with that invocation.

Using the servant locator gives the developer sufficient flexibility to implement practically any scheme for managing the lifecycle of servant objects. For example, the CORBA Components specification makes extensive use of the servant locator to implement flexible management of CORBA components—see Chapter 15, "CORBA Components."

The following sections provide an outline of the steps to implement an evictor strategy using a servant locator.

The Evictor Pattern Revisited

The section "Servant Activator POA," earlier in this chapter, describes a strategy for managing the number of servants in memory, known as the evictor pattern. However, the evictor described in that section has a significant drawback: The strategy of evicting the oldest servant in memory is fairly primitive. Moreover, it is difficult to improve on that evictor strategy using a servant activator.

The servant locator, on the other hand, provides an excellent basis for implementing more sophisticated evictor patterns. Some more efficient strategies for choosing which servants to evict are

- To evict the least recently used servant.
  This requires the developer to implement the list of active servants as an ordered list, with the least recently used servant at the front of the list. When the size of the list is about to overflow, the servant at the front of the list can be deactivated and deleted.
  The list of servants can easily be kept in the right order. Each time `preinvoke()` is called, it moves the servant identified by the `oid` argument to the back of the list.
- To evict any servant that has not received invocations within a specified period of time.
  This requires the developer to implement a list that has a time stamp for each servant. The time stamp records the time of the last invocation on a servant. If the period elapsed between the time stamp and the current time is greater than a specified amount, the servant, considered dormant, is deactivated and deleted.
  The time stamps can easily be kept up-to-date by the `preinvoke()` function. Each time `preinvoke()` is called, it can update a servant's time stamp to the current time.

Both of these evictor strategies are straightforward to implement using a servant locator.

Creating the POA

The code to create a POA that uses a `ServantLocator` is conveniently encapsulated in the `create_servant_locator_POA()` function, shown in Listing 7.42 and Listing 7.43.

Listing 7.42 C++ Creating a POA That Uses a Servant Locator

```
//C++
PortableServer::POA_ptr
POAUtility::create_servant_locator_POA(
    PortableServer::POA_ptr           parentPOAP,
    PortableServer::POAManager_ptr    POAManagerP,
    char *                            POAName,
    CORBA::Boolean                    isMultiThread,
    CORBA::Boolean                    isPersistent
)
{
    // Create a policy list.
    CORBA::PolicyList policies;
    policies.length(5);
    CORBA::ULong i = 0;

    // Thread Policy
    PortableServer::ThreadPolicyValue threadPolicy;

    if (isMultiThread) {
        threadPolicy = PortableServer::ORB_CTRL_MODEL;
    }
    else {
        threadPolicy = PortableServer::SINGLE_THREAD_MODEL;
    }
    policies[i] = parentPOAP->create_thread_policy(threadPolicy);

    PortableServer::LifespanPolicyValue     lifeSpanPolicy;
    PortableServer::IdAssignmentPolicyValue idAssignPolicy;

    // Lifespan and IdAssignment Policies
    if (isPersistent) {
        // Policies for 'Entity' objects
        lifeSpanPolicy = PortableServer::PERSISTENT;
        idAssignPolicy = PortableServer::USER_ID;
    }
    else {
        // Policies for 'Session' objects
        lifeSpanPolicy = PortableServer::TRANSIENT;
        idAssignPolicy = PortableServer::SYSTEM_ID;
    }
```

Listing 7.42 continued

```
    // Lifespan Policy
    i++;
    policies[i] = parentPOAP->create_lifespan_policy(lifeSpanPolicy);

    // IdAssignment Policy
    i++;
    policies[i] = parentPOAP->create_id_assignment_policy(idAssignPolicy);

    // IdUniqueness Policy         -  Default = UNIQUE_ID

    // ImplicitActivation Policy  -  Default = NO_IMPLICIT_ACTIVATION

    // RequestProcessing Policy
    i++;
    policies[i] = parentPOAP->create_request_processing_policy(
        PortableServer::USE_SERVANT_MANAGER
    );

    // ServantRetention Policy
    i++;
    policies[i] = parentPOAP->create_servant_retention_policy(
        PortableServer::NON_RETAIN
    );

    return parentPOAP->create_POA(POAName,  POAManagerP, policies);
}
```

Listing 7.43 Java Creating a POA That Uses a Servant Locator

```
//Java
package Pure.Util;
import org.omg.PortableServer.*;

public class POAUtility {
  //...
  public static org.omg.PortableServer.POA
  create_servant_locator_POA(
        org.omg.PortableServer.POA        parentPOA,
        org.omg.PortableServer.POAManager POAManager,
        String                            POAName,
        boolean                           isMultiThread,
        boolean                           isPersistent
  )
  throws org.omg.PortableServer.POAPackage.InvalidPolicy,
         org.omg.PortableServer.POAPackage.AdapterAlreadyExists
  {
    // Create a policy list.
    org.omg.CORBA.Policy policies[] = new org.omg.CORBA.Policy[5];
    int i = 0;
```

Listing 7.43 continued

```
// Thread Policy
org.omg.PortableServer.ThreadPolicyValue threadPolicy = null;

if (isMultiThread) {
    threadPolicy = ThreadPolicyValue.ORB_CTRL_MODEL;
}
else {
    threadPolicy = ThreadPolicyValue.SINGLE_THREAD_MODEL;
}
policies[i] = parentPOA.create_thread_policy(threadPolicy);

org.omg.PortableServer.LifespanPolicyValue     lifeSpanPolicy = null;
org.omg.PortableServer.IdAssignmentPolicyValue idAssignPolicy = null;

// Lifespan and IdAssignment Policies
if (isPersistent) {
    // Policies for 'Entity' objects
    lifeSpanPolicy = LifespanPolicyValue.PERSISTENT;
    idAssignPolicy = IdAssignmentPolicyValue.USER_ID;
}
else {
    // Policies for 'Session' objects
    lifeSpanPolicy = LifespanPolicyValue.TRANSIENT;
    idAssignPolicy = IdAssignmentPolicyValue.SYSTEM_ID;
}

// Lifespan Policy
i++;
policies[i] = parentPOA.create_lifespan_policy(lifeSpanPolicy);

// IdAssignment Policy
i++;
policies[i] = parentPOA.create_id_assignment_policy(idAssignPolicy);

// IdUniqueness Policy        -  Default = UNIQUE_ID

// ImplicitActivation Policy  -  Default = NO_IMPLICIT_ACTIVATION

// RequestProcessing Policy
i++;
policies[i] = parentPOA.create_request_processing_policy(
    RequestProcessingPolicyValue.USE_SERVANT_MANAGER
);

// ServantRetention Policy
i++;
policies[i] = parentPOA.create_servant_retention_policy(
```

Listing 7.43 continued

```
        ServantRetentionPolicyValue.NON_RETAIN
    );

    return parentPOA.create_POA(POAName,  POAManager, policies);
  }
}
```

Two policies are particularly relevant to the use of a `ServantLocator`: the *servant retention policy* and the *request processing policy*. The policy values that must be used in combination with a `ServantLocator` are shown in Table 7.7.

Table 7.7 POA Policy Values Used with a **`ServantLocator`**

Policy Name	Policy Value
`RequestProcessingPolicy`	`USE_SERVANT_MANAGER`
`ServantRetentionPolicy`	`NON_RETAIN`

The `NON_RETAIN` policy value specifies that this POA does not use an active object map. For details of these two POA policies, see the earlier section, "Servant Activator POA."

Mapping for `PortableServer::ServantLocator`

The mapping of the IDL `ServantLocator` interface to C++ and Java is shown in Listing 7.44 and Listing 7.45, respectively.

Listing 7.44 C++ Mapping of the **`ServantLocator`** ***Class***

```
//C++
#include <omg/PortableServerS.hh>

class AccountServantLocatorImpl :
    public PortableServer::ServantLocator,
    public CORBA::LocalObject
{
  public:
    PortableServer::Servant
    preinvoke(
        const PortableServer::ObjectId &        oid,
        PortableServer::POA_ptr                 adapter,
        const char*                             operation,
        PortableServer::ServantLocator::Cookie& the_cookie
    )
    throw (CORBA::SystemException, PortableServer::ForwardRequest);

    void
    postinvoke(
        const PortableServer::ObjectId &       oid,
        PortableServer::POA_ptr                adapter,
        const char*                            operation,
```

Listing 7.44 C++ Mapping of the `ServantLocator` Class

```
        PortableServer::ServantLocator::Cookie the_cookie,
        PortableServer::Servant                the_servant
    )
    throw (CORBA::SystemException);
    //...
};
```

Listing 7.45 Java Mapping of the `ServantLocator` Class

```
//Java
import org.omg.CORBA.*;
import org.omg.CORBA.portable.*;
import org.omg.PortableServer.POA.*;
import org.omg.PortableServer.*;
import org.omg.PortableServer.ServantLocatorPackage.*;

import java.io.*;

public class AccountServantLocatorImpl
  extends LocalObject
  implements ServantLocator
{
  public org.omg.PortableServer.Servant
  preinvoke(
      byte[] oid,
      POA adapter,
      String operation,
      CookieHolder the_cookie
  )
  throws ForwardRequest
  {
    // Implementation not shown...
  }

  public void
  postinvoke(
    byte[] oid,
    POA adapter,
    String operation,
    java.lang.Object the_cookie,
    org.omg.PortableServer.Servant the_servant
  )
  {
    // Implementation not shown...
  }
  //...
}
```

To implement your own servant locator, perform the following steps:

1. Declare a new class that inherits from `ServantLocator`.
2. In the new class, override the `preinvoke()` and `postinvoke()` functions, providing your own implementation.
3. Create an instance of the new `ServantLocator` class and register it with a POA that has the `USE_SERVANT_MANAGER` and `NON_RETAIN` policy values set. Register the `ServantLocator` object in the same way you would register a `ServantActivator` object, using the `PortableServer::POA::set_servant_manager()` operation. See the section "Servant Activator POA."

Default Servant POA

A *default servant* is a single servant object that provides the implementation for many CORBA objects. In a sense, it is an extension of the concept of a service object (see the section "POA for Service Objects"). However, it is implemented using a different set of POA policies and does not require an active object map.

The following list gives some typical uses for a default servant:

- A default servant is useful for implementing stateless CORBA objects. It could be used to implement service objects, for example, instead of using the `MULTIPLE_ID` policy value.
- A default servant can be used to implement entity objects where the state of the entity object is *not* cached in the servant's member variables. That is, every operation on the object's state would require a database read or write operation. This is slower than a conventional entity object implementation, but it saves memory in the server process.
- A default servant can be used to implement the dynamic skeleton interface (see Chapter 22).

The POA policies that are relevant to the use of default servants are the `RequestProcessingPolicy` and the `ServantRetentionPolicy`.

Table 7.8 shows the POA policy values that should be chosen when using a default servant together with an active object map. When an invocation request arrives at a POA having these policies, the POA first searches its active object map to see if there is a matching `ObjectId`. If the `ObjectId` is not found in the active object map, the invocation is made on the default servant instead.

Table 7.8 Default Servant POA Policies—With Active Object Map

Policy Name	Policy Value
`RequestProcessingPolicy`	`USE_DEFAULT_SERVANT`
`ServantRetentionPolicy`	`RETAIN`

Table 7.9 shows the POA policy values that should be chosen when using a default servant on its own, without the active object map. When an invocation request arrives at a POA having these policies, the invocation is made on the default servant.

Table 7.9 Default Servant POA Policies—No Active Object Map

Policy Name	Policy Value
RequestProcessingPolicy	USE_DEFAULT_SERVANT
ServantRetentionPolicy	NON_RETAIN

In both cases, for `RETAIN` and `NON_RETAIN` policy values, if the default servant is of the wrong type, an unspecified system exception is thrown. If there is no default servant registered with the POA, the `CORBA::OBJ_ADAPTER` system exception is thrown.

The IDL in Listing 7.46 gives the operations associated with registering a default servant.

Listing 7.46 IDL Operations to Register a Default Servant

```
//IDL
module PortableServer {
    interface POA {
        //...
        // operations for the USE_DEFAULT_SERVANT policy
        Servant get_servant()
        raises (NoServant, WrongPolicy);

        void set_servant(in Servant p_servant)
        raises (WrongPolicy);
        //...
    };
    //...
};
```

The `POA::set_servant()` operation registers a default servant. It can be invoked only on a POA that has the `USE_DEFAULT_SERVANT RequestProcessingPolicy` value. Otherwise, the `WrongPolicy` user exception is raised.

The `POA::get_servant()` operation gets a reference to a registered default servant. If the POA does not have the `USE_DEFAULT_SERVANT RequestProcessingPolicy` value, the `WrongPolicy` user exception is raised. If no default servant has yet been registered, the `NoServant` user exception is raised.

Two Kinds of Default Servant

There are two basic kinds of default servant:

- A default servant using static skeleton code.
  This kind of default servant implements a single IDL interface. The default servant class inherits from `POA_`*`InterfaceName`* (C++) or *`InterfaceName`*`POA` (Java). Alternatively, it can be implemented using the tie approach.

The steps involved in implementing this kind of servant are described in the next section, "Implementing a Default Servant."

- A default servant using the dynamic skeleton interface (DSI).
  This kind of default servant can implement any number of IDL interfaces. The default servant class inherits from the `PortableServer::DynamicImplementation` (C++) or `org.omg.PortableServer.DynamicImplementation` (Java) class.
  The DSI is typically used for building CORBA bridges or other types of dynamic application for which compiled-in skeleton code is not available. It is described in detail in Chapter 22.

Implementing a Default Servant

The implementation of a default servant using static skeleton code has some similarities to the implementation of a conventional servant object:

- Inheritance from a generated skeleton class can be used to implement the default servant. The default servant class can inherit from the `POA_`*`InterfaceName`* (C++) or *`InterfaceName`*`POA` (Java) class. Alternatively, the default servant can be implemented using the tie approach.
- The *`InterfaceName`* operations are implemented by overriding the member functions of the same name.

The implementation also differs from a conventional servant object implementation:

- Because a default servant is associated with many CORBA object instances, it is inconvenient to cache the state of a CORBA object in the default servant. To do so, you would have to define the servant member variables as arrays indexed by the target object's `ObjectId`. It is better to avoid using a default servant in this way.
- A servant object governed by the `UNIQUE_ID` policy value identifies the target CORBA object either by caching the object identity in a member variable or by calling `PortableServer::POA::servant_to_id()`. A default servant, by contrast, must use the `PortableServer::Current` interface to establish the identity of the target CORBA object.

The `PortableServer::Current` interface is defined by the IDL in Listing 7.47.

Listing 7.47 IDL Definition of the `PortableServer::Current` *Interface*

```
//IDL
module PortableServer {
    //...
    // Current interface
    interface Current : CORBA::Current {
        exception NoContext { };

        POA      get_POA() raises (NoContext);

        ObjectId get_object_id() raises (NoContext);
    };
};
```

A reference to the PortableServer::Current interface is obtained by invoking the resolve_initial_references() operation on the ORB, passing in the string POACurrent. The returned object reference is then narrowed to the PortableServer::Current_ptr type.

The PortableServer::Current operations get_POA() and get_object_id() can be called only in the context of a dispatched invocation. In other words, get_object_id() could be called in the body of a servant method that implements an IDL operation, assuming that the method was called in the context of a CORBA invocation.

If the PortableServer::Current operations are called outside the context of a CORBA invocation, the NoContext user exception is raised.

A factory that creates CORBA objects implemented by a default servant should follow the pattern for a *lazy factory class*, as described in the section "Implementing a Lazy Factory." This involves the use of the POA::create_reference_with_id() operation to generate object references independently of the servant object.

Implicit Activation

The IMPLICIT_ACTIVATION policy value enables you to activate a CORBA object and create a corresponding object reference from the servant object in a single step using the servant's _this() function.

To enable implicit activation, the POA policies shown in Table 7.10 must be used together.

Table 7.10 Policy Values Required for Implicit Activation

POA Policy Type	Policy Value
ImplicitActivationPolicy	IMPLICIT_ACTIVATION
IdAssignmentPolicy	SYSTEM_ID
ServantRetentionPolicy	RETAIN

If you attempt to set the IMPLICIT_ACTIVATION policy value without using the SYSTEM_ID and RETAIN policy values as well, the POA::create_POA() operation raises the InvalidPolicy user exception.

Consider, for example, the RecycleBroker::BranchOffice interface, whose definition is given in Listing 7.2. The C++ signature of the _this() member function is

```
//C++
RecycleBroker::BranchOffice_ptr  POA_RecycleBroker::BranchOffice::_this();
```

and the Java signature of the _this() method is

```
//Java
RecycleBroker.BranchOffice  RecycleBroker.BranchOfficePOA._this();
```

Java mapping also supports an equivalent method that has the `org.omg.CORBA.Object` return type:

```
//Java
org.omg.CORBA.Object org.omg.PortableServer.Servant._this_object();
```

It is important to understand that the behavior of `_this()` depends on whether it is invoked within or outside the context of an invocation dispatch. In fact, the difference is fairly radical:

- The `_this()` function *within* the context of invocation dispatch arises, for example, where the `_this()` function is called in the body of a servant method. The `_this()` function derives the associated POA and `ObjectId` from the context of the invocation (that is, from the `PortableServer::Current` interface). The POA and `ObjectId` are used to create the object reference for the current target object. This use of the `_this()` function is *not* connected with implicit activation and can be used when either the `NO_IMPLICIT_ACTIVATION` or `IMPLICIT_ACTIVATION` policy value is in force.
- The `_this()` function *outside* the context of invocation dispatch arises when the `_this()` function is invoked directly on a servant instance in a CORBA server, as a shortcut to activating a CORBA object. There is no invocation context in this case and no possibility of obtaining the POA and `ObjectId` from the `PortableServer::Current` interface. Instead, the POA is obtained by calling the `_default_POA()` function, and the `ObjectId` is generated automatically (the `SYSTEM_ID` policy value is in force).
  This use of the `_this()` function requires implicit activation and can be used only when the `IMPLICIT_ACTIVATION` policy value is in force.

In the first case, the `_this()` function straightforwardly generates an object reference without causing implicit activation or any other side effects. Hence, this case needs no elaboration.

The following subsections discuss the second case in detail: how to use `_this()` to perform implicit activation.

Implicit Activation Using `_this()`

Because the root POA is an example of a POA that supports implicit activation, it is used for the examples in this section. Implicit activation allows you to activate and create CORBA objects using `_this()` as a shortcut. Listing 7.48 and Listing 7.49 show both the shortcut approach and the longhand equivalent in C++ and Java, respectively. The examples show the activation and creation of the `RecycleBroker::BranchOffice` CORBA object.

Listing 7.48 C++ Activating and Creating a CORBA Object Using `_this()` and Equivalent Code

```
//C++
//-------------------------------------------------------------
// Shortcut Approach
```

Listing 7.48 continued

```
//-----------------------------------------------------------
PortableServer::ServantBase_var theBranchOfficeV;
CORBA::Object_var refV;

the_BranchOfficeV = new RecycleBroker_BranchOffice_i( ... );
refV = the_BranchOfficeV->_this();


...
//-----------------------------------------------------------
// Longhand Equivalent
//-----------------------------------------------------------
PortableServer::ServantBase_var theBranchOfficeV;
PortableServer::POA_var poaV;
PortableServer::ObjectId_var oidV;
CORBA::Object_var refV;

the_BranchOfficeV = new RecycleBroker_BranchOffice_i( ... );
poaV = the_BranchOfficeV->_default_POA();
oidV = poaV->activate_object(the_BranchOfficeV.in());
refV = poaV->id_to_reference(oidV);
```

Listing 7.49 Java Activating and Creating a CORBA Object Using `_this()` and Equivalent Code

```
//Java
//-----------------------------------------------------------
// Shortcut Approach
//-----------------------------------------------------------
org.omg.PortableServer.Servant the_BranchOffice = null;
org.omg.CORBA.Object ref = null;

the_BranchOffice = new RecycleBroker_BranchOffice_i( ... );
ref = the_BranchOffice._this();


...
//-----------------------------------------------------------
// Longhand Equivalent
//-----------------------------------------------------------
org.omg.PortableServer.Servant the_BranchOffice = null;
org.omg.PortableServer.POA     poa = null;
byte[] oid = null;
org.omg.CORBA.Object ref = null;

the_BranchOffice = new RecycleBroker_BranchOffice_i( ... );
poa = the_BranchOffice._default_POA();
oid = poa.activate_object(the_BranchOffice);
ref = poa.id_to_reference(oid);
```

The CORBA specification mandates that _this() obtain a POA by calling _default_POA() on the servant, as shown explicitly in the equivalent code. The default implementation of _default_POA() returns the root POA. If you are not using the root POA to activate your servants, it is essential to override the definition of _default_POA() to return a reference to the correct POA, instead.

Overriding the _default_POA() Function

The default implementation of _default_POA(), which returns a reference to the root POA, is dangerous. If you do not override the definition of _default_POA(), it could happen that some part of the code calls _default_POA() and erroneously uses the root POA to activate one of your CORBA objects.

In particular, if you do not override _default_POA(), the _this() function activates objects erroneously, using the root POA instead of the POA you intended. Because of the potential for confusion and error, it is recommended that you always override the definition of _default_POA() in servant implementations.

The POAManager

The POAManager is used to control the flow of invocation requests into one or more associated POA objects. It is needed particularly as the server application is being started up or shut down. When the server starts up, the POAManager can ensure that requests are not passed to a POA until it is ready to process them. When the server shuts down, the POAManager enables you to specify when request processing should cease.

The remainder of this section is divided into the following parts:

- The lifecycle of a POAManager
- POAManager states
- POAManager state transitions

Lifecycle of a POAManager

A POA manager is created as follows:

- The *root POA manager* is implicitly created at the same time as the root POA, when resolve_initial_references() is called with the "RootPOA" argument. A reference to the root POA manager can be obtained by invoking the POA::the_POAManager attribute on the root POA object.
- A new POA manager object is implicitly created whenever POA::create_POA() is invoked with a nil second argument. The newly created POA object is implicitly associated with a new POA manager.
  A reference to the new POA manager can be obtained by invoking the POA::the_POAManager attribute on the POA object.

If you allow a new POA manager to be implicitly created along with every new POA, you end up with a server architecture like that shown in Figure 7.11(a). Each POA is associated with its own POAManager, allowing the flow of requests into each POA to be independently controlled.

On the other hand, you can also arrange for a single `POAManager` to control the flow of requests into several POA objects, as shown in Figure 7.11(b). A reference to the same `POAManager` object is passed as the second argument of `create_POA()` for each POA object.

In the examples shown in this chapter, all of the POA objects are associated with the root POA manager object. This conveniently allows the flow of requests into POA objects to be simultaneously controlled and is the preferred approach for normal CORBA applications.

Because a single POA manager object provides uniform control over the flow of messages, it is natural for ORB implementations to identify a POA manager with a single communications channel. For example, an ORB implementation with a TCP/IP transport layer might identify a POA manager with a single server IP port. Whether or not this is done in practice is an ORB-specific implementation detail.

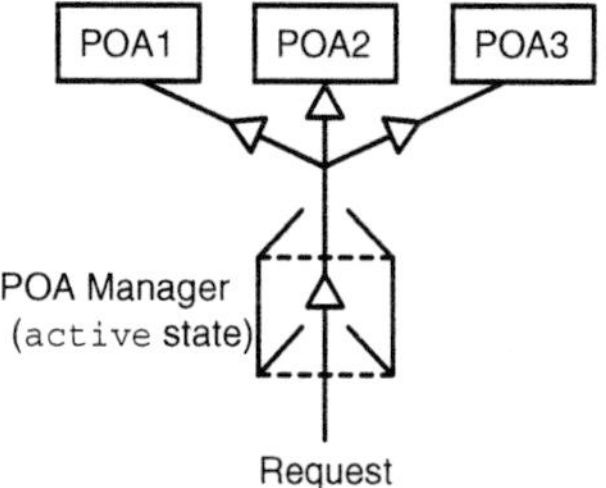

(a) One POA manager for Many POAs

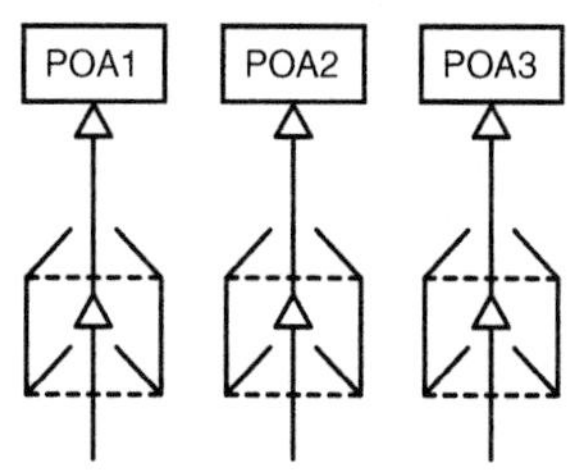

(b) One POA manager per POA Instance

Figure 7.11

Associating POAs and `POAManagers`.

A `POAManager` object is implicitly destroyed when all of its associated POA objects are destroyed.

POAManager States

A `POAManager` object can be in one of four states: `HOLDING`, `ACTIVE`, `DISCARDING`, or `INACTIVE`. These four states are described as follows:

- **`HOLDING`** When a POA manager is in the holding state, no requests are passed on to its associated POAs. Incoming requests are held in a message queue and are processed after the POA manager makes a transition to the active state. A newly created POA manager is initially put into the holding state.
  One of the uses of the holding state is to ensure that server startup proceeds smoothly. There is usually some short delay between the time when a server is physically able to receive messages from the network (for example, when it begins listening on an IP port) and the time when a POA is able to process the requests. The holding state allows the requests to be buffered until the POA is ready to process them.
- **`ACTIVE`** When a POA manager is in the active state, incoming requests are passed on to all of its associated POAs. This is the normal state of the POA manager in a running server application.
- **`DISCARDING`** When a POA manager is in the discarding state, the ORB responds to incoming requests by raising a `CORBA::TRANSIENT` system exception back to the client. The requests are neither processed nor stored in a message queue. However, any processing of requests that began before the `POAManager` entered the discarding state will be allowed to finish.
  The discarding state can be useful as a means of controlling the flow of requests into a heavily loaded server. If the load on the server becomes unmanageable, the POA manager can be put into the discarding state temporarily.
- **`INACTIVE`** A POA manager in the inactive state rejects all incoming requests. The way in which requests are rejected is specific to the ORB implementation. It is impossible to make a transition to any other state from the inactive state. A POA manager typically enters the inactive state just prior to server shutdown. No new requests can be processed by its associated POA objects.

POAManager State Transitions

Figure 7.12 shows the allowed transitions between these states and the IDL operations that effect the transitions.

The operations used to change from one state to another are given by the IDL in Listing 7.50.

Listing 7.50 IDL for the `PortableServer::POAManager` Interface

```
//IDL
module PortableServer {
    //...
    // POAManager interface
    interface POAManager {
        exception AdapterInactive{};
```

Listing 7.50 continued

```
        enum State {HOLDING, ACTIVE, DISCARDING, INACTIVE};

        void activate()
        raises(AdapterInactive);

        void hold_requests(in boolean wait_for_completion)
        raises(AdapterInactive);

        void discard_requests(in boolean wait_for_completion)
        raises(AdapterInactive);

        void deactivate(
            in boolean etherealize_objects,
            in boolean wait_for_completion
        )
        raises(AdapterInactive);

        State get_state();
    };
};
```

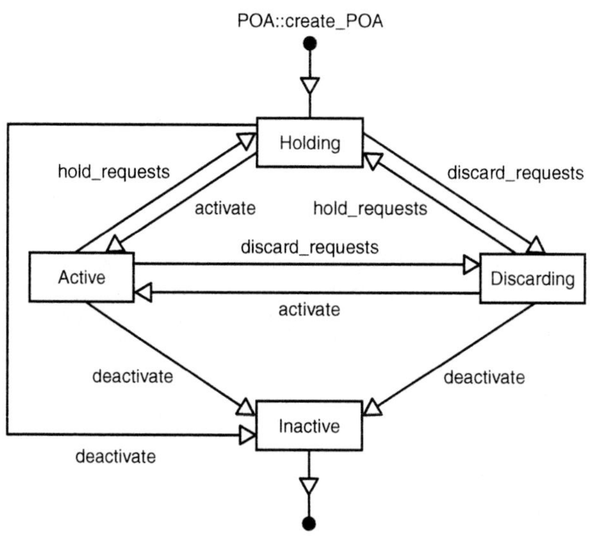

Figure 7.12

A `POAManager` *state transition diagram.*

The four operations for making state transitions are `activate()`, `hold_requests()`, `discard_requests()`, and `deactivate()`.

The AdapterInactive user exception can be raised by any of the four state transition operations if they are invoked on a POA manager in the INACTIVE state. An INACTIVE POA manager is not allowed to undergo any further state transitions (not even the INACTIVE to INACTIVE state transition).

Three of the four state transition operations take a wait_for_complete flag as an argument. When the POA manager is making a transition from the ACTIVE state to one of the other states, it may take some time before the associated POA objects finish processing the outstanding requests. If the wait_for_complete flag is TRUE, an operation will wait for outstanding requests to finish processing. Otherwise, the operation returns straightaway.

Calling an operation with the wait_for_complete flag equal to TRUE, theoretically, could lead to deadlock if called in the same thread that is actually processing the associated requests. If this is liable to occur, the ORB will throw the CORBA::BAD_INV_ORDER system exception instead, and the state transition will not take place.

The deactivate() operation takes an etherealize_objects flag as its first parameter. This option affects only POAs that have a ServantActivator installed (see the section "Servant Activator POA," earlier in this chapter). The option instructs the servant activator POAs to call etherealize() for every entry in their active object maps. The etherealize_objects flag should normally be set equal to TRUE. A value of FALSE is used only in case of abnormal server shutdown.

POA Activation

Occasionally, it is necessary to develop a server in such a way that POA objects are created only when they are needed. For example, certain kinds of bridges built using the dynamic skeleton interface might be required to construct POA hierarchies dynamically.

To support dynamic creation of POA objects, the PortableServer module provides an AdapterActivator interface. The developer implements the AdapterActivator interface by providing code that can create POA objects on demand.

Listing 7.51 shows extracts from the PortableServer module that are relevant to the AdapterActivator.

Listing 7.51 IDL Definition of the **PortableServer::AdapterActivator** *Interface*

```
//IDL
module PortableServer {
    //...
    // AdapterActivator interface
    interface AdapterActivator {
        boolean unknown_adapter(
            in POA parent,
            in string name
```

Listing 7.51 continued

```
        );
    };

    // POA interface
    interface POA {
        exception AdapterNonExistent {};
        //...
        attribute AdapterActivator the_activator;
        //...
        POA find_POA(in string adapter_name, in boolean activate_it)
        raises (AdapterNonExistent);
        //...
    };
};
```

The `AdapterActivator` interface is implemented by the developer and installed in one or more existing POA objects. The POA objects created by an `AdapterActivator` are the direct children of the POA in which the `AdapterActivator` is installed, the parent POA.

The `AdapterActivator::unknown_adapter()` operation is used to create new POA instances. It is invoked automatically when an invocation request arrives at the parent POA and the parent POA cannot find the appropriate child. The `parent` argument is a reference to the POA that received the invocation request. The `name` argument identifies the child POA sought by the parent.

The `POA::the_activator` attribute is used either to install an `AdapterActivator` in a POA (modifier method) or to obtain a reference to an already installed `AdapterActivator` object (accessor method).

The `POA::find_POA()` operation is used sto obtain a reference to a child POA. The operation returns a reference to the child POA whose name is given by the `adapter_name` argument. If an active POA with the `adapter_name` name cannot be found, the outcome depends on the value of the Boolean `activate_it` argument:

- If the `activate_it` argument is `FALSE`, the `AdapterNonExistent` user exception is raised.
- If the `activate_it` argument is `TRUE`, an attempt is made to create the child POA using the `AdapterActivator` (if one is installed). If this attempt fails, the `AdapterNonExistent` user exception is raised.

An `AdapterActivator` object is implemented as a locality-constrained CORBA object. Listing 7.52 and Listing 7.53 show the declaration of a `MyAdapterActivator` example class in C++ and Java, respectively.

Listing 7.52 C++ Declaration of `MyAdapterActivator` *Class*

```
//C++
class MyAdapterActivator :
    public PortableServer::AdapterActivator,
    public CORBA::LocalObject
{
  public:
    //...

    // Developer must override this function:
    virtual CORBA::Boolean
    unknown_adapter(
        PortableServer::POA_ptr  parent,
        const char*  name
    )
    throw (CORBA::SystemException);
};
```

Listing 7.53 Java Declaration of `MyAdapterActivator` *Class*

```
//Java
class MyAdapterActivator
      implements org.omg.PortableServer.AdapterActivator
      extends org.omg.CORBA.LocalObject
{
    //...

    // Developer must override this function:
    boolean unknown_adapter(
        org.omg.PortableServer.POA parent,
        java.lang.String name
    );
}
```

The `unknown_adapter()` typically implements the following algorithm:

1. Decide whether or not to create the child POA called `name`. If the child POA is not to be created, return `FALSE`.
2. Invoke `create_POA()` on the `parent` POA, passing `name` as the first argument.
3. If the newly created child POA also needs to be associated with an `AdapterActivator`, install an `AdapterActivator` using the `the_activator` modifier method.
4. If the `name` child POA was successfully created, return `TRUE`.

At least one POA object has to exist in the server before any invocation requests can be processed. At a minimum, you can get away with creating just the root POA object. An `AdapterActivator` object can be installed in the root POA to senable further POA objects to be created on demand.

Recall that POA hierarchies can potentially be nested. For example, an invocation request arriving at the root POA might be targeted at a CORBA object that lives at the bottom of a POA hierarchy `firstPOA/secondPOA`. This request results in a cascade of POA activations: The root POA's `AdapterActivator` creates the `firstPOA` POA, and the `firstPOA` POA's `AdapterActivator` creates the `secondPOA` POA. The `secondPOA` POA then s handles the processing of the request.

Summary

This chapter has outlined all of the features provided by the portable object adapter. It is not necessary to master all of the POA functionality at once, however. A simple CORBA application typically needs only two different kinds of POAs: one for session objects and one for entity objects, as described in the earlier sections of this chapter.

For more advanced applications, particularly for applications supporting very many objects, the servant activator, servant locator, and default servant features are invaluable. For example, in the CORBA Components specification, described in Chapter 15, extensive use is made of the servant locator, which allows the lifecycle of CORBA objects to be managed with maximum flexibility.

CHAPTER 8

The any Type

The any type provides support for dynamic typing in IDL. Specifying a parameter or return value to be of type any allows you to decide at runtime what type of data is sent.

Introduction to the any Type

The any type is a built-in CORBA data type that can be used as a parameter or return value of an IDL operation. It can also be nested inside other data types; for example, you could have a sequence of anys, a struct containing an any, or even an any containing an any. The following IDL fragment shows an example of its use:

```
//IDL
typedef sequence<any> AnySeq;

interface BlobStack {
    readonly attribute size;
    void push(in any blob);
    void pop(out any blob);
    void popNBlobs(in long n, out AnySeq blobs);
};
```

The BlobStack interface describes a stack whose elements can be of arbitrary type. Elements of the stack are added and removed using push() and pop(), respectively. The popNBlobs() operation returns an out parameter of type AnySeq, allowing you to remove an arbitrary number of stack elements at a time.

The any type is not an escape hatch for sending arbitrarily formatted data—it is possible to send only built-in IDL types or user-defined IDL types. The type of data sent in the any must be declared somewhere in IDL, and this declaration must be accessible to both client and server so that they can marshal the any.

The marshalling of an any is somewhat different from ordinary data types. When an ordinary data type is sent as a parameter, only the value of the data is marshalled. When an any is sent as a parameter, two pieces of information are sent:

- value—This is the data contained in the any.
- type—This is a type code that completely describes the layout of the any data.

The inclusion of type information makes the any completely self describing.

Because an any is self describing, it is possible to marshal and parse its data without having access to the original IDL. However, this requires advanced features of dynamic CORBA: dynamic anys and dynamic creation of TypeCodes. See Chapter 19, "DynAny Type."

When to Use the any Type

There are two common situations when you might need to use the any type:

- In operations that must handle a variety of data types.
  The best way to use an any is as a parameter that handles a wide variety of data types. An example of this can be found in messaging services. The IDL that describes the CORBA Events Service needs to be able to propagate messages of an arbitrary type. The any type is therefore used to declare the messages that are passed as parameters.
- In recursive data structures.
  Because an any can contain data of an arbitrary type, it is possible to build flexible, recursive data structures using them. This is a powerful feature, but there is likely to be some performance cost associated with this kind of use.

The difficulty or ease in implementing an application using anys depends strongly on the predictability of any data. If it is known that a limited number of data types will be sent in the any, it is much easier to identify the any's contents and extract the data.

When Not to Use the any Type

Just as important as knowing when to use anys is knowing when not to use them. It is best to avoid the unnecessary use of anys, because of the extra marshalling overhead, which can affect performance.

A common wrong use of an any is to declare a parameter as an any because the declaration of that parameter type is unclear at the outset and subject to change during application development. For example, in a financial application you might want to pass the state of an Account object from the server to the client. A sample IDL is

```
//IDL
struct AccountDetails {
    long        accountNumber;
    string      name;
    fixed<8,2> balance;
};
```

```
interface Account {
   void getDetails(in long accNumber, out AccountDetails details);
};
```

In this example, `AccountDetails` represents the state of an `Account` object. Unfortunately, if the server wants to pass an object's state to the client, it is impossible to hide this state. You could declare the second parameter of `getDetails()` to be an `any`, but you still have to declare the `AccountDetails` struct that will be passed in the `any`.

This example demonstrates that distributed programming sometimes meshes imperfectly with object orientation. The example breaks the object-oriented principle of data hiding. There is no magic solution to this problem, and declaring `details` to be of type `any` instead of type `AccountDetails` does not solve it. In a multi-platform, multi-language architecture such as CORBA, an object that has its state passed from place to place must have that state declared in the IDL.

A Sample IDL Module

For the sections that follow it is helpful to have a sample of CORBA data types at hand to illustrate insertion from and extraction to an `any`. The IDL module `SampleTypes`, seen in Listing 8.1, declares a representative set of types—this is essentially the same set as used in Chapter 4, "Memory Management."

Listing 8.1 Sample IDL Data Types Used by `any` *Examples*

```
// IDL
#pragma prefix "pure-corba-3.com"

module SampleTypes {
     typedef string< 64 >   BoundedString;
     typedef wstring< 128 > BoundedWString;

     struct FixLen {
          short theShort;
          float theFloat;
     };
     struct VarLen {
          string theString;
          long theLong;
     };
     typedef sequence< FixLen > SeqOfFixLen;
     typedef sequence< VarLen > SeqOfVarLen;
     typedef sequence< VarLen, 5 > BSeqOfVarLen;

     typedef fixed<6,2> Money;

     union Poly switch(short) {
          case 1: short theShort;
          case 2: string theString;
     };
```

Listing 8.1 continued

```
    typedef FixLen ArrOfFixLen[10];
    typedef VarLen ArrOfVarLen[10];

    exception GenericExc {
        string reason;
    };

    interface Foo {
        ...
    }; // interface Foo

}; // module SampleTypes
```

This IDL declares a number of compound types—structs, sequences, and arrays—as well as `typedef`s of some basic types.

C++ Example of Passing `any`s

C++ mapping maps the IDL type `any` to the C++ class `CORBA::Any`. A corresponding `_var` class, `CORBA::Any_var`, is also generated. The C++ mapping of the `any` is focussed on the definition of the following two operators: the insertion operator `<<=` (left-shift assignment) and the extraction operator `>>=` (right-shift assignment).

The motivation for using operators for insertion and extraction is to take advantage of the C++ overloading mechanism. With the help of operator overloading, the appropriate function is chosen automatically by the C++ compiler according to the type of data being inserted or extracted.

For a variety of reasons, however, overloading cannot automatically cope with the full range of CORBA data types. This gives rise to exceptions to the simple insertion and extraction syntax. Additional helper types are used to insert and extract many of the CORBA data types.

The `AnyPasser` Interface

Consider the following sample IDL, which introduces the interface `AnyPasser`:

```
// IDL
interface AnyPasser {
    void sendEvent(in any item);
};
```

The `sendEvent()` operation can be used to send an `any` from a client to a server. The next two sections show client code and server code that make use of the interface `AnyPasser`.

C++ Client for `AnyPasser` Interface

Suppose that you are writing a client of the `AnyPasser` interface that sends only one of the IDL types `long` and `string` and the user-defined type `SampleTypes::VarLen`. (See the section "A Sample IDL Module," earlier in this chapter.) The operation `sendEvent()` can be invoked, as shown in Listing 8.2.

Listing 8.2 C++ Invocation of `sendEvent()`

```
// C++
//-------------------
// Initialize the object reference and the 'any'.
//
AnyPasser_var theAnyPasserV = /* initialize 'AnyPasser' object reference */;
CORBA::Any theItem;

// Pass a 'long' using operation 'sendEvent()'
theItem <<= (CORBA::Long) 10001;
theAnyPasserV->sendEvent(theItem);
...
// Pass a 'string' using operation 'sendEvent()'
theItem <<= "A string item.";
theAnyPasserV->sendEvent(theItem);
...
// Pass a 'SampleTypes::VarLen' struct using operation 'sendEvent()'
SampleTypes::VarLen_var theVarLenV = new SampleTypes::VarLen();
theVarLenV->theString = CORBA::string_dup("String member");
theVarLenV->theLong   = (CORBA::Long) 123;
theItem <<= theVarLenV._ retn();
theAnyPasserV->sendEvent(theItem);
```

Insertion of the types `long` and `string` into the any is straightforward. When inserting the type `SampleTypes::VarLen`, the call to `_retn()` causes the `_var` to give up ownership of the data it references. After insertion, the instance `theItem` owns the memory, instead.

C++ Server for `AnyPasser` Interface

Suppose that the server developer works in close collaboration with the developer of the preceding client. In that case, the server developer knows that there are only three possible values for the any: a `long`, a `string`, or a `SampleTypes::VarLen`. Given that the implementation class is called `AnyPasserImpl`, the implementation of the operation `sendEvent()` can be written as shown in Listing 8.3.

Listing 8.3 C++ Implementation of `sendEvent()`

```
// C++
...
AnyPasserImpl::sendEvent(const CORBA::Any& item) {
     CORBA::Long l;
     char * s;
     SampleTypes::VarLen * vlP;

     if (item >>= l) {
          // value is of type 'long'
```

Listing 8.3 continued

```
            cout << "Received long = " << l << endl;
        }
        else if (item >>= s) {
            // value is of type 'string'
            cout << "Received string = " << s << endl;
        }
        else if (item >>= vlP) {
            // value is of type 'SampleTypes::VarLen'
            cout << "Received VarLen = {" << endl
                << "\ttheString = " << vlP->theString << endl
                << "\ttheLong   = " << vlP->theLong   << endl
                << "}" << endl;
        }
        else {
            // value is of unexpected type!
            // probably should raise an exception in this case.
            cout << "Received unexpected type in any" << endl;
        }
}
```

The expression that is used to extract an any, for example `item >>= l`, has a return type of `CORBA::Boolean`. If the type of the extracted variable (in this case `l`) matches the type of the data in the any, the expression returns `TRUE`. Otherwise, the expression returns `FALSE`, and the extraction fails to take place.

The return status of the extraction expression facilitates a simple method for checking the contents of the any. As shown in the example above, a series of `if-then-else` clauses can be used to attempt extraction into a fixed set of alternative data types. In many cases, this simple approach is adequate.

There are times when this approach is unsatisfactory: There might be such a large number of alternatives that the linear search (as used above) affects performance, or you might not know in advance what types will be sent in the any. In both of these cases, you have to learn about type code parsing to make further progress. This topic is beyond the scope of this chapter—reference material on type codes can be found in Chapter 17, "IDL Data Types." See also Chapter 19, "DynAny Type."

C++ Insertion into `CORBA::Any`

This section provides sample code that shows how a variety of data types are inserted into a `CORBA::Any`. Some special cases of insertion are discussed in more detail as they arise.

Insertion of Basic Types

Insertion of most basic types `T` is accomplished using the following operator:

```
// C++
void operator<<=(CORBA::Any&, T);      // Copying insertion
```

This is sufficient for most data types `T` that are normally passed by value, such as `short`, `long`, and `float`.

Insertion of Compound Types

Insertion of most compound types `T` is accomplished using the following pair of operators:

```
// C++
void operator<<=(CORBA::Any&, const T&);      // Copying insertion
void operator<<=(CORBA::Any&, T*);            // Consuming insertion
```

These two operators give you the choice of making either a copying insertion or a consuming insertion. This applies to most compound data types, except for arrays and object references.

Copying Insertion

A copying insertion is an insertion that creates a deep copy of the data and puts the copied data under the ownership of the any.

The copying insertion of a compound type `T` is illustrated in Figure 8.1.

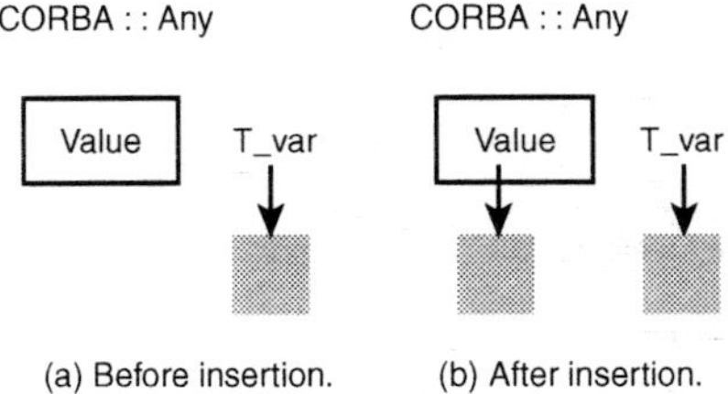

Figure 8.1

A copying insertion into `CORBA::Any`.

With this type of insertion, the `CORBA::Any` creates and owns a deep copy of the data. Deallocation of the original data remains the responsibility of the original reference. Deallocation of the inserted copy is the responsibility of the `CORBA::Any`.

The `CORBA::Any` deletes the inserted copy when either of the following happens:

- The `CORBA::Any` itself is deleted.
- A new value is inserted into the `CORBA::Any`.

This ensures that the memory associated with the inserted copy is not leaked.

Consider the following code fragment, which shows two examples of a copying insertion. The fragment uses the IDL struct `SampleTypes::VarLen`, previously defined in the section "A Sample IDL Module":

```
// C++
//-----------------------------------------------------------------
```

```
// Inserting Struct - Copying insertion
//
// Uses: //IDL
//       //...in module 'SampleTypes'
//            struct VarLen {
//                 string theString;
//                 long theLong;
//            };
//
CORBA::Any theAny;      // 'theAny' is initially empty
SampleTypes::VarLen theVarLen;
theVarLen.theString = CORBA::string_dup("Insert me!");
theVarLen.theLong   = (CORBA::Long) 123;

// 'theAny' makes a deep copy of the struct 'theVarLen'
theAny <<= theVarLen;                          // Copying insertion

SampleTypes::VarLen_var theVarLenV = new SampleTypes::VarLen();
theVarLenV->theString = CORBA::string_dup("Insert me!");
theVarLenV->theLong   = (CORBA::Long) 123;

// The insertion occurs as follows:
// i)  The data currently referenced by the 'any' is deleted.
// ii) The 'any' makes a deep copy of '*theVarLenV'.
theAny <<= *theVarLenV;                        // Copying insertion
```

This shows `theVarLen` and `*theVarLenV` being inserted into a `CORBA::Any`. In both cases, the `VarLen` struct is passed by value, and this results in a copying insertion.

This is a general rule: Passing by value to the insertion operator <<= indicates copying insertion. Types naturally represented as pointers—strings, arrays, and object references—are treated as a special case.

Consuming Insertion

A consuming insertion is an insertion that puts the original data under the ownership of the any. No copy of the data is made.

The consuming insertion of a compound type `T` is illustrated in Figure 8.2.

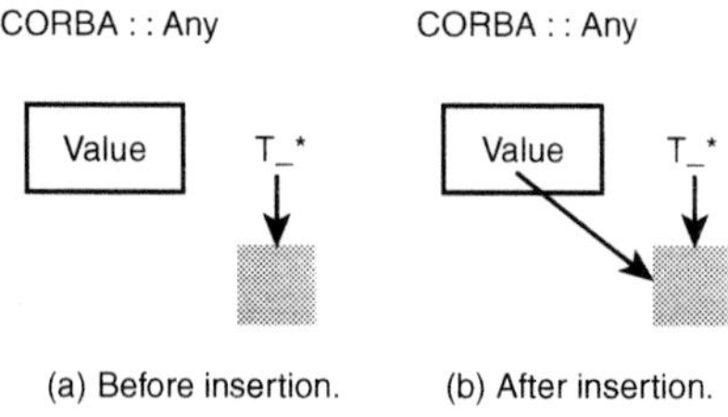

Figure 8.2

A consuming insertion into `CORBA::Any`.

With this type of insertion, the CORBA::Any does not create a new copy of the data. Instead, the value of the CORBA::Any is initialized so as to reference the original copy of the data. The CORBA::Any takes over ownership of the inserted data and has responsibility for deallocating it. The original reference loses ownership of the data, and it should not attempt to write to or read from the data any longer.

The CORBA::Any deletes the inserted data when either of the following happens:

- The CORBA::Any itself is deleted.
- A new value is inserted into the CORBA::Any.

This ensures that the memory associated with the inserted data is not leaked.

Consider the following code fragment, which shows two examples of a consuming insertion. The fragment uses the same IDL struct as the previous example (SampleTypes::VarLen, defined in the previous section "A Sample IDL Module"):

```
// C++
//-------------------------------------------------------------------
// Inserting Struct - Consuming insertion
//
// (Uses same IDL as in previous section)
//
CORBA::Any theAny;      // 'theAny' is initially empty
SampleTypes::VarLen * theVarLenP = new SampleTypes::VarLen();
theVarLenP->theString = CORBA::string_dup("Insert me!");
theVarLenP->theLong   = (CORBA::Long) 123;

// 'theAny' makes a shallow copy of the struct 'VarLen'
// and assumes ownership of the data
theAny <<= theVarLenP;                     // Consuming insertion

SampleTypes::VarLen_var theVarLenV = new SampleTypes::VarLen();
theVarLenV->theString = CORBA::string_dup("Insert me!");
theVarLenV->theLong   = (CORBA::Long) 123;

// The insertion occurs as follows:
//    i)   'theVarLenV' gives up ownership of the data by invoking '_retn()'
//    ii)  The data currently referenced by the 'any' is automatically deleted
//    iii) The 'any' assumes ownership of the data
//         referenced by 'theVarLenV'
theAny <<= theVarLenV._retn();             // Consuming insertion
```

In the first case, a dumb pointer theVarLenP is inserted into the CORBA::Any. The fact that theVarLenP is passed as a pointer indicates that a consuming insertion is intended. The CORBA::Any makes a shallow copy of the pointer and takes ownership of the referenced data.

In the second case, a smart pointer theVarLenV is used to reference the data before insertion. In order for a _var type to be inserted into a CORBA::Any, it is essential that the _var give up ownership of the data it references. Therefore, in the above example, the _retn() method is invoked on the _var. This returns a simple pointer to the data and relinquishes ownership.

The general rule is this: Passing a pointer to the insertion operator indicates consuming insertion. Exceptions to this pattern are types that are naturally represented as pointers—strings, arrays, and object references.

CAUTION

Never insert a _var directly into a CORBA::Any. That would result in both the _var and the CORBA::Any owning the data. Disastrous results would occur when they both subsequently tried to delete the same block of memory.

Inserting _var Types

If you want to make a consuming insertion of a _var type, you have to be careful. A _var type cannot be inserted directly or you would have a situation in which both the _var and the CORBA::Any own the associated data, leading to double deletion of the data. The correct way to make a consuming insertion, taking the example of a struct, is as follows:

```
//C++
SampleTypes::VarLen_var theVarLenV = new SampleTypes::VarLen();
theVarLenV->theString = CORBA::string_dup("Insert me!");
theVarLenV->theLong   = (CORBA::Long)123;
theAny <<= theVarLenV._retn();                    // Consuming insertion
```

The trick is to use the _retn() method of the _var class in the insertion statement (note that it is invoked as theVarLenV._retn(), not theVarLenV->_retn()). The return value of _retn() is a plain pointer of type SampleTypes::VarLen*. Critically, a side effect of calling _retn() is that the _var gives up ownership of the data. Afterward, the CORBA::Any is the sole owner of the data.

Inserting Unambiguous Basic Types

The code in Listing 8.4 shows how unambiguous basic types are inserted into an any.

Listing 8.4 C++ Examples of Inserting Unambiguous Basic Types

```
//C++
//-----------------------------------------------------------------
// Declaration of 'CORBA::Any' on the stack
//
CORBA::Any theAny;

//-----------------------------------------------------------------
// Inserting unambiguous Basic Types
//
```

Listing 8.4 continued

```
// Inserting a 'short'
theAny <<= (CORBA::Short) -33;              // Copying insertion

CORBA::Short s = -33;
theAny <<= s;                               // Copying insertion

// Inserting an 'unsigned short'
theAny <<= (CORBA::UShort) 44;              // Copying insertion

CORBA::UShort us = 44;
theAny <<= us;                              // Copying insertion

// Inserting a 'long'
theAny <<= (CORBA::Long) -1000000;          // Copying insertion

CORBA::Long l = -1000000;
theAny <<= l;                               // Copying insertion

// Inserting an 'unsigned long'
theAny <<= (CORBA::ULong) 2000123;          // Copying insertion

CORBA::ULong ul = 2000123;
theAny <<= ul;                              // Copying insertion

// Inserting a 'long long'
theAny <<= (CORBA::LongLong) -1234;         // Copying insertion

CORBA::LongLong ll = -1234;
theAny <<= ll;                              // Copying insertion

// Inserting an 'unsigned long long'
theAny <<= (CORBA::ULongLong) 1234;         // Copying insertion

CORBA::ULongLong ull = 1234;
theAny <<= ull;                             // Copying insertion

// Inserting a 'float'
theAny <<= (CORBA::Float) 2.567;            // Copying insertion

CORBA::Float f = 2.567;
theAny <<= f;                               // Copying insertion

// Inserting a 'double'
theAny <<= (CORBA::Double) 2.567891;        // Copying insertion

CORBA::Double d = 2.567891;
theAny <<= d;                               // Copying insertion
```

Listing 8.4 continued

```
// Inserting a 'long double'
theAny <<= (CORBA::LongDouble) 1e-40;        // Copying insertion

CORBA::LongDouble ld = 1e-40;
theAny <<= ld;  // Copying insertion
```

Inserting Ambiguous Basic Types

The CORBA specification does not require `boolean`, `octet`, `char`, and `wchar` to map to distinct types. For example, it is possible that the IDL types `unsigned char` and `octet` both map to the C++ type `unsigned char`. It follows that operator overloading cannot be relied on to insert those types.

A set of helper types, `CORBA::Any::from_boolean`, `CORBA::Any::from_octet`, `CORBA::Any::from_char`, and `CORBA::Any::from_wchar`, are defined to aid the insertion of these types.

The code in Listing 8.5 shows how ambiguous basic types are inserted into an `any`.

Listing 8.5 C++ Examples of Inserting Ambiguous Basic Types

```
//-----------------------------------------------------------------------
// Inserting Ambiguous Basic Types
//

// Inserting a 'boolean'
CORBA::Boolean b = 1;
theAny <<= CORBA::Any::from_boolean(b);      // Copying insertion

// Inserting an 'octet'
CORBA::Octet o = 0xf3;
theAny <<= CORBA::Any::from_octet(o);        // Copying insertion

// Inserting a 'char'
CORBA::Char c = 'q';
theAny <<= CORBA::Any::from_char(c);         // Copying insertion

// Inserting a 'wchar;
CORBA::WChar wc = L'q';
theAny <<= CORBA::Any::from_wchar(wc);  // Copying insertion
```

Inserting String Types

To insert bounded strings into a `CORBA::Any`, there has to be some way of specifying the bound as the string is inserted. For this reason, the helper type `CORBA::Any::from_string` is defined. Two constructors for this helper type are declared:

```
// C++
CORBA::Any::from_string(char * s,                  // string to insert
                        CORBA::ULong b,            // bound, as declared in IDL
```

```
                        CORBA::Boolean n=FALSE    // no-copy flag
            );

// Constructor for const strings
CORBA::Any::from_string(const char * s,           // const string to insert
                        CORBA::ULong b            // bound, as declared in IDL
            );
```

A bound of `0`, passed as the second argument, indicates that the string is unbounded. When the no-copy flag is set to `TRUE`, a consuming insertion is made.

The code in Listing 8.6 shows how string types are inserted into an `any`. Three kinds of string are considered:

- Unbounded strings
- Bounded strings
- Aliases of a bounded string

Listing 8.6 C++ Examples of Inserting String Types

```
//-----------------------------------------------------------------
// Inserting Unbounded Strings
//

theAny <<= "Insert me!";                       // Copying insertion

char * theString = "Insert me!";
theAny <<= theString;                          // Copying insertion

const char * theConstString = "Insert me!";
theAny <<= theConstString;                     // Copying insertion

// Note: There is no special insertion operator for '_var' types
//       so we convert it to a 'char *' using the 'in()' method.
CORBA::String_var theStringV = CORBA::string_dup("Insert me!");
theAny <<= theStringV.in();                    // Copying insertion

theAny <<= CORBA::Any::from_string("Insert me!", 0);
                                               // Copying insertion

char * theStringP = CORBA::string_dup("Insert me!");
theAny <<= CORBA::Any::from_string(theStringP, 0, 1);
                                               // Consuming insertion

theStringV = CORBA::string_dup("Insert me!");
theAny <<= CORBA::Any::from_string(theStringV._retn(), 0, 1);
                                               // Consuming insertion

// Beware! Do not make a consuming insertion of a string literal.
```

Listing 8.6 continued

```
//-----------------------------------------------------------------------
// Inserting Bounded Strings
//
// These examples use the bounded string of type 'string<64>'.
//
char * theBString = "Insert me!";
theAny <<= CORBA::Any::from_string(theBString, 64);
                                              // Copying insertion

const char * theConstBString = "Insert me!";
theAny <<= CORBA::Any::from_string(theConstBString, 64);
                                              // Copying insertion

// Note: There is no special insertion operator for '_var' types
//       so convert it to a 'char *' using the 'in()' method.
CORBA::String_var theBStringV = CORBA::string_dup("Insert me!");
theAny <<= CORBA::Any::from_string(theBStringV.in(), 64);
                                              // Copying insertion

theAny <<= CORBA::Any::from_string("Insert me!", 64);
                                              // Copying insertion

char * theBStringP = CORBA::string_dup("Insert me!");
theAny <<= CORBA::Any::from_string(theBStringP, 64, 1);
                                              // Consuming insertion

theBStringV = CORBA::string_dup("Insert me!");
theAny <<= CORBA::Any::from_string(theBStringV._retn(), 64, 1);
                                              // Consuming insertion

// Beware! Do not make a consuming insertion of a string literal.

//-----------------------------------------------------------------------
// Inserting Alias of Bounded String
//
// Uses 'typedef string<64> BoundedString'
//
theAny <<= CORBA::Any::from_string("Insert me!", 64);
                                              // Copying insertion
// Explicitly set type code
theAny.type(SampleTypes::_tc_BoundedString);
```

Inserting Wide String Types

A helper type `CORBA::Any::from_wstring` is defined for wide strings. Two constructors for this helper type are declared:

```
// C++
CORBA::Any::from_wstring(CORBA::WChar * s,        // string to insert
                         CORBA::ULong b,          // bound, as declared in IDL
                         CORBA::Boolean n=FALSE   // no-copy flag
           );

// Constructor for const strings
CORBA::Any::from_wstring(const CORBA::WChar * s,  // const string to insert
                         CORBA::ULong b           // bound, as declared in IDL
           );
```

A bound of 0, passed as the second argument, indicates that the wide string is unbounded. When the no-copy flag is set to TRUE, a consuming insertion is made.

The code in Listing 8.7 shows how wide string types are inserted into an any. Three kinds of wide string are considered:

- Unbounded wide strings
- Bounded wide strings
- Aliases of a bounded wide string

Listing 8.7 C++ Examples of Inserting Wide String Types

```
//-----------------------------------------------------------------
// Inserting Unbounded Wide Strings
//

theAny <<= L"Insert me!";                     // Copying insertion

CORBA::WChar * theWString = L"Insert me!";
theAny <<= theWString;                        // Copying insertion

const CORBA::WChar * theConstWString = L"Insert me!";
theAny <<= theConstWString;                   // Copying insertion

// Note: There is no special insertion operator for '_var' types
//       so convert it to a 'CORBA::WChar *' using the 'in()' method.
CORBA::WString_var theWStringV = CORBA::wstring_dup(L"Insert me!");
theAny <<= theWStringV.in();                  // Copying insertion

theAny <<= CORBA::Any::from_wstring(L"Insert me!", 0);
                                              // Copying insertion

CORBA::WChar * theWStringP = CORBA::wstring_dup(L"Insert me!");
theAny <<= CORBA::Any::from_wstring(theWStringP, 0, 1);
                                              // Consuming insertion

theWStringV = CORBA::wstring_dup(L"Insert me!");
theAny <<= CORBA::Any::from_wstring(theWStringV._retn(), 0, 1);
                                              // Consuming insertion
```

Listing 8.7 continued

```
// Beware! Do not make a consuming insertion of a string literal.

//--------------------------------------------------------------------
// Inserting Bounded Wide Strings
//
// These examples use the bounded wide string of type 'wstring<128>'.
//
CORBA::WChar * theBWStringP = L"Insert me!";
theAny <<= CORBA::Any::from_wstring(theBWStringP, 128);
                                              // Copying insertion

const CORBA::WChar * theConstBWStringP = L"Insert me!";
theAny <<= CORBA::Any::from_wstring(theConstBWStringP, 128);
                                              // Copying insertion

// Note: There is no special insertion operator for '_var' types
//       so convert it to a 'CORBA::WChar *' using the 'in()' method.
CORBA::WString_var theBWStringV = CORBA::wstring_dup(L"Insert me!");
theAny <<= CORBA::Any::from_wstring(theBWStringV.in(), 128);
                                              // Copying insertion

theAny <<= CORBA::Any::from_wstring(L"Insert me!", 128);
                                              // Copying insertion

CORBA::WChar * wp = CORBA::wstring_dup(L"Insert me!");
theAny <<= CORBA::Any::from_wstring(wp, 128, 1);
                                              // Consuming insertion

theBWStringV = CORBA::wstring_dup(L"Insert me!");
theAny <<= CORBA::Any::from_wstring(theBWStringV._retn(), 128, 1);
                                              // Consuming insertion

// Beware! Do not make a consuming insertion of a string literal.

//--------------------------------------------------------------------
// Inserting Alias of Bounded Wide String
//
// Uses 'typedef wstring<128> BoundedWString'
//
theAny <<= CORBA::Any::from_wstring(L"Insert me!", 128);
                                              // Copying insertion
// Explicitly set type code
theAny.type(SampleTypes::_tc_BoundedWString);
```

Inserting Struct Types

The code in Listing 8.8 shows how struct types are inserted into an any.

Listing 8.8 C++ Examples of Inserting Struct Types

```
//----------------------------------------------------------------------
// Inserting Structs
//
// Uses: //IDL
//       //...in module 'SampleTypes'
//            struct VarLen {
//                 string theString;
//                 long theLong;
//            };
//
SampleTypes::VarLen theVarLen;
theVarLen.theString = CORBA::string_dup("Insert me!");
theVarLen.theLong   = (CORBA::Long)123;
theAny <<= theVarLen;                     // Copying insertion

SampleTypes::VarLen_var theVarLenV = new SampleTypes::VarLen();
theVarLenV->theString = CORBA::string_dup("Insert me!");
theVarLenV->theLong   = (CORBA::Long)123;
theAny <<= *theVarLenV;                   // Copying insertion

SampleTypes::VarLen * theVarLenP = new SampleTypes::VarLen();
theVarLenP->theString = CORBA::string_dup("Insert me!");
theVarLenP->theLong   = (CORBA::Long)123;
theAny <<= theVarLenP;                    // Consuming insertion

theAny <<= theVarLenV._retn(); // Consuming insertion
```

Inserting Sequence Types

The code in Listing 8.9 shows how sequence types are inserted into an any.

Listing 8.9 C++ Examples of Inserting Sequence Types

```
//----------------------------------------------------------------------
// Inserting Sequences
//
// Uses: //IDL
//       //...in module 'SampleTypes'
//            typedef sequence< VarLen > SeqOfVarLen;
//
SampleTypes::SeqOfVarLen theSeqOfVarLen(1);  //maximum = 1
                                             //length = 0
theSeqOfVarLen.length(1);
theSeqOfVarLen[0].theString = CORBA::string_dup("Insert me!");
theSeqOfVarLen[0].theLong   = (CORBA::Long)123;
theAny <<= theSeqOfVarLen;                // Copying insertion
```

Listing 8.9 continued

```
SampleTypes::SeqOfVarLen_var theSeqOfVarLenV
     = new SampleTypes::SeqOfVarLen(1);      //maximum = 1
                                             //length = 0
theSeqOfVarLenV->length(1);
(*theSeqOfVarLenV)[0].theString = CORBA::string_dup("Insert me!");
(*theSeqOfVarLenV)[0].theLong   = (CORBA::Long) 123;
theAny <<= *theSeqOfVarLenV;                 // Copying insertion

SampleTypes::SeqOfVarLen * theSeqOfVarLenP
     = new SampleTypes::SeqOfVarLen(1);      //maximum = 1
                                             //length = 0
theSeqOfVarLenP->length(1);
(*theSeqOfVarLenP)[0].theString = CORBA::string_dup("Insert me!");
(*theSeqOfVarLenP)[0].theLong   = (CORBA::Long) 123;
theAny <<= theSeqOfVarLenP;                  // Consuming insertion


theSeqOfVarLenV->length(1);
(*theSeqOfVarLenV)[0].theString = CORBA::string_dup("Insert me!");
(*theSeqOfVarLenV)[0].theLong   = (CORBA::Long) 123;
theAny <<= theSeqOfVarLenV._retn();         // Consuming insertion
```

Inserting Fixed Precision Numbers

The code in Listing 8.10 shows how fixed types are inserted into an any.

Listing 8.10 C++ Examples of Inserting Fixed Types

```
//-----------------------------------------------------------------
// Inserting Fixed Precision Numbers
//
// Uses: Type 'fixed<6, 2>'
//
CORBA::Fixed fx = "-1234.56";  // Use 6 digits and 2 decimal places
theAny <<= CORBA::Any::from_fixed(fx, 6, 2);            // Copying insertion

// Note: There is no such type as a 'CORBA::Fixed_var'. The 'fixed' type
//       is always passed by value.
```

Inserting Union Types

The code in Listing 8.11 shows how union types are inserted into an any.

Listing 8.11 C++ Examples of Inserting Union Types

```
//-----------------------------------------------------------------
// Inserting Unions
//
// Uses: //IDL
//       //...in module 'SampleTypes'
//            union Poly switch(short) {
//                 case 1: short theShort;
```

```
//                  case 2: string theString;
//              };
//
SampleTypes::Poly thePoly;
thePoly.theString((const char*) "Insert me!");
theAny <<= thePoly;                           // Copying insertion

SampleTypes::Poly_var thePolyV = new SampleTypes::Poly();
thePolyV->theString((const char*) "Insert me!");
theAny <<= *thePolyV;                         // Copying insertion

SampleTypes::Poly * thePolyP = new SampleTypes::Poly();
thePolyP->theString((const char*) "Insert me!");
theAny <<= thePolyP;                          // Consuming insertion

theAny <<= thePolyV._retn();   // Consuming insertion
```

Inserting Array Types

A helper type is needed for array types because insertion of an array pointer alone offers no way of determining the array bounds. For every array *arrayName*, a corresponding helper type *arrayName*_forany is generated, having the following constructor:

```
// C++
arrayName_forany(arrayName_slice * a, CORBA::Boolean nocopy=FALSE );
```

When the nocopy flag is set to TRUE, a consuming insertion is made.

The code in Listing 8.12 shows how array types are inserted into an any.

Listing 8.12 C++ Examples of Inserting Array Types

```
//-----------------------------------------------------------------
// Inserting Arrays
//
// Uses: //IDL
//       //... in module 'SampleTypes'
//            typedef VarLen ArrOfVarLen[10];
//
SampleTypes::ArrOfVarLen theArr;
//...initialize the array 'theArr'
theAny <<= SampleTypes::ArrOfVarLen_forany(theArr);      // Copying insertion

SampleTypes::ArrOfVarLen_var theArrV = SampleTypes::ArrOfVarLen_alloc();
//...initialize the array 'theArrV'
theAny <<= SampleTypes::ArrOfVarLen_forany(theArrV.in() ); // Copying insertion

SampleTypes::ArrOfVarLen_slice * theArrP = SampleTypes::ArrOfVarLen_alloc();
//...initialize the array 'theArrP'
theAny <<= SampleTypes::ArrOfVarLen_forany(theArrP, 1);  // Consuming insertion

theAny <<= SampleTypes::ArrOfVarLen_forany(theArrV._retn(), 1);
                                              // Consuming insertion
```

Inserting Exception Types

The code in Listing 8.13 shows how exception types are inserted into an any.

Listing 8.13 C++ Examples of Inserting Exception Types

```
//-----------------------------------------------------------------
// Inserting Exceptions
//
// Uses: //IDL
//      //... in module 'SampleTypes'
//           exception GenericExc {
//                string reason;
//           };
//

SampleTypes::GenericExc theExc("This is the reason.");
theAny <<= theExc;                           // Copying insertion

//Exceptions are normally declared on the stack.
```

Inserting Object References

For a given interface *intfName*, a pair of insertion operators are generated:

```
// C++
void operator<<=(CORBA::Any&, intfName_ptr)   // Copying insertion
void operator<<=(CORBA::Any&, intfName_ptr*)  // Consuming insertion
```

For a consuming insertion, you effectively pass a pointer to a pointer.

The code in Listing 8.14 shows how object references are inserted into an any.

Listing 8.14 C++ Examples of Inserting Object References

```
//-----------------------------------------------------------------
// Inserting Object References
//

SampleTypes::Foo_var theFooV;
// ...initialize 'theFooV'
theAny <<= theFooV;                          // Copying insertion

SampleTypes::Foo_ptr theFooP;
// ...initialize 'theFooP'
theAny <<= theFooP;                          // Copying insertion

theAny <<= &theFooP;                         // Consuming insertion
```

Inserting any Types

The code in Listing 8.15 shows how any types are inserted into an any.

Listing 8.15 C++ Examples of Inserting any Types

```
//-----------------------------------------------------------------
// Inserting Anys
//
CORBA::Any anyToBeInserted;
anyToBeInserted <<= (CORBA::Long) 123;
theAny <<= anyToBeInserted;                    // Copying insertion

CORBA::Any_var anyToBeInsertedV = new CORBA::Any();
*anyToBeInsertedV <<= (CORBA::Long) 123;
theAny <<= *anyToBeInsertedV;                  // Copying insertion

CORBA::Any * anyToBeInsertedP = new CORBA::Any();
*anyToBeInsertedP <<= (CORBA::Long) 123;
theAny <<= anyToBeInsertedP;                   // Consuming insertion

theAny <<= anyToBeInsertedV. _retn();          // Consuming insertion
```

C++ Extraction from CORBA::Any

This section provides sample code that shows how a variety of data types are extracted from a CORBA::Any. Some special cases of extraction are discussed in more detail at the end of this section.

Extraction of Basic Types

Extraction of most (but not all) basic types T is accomplished using the following operator:

```
// C++
CORBA::Boolean operator>>=(const CORBA::Any&, T&);      // Simple extraction
```

This is sufficient for most data types T that are passed by value, such as short, long, and float.

Extraction of Compound Types

Extraction of most (but not all) compound types T is accomplished using the following operator:

```
// C++
void operator>>=(const CORBA::Any&, const T*&);      // Read-only extraction
```

This is sufficient for most compound data types, except for arrays and object references.

Read-Only Extraction

When a compound type is extracted from a `CORBA::Any`, there is only one option: a read-only extraction. The read-only extraction of a compound type `T` is illustrated in Figure 8.3.

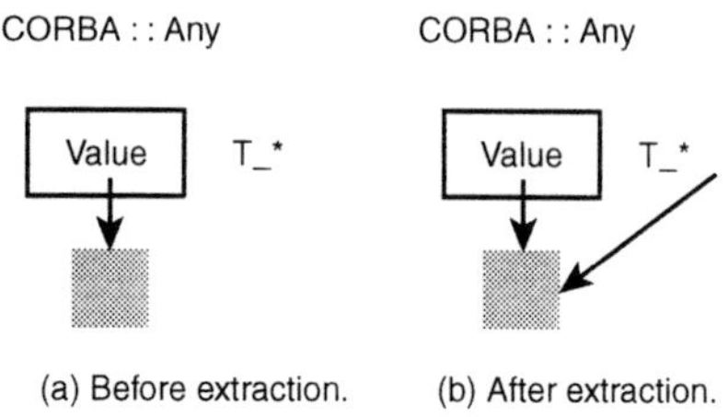

Figure 8.3

A read-only extraction from `CORBA::Any`.

When data is extracted from the `CORBA::Any`, the extraction operator makes a shallow copy of the pointer to the data. No new copy of the data is made, and the extracted pointer references data inside the `CORBA::Any`. The `CORBA::Any` retains ownership of the inserted data and has responsibility for deallocating it. The extracted reference is granted only read-only access to the `CORBA::Any`'s data. It is essential that the extracted pointer not attempt to deallocate the data or modify it in any way.

Consider the following code fragment, which shows an example of a read-only extraction. The fragment uses the same IDL struct as the previous example (`SampleTypes::VarLen`, defined in the earlier section "A Sample IDL Module"):

```
// C++
//--------------------------------------------------------------
// Inserting Struct - Consuming insertion
//
// (Uses same IDL as in previous section)
//
// Given 'theAny' which contains a 'VarLen' struct
SampleTypes::VarLen * theVarLenP;
extractSucceeds = (theAny >>= theVarLenP);  // Read-only extraction

// Make a modifiable copy of 'theVarLenP'
SampleTypes::VarLen theVarLenCopy;          // Allocated on the stack
theVarLenCopy = *theVarLenP;
...
```

The contents of the `CORBA::Any` are shallow-copied to the pointer `theVarLenP`. You therefore have only read-only access to the `CORBA::Any`'s data via this pointer. A new copy of the data is made in case you need to modify it.

Extracting Unambiguous Basic Types

The code in Listing 8.16 shows how unambiguous basic types are extracted from an any.

Listing 8.16 C++ Examples of Extracting Unambiguous Basic Types

```
//C++
//-----------------------------------------------------------------
// Declaration of 'CORBA::Any' on the stack
//

CORBA::Any theAny;

//-----------------------------------------------------------------
// Declaration of 'CORBA::Boolean' status
//      TRUE  => attempted extraction succeeded
//      FALSE => attempted extraction failed

CORBA::Boolean extractSucceeds;

//-----------------------------------------------------------------
// Extracting unambiguous Basic Types
//
...
// Extracting a 'short'
CORBA::Short s;
extractSucceeds = (theAny >>= s);          // Simple extraction
...
// Extracting an 'unsigned short'
CORBA::UShort us;
extractSucceeds = (theAny >>= us);         // Simple extraction
...
// Extracting a 'long'
CORBA::Long l;
extractSucceeds = (theAny >>= l);          // Simple extraction
...
// Extracting an 'unsigned long'
CORBA::ULong ul;
extractSucceeds = (theAny >>= ul);         // Simple extraction
...
// Extracting a 'long long'
CORBA::LongLong ll;
extractSucceeds = (theAny >>= ll);         // Simple extraction
...
// Extracting an 'unsigned long long'
CORBA::ULongLong ull;
extractSucceeds = (theAny >>= ull);        // Simple extraction
...
```

Listing 8.16 continued

```
// Extracting a 'float'
CORBA::Float f;
extractSucceeds = (theAny >>= f);          // Simple extraction
...
// Extracting a 'double'
CORBA::Double d;
extractSucceeds = (theAny >>= d);          // Simple extraction
...
// Extracting a 'long double'
CORBA::LongDouble ld;
extractSucceeds = (theAny >>= ld);         // Simple extraction
```

Extracting Ambiguous Basic Types

The CORBA specification does not require `boolean`, `octet`, `char`, and `wchar` to map to distinct types. Therefore, operator overloading cannot be relied on to extract these types.

A set of helper types, `CORBA::Any::to_boolean`, `CORBA::Any::to_octet`, `CORBA::Any::to_char`, and `CORBA::Any::to_wchar`, are defined to aid in the extraction of these types.

The code in Listing 8.17 shows how ambiguous basic types are extracted from an `any`.

Listing 8.17 C++ Examples of Extracting Ambiguous Basic Types

```
//C++
//-------------------------------------------------------------------
// Extracting Ambiguous Basic Types
//
...
// Extracting a 'boolean'
CORBA::Boolean b;
extractSucceeds = (theAny >>= CORBA::Any::to_boolean(b));
                                           // Simple extraction
...
// Extracting an 'octet'
CORBA::Octet o;
extractSucceeds = (theAny >>= CORBA::Any::to_octet(o));
                                           // Simple extraction
...
// Extracting a 'char'
CORBA::Char c;
extractSucceeds = (theAny >>= CORBA::Any::to_char(c));
                                           // Simple extraction
...
// Extracting a 'wchar;
CORBA::WChar wc;
extractSucceeds = (theAny >>= CORBA::Any::to_wchar(wc));
                                           // Simple extraction
```

Extracting String Types

To extract bounded strings from a `CORBA::Any`, there has to be some way of specifying the bound as the string is extracted. For this reason, the helper type `CORBA::Any::to_string` is defined. The constructor for this helper type is

```
// C++
CORBA::Any::to_string(const char *& s,          // string to extract
                      CORBA::ULong b            // bound, as declared in IDL
           );
```

A bound of `0`, passed as the second argument, indicates that the string is unbounded.

The code in Listing 8.18 shows how string types are extracted from an `any`. Three kinds of string are considered:

- Unbounded strings
- Bounded strings
- Aliases of a bounded string

Listing 8.18 C++ Examples of Extracting String Types

```
//C++
//-----------------------------------------------------------------
// Extracting Unbounded Strings
//
...
const char * theStringP;
extractSucceeds = (theAny >>= theStringP);  // Read-only extraction
...
const char * theStringP;
extractSucceeds = (theAny >>= CORBA::Any::to_string(theStringP, 0));
                                            // Read-only extraction

// Make a modifiable copy of the string
CORBA::String_var theStringCopyV = CORBA::string_dup(theStringP);
...
//-----------------------------------------------------------------
// Extracting Bounded Strings
//
// Assume that the 'any' contains a string of type 'string< 64 >'.
//
...
const char * theBStringP;
extractSucceeds = (theAny >>= CORBA::Any::to_string(theBStringP, 64));
                                            // Read-only extraction
...
// Make a modifiable copy of the string
CORBA::String_var theBStringCopyV = CORBA::string_dup(theBStringP);
...
```

Listing 8.18 continued

```
//-----------------------------------------------------------------
// Extracting Alias of Bounded String
//
// Uses 'typedef string<64> BoundedString'
//
...
const char * theBStringP;
// Make a more stringent check to ensure that the type is 'BoundedString'
if ( (theAny.type()).equal(CORBA::_tc_BoundedString) ) {
     extractSucceeds = (theAny >>= CORBA::Any::to_string(theBStringP, 64));
                                                  // Read-only extraction
}
```

Extracting Wide String Types

To extract bounded wide strings from a `CORBA::Any`, there has to be some way of specifying the bound as the wide string is extracted. For this reason, the helper type `CORBA::Any::to_wstring` is defined. The constructor for this helper type is

```
// C++
CORBA::Any::to_wstring(const CORBA::WChar *& ws,  // wide string to extract
                       CORBA::ULong b             // bound, as declared in IDL
            );
```

A bound of `0`, passed as the second argument, indicates that the wide string is unbounded.

The code in Listing 8.19 shows how wide string types are extracted from an any. Three kinds of wide string are considered:

- Unbounded wide strings
- Bounded wide strings
- Aliases of a bounded wide string

Listing 8.19 C++ Examples of Extracting Wide String Types

```
//C++
//-----------------------------------------------------------------
// Extracting Unbounded Wide Strings
//
...
const CORBA::WChar * theWStringP;
extractSucceeds = (theAny >>= theWStringP); // Read-only extraction
...
const CORBA::WChar * theWStringP;
extractSucceeds = (theAny >>= CORBA::Any::to_wstring(theWStringP, 0));
                                                  // Read-only extraction

// Make a modifiable copy of the string
CORBA::WString_var theWStringCopyV = CORBA::wstring_dup(theWStringP);
...
```

Listing 8.19 continued

```
//-----------------------------------------------------------------
// Extracting Bounded Wide Strings
//
// Assume that the 'any' contains a wide string of type 'string<128>'.
//
...
const CORBA::WChar * theBWStringP;
extractSucceeds = (theAny >>= CORBA::Any::to_wstring(theBWStringP, 128));
                                                // Read-only extraction

// Make a modifiable copy of the wide string
CORBA::WString_var theBWStringCopyV = CORBA::wstring_dup(theBWStringP);
...
//-----------------------------------------------------------------
// Extracting Alias of Bounded Wide String
//
// Uses 'typedef wstring<128> BoundedWString'
//
...
const CORBA::WChar * theBWStringP;
// Make a more stringent check to ensure that the type is 'BoundedWString'
if ( (theAny.type()).equal(CORBA::_tc_BoundedWString) ) {
     extractSucceeds = (theAny >>= CORBA::Any::to_wstring(theBWStringP, 128));
                                                // Read-only extraction
}
```

Extracting Struct Types

The code in Listing 8.20 shows how struct types are extracted from an any.

Listing 8.20 C++ Examples of Extracting Struct Types

```
//C++
//-----------------------------------------------------------------
// Extracting Structs
//
// Uses: //IDL
//       //...in module 'SampleTypes'
//            struct VarLen {
//                 string theString;
//                 long theLong;
//            };
//
...
SampleTypes::VarLen * theVarLenP;
extractSucceeds = (theAny >>= theVarLenP);  // Read-only extraction

// Make a modifiable copy of 'theVarLenP'
SampleTypes::VarLen theVarLenCopy;          // Allocated on the stack
theVarLenCopy = *theVarLenP;
```

Extracting Sequence Types

The code in Listing 8.21 shows how sequence types are extracted from an any.

Listing 8.21 C++ Examples of Extracting Sequence Types

```
//------------------------------------------------------------------
// Extracting Sequences
//
// Uses: //IDL
//       //...in module 'SampleTypes'
//            typedef sequence< VarLen > SeqOfVarLen;
//
...
SampleTypes::SeqOfVarLen * theSeqOfVarLenP;
extractSucceeds = (theAny >>= theSeqOfVarLenP);
                                              // Read-only extraction

// Make a modifiable copy of 'theSeqOfVarLenP'
SampleTypes::SeqOfVarLen theSeqOfVarLenCopy;  // Allocated on the stack
theSeqOfVarLenCopy = *theSeqOfVarLenP;
```

Extracting Fixed Precision Numbers

The code in Listing 8.22 shows how fixed types are extracted from an any.

Listing 8.22 C++ Examples of Extracting Fixed Types

```
//C++
//------------------------------------------------------------------
// Extracting Fixed Precision Numbers
//
// Uses: Type 'fixed<6, 2>'
//
...
CORBA::Fixed fx;
extractSucceeds = (theAny >>= CORBA::Any::to_fixed(fx, 6, 2));
                                              // Read-only extraction
...
// Note: You do not use a 'CORBA::fixed *' here. The 'fixed' type
//       is always passed by value --- it is a basic type.
```

Extracting Union Types

The code in Listing 8.23 shows how union types are extracted from an any.

Listing 8.23 C++ Examples of Extracting Union Types

```
//C++
//------------------------------------------------------------------
// Extracting Unions
//
// Uses: //IDL
```

Listing 8.23 continued

```
//        //...in module 'SampleTypes'
//             union Poly switch(short) {
//                  case 1: short theShort;
//                  case 2: string theString;
//             };
//
...
SampleTypes::Poly * thePolyP;
extractSucceeds = (theAny >>= thePolyP);
                                                  // Read-only extraction

// Make a modifiable copy of 'thePolyP' union
SampleTypes::Poly thePolyCopy;                    // Allocated on the stack
thePolyCopy = *thePolyP;
```

Extracting Array Types

A helper type is needed for array types because extraction of an array pointer alone offers no way of determining the array bounds. For every array *arrayName*, a corresponding helper type *arrayName*_forany is generated. This is the same helper type that is generated to aid the insertion of arrays.

The type *arrayName*_forany does not own the memory it references (remember that data extracted from an array is read-only). This is a fundamental difference between it and the _var types. However, in almost every other respect it is identical to the *arrayName*_var type, even including support for an indexing operator.

The code in Listing 8.24 shows how array types are extracted from an any.

Listing 8.24 C++ Examples of Extracting Array Types

```
//C++
//---------------------------------------------------------------------
// Extracting Arrays
//
// Uses: //IDL
//        //... in module 'SampleTypes'
//             typedef VarLen ArrOfVarLen[10];
//
...
SampleTypes::ArrOfVarLen_forany theForany;
extractSucceeds = (theAny >>= theForany);   // Read-only extraction

// The type 'SampleTypes::ArrOfCVarLen_forany' also overloads
// the subscripting 'operator[]'
cout << theForany[9].theString << endl;     // Use as read-only

// Make a modifiable copy of 'theForany' array
SampleTypes::ArrOfVarLen theArrCopy;        // Allocate on the stack
SampleTypes::ArrOfVarLen_copy(theArrCopy, theForany);
```

Extracting Exception Types

The code in Listing 8.25 shows how exception types are extracted from an any.

Listing 8.25 C++ Examples of Extracting Exception Types

```
//C++
//-----------------------------------------------------------------
// Extracting Exceptions
//
// Uses: //IDL
//       //... in module 'SampleTypes'
//           exception GenericExc {
//               string reason;
//           };
//
...
SampleTypes::GenericExc * theExcP;
extractSucceeds = (theAny >>= theExcP);   // Read-only extraction
```

Extracting Object References

For a given interface *intfName*, the following extraction operator is generated:

```
// C++
CORBA::Boolean operator>>=(const CORBA::Any&, intfName_ptr&)
➥   // Read-only extraction
```

A special case arises when you want to make a widening extraction of an object reference. For example, consider the following fragment of IDL:

```
// IDL
interface Base { };
interface Derived : Base { };
```

An instance of a `Derived` object reference is inserted into a `CORBA::Any` as follows:

```
// C++
// Given an initialized object reference 'theDerivedP' of type 'Derived_ptr'
CORBA::Any theAny;
theAny <<= &theDerivedP;  // Consuming insertion
```

If you attempt to extract the object reference as a `Base` type, as follows

```
// C++
Base_ptr theBaseP;
CORBA::Boolean succeeds = (theAny >>= theBaseP);  // Extraction fails!
```

the extraction fails. Extraction of an object reference succeeds only if the extracted type exactly matches the inserted type. If you need to perform a widening extraction, it can be done using the helper type `CORBA::Any::to_object` as follows:

```
// C++
CORBA::Object_var objV;
Base_var theBaseV;

CORBA::Boolean succeeds = (theAny >>= CORBA::Any::to_object(objV) );
                                              // Widening extraction
theBaseV = Base::_narrow(objV);
if (CORBA::is_nil(theBaseV.in()) ) {
     cerr << "Narrow failed" << endl;
}
else {
     cout << "Base object successfully extracted" << endl;
}
```

Note that extraction using `CORBA::Any::to_object()` is a special case with regard to memory management. The extracted reference must be explicitly released, and it is therefore extracted into the _`var` type `objV`. Since _`narrow()` implicitly duplicates the object reference, it is also necessary to make the reference `theBaseV` a _`var` type.

The code in Listing 8.26 shows how object references are extracted from an `any`.

Listing 8.26 C++ Examples of Extracting Object References

```
//C++
//-------------------------------------------------------------------
// Extracting Object References
//
...
SampleTypes::Foo_ptr theFooP;
extractSucceeds = (theAny >>= theFooP);     // Read-only extraction
```

Extracting Any Types

The code in Listing 8.27 shows how any types are extracted from an `any`.

Listing 8.27 C++ Examples of Extracting `any` Types

```
//C++
//-------------------------------------------------------------------
// Extracting Anys
//
// Assume that the extracted 'any' contains a 'CORBA::Long'
...
CORBA::Any * anyToExtractP;
extractSucceeds = (theAny >>= anyToExtractP);
                                              // Read-only extraction
if (extractSucceeds) {
     CORBA::Long theLong;
     if (*anyToExtractP >>= theLong) {
          cout << "any(any(long)) = " << theLong << endl;
     }
}
```

Java Example of Passing anys

Java mapping maps the IDL type any to the Java class `org.omg.CORBA.Any`. There are two styles of access to `CORBA.Any` when inserting or extracting data: the API for built-in types and the API for user-defined types.

Insertion or extraction of built-in types is performed by invoking methods directly on `CORBA.Any`. For example, the IDL type `long` is inserted and extracted using the following methods:

```
// Java
void org.omg.CORBA.Any.insert_long(int l)
int org.omg.CORBA.Any.extract_long()
```

Insertion or extraction of user-defined types is performed by invoking methods defined on the `Helper` classes. For example, an IDL user-defined struct called `Foo` would be inserted and extracted using the following methods:

```
// Java
void FooHelper.insert(org.omg.CORBA.Any a, Foo f)
Foo FooHelper.extract(org.omg.CORBA.Any a)
```

The following sections show how these operations are used in practice.

The `AnyPasser` Interface

Consider a sample IDL interface that illustrates use of the any type:

```
// IDL
interface AnyPasser {
    void sendEvent(in any item);
};
```

The next two sections show client and server code that uses the interface `AnyPasser`.

Java Client for the `AnyPasser` Interface

Suppose that you are writing a client of the `AnyPasser` interface that sends only one of the IDL types `long` or `string` or the user-defined type `SampleTypes::VarLen` (see the section "A Sample IDL Module," earlier in this chapter). The operation `sendEvent()` can be invoked as shown in Listing 8.28.

***Listing 8.28 A Java Invocation of* `sendEvent()`**

```
// Java
//--------------------
// Initialize the object reference and the 'any'.
//
...
package Pure.AnyPasser;
```

Listing 8.28 continued

```
import java.io.*;
import org.omg.CORBA.*;
import Pure.AnyPasser.SampleTypes.*;
...
try {
    AnyPasser theAnyPasser = /* initialize 'AnyPasser' object reference */;
    org.omg.CORBA.Any theItem = org.omg.CORBA.ORB.init().create_any();

    // Pass a 'long' using operation 'sendEvent()'
    theItem.insert_long(10001);
    theAnyPasser.sendEvent(theItem);
    ...
    // Pass a 'string' using operation 'sendEvent()'
    theItem.insert_string("A string item.");
    theAnyPasser.sendEvent(theItem);
    ...
    // Pass a 'SampleTypes::VarLen' struct using operation 'sendEvent()'
    VarLen theVarLen
         = new VarLen("String member", 123);
    VarLenHelper.insert(theItem, theVarLen);
    theAnyPasser.sendEvent(theItem);
}
catch (org.omg.CORBA.SystemException sysEx) {
    System.out.println("SystemException:  " + sysEx);
}
```

Insertion of the types `long` and `string` into the any follows the pattern for built-in types. The method `insert_type()` is invoked on the any.

Insertion of the struct `VarLen` follows the pattern for user-defined types. The method `insert()` is invoked on the `SampleTypes.VarLenHelper` class.

Java Server for the `AnyPasser` Interface

Suppose that the server developer works in close collaboration with the developer of the preceding client. In that case, the server developer knows that there are only three possible values for the any parameter: a `long`, a `string`, or a `SampleTypes::VarLen`. Given that the implementation class is called `AnyPasserImpl`, the implementation of the operation `sendEvent()` can be written as shown in Listing 8.29.

Listing 8.29 A Java Implementation of `sendEvent()`

```
// Java
...
package Pure.AnyPasser;

import java.io.*;
import org.omg.CORBA.*;
```

Listing 8.29 continued

```
import org.omg.PortableServer.*;
import Pure.AnyPasser.SampleTypes.*;
...
//Declared in 'class AnyPasserImpl'
public sendEvent(org.omg.CORBA.Any item) {
      int l;
      String s;
      VarLen vl;

      if ( (item.type()).kind() == org.omg.CORBA.TCKind.tk_long) {
            // value is of type 'long'
            l = item.extract_long();
            System.out.println("Received long = " + l);
      }
      else if ( (item.type()).kind() == org.omg.CORBA.TCKind.tk_string) {
            // value is of type 'string'
            s = item.extract_string();
            System.out.println("Received string = " + s);
      }
      else if ( (item.type()).equivalent(VarLenHelper.type()) ) {
            // value is of type 'SampleTypes::VarLen'
            vl = VarLenHelper.extract(item);
            System.out.println("Received VarLen = {\n"
                  + "\ttheString = " + vl.theString + "\n"
                  + "\ttheLong   = " + vl.theLong   + "\n"
                  + "}");
      }
      else {
            // value is of unexpected type!
            // probably should raise an exception in this case.
            System.out.println("Received unexpected type in any");
      }
}
```

Before you can extract the data from the CORBA.Any, you must check the type of the any's contents. The type code for the any's contents can be accessed using the method

```
// Java
org.omg.CORBA.TypeCode  org.omg.CORBA.Any.type()
```

A complete declaration of the class TypeCode is given in Chapter 18. Two TypeCode methods are commonly used in conjunction with the CORBA.Any:

```
// Java
org.omg.CORBA.TCKind  org.omg.CORBA.TypeCode.kind()
boolean  org.omg.CORBA.TypeCode.equivalent(org.omg.CORBA.TypeCode tc)
```

For CORBA built-in types you can check the value of the type code by invoking kind(), which returns a tag of type TCKind (a complete list of tags is given in

Chapter 18). For example, Listing 8.29 shows how to check the contents of the any by comparing its type code kind with tags `tk_long` and `tk_string`.

For CORBA user-defined types, you can check the value of the type code by invoking `equivalent()` to compare it with a given type code. For example, in Listing 8.29, the any's type code is compared with `SampleTypes.VarLenHelper.type()`. For every user-defined type `Foo`, the corresponding type code is given by `FooHelper.type()`.

There are times when you might have such a large number of alternatives that the linear search (as used above) affects performance, or you might not know in advance what types will be sent in the any. In both of these cases you have to learn about type code parsing to make further progress. This topic is beyond the scope of this chapter—reference material on type codes can be found in Chapter 18. See also Chapter 20.

Java Insertion into `org.omg.CORBA.Any`

The following sections give examples of any insertion for a representative sample of CORBA data types. The IDL types used in these examples are taken from Listing 8.1.

Inserting Basic Types

The code in Listing 8.30 shows how basic types are inserted into an any.

Listing 8.30 Java Examples of Inserting Basic Types

```
// Java
//-------------------------------------------------------------------
// Declaration of ' org.omg.CORBA.Any '
// (assume that 'orb', an instance of 'org.omg.CORBA.ORB', is initialized)

org.omg.CORBA.Any theAny = org.omg.CORBA.ORB.init().create_any();

//-------------------------------------------------------------------
// Inserting Basic Types
//

// Inserting a 'short'
short s = -123;
theAny.insert_short(s);

// Inserting an 'unsigned short'
short us = 321;
theAny.insert_ushort(us);

// Inserting a 'long'
int l = -1000000;
theAny.insert_long(l);

// Inserting an 'unsigned long'
int ul = 1000000;
theAny.insert_ulong(ul);
```

Listing 8.30 continued

```
// Inserting a 'long long'
long ll = -1000;
theAny.insert_longlong(ll);

// Inserting an 'unsigned long long'
long ull = 1000;
theAny.insert_ulonglong(ull);

// Inserting a 'float'
float f = 0.432f;
theAny.insert_float(f);

// Inserting a 'double'
double d = 0.0000123;
theAny.insert_double(d);

// Inserting a 'long double'
// Not available in the CORBA 2.3 IDL-to-Java mapping

// Inserting a 'boolean'
boolean b = true;
theAny.insert_boolean(b);

// Inserting an 'octet'
byte o = 0x3f;
theAny.insert_octet(o);

// Inserting a 'char'
char c = 'H';
theAny.insert_char(c);

// Inserting a 'wchar'
char wc = 'H';
theAny.insert_wchar(wc);
```

Inserting Strings and Wide Strings

Insertion of aliased bounded strings is different from insertion of unbounded strings. Instead of the `org.omg.CORBA.Any.insert_string()` and `org.omg.CORBA.Any.insert_wstring()` methods used for unbounded strings, you must use insert methods defined on `Helper` classes.

For example, consider the bounded string type `BoundedString` and the bounded wide string type `BoundedWString`, defined as follows:

```
//IDL
module SampleTypes {
    typedef string < 64 > BoundedString;
    typedef wstring < 128 > BoundedWString;
```

```
    ...
};
```

Insertion of `BoundedString` strings is done using

```
//Java
void SampleTypes.BoundedStringHelper.insert(
    org.omg.CORBA.Any theAny,
    String plainString
);
```

Insertion of `BoundedWString` wide strings is done using

```
//Java
void SampleTypes.BoundedWStringHelper.insert(
    org.omg.CORBA.Any theAny,
    String wideString
);
```

The code in Listing 8.31 shows how string types are inserted into an any.

Listing 8.31 Java Examples of Inserting String Types

```
//Java
//----------------------------------------------------------------------
// Inserting Unbounded Strings
//
String s = "Insert me!";
theAny.insert_string(s);

//----------------------------------------------------------------------
// Inserting Bounded Strings
//
// Uses: 'string<64>'
//
// (In Java, insertion of unaliased bounded strings is NOT SUPPORTED.)
// (The dynamic any interface can be used to work around this limitation.)

//----------------------------------------------------------------------
// Inserting Alias of Bounded String
//
// Uses 'typedef string<64> BoundedString'
//
String s = "Insert me!";
BoundedStringHelper.insert(theAny, s);

//----------------------------------------------------------------------
// Inserting Unbounded Wide Strings
//
String ws = "Insert me!";
theAny.insert_wstring(ws);

//----------------------------------------------------------------------
```

Listing 8.31 continued

```
// Inserting Bounded Wide Strings
//
// Uses: 'wstring<64>'
//
// (In Java, insertion of unaliased bounded strings is NOT SUPPORTED.)
// (The dynamic any interface can be used to work around this limitation.)

//-----------------------------------------------------------------------
// Inserting Alias of Bounded Wide String
//
// Uses 'typedef wstring<128> BoundedWString'
//
String ws = "Insert me!";
BoundedWStringHelper.insert(theAny, ws);
```

Inserting Struct Types

The code in Listing 8.32 shows how struct types are inserted into an any.

Listing 8.32 Java Examples of Inserting Struct Types

```
//Java
//-----------------------------------------------------------------------
// Inserting Structs
//
// Uses: //IDL
//       //...in module 'SampleTypes'
//            struct VarLen {
//                 string theString;
//                 long theLong;
//            };
//
SampleTypes.VarLen theVarLen;
theVarLen = new SampleTypes.VarLen("Insert me!", 123);
SampleTypes.VarLenHelper.insert(theAny,  theVarLen);
```

Inserting Sequence Types

The code in Listing 8.33 shows how sequence types are inserted into an any.

Listing 8.33 Java Examples of Inserting Sequence Types

```
//-----------------------------------------------------------------------
// Inserting Sequences
//
// Uses: //IDL
//       //...in module 'SampleTypes'
//            typedef sequence< VarLen > SeqOfVarLen;
//
SampleTypes.VarLen theSeqOfVarLen[] = new SampleTypes.VarLen[1];
theSeqOfVarLen[0] = new SampleTypes.VarLen("Insert me!", 123);
SampleTypes.SeqOfVarLenHelper.insert(theAny, theSeqOfVarLen);
```

Inserting Fixed Precision Numbers

The code in Listing 8.34 shows how fixed types are inserted into an any.

Listing 8.34 Java Examples of Inserting Fixed Types

```
//Java
//------------------------------------------------------------------
// Inserting Fixed Precision Numbers
//
// Uses: Type 'fixed<6, 2>'
//
java.math.BigDecimal fx = new java.math.BigDecimal("1234.02");
theAny.insert_fixed(fx);
```

Inserting Union Types

The code in Listing 8.35 shows how union types are inserted into an any.

Listing 8.35 Java Examples of Inserting Union Types

```
//Java
//------------------------------------------------------------------
// Inserting Unions
//
// Uses: //IDL
//       //...in module 'SampleTypes'
//            union Poly switch(short) {
//                 case 1: short theShort;
//                 case 2: string theString;
//            };
//
SampleTypes.Poly thePoly = new SampleTypes.Poly();
thePoly.theString("Insert me!");
SampleTypes.PolyHelper.insert(theAny, thePoly);
```

Inserting Array Types

The code in Listing 8.36 shows how array types are inserted into an any.

Listing 8.36 Java Examples of Inserting Array Types

```
//Java
//------------------------------------------------------------------
// Inserting Arrays
//
// Uses: //IDL
//       //... in module 'SampleTypes'
//            typedef VarLen ArrOfVarLen[10];
//
SampleTypes.VarLen theArrOfVarLen[] = new SampleTypes.VarLen[10];
theArrOfVarLen[0] = new SampleTypes.VarLen("Insert me!", 123);
... // Initialize each of 10 elements.
SampleTypes.ArrOfVarLenHelper.insert(theAny, theArrOfVarLen);
```

Inserting Exception Types

The code in Listing 8.37 shows how exception types are inserted into an any.

Listing 8.37 Java Examples of Inserting Exception Types

```
//Java
//------------------------------------------------------------------
// Inserting Exceptions
//
// Uses: //IDL
//       //... in module 'SampleTypes'
//           exception GenericExc {
//               string reason;
//           };
//
SampleTypes.GenericExc theExc;
theExc = new SampleTypes.GenericExc("This is the reason field.");
SampleTypes. GenericExcHelper.insert(theAny, theExc);
```

Inserting Object References

There are two approaches supported for inserting an object reference into an any.

The first approach is to use the insert() method of the Helper class. For example, in Listing 8.38, the method SampleTypes.FooHelper.insert() is used to insert a Foo object reference.

The second approach is to use one of the generic insert_Object() methods:

```
//Java
package org.omg.CORBA;

void Any.insert_Object(org.omg.CORBA.Object obj);
void Any.insert_Object(org.omg.CORBA.Object obj, org.omg.CORBA.TypeCode t)
        throws org.omg.CORBA.BAD_PARAM;
```

The second form of insert_Object() throws the BAD_PARAM system exception if the type code t is inconsistent with the type of the object reference obj.

The code in Listing 8.38 shows how object references are inserted into an any.

Listing 8.38 Java Examples of Inserting Object References

```
//Java
//------------------------------------------------------------------
// Inserting Object References
//

SampleTypes.Foo theFoo = /* Initialize object reference */;

// Method 1. - Insert as derived type
SampleTypes.FooHelper.insert(theAny, theFoo);
```

```
// Method 2. - Insert as org.omg.CORBA.Object
SampleTypes.Foo theFoo = /* Initialize object reference */;
theAny.insert_Object(theFoo, SampleTypes.FooHelper.type());
```

Inserting any and TypeCode Types

The code in Listing 8.39 shows how any and TypeCode types are inserted into an any.

Listing 8.39 Java Examples of Inserting any and TypeCode Types

```
//-------------------------------------------------------------------
// Inserting Anys
//
org.omg.CORBA.Any anyToBeInserted = org.omg.CORBA.ORB.init().create_any();
anyToBeInserted.insert_long(123);
theAny.insert_any(anyToBeInserted);

//-------------------------------------------------------------------
// Inserting TypeCodes
//
org.omg.CORBA.TypeCode theTypeCode = /* Initialize the TypeCode */;
theAny.insert_TypeCode(theTypeCode);
```

Extraction from org.omg.CORBA.Any

The following sections give examples of any extraction for a representative sample of CORBA data types. The IDL types used in these examples are taken from Listing 8.1.

Extracting Basic Types

The code in Listing 8.40 shows how basic types are extracted from an any.

Listing 8.40 Java Examples of Extracting Basic Types

```
// Java
//-------------------------------------------------------------------
// Declaration of ' org.omg.CORBA.Any '
//

org.omg.CORBA.Any theAny = org.omg.CORBA.ORB.init().create_any();

//-------------------------------------------------------------------
// Extracting Basic Types
//

// Extracting a 'short'
short s;
if ( (theAny.type()).kind() == org.omg.CORBA.TCKind.tk_short) {
     s = theAny.extract_short();
}

// Extracting an 'unsigned short'
short us;
```

Listing 8.40 continued

```
if ( (theAny.type()).kind() == org.omg.CORBA.TCKind.tk_ushort) {
     us = theAny.extract_ushort();
}

// Extracting a 'long'
int l;
if ( (theAny.type()).kind() == org.omg.CORBA.TCKind.tk_long) {
     l = theAny.extract_long();
}

// Extracting an 'unsigned long'
int ul;
if ( (theAny.type()).kind() == org.omg.CORBA.TCKind.tk_ulong) {
     ul = theAny.extract_ulong();
}

// Extracting a 'long long'
long ll;
if ( (theAny.type()).kind() == org.omg.CORBA.TCKind.tk_longlong) {
     ll = theAny.extract_longlong();
}

// Extracting an 'unsigned long long'
long ull;
if ( (theAny.type()).kind() == org.omg.CORBA.TCKind.tk_ulonglong) {
     ull = theAny.extract_ulonglong();
}

// Extracting a 'float'
float f;
if ( (theAny.type()).kind() == org.omg.CORBA.TCKind.tk_float) {
     f = theAny.extract_float();
}

// Extracting a 'double'
double d;
if ( (theAny.type()).kind() == org.omg.CORBA.TCKind.tk_double) {
     d = theAny.extract_double();
}

// Extracting a 'long double'
// Not available in the CORBA 2.3 IDL-to-Java mapping

// Extracting a 'boolean'
boolean b;
if ( (theAny.type()).kind() == org.omg.CORBA.TCKind.tk_boolean) {
     b = theAny.extract_boolean();
}
```

Listing 8.40 continued

```
// Extracting an 'octet'
byte o;
if ( (theAny.type()).kind() == org.omg.CORBA.TCKind.tk_octet) {
     o = theAny.extract_octet();
}

// Extracting a 'char'
char c;
if ( (theAny.type()).kind() == org.omg.CORBA.TCKind.tk_char) {
     c = theAny.extract_char();
}

// Extracting a 'wchar'
char wc;
if ( (theAny.type()).kind() == org.omg.CORBA.TCKind.tk_wchar) {
     wc = theAny.extract_wchar();
}
```

Extracting Strings and Wide Strings

Extraction of aliased bounded strings is different from extraction of unbounded strings. Instead of the `org.omg.CORBA.Any.extract_string()` and `org.omg.CORBA.Any.extract_wstring()` methods used for unbounded strings, you must use extraction methods defined on `Helper` classes.

For example, consider the bounded string type `BoundedString` and the bounded wide string type `BoundedWString`, defined as follows:

```
//IDL
module SampleTypes {
    typedef string < 64 > BoundedString;
    typedef wstring < 128 > BoundedWString;
    ...
};
```

Extraction of `BoundedString` strings is done using

```
//Java
String SampleTypes.BoundedStringHelper.extract(
    org.omg.CORBA.Any theAny
);
```

Extraction of `BoundedWString` wide strings is done using

```
//Java
String SampleTypes.BoundedWStringHelper.extract(
    org.omg.CORBA.Any theAny
);
```

The code in Listing 8.41 shows how string types are extracted from an any.

Listing 8.41 Java Examples of Extracting String Types

```
//Java
//-----------------------------------------------------------------------
// Extracting Unbounded Strings
//
String s;
if ( (theAny.type()).kind() == org.omg.CORBA.TCKind.tk_string) {
     s = theAny.extract_string();
}

//-----------------------------------------------------------------------
// Extracting Bounded Strings
//
// Uses: 'string<64>'
//
// (In Java, extraction of unaliased bounded strings is NOT SUPPORTED.)
// (The dynamic any interface can be used to work around this limitation.)

//-----------------------------------------------------------------------
// Extracting Alias of Bounded String
//
// Uses 'typedef string<64> BoundedString'
//
String s;
if (  (theAny.type()).equal(BoundedStringHelper.type()) ) {
     s = BoundedStringHelper.extract(theAny);
}

//-----------------------------------------------------------------------
// Extracting Unbounded Wide Strings
//
String ws;
if ( (theAny.type()).kind() == org.omg.CORBA.TCKind.tk_wstring) {
     ws = theAny.extract_wstring();
}

//-----------------------------------------------------------------------
// Extracting Bounded Wide Strings
//
// Uses: 'wstring<64>'
//
// (In Java, extraction of unaliased bounded strings is NOT SUPPORTED.)
// (The dynamic any interface can be used to work around this limitation.)

//-----------------------------------------------------------------------
// Extracting Alias of Bounded Wide String
//
```

Listing 8.41 continued

```
// Uses 'typedef wstring<128> BoundedWString'
//
String ws;
if (  (theAny.type()).equal(BoundedWStringHelper.type()) ) {
     ws = BoundedWStringHelper.extract(theAny);
}
```

Extracting Struct Types

The code in Listing 8.42 shows how struct types are extracted from an any.

Listing 8.42 Java Examples of Extracting Struct Types

```
//Java
//--------------------------------------------------------------------
// Extracting Structs
//
// Uses: //IDL
//       //...in module 'SampleTypes'
//            struct VarLen {
//                 string theString;
//                 long theLong;
//            };
//
SampleTypes.VarLen theVarLen;
if ( (theAny.type()).equivalent(SampleTypes.VarLenHelper.type()) ) {
     theVarLen = SampleTypes.VarLenHelper.extract(theAny);
}
```

Extracting Sequence Types

The code in Listing 8.43 shows how sequence types are extracted from an any.

Listing 8.43 Java Examples of Extracting Sequence Types

```
//Java
//--------------------------------------------------------------------
// Extracting Sequences
//
// Uses: //IDL
//       //...in module 'SampleTypes'
//            typedef sequence< VarLen > SeqOfVarLen;
//
SampleTypes.VarLen theSeqOfVarLen[];
if ( (theAny.type()).equivalent(SampleTypes.SeqOfVarLenHelper.type()) ) {
     theSeqOfVarLen = SampleTypes.SeqOfVarLenHelper.extract(theAny);
}
```

Extracting Fixed Precision Numbers

The code in Listing 8.44 shows how fixed types are extracted from an any.

Listing 8.44 Java Examples of Extracting Fixed Types

```
//Java
//-----------------------------------------------------------------
// Extracting Fixed Precision Numbers
//
// Uses: Type 'fixed<6, 2>'
//
java.math.BigDecimal fx;
if ( (theAny.type()).kind() == org.omg.CORBA.TCKind.tk_fixed) {
     fx = theAny.extract_fixed();
}
```

Extracting Union Types

The code in Listing 8.45 shows how union types are extracted from an any.

Listing 8.45 Java Examples of Extracting Union Types

```
//Java
//-----------------------------------------------------------------
// Extracting Unions
//
// Uses: //IDL
//        //...in module 'SampleTypes'
//             union Poly switch(short) {
//                  case 1: short theShort;
//                  case 2: string theString;
//             };
//
SampleTypes.Poly thePoly = new SampleTypes.Poly();
if ( (theAny.type()).equivalent(SampleTypes.PolyHelper.type()) ) {
     thePoly = SampleTypes.PolyHelper.extract(theAny);
}
```

Extracting Array Types

The code in Listing 8.46 shows how array types are extracted from an any.

Listing 8.46 Java Examples of Extracting Array Types

```
//Java
//-----------------------------------------------------------------
// Extracting Arrays
//
// Uses: //IDL
//        //... in module 'SampleTypes'
//             typedef VarLen ArrOfVarLen[10];
//
```

Listing 8.46 continued

```
SampleTypes.VarLen theArrOfVarLen[];
if ( (theAny.type()).equivalent(SampleTypes.ArrOfVarLenHelper.type()) ) {
     theArrOfVarLen = SampleTypes.ArrOfVarLenHelper.extract(theAny);
}
```

Extracting Exception Types

The code in Listing 8.47 shows how exception types are extracted from an any.

Listing 8.47 Java Examples of Extracting Exception Types

```
//Java
//-----------------------------------------------------------------
// Extracting Exceptions
//
// Uses: //IDL
//       //... in module 'SampleTypes'
//            exception GenericExc {
//                 string reason;
//            };
//
SampleTypes.GenericExc theExc;
if ( (theAny.type()).equivalent(SampleTypes.GenericExcHelper.type()) ) {
     theExc = SampleTypes.GenericExcHelper.extract(theAny);
}
```

Extracting Object References

There are two approaches to extracting an object reference from an any.

The first approach is to use the `extract()` method of the `Helper` class. For example, in Listing 8.48, the method `SampleTypes.FooHelper.extract()` is used to extract a `Foo` object reference.

The second approach is to use the generic `extract_Object()` method:

```
//Java
package org.omg.CORBA;

org.omg.CORBA.Object Any.extract_Object()
          throws org.omg.CORBA.BAD_OPERATION;
```

Because the return type of `extract_Object()` is the base class `org.omg.CORBA.Object`, it is typically necessary to narrow the returned object reference to the correct type.

The code in Listing 8.48 shows how object references are extracted from an any.

Listing 8.48 Java Examples of Extracting Object References

```
//Java
//-----------------------------------------------------------------
// Extracting Object References
```

Listing 8.48 continued

```
//
// Method 1. - Extract derived type
SampleTypes.Foo theFoo;
if ( (theAny.type()).equivalent(SampleTypes.FooHelper.type()) ) {
     theFoo = SampleTypes.FooHelper.extract(theAny);
}

// Method 2. - Extract base type
SampleTypes.Foo theFoo;
org.omg.CORBA.Object theObj;
if ( (theAny.type()).kind() == org.omg.CORBA.TCKind.tk_objref) {
     theObj = theAny.extract_Object();
     theFoo = SampleTypes.FooHelper.narrow(theObj);
}
```

Extracting `any` and `TypeCode` Types

The code in Listing 8.49 shows how any and `TypeCode` types are extracted from an any.

Listing 8.49 Java Examples of Extracting `any` *and* `TypeCode` *Types*

```
//Java
//-------------------------------------------------------------------
// Extracting Anys
//
// Given an 'Any' that contains an 'Any' that contains a 'long':
//
org.omg.CORBA.Any extractedAny;
if ( (theAny.type()).kind() == org.omg.CORBA.TCKind.tk_any) {
     extractedAny = theAny.extract_any();
     long extractedLong = extractedAny.extract_long();
}

//-------------------------------------------------------------------
// Extracting TypeCodes
//
org.omg.CORBA.TypeCode theTypeCode;
if ( (theAny.type()).kind() == org.omg.CORBA.TCKind.tk_TypeCode) {
     theTypeCode = theAny.extract_TypeCode();
}
```

Type Codes

Type codes are an essential part of the dynamic typing mechanism of CORBA. They are described by the pseudo-IDL interface `CORBA::TypeCode`, which maps to the class `CORBA::TypeCode` in C++ and `org.omg.CORBA.TypeCode` in Java.

A type code can provide a complete description of built-in IDL types or user-defined IDL types. Usually, it is possible to re-create the exact IDL declaration of a given user-defined type by querying the properties of the corresponding type code.

Most of the time you do not need to know much about the structure of type codes because the IDL compiler generates predefined type codes for you. Often the only operation you will need to perform on type codes is to make comparisons. Comparisons can be made using the operations `equal()` and `equivalent()`, as described in the section "Comparison of Type Codes," later in this chapter. If you need to use type codes in a more sophisticated way, consult Chapter 17 and Chapter 19.

C++ Type Code Constants

The C++ language mapping provides a predefined set of type code constants. Type code constants are predefined for

- All built-in CORBA types.
- All user-defined types for which stub code is available.

If your application does not have the stub code for an IDL type, the corresponding type code constant will not be available. In that case, you could use the operations defined on `CORBA::ORB` to create the type code dynamically (see Chapter 18 and Chapter 20).

Built-In CORBA Types

The constants provided for built-in types are listed in Table 8.1.

Table 8.1 Type Codes for Built-In Types

IDL Type	Type Code Constant
no type	CORBA::_tc_null
void	CORBA::_tc_void
short	CORBA::_tc_short
long	CORBA::_tc_long
unsigned short	CORBA::_tc_ushort
unsigned long	CORBA::_tc_ulong
float	CORBA::_tc_float
double	CORBA::_tc_double
boolean	CORBA::_tc_boolean
char	CORBA::_tc_char
octet	CORBA::_tc_octet
any	CORBA::_tc_any
TypeCode	CORBA::_tc_TypeCode
Principal	CORBA::_tc_Principal
Object	CORBA::_tc_Object
string	CORBA::_tc_string
long long	CORBA::_tc_longlong
unsigned long long	CORBA::_tc_ulonglong
long double	CORBA::_tc_longdouble
wchar	CORBA::_tc_wchar
wstring	CORBA::_tc_wstring
fixed<>	CORBA::_tc_fixed

The type code constants are object references of type CORBA::TypeCode_ptr. The corresponding objects, of type CORBA::TypeCode, are local objects (technically, these are locality-constrained CORBA objects).

There are a few special cases among the built-in type codes. The constant CORBA::_tc_null does not correspond to any IDL type. It merely represents the value of a type code that is in an uninitialized state.

As an example of a type code constant in use, consider the following code fragment.

```
// C++
CORBA::Any theAny;
...
// Given that 'theAny' contains a 'float' value:

CORBA::Float f;
CORBA::Boolean succeeds;
if ( (theAny.type())->equivalent(CORBA::_tc_float) ) { // Redundant check
     succeeds = theAny >>= f;
}
```

The method CORBA::TypeCode::equivalent() is used to compare the type code of theAny with CORBA::_tc_float. Note that it would be an error to attempt to compare two type codes using the == operator.

In fact, checking the type code of the CORBA::Any in this way is redundant. The extraction operator >>= performs the type check anyway. The return value of the extraction expression is TRUE if the types match.

User-Defined CORBA Types

Constants are also defined for user-defined CORBA types. For example, the struct SampleTypes::VarLen (defined in Listing 8.1) has a corresponding type code constant called SampleTypes::_tc_VarLen.

The following code fragment shows SampleTypes::_tc_VarLen being used to check the type of the data inside a CORBA::Any.

```
// C++
CORBA::Any theAny;
...
// Given that 'theAny' contains a 'SampleTypes::VarLen' struct

SampleTypes::VarLen * theVarLenP;
CORBA::Boolean succeeds;
if ( (theAny.type())->equivalent(SampleTypes::_tc_VarLen) ) { //Redundant check
     succeeds = theAny >>= theVarLenP;  // Read-only extraction
}
```

The method CORBA::TypeCode::equivalent() is used to compare the type code of theAny with SampleTypes::_tc_VarLen. Once again, the explicit check of the CORBA::Any's type is redundant.

Typedefs of CORBA Types

Type code constants are also generated for aliases of CORBA types. For example, if the following lines appear in your IDL file

```
// IDL
...
typedef string AliasString;
typedef VarLen AliasStruct;
```

this results in the generation of constants `_tc_AliasString` and `_tc_AliasStruct` when mapped to C++.

Type Code Representations

Type codes can be fairly complex and bulky. In the interest of efficiency, it is worth considering how some of the bulk can be discarded. There is one important case in which the bulk of the type code *can* be reduced: a type code that describes the layout of data for marshalling or unmarshalling. In this case, most identifiers appearing in the type definition are redundant.

For reasons of efficiency, therefore, two representations of a type code are supported:

- Complete type code
- Compact type code

These representations are discussed in the following sections.

Complete Type Codes

A complete type code contains enough information to re-create the fragment of IDL that describes the type. Consider `SampleTypes::VarLen`, defined in Listing 8.1. The corresponding type code consists of a repository ID and other details.

Some types have no need of a repository ID. These are known as *unnamed types*, and for these types the repository ID is left blank. For example, there is no need to provide a repository ID for trivial IDL types like `short` or `float`.

Using the operations of the `TypeCode` interface (Chapter 18), you can extract the following information about `VarLen`:

- The name of the struct is `VarLen`.
- There are two members.
- The first member is of type `string` and named `theString`.
- The second member is of type `long` and named `theLong`.

Putting this information together, you can re-create the original IDL:

```
// IDL

// RepositoryID = "IDL:pure-corba-3.com/SampleTypes/VarLen:1.0"
// (defined in scope 'SampleTypes')
    struct VarLen {
```

```
        string theString;
        long theLong;
    };
```

A complete type code supplies a repository ID (where appropriate) and enough structure to re-create the IDL definition exactly.

Compact Type Codes

A compact type code is derived from a complete type code in the following way:

- The repository ID remains intact.
- Alias names remain intact (that is, alternative names for the type resulting from a `typedef`).
- All other identifiers in the type code are left blank.

To obtain a compact type code, invoke the operation `CORBA::TypeCode::get_compact_typecode()` on a regular type code. For example, consider how to generate a compact type code for the type `VarLen`:

```
// C++
CORBA::TypeCode_var tcCompactV;
tcCompactV = SampleTypes::_tc_VarLen->get_compact_typecode();

// Java
org.omg.CORBA.TypeCode tcCompact;
tcCompact = SampleTypes.VarLenHelper.type().get_compact_typecode();
```

For a compact type code, the operations of the `TypeCode` interface (see Chapter 18) allow you to reconstruct only a bare outline of the original IDL declaration:

```
// IDL

// RepositoryID = "IDL:pure-corba-3.com/SampleTypes/VarLen:1.0"
// (defined in scope 'SampleTypes')
    struct blank {
        string blank;
        long blank;
    };
```

The compact type code has an intact repository ID, but it provides only a bare type code structure that is stripped of identifier names.

Inserting and Extracting Type Aliases

In the C++ mapping of `any`, it is necessary to set the `type()` field of the `any` explicitly when inserting type aliases into the `any`.

Consider the following fragment of IDL:

```
// IDL
typedef string Alias1;
typedef string Alias2;
```

This defines the two alias types Alias1 and Alias2.

To insert an aliased string, Alias1, the usual C++ expression, theAny <<= "Inserted", is not adequate. The generic API does not specify the exact type of the any's data. This difficulty is solved by explicitly calling the type() modifier method of CORBA::Any after the string has been inserted.

The way to insert a string alias in C++ and in Java is as follows:

```
// C++
...
theAny <<= "Insert me as an Alias1";  // Copying insertion
theAny.type(_tc_Alias1);              // Explicitly set type code

// Java
...
Alias1Helper.insert(theAny,"Insert me as an Alias1");
```

The C++ code fragment shows that you can set the type of the any explicitly after inserting the string.

The Java code fragment uses the insert() method of the Alias1Helper class to insert the string alias into the any.

Suppose you have a piece of code that expects to receive an any containing either Alias1 or Alias2:

```
// C++
// Given 'theAny' containing either 'Alias1' or 'Alias2'
...
if ( (theAny.type()).equal(_tc_Alias1)) {
     // Perform actions for 'Alias1'
}
else if ( (theAny.type()).equal(_tc_Alias2)) {
     // Perform actions for 'Alias2'
}

// Java
// Given 'theAny' containing either 'Alias1' or 'Alias2'
...
if ( (theAny.type()).equal(Alias1Helper.type()) ) {
     // Perform actions for 'Alias1'
}
else if ( (theAny.type()).equal(Alias2Helper.type()) ) {
     // Perform actions for 'Alias2'
}
```

This code fragment is sensitive to the exact type contained in the any. It is therefore essential to use equal() here and not equivalent(), because the equivalent() method cannot distinguish between aliases.

Comparison of Type Codes

There are times when the distinction between a type alias (defined using an IDL `typedef` statement) and the original type is important. At other times the distinction is unimportant. The `CORBA::TypeCode` interface, therefore, provides two comparison operations that treat type aliases in different ways:

- `CORBA::TypeCode::equal()`—Returns `TRUE` if and only if the target type code and the type code passed as an argument are identical in every respect.
- `CORBA::TypeCode::equivalent()`—Returns `TRUE` if the type codes being compared are derived from the same original type code, ignoring aliases. Comparison using `equivalent()` is also tolerant of compact type codes. When comparing a type code with its compact representation, `equivalent()` returns `TRUE`.

The difference between an `equal()` comparison and an `equivalent()` comparison can be illustrated by an example. Consider the following fragment of IDL that defines aliases of the `string` type:

```
// IDL
typedef string FirstAlias;
typedef FirstAlias SecondAlias;
typedef SecondAlias ThirdAlias;

typedef string OtherAlias;
```

The following sections show the results of comparing the type `string` with the type `ThirdAlias`, using first the `equal()` operation and then the `equivalent()` operation.

Comparison Using `CORBA::TypeCode::equal()`

The following code fragments, in C++ and Java, define two anys: `anyForString`, which holds a plain `string`, and `anyForThirdAlias`, which holds a string of type `ThirdAlias`. A strict comparison of the `type()` fields is made using `CORBA::TypeCode::equal()`.

```
// C++
// Initialize 'anyForString' and 'anyForThirdAlias'
CORBA::Any anyForString <<= "Any old string";
CORBA::Any anyForThirdAlias <<= "and another string";
anyForThirdAlias.type(_tc_ThirdAlias);

// Strict Comparison, using 'equal()'.
CORBA::Boolean isEqual;
isEqual = (anyForString.type()).equal(anyForThirdAlias.type());
// --------> Result: isEqual == FALSE

// Java
// Initialize 'anyForString' and 'anyForThirdAlias'
org.omg.CORBA.Any anyForString = org.omg.CORBA.ORB.init().create_any();
```

```
anyForString.insert_string("Any old string");
org.omg.CORBA.Any anyForThirdAlias = org.omg.CORBA.ORB.init().create_any();
ThirdAliasHelper.insert(anyForThirdAlias, "and another string");

// Strict Comparison, using 'equal()'.
boolean isEqual;
isEqual = (anyForString.type()).equal(anyForThirdAlias.type());
// --------> Result: isEqual == FALSE
```

The comparison using `equal()` returns `FALSE` because an original type and its alias are considered to be distinct by the `equal()` operation.

Comparison Using CORBA::TypeCode::equivalent()

The following code fragments, in C++ and Java, define two anys: `anyForString`, which holds a plain `string`, and `anyForThirdAlias`, which holds a string of type `ThirdAlias`. A loose comparison of the `type()` fields is made using `CORBA::TypeCode::equivalent()`.

```
// C++
// Initialize 'anyForString' and 'anyForThirdAlias'
CORBA::Any anyForString <<= "Any old string";
CORBA::Any anyForThirdAlias <<= "and another string";
anyForThirdAlias.type(_tc_ThirdAlias);

// Loose Comparison using, 'equivalent()'.
CORBA::Boolean isEquiv;
isEquiv = (anyForString.type()).equivalent(anyForThirdAlias.type());
// --------> Result: isEquiv == TRUE

// Java
// Initialize 'anyForString' and 'anyForThirdAlias'
org.omg.CORBA.Any anyForString = org.omg.CORBA.ORB.init().create_any();
anyForString.insert_string("Any old string");
org.omg.CORBA.Any anyForThirdAlias = org.omg.CORBA.ORB.init().create_any();
ThirdAliasHelper.insert(anyForThirdAlias, "and another string");

// Loose Comparison using, 'equivalent()'.
boolean isEquiv;
isEquiv = (anyForString.type()).equivalent(anyForThirdAlias.type());
// --------> Result: isEquiv == TRUE
```

The comparison using `equivalent()` returns `TRUE` because `equivalent()` implicitly *unwinds* the aliases `ThirdAlias`, `SecondAlias`, and `FirstAlias` until it arrives at the basic type `string`. The unwinding of aliases is performed on both arguments before type comparison is made. Therefore, comparison between any permutation of `string`, `FirstAlias`, `SecondAlias`, `ThirdAlias`, and `OtherAlias` would return `TRUE` when `equivalent()` is used.

Summary

This chapter has covered the syntax and semantics of insertion into and extraction from the `any` type. To use the `any` type effectively, you also need to have some understanding of CORBA type codes. The following aspects of type codes were discussed in this chapter:

- Type code constants
- Comparison of type codes

The contents of an `any` can easily be checked by examining its `type()` field.

The use of the `any` type in this chapter is restricted to cases in which you have stub code to support the data types contained in the `any`. There are applications, however, that need to manipulate the `any`'s contents even without stub code. The `DynamicAny` module is provided by CORBA for this sort of application. It is discussed in detail in Chapter 20.

CHAPTER 9

Callbacks

Many simple CORBA applications exhibit a clear distinction between client and server roles. The server plays a passive role, responding to invocation requests from clients, while the client plays an active role, initiating invocations on the server.

Sometimes, however, the roles need to be reversed. If a server logs an important event, it might need to take the initiative to notify interested clients in a timely manner. An example of this is a system for monitoring stock prices. A server that monitors stock prices must send out notifications to enable traders to track the latest price movements in stocks that interest them.

This kind of system requires the direction of the invocations to be reversed so that a server invokes on a client. The client application must implement and instantiate a CORBA object, a *callback object*, to receive the invocations. The client, therefore, takes on some of the characteristics of a server—it is a hybrid in many respects. This chapter describes the features of a callback client and provides a simple example of a system that uses callbacks. There is nothing fundamentally new, in terms of CORBA programming, described here. However, the use of callbacks is a common pattern that illustrates a number of principles of CORBA programming, including how to avoid distributed deadlock.

Processing Invocations in a Client

Implementing a callback object in a client is similar to implementing a regular CORBA object in a server (a callback object is just a CORBA object that lives in the client). To implement a callback, perform the following steps:

1. Implement a servant class for the callback's IDL interface.

2. Instantiate and activate the callback servant in the same way as in a server.
3. Configure the POA that activates the callback object to have the TRANSIENT lifespan policy value.
   An application that supports only TRANSIENT objects does not need to be registered with the ORB's activation mechanism (activation in the sense of launching a process).
   Most ORB implementations optimize the interoperable object references (IORs) associated with TRANSIENT objects. TRANSIENT IORs typically contain the host and port of the application that generated the IOR.
4. Implement the callback client to process incoming invocations within an event loop.
5. Generate skeleton code from the callback's IDL interface and link it with the client application.

You could call CORBA::ORB::run() to process events, but this is not satisfactory in a client application because the run() operation blocks, preventing all other activities apart from processing invocations. There are two alternative approaches to processing invocations in a client application:

- **Single-threaded client** Use the CORBA::ORB::perform_work() operation instead of CORBA::ORB::run(). The perform_work() operation does not block indefinitely and returns after a certain number of invocations have been processed (the exact behavior of perform_work() is implementation dependent). This allows you to write an event loop to integrate with the other activities of the client application. For example, the following listings outline a simple client event loop in C++ and Java:

  Listing 9.1 C++ Sample Event Loop

```
//C++
    ...
    while (keep_running) {
        if (orb->work_pending() ) { orb->perform_work(); }
        process_user_input();
    }
```

  Listing 9.2 Java Sample Event Loop

```
//Java
    ...
    while (keep_running) {
        if (orb.work_pending() ) { orb.perform_work(); }
        process_user_input();
    }
```

  The process_user_input() function processes events from the user's keyboard and mouse.
  The drawback with this approach is that it often makes the client unresponsive. If an invocation takes a long time to process, the user is frozen out by the perform_work() operation, and the client application cannot respond to the keyboard or mouse.

- **Multithreaded client** In this case you reserve one thread for processing CORBA invocations, and within this thread you can call the `CORBA::ORB::run()` operation. A second thread is created to respond to user input and perform other tasks.

Of the two approaches to invocation processing in the client, the multithreaded approach is preferable because it ensures a reasonable degree of responsiveness to user input. However, if you are adding callback functionality to an existing single-threaded application, it is preferable to avoid multithreading. Retrofitting multithreading to a legacy application can be a fairly complex task that carries with it a risk of destabilizing the application.

Avoiding Deadlock in Callbacks

Callbacks can easily manifest the phenomenon of *distributed deadlock*. Consider the system shown in Figure 9.1, where a client with a callback object makes an invocation on a CORBA object in a server. Both client and server are single threaded.

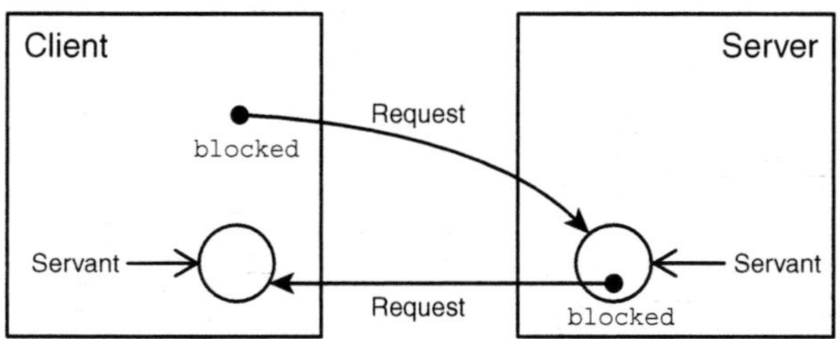

Figure 9.1

Deadlock in a system using callbacks.

Because the client is single threaded, it uses an event loop, as shown in Listing 9.1 and Listing 9.2. In the course of executing the `process_user_input()` function, the client makes a remote invocation on the server's CORBA object. Consider what happens if the server calls back on the client's CORBA object while processing this invocation. Ordinary CORBA invocations are synchronous, and therefore the server is blocked while it awaits a reply from the client. But the client will never send the reply, because it is also blocked, waiting for the reply from the invocation it made on the server. This is distributed deadlock.

There are two ways of avoiding the deadlock in this system:

- **Client is single threaded** Declare the operations on the callback object to be `oneway` operations in your IDL. Because `oneway` operations expect no reply, the callback invocation returns right away, thereby avoiding the deadlock.
- **Client is multithreaded** Using a separate thread for processing invocations in the client avoids the deadlock, assuming that the initial client invocation is made from another thread.

> To be really safe against deadlock, however, it might be necessary to activate the callback object using a POA that supports the `ORB_CTRL_MODEL` multithreading policy. The client will then be protected against deadlock even if the initial invocation originates from a thread that is processing invocations.

The example in the next section shows how to use the first approach (using `oneways`) to implement a simple callback application.

Callback Example Using `oneway` Operations

The example in this section is based on the `RecycleBroker` IDL described in Chapter 3, "A Sample CORBA System." Listing 9.3 shows an enhancement to the `RecycleBroker` system that enables users of the system to be notified as soon as a new waste item is offered for sale.

Listing 9.3 IDL for a Callback That Uses a `oneway` Operation

```
//IDL
module RecycleBroker {
    typedef long        KeyType;

    enum WasteType {
        BROWN_GLASS, GREEN_GLASS, CLEAR_GLASS, SCRAP_STEEL,
        ALUMINIUM_CANS, PLASTIC_BOTTLES, WASTE_PAPER
    };

    // Implemented by the Client.
    interface WasteItemCallback {
        oneway void notify(in KeyType wasteitem_id, in WasteType waste);
    };

    // Implemented by the Server.
    interface WasteItemRegister {
        void reg_callback(in WasteItemCallback obj, in WasteType waste);
        void dereg_callback(in WasteItemCallback obj, in WasteType waste);
    };
};
```

Two new interfaces are defined to support this feature: `WasteItemCallback` and `WasteItemRegister`.

The `WasteItemCallback` interface is implemented by client applications. It provides a single `notify()` operation, which a server can call to notify a client that a new waste item is up for sale. The `wasteitem_id` argument uniquely identifies the new item, and the `waste` argument indicates the type of waste. The `notify()` operation is declared `oneway` to avoid the possibility of deadlock, as explained in the section "Avoiding Deadlock in Callbacks," earlier in this chapter.

The `WasteItemRegister` interface is implemented by server applications. The `reg_callback()` operation allows clients to register their interest in receiving notifications about certain kinds of waste item. The `obj` argument is a reference to a

WasteItemCallback object in the client, and the waste argument specifies the type of waste item. The dereg_callback() operation is used by the client to tell the server to stop sending notifications to the obj object.

Limitations of oneway Operations

Although oneway operations are convenient to use with callbacks, they do have limitations. A oneway operation

- Must have a void return type and can have only in parameters.
- Cannot raise any exceptions, either user or system exceptions, back to the caller.
- Is not always a oneway operation. One of the peculiar features of version 1.2 of the general inter-ORB protocol (GIOP) standard is that it allows the semantics of oneway operations to be overridden by the ORB configuration. If your ORB supports GIOP 1.2 and is configured to make all invocations synchronous, the oneway directive is ignored, and callbacks can become deadlocked after all. The solution, obviously, is to reconfigure your ORB to treat oneways normally.

Because of these limitations, using oneways might not be appropriate in all circumstances. You should also bear in mind that, in general, it is easier to design and implement applications that rely on synchronous invocations, which are processed in a definite sequence. It is not a good idea to use oneways extensively—in this chapter oneways are used solely when needed to avoid deadlock.

Callback Sample Implementation

This section presents a sample implementation of the callback IDL in Listing 9.3. The sample code is a test implementation that illustrates the mechanics of making a callback—it is not intended to be a realistic implementation.

The implementation of the WasteItemRegister interface is shown in Listing 9.4 and Listing 9.5 for C++ and Java, respectively.

Listing 9.4 C++ Implementation of **RecycleBroker::WasteItemRegister** *Interface*

```
//C++
// Part of 'server' application.

// reg_callback()
// Implements IDL operation "RecycleBroker::WasteItemRegister::reg_callback".
void
RecycleBroker_WasteItemRegister_i::reg_callback(
    RecycleBroker::WasteItemCallback_ptr obj,
    RecycleBroker::WasteType           waste
)
throw (CORBA::SystemException)
{
    m_callback_objV = RecycleBroker::WasteItemCallback::_duplicate(obj);
    m_waste_type    = waste;
```

Listing 9.4 continued

```
    if (!CORBA::is_nil(m_callback_objV.in()) ) {
        // Do some notifications to test the callback:
        m_callback_objV->notify((CORBA::Long) 1234, m_waste_type);
        m_callback_objV->notify((CORBA::Long) 2345, m_waste_type);
        m_callback_objV->notify((CORBA::Long) 6543, m_waste_type);
    }
}

// dereg_callback()
// Implements IDL operation "RecycleBroker::WasteItemRegister::dereg_callback".
void
RecycleBroker_WasteItemRegister_i::dereg_callback(
    RecycleBroker::WasteItemCallback_ptr obj,
    RecycleBroker::WasteType        waste
)
throw (CORBA::SystemException)
{
    if (m_callback_objV->_is_equivalent(obj) ) {
        m_callback_objV = RecycleBroker::WasteItemCallback:: _nil();
    }
}
```

Listing 9.5 Java Implementation of **RecycleBroker::WasteItemRegister** *Interface*

```
//Java
package Pure.CallbackDemo.RecycleBroker;

public class WasteItemRegister_i extends WasteItemRegisterPOA
{
    ...
    public void reg_callback(
        Pure.CallbackDemo.RecycleBroker.WasteItemCallback obj,
        Pure.CallbackDemo.RecycleBroker.WasteType waste
    )
    {
        System.out.println("WasteItemRegister_i.reg_callback(): called.");
        m_callback_obj = obj;
        m_waste_type   = waste;

        if (m_callback_obj != null) {
            // Do some notifications:
            System.out.println(
                "info: about to call back with wasteitem_id = \"1234\""
            );
            m_callback_obj._notify(1234, m_waste_type);
            m_callback_obj._notify(2345, m_waste_type);
            m_callback_obj._notify(6543, m_waste_type);
        }
    }
```

Listing 9.5 continued

```
     public void dereg_callback(
        Pure.CallbackDemo.RecycleBroker.WasteItemCallback obj,
        Pure.CallbackDemo.RecycleBroker.WasteType waste
    )
    {
        System.out.println("WasteItemRegister_i.dereg_callback(): called.");
        if (m_callback_obj._is_equivalent(obj) ) {
            m_callback_obj = null;
        }
    }
    ...
    private WasteItemCallback               m_callback_obj;
    private WasteType                       m_waste_type;
}
```

The `reg_callback()` operation allows clients to register an interest in receiving callbacks about a particular waste type. This simple example allows only a single client to register a callback. The reference to the callback object is stored in the private member variable `m_callback_objV` (C++) or `m_callback_obj` (Java), and the waste type is stored in `m_waste_type`.

The `reg_callback()` implementation tests the callback by making a few `notify()` invocations with random arguments.

NOTE

> The `WasteItemCallback::notify()` operation is mapped to `_notify()` in Java because it clashes with a Java keyword. The convention used in IDL-to-Java mapping is to prefix clashing identifiers with an underscore character.

The `dereg_callback()` operation clears the value in the `m_callback_objV` (C++) or `m_callback_obj` (Java) member variable if it is equal to the supplied `obj` object reference.

The implementation of the `WasteItemCallback` interface is shown in Listing 9.6 and Listing 9.7. This code represents the callback object, and it is compiled and linked with the client application.

Listing 9.6 C++ Implementation of* `RecycleBroker::WasteItemCallback` *Interface

```
//C++
// Part of 'client' application

// notify()
// Implements IDL operation "RecycleBroker::WasteItemCallback::notify".
void
RecycleBroker_WasteItemCallback_i::notify(
    RecycleBroker::KeyType              wasteitem_id,
```

Listing 9.6 continued

```
    RecycleBroker::WasteType        waste
)
throw (CORBA::SystemException)
{
    cout << "RecycleBroker_WasteItemCallback_i::notify(): called." << endl;
    cout << "        wasteitem_id = " << wasteitem_id << endl;
}
```

Listing 9.7 Java Implementation of `RecycleBroker::WasteItemCallback` Interface

```
//Java
package Pure.CallbackDemo.RecycleBroker;

public class WasteItemCallback_i extends WasteItemCallbackPOA
{
    ...
    public void _notify(
        int wasteitem_id,
        Pure.CallbackDemo.RecycleBroker.WasteType waste
    )
    {
        System.out.println("WasteItemCallback::notify(): called.");
        System.out.println("  wasteitem_id = " + wasteitem_id);
    }
    ...
}
```

For testing purposes, `WasteItemCallback::notify()` prints out the value of the `wasteitem_id` parameter to let you verify that the callback has been processed.

The `main()` function of the callback client is shown in Listing 9.8 and Listing 9.9. In many respects, it resembles the `main()` function of a CORBA server, but there are a couple of differences.

Listing 9.8 C++ Callback Client `main()` Function

```
//C++
...
#include "RecycleBroker_WasteItemCallback_i.h"
#include "POAUtility.h"
...
int
main(int argc, char **argv)
{
    int exit_status = 0;            // Return code from main.

    PortableServer::Servant the_RecycleBroker_WasteItemCallback = 0;
```

Listing 9.8 continued

```
try
{
    // For temporary object references.
    CORBA::Object_var tmp_ref;
    // Reference to Callback object.
    RecycleBroker::WasteItemCallback_var callback_refV;

    // Initialise the ORB and Root POA.
    cout << "Initializing the ORB" << endl;
    global_orb = CORBA::ORB_init(argc, argv);
    tmp_ref = global_orb->resolve_initial_references("RootPOA");
    PortableServer::POA_var root_poaV =
        PortableServer::POA::_narrow(tmp_ref);
    PortableServer::POAManager_var root_poa_managerV
        = root_poaV->the_POAManager();

    // Create a POA for TRANSIENT (session) objects.
    PortableServer::POA_var my_poa =
        POAUtility::create_basic_POA(
            root_poaV.in(),
            root_poa_managerV.in(),
            "my_poa",
            0,                  // Single threaded
            0                   // for 'Session' objects
        );
    PortableServer::ObjectId_var oid;

    // Create a servant for interface RecycleBroker::WasteItemCallback.
    the_RecycleBroker_WasteItemCallback =
        new RecycleBroker_WasteItemCallback_i(my_poa);

    // Activate the 'WasteItemCallback' object.
    oid = my_poa->activate_object(the_RecycleBroker_WasteItemCallback);
    tmp_ref = my_poa->id_to_reference(oid);
    callback_refV = RecycleBroker::WasteItemCallback::_narrow(tmp_ref);
    if (CORBA::is_nil(callback_refV.in()) ) {
        cerr << "error: failed to narrow to 'WasteItemCallback' object"
             << endl;
        exit(1);
    }

    // Activate the POA Manager
    // NB: The POA Manager must be activated before the 'WasteItemCallback'
    // object can service callback invocations.
    root_poa_managerV->activate();
```

Listing 9.8 continued

```
        tmp_ref = // Get a reference to a 'WasteItemRegister' object
                  // using the Naming Service or some other means.
        RecycleBroker::WasteItemRegister_var WasteItemRegister2 =
            RecycleBroker::WasteItemRegister::_narrow(tmp_ref);
        if (CORBA::is_nil(WasteItemRegister2))
        {
            cerr << "Could not narrow reference to interface "
                 << "RecycleBroker::WasteItemRegister" << endl;
            exit(1);
        }
        WasteItemRegister2->reg_callback(
            callback_refV.in(),
            RecycleBroker::BROWN_GLASS
        );

        // Begin event loop...
        keep_running = 1;
        while (keep_running) {
            if (orb->work_pending() ) { orb->perform_work(); }
            process_user_input();
        }
    }
    catch (CORBA::Exception& e)
    {
        cout << "Unexpected CORBA exception: " << e << endl;
        exit_status = 1;
    }
    // Delete the servants.
    the_RecycleBroker_WasteItemCallback->_remove_ref();

    // Ensure that the ORB is properly shutdown and cleaned up.
    try
    {
        global_orb->shutdown(1);
        global_orb->destroy();
    }
    catch (...)
    {
        // Do nothing.
    }
    return exit_status;
}
```

Listing 9.9 Java Callback Client `main()` Function

```
//Java
package Pure.CallbackDemo;

import java.io.*;
```

Listing 9.9 continued

```
import org.omg.CORBA.*;
import org.omg.PortableServer.*;
import Pure.CallbackDemo.RecycleBroker.*;

public class callback
{
  public static ORB global_orb;

  public static void main(String args[])
  {
    try
    {
        System.out.println("Initializing the ORB");

        global_orb = ORB.init(args, null);
        org.omg.CORBA.Object poa_obj
          = global_orb.resolve_initial_references("RootPOA");
        org.omg.PortableServer.POA root_poa
          = org.omg.PortableServer.POAHelper.narrow(poa_obj);
        org.omg.PortableServer.POAManager root_poa_manager
            = root_poa.the_POAManager();

        // Create a basic POA for 'Session' objects.
        System.out.println("Creating basic session POA");
        POA basic_session_poa =
            Pure.Util.POAUtility.create_basic_POA(
                root_poa,
                root_poa_manager,
                "basic_session_poa",
                false,                      // Single threaded
                false                       // for 'Session' objects
            );

        byte[] oid = null;
        org.omg.CORBA.Object ref = null;

        // Create a servant for interface WasteItemCallback.
        Servant the_WasteItemCallback = new WasteItemCallback_i(
            basic_session_poa                  //Default POA
        );
        oid = basic_session_poa.activate_object(the_WasteItemCallback);
        ref = basic_session_poa.id_to_reference(oid);
        WasteItemCallback the_callback
            = WasteItemCallbackHelper.narrow(ref);

        // Activate the POA Manager
        // NB: The POA Manager must be activated before the 'WasteItemCallback'
```

Listing 9.9 continued

```
        // object can service callback invocations.
        root_poa_manager.activate();

        ref = // Get a reference to a 'WasteItemRegister' object
              // using the Naming Service or some other means.
        WasteItemRegister the_reg = WasteItemRegisterHelper.narrow(ref);
        the_reg.reg_callback(the_callback, WasteType.BROWN_GLASS);

        // Begin event loop...
        keep_running = 1;
        while (keep_running) {
            if (orb.work_pending() ) { orb.perform_work(); }
            process_user_input();
        }
    }
    catch (org.omg.CORBA.SystemException sysEx) {
        System.out.println("SystemException: " + sysEx);
    }
    catch (Exception ex) {
        System.out.println("Exception: " + ex);
    }

    System.out.println("Done");
    orb.shutdown(true);
  }
}
```

The callback client `main()` function follows the standard steps for a server `main()` function up to the point where it creates and activates the `WasteItemCallback` object. The next step the client makes is to activate the POA Manager by calling `PortableServer::POAManager::activate()`. It is essential for the client to call `activate()` before making remote invocations because the client is not able to receive callbacks when the POA Manager is not in the active state.

The client gets a reference to the `WasteItemRegister` object, the CORBA object that lives in the server, and invokes the `reg_callback()` operation on it. The following sequence of events occurs:

1. The client ORB sends a request message to the server to invoke the `reg_callback()` operation.
2. In the course of processing the `reg_callback()` operation, the server calls back on the client by invoking the `notify()` operation (refer to Listing 9.6 and Listing 9.7).
3. Upon the first invocation of `notify()`, the server establishes a new network connection to the client.

   IIOP specifies that invocations can be made in only one direction along a network connection. Therefore, the existing connection from the client to the server cannot be reused for callback invocations.

4. Because `notify()` is a `oneway` operation, a request is sent to the client, and `notify()` returns immediately without waiting for a reply. This is the step that breaks the deadlock.
   The `oneway` requests are stored in a queue on the client side. Typically, an ORB creates internal threads to deal with requests incoming from the network.
5. The `reg_callback()` operation finishes executing, and a reply message is sent back to the client.
6. Control returns to the client `main()` function. The `reg_callback()` invocation has returned, so the client can proceed to its event loop.
   Once the `perform_work()` function is called, the queued `notify()` requests start to be processed on the client side.

In this way, the problem of deadlock is resolved without resorting to the use of application level threads.

Summary

The use of callbacks introduces the risk of distributed deadlock, and this has to be resolved either using multithreading or by declaring the callback operations as `oneway`. The callback pattern is particularly useful in applications that use messaging services. Two of the CORBA services, the CORBA Event Service and the CORBA Notification Service, provide messaging infrastructures based on a callback pattern.

CHAPTER 10

Interceptors

The ORB core is defined in the CORBA architecture as "that part of the ORB that provides the basic representation of objects and communication of requests." ORB Services, such as the security or transaction, are built on this core and provide a higher-level ORB environment to distributed object applications. The function of an ORB service is specified as a transformation of a given message (a request, reply, or derivation thereof), in terms of service contexts. A client may generate an object request. ORB services require hooks into the ORB in order to necessitate some transformation of that request.

Interceptors provide hooks into the ORB or interception points within the request/reply sequence, through which ORB services can query request/reply data and transfer service contexts between clients and servers. They are a means of structuring an ORB's interactions with extra-ORB services.

The concept of interceptors in CORBA 2.2 was underspecified and the interfaces for dealing with service context were not portable. For example, service implementations must negotiate interfaces with each ORB vendor in order to pass service context. This makes them largely useless as a mechanism for third parties, who offer services to "plug in to" an ORB.

The OMG issued a request for proposal (RFP) for a specification of portable Interceptors, which aims to solve this problem. Portable Interceptors are hooks into the ORB through which ORB services can intercept the normal flow of execution of the ORB. Portable Interceptors presented in this chapter are based on the adopted draft specification for CORBA v2.4+, which defines two classes of portable Interceptors: request Interceptors and IOR Interceptors. Request Interceptors are concerned with service contexts and are called during request mediation. IOR Interceptors are concerned with adding service specific information related to an object or server into tagged components of the profile in the IOR when the IOR is created.

The rest of the chapter provides an overview of the portable Interceptor interface specification and covers two types of portable Interceptors including request and IOR Interceptors. It also covers the Portable Interceptor Current, which can provide service context, and Policy Factory, which provides the policies used to create a POA and influences the set of tagged components within the profiles of any IOR created by that POA. Registering Interceptors are discussed, and writing and using Interceptors are demonstrated with a simple example in both C++ and Java.

Portable Interceptor Interface

The module `PortableInterceptor` defines portable Interceptor interfaces and related types.

```
module PortableInterceptor{
    local interface Interceptor{
        readonly attribute string name;
        void destroy();
};
};
```

All portable Interceptors inherit from the local interface Interceptor. This means all portable Interceptors must be declared local and invocations on local objects that implement interceptors are not ORB mediated.

Each interceptor may have a name or have an empty string as the name attribute. Only one Interceptor of a given name can be registered with ORB for each Interceptor type. An Interceptor with empty string as the name is anonymous. Any number of anonymous Interceptors may be registered with ORB. `Interceptor::destroy` is called during `ORB::destroy`.

As mentioned earlier, there are two classes of Interceptors: request Interceptors and IOR Interceptors.

Request Interceptors

A request Interceptor is designed to intercept the flow of a request/reply sequence through the ORB at specific points so that the services can query the request information and manipulate the service contexts, which are propagated between clients and servers.

The main function of request Interceptors is to allow ORB services to transfer service context information between clients and servers.

There are two types of request Interceptors. One is the client-side Interceptor and the other is the server-side Interceptor. Both client- and server-side Interceptors are registered with the ORB. The ORB logically maintains an ordered list of these Interceptors.

Each request Interceptor is called at a number of interception points within the flow of request/reply sequence. The interception points are shown in Figure 10.1.

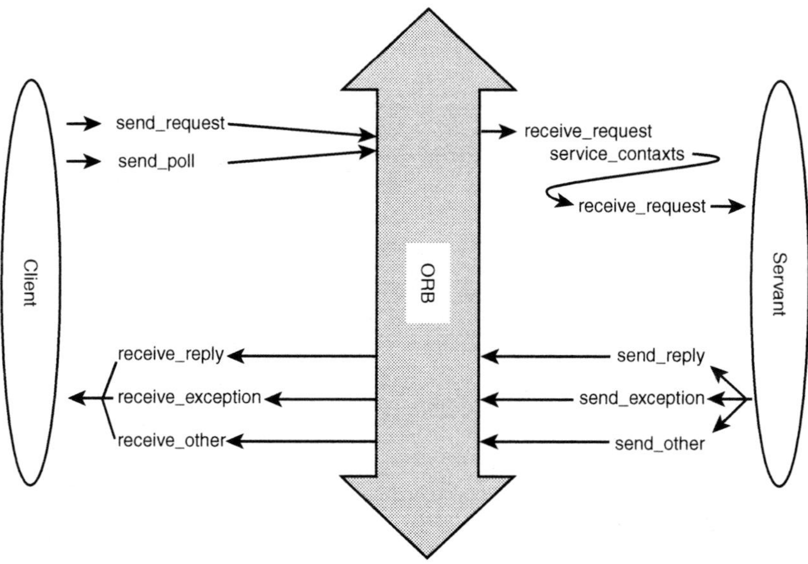

Figure 10.1

Request interceptor points.

Client-Side Interceptor

```
local interface ClientRequestInterceptor: Interceptor {
    void send_request (in ClientRequestInfo ri) raises (ForwardRequest);
    void send_poll (in ClientRequestInfo ri);
    void receive_reply (in ClientRequestInfo ri);
    void receive_exception (in ClientRequestInfo ri) raises (ForwardRequest);
    void receive_other (in ClientRequestInfo ri)    raises (ForwardRequest);
};
```

The local interface `ClientRequestInterceptor` defines a number of operations that correspond to the client-side interception points as shown in Figure 10.1.

Client-Side Interception Points

At the client-side, there are five interception points:

- `send_request`
- `send_poll`
- `receive_reply`
- `receive_exception`
- `receive_other`

The send_request interception point allows an Interceptor to query request information and modify the service context before the request is sent to the server. A system exception may be raised at this point. In this case, no other Interceptor's send_request operations are called. Rather, receive_exception interception points are called instead. The Interceptor may also raise a ForwardRequest exception. In this case, no other Interceptor's send_request operations are called. Instead, receive_other interception points are called to signal the ForwardRequest exception. The completion_status will be COMPLETED_NO if a system exception is raised.

The send_poll interception point allows an Interceptor to query an asynchronously invoked request when the client polls for results of the deferred synchronous invocations. This poll is reported to Interceptors through the send_poll interception points and a response is returned through the receive_reply or receive_exception interceptor points. If the response is not available before the polling timeout expires, the system exception TIMEOUT is raised and receive_exception is called with this exception. A system exception may be raised at this point. In this case, no other Interceptor's send_poll operations are called whereas receive_exception interception points are called, and the completion_status will be COMPLETED_NO.

The receive_reply interception point allows an Interceptor to query the information on a reply after it is returned from the server and before control is returned to the client. A system exception may be raised at this point. In this case, no other Interceptor's receive_reply operations are called. Rather, receive_exception interception points are called, and the completion_status will be COMPLETED_YES.

When an exception occurs, the receive_exception interception is called. It allows an Interceptor to query the exception's information before it is passed to the client. This operation may raise a system exception. As successive Interceptors may change the exception while receiving their calls to receive_exception, the exception raised to the client will be the last exception raised by the interceptor, or the original exception if no Interceptor changes the exception. This operation may also raise a ForwardRequest exception. If an Interceptor raises this exception, no other Interceptors' receive_exception will be called. Rather, receive_other will be called. If the original exception is a system exception, the completion_status of the new exception will be the same as the original. If the original exception is a user exception, then the completion_status of the new exception is COMPLETED_YES. Under some conditions, depending on what policies are in effect, an exception such as COMM_FAILURE may result in a retry of the request. Because this retry is a new request with respect to Interceptors, but control has not returned to the client, the PortableInterceptor::Current will be the same for the original request and the retry request.

The receive_other interceptor point allows an Interceptor to query the information available when a request results in something other than a normal reply or an exception—for example, a retry or an asynchronous call. The reply does not immediately follow the request, but the control will return to the client and an ending interception point will be called. For a retry, that is a new request with respect to Interceptors; if it does follow the original request, the request scoped `PortableInterceptor::Current` will be the same for the original request and the retrying request. This interception point may raise a system exception. If it does, no other Interceptors' `receive_other` will be called. Rather, `receive_exception` will be called. It may also raise a `ForwardRequest` exception. If it happens, successive interceptors' `receive_other` will be called with the new information provided by the `ForwardRequest` exception. The `completion_status` will be `COMPLETED_NO`. If the target invocation had completed, this interception point would not be called.

Client-Side Interception Point Flow

The `send_request` and `send_poll` are starting interception points. The `receive_reply`, `receive_exception`, and `receive_other` are ending interception points. On any given request/reply sequence, only one of the starting interception points and one of the ending points is called. There is no intermediate exception point. Only when `send_request` or `send_poll` runs to completion is an ending interception point called.

A `ClientRequestInterceptor` instance is registered with ORB. When multiple interceptors are registered on a client, the ORB maintains an ordered list. The Interceptor list is traversed in order on send interception points and in reverse order for receive interception points.

The following scenarios assume there are three Interceptors: A, B, and C. On the send interception points they are called in the order A, B, C. On the receive interception points they are called in the order C, B, A.

Scenario 1: Request/reply sequence is successful. The interception point flow is shown in Figure 10.2. The flow for each Interceptor follows the rules: the `send_request` followed by `receive_reply`—that is, a start point is followed by an end point.

Scenario 2: `B.send_request` raises an exception. As shown in Figure 10.3, the flow for A is `send_request` followed by `receive_exception`. The flow for B is `send_request`; as the start point did not complete, so no end point is called. The interceptor C is never called. The exception aborts the interception flow.

Scenario 3: A reply returns successfully from the server, but `B.receive_reply` raises an exception. From the interception point flow shown in Figure 10.4, it can be seen that the flow for B and C is `send_request` followed by `receive_reply`. Because `receive_reply` of B raises an exception, the flow for A is `send_request` followed by `receive_exception`.

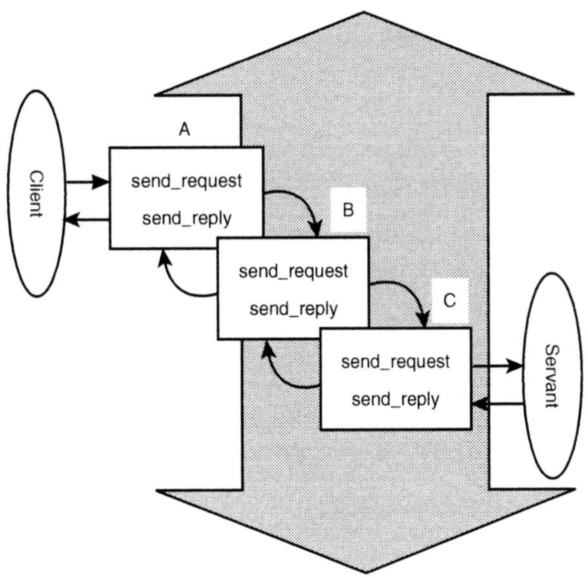

Figure 10.2

Request/reply sequence is successful.

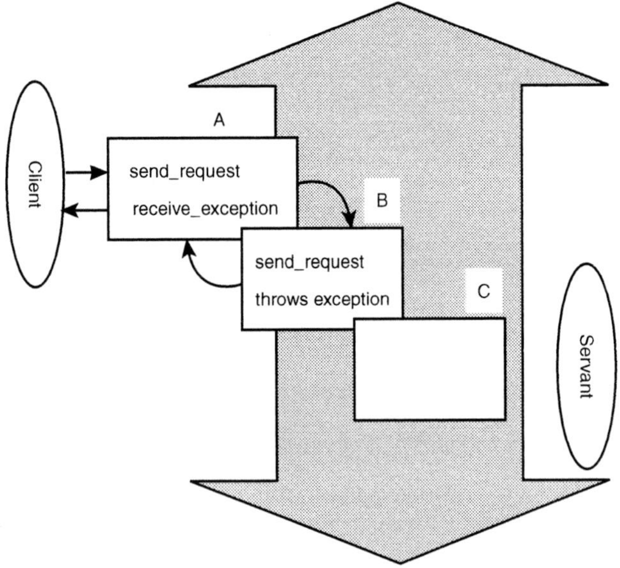

Figure 10.3

`B.send_request` *raises an exception.*

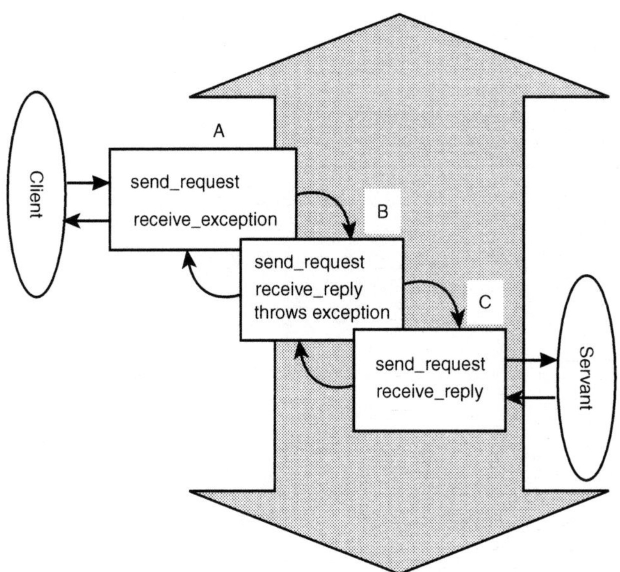

Figure 10.4

`B.receive_reply` *throws an exception.*

Scenario 4: An exception X is thrown by `C.receive_reply`, but `B.receive_exception` changes it to the exception Y. As shown in Figure 10.5, the flow for C is `send_request` followed by `receive_reply`. Because `C.receive_reply` raises the exception X, the flow for A and B is `send_request` followed by `receive_exception`, but B is handled in exception X while A is handled in exception Y.

Scenario 5: An exception arrives from the server. `C.receive_exception` raises exception `ForwardRequest` F1 and `B.receive_other` raises exception `ForwardRequest` F2. The interception point flow of this scenario is shown in Figure 10.6.

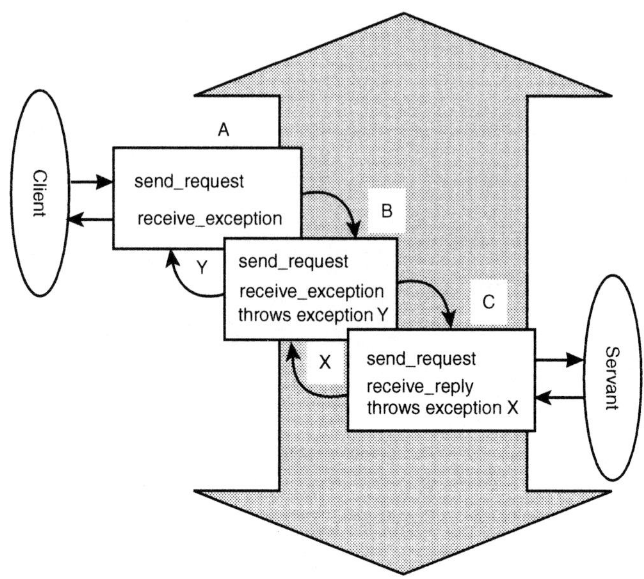

Figure 10.5

`C.receive_reply` *throws exception X and* `B.receive_exception` *throws exception Y.*

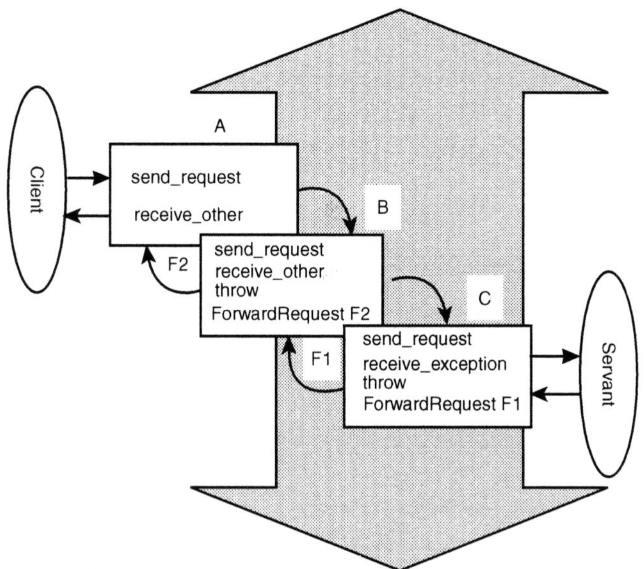

Figure 10.6

An exception arrives from the server.

Server-Side Interceptor

```
local interface ServerRequestInterceptor : Interceptor{
void receive_request_service_contexts (in ServerRequestInfo ri)
        raises (ForwardRequest);
    void receive_request (in ServerRequestInfo ri)
        raises (ForwardRequest);
    void send_reply (in ClientRequestInfo ri);
    void send_exception (in ServerRequestInfo ri)
        raises (ForwardRequest);
    void send_other (in ServerRequestInfo ri)
        raises (ForwardRequest);
};
```

A server-side Interceptor defines a number of operations that matches the server-side interception points shown in Figure 10.1.

Server-Side Interception Points

At the server-side, there are also five interception points:

- `receive_request_service_contexts`
- `receive_request`
- `send_reply`
- `send_exception`
- `send_other`

The `receive_request_service_contexts` is an interception point at which Interceptors must get their service context information from the incoming request and transfer it to `PortableInterceptor::Current`'s slots. This interception point is called before the servant manager is called. This interception point may or may not execute in the same thread as the target invocation. Operation parameters are not yet available at this point. A system exception may be raised at this interception point. If it happens, no other Interceptors' `receive_request_service_contexts` will be called. Rather, their `send_exception` interception points are called instead. A `ForwardRequest` exception may also be raised. In this case, no other Interceptors' `receive_request_service_contexts` will be called whereas their `send_other` operations are called. The `completion_status` is `COMPLTED_NO`, if a system exception is raised.

The `receive_request` interception point allows an Interceptor to query information after all the information, including operation parameters, is available. This operation executes in the same thread as the target invocation. The ORB guarantees that `receive_request` is called once, either through arguments or through `set_exception`. If it is called through `set_exception`, requesting the arguments will result in `NO_RESOURCES` being raised with a standard minor code of 1. If a system exception is raised, no other Interceptors' `receive_request` operations are called, whereas their `send_exception` interception points are called instead. A `ForwardRequest` exception may also be raised. In this case, no other Interceptors' `receive_request` operations are called. Rather, their `send_other` interception points are called instead. If a system exception has been raised, the `completion_status` is `COMPLETED_NO`.

The `send_reply` interception point allows an Interceptor to query information and modify the reply service context after the target operation has been invoked and before the reply is returned to the client. If a system exception is raised, no other Interceptors' `receive_reply` operations are called whereas their `send_exception` interception points are called instead. Even if a system exception is raised, the `completion_status` will be `COMLETED_YES`.

The `send_exception` interception point is called when an exception occurs. It allows an Interceptor to query the exception information and modifies the service context before the exception is raised to the client. A system exception may be raised. Successive Interceptors may receive calls on `send_exception`. The exception raised to the client will be the last exception raised by an Interceptor, or the original exception if no Interceptor change the exception. A `ForwardRequest` exception may also be raised at this point. In this case, no other Interceptors' `send_exception` operations are called. Rather, their `send_other` interception points are called instead. When a system exception has been raised, if the original exception is a system exception, the `completion_status` of the new exception is the same as the original one. If the original exception is a user exception, then the `completion_status` of the new exception is `COMPLETED_YES`.

The `send_other` interception point allows an Interceptor to query the information available when a request results in something other than a normal reply or an exception, for instance, a retry. At this interception point, a system exception may be raised. If it happens, no other Interceptors' `send_other` operations are called. The remaining Interceptors will have their `send_exception` interception points called. A `ForwardRequest` exceptionmay also be raised at this interception point. If an interceptor raises this exception, successive Interceptors' `send_other` operations are called with the new information provided by the `ForwardRequest` exception. If a system exception has been raised, the `completion_status` is `COMPLETED_NO`.

Server-Side Interception Point Flow

The `receive_request_service_contexts` is the starting interception point. It is called on any given request/reply sequence. The `send_reply`, `send_exception`, and `send_other` are the ending interception points. Only one of these is called on any given request/reply sequence. The `receive_request` is the intermediate interception point. It is called after `receive_request_service_contexts` and before an ending interception point. On an exception, `receive_request` may not be called. If and only if `receive_request_service_context` runs to completion is an ending interception point called. For a successful invocation, the chain of interception points is in order of `receive_request_service_context`, `receive_request`, and `send_reply`, that is, a start point is followed by an intermediate point that is followed by an end point.

A `ServerRequestInterceptor` instance is registered with the ORB. When multiple server-side Interceptors are registered, the ORB logically maintains an ordered list. The

Interceptor list is traversed in order on the receiving interception points and in reverse order on sending interception points. The following scenarios assume there are three Interceptors: A, B, and C. On the receive interception points they are called in order A, B, C; on the send interception points, they are called in the order C, B, A.

Scenario 6: The target invocation returns successfully, but `B.send_reply` raises an exception. The server-side point flow is shown in Figure 10.7. The flow for B and C is `receive_request_service_contexts` followed by `receive_request` that is followed by `send_reply`. Because `send_reply` of B raised an exception, the flow for A is `receive_request_service_contexts` followed by `receive_request` that is followed by `send_exception`.

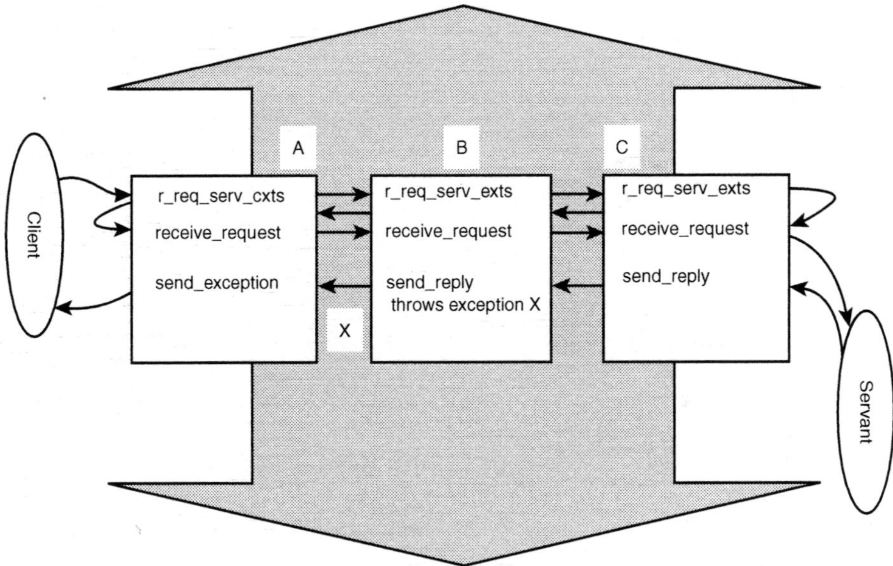

Figure 10.7

The target invocation returns successfully, and `B.send_reply` *raises an exception.*

Scenario 7: `B.receive_request` raises an exception. As shown in Figure 10.8, when `B.receive_request` raises an exception, `C.receive_request` will not be called and all Interceptors have the end point `send_exception`.

Scenario 8: `B.receive_request_service_contexts` raises an exception. The interception point flow is shown in Figure 10.9. Because B's `receive_request_service_contexts` did not complete, no end point of B was called. The flow for A is `receive_request_service_contexts` followed by `send_exception`; no intermediate points are called. The flow for C did not exist because the exception occurred before any of C's interception points were called.

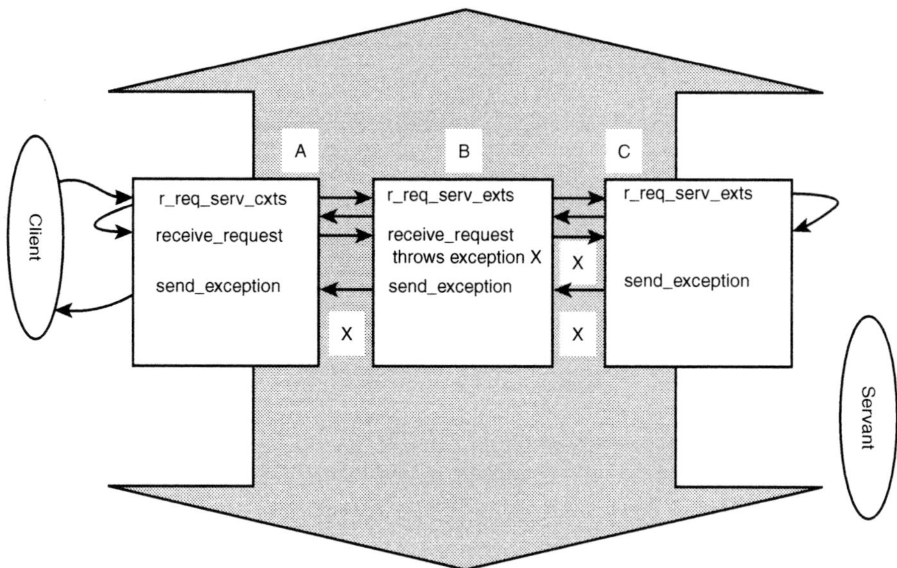

Figure 10.8

`B.receive_request` *throws exception X.*

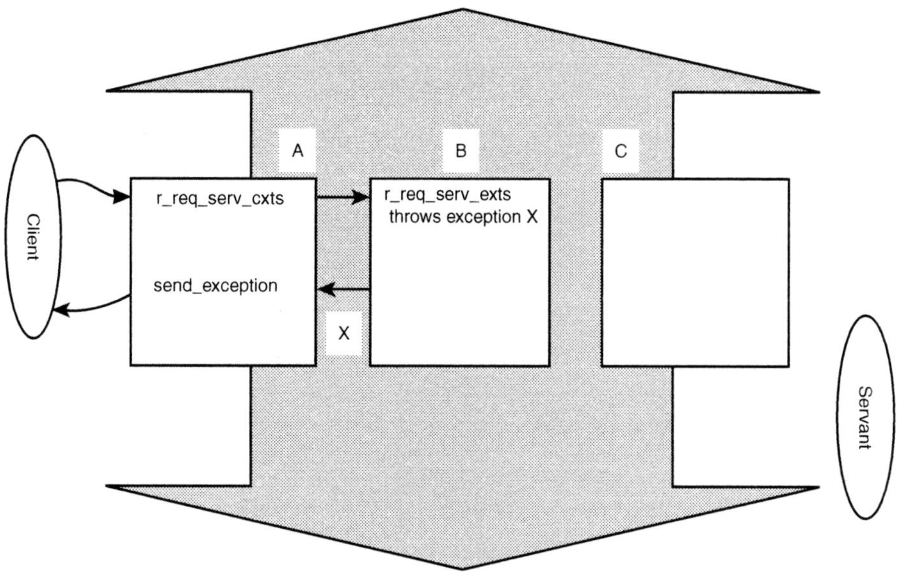

Figure 10.9

`B.receive_request_service_contexts` *throws an exception.*

Scenario 9: `C.receive_request` throws exception X and `B.send_exception` throws exception Y. The interception point flow is shown in Figure 10.10. When the exception X is raised by `C.receive_request`, the flows for A, B and C are the same: `receive_request_service_contexts` and `receive_request`, followed by `send_exception`. But B is handled in exception X while A is handled in exception Y because `B.send_exception` changed the exception.

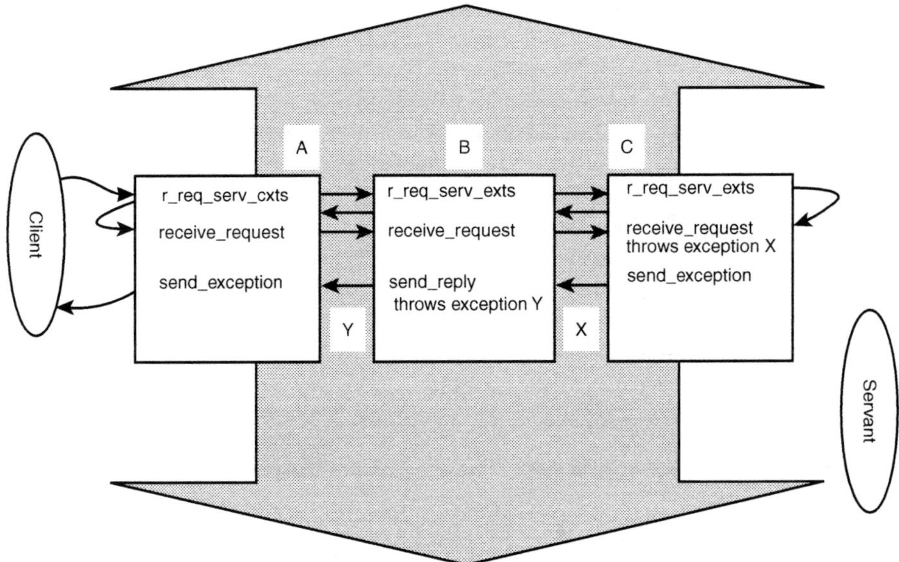

Figure 10.10

`C.receive_request` *throws exception X and* `B.send_exception` *throws exception Y.*

Request Information

Each interception point is given an object of `ClientRequestInfo` or `ServerRequestInfo` through which the Interceptor can access request information. Client-side and server-side have different information: `ClientRequestInfo` and `ServerRequestInfo`. They inherit from a common interface: `RequestInfo` which provides general request information that is common to both.

`RequestInfo` Interface is defined as follows:

```
local interface RequestInfo {
    readonly attribute unsigned long request-id;
    readonly attribute string operation;
    readonly attribute Dynamic::ParameterList arguments;
    readonly attribute Dynamic::ExceptionList exceptions;
    readonly attribute Dynamic::ContextList contexts;
```

```
    readonly attribute Dynamic::RequestContext operation_context;
    readonly attribute any result;
    readonly attribute boolean response_exepcted;
    readonly attribute Messaging::SyncScope sync_scope;
    readonly attribute ReplyStatus reply_status;
    readonly attribute Object forward_reference;
    any get_slot (in SlotId id) raises (InvalidSlot);
    IOP::ServiceContext get_request_service_context(in IOP::ServiceId id);
    IOP::ServiceContext get_reply_service_context(in IOP::ServiceId id);
};
```

All the attributes defined in this interface are read-only. This means that Interceptors cannot change attribute values. Attributes and operations provide the general request information: the `request_id` that uniquely identifies an active request/reply sequence, a name of the operation and the arguments on the operation being invoked, contexts being passed on the operation invocation, `operation_context` being sent on the request and the result of the operation invocation. In addition, the Boolean attribute `response_expected` indicates whether a response is expected. When it is false the `sync_scope` defines how far the request is passed before the control is returned to the client. It can have one of the following values:

`Messaging::SYNC_NONE`

`Messaging::SYNC_WITH_TRANSPORT`

`Messaging::SYNC_WITH_SERVER`

`Messaging::SYNC_WITH_TARGET`

The attribute `reply_status` gives the state of the result of the operation invocation. It takes one of the following values:

`PortableInterceptor::SUCCESSFUL`

`PortableInterceptor::SYSTEM_EXCEPTION`

`PortableInterceptor::USER_EXCEPTION`

`PortableInterceptor::LOCATION_FORWARD`

`PortableInterceptor::TRANSPORT_ENTRY`

If the `reply_status` is `LOCATION_FORWARD`, the attribute will contain the object to which the request will be forwarded.

The operation `get_slot` allows an Interceptor to access the data from the given slot in the `PortableInterceptor::Current`. The operation `get_request_service_context` returns a copy of the service context with the given ID that is associated with the request. The operation `get_reply_service_context` returns a copy of the service context with the given the ID that is associated with the reply.

ClientRequestInfo inherits from RequestInfo and provides more specific information on client request which Client Request Interceptor can access and modify:

```
local interface ClientRequestInfo : RequestInfo {
    readonly attribute Object target;
    readonly attribute Object effective_target;
    readonly attribute IOP::TaggedProfile effective_profile;
    readonly attribute any received_exception;
    readonly attribute CORBA::RepositoryId received_exception_id;
    IOR::TaggedComponent get_effective_component(in IOP::ComponentId id);
    IOP_N::TaggedComponentSeq get_effective_components(in IOP::Componentd id);
    CORBA::Policy get_request_policy (in CORBA::PolicyType type);
    void add_request_service_context(in IOP::ServiceContext service_context,
                                      in boolean replace);
};
```

Not all attributes and operations on ClientRequestInfo are valid at all client-side interception points. Table 10.1 shows which attributes and operations are valid to each client-side interception point. If it is not valid, attempting to access it will throw a BAD_INV_ORDER exception with minor code of 14.

Table 10.1 **ClientRequestInfo** ***Validity for Client-side Interception Points***

	Send_ request	**send_ poll**	**receive_ reply**	**Receive_ exception**	**receive_ other**
Request_id	Yes	Yes	Yes	Yes	Yes
Operation	Yes	Yes	Yes	Yes	Yes
Arguments	Yes[a]	No	Yes	No	No
Exceptions	Yes	No	Yes	Yes	Yes
Contexts	Yes	No	Yes	Yes	Yes
Operation_context	Yes	No	Yes	Yes	Yes
Result	No	No	Yes	No	No
Response_expected	Yes	Yes	Yes	Yes	Yes
Sync_scope	Yes	No	Yes	Yes	Yes
Reply_status	No	No	Yes	Yes	Yes
Forward_reference	No	No	No	No	Yes[b]
Get_slot	Yes	Yes	Yes	Yes	Yes
Get_request_ Service_context	Yes	No	Yes	Yes	Yes
Get_reply_ Service_context	No	No	Yes	Yes	Yes
Target	Yes	Yes	Yes	Yes	Yes
Effective_target	Yes	Yes	Yes	Yes	Yes
Effective_profile	Yes	Yes	Yes	Yes	Yes
Received_exception	No	No	No	Yes	No
Receive_exception_id	No	No	No	Yes	No

Table 10.1 continued

	Send_ request	**send_ poll**	**receive_ reply**	**Receive_ exception**	**receive_ other**
Get_effective_ Component	Yes	No	Yes	Yes	Yes
Get_effective_ Components	Yes	No	Yes	Yes	Yes
Get_request_policy	Yes	No	Yes	Yes	Yes
Add_request Service_context	Yes	No	No	No	No

a. When `ClientRequestInfo` *is passed to* `Send_request`, *there is an entry in the list for every argument, but only* `in` *and* `inout` *arguments are available.*

b. If the `reply_status` *attribute is not* `LOCATION_FORWARD`, *accessing this attribute will throw* `BAD_INV_ORDER` *with a minor code of 14.*

The attribute target is an object which the client called to perform the operation. The `effective_target` indicates the actual object on which the operation is invoked. If the `reply_status` is `LOCATION_FORWARD`, then on the subsequent requests, `effective_target` will contain the forwarded IOR while target remains unchanged. The attribute `effective_profile` is the profile being used to send the request. The attributes `received_exception` and `received_exception_id` provide the exception and its ID returned to the client. The operation `get_effective_component` returns the `IOP::TaggedComponent` with the given ID from the profile selected for the request and the operation `get_effective_components` returns all the tagged components. With operation `get_request_policy`, the given policy in effect for this operation is obtained. Interceptors can add service contexts to the request using operation `add_request_service_context`.

The interface `ServerRequestInfo` inherits from `RequestInfo` and provides more specific information on server request that a server-side request Interceptor can access and modify:

```
local interface ServerRequestInfo : RequestInfo {
    readonly attribute any sending_exception;
    readonly attribute CORBA::OctetSeq object_id;
    readonly attribute CORBA::OctetSeq adapter_id;
    readonly attribute CORBA::RepositoryId target_most_derived_interface;
    CORBA::Policy get_server_policy (in CORBA::PolicyType type);
    void  set_slot(in SlotId, in any data) raises (InvalidSlot);
    boolean target_is_a (in CORBA::RepositoryId id);
    void add_reply_service_context(in IOP::ServiceContext service_context,
                                   in boolean replace);
};
```

Not all attributes and operations on ClientRequestInfo are valid at all server-side interception points. Table 10.2 shows which attributes and operations are valid to each server-side interception point. If it is not valid, attempting to access it will throw a BAD_INV_ORDER exception with minor code of 14.

Table 10.2* ServerRequestInfo *Validity for Server-side Interception Points

	Receive_request_Service_contexts	receive_request	send_reply	send_exception	send_other
Request_id	Yes	Yes	Yes	Yes	Yes
Operation	Yes	Yes	Yes	Yes	Yes
Arguments	No	Yes[a]	Yes	No[b]	No[b]
Exceptions	No	Yes	Yes	Yes	Yes
Contexts	No	Yes	Yes	Yes	Yes
Operation_context	No	Yes	Yes	No	No
Result	No	No	Yes	No	No
Response_expected	Yes	Yes	Yes	Yes	Yes
Sync_scope	Yes	Yes	Yes	Yes	Yes
Reply_status	No	No	Yes	Yes	Yes
Forward_reference	No	No	No	No	Yes[b]
Get_slot	Yes	Yes	Yes	Yes	Yes
Get_request_Service_context	Yes	No	Yes	Yes	Yes
Get_reply_Service_context	No	No	Yes	Yes	Yes
Sending_exception	No	No	No	Yes	No
Object_id	No	Yes	Yes	Yes[c]	Yes[c]
Adapter_id	No	Yes	Yes	Yes[c]	Yes[c]
Target_most_Derived_interface	No	Yes	No[d]	No[d]	No[d]
Get_server_policy	Yes	Yes	Yes	Yes	Yes
Set_slot	Yes	Yes	Yes	Yes	Yes
Target_is_a	No	Yes	No[d]	No[d]	No[d]
Add_reply_Service_context	Yes	Yes	Yes	Yes	Yes

a. When ServerRequestInfo *is passed to* receive_request, *there is an entry in the list for every argument, but only* in *and* inout *arguments are available.*

b. If the reply_status *attribute is not* LOCATION_FORWARD, *accessing this attribute will throw* BAD_INV_ORDER *with a minor code of 14.*

c. If the servant locator caused a location forward, or raised an exception, this attribute/operation may not be available in this interception point. If it is not available, NO_RESOURCES *with a standard minor code of 1 will be raised.*

d. When the necessary information requires access to the target object's servant that may no longer available to the ORB, the operation is not available in this interception point.

The attribute object_id and adaptor_id provide target object and object adapter information. The attribute RepositoryId is the most derived interface of servant that allows the method target_is_a to determine other target types. The attribute sending_exception contains the exception in any type to be returned to the client. If the exception is a user exception, which cannot be inserted into an any, the attribute will be an any containing the system exception UNKNOWN with a standard minor code of 1. The get_server_policy returns the policy in effect of a given policy type. An Interceptor can set a slot in the PortableInterceptor::Current that is in the scope of the request using the set_slot operation. With add_reply_service_context operation, an Interceptor can add service contexts to the request.

Portable Interceptor Current

The object PortableInterceptor::Current (PICurrent) is a Current object used by portable Interceptors to transfer thread context information to a request context if the information from a client's thread context is required at an Interceptor's interception points. Portable Interceptors are not required to use PICurrent. But if information from a client's thread is required at an Interceptor's interception points, PICurrent can be used to propagate that information. On the client side, this information includes, but is not limited to, thread context information that will be propagated to the server via a service context. On the server side, this information includes, but is not limited to, service context information received from the client that will be propagated to the target's thread context. PICurrent allows portable service code to be written regardless of an ORB's threading model. The definition of the portable Interceptor Current interface is as follows:

```
module PortableInterceptor{
    typedef unsinged long SlotId;
    exception InvalidSlot{};

    local interface Current : CORBA::Current{
    any get_slot(inSlotIf id) raises(InvalidSlot);
    void set_slot (in SlotId id, in any data) raises (InvalidSlot);
        };
};
```

It defines a table of slots which are used by each service to transfer their context data between their context and request's or reply's service context. Via the operation set_slot, a service sets data in a slot in the form of any. If the data already exists in that slot, it is overwritten. If a slot that is called on has not been allocated, InvalidSlot is raised. With the operation get_slot a service can get the slot data set in PICurrent. If the given slot has not been set, an any contains a type code with a TCKind value of tk_null. No value is returned. If the slot that is called on has not been allocated, InvalidSlot is raised.

Each service which wishes to use PICurrent reserves a lot of slots at initialization time and uses those slots during the processing of requests and replies.

`PICurrent` is obtained via a call to `ORB::resolve_initial_references ("PICurrent")`.

IOR Interceptor

The IOR Interceptor allows services to add the information that describes the server's or object's ORB service related capabilities to object references when the reference is created. This information is included in tagged components in the profile within an IOR.

```
local interface IORInterceptor : Interceptor {
    void establish_components(in IORInfo info);
};
```

The ORB calls `establish_components` on all registered IOR Interceptors when it is assembling the list of components that will be included in the profile or profiles of an object reference. The object `IORInfo` is passed as an argument of the operation to establish these components. This operation is not allowed to throw exceptions.

The `IORInfo` interface provides the sever-side ORB service with access to the applicable policies during IOR construction and the ability to add components:

```
local interface IORInfo {
    CORBA::Policy get_effective_policy(in CORBA::PolicyType type);
    void add_ior_component(in IOP::TaggedComponent a_component);
    void add_ior_component_to_profile (
        in IOP::TaggedComponenet a_component,
        in IOP::ProfileId profile);
};
```

A call to the `get_effective_policy` operation will return the effective server-side policy of a particular type for an IOR being constructed. If the IOR being constructed is for an object implemented using a POA, all Policy objects passed to the `PortableServer::POA::create_POA` call that created that POA are accessible via `get_effective_policy`. If a policy for a given type is not known to the ORB, this operation will raise `INV_POLICY` exception. If the given policy type is known, but no policy of that type is in effect, the operation will return a nil object reference.

The operation `add_ior_component` allows adding a tagged component to all profiles. The operation `add_ior_component_to_profile` allows adding a tagged component into a specified profile. Any number of components may exist with the same component ID. If the given profile ID does not define a known profile or it is impossible to add components to that profile, `BAD_PARAM` exception will be raised with a standard minor code of 29.

PolicyFactory Interface

An IOR that represents an object is created by POA. The policies used to create a POA affect the tagged components in the profile of the IOR. ORB services may introduce new polices related to their services. The interface PolicyFactory allows to create these new policies:

```
module PortableInterceptor
{
    local interface PolicyFactory{
        CORBA::Policy create_policy(
            in CORBA::PolicyType type,
            in any value)
        raises (CORBA::PolicyError);
    };
};
```

The interface PolicyFactory has one operation, create_policy. During ORB initialization, a portable service implementation registers an instance of the PolicyFactory interface. When CORBA::ORB::create_policy is called for the PolicyType under which the PolicyFactory is registered, a ORB calls the create_policy on a registered PolicyFactory instance. The create_policy returns an instance of the appropriate interface derived from CORBA::Policy of type any. If it cannot, it will raise an exception.

Registering Interceptors

Interceptors provide a means for ORB services to access ORB processing. They become part of the ORB and are therefore required to register with the ORB. When ORB_init returns an ORB, they will have been registered. Interceptors cannot be registered on an ORB after it has been returned by a call to ORB_init.

An Interceptor is registered by registering an associated ORBInitializer object which implements the ORBInitializer interface. When an ORB is initializing, it calls registered ORBInitializer, passing it an ORBInitInfo object that is used to register its Interceptor:

```
module PortableInterceptor {
    local interface ORBInitializer {
        void pre_init (in ORBInitInfo info);
        void post_init(in ORBInitInfo info);
    };
};
```

The operations pre_init and post_init are called during ORB initialization. If initial services registered by an Interceptor are expected to be used by other interceptors, then these initial services are registered at the point of pre_init via calls to ORBInitInfo::register_initial_reference. If a service must resolve initial references as part of its initialization, it can assume that all initial references are available at the point of post_init.

ORBInitInfo object is passed that provides initialization attributes and operations by which Interceptors can be registered. It is defined by ORBInitInfo interface:

```
module PortableInterceptor {
    local interface ORBInitInfo {
    typedef string ObjectId;
    exception DuplicateName {
        string name;
    };

    exception InvalidName{};
    readonly attribute CORBA::StringSeq arguments;
    readonly attribute string orb_id;
    readonly attribute IOP::CodecFactory codec_factory;

    void register_initial_reference (in ObjectId id, in Object obj)
        raises (InvalidName);
    void resolve_initial_references(in ObjectId id)
        raises (InvalidName);
    void add_client_request_interceptor (in ClientRequestInterceptor
➥interceptor)
        raises(DuplicateName);
    void add_server_request_interceptor (in ServerRequestInterceptor
➥interceptor)
        raises(DuplicateName);
    void add_ior_interceptor (in IORInterceptor interceptor)
        raises(DuplicateName);
    SlotId allocate_slot_id();
    void register_policy_factory (in CORBA::PolicyType type,
        in PolicyFactory policy_factory);
    };
};
```

Only one Interceptor of a given name can be registered with the ORB for each Interceptor type. An attempt to register a second Interceptor with the same name will raise `DuplicateName` exception. An Interceptor may be anonymous, that is, having an empty string as the name attribute. As any number of anonymous Interceptors can be registered with the ORB, registering an anonymous Interceptor will not raise `DuplicateName` exception.

In order to register an `OBRInitializer`, an operation `register_orb_initializer` is provided. It resides in `PortableInterceptor` module:

```
module PortableInterceptor {
void register_orb_initializer (in ORBInitializer init);
};
```

Each service that implements Interceptors will provide an instance of `ORBInitializer`. To use a service, an application first calls `register_orb_initializer`, passing in the service's `ORBInitializer`. After this is complete, the application will make an instantiating `ORB_init` call. This instantiating `ORB_init` call calls each registers `ORBInitializer`. The returned ORB will contain any Interceptors that the service requires.

The `register_orb_initializer` is a global operation. An `ORBInitializer` registered at a given point in time will be called by all instantiating `ORB_init` calls that occur after that point in time.

In C++, the `register_orb_initializer` is defined in the `PortableInterceptor` name space as

```
Namespace PortableInterceptor {
    static void register_orb_initializer (
    PortableInterceptor::ORBInitializer_ptr init);
    };
```

In Java, as the global operation `register_orb_initializer` would break applet security with respect to ORB, `ORBInitializers` are registered via Java ORB properties. The new property names are of the form

```
org.omg.PortableInterceptor.ORBInitializerClass.Service
```

where *`Service`* is the string name of a class which implements `org.omg.PortableInterceptor.ORBInitializer` (see the example in the following section).

Request Interceptors are registered on a per-ORB basis. Virtual per-object Interceptors can be achieved by querying the policies on each target from within the interception points to determine whether they should do any work. Virtual per-POA Interceptors can be achieved by instantiating each POA with a different ORB.

Writing and Using Portable Interceptors

To illustrate writing and using the Portable Interceptors, we consider a simple example of server-side logging service. It observes every invocation call from a client and prints the `RepositoryID` for the most derived interface of the called servant, the operation name, the time of the incoming request, and the time when the reply is returned to the client.

Writing a Server-Side Interceptor

To provide the above logging service, we write a server-side request Interceptor that implements the `ServerRequestInterceptor` interface and extends `LocalObject` in case of Java (for example, ORBIX, OpenORB), or `IT_CORBA::RefCountedLocalObject` in case of C++ (for example, ORBIX). The logging functionality is implemented by the two methods: `receive_request()` and `send_reply()`. The other three methods are empty.

```
//C++
//in server_interceptor_impl.hh

#include <omg/PortableInterceptor.hh>
#include <orbix/corba.hh> //in case of using Orbix2000
```

```
class ServerInterceptorImpl :
    public PortableInterceptor::ServerRequestInterceptor,
    public IT_CORBA::RefCountedLocalObject
{
  public:
    ServerInterceptorImpl();

    //declaration of the five methods defined by IDL
    void
    receive_request_service_contexts(
    PortableInterceptor::ServerRequestInfo_ptr  ri
    ) throw(CORBA::SystemException, PortableInterceptor::ForwardRequest));
    //......
}

//in server_interceptor_impl.cc

#include <time.h>
#include <iostream.h>
#include "server_interceptor_impl.hh"

ServerInterceptorImpl::ServerInterceptorImpl()
{
}

char*
ServerInterceptorImpl::name(
) throw(CORBA::SystemException)
{
    return CORBA::String_dup("ServerInterceptorDemo");
}

void
ServerInterceptorImpl::receive_request_service_contexts(
    PortableInterceptor::ServerRequestInfo_ptr ri
) throw(CORBA::SystemException, PortableInterceptor::ForwardRequest)
{
    // do nothing
}

void
ServerInterceptorImpl::receive_request(
    PortableInterceptor::ServerRequestInfo_ptr ri
) throw (CORBA::SystemException,  PortableInterceptor::ForwardRequest)
{
    cout<<"Receives a request << endl;
    cout<< "    for an object: " << ri->target_most_derived_interface()<<endl;
    cout <<"    on operation: " + ri->operation()<<endl;
```

```
    time_t t_now=time(0);
    cout <<"    at time: " << ctime(&t_now)<<endl;
}

void
ServerInterceptorImpl::send_reply(
    PortableInterceptor::ServerRequestInfo_ptr ri
) throw(CORBA::SystemException)
{
    cout<<"Sends a reply" << endl;
    cout<< "    for an object: " << ri->target_most_derived_interface()<<endl;
    cout <<"    on operation: " + ri->operation()<<endl;
    time_t t_now=time(0);
    cout <<"    at time: " << ctime(&t_now)<<endl;
}

void
ServerInterceptorImpl::send_exception(
    PortableInterceptor::ServerRequestInfo_ptr ri
) throw(CORBA::SystemException, PortableInterceptor::ForwardRequest)
{
    // do nothing
}

void
ServerInterceptorImpl::send_other(
    PortableInterceptor::ServerRequestInfo_ptr ri
) throw(CORBA::SystemException, PortableInterceptor::ForwardRequest)
{
    // do nothing
}

//java
//in ServerInterceptorImpl.java

package Pure.InterceptorDemo;

import org.omg.CORBA.LocalObject;
import org.omg.PortableInterceptor.*;
import java.util.*;

public class ServerInterceptorImpl
    extends LocalObject
    implements ServerRequestInterceptor
{
public void receive_request_service_contexts(ServerRequestInfo ri)
    throws ForwardRequest
    {
```

```
    //do nothing
    }

    public void receive_request(ServerRequestInfo ri)
        throws ForwardRequest
    {
        System.out.println("Receives a request \n"
               + "\t for an object: "
               + ri.target_most_derived_interface() +"\n"
               + "\t on operation: " + ri.operation() + "\n"
               + "\t at time: " + new Date(System.currentTimeMillis()) +"\n");

    }

    public void send_reply(ServerRequestInfo ri)
    {
        System.out.println("Sends a reply \n"
            + "\t for operation: " + ri.operation() +"\n"
            + "\t at time: " + new Date(System.currentTimeMillis()));

    }

    public void send_exception(ServerRequestInfo ri)
        throws ForwardRequest
    {
    //do nothing
    }

    public void send_other(ServerRequestInfo ri)
        throws ForwardRequest
    {
    //do nothing
    }

    public java.lang.String name()
    {
        return "ServerInterceptorDemo";
    }
}
```

Registering the Interceptor

To use the Interceptor, you need to register it with the ORB by writing `ORBInitializerImpl` that implements the `ORBInitializer` interface. When an ORB is initializing, it calls the registered `ORBInitializerImpl` object and passes it an `ORBInitInfo` object that is used to register the Interceptor.

```
//C++
//in initializer_impl.hh
```

```
#include <omg/PortableInterceptor.hh>
#include <orbix/corba.hh> //in case of using Orbix2000

class ORBInitializerImpl :
    public PortableInterceptor::ORBInitializer,
    public IT_CORBA::RefCountedLocalObject
{
  public:
    ORBInitializerImpl();

    void
    pre_init(
    PortableInterceptor::ORBInitInfo_ptr  info
    ) throw (CORBA::SystemException);

    void
    post_init(
    PortableInterceptor::ORBInitInfo_ptr  info
    ) throw (CORBA::SystemException);
};


//in initializer_impl.cc

#include "initializer_impl.hh"
#include "server_interceptor_impl.hh"
#include <iostream.h>

ORBInitializerImpl::ORBInitializerImpl()
{
}

void
ORBInitializerImpl::pre_init(
    PortableInterceptor::ORBInitInfo_ptr info)
{
    try{
    // Create and Register server interceptor
       PortableInterceptor::ServerRequestInterceptor_var
➥server_interceptor
          = new ServerInterceptorImpl();
       info->add_server_request_interceptor(server_interceptor);
    }
    catch (DuplicateName &){
    // ....
    }
}
```

```
void
ORBInitializerImpl::post_init(
    PortableInterceptor::ORBInitInfo_ptr  info
)
{
// we do not need to do anything here
}

//java
//in ORBInitializerImpl.java

package Pure.InterceptorDemo;

import org.omg.CORBA.LocalObject;
import org.omg.PortableInterceptor.*;
import org.omg.PortableInterceptor.ORBInitInfoPackage.*;

public class ORBInitializerImpl extends LocalObject implements
➥ORBInitializer
{
    public void pre_init(ORBInitInfo info)
    {
        ServerInterceptorImpl serverInterceptor = new
➥ServerInterceptorImpl();

        try{
            System.out.println("Registering Interceptors");
            info.add_server_request_interceptor(serverInterceptor);
        }
        catch (DuplicateName dn) {
            System.out.println("DuplicateName " + dn.getMessage());
        }
    }

    public void post_init(ORBInitInfo info)
    {
    //we do not need to do anything here
    }
}
```

Running an Application Using the Interceptor

The logging service can be used by a CORBA server program. Suppose you have a very simple application defined by the IDL:

```
module MyApp
{
    interface SimpleObject
    {
```

```
    void
    print_message(in string message);
    };
};
```

To use the logging service, you need to register the `ORBInitializerImpl` object. In C++, registering `ORBInitializerImpl` object is done by calling `register_orb_initializer (PortableInterceptor::ORBInitializer_ptr init)`. In Java the registration is done by setting a Java property. For example, when you run the server program that is implemented by using `OpenORB`, type

```
Java -Dorg.omg.PortableInterceptor.ORBInitializerClass.
Pure.InterceptorDemo.ORBInitializerImpl
=Pure.InterceptorDemo.ORBInitializerImpl
Pure.InterceptorDemo.Server
```

When it is called by a client, it will print the following logging message:

```
Receives a request
         for an object : IDL:MyApp/SimpleObject:1.0
         on operation : print_message
         at time: Wed May 23 10:54:07 BST 2001

Sends a reply
         for operation: print_message
         at time: Wed May 23 10:54:07 BST 2001
```

Without specifying this Java property, the application will work without using the logging service, that is, no logging message is printed out.

Summary

ORB services such as security or transaction require hooks into the ORB in order to be able to fulfill their goals. Portable Interceptors provide such hooks into the ORB, or interception points within a request/reply sequence, through which ORB services can intercept the normal flow of execution of the ORB. There are two classes of interceptors: request Interceptors and IOR Interceptors. A request Interceptor allows intercepting the flow of a request/reply sequence through the ORB at specific points so that the services can query the request/reply information and transfer the service contexts between clients and servers. The IOR Interceptor allows services to add the information into tagged components in the profile within an IOR when the IOR is created. This information describes the IOR represented server's or object's ORB service related capabilities.

Each interception point is given an object `ClientRequestInfo` or `ServerRequestInfo` through which an Interceptor can access request information. Service contexts of the request are populated from information in a service's `Current` object, from effective policies, and from information in the tagged components on an Igor's profile. Interfaces `Current`, `PolicyFactory`, and `IORInfo` necessitate this population.

CHAPTER 11

Objects by Value

The CORBA objects by value specification enables you to define objects that can be passed by value when transmitted as a parameter or return value of an operation. The value objects can have an associated state and behavior, which is declared in IDL.

Pass by value semantics are most useful between tightly integrated applications that are written in the same language. Because sender and receiver must both provide an implementation of every transmitted value type, it is generally not practical to transmit value types across a language barrier.

This chapter provides a basic introduction to programming with value types.

Overview of Value Semantics

A value type combines the characteristics of an IDL struct and an IDL interface. A regular value can declare state members (displaying struct-like character) and operations and attributes (displaying interface-like character). For example, an `AccountVal` type could be declared as a regular value, as shown in Listing 11.1.

Listing 11.1 An `AccountVal` Type Declared as a Regular Value

```
//IDL
valuetype AccountVal {
    // state members
    public  long   m_account_id;
    public  string m_owner;
    private long   m_balance;

    // operations
    boolean withdraw(in long amount);
    void    pay_in(in long amount);
};
```

The AccountVal value type could represent a cached database record in a server. The state members of AccountVal—that is, m_account_id, m_owner, and m_balance—are declared in a similar manner to struct members, except that each member declaration must be preceded by one of the keywords public or private. The public or private keyword directs a language mapping (for example, IDL to C++, or IDL to Java) to make the mapped state member, respectively, either accessible or inaccessible to the general application code. The operations of AccountVal are defined with the same syntax as ordinary interface operations.

Regular values exhibit a mixture of behavior and state—both are explicitly declared in IDL. Some values exhibit only behavior (operations and attributes) and other values exhibit only state. The balance between state and behavior has an important bearing on how a value is used because it affects inheritance (see "Summary of Inheritance Rules," later in this chapter) and the relative difficulty of implementing the value. It is helpful, therefore, to distinguish between the following kinds of regular value:

- Pure state (character of a struct). For example, the following NameData value type has only state members:

```
//IDL
valuetype NameData {
    public string FirstName;
    public string SecondName;
};
```

- Pure behavior (character of an IDL interface). For example, the following UserAccount value type has only operations:

```
//IDL
valuetype UserAccount {
    boolean logon(in NameData user, in string passwd);
    void logoff();
};
```

- State and behavior. This is illustrated by the AccountVal value type from Listing 11.1.

You could regard a value type either as an enhanced struct or an enhanced IDL interface, depending on your point of view. The defining feature of a value type, however, is that it can support pass by value semantics when passed as a parameter or return value of an IDL operation. In this respect, a value type resembles a struct more than it does an IDL interface. Pass by value semantics are discussed in the next section.

Pass by Value Semantics

If you look at the motivation for value types, you can see that they were introduced partly to remedy the deficiencies of structs (which cannot support inheritance), and partly to remedy the limitations of interfaces (which do not allow CORBA objects to be passed by value). A regular value type lets you create *value objects* that can be passed by value and combines characteristics from structs and interfaces.

TIP

A value object is *not* a CORBA object. Consequently, a value object is not associated with an ORB, is not associated with a POA, and does not have an associated object ID. In fact, there is a much closer analogy between a value type and a struct than between a value type and an IDL interface.

For an example of passing by value, consider the `PassByValue` IDL interface defined in Listing 11.2, which declares a single operation, `pass_account_val()`.

Listing 11.2 The `PassByValue` Interface That Enables `AccountVal` Value Object to Be Passed by Value

```
//IDL
valuetype AccountVal;    // Forward reference.

interface PassByValue {
    void pass_account_val(in AccountVal val);
};
```

The `pass_account_val()` operation can pass a value object, `val`, of `AccountVal` value type (as defined in Listing 11.1). Because it is declared as a value type, the `val` parameter is passed by value. Figure 11.1 shows what happens when a server A passes an `AccountVal` value object to server B by invoking the `pass_account_val()` operation on a `PassByValue` CORBA object.

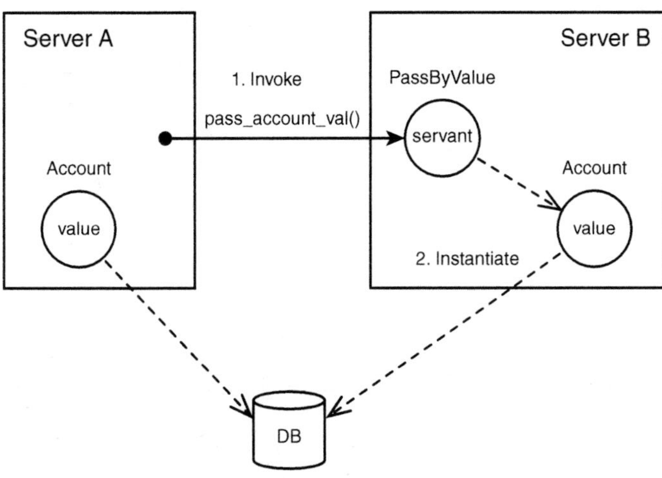

Figure 11.1

Passing an `AccountVal` value object by value.

In this example, the `AccountVal` value object might represent the cached value of a record stored in a central database, also shown in Figure 11.1. The `PassByValue` interface might prove useful if, for example, server A is shutting down for maintenance reasons and server B is a standby process that is running in parallel to A. When server A shuts down, it can pass all its currently active `AccountVal` value objects to server B by calling `pass_account_val()` for each object. (Of course, in a real system, it would be more efficient to pass a sequence of `AccountVal` value objects.)

When server A invokes `pass_account_val()` on the `PassByValue` CORBA object in server B, the `AccountVal` value object is passed as follows:

1. When `pass_account_val()` is invoked, the ORB automatically marshals the `AccountVal` state members and sends them in a request message to server B.
2. When the ORB receives the request message, it creates a new `AccountVal` value object and initializes the value object with the state members read from the request message. The `val` parameter of `pass_account_val()` is initialized as a pointer to the local copy of the `AccountVal` value object.

The `val` parameter received by server B is, therefore, used strictly for accessing the local copy of the `AccountVal` value object. Any operations invoked on `val`—for example, `pay_in()`—are called only on the local copy of the object. Consequently, the semantics of calling a value type operation are different from the semantics of calling an interface operation. Table 11.1 highlights some of the semantic differences.

Table 11.1 Differences Between Value Type Operations and Interface Operations

Value Type Operations	Interface Operations
Always called locally	Called locally or remotely
Invoked on a pointer that points directly at a value object	Invoked on an object reference that indirectly propagates the invocation through an ORB
Called on a local copy of a value object	Called on a unique, original copy of a CORBA object

The preceding description of passing by value, as shown in Figure 11.1, omits some important details. In particular, there are certain prerequisites for server B to be able to unmarshal the `AccountVal` value object:

- The implementation code for the `AccountVal` value type must be available on server B, as well as on server A
- The server B ORB must have the capability to create new instances of `AccountVal` value objects in order to perform unmarshalling of `AccountVal` value parameters

The capability to create new `AccountVal` value objects is satisfied by implementing and registering value factories, as described in the sections "Implementing a Value

Factory" and "Registering the Value Factory," later in this chapter. The following section describes the role played by a value factory in unmarshalling its associated value type.

Value Factories

Value factories are the key to supporting pass by value semantics. To have the capability to unmarshal a particular value type, you must provide a local implementation of both the value type and its associated value factory. On the other hand, if you have a local value type that will *not* be passed between processes, there is no need to implement an accompanying value factory. The unmarshalling mechanism is required only when dealing with a value type that is passed between applications—otherwise the value type is used locally within the application.

To support the unmarshalling of value types, each ORB instance maintains its own value factory table. The purpose of the value factory table is to enable the ORB to find the appropriate value factory while it unmarshals a value type. Entries in the value factory table consist of a value type repository ID (for example, a string such as `IDL:AccountVal:1.0`) and an associated pointer to a value factory. The ORB provides operations for creating an entry in the table (registering a value factory) and removing an entry from the table (unregistering a value factory).

Value type unmarshalling support has the following pre-requisites:

- A value type implementation must be provided locally.
- A corresponding value factory implementation must be provided locally.
- An instance of the value factory must be registered with the ORB.

For example, given the preceding conditions, Figure 11.2 shows the steps performed by the ORB to unmarshal an `AccountVal` value object passed as a parameter to the `pass_account_val()` operation.

An `AccountVal` value object is unmarshalled, as follows:

1. A remote application invokes the `pass_account_val()` operation on the `PassByValue` CORBA object in server B, which causes a request message to be sent to server B.
2. When the request message reaches the ORB object in server B, the ORB reads the repository ID of the `val` parameter from the request message (in this example, the string `IDL:AccountVal:1.0`). The ORB looks up the `IDL:AccountVal:1.0` repository ID in its value factory table to find the associated value factory. If no value factory can be found, the ORB raises the `CORBA::MARSHAL` system exception.
3. The ORB calls the `create_for_unmarshal()` function (C++) or the `read_value()` method (Java) on the value factory to create a new, uninitialized `AccountVal` value object.

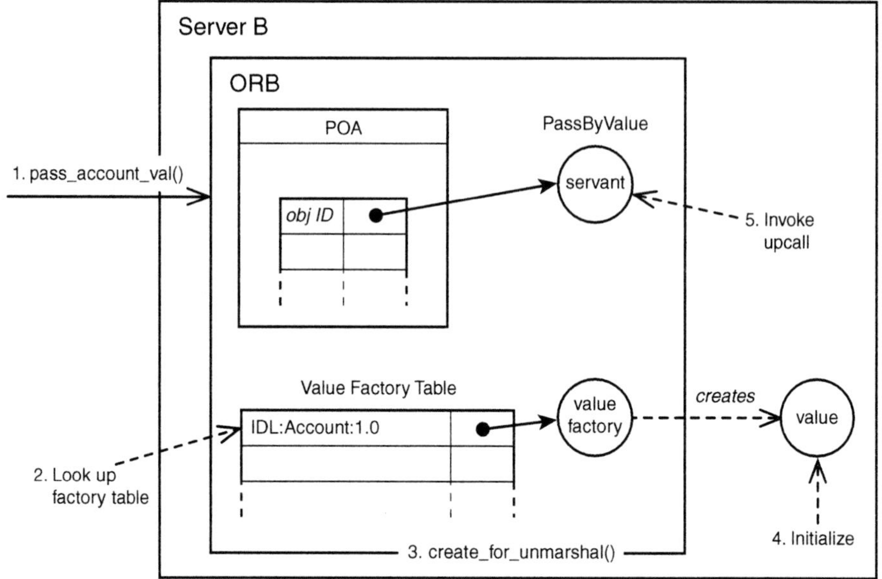

Figure 11.2

Unmarshalling an `AccountVal` value object with the assistance of a value factory.

4. The ORB initializes the new `AccountVal` value object by reading the state members from the request message (both `public` and `private`) and setting the corresponding members of the value object.
5. The `pass_account_val()` upcall is made on the target object, with the `val` parameter pointing at the local copy of the `AccountVal` value object.

It is, therefore, appropriate to use pass by value semantics when the client requires a separate, local instance of the value object. If a client requires access to a remote copy of a value object, pass by reference semantics are used instead (as discussed in the next section).

Pass by Reference Semantics

There are circumstances in which it is more convenient for a value to support pass by reference semantics—in other words, to behave more like a conventional CORBA object. For example, although it is convenient for server-side applications to pass around `AccountVal` values, which represent cached database records, it makes no sense to expose this kind of entity to a client-side application because the client has no access to the database. A better solution would be to expose the account record to a client using a conventional IDL interface; for example, `Account`.

The object by value specification solves this problem by allowing a value type to inherit from a single ordinary IDL interface, using the `supports` keyword. This inheritance feature effectively allows you to create hybrid objects that combine the personality of a value type, which supports pass by value semantics, with the personality of a CORBA object, which supports pass by reference semantics. For example, Listing 11.3 shows how the AccountVal type can be refactored to take advantage of this inheritance feature. This involves declaring a new IDL interface, Account, and deriving the AccountVal value type from this interface using the supports keyword.

Listing 11.3 Definition of the `Account` *Interface and the Refactored Definition of the* `AccountVal` *Value Type*

```
//IDL
interface Account {
    // attributes
    readonly attribute account_id;
    readonly attribute owner;
    readonly attribute balance;

    // operations
    boolean withdraw(in long amount);
    void    pay_in(in long amount);
};

valuetype AccountVal supports Account {
    // state members
    public  long   m_account_id;
    public  string m_owner;
    private long   m_balance;
};
```

In the refactored code, the IDL operations are moved from the AccountVal scope into the Account scope so that clients of the Account interface can call these operations remotely.

To pass a reference to an AccountVal object, you must simply refer to it as an Account object in IDL. For example, Listing 11.4 shows the definition of a PassByReference interface, which provides a single get_account() operation.

Listing 11.4 Definition of the `PassByReference` *Interface That Defines an Operation to Return a Reference to an* `AccountVal` *Object*

```
//IDL
interface PassByReference {
    Account get_account(in long account_id);
};
```

When the get_account() operation is invoked, it returns an ordinary Account object reference, which provides the client with remote access to an AccountVal value. The returned object reference supports only the operations and attributes defined in the Account interface—it cannot be narrowed to the AccountVal type.

To enable the AccountVal type to be passed by reference, it is not enough just to refactor the IDL as shown in Listing 11.3. It is also necessary to modify the implementation of the server so that an AccountVal object is initialized in the same way as a CORBA object. Figure 11.3 shows a schematic example of an AccountVal object that is configured to support pass by reference semantics. The following objects are shown in Figure 11.3:

- PassByReference servant—provides an implementation of the PassByReference interface that can pass AccountVal objects by reference.
- AccountVal value object—is both a value object and a servant at the same time. It can be passed either by value or by reference.
- Value factory object—is provided to enable unmarshalling of AccountVal values. The value factory is not needed for pass by reference semantics, however.

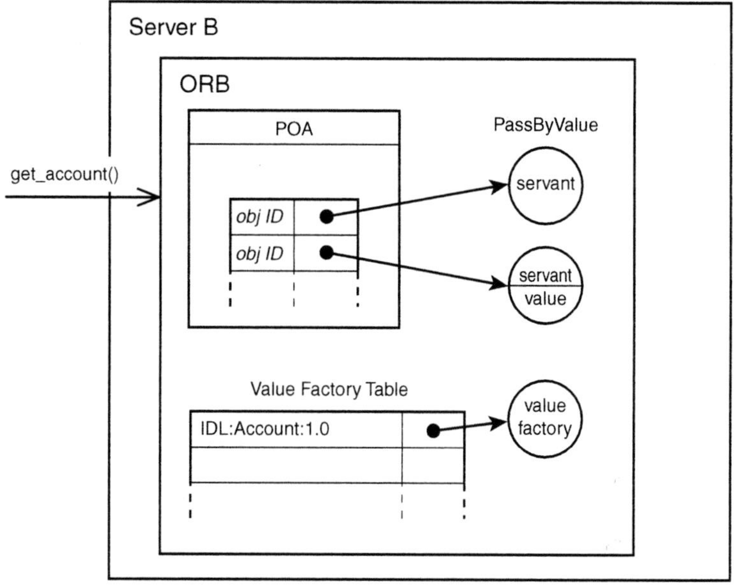

Figure 11.3

Configuring a value to support pass by reference semantics.

When the AccountVal object is created, it can be activated with a POA instance, just like any servant object. The activated value object then has a dual personality:

- **CORBA object** If the AccountVal object is passed by reference (as an Account type), it is treated like a CORBA object and operation invocations are mediated by the ORB.
- **Value type** If the AccountVal object is passed by value (as an AccountVal type), it is treated like a value type and operations are invoked directly on the value object.

If the AccountVal object is not activated, it displays only the personality of a value type. The AccountVal object can then be passed by value, but not by reference.

Regular Value Type

There are several different kinds of value type. This section focuses on the *regular value type*, which is used to define concrete value objects. Some of the other kinds of value type—abstract value types and abstract interfaces—are primarily useful for constructing complex inheritance hierarchies. They are discussed in the section "Other Kinds of Value Type," later in this chapter.

The following subsections describe the IDL syntax and the language mappings for regular value types.

IDL Syntax

This section describes the IDL syntax for regular value types excluding the syntax for value type inheritance, which is discussed in the section "Summary of Inheritance Rules." Listing 11.5 shows the basic IDL syntax for a regular value type.

Listing 11.5 Syntax of a Regular Value Type (Without Inheritance)

```
//IDL
valuetype ValueName  [: OtherValueName] [supports IntfName] {
    //-----------------------------------------
    // Syntax Specific to Valuetypes
    //-----------------------------------------
    // public state members
    public TypeSpec MemberList;
    ...
    // private state members
    private TypeSpec MemberList;
    ...
    // initializers
    factory InitializerName(in Param, in Param, ...);
    ...

    //-----------------------------------------
    // Syntax Common to Interfaces and Valuetypes
    //-----------------------------------------
    // operations
    ...
    // attributes
    ...
    // type declarations
    ...
    // exception declarations
    ...
    // constant declarations
    ...
};
```

The value type definition in Listing 11.5 defines a new value type, *ValueName*, which can then be used as a type specifier in subsequent IDL definitions. The body of the value type can contain zero or more elements, and all the element kinds familiar from the IDL interface syntax are allowed within the scope of the value type. For example, you can include ordinary operations, attributes, and type declarations. In addition, a value type allows you to define the following kinds of element:

- **State member** (both `public` and `private`) Has the syntax of a `struct` member prefixed by either of the keywords `public` or `private`.
- **Initializer** Has the syntax of an IDL operation in which the return type specifier is replaced by the `factory` keyword and all the parameters are declared as `in` parameters. This element is analogous to a constructor in C++ or Java. When the initializer is mapped from IDL to a target language, the initializer return type is declared to be the mapped *ValueName* type.

C++ Mapping

When a value type, *ValueName*, is mapped to C++, several C++ classes are generated as described in Table 11.2.

***Table 11.2** C++ Classes Generated from the `ValueName` Value Type*

Generated C++ Class	Description
ValueName	An abstract base class that can reference instances of the *ValueName* value type. A plain pointer, *ValueName**, can be used to point at value objects. Every *ValueName* class inherits from the common `CORBA::ValueBase` class.
*ValueName*_var	A smart pointer for *ValueName* types that manages reference counting in a similar manner to object reference `_var` types (see Chapter 5, "Object References").
OBV_*ValueName*	A partial implementation of the *ValueName* class, which provides implementations for all `public` and `private` value state members.
*ValueName*_init	An abstract base class for the *ValueName* value factory. This class inherits from `CORBA::ValueFactoryBase` and defines virtual abstract member functions for each initializer declared in IDL. This class is generated only if the IDL definition of *ValueName* declares at least one initializer.

The state members of a value type are mapped to accessor and modifier member functions of the *ValueName* class. For example, Listing 11.6 shows how you can access the public state members of the `AccountVal` value type previously defined in Listing 11.1.

Listing 11.6 Accessing the Public Members of `AccountVal`

```
//C++
AccountVal_var acc_valV = // get a pointer to an AccountVal object.

cout << "Account ID = " << acc_valV->m_account_id() << endl;

// Note: In contrast to an attribute accessor, the following line
//       does NOT cause a memory leak. The value returned by m_owner() is
//       a const char * pointer to memory owned by the value object.
cout << "Owner      = " << acc_valV->m_owner() << endl;
```

Listing 11.7 shows how you can set the public state members of the `AccountVal` value type.

Listing 11.7 Setting the Public Members of `AccountVal`

```
//C++
AccountVal_var acc_valV = // get a pointer to an AccountVal object.

acc_valV->m_account_id(1234);

// Note: The following call makes a copy of the "Mr. New Owner" string.
acc_valV->m_owner("Mr. New Owner");

char * new_ownerP = CORBA::string_dup("Yet another owner");
// Note: In the following call, acc_valV assumes ownership of
//       the new_ownerP string.
acc_valV->m_owner(new_ownerP);
```

The C++ mapping of `valuetype` state members to C++ accessor and modifier functions is based directly on the C++ mapping of `union` members. The C++ syntax and semantics are the same in both cases.

To implement a value type, *`ValueName`*, in C++, you must inherit from the generated `OBV_`*`ValueName`* class and you can optionally inherit from the `CORBA::DefaultValueRefCountBase` class. Listing 11.8 shows the outline of a class, *`ValueName`*`Impl`, that implements a value type.

Listing 11.8 Outline of a Value Implementation Class, *`ValueName`*`Impl`

```
//C++
class ValueNameImpl :
    public virtual OBV_ValueName,
    public virtual CORBA::DefaultValueRefCountBase
{
    // Override virtual functions to implement IDL operations and attributes.
    ...  // (not shown)

    // Override the standard _copy_value() function.
    virtual CORBA::ValueBase* _copy_value();
};
```

The OBV_*ValueName* class provides the implementation of state members and the CORBA::DefaultValueRefCountBase mix-in class supplies the missing implementation of reference counting. The value type's operations and attributes can be implemented using the same syntax as for operations and attributes defined in ordinary IDL interfaces.

The _copy_value() function, which returns a deep copy of the value object, is inherited from the CORBA::ValueBase class. An implementation of the _copy_value() function must be provided.

Implementing a value type that inherits from an IDL interface is a special case that is discussed in the section "Values That Inherit from an Interface," later in this chapter.

The process of implementing a value factory, *ValueName*Factory, depends on whether the *ValueName* value type defines any initializers:

- If the *ValueName* value type does not declare any initializers, a value factory implementation must be defined by inheriting directly from the CORBA::ValueFactoryBase class. For example, the following code outlines the declaration of a value factory implementation class, *ValueName*Factory:

```
//C++
class ValueNameFactory :
    public virtual CORBA::ValueFactoryBase
{
    // Override the 'create_for_unmarshal()' virtual function.
    virtual CORBA::ValueBase* create_for_unmarshal();
};
```

  The CORBA::ValueFactoryBase class has built-in support for reference counting, so there is no need to inherit a reference-counting mix-in class here.

- If the *ValueName* value type declares at least one initializer, a value factory implementation is defined by inheriting from the generated *ValueName*_init class. For example, the following code outlines the declaration of a value factory implementation class, *ValueName*Factory:

```
//C++
class ValueNameFactory :
    public virtual ValueName_init
{
    // Override the 'create_for_unmarshal()' virtual function.
    virtual CORBA::ValueBase* create_for_unmarshal();

    // Override the initializer virtual functions
    ...  // (not shown)
};
```

Implementing value factories is described in more detail in the later section "Implementing the Value Factory."

Value types provide support for reference counting that works in a similar way to reference counting for object references (see Chapter 5). Table 11.3 shows the functions that are provided to manipulate the reference count of value objects.

Table 11.3 Value Type Reference Counting Functions

Function Name	Description
`ValueName::_add_ref()`	Increment the reference count (usually implemented by a mix-in class)
`ValueName::_remove_ref()`	Decrement the reference count (usually implemented by a mix-in class)
`ValueName::_refcount_value()`	Return the current reference count (usually implemented by a mix-in class)
`CORBA::add_ref( CORBA::ValueBase* )`	Increment the reference count
`CORBA::remove_ref( CORBA::ValueBase* )`	Decrement the reference count

The functions in Table 11.3 are useful for manually manipulating reference counts. The usual way of managing reference counts, however, is to assign `ValueName` pointers to a `ValueName_var` smart pointer type. Reference counting (and, hence, memory management) of the value object is then taken care of automatically.

Java Mapping

When a value type, `ValueName`, is mapped to Java, several Java classes and interfaces are generated as described in Table 11.4.

Table 11.4 Java Classes Generated from the `ValueName` Value Type

Generated Java Class	Description
`ValueName`	An abstract Java class that can reference instances of the `ValueName` value type.
`ValueNameHelper`	The Helper class that is associated with the `ValueName` value type.
`ValueNameHolder`	The Holder class that is associated with the `ValueName` value type.
`ValueNameValueFactory`	A Java interface for the `ValueName` value factory. This class inherits from `org.omg.CORBA.portable.ValueFactory` and defines methods for each initializer declared in IDL. This interface is generated only if the IDL definition of `ValueName` declares at least one initializer.

The public and private state members of a value type are mapped, respectively, to public and private member variables of the *ValueName* Java interface. For example, Listing 11.9 shows how to access the public state members of the AccountVal value type previously defined in Listing 11.1.

Listing 11.9 Accessing the Public Members of AccountVal

```
//Java
AccountVal acc_val = // get a reference to an AccountVal object.
System.out.println("Account ID = " + acc_val.m_account_id);

System.out.println("Owner      = " + acc_val.m_owner);
```

Listing 11.10 shows how to set the public state members of the AccountVal value type.

Listing 11.10 Setting the Public Members of AccountVal

```
//Java
AccountVal acc_val = // get a reference to an AccountVal object.
acc_val.m_account_id = (int) 1234;
acc_val.m_owner      = "Mr. New Owner";
```

The process of implementing a value type, *ValueName*, in Java requires you to extend and implement the generated *ValueName* abstract Java class as shown in Listing 11.11.

Listing 11.11 Implementing a ValueName *Value Type in Java*

```
//Java
public class ValueNameImpl extends ValueName
{
    // Implement all IDL operations and attributes.
    ...  // (not shown)
}
```

Implementing a value type that inherits from an IDL interface is a special case that is discussed in the section "Values that Inherit from an Interface," later in this chapter.

The process of implementing a value factory, *ValueName*FactoryImpl, in Java, depends on whether the *ValueName* value type defines any initializers:

- If the *ValueName* value type does not declare any initializers, a value factory implementation must be defined by implementing the org.omg.CORBA.portable.ValueFactory class. For example, the following code outlines the declaration of a value factory implementation class, *ValueName*FactoryImpl:

  ```
  //Java
  public class ValueNameFactoryImpl
      implements org.omg.CORBA.portable.ValueFactory
  {
      // Override the factory's 'read_value()' method.
  ```

```
        public java.io.Serializable
        read_value(org.omg.CORBA_2_3.portable.InputStream is) {
            return is.read_value((java.io.Serializable) new ValueNameImpl());
        }
    }
```

You must override the ValueFactory's `read_value()` method as shown.

- If the *`ValueName`* value type declares at least one initializer, a value factory implementation is defined by implementing the generated *`ValueName`*`ValueFactory` class. For example, the following code outlines the declaration of a value factory implementation class, *`ValueName`*`FactoryImpl`:

```
//Java
public class ValueNameFactoryImpl
    implements ValueNameValueFactory
{
    // Override the factory's 'read_value()' method.
    public java.io.Serializable
    read_value(org.omg.CORBA_2_3.portable.InputStream is) {
        return is.read_value((java.io.Serializable) new ValueNameImpl());
    }

    // Override the mapped initializer methods.
    ...  // (not shown)
}
```

Implementing value factories is described in more detail in the next section.

Example of a Regular Value Implementation

The following subsections describe in detail how to implement a regular value type in C++ and Java. The example is based on the Recycle Broker application of Chapter 3, "A Sample CORBA System." In the original definition of the `RecycleBroker` IDL module (Listing 3.1), struct types—for example, `CustomerDetails` and `WasteItemDetails`—are used to represent the state of objects. The Recycle Broker code can be refactored to replace those structs with value types instead. This section describes how to re-implement `WasteItemDetails` as a value type.

Example IDL

A partial listing of the `RecycleBroker` module refactored from Listing 3.1 is shown in Listing 11.12. The Listing 11.12 shows only the IDL definitions relevant to the `WasteItemDetails` value type.

Listing 11.12 Refactored IDL Definition of the `WasteItemDetails` _Value Type_

```
//IDL
module RecycleBroker {
    typedef float        PriceType;
```

Listing 11.12 Continued

```
    enum WasteType {
        BROWN_GLASS, GREEN_GLASS, CLEAR_GLASS, SCRAP_STEEL,
        ALUMINIUM_CANS, PLASTIC_BOTTLES, WASTE_PAPER
    };

    // valuetype RecycleBroker::WasteItemDetails
    valuetype WasteItemDetails {
        // public members
        public WasteType        waste;
        public long             quantity;
        public PriceType        price_per_kilo;
        factory create(in WasteType w, in long q, in PriceType p);
    };

    interface WasteItemAdmin {
        WasteItemDetails get_item_details(in KeyType wasteitem_id);
    };
};
```

The original `WasteItemDetails` struct from Listing 3.1 is refactored as a `WasteItemDetails` value type by prefixing the `public` keyword to each of the state members and adding a single value type initializer, `create()`.

The `WasteItemAdmin` IDL interface is abbreviated here to show just the single operation, `get_item_details()`, that is needed for the example.

Implementing a Regular Value

The implementation of the `WasteItemDetails` value type follows the general pattern described for the C++ mapping and the Java mapping in the preceding section "Regular Value Type."

In this example, the `WasteItemDetails` value type is implemented by the `RecycleBroker_WasteItemDetailsImpl` class in C++ (Listing 11.13 and Listing 11.14) and the `RecycleBroker.WasteItemDetailsImpl` class in Java (Listing 11.15).

Listing 11.13 shows the C++ declaration of the `RecycleBroker_WasteItemDetailsImpl` class.

Listing 11.13 C++ `RecycleBroker_WasteItemDetailsImpl` Class Declaration

```
//C++
...
class RecycleBroker_WasteItemDetailsImpl :
    public virtual OBV_RecycleBroker::WasteItemDetails,
    public virtual CORBA::DefaultValueRefCountBase
{
```

Listing 11.13 Continued

```
public:
    RecycleBroker_WasteItemDetailsImpl();
    virtual ~RecycleBroker_WasteItemDetailsImpl();

    RecycleBroker_WasteItemDetailsImpl(
        RecycleBroker::WasteType         _waste,
        CORBA::Long                      _quantity,
        RecycleBroker::PriceType         _price_per_kilo
    );

    // Override the standard _copy_value() function.
    virtual CORBA::ValueBase* _copy_value();

private:
    ... //  (not shown)
};
```

In C++, the implementation inherits from `OBV_RecycleBroker::WasteItemDetails`, which supplies the definitions of the state member accessor and modifier functions, and `CORBA::DefaultValueRefCountBase`, which supplies the definitions of the reference counting functions.

Because the `WasteItemDetails` value type does not define IDL operations or attributes, there is little additional functionality to define. The required `_copy_value()` function is declared and an additional constructor also, for convenience. Listing 11.14 shows the definition of these C++ functions.

Listing 11.14 C++ `RecycleBroker_WasteItemDetailsImpl` Class Definition

```
//C++
...
RecycleBroker_WasteItemDetailsImpl::RecycleBroker_WasteItemDetailsImpl()  { }

RecycleBroker_WasteItemDetailsImpl::~RecycleBroker_WasteItemDetailsImpl()  { }

RecycleBroker_WasteItemDetailsImpl::RecycleBroker_WasteItemDetailsImpl(
    RecycleBroker::WasteType         _waste,
    CORBA::Long                      _quantity,
    RecycleBroker::PriceType         _price_per_kilo
)
{
    waste(_waste);
    quantity(_quantity);
    price_per_kilo(_price_per_kilo);
}

// Override the standard _copy_value() function.
CORBA::ValueBase*
```

Listing 11.14 Continued

```
RecycleBroker_WasteItemDetailsImpl::_copy_value()
{
    return new RecycleBroker_WasteItemDetailsImpl(
        waste(),
        quantity(),
        price_per_kilo()
    );
}
```

The extra constructor enables all the state members to be initialized at construction time. Recall that for complex data types, a state modifier function makes a deep copy of its argument. The `_copy_value()` function is implemented to return a deep copy of the `WasteItemDetails` value type.

Listing 11.15 shows the Java definition of the `RecycleBroker.WasteItemDetailsImpl` class.

Listing 11.15 Java `WasteItemDetailsImpl` Class Definition

```
//Java
package RecycleBroker;

public class WasteItemDetailsImpl
    extends WasteItemDetails
{
    WasteItemDetailsImpl () {  }
}
```

The definition of `WasteItemDetailsImpl` is trivial because the state members, `waste`, `quantity`, and `price_per_kilo`, are already defined in the IDL-compiler generated abstract class `WasteItemDetails`. You are not required to implement a copy method for value objects in Java, but you could, optionally, specify that `WasteItemDetailsImpl` implements the `java.lang.Cloneable` interface and implement the `clone()` method.

Implementing a Value Factory

The implementation of the value factory for `WasteItemDetails` follows the pattern for a value type that declares at least one initializer, as described in the preceding section "Regular Value Types." On account of the initializer's presence in the value type declaration, the IDL compiler generates an extra definition, a `RecycleBroker::WasteItemDetails_init` class in C++ and a `RecycleBroker.WasteItemDetailsValueFactory` interface in Java, which serves as the base for the value factory implementation.

In this example, the value factory is implemented by the `RecycleBroker_WasteItemDetailsFactory` class in C++ (Listing 11.16 and Listing 11.17) and the `RecycleBroker.WasteItemDetailsFactoryImpl` class in Java (Listing 11.18).

Listing 11.16 shows the C++ declaration of the `RecycleBroker_WasteItemDetailsFactory` class.

Listing 11.16 C++ `RecycleBroker_WasteItemDetailsFactory` *Class Declaration*

```
//C++
class RecycleBroker_WasteItemDetailsFactory :
    public virtual RecycleBroker::WasteItemDetails_init {
public:
    virtual CORBA::ValueBase* create_for_unmarshal();

    virtual RecycleBroker::WasteItemDetails*
    create(
        RecycleBroker::WasteType        w,
        CORBA::Long                     q,
        RecycleBroker::PriceType        p
    );
};
```

In C++, the factory implementation inherits from `RecycleBroker::WasteItemDetails_init`, which includes pure virtual function declarations corresponding to each of the initializers declared in IDL.

The `create_for_unmarshal()` function must be implemented to enable a transmitted `WasteItemDetails` value object to be unmarshalled at the receiving end. The `create()` function is the C++ mapping of the `create()` initializer declared in IDL. Listing 11.17 shows the definition of these C++ functions.

Listing 11.17 C++ `RecycleBroker_WasteItemDetailsFactory` *Class Definition*

```
//C++
CORBA::ValueBase*
RecycleBroker_WasteItemDetailsFactory::create_for_unmarshal()
{
    return new RecycleBroker_WasteItemDetailsImpl();
}

RecycleBroker::WasteItemDetails*
RecycleBroker_WasteItemDetailsFactory::create(
    RecycleBroker::WasteType        w,
    CORBA::Long                     q,
    RecycleBroker::PriceType        p
)
{
    return new RecycleBroker_WasteItemDetailsImpl(w, q, p);
}
```

In Java, the factory class implements the `WasteItemDetailsValueFactory` Java interface, which includes method declarations corresponding to each of the initializers declared in IDL. The definition of the `WasteItemDetailsValueFactory` class is given in Listing 11.18.

Listing 11.18 ***Java*** **`WasteItemDetailsFactoryImpl`** ***Class Definition***

```
//Java
package RecycleBroker;

public class WasteItemDetailsFactoryImpl
    implements WasteItemDetailsValueFactory
{
    public java.io.Serializable read_value(
        org.omg.CORBA_2_3.portable.InputStream is
    )
    {
        return is.read_value(
                   (java.io.Serializable)new WasteItemDetailsImpl()
               );
    }

    public WasteItemDetails create(RecycleBroker.WasteType w, int q, float p) {
        return new WasteItemDetailsImpl(w,q,p);
    }
}
```

The `read_value()` method must be implemented to enable a transmitted `WasteItemDetails` value object to be unmarshalled at the receiving end. The `create()` method is the Java mapping of the `create()` initializer declared in IDL.

Registering the Value Factory

To enable an application (client or server) to receive `WasteItemDetails` value objects as parameters or return values, it is necessary to register the value factory with your ORB instance beforehand. In the case of an application with multiple ORB instances, it would be necessary to register the value factory with each ORB. Listing 11.19 and Listing 11.20 show how to register a value factory with an ORB instance in C++ and Java respectively.

Listing 11.19 ***C++ Registration of the*** **`RecycleBroker_WasteItemDetailsFactory`** ***Value Factory***

```
//C++
...
// global_orb
CORBA::ORB_var global_orb = CORBA::ORB::_nil();

int main(int argc, char **argv)
{
```

Listing 11.19 Continued

```
    ...
    try
    {
    ...
        // Initialise the ORB.
        global_orb = CORBA::ORB_init(argc, argv);

        // Register valuetype factories:
        CORBA::ValueFactoryBase_var vf
            = new RecycleBroker_WasteItemDetailsFactory();
        CORBA::String_var repIdV = RecycleBroker::_tc_WasteItemDetails->id();
        orb->register_value_factory(
            repIdV.in(),
            vf.in()
        );
        ...
    }
    catch (CORBA::Exception) {
        // Deal with exceptions...
    }
}
```

Listing 11.20 Java Registration of the `WasteItemDetailsFactoryImpl` *Value Factory*

```
//Java
...
public class client
{
    // global_orb
    public static org.omg.CORBA_2_3.ORB global_orb = null;

    public static void main (String args[])
    {
        try
        {
            ...
            global_orb = (org.omg.CORBA_2_3.ORB) ORB.init(args, null);

            // Register valuetype factories:
            global_orb.register_value_factory(
                 Pure.RecycleBroker.WasteItemDetailsHelper.id(),
                 new Pure.RecycleBroker.WasteItemDetailsFactoryImpl()
            );
            ...
        }
        catch (org.omg.CORBA.SystemException ex) {
```

Listing 11.20 Continued

```
            // Handle exceptions here...
        }
    ...
    }
    ...
}
```

In C++, registration is performed by calling the `register_value_factory()` operation, passing the `WasteItemDetails` repository ID as the first parameter and a pointer to a new value factory instance.

CAUTION

In C++, assigning the newly created value factory object to a `_var` object, `vf`, is essential to avoid leaking memory in Listing 11.19.

In Java, registration is performed by calling the `register_value_factory()` operation, passing the `WasteItemDetails` repository ID as the first parameter and a reference to a new value factory instance. Because the mapped Java `register_value_factory()` method is declared by the `org.omg.CORBA_2_3.ORB` subtype, it is necessary, first of all, to cast the ORB instance to the `org.omg.CORBA_2_3.ORB` type.

Passing the Value as a Return Value

The `WasteItemAdmin::get_item_details()` operation provides a demonstration of how to pass a value object as the return value of an IDL operation. The implementation of `get_item_details()` is given in Listing 11.21 and Listing 11.22 for C++ and Java respectively.

Listing 11.21 C++ Implementation of the **`WasteItemAdmin::get_item_details()`** ***Operation***

```
//C++
RecycleBroker::WasteItemDetails*
RecycleBroker_WasteItemAdminImpl::get_item_details(
    RecycleBroker::KeyType          wasteitem_id
) throws (CORBA::SystemException)
{
    // TEST IMPLEMENTATION - return a sample value:
    RecycleBroker::WasteItemDetails* _result
        = new RecycleBroker_WasteItemDetailsImpl();
    _result->waste(RecycleBroker::BROWN_GLASS);
    _result->quantity(1000);
    _result->price_per_kilo(2.4f);

    return _result;
}
```

Listing 11.22 Java Implementation of the **`WasteItemAdmin::get_item_details()`** ***Operation***

```
//Java
package RecycleBroker;

public interface WasteItemAdminImpl
    extends WasteItemAdminPOA
{
     Pure.RecycleBroker.WasteItemDetails get_item_details(
        int wasteitem_id
    )
    {
        // TEST IMPLEMENTATION - return a sample value:
        WasteItemDetails _result = new WasteItemDetailsImpl();
        _result.waste          = WasteType.BROWN_GLASS;
        _result.quantity       = (int)1000;
        _result.price_per_kilo = (float)2.4;

        return _result;
    }
}
```

In C++, a value object is created and a pointer to the object is returned. In Java, a value object is created and a reference to the object is returned. This resembles the way that an ordinary complex type, such as a struct, is returned, but constrasts markedly with the way that a CORBA object is returned. In this context, therefore, a value object is more like a struct than a CORBA object.

Other Kinds of Value Type

In addition to regular value types, which can correspond directly to concrete implementations, the value type specification defines `abstract value` and `abstract interface` types, which can be used only as base types in the context of an inheritance hierarchy.

Value types support a relatively rich syntax for defining inheritance relationships. This section describes the different kinds of value type that result from applying the various inheritance rules and, at the end, a summary of the inheritance rules is presented.

Values That Inherit from a Value

A regular value can inherit from another regular value subject to a limit of *single* inheritance. This brings a valuable element of flexibility to defining complex types. Consider, for example, the original definition of the `RecycleBroker` IDL module from Listing 3.1 where `WasteItemDetails` and `WasteItemDetailsFull` are both declared as structs. Although these structs are clearly related to each other, in the sense that `WasteItemDetailsFull` extends `WasteItemDetails`, the only way of expressing the relationship prior to the introduction of value types was to declare a `WasteItemDetails` member within the scope of `WasteItemDetailsFull`.

The relationship between `WasteItemDetails` and `WasteItemDetailsFull` can, however, be expressed more elegantly using inheritance after the `RecycleBroker` module has been refactored using value types, as shown in Listing 11.23.

Listing 11.23 Refactored Definition of the `WasteItemDetailsFull` *Value Type Using Inheritance*

```
//IDL
module RecycleBroker {
    typedef long        KeyType;
    typedef float       PriceType;

    enum WasteType {
        BROWN_GLASS, GREEN_GLASS, CLEAR_GLASS, SCRAP_STEEL,
        ALUMINIUM_CANS, PLASTIC_BOTTLES, WASTE_PAPER
    };

    valuetype WasteItemDetails {
        // public members
        public WasteType        waste;
        public long             quantity;
        public PriceType        price_per_kilo;
        // initializer
        factory create(in WasteType w, in long q, in PriceType p);
    };

    valuetype WasteItemDetailsFull : WasteItemDetails {
        // private members
        private KeyType          branch_id;
        private KeyType          customer_id;
        private KeyType          wasteitem_id;
        // operations
        void reassign_branch(in KeyType new_branch_id);
        void delete_record();
        // initializer
        factory create(in KeyType branch_id,  in KeyType customer_id);
    };

    interface WasteItemAdmin {
        WasteItemDetails get_item_details(in KeyType wasteitem_id);
    };
};
```

In Listing 11.23, the `WasteItemDetailsFull` value type inherits state members, operations, attributes, exceptions, and type definitions from `WasteItemDetails`.

NOTE

Initializers are *not* inherited between value types. Hence, in Listing 11.23, there is no identifier clash between the `create()` initializer defined within the `WasteItemDetails` scope and the `create()` initializer defined within the `WasteItemDetailsFull` scope.

The `WasteItemAdmin::get_item_details()` operation, which returns `WasteItemDetails`, supports a kind of polymorphism in the sense that either a `WasteItemDetails` or a `WasteItemDetailsFull` value object can be returned from the `get_item_details()` operation. When a value object is transmitted as a return value from `get_item_details()`, the receiving application reads the object's repository ID from the incoming reply message to identify the value type. The ORB then looks up the value factory table to find the appropriate kind of factory, for either `WasteItemDetails` value objects or `WasteItemDetailsFull` value objects. If the matching value factory cannot be found, the ORB normally throws a `CORBA::MARSHAL` system exception.

Value types also support a special form of inheritance that allows unmarshalling to succeed even if the matching value factory cannot be found. Listing 11.24 illustrates the syntax of *truncatable inheritance* in the definition of the `WasteItemDetailsFull` value type.

Listing 11.24 *The* `WasteItemDetailsFull` *Value Type Inherits "Truncatably" from* `WasteItemDetails`

```
//IDL
module RecycleBroker {
    ...
    valuetype WasteItemDetails {
        ...
    };

    valuetype WasteItemDetailsFull : truncatable WasteItemDetails {
        ...
    };

    interface WasteItemAdmin {
        WasteItemDetails get_item_details(in KeyType wasteitem_id);
    };
};
```

When a truncatable `WasteItemDetailsFull` value object is transmitted as the return value from `get_item_details()`, the unmarshalling can now succeed in the receiving application even if just the `WasteItemDetails` value factory is registered. The ORB initially looks for the value factory for `WasteItemDetailsFull` value objects. If that factory is not found, the ORB then looks for the value factory for `WasteItemDetails` value objects instead and discards the state members—branch_id, customer_id, and wasteitem_id—specific to WasteItemDetailsFull.

CAUTION

Use truncatability with some discretion. Unless your application is designed specifically with truncatability in mind, truncatable inheritance can lead to bugs in which value objects are unexpectedly and erroneously truncated.

Using value type inheritance has an impact on the inheritance hierarchy of implementation classes, which is discussed briefly in the following two subsections, for C++ and Java, respectively.

C++ Mapping

Listing 11.25 shows the effect that value type inheritance has on the C++ inheritance hierarchy when a regular value, WasteItemDetails, inherits from another regular value, WasteItemDetailsFull.

Listing 11.25 C++ Inheritance Hierarchy for a Value That Inherits from Another Value

```
//C++
class RecycleBroker_WasteItemDetailsImpl :
    public virtual OBV_RecycleBroker::WasteItemDetails,
    public virtual CORBA::DefaultValueRefCountBase
{
public:
    ...
};

class RecycleBroker_WasteItemDetailsFullImpl :
    public virtual OBV_RecycleBroker::WasteItemDetailsFull,
    public virtual RecycleBroker_WasteItemDetailsImpl
{
public:
    ...
};
```

The base value type, WasteItemDetails, is implemented as normal. The derived value type, WasteItemDetailsFull, is conveniently implemented by letting the implementation class inherit from the WasteItemDetails implementation class. This ensures that existing operation and attribute implementations are inherited by the derived implementation.

Java Mapping

Listing 11.26 shows the effect that value type inheritance has on the Java inheritance hierarchy when a regular value, WasteItemDetails, inherits from another regular value, WasteItemDetailsFull.

Listing 11.26 Java Inheritance Hierarchy for a Value That Inherits from Another Value

```
//Java
package RecycleBroker;

public class WasteItemDetailsImpl
    extends WasteItemDetails
{
    ...
}

public class WasteItemDetailsFullImpl
    extends WasteItemDetailsFull
{
    ...
}
```

Both the base value type, `WasteItemDetails`, and the derived value type, `WasteItemDetailsFull`, are implemented as normal. The disadvantage of this arrangement is that the derived implementation class does not inherit existing operations and attributes from the `WasteItemDetails` implementation class. This implies that existing operation and attribute implementations must be redefined by the derived implementation.

Values That Inherit from an Interface

A regular value can inherit from an ordinary IDL interface subject to a limit of *single* inheritance. This feature is the key to enabling pass by reference semantics for value types, as discussed in the earlier section "Pass by Reference Semantics." An instance of a regular value type that inherits from an ordinary IDL interface can be both a CORBA object and a value object.

Listing 11.27 shows an extract from the `RecycleBroker` IDL module that is refactored to make the `WasteItemDetailsFull` value type support the `WasteItem` IDL interface.

Listing 11.27 Refactoring the `WasteItemDetailsFull` *Value Type to Support the IDL Interface,* `WasteItem`

```
//IDL
module RecycleBroker {
    typedef long        KeyType;
    typedef float       PriceType;

    enum WasteType {
        BROWN_GLASS, GREEN_GLASS, CLEAR_GLASS, SCRAP_STEEL,
        ALUMINIUM_CANS, PLASTIC_BOTTLES, WASTE_PAPER
    };

    valuetype WasteItemDetails;
```

Listing 11.27 Continued

```
    interface WasteItem {
        WasteType    get_waste();
        void         set_waste(in WasteType w);
        long         get_quantity();
        void         set_quantity(in long q);
        PriceType    get_price_per_kilo();
        void         set_price_per_kilo(in PriceType pt);

        KeyType get_branch_id();
        KeyType get_customer_id();
        KeyType get_wasteitem_id();

        // operations
        WasteItemDetails get_details();
    };

    valuetype WasteItemDetails {
        // public members
        public WasteType        waste;
        public long             quantity;
        public PriceType        price_per_kilo;
    };

    valuetype WasteItemDetailsFull
        : WasteItemDetails
        supports WasteItem
    {
        // private members
        private KeyType          branch_id;
        private KeyType          customer_id;
        private KeyType          wasteitem_id;
        // operations
        void reassign_branch(in KeyType new_branch_id);
        void delete_record();
        // initializers
        factory create(in KeyType branch_id, in KeyType customer_id);
    };

    interface WasteItemAdmin {
        WasteItemDetails get_item_details(in KeyType wasteitem_id);
        WasteItem        get_waste_item(in KeyType wasteitem_id);
    };
};
```

Because `WasteItemDetailsFull` supports the `WasteItem` interface, it can now be passed either as a value type or as an object reference, depending on how it is declared in IDL. For example, when a `WasteItemDetailsFull` object is returned from the

WasteItemAdmin::get_item_details() operation, it is passed by value. On the other hand, when a WasteItemDetailsFull object is returned from the WasteItemAdmin::get_waste_item() operation it is passed by reference (as a WasteItem object reference).

If you need the flexibility to choose between pass by value and pass by reference semantics at runtime, you should consider using abstract interfaces—see the later section, "Abstract Interfaces."

Making value types inherit from an IDL interface has an impact on the inheritance hierarchy of implementation classes, which is discussed briefly in the following two subsections, for C++ and Java, respectively.

C++ Mapping

Listing 11.28 shows the inheritance hierarchy of C++ implementation classes that result when a regular value, WasteItemDetailsFull, inherits from an ordinary IDL interface, WasteItem.

Listing 11.28 C++ Inheritance Hierarchy for a Value That Inherits from an Ordinary IDL Interface

```
//C++
class RecycleBroker_WasteItemDetailsImpl :
    public virtual OBV_RecycleBroker::WasteItemDetails,
    public virtual CORBA::DefaultValueRefCountBase
{
public:
    ...
};

class RecycleBroker_WasteItemDetailsFullImpl :
    public virtual RecycleBroker_WasteItemDetailsImpl,
    public virtual OBV_RecycleBroker::WasteItemDetailsFull,
    public virtual PortableServer::ValueRefCountBase,
    public virtual POA_RecycleBroker::WasteItem
{
public:
    ...
};
```

To enable the WasteItemDetailsFullImpl class to be used as a servant class and to support pass by reference semantics, the WasteItemDetailsFullImpl class must inherit from the following:

- POA_RecycleBroker::WasteItem This is the usual POA class generated for the WasteItem interface.
- PortableServer::ValueRefCountBase This is a special implementation of a reference counting mix-in class that *must* appear as a base class when a value type implements an IDL interface using the inheritance approach.

Java Mapping

To implement the inheritance hierarchy built using `WasteItem`, `WasteItemDetails`, and `WasteItemDetailsFull` from Listing 11.27, you can define the Java implementation classes as defined in Listing 11.29.

Listing 11.29 Java Inheritance Hierarchy for a Value That Inherits from Another Value

```
//Java
package RecycleBroker;

public class WasteItemDetailsImpl
    extends WasteItemDetails
{
    ...
}

public class WasteItemDetailsFullImpl
    extends WasteItemDetailsFull
    implements WasteItemOperations
{
    ...
}
```

You immediately run into a problem, however, when you consider how to make the `WasteItemDetailsFullImpl` class support the `WasteItem` interface because the sole inheritance slot is filled by the `WasteItemDetailsFull` class. The solution is to implement the `WasteItem` interface using the Tie approach—hence the `WasteItemDetailsFull` class is defined to implement the `WasteItemOperations` interface. An instance of a `WasteItem` object can now be created and activated as shown in Listing 11.30.

Listing 11.30 Java Creating a `WasteItem` Instance Using the Tie Approach

```
//Java
package RecycleBroker;

// Create a value object and its associated TIE object.
WasteItemDetailsFullImpl value_object = new WasteItemDetailsFullImpl();
WasteItemPOATie the_tie  = new WasteItemPOATie(value_object, my_poa);

// Activate the TIE object (servant object).
byte[]                oid = my_poa.activate_object(the_tie);
org.omg.CORBA.Object obj = obj = my_poa.id_to_reference(oid);
...
```

Abstract Values

An abstract value type, which is introduced by the `abstract` keyword in IDL, restricts the syntax and semantics of a value type as follows:

- No state members can be declared.
- No initializers can be declared.
- An abstract value type cannot be directly implemented in the target language. Only concrete value types that derive from the abstract value can be implemented.

The effect of the syntax restrictions is shown in Listing 11.31, which summarizes the IDL syntax for abstract value type. The IDL inheritance syntax is described later, in the section "Summary of Inheritance Rules."

Listing 11.31 Syntax of an Abstract Value Type

```
//IDL
abstract valuetype AbstractValueName
    [: OtherAbstractValue, OtherAbstractValue ...]
    [supports AbstractIntf, AbstractIntf ...]
{
    // NO public state members
    // NO private state members
    // NO initializers

    // operations
    ...
    // attributes
    ...
    // type declarations
    ...
    // exception declarations
    ...
    // constant declarations
    ...
};
```

Abstract value types are typically used to define bundles of operation signatures, which are then inherited by regular value types. Forward declarations of abstract value types are also permitted, for example:

```
//IDL
abstract valuetype AbstractValueName;
```

Abstract Interfaces

An abstract interface is useful in circumstances where you need to pass *either* an interface *or* a value type, but you cannot know which until the application is running. Semantically, an abstract interface is similar to a special kind of `union` or `any` type in that it allows alternative types to be passed. The advantage of using an abstract interface, however, is that it offers greater syntactical convenience.

An abstract interface type, which is introduced by the `abstract` keyword in IDL, can contain the same kinds of declaration as an ordinary IDL interface. The IDL syntax (apart from inheritance) is shown in Listing 11.32.

Listing 11.32 Syntax of an Abstract Interface Type

```
//IDL
abstract interface AbstractIntfName
    [: OtherAbstractIntf, OtherAbstractIntf ...]
{
    // operations
    ...
    // attributes
    ...
    // type declarations
    ...
    // exception declarations
    ...
    // constant declarations
    ...
};
```

There are a couple of different patterns for using abstract interfaces. One pattern is to use the abstract interface as a polymorphic base class that serves as a base class for interfaces or value types. This usage is illustrated by the following IDL fragment:

```
//IDL
abstract interface AdminStuff;

interface MainApplication {
    AdminStuff get_admin_stuff(in string objID);
    ...
};

abstract interface AdminStuff {
    // could define some operations here...
};

valuetype Status supports AdminStuff {
    ... // (some useful info)
};

interface ShutdownTool : AdminStuff {
    void shutdown();
};
```

In the preceding IDL example, the `AdminStuff` abstract interface represents a miscellaneous collection of administration objects. Some of these objects—for example, the `Status` value type—consist mainly of state and can be passed by value. Other objects—for example, the `ShutdownTool` interface—represent a service provided by the remote application and are therefore passed by reference.

Another usage pattern can be illustrated by modifying the `WasteItem` interface declared in Listing 11.27 to make it inherit from an abstract interface, `AbstractWasteItem`, as follows:

```
//IDL
module RecycleBroker {
    ...
    abstract interface AbstractWasteItem;

    interface WasteItemAdmin {
        AbstractWasteItem        get_abstract(in KeyType wasteitem_id);
    };

    abstract interface AbstractWasteItem { };
    interface WasteItem : AbstractWasteItem { ... };
    ...
    valuetype WasteItemDetails { ... };
    valuetype WasteItemDetailsFull
        : WasteItemDetails supports WasteItem { ... };
};
```

In the preceding IDL example, a client that invokes the `WasteItemAdmin::get_abstract()` operation could receive either a `WasteItem` object reference or a `WasteItemDetailsFull` value object. In this example, the abstract interface lets the server return two alternative views of the *same* underlying object. One view, the `WasteItem` object reference, is appropriate for remote clients, and the other view, the `WasteItemDetailsFull` value object, is appropriate for other server applications.

Summary of Inheritance Rules

The syntax for defining regular value inheritance from other value types and interfaces is as follows:

```
//IDL
valuetype RegValueName
    [: OtherRegValueName, AbstractValueName, AbstractValueName ...]
    [supports IntfName, AbstractIntfName, AbstractIntfName ...]
{
    // Value members
};
```

The value type inheritance rules state that a regular value type, *RegValueName*, can inherit from any of the following:

- At most, one other regular value, *OtherRegValueName*, and any number of abstract value types, *AbstractValueName*
- At most, one ordinary IDL interface, *IntfName*, and any number of abstract interfaces, *AbstractIntfName*

There are, in addition, specific inheritance rules that govern every possible inheritance relationship between values and interfaces. Generally, the different kinds of value and interface can be placed in a sequence that runs from the most abstract to the most concrete entity, as follows:

1. `abstract interface`
2. `interface`
3. `abstract valuetype`
4. `valuetype`

An entity in this list can inherit from, or support, any one of the preceding (more abstract) entities in the list, but not the other way around. Thus, a `valuetype` can support an `abstract interface`, but an `abstract interface` cannot support or inherit from a `valuetype`.

In addition to this basic rule, there are additional constraints that specify when single or multiple inheritance is allowed. The complete set of inheritance rules are summarized in Figure 11.4, in which each inheritance relationship is labeled with one of the following kinds of inheritance: *inherit single*, *inherit multiple*, *support single*, and *support multiple*.

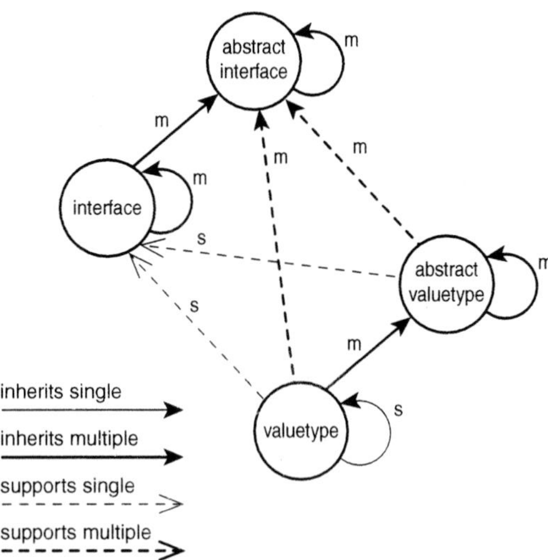

Figure 11.4

Allowed inheritance relationships for value types and interfaces.

Summary

This chapter has described how to define and implement regular value types, including cases in which a regular value type inherits from another regular value type or supports an IDL interface. Other types that can be used as part of an inheritance hierarchy—`abstract valuetype` and `abstract interface`—are also briefly described.

Other special features of value types are not covered in this chapter; specifically, transmission of value graphs and transmission of custom value types are not discussed.

The transmission of value graphs is a useful feature for programmers who want to transmit large, complex graphs of objects. Value types support an optimized encoding to minimize the overhead of transmitting value graphs.

The transmission of custom value types is currently not widely supported—it requires an application programmer to implement custom marshalling code for a value type using an approach that is not specified by CORBA.

CHAPTER 12

Events Service

Most communication in a CORBA system is done synchronously. This means that an operation will block until a return value is returned from the target object, or until an exception is thrown by the ORB. It also means that the two parties in the communication must be in direct contact with one another via the ORB. In most instances, this is desired behavior.

There are occasions, however, when indirectand asynchronous communication is indicated, such as when two objects do not want to or cannot have direct knowledge of one another. Other reasons indirect or asynchronous communication may be desired include whenever an object does not want to wait until the message is received by the recipient or when one object wishes to deliver a message to a collection of potentially unknown recipients.

A pattern known as the Mediator (see Figure 12.1) facilitates the design of such asynchronous communication by promoting loose coupling between the two parties in the communication. The Mediator pattern encapsulates the communication between objects into a common object, and each party then communicates with that common object directly. This requires the parties on either end of the communication to know only about the Mediator object, and not about each other directly. Such a pattern implements the OO principles of loose coupling of objects, as well as tight cohesion in the Mediator object itself, as it encapsulates the communication between the two objects into a common object. A Mediator object is responsible for mediating the communication between two or more collaborating objects. Through the use of a Mediator, collaborators are decoupled and their communication is abstracted and encapsulated into a single controller object. The Mediator thus centralizes the management of the communication and acts as a forwarder of information from one collaborating object to another.

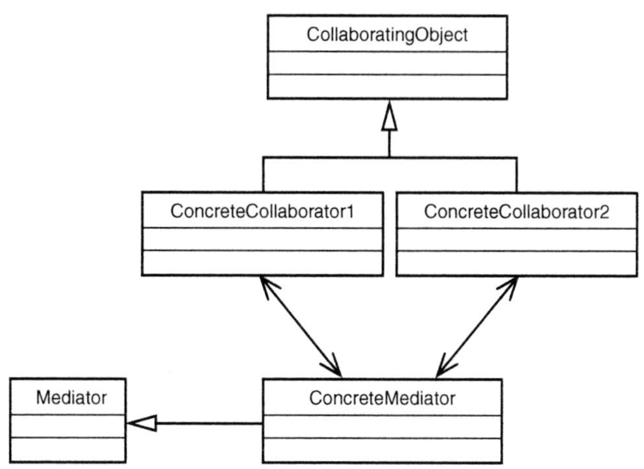

Figure 12.1
The Mediator pattern.

CORBA Event Service Patterns

The CORBA Event Service is one implementation of the Mediator pattern. The OMG Event Service specification provides for decoupled message transfer between CORBA objects. The decoupling of communication provided by the Event Service enables variability in terms of the communication modes and methods. Specifically, it gives one object (the Supplier) the capability to send messages to another object (the Consumer) that is interested in receiving those messages without having to know where the receiver is or even whether the receiver is listening. This decoupling provides several important benefits:

- Suppliers and Consumers do not themselves physically have to handle the communication, nor must they have any specific knowledge of each other. They simply connect to the Event Service, which mediates their communication.
- Message passing between the Supplier and Consumer takes place asynchronously. Message delivery does not need to entail blocking (although a pull Consumer may choose to block if it wishes, as will be seen in the "Pull Model" section of this chapter). Event Channels may be set up to be either typed or untyped (not all ORB implementations support typed events).
- Event Channels will automatically buffer events they receive until a suitable Consumer expresses interest in the events. (Note that this does not imply either persistence or store and forward capabilities.) Generally, an independent queue

in the Event Channel will be devoted to each Consumer. These internal queues usually operate on a last in, first out (LIFO) basis, with older messages being disposed of if the buffer is full and new messages arrive without a Consumer extracting the messages fast enough. Most ORBs will allow the maximum queue length to be set.

- Events may be confirmed and their delivery guaranteed if the vendor has implemented this capability.
- Suppliers can choose either to push events onto the channel (push) or have the channel itself request events from them (pull). Similarly, a Consumer may request to either synchronously or asynchronously obtain (pull) events from the channel or to have the channel deliver (push) events to them.
- A one-to-one correspondence between Suppliers and Consumers is not necessary; there can be multiple Suppliers connected to a single Consumer via the Event Service, as well as a single Supplier connected to one or more Consumers.

Event Flow Models

As alluded to above, there are two primary styles of interaction between Suppliers and Consumers and the Event Channel. These two styles are known as the Push and Pull models. Although the flow of events is always from Supplier to Consumer, the direction of a method call by which an event is transmitted may be either from Supplier to Consumer or vice versa. Figure 12.2 illustrates this concept of event flow.

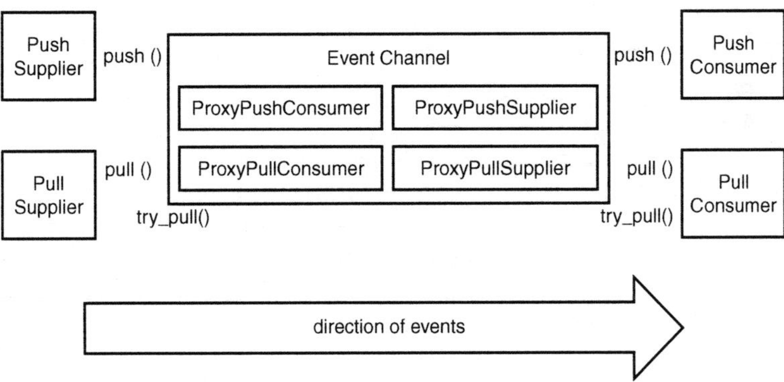

Figure 12.2

Event flow.

Push Model

In the Push model, a Supplier connects to the Event Channel and initiates a push of an event onto the Event Channel whenever it is ready to do so. It is the Event Channel's responsibility to buffer those events until they are delivered to one or more interested Consumers. When a Supplier wants to connect to an Event Channel, it needs an object within the Event Channel to pretend it is a Consumer. This enables the Supplier simply to deliver events to its consumer, when in reality, this consumer is simply a proxy for the actual Consumer, which is outside of the Event Channel. It is to this proxy consumer that the Push Supplier pushes events. Thus, the Proxy object is not a real Consumer, merely an object within the Event Channel that provides a delivery mechanism through which the Supplier can deliver messages.

A Push Consumer likewise connects to a proxy object, a proxy that represents the Push Supplier. When the Event Channel has a message available, the Push Supplier Proxy delivers (pushes) the message to the actual Consumer object. The message path is from the actual Push Supplier, through its Proxy Push Consumer, to the Proxy Push Supplier, and finally to the Push Consumer itself. There are other variations of this, as the example used throughout the "Using an Event Channel" section shows.

NOTE

A *proxy,* or *surrogate,* is a pattern in which an object acts as a placeholder for another object. As far as the user of a proxy is concerned, the proxy is responsible for providing the requested functionality, when in actuality, the proxy simply delegates the functionality to some third party.

Pull Model

In the Pull model, the Event Channel pulls data from the Supplier. In the Pull model, it is the Consumer that drives the delivery of messages. A Pull Supplier connects to a Proxy Pull Consumer. Again, as far as the Pull Supplier is concerned, it can consider this proxy object a real Consumer, which requests events from it periodically. An interested Pull Consumer object then connects on the other end of the Event Channel to a Proxy Pull Supplier. When a Pull Consumer is ready to receive an event, it initiates either a `pull()` (which will block until an event is available to be consumed) or `try_pull()` (which will retrieve an event for consumption if one is available, but will not block if one is not) on its Proxy Pull Supplier, which in turn queries the Proxy Pull Consumer connected to the actual Pull Supplier to request that another event be delivered. In this way, the Consumer drives the data when it is ready to process another message. Some implementations of the `pull()` method allow the Proxy Pull Supplier to pull events from the Supplier at regular intervals, to try to keep a buffer full of events for Consumers when they request delivery.

The nice thing about the Event Channel abstraction is that a communication does not need to be either entirely Push model or Pull model. A Push Supplier may indirectly connect to one or more Pull Consumers, and several Pull Suppliers may connect to one or more Push Consumers. It is the Event Channel logic itself that enables such disproportional interrelationships among objects. It is the application design itself that drives the decisions concerning suppliers and consumers and their numbers.

Using an Event Channel

Regardless of the relationship among suppliers and consumers, to establish a connection and deliver events through the Event Channel, five steps must be taken:

1. The client (Supplier or Consumer) first binds to the Event Channel (which must be created by someone already, perhaps the client itself).
2. The client obtains an Admin object from the Event Channel. A Consumer needs a `ConsumerAdmin` object, and a Supplier needs a `SupplierAdmin` object.
3. The client obtains a proxy object from the Admin object (a Consumer Proxy for a Supplier client, and a Supplier Proxy for a Consumer client).
4. The client adds the Supplier or Consumer to the Event Channel via a `connect()` call.
5. The client and/or the Event Channel transfer data via the `push()`, `pull()`, and/or `try_pull()` calls.

When messages are delivered through the Event Channel, they can be either typed or untyped. Typed messages are those defined in an IDL that are type-checked at compile time. Untyped events, the most common, adhere to the standard Event Services interfaces and are packaged as type `CORBA::Any`, which is a wrapper around all known CORBA types. It is this `Any` type that is actually sent from a Supplier object to a Consumer object. The Supplier constructs an `Any`, and the Consumer, upon receipt of the message, derives the true value from the `Any` wrapper. This enables great flexibility in delivering messages because a Supplier may (for example) pass a `string` first, a `long` value second, and an array third, all through packaging the values into an `Any`. The following supplier and consumer examples show how to create, embed, and extract values from `Any` types (refer back to Chapter 8, "The `any` Type," for more on `Any` types).

This example incorporates an implementation of a Supplier and a Consumer interacting through the use of the Event Service. The Supplier implements the Push Supplier model and the Consumer implements the Pull Consumer model, thus illustrating that the models themselves do not have to be all of one type. The example is implemented both in Java and C++. Listings 12.1 and 12.2 contain the Java implementations of consumer and supplier, respectively; Listings 12.3 and 12.4 show the corresponding C++ implementations.

Listing 12.1 `PurePullConsumer.java`

```
// Java

import org.omg.CORBA.Any;
import org.omg.CORBA.BooleanHolder;
import org.omg.CORBA.ORB;
import org.omg.CORBA.Policy;
import org.omg.CORBA.SystemException;
import org.omg.CORBA.TCKind;
import org.omg.CosEventChannelAdmin.EventChannel;
import org.omg.CosEventChannelAdmin.EventChannelHelper;
```

Listing 12.1 continued

```
import org.omg.CosEventChannelAdmin.ProxyPullSupplier;
import org.omg.CosEventChannelAdmin.ConsumerAdmin;
import org.omg.CosEventComm.Disconnected;
import org.omg.CosEventComm.PullSupplier;
import org.omg.CosEventComm.PullConsumerPOA;
import org.omg.PortableServer.LifespanPolicyValue;
import org.omg.PortableServer.POA;
import org.omg.PortableServer.POAHelper;
import org.omg.PortableServer.POAManager;

public class PurePullConsumer extends PullConsumerPOA {

    private POA _poa;
    PullSupplier _pullSupplier;

    public PurePullConsumer(PullSupplier pullSupplier, POA poa) {

        _pullSupplier = pullSupplier;
        _poa = poa;
    }

    public void start() throws InterruptedException {

        Any anyVal = null;
        long longVal;
        short shortVal;
        double doubleVal;
        String stringVal;
        boolean hasEvent = false;
        BooleanHolder hasEventHolder = new BooleanHolder();

        System.out.println("Consumer in start of thread, sleeping...");
        Thread.currentThread().sleep(2000);
        while (true) {
            try {
                while (!hasEvent) {
                    Thread.currentThread().sleep(1000);
                    System.out.println("Consumer calling try_pull");
                    try {
                        anyVal = _pullSupplier.try_pull(hasEventHolder);
                        hasEvent = hasEventHolder.value;
                    } catch (SystemException se) {
                        System.err.println("Consumer caught CORBA " +
                                "SystemException: " + se);
                        return;
                    }
                }
```

Listing 12.1 continued

```
                System.out.println("Consumer got event");
                TCKind kind = anyVal.type().kind();
                if (kind == TCKind.tk_long) {
                    longVal = anyVal.extract_long();
                    System.out.println("Consumer pulled long: " +
                            longVal);
                    if (longVal == 13) {
                        System.out.println("Consumer received #13, " +
                                "exiting...");
                        _pullSupplier.disconnect_pull_supplier();
                        return;
                    }
                } else if (kind == TCKind.tk_short) {
                    shortVal = anyVal.extract_short();
                    System.out.println("Consumer pulled short: " +
                            shortVal);
                } else if (kind == TCKind.tk_double) {
                    doubleVal = anyVal.extract_double();
                    System.out.println("Consumer pulled double: " +
                            doubleVal);
                } else if (kind == TCKind.tk_string) {
                    stringVal = anyVal.extract_string();
                    System.out.println("Consumer pulled string: " +
                            stringVal);
                 }
                 hasEvent = false;
            } catch (Disconnected d) {
                System.err.println("Consumer caught Disconnected " +
                        "Exception");
                return;
            }
        }
    }

    public void disconnect_pull_consumer() {

        System.out.println("PurePullConsumer." +
                "disconnect_pull_consumer()");

        try {
            byte[] objId = "PurePullConsumer".getBytes();
            _poa.deactivate_object(objId);
        } catch (Exception e) {
            System.err.println(e);
```

Listing 12.1 continued

```
        }
    }

    public static void main(String[] args) {

        try {
            // initialize the ORB
            ORB orb = ORB.init(args, null);

            // 1. The client (Supplier or Consumer) first binds to the
            // Event Channel (which must be created by someone already,
            // perhaps the client itself).
            org.omg.CORBA.Object obj = orb.
                    resolve_initial_references("EventService");
            EventChannel eventChannel = EventChannelHelper.narrow(obj);
            if (eventChannel == null) {
                System.err.println("could not find EventChannel");
                return;
            }
            System.out.println("found the EventChannel");

            // 2. The client obtains an Admin object from the Event
            // Channel. A Consumer needs a ConsumerAdmin object, and a
            // Supplier needs a SupplierAdmin object.
            ConsumerAdmin consumerAdmin = eventChannel.for_consumers();

            // 3. The client obtains a proxy object from the Admin
            // object (a Consumer Proxy for a Supplier client, and a
            // Supplier Proxy for a Consumer client).
            ProxyPullSupplier proxySupplier = consumerAdmin.
                    obtain_pull_supplier();
            System.out.println("got a ProxyPullSupplier");

            // obtain a reference to the Root POA
            obj = orb.resolve_initial_references("RootPOA");
            POA rootPOA = POAHelper.narrow(obj);

            // create the policies for the push supplier POA
            Policy[] policies = new Policy[1];
            policies[0] = rootPOA.
                    create_lifespan_policy(LifespanPolicyValue.
                    PERSISTENT);

            // create the push supplier POA
            POAManager poaManager = rootPOA.the_POAManager();
```

Listing 12.1 continued

```
            POA consumerPOA = rootPOA.create_POA("PullConsumerPOA",
                    poaManager, policies);

            // create and activate the push supplier
            PurePullConsumer pullConsumer = new
                    PurePullConsumer(proxySupplier, consumerPOA);
            String consumerName = "PurePullConsumer";
            byte[] objId = consumerName.getBytes();
            consumerPOA.activate_object_with_id(objId,  pullConsumer);
            consumerPOA.the_POAManager().activate();
            consumerPOA.servant_to_reference(pullConsumer);

            // 4. The client adds the Supplier or Consumer to the Event
            // Channel via a connect() call.
            proxySupplier.connect_pull_consumer(pullConsumer._this());

            // 5. The client and/or the Event Channel transfer data via
            // the push(), pull(), and/or try_pull() calls.
            pullConsumer.start();

            System.out.println("Consumer is ending");
        } catch (Exception e) {
            System.err.println(e);
        }
    }
}
```

Listing 12.2 **PurePushSupplier.java**

```
// Java

import org.omg.CORBA.Any;
import org.omg.CORBA.ORB;
import org.omg.CORBA.Policy;
import org.omg.CORBA.SystemException;
import org.omg.CosEventChannelAdmin.EventChannel;
import org.omg.CosEventChannelAdmin.EventChannelHelper;
import org.omg.CosEventChannelAdmin.ProxyPushConsumer;
import org.omg.CosEventChannelAdmin.SupplierAdmin;
import org.omg.CosEventComm.Disconnected;
import org.omg.CosEventComm.PushConsumer;
import org.omg.CosEventComm.PushSupplierPOA;
import org.omg.PortableServer.LifespanPolicyValue;
import org.omg.PortableServer.POA;
```

Listing 12.2 continued

```
import org.omg.PortableServer.POAHelper;
import org.omg.PortableServer.POAManager;

public class PurePushSupplier extends PushSupplierPOA {

    private ORB _orb;
    private POA _poa;
    private PushConsumer _pushConsumer;

    public PurePushSupplier(PushConsumer pushConsumer, ORB orb, POA poa)
            {

        _pushConsumer = pushConsumer;
        _orb = orb;
        _poa = poa;
    }

    public void start() throws Disconnected, InterruptedException {

        Any any = _orb.create_any();

        // push some events to the channel

        any.insert_long(555555555);
        _pushConsumer.push(any);
        System.out.println("Supplier: just pushed a long value");
        Thread.currentThread().sleep(1000);

        any.insert_short((short)100);
        _pushConsumer.push(any);
        System.out.println("Supplier: just pushed a short value");

        any.insert_double(999999.999999);
        _pushConsumer.push(any);
        System.out.println("Supplier: just pushed a double value");

        any.insert_string("And the ubiquitous Hello World!");
        _pushConsumer.push(any);
        System.out.println("Supplier: just pushed a string");
        Thread.currentThread().sleep(5000);

        any.insert_long(13);
        _pushConsumer.push(any);

        _pushConsumer.disconnect_push_consumer();
    }
```

Listing 12.2 continued

```
public void disconnect_push_supplier() {

    System.out.println("PurePushSupplier." +
            "disconnect_push_supplier()");

    try {
        byte[] objId = "PurePushSupplier".getBytes();
        _poa.deactivate_object(objId);
    } catch (Exception e) {
        System.out.println(e);
    }
}

public static void main(String[] args) {

    try {
        // initialize the ORB
        ORB orb = ORB.init(args, null);

        // 1. The client (Supplier or Consumer) first binds to the
        // Event Channel (which must be created by someone already,
        // perhaps the client itself).
        org.omg.CORBA.Object obj = orb.
                resolve_initial_references("EventService");
        EventChannel eventChannel = EventChannelHelper.narrow(obj);
        if (eventChannel == null) {
            System.err.println("could not find EventChannel");
            return;
        }
        System.out.println("found the EventChannel");

        // 2. The client obtains an Admin object from the Event
        // Channel. A Consumer needs a ConsumerAdmin object, and a
        // Supplier needs a SupplierAdmin object.
        SupplierAdmin supplierAdmin = eventChannel.for_suppliers();

        // 3. The client obtains a proxy object from the Admin
        // object (a Consumer Proxy for a Supplier client, and a
        // Supplier Proxy for a Consumer client).
        ProxyPushConsumer proxyConsumer = supplierAdmin.
                obtain_push_consumer();
        System.out.println("got a ProxyPushConsumer");

        // obtain a reference to the Root POA
        obj = orb.resolve_initial_references("RootPOA");
        POA rootPOA = POAHelper.narrow(obj);
```

Listing 12.2 continued

```
            // create the policies for the push supplier POA
            Policy[] policies = new Policy[1];
            policies[0] = rootPOA.
                    create_lifespan_policy(LifespanPolicyValue.
                    PERSISTENT);

            // create the push supplier POA
            POAManager poaManager = rootPOA.the_POAManager();
            POA supplierPOA = rootPOA.create_POA("pushSupplierPOA",
                    poaManager, policies);

            // create and activate the push supplier
            PurePushSupplier  pushSupplier = new
                    PurePushSupplier(proxyConsumer, orb, supplierPOA);
            String supplierName = "PurePushSupplier";
            byte[] objId = supplierName.getBytes();
            supplierPOA.activate_object_with_id(objId, pushSupplier);
            supplierPOA.the_POAManager().activate();
            supplierPOA.servant_to_reference(pushSupplier);

            // 4. The client adds the Supplier or Consumer to the Event
            // Channel via a connect() call.
            proxyConsumer.connect_push_supplier(pushSupplier. _this());

            // 5. The client and/or the Event Channel transfer data via
            // the push(), pull(), and/or try_pull() calls.
            pushSupplier.start();

            System.out.println("Supplier is ending");
        } catch (Exception e) {
            System.err.println(e);
        }
    }
}
```

Listing 12.3 **PurePullConsumer.C**

```
// C++

#include <unistd.h>
#include <iostream.h>
#include <iomanip.h>
#include <corba.h>
#include <CosEventComm_s.hh>
#include <CosEventChannelAdmin_c.hh>
```

Listing 12.3 continued

```
class PurePullConsumer : public POA_CosEventComm::PullConsumer {

public:
    PurePullConsumer(CosEventComm::PullSupplier_ptr pullSupplier,
            PortableServer::POA_ptr poa) : _pullSupplier(pullSupplier),
            _poa(poa) { }

    void start() {

        CORBA::Any* anyVal;
        CORBA::ULong longVal;
        CORBA::Short shortVal;
        CORBA::Double doubleVal;
        char* stringVal;
        CORBA::Boolean hasEvent = 0;

        cout << "Consumer in start of thread, sleeping..." << endl;
        sleep(2);
        while (1) {
            try {
                while (!hasEvent) {
                    sleep(1);
                    cout << "Consumer calling try_pull" << endl;
                    try {
                        anyVal = _pullSupplier->try_pull(hasEvent);
                    } catch (const CORBA::Exception& e) {
                        cerr << "Consumer caught CORBA::Exception: " <<
                                e << endl;
                        return;
                    }
                }
                cout << "Consumer got event" << endl;
                if (*anyVal >>= longVal) {
                    cout << "Consumer pulled long: " << longVal << endl;
                    if (longVal == 13) {
                        cout << "Consumer received #13, exiting..." <<
                                endl;
                        _pullSupplier->disconnect_pull_supplier();
                        return;
                    }
                } else if (*anyVal >>= shortVal) {
                    cout << "Consumer pulled short: " << shortVal <<
                            endl;
                } else if (*anyVal >>= doubleVal) {
                    cout << setiosflags(ios::fixed);
                    cout << "Consumer: pulled double: " << doubleVal <<
                            endl;
```

Listing 12.3 continued

```
                } else if (*anyVal >>= stringVal) {
                    cout << "Consumer: pulled string: " << stringVal <<
                            endl;
                    CORBA::string_free(stringVal);
                }
                hasEvent = 0;
            } catch (const CosEventComm::Disconnected& e) {
                cerr << "Consumer caught Disconnected Exception" <<
                        endl;
                return;
            } catch (const CORBA::Exception& e) {
                cerr << "Consumer caught CORBA::Exception: " << e <<
                        endl;
                return;
            }
        }
    }

    void disconnect_pull_consumer() {

        cout << "PurePullConsumer::disconnect_pull_consumer()" << endl;

        try {
            PortableServer::ObjectId_var objId = PortableServer::
                    string_to_ObjectId("PurePullConsumer");
            _poa->deactivate_object(objId);
        } catch (const CORBA::Exception& e) {
            cout << e << endl;
        }
    }

private:
    PortableServer::POA_var _poa;
    CosEventComm::PullSupplier_var _pullSupplier;
};

int main(int argc, char** argv) {

    // initialize the ORB
    CORBA::ORB_var orb = CORBA::ORB_init(argc, argv);

    // 1. The client (Supplier or Consumer) first binds to the Event
    // Channel (which must be created by someone already, perhaps the
    // client itself).
    CORBA::Object_var obj = orb->
            resolve_initial_references("EventService");
```

Listing 12.3 continued

```
CosEventChannelAdmin::EventChannel_var eventChannel =
        CosEventChannelAdmin::EventChannel::_narrow(obj);
if (eventChannel == NULL) {
    cerr << "could not find EventChannel" << endl;
    return -1;
}
cout << "found the EventChannel" << endl;

// 2. The client obtains an Admin object from the Event Channel. A
// Consumer needs a ConsumerAdmin object, and a Supplier needs a
// SupplierAdmin object.
CosEventChannelAdmin::ConsumerAdmin_var consumerAdmin =
        eventChannel->for_consumers();

// 3. The client obtains a proxy object from the Admin object (a
// Consumer Proxy for a Supplier client, and a Supplier Proxy for a
// Consumer client).
CosEventChannelAdmin::ProxyPullSupplier_var proxySupplier =
        consumerAdmin->obtain_pull_supplier();
cout << "got a ProxyPullSupplier" << endl;

// obtain a reference to the Root POA
obj = orb->resolve_initial_references("RootPOA");
PortableServer::POA_var rootPOA = PortableServer::POA::_narrow(obj);

// create the policies for the push supplier POA
CORBA::PolicyList policies;
policies.length(1);
policies[0] = rootPOA->create_lifespan_policy(PortableServer::
        PERSISTENT);

// create the push supplier POA
PortableServer::POAManager_var poaManager = rootPOA->
        the_POAManager();
PortableServer::POA_var consumerPOA = rootPOA->
        create_POA("PullConsumerPOA", poaManager, policies);

// create and activate the push supplier
PurePullConsumer* pullConsumer = new PurePullConsumer(proxySupplier,
        consumerPOA);
CORBA::String_var consumerName(CORBA::
        string_dup("PurePullConsumer"));
PortableServer::ObjectId_var objId = PortableServer::
        string_to_ObjectId(consumerName);
consumerPOA->activate_object_with_id(objId, pullConsumer);
```

Listing 12.3 continued

```
    consumerPOA->the_POAManager()->activate();
    consumerPOA->servant_to_reference(pullConsumer);

    // 4. The client adds the Supplier or Consumer to the Event Channel
    // via a connect() call.
    proxySupplier->connect_pull_consumer(pullConsumer->_this());

    // 5. The client and/or the Event Channel transfer data via the\
    // push(), pull(), and/or try_pull() calls.
    pullConsumer->start();

    cout << "Consumer is ending" << endl;
    return 0;
}
```

Listing 12.4 **PurePushSupplier.C**

```
// C++

#include <unistd.h>
#include <iostream.h>
#include <corba.h>
#include <CosEventComm_s.hh>
#include <CosEventChannelAdmin_c.hh>

class PurePushSupplier : public POA_CosEventComm::PushSupplier {

public:
    PurePushSupplier(CosEventComm::PushConsumer_ptr pushConsumer,
            PortableServer::POA_ptr poa) : _pushConsumer(pushConsumer),
            _poa(poa) { }

    void start() {

        CORBA::Any any;

        // push some events to the channel

        any <<= (CORBA::ULong)555555555;
        _pushConsumer->push(any);
        cout << "Supplier: just pushed a long value" << endl;
        sleep(1);

        any <<= (CORBA::Short)100;
        _pushConsumer->push(any);
        cout << "Supplier: just pushed a short value" << endl;
```

Listing 12.4 continued

```
        any <<= (CORBA::Double)999999.999999;
        _pushConsumer->push(any);
        cout << "Supplier: just pushed a double value" << endl;

        CORBA::String_var str = CORBA::string_dup("And the ubiquitous "
                "Hello World!");
        any <<= str;
        _pushConsumer->push(any);
        cout << "Supplier: just pushed a string" << endl;
        sleep(5);

        any <<= (CORBA::ULong)13;
        _pushConsumer->push(any);

        _pushConsumer->disconnect_push_consumer();
    }

    void disconnect_push_supplier() {

        cout << "PurePushSupplier::disconnect_push_supplier()" << endl;

        try {
            PortableServer::ObjectId_var objId = PortableServer::
                    string_to_ObjectId("PurePushSupplier");
            _poa->deactivate_object(objId);
        } catch (const CORBA::Exception& e) {
            cout << e << endl;
        }
    }

private:
    PortableServer::POA_var _poa;
    CosEventComm::PushConsumer_var _pushConsumer;
};

int main(int argc, char** argv) {

    // initialize the ORB
    CORBA::ORB_var orb = CORBA::ORB_init(argc, argv);

    // 1. The client (Supplier or Consumer) first binds to the Event
    // Channel (which must be created by someone already, perhaps the
    // client itself).
    CORBA::Object_var obj = orb->
            resolve_initial_references("EventService");
    CosEventChannelAdmin::EventChannel_var eventChannel =
            CosEventChannelAdmin::EventChannel::_narrow(obj);
```

Listing 12.4 continued

```
if (eventChannel == NULL) {
    cerr << "could not find EventChannel" << endl;
    return -1;
}
cout << "found the EventChannel" << endl;

// 2. The client obtains an Admin object from the Event Channel. A
// Consumer needs a ConsumerAdmin object, and a Supplier needs a
// SupplierAdmin object.
CosEventChannelAdmin::SupplierAdmin_var supplierAdmin =
        eventChannel->for_suppliers();

// 3. The client obtains a proxy object from the Admin object (a
// Consumer Proxy for a Supplier client, and a Supplier Proxy for a
// Consumer client).
CosEventChannelAdmin::ProxyPushConsumer_var proxyConsumer =
        supplierAdmin->obtain_push_consumer();
cout << "got a ProxyPushConsumer" << endl;

// obtain a reference to the Root POA
obj = orb->resolve_initial_references("RootPOA");
PortableServer::POA_var rootPOA = PortableServer::POA::_narrow(obj);

// create the policies for the push supplier POA
CORBA::PolicyList policies;
policies.length(1);
policies[0] = rootPOA->create_lifespan_policy(PortableServer::
        PERSISTENT);

// create the push supplier POA
PortableServer::POAManager_var poaManager = rootPOA->
        the_POAManager();
PortableServer::POA_var supplierPOA = rootPOA->
        create_POA("pushSupplierPOA", poaManager, policies);

// create and activate the push supplier
PurePushSupplier* pushSupplier = new PurePushSupplier(proxyConsumer,
        supplierPOA);
CORBA::String_var supplierName(CORBA::
        string_dup("PurePushSupplier"));
PortableServer::ObjectId_var objId = PortableServer::
        string_to_ObjectId(supplierName);
supplierPOA->activate_object_with_id(objId, pushSupplier);
supplierPOA->the_POAManager()->activate();
supplierPOA->servant_to_reference(pushSupplier);

// 4. The client adds the Supplier or Consumer to the Event Channel
// via a connect() call.
```

Listing 12.4 continued

```
    proxyConsumer->connect_push_supplier(pushSupplier->_this());

    // 5. The client and/or the Event Channel transfer data via the
    // push(), pull(), and/or try_pull() calls.
    pushSupplier->start();

    cout << "Supplier is ending" << endl;
    return 0;
}
```

In the first step, the client (Consumer or Supplier) must bind to the Event Channel, which is assumed to have been created already. This is accomplished by calling `resolve_initial_references()` with the string `"EventService"` as a parameter. For the Event Service, the object returned from `resolve_initial_references()` will be an instance of an `EventChannel`. This is performed as follows in Java (assuming the ORB has already been initialized):

```
// Java
org.omg.CORBA.Object obj = orb.resolve_initial_references("EventService");
EventChannel eventChannel = EventChannelHelper.narrow(obj);
if (eventChannel == null) {
    System.err.println("could not find EventChannel");
    return;
}
System.out.println("found the EventChannel");
```

and in C++ as follows:

```
// C++
CORBA::Object_var obj = orb->resolve_initial_references("EventService");
CosEventChannelAdmin::EventChannel_var eventChannel = CosEventChannelAdmin::
        EventChannel::_narrow(obj);
if (eventChannel == NULL) {
    cerr << "could not find EventChannel" << endl;
    return -1;
}
cout << "found the EventChannel" << endl;
```

NOTE

Although the ORB provides a standard mechanism for application code to obtain a reference to certain standard CORBA services such as the Event Service, the standard does not specify how the ORB is to determine what instance of the Event Service to use. It is up to the specific ORB implementation to provide a mechanism for mapping, for example, the "EventService" initial reference to an actual object reference. Typically, this is accomplished through the use of properties, command line arguments, or configuration files.

Implementing a Consumer

Once a reference to the Event Channel has been obtained, the Event Channel object (the eventChannel variable in the example) is used to obtain a reference to a ConsumerAdmin object through the for_consumers() function. The ConsumerAdmin object provides the proxies for the Consumer clients of the Event Channel. It enables the Consumer to obtain the appropriate Supplier Proxy. In this case, the ConsumerAdmin object provides the Pull Consumer with a proxy Pull Supplier. This enables the Consumer object to act as if it were communicating directly with a Supplier that expects the Consumer to be "pulling" events from it. Of course, that's not actually the case. The Supplier is really a Push Supplier that itself pushes events onto the Event Channel. The proxies decouple the Consumer and Supplier objects and enable them to function as if they were directly connected, when in fact their connection is entirely indirect. Once the ConsumerAdmin is obtained, it is used to create the Pull Supplier Proxy, as shown in the following example:

```
// Java
ConsumerAdmin consumerAdmin = eventChannel.for_consumers();
ProxyPullSupplier proxySupplier = consumerAdmin.obtain_pull_supplier();
System.out.println("got a ProxyPullSupplier");

// C++
CosEventChannelAdmin::ConsumerAdmin_var consumerAdmin = eventChannel->
        for_consumers();
CosEventChannelAdmin::ProxyPullSupplier_var proxySupplier =
        consumerAdmin->obtain_pull_supplier();
cout << "got a ProxyPullSupplier" << endl;
```

Once the Consumer has obtained a reference to its Supplier Proxy, it then notifies the Event Channel of its interest in receiving events from it through a call to the Proxy's connect_pull_consumer() method. An implementation of the Event Service's Pull Consumer interface (the creation of this implementation is not shown here) is passed into the proxy_supplier to make the connection.

```
// Java
proxySupplier.connect_pull_consumer(pullConsumer._this());

// C++
proxySupplier->connect_pull_consumer(pullConsumer->_this());
```

Once connected, calls can be made on the Proxy Pull Supplier's pull() or try_pull() functions. The interface for the PullSupplier is shown here:

```
// IDL
interface PullSupplier  {
    any pull() raises(Disconnected);
    any try_pull(out boolean has_event) raises(Disconnected);
    void disconnect_pull_supplier();
};
```

In this case, the Consumer's main thread makes the `try_pull()` call. The `try_pull()` call is an asynchronous polling mechanism that enables the Consumer to contact the Event Channel and "check for mail," so to speak. If there is a message in the Event Channel, that message will be returned as a `CORBA::Any` value, and the `try_pull()`'s `CORBA::Boolean` flag `hasEvent` will be set to true. The `try_pull()` call is thus made from within the Consumer's `start()` method (the `_pullSupplier` variable contains a reference to the `ProxyPullSupplier` obtained earlier):

```
// Java
Any anyVal = null;
BooleanHolder hasEventHolder = new BooleanHolder();
...
anyVal = _pullSupplier.try_pull(hasEventHolder);
hasEvent = hasEventHolder.value;

// C++
CORBA::Any* anyVal;
CORBA::Boolean hasEvent = 0;
...
anyVal = _pullSupplier->try_pull(hasEvent);
```

If there is no event waiting, the `hasEvent` flag is set to false and no value is returned. The call does not block (as the `pull()` function does); it returns to the client immediately. This enables the client to continue doing other work while periodically checking to see if a new event message is waiting in the Event Channel's queue.

Once the `hasEvent` value is true and an `Any` value is retrieved, the Consumer must decide first what type it is and then extract that value from the `Any` wrapper in order to use it. (The `Any` type is discussed in great detail in Chapter 8). For the purposes of this example, the value is extracted from the `Any` as follows:

```
// Java
TCKind kind = anyVal.type().kind();
if (kind == TCKind.tk_short) {
    shortVal = anyVal.extract_short();
    System.out.println("Consumer pulled short: " + shortVal);
} else if (kind == TCKind.tk_double) {
    doubleVal = anyVal.extract_double();
    System.out.println("Consumer pulled double: " + doubleVal);
}

// C++
if (*anyVal >>= shortVal) {
    cout << "Consumer pulled short: " << shortVal << endl;
} else if (*anyVal >>= doubleVal) {
    cout << setiosflags(ios::fixed);
    cout << "Consumer: pulled double: " << doubleVal << endl;
}
```

In this case, when the Consumer extracts the correct type from the Any, it prints its value out and immediately begins again checking for events through the try_pull() call.

Implementing a Supplier

The Supplier implementation is a bit simpler. After binding to the ORB, it creates an implementation of a class that implements the CORBA PushSupplier IDL:

```
// Java
public class PurePushSupplier extends PushSupplierPOA {
    public PurePushSupplier(PushConsumer pushConsumer, ORB orb, POA poa)
            {
        ...
    }
    ...
    public void disconnect_push_supplier() {
        ...
    }
}

// (creation of proxy consumer and appropriate POA precedes)
PurePushSupplier  pushSupplier = new PurePushSupplier(proxyConsumer,
        orb, supplierPOA);
// (activation of servant follows)

// C++
class PurePushSupplier : public POA_CosEventComm::PushSupplier {
    ...
    void disconnect_push_supplier();
};

// (creation of proxy consumer and appropriate POA precedes)
PurePushSupplier* pushSupplier = new PurePushSupplier(proxyConsumer,
        supplierPOA);
// (activation of servant follows)
```

This class implements the IDL PushSupplier interface, which only has a single function to implement: disconnect_push_supplier(). The pushSupplier servant will be used later to connect to the Event Channel and register its interest in supplying events to the Channel.

Just as the Consumer started by locating the Event Service, our Supplier begins by calling resolve_initial_references(). Using the IOR returned by resolve_initial_references(), the Supplier can then narrow to the EventChannel object. The mechanism for doing so is exactly the same as in the Consumer. Once a reference to the EventChannel is obtained, the Supplier attempts to retrieve a SupplierAdmin object through a call to the event channel's for_suppliers() function:

```
// Java
SupplierAdmin supplierAdmin = eventChannel.for_suppliers();

// C++
CosEventChannelAdmin::SupplierAdmin_var supplierAdmin = eventChannel->
        for_suppliers();
```

Once the SupplierAdmin object is retrieved, its obtain_push_consumer() function is called in order for the Supplier to obtain a Proxy PushConsumer with which to communicate.

```
// Java
ProxyPushConsumer proxyConsumer = supplierAdmin.obtain_push_consumer();

// C++
CosEventChannelAdmin::ProxyPushConsumer_var proxyConsumer =
        supplierAdmin->obtain_push_consumer();
```

Once a proxy is obtained, the Supplier then needs to connect to the proxy through this call:

```
// Java
proxyConsumer.connect_push_supplier(pushSupplier._this());

// C++
proxyConsumer->connect_push_supplier(pushSupplier->_this());
```

This call registers the Supplier's interest in providing the Event Channel with events. The IDL interface for the PushConsumer (from which ProxyPushConsumer inherits) is

```
// IDL
interface PushConsumer {
    void push(in any data) raises(Disconnected);
    void disconnect_push_consumer();
};
```

Once a proxy push Consumer has been obtained, calls may be made on its push() function, passing in a CORBA::Any value. That is done quite simply:

```
// Java
Any any = _orb.create_any();
any.insert_long(555555555);
_pushConsumer.push(any);

// C++
CORBA::Any any;
any <<= (CORBA::ULong)555555555;
_pushConsumer->push(any);
```

At this point, the `Any` value is delivered to the Event Channel, which is responsible for making that event message available to the `try_pull()` calls of the Consumer, which was described above. Thus, the discussion of the Supplier/Consumer roles in interacting with the Event Service has come full circle.

When the Consumer and Supplier executables are run, the progress of the Supplier writing messages to the Event Channel will be visible. Also, the Consumer can be seen extracting the messages from the Event Channel and printing out their contents. The Supplier pushes, in succession, a `long`, a `short`, a `double`, a `string`, and finally, another `long` (the number 13), which signals to the Consumer that it is finished. At that point, the Consumer thread terminates and both applications exit.

Summary

This chapter introduced the CORBA Events Service. This service realizes the well-known Mediator pattern, which decouples two objects for which direct knowledge of each other is undesirable. In this case, it is preferred that suppliers and consumers of events should not have direct knowledge of each other. Hence the concept of an Event Channel, which mediates the relationship between suppliers and consumers, was introduced.

The chapter then demonstrated that the CORBA Events Service defines two types each of suppliers and consumers: both push and pull. A Push Supplier pushes events asynchronously to the Event Channel; similarly, a Push Consumer receives events asynchronously from the Event Channel. Conversely, a Pull Supplier is periodically polled by the Event Channel for events; a Pull Consumer likewise periodically polls the Event Channel for events.

Finally, the actual use of the Event Channel was discussed, including the implementation of consumers and suppliers. The actual events themselves are realized as `CORBA::Any` values, and thus may contain any data type that can be expressed in IDL.

Listings 12.5–8 contain the IDL definitions for the Event Service, as defined by the OMG, provided here for reference. Listing 12.5 contains the definitions for the administration interfaces and the event channel itself, as well as for the proxy consumers and suppliers. (These interfaces are typically implemented by the vendor of an Event Service implementation.) Listing 12.6 contains the definitions for consumers and suppliers, which are typically implemented by users of the Event Service. Listings 12.7 and 12.8 contain similar definitions again, but for typed event channels.

Listing 12.5 **`CosEventChannelAdmin.idl`**

```
// IDL

//File: CosEventChannelAdmin.idl
//Part of the Event Service
```

Listing 12.5 continued

```
#ifndef _COS_EVENT_CHANNEL_ADMIN_IDL_
#define _COS_EVENT_CHANNEL_ADMIN_IDL_

#include <CosEventComm.idl>

#pragma prefix "omg.org"

module CosEventChannelAdmin {

    exception AlreadyConnected {};
    exception TypeError {};

    interface ProxyPushConsumer: CosEventComm::PushConsumer {
        void connect_push_supplier(
                in CosEventComm::PushSupplier push_supplier)
            raises(AlreadyConnected);
    };

    interface ProxyPullSupplier: CosEventComm::PullSupplier {
        void connect_pull_consumer(
                in CosEventComm::PullConsumer pull_consumer)
            raises(AlreadyConnected);
    };

    interface ProxyPullConsumer: CosEventComm::PullConsumer {
        void connect_pull_supplier(
                in CosEventComm::PullSupplier pull_supplier)
            raises(AlreadyConnected,TypeError);
    };

    interface ProxyPushSupplier: CosEventComm::PushSupplier {
        void connect_push_consumer(
                in CosEventComm::PushConsumer push_consumer)
            raises(AlreadyConnected, TypeError);

    };

    interface ConsumerAdmin {
        ProxyPushSupplier obtain_push_supplier();
        ProxyPullSupplier obtain_pull_supplier();
    };

    interface SupplierAdmin {
        ProxyPushConsumer obtain_push_consumer();
        ProxyPullConsumer obtain_pull_consumer();
    };
```

Listing 12.5 continued

```
    interface EventChannel {
        ConsumerAdmin for_consumers();
        SupplierAdmin for_suppliers();
        void destroy();
    };
};
#endif /* ifndef _COS_EVENT_CHANNEL_ADMIN_IDL_ */
```

Listing 12.6 **CosEventComm.idl**

```
// IDL

//File: CosEventComm.idl
//Part of the Event Service

#ifndef _COS_EVENT_COMM_IDL_
#define _COS_EVENT_COMM_IDL_
#pragma prefix "omg.org"

module CosEventComm {

    exception Disconnected{};

    interface PushConsumer {
        void push (in any data) raises(Disconnected);
        void disconnect_push_consumer();
    };

    interface PushSupplier {
        void disconnect_push_supplier();
    };

    interface PullSupplier {
        any pull () raises(Disconnected);
        any try_pull (out boolean has_event)
            raises(Disconnected);
        void disconnect_pull_supplier();
    };

    interface PullConsumer {
        void disconnect_pull_consumer();
    };

};
#endif /* ifndef _COS_EVENT_COMM_IDL_ */
```

Listing 12.7 **CosTypedEventChannelAdmin.idl**

```
// IDL

//File: CosTypedEventChannelAdmin.idl
//Part of the Event Service
//Updated to reflect version 1.1 - March 2001

#ifndef _COS_TYPED_EVENT_CHANNEL_ADMIN_IDL_
#define _COS_TYPED_EVENT_CHANNEL_ADMIN_IDL_

#include <CosEventChannelAdmin.idl>
#include <CosTypedEventComm.idl>

#pragma prefix "omg.org"

module CosTypedEventChannelAdmin {

    exception InterfaceNotSupported {};
    exception NoSuchImplementation {};
    typedef string Key;                             //Repository ID

    interface TypedProxyPushConsumer :
            CosEventChannelAdmin::ProxyPushConsumer,
            CosTypedEventComm::TypedPushConsumer  { };

    interface TypedProxyPullSupplier :
             CosEventChannelAdmin::ProxyPullSupplier,
            CosTypedEventComm::TypedPullSupplier { };

    interface TypedSupplierAdmin :
            CosEventChannelAdmin::SupplierAdmin {
        TypedProxyPushConsumer obtain_typed_push_consumer(
                 in Key supported_interface)
            raises(InterfaceNotSupported);
        CosEventChannelAdmin::ProxyPullConsumer obtain_typed_pull_consumer (
                in Key uses_interface)
             raises(NoSuchImplementation);
    };

    interface TypedConsumerAdmin :
            CosEventChannelAdmin::ConsumerAdmin {
        TypedProxyPullSupplier obtain_typed_pull_supplier(
                in Key supported_interface)
            raises (InterfaceNotSupported);
        CosEventChannelAdmin::ProxyPushSupplier obtain_typed_push_supplier(
                in Key uses_interface)
```

Listing 12.7 continued

```
            raises(NoSuchImplementation);
    };

    interface TypedEventChannel {
        TypedConsumerAdmin for_consumers();
        TypedSupplierAdmin for_suppliers();
        void destroy ();
    };
};

#endif /* ifndef _COS_TYPED_EVENT_CHANNEL_ADMIN_IDL_ */
```

Listing 12.8 **CosTypedEventComm.idl**

```
// IDL

//File: CosTypedEventComm.idl
//Part of the Event Service

#ifndef _COS_TYPED_EVENT_COMM_IDL_
#define _COS_TYPED_EVENT_COMM_IDL_

#include <CosEventComm.idl>

#pragma prefix "omg.org"

module CosTypedEventComm {

    interface TypedPushConsumer : CosEventComm::PushConsumer {
        Object get_typed_consumer();
    };

    interface TypedPullSupplier : CosEventComm::PullSupplier {
        Object get_typed_supplier();
    };

};

#endif /* ifndef _COS_TYPED_EVENT_COMM_IDL_ */
```

CHAPTER 13

CORBA Components

A *CORBA component* is an extension of a CORBA object, which is based on a different server programming model. The *CORBA Component Model (CCM)* is the framework for defining, implementing, and deploying CORBA components. It addresses all the stages of application development, from the design of components to the deployment of a component-based application.

The primary purpose of the CCM is to reduce the effort needed to develop and deploy CORBA servers. The CCM simplifies the development of CORBA servers in the following ways:

- **Abstraction of POA functionality** POA functionality is made available to components through a container. A container is responsible for managing the life-cycle of CORBA components, freeing developers from this task.
- **Provision of CORBA services** CORBA services typically required by enterprise applications include security, transactions, and events. The CCM specifies that these services should be made available to components and defines simplified interfaces covering the most commonly used features for the services.
- **Support for ready-made components** The CCM supports the development of reusable, general-purpose CORBA components. A clean separation can be made between the component logic and CORBA functionality.

  The CCM's support for configuration and assembly also makes it easier to integrate ready-made components into a new application.

Consider, for example, the code appearing in Chapter 7, "The Portable Object Adapter." Much of the code is concerned purely with CORBA-related housekeeping tasks—for example, creating POA objects and managing the life-cycle of CORBA objects. From the perspective of an application developer, writing this CORBA-related code is an unwelcome burden that adds nothing to the core business functionality. The CCM eliminates this burden by providing a container with ready-made life-cycle management.

There are many similarities between the CCM and the Enterprise Java Beans (EJB) specification from Sun. This is not accidental—the OMG committee that drafted the CCM specification made a deliberate effort to make the CCM consistent with EJB. To optimize compatibility with EJB, it was necessary to split the CCM into two levels: the *basic level* and the *extended level*.

The basic level contains the elements of the CCM that are fully compatible with EJB. Servers conforming to the basic level of the CCM are fully interoperable with EJB.

The extended level adds elements that have no parallel in EJB. Servers that use features from the extended level might not be compatible with EJB. See the section "Extended Components," later in this chapter, for an outline of the extra features supported at that level.

NOTE

This chapter focuses mainly on the basic level of the CCM, which is fully consistent with EJB.

Basic Architecture

The basic architecture of the CCM is shown in Figure 13.1.

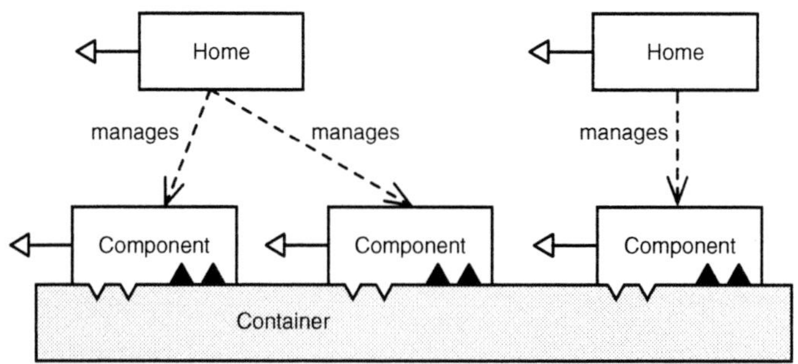

Figure 13.1

The CORBA Component Model architecture.

The architecture consists of the following elements:

- **Components** The basic building blocks for server applications.
- **Component homes** Factory objects that create and manage components.
- **Containers** The environments that support components, enabling them to run.

These basic architectural elements are discussed in the following sections.

Components

There are two types of component:

- **Basic components** These conform to the basic level of the CCM. They are conceptually similar to CORBA objects. Each instance of a component *supports* one or more IDL interfaces (similar to IDL interface inheritance). Application developers implement the component's operations and attributes. The main difference between a basic component and a CORBA object is the context in which each is used. A component is used in the context of the CCM and uses the programming interfaces exposed by the container in which it resides.
- **Extended components** These conform to the extended level of the CCM. They have additional features—ports—that are supported neither by basic components nor CORBA objects. Component ports are described in the section "Extended Components," later in this chapter.
  One noteworthy feature of an extended component is that it can support multiple distinct (unrelated by IDL inheritance) IDL interfaces, known as *facets*. A navigation mechanism is also provided that enables clients of a component to move between facets.

Component Homes

A component home is an object that manages a particular type of component. Every component type is managed by at least one component home type. Conversely, each component home manages one, and only one, component type. For example, a `WasteItemC` component type might be managed by a `WasteItemCH` component home.

A component home typically enables you to perform the following actions on a managed component type:

- Creating instances
- Finding instances
- Removing instances

Component homes are analogous to factory objects, as defined in Chapter 7.

The motivation for introducing component homes is to hide code that manages the life-cycle of components within the server. You may recall from Chapter 7 that the analogous factory code for managing the life-cycle of CORBA objects varies greatly, depending on what kind of life-cycle policy you are implementing.

Using component homes offers the following advantages:

- It frees you from writing the code associated with a component's life-cycle management.
- It insulates the rest of your code from the effect of changing a component's life-cycle management policy.
- It facilitates tools that can automatically generate implementations for component homes.

Containers

A container is the environment in which components are embedded, including interfaces to standard services such as transactions and security. The container is layered above the POA and offers ready-made life-cycle management policies for components. Direct access to POA objects is not allowed, however, because the container layer replaces the POA layer.

There is a two-way interaction between a container and its components:

- **Component-invoking operations on the container** A component can use the services supplied by the container or invoke operations on a `Components::CCMContext` object, which returns details about the context of the current invocation.
- **Container-invoking operations on the component** Every component inherits from a base interface, `Components::SessionComponent` or `Components::EntityComponent`, that defines callback operations for the container to invoke.

A number of IDL interfaces are defined to mediate interaction between the container and its embedded components—see the section "Container Programming Environment," later in this chapter, for details.

Component Categories

The CCM component categories are common patterns for implementing components. An application developer must choose one of the following allowed component categories before starting to implement a component:

- Session
- Service
- Entity
- Process

The following sections describe the basic characteristics of each component category.

Session Components

A session component, which is similar to an EJB stateful session bean, has the following basic characteristics:

- Transient state
- Transient identity
- Cannot participate in an OTS transaction

A session component is typically a temporary object that does some work on behalf of a client. For example, an instance of a particular type of session component is often created for each client that connects to the server. After a client disconnects from the server, its session components are no longer needed and can be discarded.

Service Components

A service component, which is similar to an EJB stateless session bean, has the following basic characteristics:

- No state
- No identity
- Cannot participate in an OTS transaction

A service component—like a session component—is also a temporary object that does some work on behalf of a client. However, a service component is particularly simple because it has no state. It follows that a single service component can service any number of clients.

Entity Components

An entity component, which is similar to an EJB entity bean, has the following basic characteristics:

- Persistent state
- Persistent identity, which is automatically visible to clients
- Can participate in an OTS transaction

An entity component can be used to represent data stored in a database. For example, objects such as customers, products for sale, and so on, could be modelled as entity components. The component container has to manage the entity component's state, loading and saving it as necessary.

Process Components

A process component has the following basic characteristics:

- Persistent state
- Persistent identity, which is *not* automatically visible to clients
- Can participate in an OTS transaction

The main difference between an entity component and a process component is the accessibility of the component identity. A process component does not expose its identity to clients.

A process component is used to represent business processes, such as buying or selling items, where the state of the process needs to be stored persistently or the process has to participate in a distributed transaction. In cases where neither persistence nor distributed transactions are needed, however, a session component can be used instead.

Defining IDL for Components

The first step in developing a component server is to define the components and their associated component homes, using extended IDL. Extended IDL is equivalent to ordinary IDL augmented by syntax that defines components and component homes. Component and component home definitions are introduced by the `component` and `home` IDL keywords, respectively.

There is a close relationship between components and IDL interfaces. In fact, component and component home definitions are mapped to ordinary IDL, *equivalent IDL*, as an intermediate step in the compilation of extended IDL. This compilation process is illustrated in Figure 13.2.

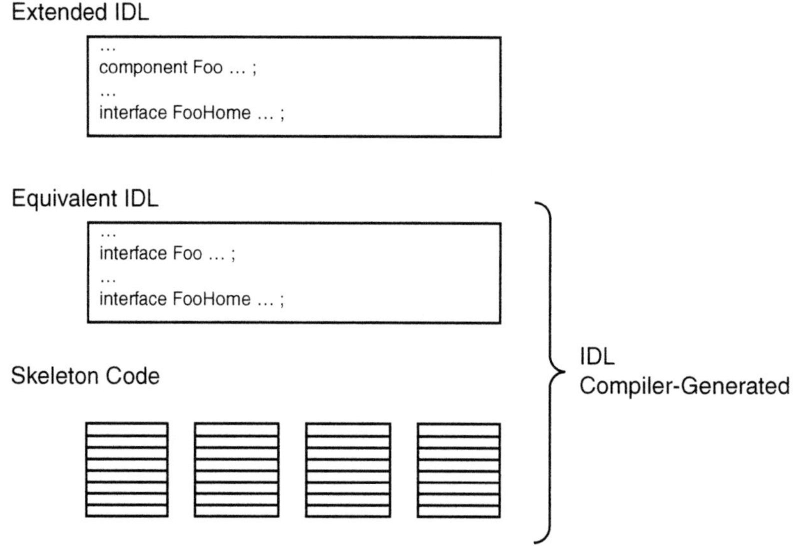

Figure 13.2

Compilation of extended IDL.

Figure 13.2 shows that under IDL compilation the extended IDL is transformed first to equivalent IDL, and then skeleton code is generated from the equivalent IDL. The following sections define the extended IDL syntax for declaring components and component homes. The mapping of the extended IDL to equivalent IDL is also presented.

Basic Component Declarations

Basic components are subject to a number of restrictions:

- Only attribute declarations can appear in the body of a component declaration.
- No other ports can be declared in a basic component (see the section "Extended Components," later in this chapter, for details about ports).
- A basic component cannot inherit from other components.

The following subsections describe the syntax of basic components, within the limits of these restrictions, and the mapping to equivalent IDL.

Basic Component Syntax

In extended IDL, basic components have the syntax shown in Listing 13.1.

Listing 13.1 Syntax for Basic Component Declarations

```
//IDL
component component_name [supports interface1, interface2, ...]
{
    [attribute_declarations]
};
```

The optional `supports` clause is followed by a comma-separated list of ordinary interface names, *`interface1`*, *`interface2`*, and so on. The body of the basic component optionally can contain attribute c declarations.

Extended Attribute Syntax

The syntax of attributes is extended by the CCM to allow attributes to raise CORBA user exceptions. This new syntax is made available both in extended IDL and in ordinary IDL.

Writable attributes have the following IDL syntax:

```
attribute attr_name [getRaises (excG1, excG2, ...)]
                    [setRaises (excS1, excS2, ...)] ;
```

The optional `getRaises` clause specifies the list of CORBA user exceptions that can be raised when the attribute is read. The optional `setRaises` clause specifies the list of CORBA user exceptions that can be raised when the attribute is written.

Read-only attributes have the following IDL syntax:

```
readonly attribute attr_name [getRaises (excG1, excG2, ...)] ;
```

Only the `getRaises` clause can appear in a `readonly attribute` declaration.

Component Example

Consider the `RecycleBroker::WasteItem` IDL interface that was introduced in the Recycle Broker application from Chapter 3, "A Sample CORBA System." To implement the `WasteItem` IDL interface in the CCM, you could declare a component, `RecycleBroker::WasteItemC`, as shown in Listing 13.2.

Listing 13.2 Declaration of the `WasteItemC` Component

```
//IDL
#include "RecycleBroker.idl"

// Re-open the 'RecycleBroker' module...
module RecyleBroker {
    ...
    // Use extended IDL syntax to declare a component.
    component WasteItemC supports WasteItem { };
    ...
};
```

The `WasteItemC` component inherits all of the operations, attributes, and definitions from the `WasteItem` IDL interface.

You can also declare attributes in the body of the component. Typically, such attributes are used for configuration or initialization of the component.

Mapping to Equivalent IDL

The syntax for components, previously shown in Listing 13.1, is mapped to equivalent IDL as shown in Listing 13.3.

Listing 13.3 Equivalent IDL for Basic Component Declarations

```
//IDL
interface component_name : Components::CCMObject, interface1, interface2, ...
{
    [attribute_declarations]
};
```

For example, the result of mapping the `RecycleBroker::WasteItemC` component to equivalent IDL is shown in Listing 13.4.

Listing 13.4 Equivalent IDL for the `WasteItemC` Component

```
//IDL
#include "RecycleBroker.idl"

module RecycleBroker {
    ...
    // Equivalent interface for 'WasteItemC' component
    interface WasteItemC : Components::CCMObject, WasteItem { };
    ...
};
```

Basic Component Home Declarations

The purpose of a component home is to manage a particular component type. Instances of the managed component type are created and destroyed using the component home. Some component homes also provide search operations to find components.

There are two kinds of component home, as follows:

- **Keyfull component homes** are associated with a primary key. A *primary key* is a long-lived, unique identifier for components that are stored persistently.
- **Keyless component homes** are not associated with a primary key.

Primary keys typically are derived from a database key or keys. Although not the same thing, there is an implicit connection between object IDs and primary keys. The container implicitly defines a private map between object IDs and primary keys.

A primary key is declared as a value type in IDL, subject to the following constraints:

- It is declared as a `valuetype` that inherits from `Components::PrimaryKeyBase`.
- All state members must be public.
- There must be at least one state member.
- None of the state members can be object references, nor can any of the state members be data types that contain object references.

The following sections describe the syntax of component homes, both keyfull and keyless, and the mapping to equivalent IDL.

Basic Component Home Syntax

In extended IDL, basic component homes have the syntax shown in Listing 13.5.

Listing 13.5 Syntax for Basic Component Home Declarations

```
//IDL
home home_name [ : base_home_name]
               manages component_name
               [ primaryKey key_type]
{
    [factory_declarations]
    [finder_declarations]
    [operation_declarations]
    [attribute declarations]
};
```

The header of a component home must always specify the component type, *`component_name`*, that it manages and can optionally specify inheritance from another home, *`base_home_name`*, and use of a primary key, *`key_type`*.

The body of a component home optionally can contain factory declarations, finder declarations, and ordinary attribute and operation declarations. The factory and finder declaration syntax is presented in the next section.

Factory and Finder Operation Syntax

Factory operations have the following IDL syntax:

```
factory factory_name(param1, param2, ...) [raises (exc1, exc2, ...)] ;
```

The syntax is similar to that of an ordinary IDL operation except that the keyword, `factory`, appears in place of a return type. The return type of the factory operation is implicitly defined to be the component type managed by the component home.

Finder operations have the following IDL syntax:

```
finder finder_name(param1, param2, ...) [raises (exc1, exc2, ...)] ;
```

The return type of the finder operation is implicitly defined to be the component type managed by the component home.

Example of a Keyless Component Home

A keyless component home is one that omits a `primaryKey` clause in its declaration. It is used to manage components that belong to the session, service, or process component category.

Consider the `RecycleBroker::Buying` IDL interface that was introduced in the Recycle Broker application from Chapter 3. A component, `BuyingC`, and component home, `BuyingCH`, can be declared for the `Buying` IDL interface, as shown in Listing 13.6.

Listing 13.6 Declaration of the `BuyingCH` *Keyless Component Home*

```
//IDL
#include "RecycleBroker.idl"

// Re-open the 'RecycleBroker' module...
module RecyleBroker {
    ...
    // Use extended IDL syntax to declare the 'BuyingC' component.
    component BuyingC         supports Buying { };

    // Use extended IDL syntax to declare the 'BuyingCH' component home.
    home      BuyingCH        manages BuyingC
    {
        // Implicitly defined factory operation:
        // factory create();

        // Explicitly defined operations:
        factory create_from_initial_data(
            KeyType branch_id
        );
    };
    ...
};
```

A keyless component home always has one implicitly defined factory operation, `factory create()`, which takes no arguments.

The factory operation, `create_from_initial_data()`, initializes the state of the `BuyingC` component with the identity of the ACME Recycling branch where the items are bought, `branch_id`.

Example of a Keyfull Component Home

A keyfull component home is one that includes a `primaryKey` clause in its declaration and is used to manage components that belong to the entity component category.

Consider the `RecycleBroker::WasteItemC` component defined in Listing 13.2. A keyless component home, `WasteItemCH`, can be declared that manages `WasteItemC` components, as shown in Listing 13.7.

Listing 13.7 Declaration of the `WasteItemCH` Keyfull Component Home

```
//IDL
#include "RecycleBroker.idl"

// Re-open the 'RecycleBroker' module...
module RecyleBroker {
    ...
    // Declaration of the primary key type 'PrimKeyType'
    valuetype PrimKeyType : Components::PrimaryKeyBase {
        public KeyType k;
    };

    // Forward declaration of WasteItemC component.
    component WasteItemC;

    // Extended IDL declaration of keyfull component home 'WasteItemCH'
    home      WasteItemCH     manages WasteItemC
                              primaryKey PrimKeyType
    {
        // Implicitly defined factory/finder operations:
        // factory create(in PrimKeyType key)
        //     raises (Components::DuplicateKeyValue, Components::InvalidKey);
        // finder  find_by_primary_key(in PrimKeyType key)
        //     raises (Components::UnknownKeyValue, Components::InvalidKey);

        // Explicitly defined operations:
        factory create_from_details(in WasteItemDetailsFull details)
            raises (Components::DuplicateKeyValue, Components::InvalidKey);

        WasteItemIdSeq find_by_waste(in WasteType waste)
            raises (NotFound);
        WasteItemIdSeq find_by_branch(in KeyType branch_id)
```

Listing 13.7 continued

```
            raises (NotFound);
        WasteItemIdSeq find_all();

        WasteItemDetailsSeq get_details(in WasteItemIdSeq id_seq)
            raises (NotFound);
    };
    ...
};
```

A primary key type, `RecycleBroker::PrimKeyType`, is defined as a value type with a single public member, `k`, which is of `RecycleBroker::KeyType` type (a typedef of `CORBA::Long`).

The `WasteItemC` component can be declared as a forward reference in advance of the full definition, as shown.

A component home, `WasteItemCH`, is declared that manages `WasteItemC` components and uses `PrimKeyType` as its primary key type.

A keyfull component home always has an implicitly defined factory operation, `factory create(in PrimKeyType key)` in this instance, and an implicitly defined finder operation, `finder find_by_primary_key(in PrimKeyType key)` in this instance.

The body of the component home, `WasteItemCH`, contains a number of explicit operation definitions. The factory operation, `create_from_details()`, creates a `WasteItemC` component whose state is initialized with a `WasteItemDetails` struct.

A number of operations—`find_by_waste()`, `find_by_branch()`, and `find_all()`—are declared that search for `WasteItemC` components. These operations are not `finder` operations. In the interests of efficiency, they are declared, instead, as ordinary operations that return a `WasteItemId` sequence (`CORBA::Long` sequence).

Given a `WasteItemId`, a client can choose to retrieve the corresponding `WasteItemC` component reference at any time. The client can wrap the `WasteItemId` in a `PrimKeyType` value type and call the implicit `finder find_by_primary_key()` operation.

Mapping Keyless Component Homes to Equivalent IDL

Consider a general keyless component home, as shown in Listing 13.8.

Listing 13.8 General Form of a Keyless Component Home

```
//IDL
home home_name manages component_name
{
    [explicit_declarations]
};
```

This is mapped to equivalent IDL as shown in Listing 13.9.

Listing 13.9 Equivalent IDL for Keyless Component Home Declarations

```
//IDL
interface home_nameImplicit : Components::KeylessCCMHome
{
    component_name create();
};
interface home_nameExplicit : Components::CCMHome
{
    [mapped_explicit_declarations]
};
interface home_name : home_nameImplicit, home_nameExplicit { };
```

Explicit declarations are mapped as follows:

- Ordinary operations and attributes are unchanged.
- For factory and finder operations, the `factory` and `finder` keywords are replaced by *`component_name`*.

For example, the result of mapping the `RecycleBroker::BuyingCH` component home, Listing 13.6, to equivalent IDL is shown in Listing 13.10.

Listing 13.10 Equivalent IDL for `RecycleBroker::BuyingCH` *Component Home*

```
//IDL
#include "RecycleBroker.idl"

module RecycleBroker {
    ...
    interface BuyingCHImplicit : Components::KeylessCCMHome
    {
        BuyingC create();
    };
    interface BuyingCHExplicit : Components::CCMHome
    {
        BuyingC create_from_initial_data(
            KeyType branch_id
        );
    };
    interface BuyingCH
        : BuyingCHExplicit,  BuyingCHImplicit { };
    ...
};
```

Mapping Keyfull Component Homes to Equivalent IDL

Consider a general keyfull component home, as shown in Listing 13.11.

Listing 13.11 General Form of a Keyfull Component Home

```
//IDL
home home_name manages    component_name
               primaryKey key_type
{
    [explicit_declarations]
};
```

This is mapped to equivalent IDL as shown in Listing 13.12.

Listing 13.12 Equivalent IDL for Keyfull Component Home Declarations

```
//IDL
interface home_nameImplicit
{
        component_name create(in key_type key)
        raises (Components::DuplicateKeyValue, Components::InvalidKey);

        component_name find_by_primary_key(in key_type key)
        raises (Components::UnknownKeyValue, Components::InvalidKey);

        void remove(in key_type key)
        raises (Components::UnknownKeyValue, Components::InvalidKey);

        key_type get_primary_key(in component_name comp);
};
interface home_nameExplicit : Components::CCMHome
{
    [mapped_explicit_declarations]
};
interface home_name : home_nameImplicit, home_nameExplicit { };
```

Explicit declarations are mapped as follows:

- Ordinary operations and attributes are unchanged.
- For factory and finder operations, the `factory` and `finder` keywords are replaced by *`component_name`*.

For example, the result of mapping the `RecycleBroker::WasteItemCH` component home, Listing 13.7, to equivalent IDL is shown in Listing 13.13.

Listing 13.13 Equivalent IDL for `RecycleBroker::WasteItemCH` *Component Home*

```
//IDL
#include "RecycleBroker.idl"

module RecycleBroker {
    ...
    interface WasteItemCHImplicit {
```

Listing 13.13 continued

```
        WasteItemC create(in PrimKeyType key)
        raises (Components::DuplicateKeyValue, Components::InvalidKey);

        WasteItemC find_by_primary_key(in PrimKeyType key)
        raises (Components::UnknownKeyValue, Components::InvalidKey);

        void remove(in PrimKeyType key)
        raises (Components::UnknownKeyValue, Components::InvalidKey);

        PrimKeyType get_primary_key(in WasteItemC comp);
    };
    interface WasteItemCHExplicit : Components::CCMHome
    {
        WasteItemC create_from_details(in WasteItemDetailsFull details)
        raises (Components::DuplicateKeyValue, Components::InvalidKey);

        WasteItemIdSeq find_by_waste(in WasteType waste)
        raises (NotFound);
        WasteItemIdSeq find_by_branch(in KeyType branch_id)
        raises (NotFound);
        WasteItemIdSeq find_all();

        WasteItemDetailsSeq get_details(in WasteItemIdSeq id_seq)
        raises (NotFound);
    };
    interface WasteItemCH :  WasteItemCHExplicit, WasteItemCHImplicit { };
    ...
};
```

Component Home Inheritance

Extended IDL supports inheritance between component homes, subject to the following restrictions:

- Single inheritance only.
- For basic components, the component type, *CType*, managed by the base and derived component homes must be identical.
- The primary key type, *KType*, declared by the base and derived component homes (if any) must be identical.

Figure 13.3 illustrates the rules of component home inheritance. A single component type, *CType*, is managed both by the base component home, `HomeBase`, and the derived component home, `HomeDeriv`. Both `HomeBase` and `HomeDeriv` use an identical primary key type, *KType*.

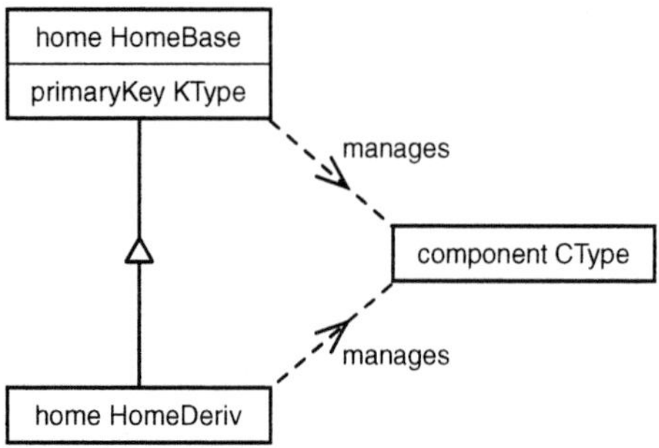

Figure 13.3

Component home inheritance.

A special case of component home inheritance arises when the base component home, `HomeBase`, declares a primary key but the derived component, `HomeDeriv`, does not. For example:

```
//IDL
component CType supports CIntf { };

// Primary key, KType, explicitly declared.
home HomeBase manages CType primaryKey KType { };

// Primary key, KType, implicitly declared because of inheritance.
home HomeDeriv : HomeBase manages CType { };
```

In this case, `HomeDeriv` becomes implicitly associated with the *`KType`* primary key, and `HomeDeriv` is treated as if the `primaryKey` *`KType`* clause is part of the component home declaration. Therefore, `HomeDeriv` is mapped to equivalent IDL in the same way as a keyfull component home.

Recycle Broker Example

Consider how to re-engineer the Recycle Broker application from Chapter 3 so that it is implemented using the CCM. The re-engineered application should be backward compatible with old recycle broker clients. This imposes the constraint that the new application must be usable by component-unaware clients.

Listing 13.14, which depends on the definitions appearing in Listing 3.1, shows the extra IDL that is needed to define the recycle broker components and component homes.

Listing 13.14 Recycle Broker Component IDL Declarations

```
//IDL
#include <components.idl>
#include "RecycleBroker.idl"
```

Listing 13.14 continued

```
module RecycleBroker {

    valuetype PrimKeyType : Components::PrimaryKeyBase {
        public KeyType k;
    };

    component CustomerC       supports Customer { };
    home      CustomerCH      manages CustomerC
                              primaryKey PrimKeyType
    {
        factory create_from_details(in CustomerDetailsFull details)
        raises (Components::DuplicateKeyValue, Components::InvalidKey);

        CustomerIdSeq find_by_name(in NameType name)
        raises (NotFound);
    };

    component WasteItemC      supports WasteItem { };
    home      WasteItemCH     manages WasteItemC
                              primaryKey PrimKeyType
    {
        factory create_from_details(in WasteItemDetailsFull details)
        raises (Components::DuplicateKeyValue, Components::InvalidKey);

        WasteItemIdSeq find_by_waste(in WasteType waste)
        raises (NotFound);
        WasteItemIdSeq find_by_branch(in KeyType branch_id)
        raises (NotFound);
        WasteItemIdSeq find_all();

        WasteItemDetailsSeq get_details(in WasteItemIdSeq id_seq)
        raises (NotFound);
    };

    component CustomerAdminC  supports CustomerAdmin { };
    home      CustomerAdminCH manages CustomerAdminC
    {
        factory create_from_initial_data(
            CORBA::Boolean hasAdminPrivileges,
            KeyType        branch_id
        );
    };

    component WasteItemAdminC  supports WasteItemAdmin { };
    home      WasteItemAdminCH manages WasteItemAdminC
    {
        factory create_from_initial_data(
```

Listing 13.14 continued

```
        CORBA::Boolean  hasAdminPrivileges,
        KeyType         branch_id,
        KeyType         customer_id
    );
};

component OfficeAdminC    supports OfficeAdmin { };
home      OfficeAdminCH   manages OfficeAdminC { };

component BrowsingC       supports Browsing { };
home      BrowsingCH      manages BrowsingC
{
    factory create_from_initial_data(
        KeyType branch_id
    );
};

component SellingC        supports Selling { };
home      SellingCH       manages SellingC
{
    factory create_from_initial_data(
        KeyType branch_id
    );
};

component BuyingC         supports Buying { };
home      BuyingCH        manages BuyingC
{
    factory create_from_initial_data(
        KeyType branch_id
    );
};

component HeadOfficeC     supports HeadOffice { };
home      HeadOfficeCH    manages HeadOfficeC
{
    factory create_from_initial_data(
        string                 address,
        KeyType branch_id
    );
};

component BranchOfficeC   supports BranchOffice { };
home      BranchOfficeCH  manages BranchOfficeC
{
    factory create_from_initial_data(
        string  address,
```

Listing 13.14 continued

```
            KeyType branch_id
        );
    };
};
```

The component definitions follow a simple pattern. For every interface, *`IntfName`*, appearing in the original recycle broker IDL, there is a corresponding *`IntfName`*`C` component type that supports *`IntfName`*.

The `CustomerCH` and `WasteItemCH` component homes, which manage `CustomerC` and `WasteItemC`, respectively, are declared with primary keys. This makes sense because both customers and waste items are long-lived entities that are held in persistent storage.

The remaining component homes are declared without primary keys.

Generating Component Skeletons

After defining your application's components and component homes in extended IDL, the next step is to put the extended IDL through an IDL compiler to generate the component skeletons.

However, the process of compiling extended IDL is more involved than compiling ordinary IDL. The aim at this stage is to generate a considerable proportion of the implementation code. The developer, therefore, has to make some choices to specify what sort of implementation should be generated.

Figure 13.4 shows a schematic depiction of the compilation process. The extended IDL and some extra information, the *implementation definition*, are supplied to the IDL compiler, which then generates component skeleton code.

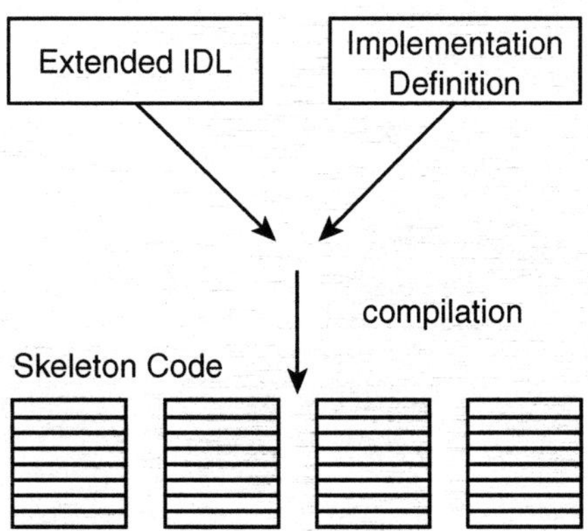

Figure 13.4

Compiling extended IDL.

There are two possible approaches to providing implementation definitions to an extended IDL compiler:

- **Using Component Implementation Definition Language (CIDL)** The CCM defines a special language, CIDL, for defining the implementation of components and component homes. The CIDL is an extension of Persistent State Definition Language (PSDL), which is used by the CORBA Persistent State Service.
  The CIDL is tightly integrated with the persistent state service and enables various operations on a component home to be delegated to the persistent state service.
- **Custom or proprietary approaches** Although at the time of this writing there are no commercially available implementations of the CCM, it seems likely that container providers will support alternative persistence mechanisms, in addition to the persistent state service.
  Proprietary approaches might enable you to specify implementation definitions using a graphical tool or XML instead of using CIDL.
  There is also likely to be a requirement to enable developers to customize component home implementations. This requires the specification of a new API. Currently, however, this kind of API is not specified as part of the CORBA standard.

The details of the CIDL lie beyond the scope of this chapter.

Apart from information about persistence, the most basic aspect of implementation definition is the choice of component category for the components. At compile time, you have to choose one of the categories—session, service, entity, or process—for the component. The choice is constrained by the kind of home that manages the component, as follows:

- **Keyless component home** The managed component can belong to the session, service, or process component category.
- **Keyfull component home** The managed component can belong only to the entity component category.

Implementing Components

The result of passing your component definitions to an extended IDL compiler is a set of partially generated classes, the executor classes. An *executor* is essentially a servant class with extra conditions imposed on it to make it fit into the CCM programming framework.

The class that implements a component is a *component executor*.

When implementing components, it is important to distinguish between container API types because the API type determines which interfaces are used to communicate with the container. There are two component API types:

- **Session API Type** applies to the session and service component categories. The relevant IDL interfaces in this case are `Components::Basic::SessionContext` and `Components::Basic::SessionComponent`. See "`Components` IDL Module" later in this chapter.
- **Entity API Type** applies to the entity and process component categories. The relevant IDL interfaces in this case are `Components::Basic::EntityContext` and `Components::Basic::EntityComponent`. See "`Components` IDL Module" later in this chapter.

The following sections give examples of how to implement components using each of the container API types.

Implementing Session and Service Components

Session and service objects belong to the same container API type, the session API type, which implies that the programming environment is similar for both. The main distinction between them is a semantic one: Session objects can assume that their operations are always invoked by the same client, so that it is all right to store client-specific state. On the other hand, a service object can have its operation invoked by several different clients, so it is not possible for it to store client-specific state.

The example in this section is based on the `RecycleBroker::BuyingC` component, which belongs to the session category. Listing 13.15 and Listing 13.16 give the declaration of the `BuyingCImpl` executor class, which implements the `BuyingC` component.

Listing 13.15 C++ Declaration of the `BuyingCImpl` *Executor Class*

```
//C++
// Class: RecycleBroker_BuyingCImpl
// A POA servant which implements of the RecycleBroker::BuyingC interface
//
#ifndef RECYCLEBROKER_BUYINGCIMPL_H_
#define RECYCLEBROKER_BUYINGCIMPL_H_

#include "recyclebrokerequivS.hh"
#include "components_basic.hh"

class RecycleBroker_BuyingCImpl :
    public virtual POA_RecycleBroker::BuyingC,
    Components::Basic::SessionComponent
{
    // ...(details not shown)
private:
    // Private member variables
    Components::Basic::SessionContext_var m_ctxV;
    //...
};

#endif
```

Listing 13.16 Java Declaration of the `BuyingCImpl` *Executor Class*

```
//Java
package RecycleBroker;

public class BuyingCImpl
implements
    RecycleBroker.BuyingCOperations,
    Components.Basic.SessionComponent
{
    //...(details shown later)
}
```

In this example, the C++ executor is implemented using the inheritance approach (Listing 13.15), and the Java executor is implemented using the delegation (tie) approach (Listing 13.16).

The `BuyingCImpl` executor exhibits the usual inheritance relationship you would expect if you were implementing a regular servant class, deriving from `POA_RecycleBroker::BuyingC` in C++ and from `RecycleBroker.BuyingCOperations` in Java.

However, the `BuyingCImpl` executor must also implement the `SessionComponent` methods, which requires that `BuyingCImpl` derives from `Components::Basic::SessionComponent` in C++ and `Components.Basic.SessionComponent` in Java. This inheritance relationship is unusual because `SessionComponent` is declared in IDL as a local interface, which implies that no POA classes are generated for it (see the section "Components IDL Module," later in this chapter).

Listing 13.17 and Listing 13.18 show the implementation of the `BuyingCImpl` executor class in C++ and Java, respectively.

Listing 13.17 C++ Implementation of the `BuyingCImpl` *Executor Class*

```
//C++

#include <stdlib.h>
#include "RecycleBroker_BuyingCImpl.h"

//----------
// Constructors and Destructors
//----------
//...

//----------
// Inherited from 'Components::CCMObject'
// (remote methods)
//----------
CORBA::IRObject_ptr
```

Listing 13.17 continued

```
RecycleBroker_BuyingCImpl::get_component_def()
throw (CORBA::SystemException)
{
    // GENERATED IMPLEMENTATION (not shown)
}

Components::CCMHome_ptr
RecycleBroker_BuyingCImpl::get_ccm_home()
throw (CORBA::SystemException)
{
    // GENERATED IMPLEMENTATION (not shown)
}

Components::PrimaryKeyBase*
RecycleBroker_BuyingCImpl::get_primary_key()
throw (CORBA::SystemException, Components::NoKeyAvailable)
{
    throw Components::NoKeyAvailable();
}

void
RecycleBroker_BuyingCImpl::configuration_complete()
throw (CORBA::SystemException, Components::InvalidConfiguration)
{
    // Actions to do at the end of config phase
}

void
RecycleBroker_BuyingCImpl::remove()
throw (CORBA::SystemException)
{
    // GENERATED IMPLEMENTATION  (not shown)
}

//----------
// Inherited from 'Components::Basic::SessionComponent'
// (local methods)
//----------
void
RecycleBroker_BuyingCImpl::set_session_context(
    Components::Basic::SessionContext_ptr  ctx
)
{
    m_ctxV = Components::Basic::SessionContext::_duplicate(ctx);
}

void
RecycleBroker_BuyingCImpl::ccm_activate()
```

Listing 13.17 continued

```
{
    // Actions to do when component is activated by Container
}

void
RecycleBroker_BuyingCImpl::ccm_passivate()
{
    // Actions to do when component is passivated by Container
}

void
RecycleBroker_BuyingCImpl::ccm_remove()
{
    // Actions to do immediately before the component is deleted.
}

//----------
// Inherited from the 'RecycleBroker::Buying' interface
// (remote methods)
//----------
//...
```

Listing 13.18 Java Implementation of the `BuyingCImpl` *Executor Class*

```
//Java
package RecycleBroker;

public class BuyingCImpl
implements
    RecycleBroker. BuyingCOperations,
    Components.Basic.SessionComponent
{
    //----------
    // Constructors
    //----------
    //...

    //----------
    // Inherited from 'Components.CCMObjectOperations'
    // (remote methods)
    //----------
    public org.omg.CORBA.IRObject get_component_def()
    {
        // GENERATED IMPLEMENTATION (not shown)
    }

    public Components.CCMHome get_ccm_home()
    {
```

Listing 13.18 continued

```
        // GENERATED IMPLEMENTATION (not shown)
    }

    public Components.PrimaryKeyBase get_primary_key()
        throws Components.NoKeyAvailable
    {
        throw new Components.NoKeyAvailable();
    }

    public void configuration_complete()
        throws Components.InvalidConfiguration
    {
        // Actions to do at the end of config phase
    }

    public void remove()
    {
        // GENERATED IMPLEMENTATION (not shown)
    }

    //----------
    // Inherited from 'Components.Basic.SessionComponent'
    // (local methods)
    //----------
    public void set_session_context(
        Components.Basic.SessionContext ctx
    ) throws Components.Basic.CCMException
    {
        m_ctx = ctx;
    }

    public void ccm_activate() throws Components.Basic.CCMException
    {
        // Actions to do when component is activated by Container
    }

    public void ccm_passivate() throws Components.Basic.CCMException
    {
        // Actions to do when component is passivated by Container
    }

    public void ccm_remove() throws Components.Basic.CCMException
    {
        // Actions to do immediately before the component is deleted.
    }

    //----------
    // Inherited from the 'RecycleBroker.BuyingOperations'
```

Listing 13.18 continued

```
    // (remote methods)
    //----------
    //...

    // Private member variables
    private Components.Basic.SessionContext m_ctx;
}
```

From a client's point of view, the important operations are the ones inherited from the `RecycleBroker::Buying` IDL interface. These operations are implemented in much the same way as for a normal servant.

The additional methods that have to be implemented for a session component derive from two different interfaces:

- The `Components::CCMObject` interface
- The `Components::Basic::SessionComponent` local interface

The methods associated with these interfaces are explained in the following sections.

`Components::CCMObject` Operations

The `get_component_def()` method returns a reference to a `CORBA::ComponentDef` object in the interface repository that provides a meta-description of the component. See Chapter 22, "Interface Repository." The body of this method is generated by the extended IDL compiler.

The `get_ccm_home()` method returns a reference to the home object associated with this component. The body of this method is generated by the extended IDL compiler.

The `get_primary_key()` method does not apply to session objects, because a session object has no primary key. Hence, the `Components::NoKeyAvailable` exception is thrown.

The `configuration_complete()` method is called by the container when the configuration phase is finished.

The `remove()` method is used to destroy a component. The body of this method is generated by the extended IDL compiler.

`Components::Basic::SessionComponent` Operations

The `set_session_context()` method is called by the container as the component is being initialized, to pass a `Components::Basic::SessionContext` reference to the component. The component can use the `SessionContext` object to communicate with the container. Here, the `SessionContext` reference is cached in a member variable.

The `ccm_activate()` method is called by the container to inform the component that it has been activated. After a component has been activated, it is liable to receive invocations.

The ccm_passivate() method is called by the container to inform the component that it is no longer activated. A passivated component does not receive any invocations.

The cmm_remove() method is called by the container to inform the component that it is about to be deleted. At this point the component should clean up the resources it is using, if any.

Implementing Entity and Process Components

Entity and process objects belong to the same container API type, the entity API type, which implies that the programming environment is similar for both. The main distinction between them relates to the use of primary keys. Entity objects use primary keys and expose their primary keys to clients—they are managed by keyfull component homes. Process objects can use primary keys, but their keys are not exposed to clients—they are managed by keyless component homes.

The example in this section is based on the RecycleBroker::WasteItemC component, which belongs to the entity category. Listing 13.19 and Listing 13.20 give the declaration of the WasteItemCImpl executor class, which implements the WasteItemC component.

Listing 13.19 C++ Declaration of the WasteItemCImpl *Executor Class*

```
//C++
#ifndef RECYCLEBROKER_WASTEITEMCIMPL_H_
#define RECYCLEBROKER_WASTEITEMCIMPL_H_

#include "recyclebrokerequivS.hh"
#include "components_basic.hh"

class RecycleBroker_WasteItemCImpl :
    public virtual POA_RecycleBroker::WasteItemC,
    Components::Basic::SessionComponent
{
    // ...(details not shown)
private:
    // Private member variables
    RecycleBroker::PrimKeyType_var       m_keyV;
    Components::Basic::EntityContext_var m_ctxV;
    //...
};

#endif
```

Listing 13.20 Java Declaration of the WasteItemCImpl *Executor Class*

```
//Java
package RecycleBroker;

public class WasteItemCImpl
implements
```

Listing 13.20 continued

```
    RecycleBroker.WasteItemCOperations,
    Components.Basic.EntityComponent
{
    //...(details shown later)
}
```

In this example, the C++ executor is implemented using the inheritance approach (Listing 13.19), and the Java executor is implemented using the delegation (tie) approach (Listing 13.20).

The `WasteItemCImpl` executor exhibits the usual inheritance relationship you would expect if you were implementing a regular servant class, deriving from `POA_RecycleBroker::WasteItemC` in C++ and from `RecycleBroker.WasteItemCOperations` in Java.

However, the `WasteItemCImpl` executor must also implement the `EntityComponent` methods, which requires that `WasteItemCImpl` derives from `Components::Basic::EntityComponent` in C++ and `Components.Basic.EntityComponent` in Java. This inheritance relationship is unusual because `EntityComponent` is declared in IDL as a local interface, which implies that no POA classes are generated for it (see the "`Components` IDL Module" section).

Listing 13.21 and Listing 13.22 show the implementation of the `WasteItemCImpl` executor class in C++ and Java, respectively.

Listing 13.21 C++ Implementation of the `WasteItemCImpl` *Executor Class*

```
//C++
#include <stdlib.h>
#include "RecycleBroker_WasteItemCImpl.h"

//----------
// Constructors and Destructors
//----------
//...

//----------
// Inherited from 'Components::CCMObject'
// (remote methods)
//----------
CORBA::IRObject_ptr
RecycleBroker_WasteItemCImpl::get_component_def()
throw (CORBA::SystemException)
{
    // GENERATED IMPLEMENTATION (not shown)
}

Components::CCMHome_ptr
RecycleBroker_WasteItemCImpl::get_ccm_home()
```

Listing 13.21 continued

```
throw (CORBA::SystemException)
{
    // GENERATED IMPLEMENTATION (not shown)
}

Components::PrimaryKeyBase*
RecycleBroker_WasteItemCImpl::get_primary_key()
throw (CORBA::SystemException, Components::NoKeyAvailable)
{
    return RecycleBroker::PrimKeyType::_duplicate(m_keyV);
}

void
RecycleBroker_WasteItemCImpl::configuration_complete()
throw (CORBA::SystemException, Components::InvalidConfiguration)
{
    // Actions to do at the end of config phase
}

void
RecycleBroker_WasteItemCImpl::remove()
throw (CORBA::SystemException)
{
    // GENERATED IMPLEMENTATION (not shown)
}

//----------
// Inherited from 'Components::Basic::EntityComponent'
// (local methods)
//----------
void
set_entity_context(
    Components::Basic::EntityContext_ptr  ctx
)
{
    m_ctxV = Components::Basic::EntityContext::_duplicate(ctx);
}

void
unset_entity_context()
{
    m_ctxV = Components::Basic::EntityContext::_nil();
}

void
ccm_activate()
{
```

Listing 13.21 continued

```
    // Actions to do when component is activated by Container
}

void
ccm_load()
{
    // Load the component's state from persistent storage,
    // if necessary.
}

void
ccm_store()
{
    // Save the component's state to persistent storage,
    // if necessary.
}

void
ccm_passivate()
{
    // Actions to do when component is passivated by Container
}

void
ccm_remove()
{
    // Actions to do immediately before the component is deleted.
}

//----------
// Inherited from the 'RecycleBroker::Buying' interface
// (remote methods)
//----------
//...
```

Listing 13.22 Java Implementation of the `WasteItemCImpl` *Executor Class*

```
//Java
package RecycleBroker;

public class WasteItemCImpl
implements
    RecycleBroker.WasteItemCOperations,
    Components.Basic.EntityComponent
{
    //----------
    // Constructors
```

Listing 13.22 continued

```
//----------
//...

//----------
// Inherited from 'Components.CCMObjectOperations'
// (remote methods)
//----------
public CORBA.IRObject get_component_def()
{
    // GENERATED IMPLEMENTATION (not shown)
}

public Components.CCMHome get_ccm_home()
{
    // GENERATED IMPLEMENTATION (not shown)
}

public Components.PrimaryKeyBase get_primary_key()
    throws Components.NoKeyAvailable
{
    return m_key;
}

public void configuration_complete()
    throws Components.InvalidConfiguration
{
    // Actions to do at the end of config phase
}

public void remove()
{
    // GENERATED IMPLEMENTATION (not shown)
}

//----------
// Inherited from 'Components.Basic.EntityComponent'
// (local methods)
//----------
public void set_entity_context(
    Components.Basic.EntityContext ctx
) throws Components.Basic.CCMException
{
    m_ctx = ctx;
}

public void unset_entity_context()
    throws Components.Basic.CCMException
```

Listing 13.22 continued

```
    {
        m_ctx = null;
    }

    public void ccm_activate()
        throws Components.Basic.CCMException
    {
        // Actions to do when component is activated by Container
    }

    public void ccm_load()
        throws Components.Basic.CCMException
    {
        // Load the component's state from persistent storage,
        // if necessary.
    }

    public void ccm_store()
        throws Components.Basic.CCMException
    {
        // Save the component's state to persistent storage,
        // if necessary.
    }

    public void ccm_passivate()
        throws Components.Basic.CCMException
    {
        // Actions to do when component is passivated by Container
    }

    public void ccm_remove()
        throws Components.Basic.CCMException
    {
        // Actions to do immediately before the component is deleted.
    }

    //----------
    // Inherited from the 'RecycleBroker.BuyingOperations'
    // (remote methods)
    //----------
    //...

    // Private member variables
    private RecycleBroker.PrimKeyType      m_key;
    private Components.Basic.EntityContext m_ctx;
}
```

From a client's point of view, the important operations are the ones inherited from the `RecycleBroker::WasteItem` IDL interface. These operations are implemented in much the same way as for a normal servant.

The additional methods that have to be implemented for a session component derive from two different interfaces:

- The `Components::CCMObject` interface
- The `Components::Basic::EntityComponent` local interface

The methods associated with these interfaces are explained in the following sections.

`Components::CCMObject` Operations

The `get_component_def()`, `get_ccm_home()`, `configuration_complete()`, and `remove()` methods have already been discussed, in the section "Implementing Session and Service Components."

The `get_primary_key()` method returns a previously cached primary key, stored as `m_keyV` in C++ and `m_key` in Java. The primary key is typically cached by the executor's constructor.

`Components::Basic::EntityComponent` Operations

The `set_entity_context()` method is called by the container as the component is being initialized to pass a `Components::Basic::EntityContext` reference to the component. The component can use the `EntityContext` object to communicate with the container. Here, the `EntityContext` reference is cached in a member variable.

The `unset_entity_context()` method is called by the container to nullify the cached `EntityContext` object. It is called just before a component instance is deleted.

The `ccm_activate()` method is called by the container to inform the component that it has been activated. After a component has been activated, it is liable to receive invocations.

The `ccm_load()` method is called by the container to tell the entity object to load its state from the underlying persistent storage. The container calls `ccm_load()` after `ccm_activate()`.

The `ccm_save()` method is called by the container to tell the entity object to save its state to the underlying persistent storage. The container calls `ccm_save()` before `ccm_passivate()`.

The `ccm_passivate()` method is called by the container to inform the component that it is no longer activated. A passivated component does not receive any invocations.

The `ccm_remove()` method is called by the container to inform the component that it is about to be deleted. At that point the component should clean up the resources it is using, if any.

Implementing Component Homes

For every component type, there is at least one component home type to implement. The class that implements a component home is a *component home executor*. In the CCM, most of the code for the component home executor is generated automatically using CIDL or some proprietary persistence mechanism. Alternatively, you might choose to customize the persistence mechanism by providing the implementation code yourself.

The examples in this section show how to implement both keyless and keyfull component homes (as defined in "Basic Component Home Declarations," earlier in this chapter).

Customizable Persistence

In the examples that follow, it is assumed that your container vendor allows you to customize the persistence mechanism for your components. However, customizing component persistence requires an API that is not specified by CORBA. Therefore, in the following examples some placeholders are used to indicate where a proprietary API would probably be needed (assuming you are not using CIDL). Table 13.1 lists the API placeholders that are used in the code examples.

Table 13.1 Placeholders for a Proprietary API

Functionality	API Placeholder
Registering a new component	`REGISTER_EXECUTOR_WITH_CONTAINER()`
Making a component reference	`GET_OBJ_REF_FROM_KEY()`
Instantiating an existing component	Component constructor

Registering a New Component

The API for registering a new component is needed when implementing factory methods for a component home. A new component is typically created as follows:

1. The developer creates and initializes a new component executor.
2. The developer registers the new component executor with the container.
3. The container activates the component whenever it is needed.

The second step requires a special API, represented by the `REGISTER_EXECUTOR_WITH_CONTAINER()` placeholder, to tell the container that a new component has been created.

Making a Component Reference

The API for making a component reference is needed when implementing finder methods for a component home. A finder method is typically implemented as follows:

1. The persistent storage is searched, using the criteria specified in the finder's parameters.
2. If a component is found, a component reference is generated from the component's primary key.
3. The component reference is returned to the caller.

The second step requires a special API, represented by the `GET_OBJ_REF_FROM_KEY()` placeholder, to convert the primary key to its corresponding component references. The mapping between primary keys and component references is managed by the container.

Instantiating an Existing Component

When a client invocation is directed at an existing component that is not in active memory, the container retrieves the component state from persistent storage and creates an instance of the component executor.

To create an instance of the component executor, the container must invoke one of the component executor's constructors. However, the form of this constructor is not specified by CORBA. To support customized persistence, the form of this constructor would have to be specified as part of a proprietary API.

Implementing Keyless Component Homes

Session, service, and process components are managed by keyless component homes. This has a direct bearing on the interfaces supported by the component home and method that have to be implemented.

The example in this section is based on the `RecycleBroker::BuyingCH` component home, which is a keyless component home that manages a session component. Listing 13.23 and Listing 13.24 give the declaration of the `BuyingCHImpl` executor class, which implements the `BuyingCH` component home.

Listing 13.23 C++ Declaration of the `BuyingCHImpl` *Executor Class*

```
//C++
#ifndef RECYCLEBROKER_BUYINGCHIMPL_H_
#define RECYCLEBROKER_BUYINGCHIMPL_H_

#include "recyclebrokerequivS.hh"
#include "components_basicS.hh"

class RecycleBroker_BuyingCHImpl :
    public virtual POA_RecycleBroker::BuyingCH
{
    // ...(details not shown)
};

#endif
```

Listing 13.24 Java Declaration of the `BuyingCHImpl` *Executor Class*

```
//Java
package RecycleBroker;

public class BuyingCHImpl
    implements RecycleBroker.BuyingCHOperations
{
    //...(details shown later)
}
```

In this example, the C++ executor is implemented using the inheritance approach (Listing 13.23), and the Java executor is implemented using the delegation (tie) approach (Listing 13.24).

The `BuyingCHImpl` executor exhibits the usual inheritance relationship you would expect if you were implementing a regular servant class, deriving from `POA_RecycleBroker::BuyingCH` in C++ and from `RecycleBroker.BuyingCHOperations` in Java.

Listing 13.25 and Listing 13.26 show the implementation of the `BuyingCHImpl` executor class in C++ and Java, respectively.

Listing 13.25 C++ Implementation of the `BuyingCHImpl` *Executor Class*

```
//C++
#include <stdlib.h>
#include "RecycleBroker_BuyingCHImpl.h"

//----------
// Constructors and Destructors
//----------
//...

//----------
// Inherited from the 'Components::CCMHome' interface
//----------
CORBA::IRObject_ptr
RecycleBroker_BuyingCHImpl::get_component_def()
throw (CORBA::SystemException)
{
    // GENERATED IMPLEMENTATION (not shown)
}

CORBA::IRObject_ptr
RecycleBroker_BuyingCHImpl::get_home_def()
throw (CORBA::SystemException)
{
```

Listing 13.25 continued

```
    // GENERATED IMPLEMENTATION (not shown)
}

void
RecycleBroker_BuyingCHImpl::remove_component(
    Components::CCMObject_ptr  comp
) throw (CORBA::SystemException)
{
    // GENERATED IMPLEMENTATION (not shown)
}

//----------
// Inherited from the 'Components::KeylessCCMHome' interface
//----------
Components::CCMObject_ptr
RecycleBroker_BuyingCHImpl::create_component()
throw (CORBA::SystemException)
{
    throw CORBA::NO_IMPLEMENT();
}

//----------
// Inherited from the 'BuyingCHImplicit' interface
//----------
RecycleBroker::BuyingC_ptr
RecycleBroker_BuyingCHImpl::create()
throw (CORBA::SystemException)
{
    throw CORBA::NO_IMPLEMENT();
}

//----------
// Inherited from the 'BuyingCHExplicit' interface
//----------
RecycleBroker::BuyingC_ptr
RecycleBroker_BuyingCHImpl::create_from_initial_data(
    RecycleBroker::KeyType branch_id
) throw (CORBA::SystemException)
{
    RecycleBroker_BuyingCImpl* _new_executor =
        new RecycleBroker_BuyingCImpl(branch_id);

    RecycleBroker::BuyingC_ptr _new_ref =
        REGISTER_EXECUTOR_WITH_CONTAINER(_new_executor);

    return _new_ref;
}
```

Listing 13.26 Java Implementation of the `BuyingCHImpl` *Executor Class*

```
//Java
package RecycleBroker;

public class BuyingCHImpl
    implements RecycleBroker.BuyingCHOperations
{
    //----------
    // Constructors
    //----------
    //...

    //----------
    // Inherited from 'Components.CCMHomeOperations'
    //----------
    public CORBA.IRObject get_component_def()
    {
        // GENERATED IMPLEMENTATION (not shown)
    }

    public CORBA.IRObject get_home_def()
    {
        // GENERATED IMPLEMENTATION (not shown)
    }

    public void remove_component(
        Components.CCMObject comp
    )
    {
        // GENERATED IMPLEMENTATION (not shown)
    }

    //----------
    // Inherited from 'Components.KeylessCCMHomeOperations'
    //----------
    public Components.CCMObject create_component()
    {
        throw new org.omg.CORBA.NO_IMPLEMENT();
    }

    //----------
    // Inherited from 'BuyingCHImplicitOperations'
    //----------
    public RecycleBroker.BuyingC create()
    {
        throw new org.omg.CORBA.NO_IMPLEMENT();
    }

    //----------
    // Inherited from 'BuyingCHExplicitOperations'
```

Listing 13.26 continued

```
    //----------
    public RecycleBroker.BuyingC create_from_initial_data(
        int branch_id
    )
    {
        RecycleBroker_BuyingCImpl _new_executor =
            new RecycleBroker_BuyingCImpl(branch_id);

        RecycleBroker.BuyingC _new_ref =
            REGISTER_EXECUTOR_WITH_CONTAINER(_new_executor);

        return _new_ref;
    }
}
```

The methods that have to be implemented for the `RecycleBroker::BuyingCH` component home derive from the following interfaces:

- `Components::CCMHome`
- `Components::KeylessCCMHome`
- `RecycleBroker::BuyingCHImplicit`
- `RecycleBroker::BuyingCHExplicit`

The methods associated with these interfaces are explained in the following sections.

The `Components::CCMHome` Interface

The `get_component_def()` method returns a reference to a `CORBA::ComponentDef` object in the interface repository that provides a meta-description of the component. See Chapter 22 for more information. The body of this method is generated by the extended IDL compiler.

The `get_home_def()` method returns a reference to a `CORBA::HomeDef` object in the interface repository that provides a meta-description of the component. The body of this method is generated by the extended IDL compiler.

The `remove_component()` method is used to destroy a component permanently. In the case of entity components, this might involve removing the component from the underlying persistent storage. The body of this method is generated by the extended IDL compiler.

The `Components::KeylessCCMHome` Interface

The `create_component()` method can be used to create a new component with a default state. In this example, it is not implemented.

The `RecycleBroker::BuyingCHImplicit` Interface

The `create()` method can be used to create a new component with a default state. It has the same effect as `create_component()` but has a different return type. In this example, it is not implemented.

The `RecycleBroker::BuyingCHExplicit` Interface

The `create_from_initial_data()` method creates a new `BuyingC` component, initializing it with the `branch_id` argument.

Implementing Keyfull Component Homes

Entity components are managed by keyfull component homes. This implies that keyfull component homes use a primary key to track the identity of the components they manage.

The example in this section is based on the `RecycleBroker::WasteItemCH` component home, which is a keyfull component home that manages a `WasteItemC` entity component. Listing 13.27 and Listing 13.28 give the declaration of the `WasteItemCHImpl` executor class, which implements the `WasteItemCH` component home.

Listing 13.27 C++ Declaration of the `WasteItemCHImpl` Executor Class

```
//C++
#ifndef RECYCLEBROKER_WASTEITEMCHIMPL_H_
#define RECYCLEBROKER_WASTEITEMCHIMPL_H_

#include "recyclebrokerequivS.hh"
#include "components_basicS.hh"

class RecycleBroker_WasteItemCHImpl :
    public virtual POA_RecycleBroker::WasteItemCH
{
    // ...(details not shown)
};

#endif
```

Listing 13.28 Java Declaration of the `WasteItemCHImpl` Executor Class

```
//Java
package RecycleBroker;

public class WasteItemCHImpl
implements RecycleBroker.WasteItemCHOperations
{
    // ...(details shown later)
}
```

In this example, the C++ executor is implemented using the inheritance approach (Listing 13.27), and the Java executor is implemented using the delegation (tie) approach (Listing 13.28).

The `WasteItemCHImpl` executor exhibits the usual inheritance relationship you would expect if you were implementing a regular servant class, deriving from `POA_RecycleBroker::WasteItemCH` in C++ and from `RecycleBroker.WasteItemCHOperations` in Java.

Listing 13.29 and Listing 13.30 show the implementation of the `WasteItemCHImpl` executor class in C++ and Java, respectively.

Listing 13.29 C++ Implementation of the `WasteItemCHImpl` *Executor Class*

```
//C++
#include <stdlib.h>
#include "RecycleBroker_WasteItemCHImpl.h"

//----------
// Constructors and Destructors
//----------
//...

//----------
// Inherited from the 'Components::CCMHome' interface
//----------
CORBA::IRObject_ptr
RecycleBroker_WasteItemCHImpl::get_component_def()
throw (CORBA::SystemException)
{
    // GENERATED IMPLEMENTATION (not shown)
}

CORBA::IRObject_ptr
RecycleBroker_WasteItemCHImpl::get_home_def()
throw (CORBA::SystemException)
{
    // GENERATED IMPLEMENTATION (not shown)
}

void
RecycleBroker_WasteItemCHImpl::remove_component(
    Components::CCMObject_ptr  comp
) throw (CORBA::SystemException)
{
    // GENERATED IMPLEMENTATION (not shown)
}

//----------
// Inherited from the 'WasteItemCHImplicit' interface
//----------
RecycleBroker::WasteItemC_ptr
RecycleBroker_WasteItemCHImpl::create(
    RecycleBroker::PrimKeyType*  key
) throw (CORBA::SystemException,
         Components::DuplicateKeyValue,
         Components::InvalidKey)
{
```

Listing 13.29 continued

```
    throw CORBA::NO_IMPLEMENT();
}

RecycleBroker::WasteItemC_ptr
RecycleBroker_WasteItemCHImpl::find_by_primary_key(
    RecycleBroker::PrimKeyType*  key
) throw (CORBA::SystemException,
         Components::UnknownKeyValue,
         Components::InvalidKey)
{
    // Search database for component identified by 'key'...
    //...

    // If 'key' is found...
    RecycleBroker::WasteItemC_ptr _new_ref =
        GET_OBJ_REF_FROM_KEY(key);

    return _new_ref;
}

void
RecycleBroker_WasteItemCHImpl::remove(
    RecycleBroker::PrimKeyType*  key
) throw (CORBA::SystemException,
         Components::UnknownKeyValue,
         Components::InvalidKey)
{
     // GENERATED IMPLEMENTATION (not shown)
}

RecycleBroker::PrimKeyType*
RecycleBroker_WasteItemCHImpl::get_primary_key(
    RecycleBroker::WasteItemC_ptr  comp
) throw (CORBA::SystemException)
{
     // GENERATED IMPLEMENTATION (not shown)
}

//----------
// Inherited from the 'WasteItemCHExplicit' interface
//----------
RecycleBroker::WasteItemC_ptr
RecycleBroker_WasteItemCHImpl::create_from_details(
    const RecycleBroker::WasteItemDetailsFull&  details
) throw (CORBA::SystemException,
         Components::DuplicateKeyValue,
         Components::InvalidKey)
{
```

Listing 13.29 continued

```
    // Implicitly create new primary key and DB record.
    // Primary key is available via the 'get_primary_key()' op.
    RecycleBroker_WasteItemCImpl* _new_executor =
        new RecycleBroker_WasteItemCImpl(details);

    RecycleBroker::WasteItemC_ptr _new_ref =
        REGISTER_EXECUTOR_WITH_CONTAINER(_new_executor);

    return _new_ref;
}

RecycleBroker::WasteItemIdSeq*
RecycleBroker_WasteItemCHImpl::find_by_waste(
    RecycleBroker::WasteType waste
) throw (CORBA::SystemException, RecycleBroker::NotFound)
{
    // Search database for a list of waste items that match the
    // given 'waste' WasteType. Return a sequence of waste IDs.
    //...
}

RecycleBroker::WasteItemIdSeq*
RecycleBroker_WasteItemCHImpl::find_by_branch(
    RecycleBroker::KeyType branch_id
) throw (CORBA::SystemException,  RecycleBroker::NotFound)
{
    // Search database for a list of waste items that match the
    // given 'branch_id'. Return a sequence of waste IDs.
    //...
}

RecycleBroker::WasteItemIdSeq*
RecycleBroker_WasteItemCHImpl::find_all()
throw (CORBA::SystemException)
{
    // Return all waste IDs.
    //...
}

RecycleBroker::WasteItemDetailsSeq*
RecycleBroker_WasteItemCHImpl::get_details(
    const RecycleBroker::WasteItemIdSeq &  id_seq
) throw (CORBA::SystemException, RecycleBroker::NotFound)
{
    // Convert the list of waste IDs, 'id_seq', into a list of
    // 'WasteItemDetails' structs.
    //...
}
```

Listing 13.30 Java Implementation of the `WasteItemCHImpl` Executor Class

```
//Java
package RecycleBroker;

public class WasteItemCHImpl
implements RecycleBroker.WasteItemCHOperations
{
    //----------
    // Inherited from 'Components.CCMHomeOperations'
    //----------
    public CORBA.IRObject get_component_def()
    {
        // GENERATED IMPLEMENTATION  (not shown)
    }

    public CORBA.IRObject get_home_def()
    {
        // GENERATED IMPLEMENTATION (not shown)
    }

    public void remove_component(
        Components.CCMObject comp
    )
    {
        // GENERATED IMPLEMENTATION  (not shown)
    }

    //----------
    // Inherited from 'WasteItemCHImplicitOperations'
    //----------
    public RecycleBroker.WasteItemC create(
        RecycleBroker.PrimKeyType key
    ) throws Components.DuplicateKeyValue, Components.InvalidKey
    {
        throw new org.omg.CORBA.NO_IMPLEMENT();
    }

    public RecycleBroker.WasteItemC find_by_primary_key(
        RecycleBroker.PrimKeyType key
    ) throws Components.UnknownKeyValue, Components.InvalidKey
    {
        // Search database for component identified by 'key'...
        //...

        // If 'key' is found...
        RecycleBroker.WasteItemC _new_ref =
            GET_OBJ_REF_FROM_KEY(key);
```

Listing 13.30 continued

```
        return _new_ref;
    }

    public void remove(
        RecycleBroker.PrimKeyType key
    ) throws Components.UnknownKeyValue, Components.InvalidKey
    {
        // GENERATED IMPLEMENTATION (not shown)
    }

    public RecycleBroker.PrimKeyType get_primary_key(
        RecycleBroker.WasteItemC comp
    )
    {
        // GENERATED IMPLEMENTATION (not shown)
    }

    //----------
    // Inherited from 'WasteItemCHExplicitOperations'
    //----------
    public RecycleBroker.WasteItemC create_from_details(
        RecycleBroker.WasteItemDetailsFull details
    ) throws Components.DuplicateKeyValue,  Components.InvalidKey
    {
        // Implicitly create new primary key and DB record.
        // Primary key is available via the 'get_primary_key()' op.
        RecycleBroker.WasteItemCImpl _new_executor =
            new RecycleBroker.WasteItemCImpl(details);

        RecycleBroker.WasteItemC _new_ref =
            REGISTER_EXECUTOR_WITH_CONTAINER(_new_executor);

        return _new_ref;
    }

    public int[] find_by_waste(
        RecycleBroker.WasteType waste
    ) throws RecycleBroker.NotFound
    {
        // Search database for a list of waste items that match the
        // given 'waste' WasteType. Return a sequence of waste IDs.
        //...
    }

    public int[] find_by_branch(
        int branch_id
```

Listing 13.30 continued

```
    ) throws RecycleBroker.NotFound
    {
        // Search database for a list of waste items that match the
        // given 'branch_id'. Return a sequence of waste IDs.
        //...
    }

    public int[] find_all()
    {
        // Return all waste IDs.
        //...
    }

    public RecycleBroker.WasteItemDetails[] get_details(
        int[] id_seq
    ) throws RecycleBroker.NotFound
    {
        // Convert the list of waste IDs, 'id_seq', into a list of
        // 'WasteItemDetails' structs.
        //...
    }
}
```

The methods that have to be implemented for the `RecycleBroker::WasteItemCH` component home derive from the following interfaces:

- `Components::CCMHome`
- `RecycleBroker::WasteItemCHImplicit`
- `RecycleBroker::WasteItemCHExplicit`

The methods associated with these interfaces are explained in the following sections.

The `Components::CCMHome` Interface

The `get_component_def()`, `get_home_def()`, and `remove_component()` methods are discussed in "Implementing Keyless Component Homes," earlier in this chapter.

The `RecycleBroker::WasteItemCHImplicit` Interface

The `create()` method can be used to create a new component with a default state, given just a primary key. In this example, it is not implemented.

The `find_by_primary_key()` method finds a component given its primary key. It is not necessary to instantiate the component executor in the course of this operation. The container can automatically instantiate a component executor when it is needed.

The `remove()` method permanently destroys the component corresponding to the given primary key. This might involve removing the component from the underlying persistent storage as well. The body of this method is generated by the extended IDL compiler.

The RecycleBroker::WasteItemCHExplicit Interface

The create_from_details() method creates a new WasteItemC component, initializing it with the details argument. The WasteItemCImpl constructor chooses the new primary key for the component and makes the primary key available using the WasteItemC::get_primary_key() member function in C++ and the WasteItemC.get_primary_key() method in Java.

The various find methods—find_by_waste(), find_by_branch(), and find_all()—are not declared as finder operations because they return a waste ID, an integer, instead of a component reference.

The find methods are meant to be used in conjunction with the get_details() method, which returns the WasteItemDetails structs associated with the waste IDs.

A waste ID can also be converted into a primary key by using it to set the k member of a RecycleBroker::PrimKeyType value. The corresponding WasteItemC component can then be found by passing the primary key to the find_by_primary_key() operation.

Implementing Clients

There are two kinds of clients that can use a component-based server:

- **Component-unaware clients** are ordinary CORBA clients that have no knowledge of the CCM. These clients have no special features beyond the ordinary capability to invoke remote operations and attributes on IDL interfaces.
  A component-unaware client treats a component reference like an ordinary object reference and sees just the operations and attributes defined on the basic component's supported IDL interfaces.
  Clients obtain component references in the same way as they obtain object references—using the naming service or the trading service or by reading a stringified object reference.
- **Component-aware clients** are those that are aware of the CCM. In practice, this means that they are linked with stub code generated from extended IDL that includes definitions of the components and their component homes. For example, to use the RecycleBroker components directly, clients would have to link against stub code generated from Listing 13.14.
  A component-aware client can see the following aspects of a basic component:
  - The operations and attributes defined on the supported IDL interfaces.
  - The attributes defined in the body of the component (although these attributes are typically meant to be used only by the CCM configuration mechanism).
  - The operations on the associated component home equivalent interface, including factory and finder operations.

  Component-aware clients have the option of obtaining component references using a component home. The clients can obtain a component home reference, for example, from the naming service or the trading service. The clients can then use the component home's factory and finder operations to obtain component references.

In general, component-unaware clients are perfectly adequate for most applications. The CCM is primarily a framework to facilitate server development—there is no need to expose the inner workings of the CCM to clients. Therefore, it is preferable to design your component-based servers so that they are usable by component-unaware clients.

Container Programming Environment

The container provides a complete programming environment for components. Interfaces are provided that enable components to interact with the container and obtain access to the container's services. The container programming environment is shown schematically in Figure 13.5.

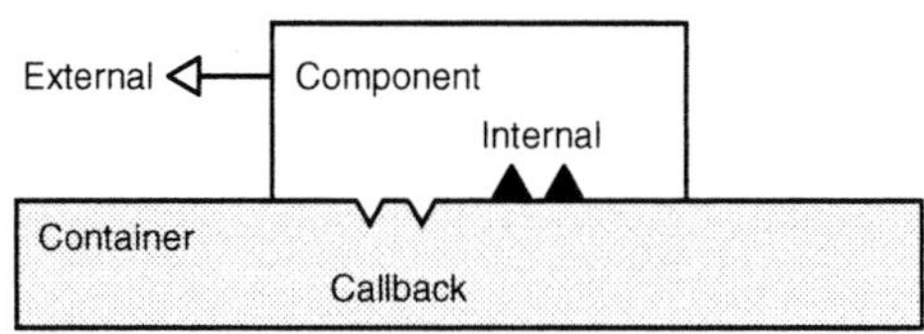

Figure 13.5

The container programming environment.

A component interacts with the world through the following sets of interfaces:

- **External interfaces** define the service provided to clients. The external interfaces include the component's supported interfaces (and facets, in the case of extended components) and are remotely accessible.
  For example, the `RecycleBroker::BuyingC` component supports the external interface, `RecycleBroker::Buying`.
- **Internal interfaces** provide access to container services. Using internal interfaces, a component can access security, transactions, and other services.
- **Callback interfaces** are used by the container to notify the component of important events and to supply the component with data.

In the case of the Recycle Broker application, the external interfaces are the IDL interfaces defined in the `RecycleBroker` module from Chapter 3. The following sections provide further details about internal interfaces and callback interfaces.

Internal Interfaces

A component accesses a container's internal interfaces using a CCM context. Listing 13.31 shows the definition of the CCM context interfaces: `CCMContext` (the base interface), `SessionContext`, and `EntityContext`.

Listing 13.31 Internal Interfaces Defined in the `Components` IDL Module

```
//IDL
...
module Components {
    ...
```

Listing 13.31 continued

```
    module Basic {
        ...
        typedef SecurityLevel2::Credentials Principal;
        exception IllegalState { };

        local interface CCMContext {
            Principal get_caller_principal();
            CCMHome get_CCM_home();
            boolean get_rollback_only()
                raises (IllegalState);
            Transaction::UserTransaction get_user_transaction()
                raises (IllegalState);
            boolean is_caller_in_role (in string role);
            void set_rollback_only()
                raises (IllegalState);
        };

        local interface SessionContext : CCMContext {
            Object get_CCM_object()
                raises (IllegalState);
        };

        local interface EntityContext : CCMContext {
            Object get_CCM_object ()
                raises (IllegalState);
            PrimaryKeyBase get_primary_key ()
                raises (IllegalState);
        };
        ...
    };
    ...
};
```

The `CCMContext` is a base interface for `SessionContext` and `EntityContext`. The `CCMContext` interface provides hooks to other internal interfaces and defines operations for some frequently used features.

The `SessionContext` interface belongs to the session API type. It is used by session and service components. When a component is instantiated, the container passes a new `SessionContext` object to the component using the `set_session_reference()` operation.

The `EntityContext` interface belongs to the entity API type. It is used by entity and process components. When a component is instantiated, the container passes a new `EntityContext` object to the component using the `set_entity_reference()` operation.

Transactional components can use the `CCMContext::get_user_transaction()` operation to get a reference to a `UserTransaction` object. The `UserTransaction` interface is an internal interface that controls transactions—see the section "`Components` IDL Module."

Callback Interfaces

A container communicates with a component using the component's callback interfaces. Listing 13.32 shows the definition of the callback interfaces: `EnterpriseComponent` (the base interface), `SessionComponent`, and `EntityComponent`.

Listing 13.32 Callback Interfaces Defined in the `Components` IDL Module

```
//IDL
...
module Components {
    ...
    module Basic {
        ...
        local interface EnterpriseComponent {};

        local interface SessionComponent : EnterpriseComponent {
            void set_session_context ( in SessionContext ctx)
                raises (CCMException);
            void ccm_activate()
                raises (CCMException);
            void ccm_passivate()
                raises (CCMException);
            void ccm_remove ()
                raises (CCMException);
        };

        local interface EntityComponent : EnterpriseComponent {
            void set_entity_context (in EntityContext ctx)
                raises (CCMException);
            void unset_entity_context ()
                raises (CCMException);
            void ccm_activate ()
                raises (CCMException);
            void ccm_load ()
                raises (CCMException);
            void ccm_store ()
                raises (CCMException);
            void ccm_passivate ()
                raises (CCMException);
            void ccm_remove ()
```

Listing 13.32 continued

```
                raises (CCMException);
        };

        local interface SessionSynchronization {
            void after_begin ()
                raises (CCMException);
            void before_completion ()
                raises (CCMException);
            void after_completion (
                in boolean committed)
                raises (CCMException);
        };
        ...
    };
    ...
};
```

`EnterpriseComponent` is a base interface for `SessionComponent` and `EntityComponent`.

The `SessionComponent` interface belongs to the session API type and must be implemented by all session and service components. For example, see the section "Implementing Session and Service Components," earlier in this chapter.

The `EntityComponent` interface belongs to the entity API type and must be implemented by all entity and process components. For example, see the section "Implementing Entity and Process Components," earlier in this chapter.

Transactional components optionally can implement the `SessionSynchronization` interface to receive callbacks that notify the component when each phase of a transaction occurs.

Extended Components

The extended level of the CCM adds a number of valuable features to components. Keep in mind, however, that using these extra features can break compatibility with EJB.

Extended components can expose a number of features to clients, collectively known as *ports*. The following port types are supported by the component model:

- **Facets** declare IDL interfaces that are implemented by the component. This gives you a way of grouping IDL interfaces together by associating them with a particular component.
- **Receptacles** implicitly declare operations that enable you to register component references with the component. This gives you a way of explicitly representing a "uses" relationship between two components.

- **Event sources** implicitly declare operations that enable you to register event consumers or event channels with the component. This enables you to express the fact that a component emits or publishes events.
- **Event sinks** implicitly declare a new facet that accepts events from event sources.
- **Attributes** are regular IDL attributes, which are also supported by basic components.

The new port types are described in the following sections.

Facets and Receptacles

For basic components (and ordinary CORBA objects), the only relationship that can be expressed directly in IDL is interface inheritance. However, there are many other relationships that could be expressed by expanding the IDL syntax.

Two new mechanisms are provided by extended components for expressing relationships:

- **Facets**—This is a mechanism for grouping interfaces together. Interfaces often can be grouped together because they offer closely related functionality or because they present different views of the same underlying object. These interfaces are not necessarily related to each other by inheritance, however. Facets offer a general way of grouping related interfaces.
- **Receptacles**—This is a mechanism for expressing the fact that one type of component uses another type of component. Components frequently cache references to other components whose operations they need to invoke on a regular basis. Receptacles provide a way of expressing this "using" relationship between component types.

Figure 13.6 shows extended components that offer facets and receptacles as part of their external interface.

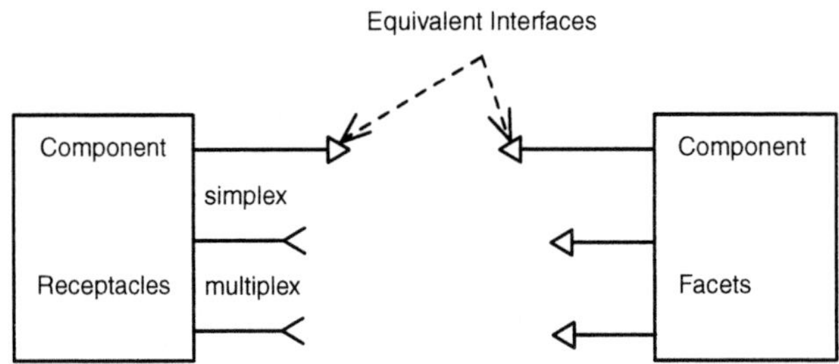

Figure 13.6

Components offering facets and receptacles.

Every component has an *equivalent interface*, which includes the operations and attributes inherited from supported interfaces, attributes declared in the component body, and a number of standard base interfaces. The equivalent interface is the only interface exposed by basic components.

Extended components can also define facets, which are additional interfaces declared by a `provides` clause in the component body. For example, the following component, `MyComponent`, provides a single facet, `MyFacet`:

```
//IDL
interface MyIntf
{
    // Operation and attribute definitions
};

interface MyFacetIntf
{
    // Operation and attribute definitions
};

component MyComponent supports MyIntf {
    provides MyFacetIntf MyFacet;
};
```

Support is provided for navigation between facets. Given a component reference, it is possible to obtain any of the facet references and, given a facet reference, it is possible to obtain the other facet references or the component reference.

Extended components can also define receptacles, which express the fact that the component caches a particular type of object reference (see Figure 13.6). Receptacles are declared by a `uses` clause in the component body. There are two kinds of receptacle:

- **Simplex receptacles** can be connected to a facet on a single component. A single object reference can be cached in the receptacle.
- **Multiplex receptacles** can be connected to facets on many components. A list of object references can be cached in the receptacle.

Event Sources and Event Sinks

Components often need the capability to notify each other of particular events and to pass messages to each other in an asynchronous fashion. The CORBA events service (see Chapter 14, "Events Service") or the CORBA notification service is generally used to support this kind of message passing between CORBA objects.

Extended components allow you to integrate the CORBA notification service into the component model. You can express the fact that components send or receive events directly in IDL. Components that send events can declare event sources, and components that receive events can declare event sinks.

The component event model has the following basic characteristics:

- The event model is layered on top of the CORBA notification service.
- Event sources are uncoupled from event sinks.
- The event model is a push model.

Figure 13.7 shows an example of a component with event sources that sends messages to a number of components with event sinks.

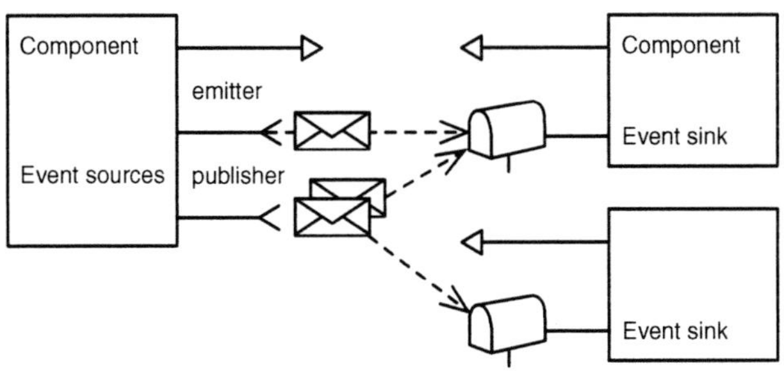

Figure 13.7

Components offering event sources and event sinks.

On the left of Figure 13.7 is a component that exposes event sources, of which there are two kinds:

- An **emitter** is an event source that can transmit events to a single event sink only. It is declared with an `emits` clause in IDL.
- A **publisher** is an event source that can transmit events to multiple event sinks. It is declared with a `publishes` clause in IDL.

The other components in Figure 13.7 expose event sinks. There is only one kind of event sink, which is declared with a `consumes` clause in IDL. There is no restriction on the number of event sources (emitters and publishers) that can connect to a single event sink.

Development and Deployment Roles

The CCM is more than just a framework for developing components. It also attempts to identify the stages along the way to reaching a working deployed application. A number of roles are defined that represent each of these stages. For each role, it is possible to define a set of tasks and responsibilities. Full-featured implementations of the CCM will provide specific tools for each role.

There are four principal roles in the CCM:

- Container provider
- Component implementor

- Component assembler
- Component deployer

These roles are discussed in the following sections.

Container Provider

A container provider is a vendor who provides the tools to deploy and run CORBA components in a container, which is the environment in which components run.

The functionality offered by the container typically covers the following areas:

- **The container API** A set of interfaces provided by the container that enable the component to interact with the container. There are two types of container API: the session API type and the entity API type, as described in the section "Implementing Components," earlier in this chapter.
- **Lifetime management** The container provides configurable policies that determine when a component is loaded into process memory and how long it remains active once it is loaded.
- **CORBA services** The container must provide a basic set of services. In particular, naming, transactions, security, and event services are typically required.
- **Assembly and deployment tools** There are many aspects of a component that are configurable. When assembling and deploying an application, the components and the relationships between those components must be configured. This is most likely to be done with the aid of proprietary graphical tools.

Component Implementor

A component implementor develops components or groups of components. The component implementor might either be a third party who develops generic components and offers them for sale. It also might be an application developer who develops components for a particular application.

One of the aims of the CCM is to encourage modular software, so that an application can be assembled from a mixture of ready-made, off-the-shelf components and custom-made application components.

A finished component is assembled as a *component package*, which consists of a library file (C++) or class file (Java), together with its CORBA component descriptor. A *CORBA component descriptor* is an XML file that contains information about the supported interfaces and the services supported by the component. A CORBA component descriptor uses `.ccd` as its file suffix.

Component Assembler

A component assembler uses a graphical tool to assemble and configure a set of CORBA components and the relationships between them. The output from the assembly step is an *assembly archive*, as shown in Figure 13.8.

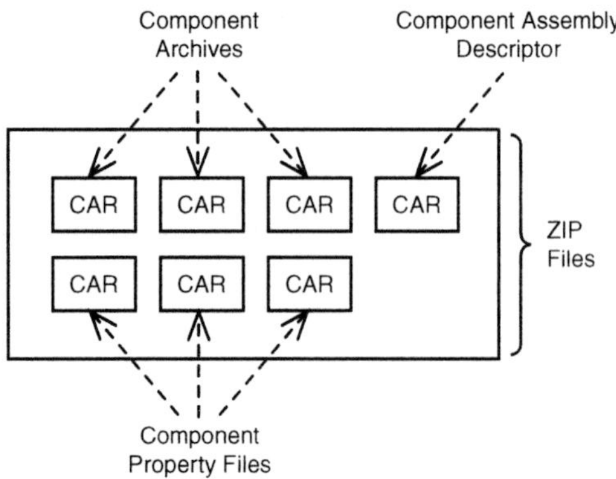

Figure 13.8

Contents of a component assembly archive file.

The assembly archive contains the following elements:

- **CORBA component archives** Each CORBA component archive consists of a component and its associated CORBA component descriptor.
- **Component property files** If you want to use the CCM configurator mechanism, you can supply a component property file for each component to be configured. A component property file uses `.cpf` as its file suffix.
- **Component assembly descriptor** This is an XML file that describes the relationships between components and provides bootstrap information for each component. For example, a component assembly descriptor can specify whether a component is to be registered with the naming service and whether a component should undergo a configuration phase at deployment time. A component assembly descriptor uses `.cad` as its file suffix.

An assembly archive can be packaged in a compressed file (Zip file), known as an *assembly archive file*, which uses `.aar` as its file suffix. When using a Zip file for the archive, the `.cad` file should be placed in a directory called `meta-inf` within the archive.

Component Deployer

A component deployer is responsible for loading components to one or more hosts where CORBA containers are available. The component deployer takes an assembly archive as input and decides how to distribute the components in the assembly across the hosts.

All of the components in the assembly are bootstrapped in an orderly fashion during the configuration phase. After the configuration phase is finished, the application is ready to service requests.

Typically, a deployment tool is provided by the ORB vendor to help the component deployer perform these tasks.

Component Assembly and Deployment

A component assembler uses the proprietary tools provided with a container to assemble and configure an application's components. Typically, this affects both the component deployment descriptors and the assembly descriptors.

Optionally, a component assembler can define component property files to configure some of the components. The data values stored in a property file are used to initialize the attributes of a component.

For example, consider the `HeadOfficeC` component with some attributes added to the component body:

```
//IDL
#include <components.idl>
#include "RecycleBroker.idl"

module RecycleBroker {
    ...
    component HeadOfficeC     supports HeadOffice
    {
        attribute string  office_location;
        attribute boolean test_mode;
    };
    ...
};
```

The `office_location` and `test_mode` attributes can be initialized from a component property file, which contains a list of name-value pairs. Each name-value pair consist of:

- ***Name*** The name of an IDL attribute.
- ***Value*** The value used to set the attribute.

The attribute types that can be configured in this way are limited to a particular subset of IDL. The types can be any combination of structs, sequences, or simple types. The simple type is one of the following: `boolean`, `char`, `octet`, `double`, `float`, `short`, `long`, `unsigned short`, `unsigned long`, `string`, and stringified object references.

The container services can also be configured using the deployment descriptors. A component assembler can specify the following policies for each component:

- Servant lifetime policies
- Transaction policies
- Security policies

These are the policies for basic components; they are discussed in more detail in the following sections. The additional policies for extended components are not discussed here.

Servant Lifetime Policies

One of the key services provided by a container is the capability to manage component lifetimes automatically. This is a fundamental service because it prevents servers from running out of memory.

Components can be activated when they are needed (loaded from persistent storage, if necessary) and then deactivated when they are no longer needed or if the server is running low on memory. Effectively, this provides a mechanism to swap objects into and out of memory.

Underlying the container are a number of POA instances that manage component lifetimes. The components themselves are implemented as servants, so the policies are called *servant lifetime policies*. The following servant lifetime policies are supported:

- **Method** The component remains active only for the duration of a single operation request.
- **Transaction** The component is activated at the beginning of a transaction in which the component takes part. The component remains active until the transaction completes (committed or rolled back).
- **Component** The component is activated in response to the first operation request and remains active until the component itself explicitly requests passivation.
- **Container** The component is activated in response to the first operation request and remains active until the container decides to passivate it.

Transaction Policies

CORBA supports two alternative approaches to managing component transactions:

- **Container-managed transactions** Transactional behavior is determined by specifying a transaction policy in the deployment descriptor. The container manages transactions according to the specified policy.
- **Self-managed transactions** No transaction policy is specified in the deployment descriptor. A component implementor can write code to manage transactions explicitly, using the CORBA transaction service.

Assuming that the component implementor chooses the container-managed transaction model, the following transaction policies are available:

- **`NOT_SUPPORTED`** If the calling code is not associated with a transaction, the invoked operation is not associated with a transaction either.
  If the calling code is associated with a transaction, `T1`, the invoked operation does not join in the transaction. The `T1` transaction is suspended for the duration of the invocation.
- **`REQUIRED`** If the calling code is not associated with a transaction, the container begins a new transaction, `T2`, and commits the `T2` transaction at the end of the invocation.

If the calling code is associated with a transaction, `T1`, the invoked operation joins the transaction.

- **`SUPPORTS`** If the calling code is not associated with a transaction, the invoked operation is not associated with a transaction either.
  If the calling code is associated with a transaction, `T1`, the invoked operation joins the transaction.
- **`REQUIRES_NEW`** If the calling code is not associated with a transaction, the container begins a new transaction, `T2`, and commits the `T2` transaction at the end of the invocation.
  If the calling code is associated with a transaction, `T1`, the container begins a new transaction, `T2`, and commits the `T2` transaction at the end of the invocation. The `T1` transaction is suspended for the duration of the invocation.
- **`MANDATORY`** If the calling code is not associated with a transaction, the container raises a `CORBA::TRANSACTION_REQUIRED` system exception.
  If the calling code is associated with a transaction, `T1`, the invoked operation joins the transaction.
- **`NEVER`** If the calling code is not associated with a transaction, the invoked operation is not associated with a transaction either.
  If the calling code is associated with a transaction, `T1`, the container raises a `CORBA::INVALID_TRANSACTION` system exception.

Security Policies

Container security depends on an underlying implementation of the CORBA security service. Some of the basic security features required by a container implementation are

- **Privacy** The transport of messages between client and server must be made secure using encryption.
- **Authentication** It must be possible to establish positively the identity and credentials of clients.
- **Integrity** There must be a way of ensuring that messages have not been tampered with.

These are the basic features required of a CORBA security service implementation.

The deployment descriptor supports the notion of required rights for invoking operations on an IDL interface. It is possible to associate any number of required rights with a particular operation.

An operation protected by required rights is invoked as follows in a secure environment:

1. When a client initially opens a secure connection to the server, the client is authenticated by the server, establishing the client's identity and credentials.
2. The client sends an encrypted request across the secure connection to invoke the operation.

3. Based on the client's credentials, the server determines whether or not the client has rights that match the operation's required rights.
4. If the client has the required rights, the operation is invoked. Otherwise, an error is returned.

Details of how a security service maps a client's credentials to the required rights is left as an implementation detail for the container provider.

Policy Constraints

Some policies are incompatible with one or more component categories. Constraints are imposed on the policy choices, depending on whether a component is in the session, service, entity, or process category.

Table 13.2 summarizes the constraints that affect lifetime and transaction policies for each of the component categories.

Table 13.2 Policy Constraints Affecting Each Component Category

Component Category	Servant Lifetime Policies	Transaction Policies
Session	any	none
Service	method	none
Entity	any	any
Process	any	any

No transaction policies can be defined for session or service components because operations on these components cannot participate in transactions. Effectively, these components behave as if the `NOT_SUPPORTED` transaction policy is in force.

Summary

The CORBA specification makes components available on two levels of functionality. This chapter focuses on the basic level, because of its compatibility with the EJB standard.

It is shown how the concept of a CORBA object is replaced by the equivalent concept of a component managed by a component home and embedded in a container. A new dialect of IDL, extended IDL, is defined that includes grammatical constructions for components, introduced by the `component` and `home` keywords.

There are four fundamental categories of component: session, service, entity, and process. The choice of component category has considerable influence on the component's implementation and life-cycle properties. For example, session and service components are transient, whereas entity and process components typically are long lived.

Some important aspects of the CCM are touched on only briefly in this chapter—for example, persistence integration, container services, and component assembly and deployment.

Components IDL Module

Listing 13.33 is a partial listing of the `Components` IDL module, containing only definitions and interfaces that are relevant to basic components.

Listing 13.33 Part of the `Components` *IDL Module—Applicable to Basic Components*

```
//IDL
#ifndef _COMPONENTS_IDL_
#define _COMPONENTS_IDL_
//import ::CORBA
//import ::SecurityLevel2
//import ::CosPersistentState
//import ::PortableServer
//import ::CosNotification
//import ::CosNotifyChannelAdmin

// ADDED
#pragma prefix "omg.org"

#include <omg/orb.idl>

module Components {
    typedef string FeatureName;
    typedef sequence<FeatureName> NameList;
    valuetype Cookie {
        private sequence<octet> cookieValue;
    };

    exception InvalidName { };
    exception InvalidConnection { };
    exception ExceededConnectionLimit { };
    exception AlreadyConnected { };
    exception NoConnection { };
    exception CookieRequired { };
    exception DuplicateKeyValue { };
    exception NoKeyAvailable { };
    exception InvalidKey { };
    exception UnknownKeyValue { };
    exception BadEventType {
        CORBA::RepositoryId expected_event_type;
    };
    exception HomeNotFound { };
    exception WrongComponentType { };
    exception InvalidConfiguration { };

    valuetype ConnectionDescription {
        public Cookie ck;
```

Listing 13.33 continued

```
        public Object objref;
    };

    typedef sequence<ConnectionDescription> ConnectedDescriptions;

    abstract valuetype PrimaryKeyBase { };

    interface CCMObject; //forward reference

    interface CCMHome {
        CORBA::IRObject get_component_def ();
        CORBA::IRObject get_home_def ();
        void remove_component ( in CCMObject comp);
    };

    interface KeylessCCMHome {
        CCMObject create_component();
    };

    interface HomeFinder {
        CCMHome find_home_by_component_type (
            in CORBA::RepositoryId comp_repid)
            raises (HomeNotFound);
        CCMHome find_home_by_home_type (
            in CORBA::RepositoryId home_repid)
            raises (HomeNotFound);
        CCMHome find_home_by_name (
            in string home_name)
            raises (HomeNotFound);
    };

    interface Configurator {
        void configure (in CCMObject comp)
            raises (WrongComponentType);
    };

    valuetype ConfigValue {
        public FeatureName name;
        public any value;
    };

    typedef sequence<ConfigValue> ConfigValues;

    interface StandardConfigurator : Configurator {
        void set_configuration (in ConfigValues descr);
    };
```

Listing 13.33 continued

```
interface HomeConfiguration : CCMHome {
    void set_configurator (in Configurator cfg);
    void set_configuration_values (
        in ConfigValues config);
    void complete_component_configuration (in boolean b);
    void disable_home_configuration();
};

interface CCMObject
    //: Navigation, Receptacles, Events
    // The preceding base interfaces are not needed
    // for basic components.
{
    CORBA::IRObject get_component_def ( );
    CCMHome get_ccm_home( );
    PrimaryKeyBase get_primary_key( )
        raises (NoKeyAvailable);
    void configuration_complete( )
        raises (InvalidConfiguration);
    void remove();
};

interface Enumeration {
    boolean has_more_elements();
    CCMObject next_element();
};

module Transaction {

    typedef sequence<octet> TranToken;

    exception NoTransaction { };
    exception NotSupported { };
    exception SystemError { };
    exception Rollback { };
    exception HeuristicMixed { };
    exception HeuristicRollback { };
    exception Security { };
    exception InvalidToken { };

    enum Status {
        ACTIVE,
        MARKED_ROLLBACK,
        PREPARED,
        COMMITTED,
        ROLLED_BACK,
        NO_TRANSACTION,
```

Listing 13.33 continued

```
        PREPARING,
        COMMITTING,
        ROLLING_BACK
    };

    local interface UserTransaction {
        void begin ()
            raises (NotSupported, SystemError);
        void commit ()
            raises (Rollback, NoTransaction,
            HeuristicMixed, HeuristicRollback,
            Security, SystemError);
        void rollback ()
            raises (NoTransaction,
            Security, SystemError);
        void set_rollback_only ()
            raises (NoTransaction, SystemError);
        Status get_status()
            raises (SystemError);
        void set_timeout (in long to)
            raises (SystemError);
        TranToken suspend ()
            raises (NoTransaction, SystemError);
        void resume (in TranToken txtoken)
            raises (InvalidToken, SystemError);
    };
};

module Basic {

    //typedef SecurityLevel2::Credentials Principal;

    enum CCMExceptionReason {
        SYSTEM_ERROR,
        CREATE_ERROR,
        REMOVE_ERROR,
        DUPLICATE_KEY,
        FIND_ERROR,
        OBJECT_NOT_FOUND,
        NO_SUCH_ENTITY
    };

    exception CCMException {
        CCMExceptionReason reason;
    };
    exception IllegalState { };
```

Listing 13.33 continued

```
local interface CCMContext {
    //Principal get_caller_principal();
    CCMHome get_CCM_home();
    boolean get_rollback_only()
        raises (IllegalState);
    Transaction::UserTransaction get_user_transaction()
        raises (IllegalState);
    boolean is_caller_in_role (in string role);
    void set_rollback_only()
        raises (IllegalState);
};

local interface EnterpriseComponent {};

local interface SessionContext : CCMContext {
    Object get_CCM_object()
        raises (IllegalState);
};

local interface SessionComponent : EnterpriseComponent {
    void set_session_context ( in SessionContext ctx)
        raises (CCMException);
    void ccm_activate()
        raises (CCMException);
    void ccm_passivate()
        raises (CCMException);
    void ccm_remove ()
        raises (CCMException);
};

local interface SessionSynchronization {
    void after_begin ()
        raises (CCMException);
    void before_completion ()
        raises (CCMException);
    void after_completion (
        in boolean committed)
        raises (CCMException);
};

local interface EntityContext : CCMContext {
    Object get_CCM_object ()
        raises (IllegalState);
    PrimaryKeyBase get_primary_key ()
        raises  (IllegalState);
};
```

Listing 13.33 continued

```
        local interface EntityComponent : EnterpriseComponent {
            void set_entity_context (in EntityContext ctx)
                raises (CCMException);
            void unset_entity_context ()
                raises (CCMException);
            void ccm_activate ()
                raises (CCMException);
            void ccm_load ()
                raises (CCMException);
            void ccm_store ()
                raises (CCMException);
            void ccm_passivate ()
                raises (CCMException);
            void ccm_remove ()
                raises (CCMException);
        };
    };

    module Deployment {

        enum AssemblyState {INACTIVE, INSERVICE};
        exception UnknownImplId { };
        exception InvalidLocation { };
        exception InvalidAssembly { };

        interface ComponentInstallation {
            boolean install(
        in string implUUID,
        in string component_loc)
                raises (InvalidLocation);
            boolean replace(
                in string implUUID,
                in string component_loc)
                raises (InvalidLocation);
            boolean remove(in string implUUID)
                raises  (UnknownImplId);
        };

        interface Assembly {
            boolean build();
            boolean tear_down();
            AssemblyState get_state();
        };

        interface AssemblyFactory {
            Cookie create(in string assembly_loc)
                raises (InvalidLocation);
```

Listing 13.33 continued

```
          Assembly lookup(in Cookie c)
              raises (InvalidAssembly);
          boolean destroy(in Cookie c)
              raises (InvalidAssembly);
      };
  };
};

#endif  /* _COMPONENTS_IDL_ */
```

CHAPTER 14

The Internet Inter-ORB Protocol

The Internet Inter-ORB Protocol is a vendor-independent communication protocol that was designed by the OMG to facilitate the transfer of CORBA requests from one ORB to another and, as such, is primarily focused on ORB-to-ORB communication. This chapter discusses the IIOP protocol, as well as the General Inter-ORB Protocol (GIOP) from which IIOP is derived, from a CORBA developer's perspective. The lower-level details (such as header structures) of the specifications are actually relevant only to those designing and implementing an ORB and are not of particular interest to CORBA application developers.

GIOP: The Basis for IIOP

Because IIOP is actually a specialization of the General Inter-ORB Protocol (GIOP), much of the behavior of IIOP is in fact inherited from the more general GIOP protocol specification. Thus it is appropriate to first discuss GIOP itself, after which the IIOP-specific specializations to GIOP can be discussed.

First, some history. The CORBA 1.1 specification published in late 1991 did not define enough of the low-level details that were necessary for one ORB to communicate effectively with another vendor's ORB, leaving many details to be decided by the various implementing vendors. Different vendors therefore developed highly proprietary ways of communication, rendering their ORBs incompatible with each other. The details that were needed to establish compatibility began to be furnished with the publication of the CORBA 2.0 specification. There are currently three versions of GIOP: 1.0, 1.1, and the latest, which is 1.2. These versions correspond to the CORBA specification revisions 2.0, 2.1, and 2.3, respectively. (So far, CORBA specifications 2.4 and beyond have not included revisions to the GIOP specification.)

As an interoperability protocol, GIOP sits on top of the fourth layer of the OSI Reference Model (the Transport layer) and, along with IIOP, which I will discuss shortly, occupies roughly both the Session and Presentation layers. The actual ORB would constitute the Application layer in the OSI model. Table 14.1 shows the relative placement of GIOP and IIOP as compared to the standard OSI Model layers.

Table 14.1 Model Layers

OSI Model	CORBA GIOP/IIOP
Application	ORB
Presentation	GIOP
Session	IIOP
Transport	TCP
Network	IP
Data Link	Data Link
Physical	Physical

GIOP Design Goals

GIOP is called a *general* protocol because it is neutral with respect to its underlying transport protocol; it can be mapped to any available connection-oriented transport. The OMG had several design goals in mind with the GIOP which, in their own word, have been pursued "vigorously." They are

- Widest possible availability: With its association with TCP/IP as its core transport, GIOP/IIOP rests on the most widely available transport mechanism and the fundamental transport of the Internet.
- Simplicity: By design, the GIOP is a simple protocol. Nothing extraneous was added that did not directly service the essential design and motivation.
- Scalability: The GIOP/IIOP protocols were designed specifically to handle the demands of individual ORB communication, as well as networked and bridged ORB communication over the Internet.
- Low cost: In keeping with its principle of simplicity, the IIOP was designed so that it could be provided as an additional transport with a minimum of effort. This can be seen in Java 1.3 with Sun's decision to substitute IIOP for the Java Remote Method Protocol (JRMP) in RMI. Among other things, this will allow an Enterprise Java Session Bean to communicate directly with a CORBA server or allow a CORBA client to use an EJB Entity Bean encapsulation.
- Generality: The GIOP message formats were designed to be transport-independent, to enable additional transport mechanisms to be defined under it, in addition to IIOP.
- Architectural neutrality: The GIOP makes no assumptions about the architecture of dependent ORBs and treats dependent ORBs as "black box" designs.

A final fundamental goal of the GIOP specification is that it only specifies the external protocol for ORB-to-ORB communication. An ORB is not required to implement IIOP as its own internal protocol (and in fact a number of commercially available ORBs do not). Thus an ORB produced by a particular vendor, for example, is free to use a proprietary protocol to communicate with other ORBs from that same vendor.

GIOP Core Elements

The OMG has defined several central requirements for interoperability between ORB implementations. First is the capability for two ORBs to communicate without one ORB needing any knowledge of the other ORB's internal mechanisms. This is a fundamental tenet of encapsulation. Second, the transport protocol must provide support for all CORBA functionality. It cannot pick and choose the functionality it wants to deliver and still conform to the specification. In addition, the transport protocol must support the integrity of content and semantics in the communication between one ORB and another.

In order to facilitate its operation, the GIOP defines three core elements that this chapter covers in turn. They are

- Common Data Representation (CDR): CDR defines a common way to express data during transport. It defines solutions to issues such as network byte ordering (big-endian versus little-endian architectures), byte alignment (byte, 2-byte, 4-byte alignment schemes), serialization ordering, and so on.
- Message Formats: With GIOP 1.2, eight message formats are defined to handle requests between ORB components, communication involving the dynamic location of agents, and communication between agents.
- Transport Assumptions: General assumptions about the transport underlying GIOP, which requires a semi-reliable connection-oriented transport that is implemented as an octet (byte) stream.

Common Data Representation (CDR)

CDR is a transfer syntax for the mapping of data defined via OMG IDL types to a low-level representation suitable for efficient and safe transport over the network. CDR supports primitive as well as constructed types, pseudo-object types such as TypeCodes and exceptions, and object references. All CDR information is transmitted as a serialized octet (8-bit byte) stream.

When addressing issues of network byte ordering, GIOP specifies that the sender must send its data in its native architecture (memory byte ordering), and it is the job of the receiver to do any order adjustment, if necessary. That way, the sender only has to send the data, and it doesn't have to know anything about the recipient architecture's byte ordering. The byte ordering (big-endian/little-endian) of the sender's architecture is encoded in a byte in the header (GIOP 1.0) or as the first bit in the flags octet in the GIOP 1.1 header structure. The recipient examines this flag and makes any modifications that are necessary in the incoming data stream. If the recipient happens to use the same network byte order as the sender, no transformation needs to be done on either side, and no time is wasted. Compare this with ONC's External Data Representation (XDR) in RPC, which uses a single-canonical format that forces all data into big endian form by default, which means that communication between two little-endian boxes must (needlessly) perform two translations, which is obviously inefficient. In CORBA, there would be no need for any conversions in byte ordering between identical architectures, making it a more efficient protocol in this regard.

Likewise, all data in the octet stream is aligned on the sender's natural boundaries. The sender does not have to make any modifications depending on whether the receiver is working on a byte, 2-byte, or 4-byte alignment architecture. As in the case of network byte ordering, it is the job of the recipient to adjust the alignment to its own needs, but again, only if necessary. This is again in contrast to XDR, which forces all XDR data to a default 4-byte alignment, using padding if necessary.

Finally, all datatypes defined in the IDL must be represented in the CDR, including pseudo-objects such as TypeCodes.

CDR assumes an agreement on the parts of both the sender and the recipient as to the types of data being transmitted. That means that both parties must know in advance the semantics of the operation (via the IDL definition itself), because GIOP will not mark the datatypes of the data being transmitted. This implicit typing is in keeping with the ONC XDR approach and is distinguished from the basic encoding rules of ASN.1, which uses explicit typing. This use of implicit typing is a common cause of the CORBA MARSHAL exception, which would be thrown if the parameter lists of an operation differ in some detail, based on either a skeleton or stub having been produced from outdated IDL information.

As mentioned previously, primitive types are encoded into an octet stream according to their natural boundaries: 1 byte for a `char`; 2 bytes for a `short`; 4 bytes for a `long`; 8 bytes for a `double`, etc. The encoded values will be padded, if necessary, either with random (uninitialized) bytes or with zeroized bytes. (CDR does not specify padding contents, so this depends on the particular ORB implementation.) An octet stream is a sequence of 8-bit values that undergo no marshaling by either the sender or recipient. An octet does not undergo network byte order conversions. Marshaling may occur before data is inserted into an octet stream. A string is encoded as a combination of an `unsigned long` length value (padded with zeros if necessary), followed by the characters of the string in a sequence of octets, followed by a `NUL`. So the string `hello` would be encoded as a 4-byte `long` value of `6` representing the length of the string plus the `NUL`, followed by the bytes `h`, `e`, `l`, `l`, `o`, followed by a `NUL`, for a total of 10 bytes. Other complex types are recursively encoded according to the same principles based on the individual types of the contained data. For example, a struct is encoded in the order of declared appearance according to each individual element's type. Sequences are encoded as an `unsigned long` value that represents the number of elements in the sequence, followed by the elements of the sequence, encoded again according to their type.

The only variability in alignment requirements is in the wchar IDL primitive type, which may be aligned on a 1-, 2-, or 4-octet alignment, depending on the byte orientation of the code set in use. For example, if the code set is byte oriented as in Shift-JIS, each wide character is represented as one or more octets. If, on the other hand, the code set is not byte oriented (as in Unicode), each wide character is represented as one or more codepoints, usually either `unsigned shorts` or `unsigned longs`.

Message Formats

GIOP message formats have a few significant features. First of all, the OMG has defined only eight message formats. This greatly simplifies the task of bringing an application to the GIOP format. These eight messages (which include the fragment format introduced in GIOP 1.1) provide for all the functional communication needs of ORBs as they communicate with one another, including advanced support for optional capabilities such as object location, dynamic agent migration, and so on. Because of this simplicity, the GIOP message formats allow ORBs to support object location and migration as an optional feature, without requiring all ORBs to support such features if that support would be inappropriate for the ORB's intended purpose (for lightweight ORBs, for instance). Finally, GIOP message formats provide full and direct support of all functions and semantics required by the CORBA specification, including exception reporting, operational context exchange, and all object reference operations for the support of remote interfaces.

The eight types of messages supported by GIOP between a client and server are (along with the originator of the message)

- `Request` (client)
- `LocateRequest` (client)
- `CancelRequest` (client)
- `MessageError` (client or server)
- `Fragment` (client or server)
- `Reply` (server)
- `LocateReply` (server)
- `CloseConnection` (server only in GIOP 1.0 and 1.1; client or server in GIOP 1.2)

The two most important messages are the `Request` and `Reply` messages, which conduct the core communication of any ORB. The `Request` message is used by the client to invoke an operation on the server. Other operations might include get and set operations for accessing interface attributes. If the client has indicated that it wants to receive a reply (by setting the Response Expected flag to `1` in the `Request` header), the server will generate a `Reply` message back to the client. Depending on the circumstances, the `Reply` message contains one of the following:

- `NO_EXCEPTION`: A normal reply, containing the return value as well as values of `out` and `inout` parameters.
- `USER_EXCEPTION`: A reply containing a CORBA user exception.

- SYSTEM_EXCEPTION: A reply containing a CORBA system exception.
- LOCATION_FORWARD: A reply containing information directing the client to a new location. The client ORB is then responsible for resending the Request to the specified location.

In addition, GIOP 1.2 adds the following Reply types:

- LOCATION_FORWARD_PERM: A reply similar semantically to LOCATION_FORWARD, except that the new location can be considered to be "permanent." (Both IORs are still valid, but the new one is preferred.) Note that use of LOCATION_ FORWARD_PERM is already deprecated, due to problems it may cause with object hashing.
- NEEDS_ADDRESSING_MODE: A reply containing a GIOP::AddressingDisposition. The client ORB is then responsible for resending the Request using the specified addressing mode.

The other messages are available to make the ORB operations more efficient. The CancelRequest message allows the client to inform a server that it is no longer interested in the results of the original request (the execution of the call is not interrupted, however). The LocateRequest and LocateReply messages allow clients to locate servers and receive an object reference or an error status as the reply. The CloseConnection message indicates that one party is closing the connection. After a CloseConnection message has been delivered, no further messages should be sent across the connection. If further communication is desired, a new connection must be established. The MessageError message is sent as a general GIOP error message, whenever a malformed message or message header has been received by the recipient. The type of the offending message is returned.

Finally, the Fragment message type allows the transfer of larger amounts of data. To fragment a message, the fragment flag in the Request message header is set to true, and subsequent fragments of that original Request message are sent in Fragment messages, with the header flag being set to true if more fragments are to follow, or false if this represents the last fragment. When the server has received the false indication, it knows that the request is complete, and it can begin to process the request.

GIOP Transport Assumptions

GIOP message transfer makes certain assumptions about the underlying transport. First, the GIOP defines a client/server architecture as it pertains to its connections. The client side of a connection always establishes the connection and sends a request to the server. The server receives requests and responds with replies. Only with the bidirectional support in GIOP 1.2 can a server actually originate a message on an existing connection established by a client. Second, an individual ORB implementation may choose to multiplex messages over a single connection to a particular server, allowing multiple clients to communicate with a single server over a single connection. This is possible because the target of each request is identified in the request itself.

GIOP makes several further general assumptions about its underlying transport. First, it assumes the transport is connection oriented, as opposed to a protocol such as the Hypertext Transfer Protocol (HTTP), which is connectionless. A connection-oriented protocol allows a client to have an open connection to a server across more than one transmission.

The second assumption made is that connections are full duplex, meaning that transmissions are bidirectional and the recipient can reply over the same connection without having to know the address of the sender. This greatly simplifies the communication. Connections are assumed to be symmetric as far as termination is concerned (and for most all messages in GIOP 1.2), in the sense that either end of the connection can close it at any time. If either party determines that a connection has terminated without being directly notified of termination (that is to say, a `CloseConnection` message was never delivered), the determining ORB must assume that an abortive disconnect has occurred and will need to handle the error.

The GIOP also assumes that the transport provides a byte stream capability, meaning that serialization of messages is not encumbered by any arbitrary size limitation, and that message fragmentation, for longer messages, may be necessary and will be supported. Finally, GIOP assumes that an error will be delivered to both ends of a connection if an error develops during transmission.

IIOP Specialization of GIOP

Recall that GIOP is independent of any particular transport and is thus an abstract protocol. The Internet Inter-ORB Protocol specifies theTransmission Control Protocol and thus is based on TCP/IP. IIOP is really not much more than GIOP implemented onto the reliable connection-oriented TCP/IP. It supports the sending of GIOP messages over TCP/IP sockets. The one thing that IIOP adds over GIOP is the definition of an IIOP profile for inclusion in an IOR. To instantiate GIOP, all IIOP has to do is define how the IIOP profile encodes the TCP/IP socket information inside the IOR, so the recipient can communicate with the sender.

Figure 14.1 illustrates the information encapsulated in an IOR.

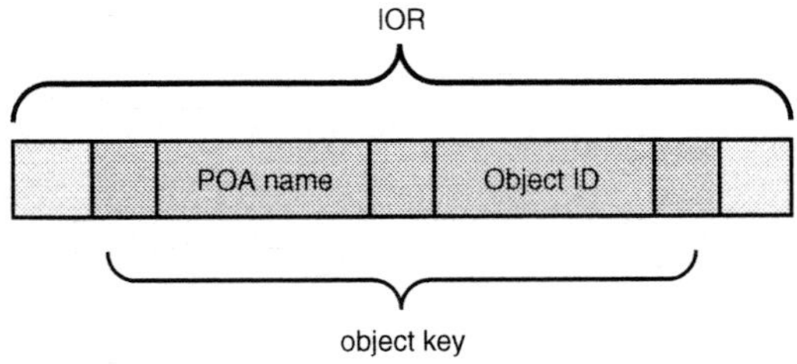

Figure 14.1

Interoperable Object Reference (IOR) Contents.

An IOR is composed of

- Repository ID: A string that identifies the object's most derived type.
- Profiles: Each profile encapsulates all of the information needed to locate and communicate with an object over a particular transport layer.

The required components of an IIOP profile include

- IIOP version: The IIOP protocol version (major and minor version numbers).
- Communication endpoint information: Information required for the client ORB to connect to the server. For TCP/IP, this includes a host identifier (either a host name or an IP address) and port number.
- Object key: An identifier which the server uses to identify the specific object (recall that a server may contain multiple objects).

In addition, an IOR may contain certain optional information, such as metadata that identifies the server's ORB (such information could be used, for example, to optimize communications between ORBs from the same vendor). Such information is contained in what are known as *profile components* or *tagged components.*

Finally, an IOR has certain properties that deserve attention:

- Can be a null reference: In other words, the IOR doesn't point to any object at all.
- Can dangle: In other words, the IOR points to an object that no longer exists.
- Is strongly typed: The type of the object to which the IOR refers can be determined from the IOR itself.
- Can be serialized: An IOR may be converted to a string which can then be written to a file, stored on an HTTP server, or otherwise made persistent for future use.
- May be persistent: A server may take certain steps to ensure that one of its objects retains an identical IOR over multiple server invocations. (Otherwise, subsequent invocations of the server executable may result in new, distinct IORs being created for its objects.)

Summary

This chapter discussed the Internet Inter-ORB Protocol (IIOP), which is actually a specialization of the General Inter-ORB Protocol (GIOP). GIOP, it was seen, was designed to combine wide availability, simplicity, scalability, and low cost. The protocol specifies a Common Data Representation (CDR) as well as eight message formats for communication between client and server ORBs. Additionally, GIOP makes some assumptions about the characteristics of the underlying transport layer.

IIOP, as its name suggests, is the protocol used to facilitate interoperability between ORBs from different vendors. It was revealed that, practically speaking, IIOP is little more than an implementation of GIOP using TCP/IP. Consequently, a discussion of GIOP suffices to provide most of the interesting details of the IIOP protocol as well. IIOP does, however, define the IIOP profile, which encapsulates the endpoint information (as well as other data) necessary to establish TCP/IP communications.

PART III

SYNTAX REFERENCE

CHAPTER 15

IDL Data Types

This chapter provides an IDL syntax and language mapping reference for all of the core IDL data types. This reference material is split across the following major sections:

- **Built-In IDL Types**—Describes basic built-in types, such as `boolean` and `long`, as well as keywords, such as `union` and `struct`, that enable the user to define new IDL data types.
- **Pseudo-IDL from the `CORBA` Module**—Describes core object types from the CORBA module, such as `CORBA::NamedValue` and `CORBA::Object`.
- **Exception Types**—Describes the C++ and Java exception base classes.
- **The `PortableServer` Module**—Describes a few types in the `PortableServer` module that have non-standard mappings to C++ and Java.
- **Java `Helper` and `Holder` Types**—Describes the templates used for generating Helper and Holder classes.

NOTE

The reference material in this chapter is based on the CORBA 2.4.2 core specification, the C++ language mapping document ptc/00-01-02, and the Java language mapping document ptc/00-02-07. All extracts from the CORBA specification appearing in this chapter are taken from those documents and used with permission of the OMG.

Built-In IDL Types

This section provides a detailed guide to most of the built-in types, describing the IDL syntax and language mappings for each one. The following categories of type are described here:

- Basic types—For example, types such as `char`, `short`, `long`, and so on.
- Constructed types—The types `struct`, `union`, and `enum`.
- Template types—The types `sequence<...>`, `fixed<...>`, `string<...>`, and `wstring<...>`.
- Complex declarator—Array types.
- Native type—Types declared using the `native` keyword.

Some built-in types are not included in this section because they are described at length elsewhere in this book. The omitted types are

- The `any` type—See Chapter 8, "The `any` Type."
- User-defined `interface` types—See Chapter 5, "Object References."
- User-defined `value` types—see Chapter 11, "Objects by Value."

Consult the relevant chapter for further details about those types.

Array Type

This section describes the IDL syntax and CDR encoding of an IDL array type. The mapping of an IDL array to C++ and to Java is also described and illustrated by example.

IDL Syntax

An array has the syntax of a declarator. It can be declared only as part of a `typedef` expression, as follows:

```
//IDL
typedef ElementTypeSpec ArrayType[DimSize][DimSize]...
```

The *`ArrayType`* is the name of the newly defined array. An integer expression in square brackets, `[`*`DimSize`*`]`, is appended for each dimension of the array. The *`ElementTypeSpec`* gives the type of the array elements and *`DimSize`* is a constant integer expression that evaluates to a positive value. For example, a two-dimensional array can be defined using a `typedef` expression, as follows:

```
//IDL
typedef long L2Array[50][100];
```

The element type of an array can, in principle, be declared using an arbitrary type specifier. From CORBA 2.4 onward, however, using anonymous type specifiers for the element type is deprecated. The following example shows the approved way to declare an array, which avoids using an anonymous type specifier for the element type:

```
//IDL
typedef string<16> String16;
typedef String16 SmallStringArr[100];
```

Contrast this with the deprecated style of array declaration in the following example, in which an anonymous type specifier is used directly to declare the element type:

```
//IDL
typedef string<16> SmallStringArr[100];    // Deprecated
```

CDR Encoding

An array is encoded by marshaling all of its elements in sequence. If the array is multidimensional, the sequence of elements is determined by letting the rightmost index vary most quickly, while the leftmost index varies most slowly.

IDL Example

The following IDL example illustrates the syntax for declaring arrays:

```
//IDL
module MyModule {
    enum CellState { EMPTY, CROSS, CIRCLE };
    typedef CellState TicTacToe[3][3];

    typedef string StringArr[2];

    interface MyInterface {
        TicTacToe useArrayFixLen(
                    in    TicTacToe ttt_in,
                    inout TicTacToe ttt_inout,
                    out   TicTacToe ttt_out
                 );
        StringArr useArrayVarLen(
                    in    StringArr sa_in,
                    inout StringArr sa_inout,
                    out   StringArr sa_out
                 );
    };
};
```

C++ Mapping

An IDL array, *<array_name>*, maps to a typedef'ed C++ array, *<c++_array_name>*. In addition, a number of other types are defined to manage the *<c++_array_name>* type in C++, as shown in Table 15.1.

Table 15.1 C++ Mapping of an Array Type

Type	Description
<c++_array_name>	A typedef of a C++ array.
<c++_array_name>_var	An array _var type is a smart pointer that manages memory for dynamically-allocated array instances.
<c++_array_name>_slice	A pointer to an array slice, <c++_array_name>_slice*, is the C++ return type of an operation that returns an array.
<c++_array_name>_forany	An array _forany type is a helper type for inserting an array into an any. See Chapter 8 "The any Type."
<c++_array_name>_out	An array _out type is the formal parameter type for an array passed as an out parameter.

For examples of how to use the array types listed in Table 15.1, see Chapter 4 "Memory Management." A number of static functions are also provided to help you to allocate, free, and copy dynamically-allocated array instances, as shown in Table 15.2.

Table 15.2 C++ Static Functions for Managing Dynamically-Allocated Arrays

Static Function	Description
<c++_array_name>_slice* <c++_array_name>_alloc()	Allocate an instance of <c++_array_name> on the heap.
void <c++_array_name>_free(<c++_array_name>_slice* arr)	Free the memory associated with arr.
<c++_array_name>_slice* <c++_array_name>_dup(const <c++_array_name> _slice arr) *	Allocate an instance of <c++_array_name> on the heap and copy the contents of arr into it.
void <c++_array_name>_copy(<c++_array_name>_slice* to const <c++_array_name>_slice* from)	Copy the contents of the from array into the to array.

For explanations and examples of using the static functions listed in Table 15.2, see Chapter 4.

The TicTacToe array defined in the preceding "IDL Example" section maps to C++ as follows:

```
//C++
namespace MyModule
{
```

```
enum CellState
{
    EMPTY,
    CROSS,
    CIRCLE
    // Possibly more members (implementation dependent)
};
...
typedef     CellState TicTacToe[3][3];
typedef     CellState TicTacToe_slice[3];

// Implementation dependent definitions generated for:
// ===>    TicTacToe_out
// ===>    _tc_TicTacToe

static TicTacToe_slice* TicTacToe_alloc();
static void             TicTacToe_free(TicTacToe_slice* );
static TicTacToe_slice* TicTacToe_dup(const TicTacToe_slice*);

static void TicTacToe_copy(
    TicTacToe_slice* _to,
    const TicTacToe_slice* _from
);

class TicTacToe_var
{
public:
    TicTacToe_var() ... { ... }
    TicTacToe_var(TicTacToe_slice*) { ... }
    TicTacToe_var(const TicTacToe_var&) { ... }

    TicTacToe_var& operator=(TicTacToe_slice*) { ... }
    TicTacToe_var& operator=(const TicTacToe_var&) { ... }

    const TicTacToe_slice* in() const { ... }
    TicTacToe_slice*       inout()    { ... }
    TicTacToe_slice*&      out()      { ... }
    TicTacToe_slice*&      _retn()    { ... }

    TicTacToe_slice& operator[](CORBA::ULong index) { ... }
    const TicTacToe_slice& operator[](CORBA::ULong index) const { ... }

    // Implementation-dependent conversion operators are included
    // to support parameter passing.
    ... // (not shown)
};

class TicTacToe_forany
{
```

```
    public:
        TicTacToe_forany() ... { ... }
        TicTacToe_forany(TicTacToe_slice*, CORBA::Boolean _nocopy = 0) { ... }
        TicTacToe_forany(const TicTacToe_forany&) { ... }

        TicTacToe_forany& operator=(TicTacToe_slice*) { ... }
        TicTacToe_forany& operator=(const TicTacToe_forany&) { ... }

        const TicTacToe_slice* in() const { ... }
        TicTacToe_slice*       inout()    { ... }
        TicTacToe_slice*&      out()      { ... }
        TicTacToe_slice*&      _retn()    { ... }

        TicTacToe_slice& operator[](CORBA::ULong index) { ... }
        const TicTacToe_slice& operator[](CORBA::ULong index) const { ... }

        // Implementation-dependent conversion operators are included
        // to support parameter passing.
        ... // (not shown)
    };
    ...
};
```

C++ Usage

The following C++ code shows how to invoke the `useArrayFixLen()` operation defined in the preceding "IDL Example" section:

```
//C++
//Assume 'obj' is an object reference of MyModule::MyInterface type.
{
// Example of using a fixed-length array.
MyModule::TicTacToe T;
T[0][0]=MyModule::CIRCLE; T[0][1]=MyModule::CIRCLE; T[0][2]=MyModule::CROSS;
T[1][0]=MyModule::EMPTY ; T[1][1]=MyModule::CROSS ; T[1][2]=MyModule::EMPTY;
T[2][0]=MyModule::CROSS; T[2][1]=MyModule::EMPTY ; T[2][2]=MyModule::EMPTY;

MyModule::TicTacToe_var InValV    = MyModule::TicTacToe_dup(T);
MyModule::TicTacToe_var InoutValV = MyModule::TicTacToe_dup(T);
// Fixed-length array => Allocate space for 'out' parameter.
MyModule::TicTacToe_var OutValV   = MyModule::TicTacToe_alloc();

MyModule::TicTacToe_var RecvValV
        = obj->useArrayFixLen(InValV, InoutValV, OutValV);

printTicTacToe(RecvValV);
printTicTacToe(InoutValV);
printTicTacToe (OutValV);
}
```

The following C++ code shows how to invoke the `useArrayVarLen()` operation defined in the preceding "IDL Example" section:

```
// Invoke the useArrayVarLen() operation
{
// Example of using a variable-length array.
MyModule::StringArr InVal;
InVal[0] = CORBA::string_dup("Zig");
InVal[1] = CORBA::string_dup("Zag");

MyModule::StringArr InoutVal;
InoutVal[0] = CORBA::string_dup("Rodge");
InoutVal[1] = CORBA::string_dup("Podge");

// Variable-length array => No allocation for 'out' parameter.
MyModule::StringArr_var OutValV;

MyModule::StringArr_var RecvValV
        = obj->useArrayVarLen(InVal, InoutVal, OutValV);

...  // Do something with *RecvValV, InoutVal,  and *OutValV
}
...
```

The `printTicTacToe()` that prints out the `TicTacToe` array function can be implemented as follows:

```
//C++
void printCellState(const MyModule::CellState cell)
{
    char result;
    switch (cell) {
        case MyModule::EMPTY  :  result = ' ';  break;
        case MyModule::CROSS  :  result = 'X';  break;
        case MyModule::CIRCLE :  result = 'O';  break;
        default :  result = ' ';  break;
    }
    cout << result;
}

void printTicTacToe(const MyModule::TicTacToe T)
{
    CORBA::ULong k;
    for (k=0; k<3; k++)
    {
        printCellState(T[k][0]);
        cout << "|";
        printCellState(T[k][1]);
        cout << "|";
```

```
        printCellState(T[k][2]);
        cout << endl;
        if (k < 2) { cout << "-----" << endl; }
    }
    cout << endl;
}
```

Java Mapping

An IDL array, *<array_name>*, with *<element_type>* elements maps directly to a Java array of the same dimensions with mapped *<java_element_type>* elements. Holder and helper classes, *<java_array_name>*`Holder` and *<java_array_name>*`Helper`, are generated according to the standard template described in the section "Java `Helper` and `Holder` Types" later in this chapter.

For example, the `MyModule.TicTacToe` IDL array maps to Java as shown in Table 15.3.

Table 15.3 Java Mapping of the **`TicTacToe`** ***Array Type***

IDL Type	Java Mapped Types
`MyModule::TicTacToe` array	`MyModule.CellState[3]`
	`MyModule.TicTacToeHolder`
	`MyModule.TicTacToeHelper`

Java Usage

The following Java code shows how to invoke the `useArrayFixLen()` operation defined in the preceding "IDL Example" section:

```
//Java
//Assume 'obj' is an object reference of MyModule::MyInterface type.
import MyModule.CellState;
{
MyModule.CellState T[][] = new MyModule.CellState[3][3];
T[0][0]=CellState.CIRCLE; T[0][1]=CellState.CIRCLE; T[0][2]=CellState.CROSS;
T[1][0]=CellState.EMPTY ; T[1][1]=CellState.CROSS ; T[1][2]=CellState.EMPTY;
T[2][0]=CellState.CROSS ; T[2][1]=CellState.EMPTY ; T[2][2]=CellState.EMPTY;

MyModule.CellState InVal[][]       = T;  // Shallow copy.
MyModule.TicTacToeHolder InoutValH = new MyModule.TicTacToeHolder(T);
MyModule.TicTacToeHolder OutValH   = new MyModule.TicTacToeHolder();

MyModule.CellState RecvVal[][]=obj.useArrayFixLen(InVal, InoutValH, OutValH);

... // Do something with RecvVal,  InoutValH.value, and OutValH.value.
}
```

The following Java code shows how to invoke the `useArrayVarLen()` operation defined in the preceding "IDL Example" section:

```
// Invoke the useArrayVarLen() operation
{
String InVal[] = new String[2];
InVal[0] = "Zig";
InVal[1] = "Zag";

String T[] = new String[2];
T[0] = "Rodge";
T[1] = "Podge";
MyModule.StringArrHolder InoutValH = new MyModule.StringArrHolder(T);
MyModule.StringArrHolder OutValH = new MyModule.StringArrHolder();

String RecvVal[] = obj.useArrayVarLen(InVal, InoutValH, OutValH);

... // Do something with RecvVal, InoutValH.value, and OutValH.value.
}
...
```

`boolean` Type

This section describes the IDL constant syntax and CDR encoding of an IDL `boolean` type. The mapping of an IDL `boolean` to C++ and to Java is also described and illustrated by example.

IDL Constant Declaration

```
//IDL
const boolean BooleanConst = BooleanLiteral;
const boolean BooleanConst = OtherBooleanConst;
```

A new `boolean` constant, *`BooleanConst`*, can be defined either in terms of a literal, *`BooleanLiteral`*, or in terms of an existing constant, *`OtherBooleanConst`*. No infix or unary operators are allowed in IDL `boolean` constant declarations.

The *`BooleanLiteral`* can be one of values shown in Table 15.4.

Table 15.4 IDL Boolean Literals

Value	Description
TRUE	Boolean literal for *true*.
FALSE	Boolean literal for *false*.

CDR Encoding

A `boolean` occupies a single octet (eight bits) and is marshaled by putting it into the next available position in an octet stream (alignment on a one-byte boundary). The value `0x01` represents TRUE and `0x00` represents FALSE.

IDL Example

The following IDL example illustrates the syntax for declaring boolean constants:

```
//IDL
const boolean GLOBAL_BOOL = TRUE;

module MyModule {
    const boolean MODULE_BOOL = FALSE;

    interface MyInterface {
        const boolean INTERFACE_BOOL = TRUE;

        boolean useBoolean(
                    in    boolean b_in,
                    inout boolean b_inout,
                    out   boolean b_out
                );
    };
};
```

C++ Mapping

The preceding "IDL Example" maps to C++ as follows:

```
//C++
const CORBA::Boolean GLOBAL_BOOL = 1;

namespace MyModule {
    const CORBA::Boolean MODULE_BOOL = 0;

    class MyInterface : public virtual CORBA::Object {
        static const CORBA::Boolean INTERFACE_BOOL;

        virtual CORBA::Boolean useBoolean(
                    CORBA::Boolean     b_in,
                    CORBA::Boolean&    b_inout,
                    CORBA::Boolean_out b_out
                ) =0;
    };
};
...
// Initialisation of 'INTERFACE_BOOL'
const CORBA::Boolean MyModule::MyInterface::INTERFACE_BOOL = 1;
...
```

C++ Usage

The following C++ code shows how to invoke the useBoolean() operation defined in the preceding "IDL Example" section:

```
//C++
//Assume 'obj' is an object reference of MyModule::MyInterface type.
CORBA::Boolean InoutVal = 0;
CORBA::Boolean OutVal;

CORBA::Boolean RecvVal = obj->useBoolean(1, InoutVal, OutVal);

cout << "Returned value = " << RecvVal << endl;
cout << "Inout value    = " << InoutVal << endl;
cout << "Out value      = " << OutVal << endl;
...
```

Java Mapping

The preceding "IDL Example" maps to Java as follows:

```
//Java
// File containing global constants:
public interface GLOBAL_BOOL {
    public static final boolean value = true;
};
...
// File containing module and interface constants:
package MyModule;

public interface MODULE_BOOL {
    public static final boolean value = false;
};

public interface MyInterfaceOperations
{
    public static final boolean INTERFACE_BOOL = true;

    boolean useBoolean(
                boolean                       b_in,
                org.omg.CORBA.BooleanHolder b_inout,
                org.omg.CORBA.BooleanHolder b_out
            );
};

public interface MyInterface
    extends MyInterfaceOperations,
    org.omg.CORBA.Object,
    org.omg.CORBA.portable.IDLEntity  { }
...
```

Java Usage

The following Java code shows how to invoke the `useBoolean()` operation defined in the preceding "IDL Example" section:

```
//Java
//Assume 'obj' is an object reference of MyModule::MyInterface type.
boolean InVal = true;
org.omg.CORBA.BooleanHolder InoutValH = new org.omg.CORBA.BooleanHolder(false);
org.omg.CORBA.BooleanHolder OutValH = new org.omg.CORBA.BooleanHolder();

boolean RecvVal = obj.useBoolean(InVal, InoutValH, OutValH);

System.out.println("Returned value = " + RecvVal);
System.out.println("Inout value    = " + InoutValH.value);
System.out.println("Out value      = " + OutValH.value);
...
```

char Type

This section describes the IDL constant syntax and CDR encoding of an IDL `char` type. The mapping of an IDL `char` to C++ and to Java is also described and illustrated by example.

IDL Constant Declaration

```
//IDL
const char CharConst = CharLiteral;
const char CharConst = OtherCharConst;
```

A new `char` constant, *`CharConst`*, can be defined either in terms of a literal, *`CharLiteral`*, or in terms of an existing constant, *`OtherCharConst`*. No infix or unary operators can be used in IDL `char` constant declarations.

The *`CharLiteral`* consists of a character enclosed in single quotes, for example `'a'`, or an escape sequence enclosed in single quotes, for example `'\n'`. See Chapter 16, "IDL Grammar" for the list of character escape sequences.

CDR Encoding

A `char` (eight bits) is marshaled by putting it into the next available position in an octet stream (alignment on a one-byte boundary). The value of a `char` is liable to undergo conversion during transmission, in accordance with the GIOP codeset conversion framework.

IDL Example

The following IDL example illustrates the syntax for declaring `char` constants:

```
//IDL
const char GLOBAL_CHAR = 'a';

module MyModule {
    const char MODULE_CHAR = '\n';
```

```
    interface MyInterface {
        const char INTERFACE_CHAR = '\x2E';

        char useChar(
                    in    char c_in,
                    inout char c_inout,
                    out   char c_out
                );
    };
};
```

C++ Mapping

The preceding "IDL Example" maps to C++ as follows:

```
//C++
const CORBA::Char GLOBAL_CHAR = 'a';

namespace MyModule {
    const CORBA::Char MODULE_CHAR = '\n';

    class MyInterface : public virtual CORBA::Object {
        static const CORBA::Char INTERFACE_CHAR;

        virtual CORBA::Char useChar(
                    CORBA::Char     c_in,
                    CORBA::Char&    c_inout,
                    CORBA::Char_out c_out
                ) =0;
    };
};
...
// Initialisation of 'INTERFACE_CHAR'
const CORBA::Char MyModule::MyInterface::INTERFACE_CHAR = '\x2E';
...
```

C++ Usage

The following C++ code shows how to invoke the `useChar()` operation defined in the preceding "IDL Example" section:

```
//C++
//Assume 'obj' is an object reference of MyModule::MyInterface type.
CORBA::Char InoutVal = 'y';
CORBA::Char OutVal;

CORBA::Char RecvVal = obj->useChar('x', InoutVal, OutVal);

cout << "Returned value = " << RecvVal << endl;
cout << "Inout value    = " << InoutVal << endl;
cout << "Out value      = " << OutVal << endl;
...
```

Java Mapping

The preceding "IDL Example" maps to Java as follows:

```
//Java
// File containing global constants:
public interface GLOBAL_CHAR {
    public static char char value = 'a';
};
...

// File containing module and interface constants:
package MyModule;

public interface MODULE_CHAR {
    public static final char value = '\n';
};

public interface MyInterfaceOperations
{
    public static final char INTERFACE_CHAR = '\u2E';

    char useChar(
             char                         c_in,
             org.omg.CORBA.CharHolder c_inout,
             org.omg.CORBA.CharHolder c_out
         );
};

public interface MyInterface
    extends MyInterfaceOperations,
    org.omg.CORBA.Object,
    org.omg.CORBA.portable.IDLEntity  { }
...
```

Java Usage

The following Java code shows how to invoke the `useChar()` operation defined in the preceding "IDL Example" section:

```
//Java
//Assume 'obj' is an object reference of MyModule::MyInterface type.
char InVal = 'x';
org.omg.CORBA.CharHolder InoutValH = new org.omg.CORBA.CharHolder('y');
org.omg.CORBA.CharHolder OutValH = new org.omg.CORBA.CharHolder();

char RecvVal = obj.useChar(InVal, InoutValH, OutValH);

System.out.println("Returned value = " + RecvVal);
System.out.println("Inout value    = " + InoutValH.value);
System.out.println("Out value      = " + OutValH.value);
...
```

double Type

This section describes the IDL constant syntax and CDR encoding of an IDL `double` type. The mapping of an IDL `double` to C++ and to Java is also described and illustrated by example.

IDL Constant Declaration

```
//IDL
const double DoubleConst = FloatingPointExpression;
```

A new `double` constant, *`DoubleConst`*, is defined in terms of a floating-point expression, *`FloatingPointExpression`*, which is composed of floating-point literals, other floating point constants, and arithmetical operators.

The `+`, `-`, `*`, `/` infix and `+`, `-` unary operators are allowed in IDL `double` constant declarations.

Literals are specified in floating point format, for example `1.6e-19`, as described in Chapter 16 "IDL Grammar."

CDR Encoding

When a `double` is appended to an octet stream, it is marshaled as eight octets (64 bits) and aligned on an eight-byte boundary. The order in which the octets are marshaled depends on the current byte-ordering of the octet stream (big-endian or little-endian).

The encoding of the `double` follows the IEEE standard for a double-precision floating point number.

IDL Example

The following IDL example illustrates the syntax for declaring `double` constants:

```
//IDL
const double GLOBAL_DOUBLE = 2E30;

module MyModule {
    const double MODULE_DOUBLE = 3.14;

    interface MyInterface {
        const double INTERFACE_DOUBLE = 6.0 * MODULE_DOUBLE;

        double useDouble(
                    in    double d_in,
                    inout double d_inout,
                    out   double d_out
                );
    };
};
```

C++ Mapping

The preceding "IDL Example" maps to C++ as follows:

```
//C++
const CORBA::Double GLOBAL_DOUBLE = 2.0e30;

namespace MyModule {
    const CORBA::Double MODULE_DOUBLE = 3.14;

    class MyInterface : public virtual CORBA::Object {
        static const CORBA::Double INTERFACE_DOUBLE;

        virtual CORBA::Double useDouble(
                    CORBA::Double     d_in,
                    CORBA::Double&    d_inout,
                    CORBA::Double_out d_out
                ) =0;
    };
};
...
// Initialisation of 'INTERFACE_DOUBLE'
const CORBA::Double MyModule::MyInterface::INTERFACE_DOUBLE
                                  = 6.0*MyModule::MODULE_DOUBLE;
...
```

C++ Usage

The following C++ code shows how to invoke the `useDouble()` operation defined in the preceding "IDL Example" section:

```
//C++
//Assume 'obj' is an object reference of MyModule::MyInterface type.
CORBA::Double InoutVal = 1.23456;
CORBA::Double OutVal;

CORBA::Double RecvVal = obj->useDouble(1.0e10, InoutVal, OutVal);

cout << "Returned value = " << RecvVal << endl;
cout << "Inout value    = " << InoutVal << endl;
cout << "Out value      = " << OutVal << endl;
...
```

Java Mapping

The preceding "IDL Example" maps to Java as follows:

```
//Java
// File containing global constants:
public interface GLOBAL_DOUBLE {
    public static final double value = (double) 2.0e30;
```

```
};
...

// File containing module and interface constants:
package MyModule;

public interface MODULE_DOUBLE {
    public static final double value = (double) 3.14;
};

public interface MyInterfaceOperations
{
    public static final double INTERFACE_DOUBLE = (double) 18.84;

    double useDouble(
                double                        d_in,
                org.omg.CORBA.DoubleHolder d_inout,
                org.omg.CORBA.DoubleHolder d_out
            );
};

public interface MyInterface
    extends MyInterfaceOperations,
    org.omg.CORBA.Object,
    org.omg.CORBA.portable.IDLEntity  { }
...
```

Java Usage

The following Java code shows how to invoke the `useDouble()` operation defined in the preceding "IDL Example" section:

```
//Java
//Assume 'obj' is an object reference of MyModule::MyInterface type.
double InVal = 1.0e10;
org.omg.CORBA.DoubleHolder InoutValH = new org.omg.CORBA.DoubleHolder(1.23456);
org.omg.CORBA.DoubleHolder OutValH = new org.omg.CORBA.DoubleHolder();

double RecvVal = obj.useDouble(InVal, InoutValH, OutValH);

System.out.println("Returned value = " + RecvVal);
System.out.println("Inout value    = " + InoutValH.value);
System.out.println("Out value      = " + OutValH.value);
...
```

`enum` Type

This section describes the IDL syntax, IDL constant syntax, and CDR encoding of an IDL enumerated type. The mapping of an IDL `enum` to C++ and to Java is also described and illustrated by example.

IDL Syntax

An enum can stand on its own as a type declaration, in which case it is terminated by a semicolon:

```
//IDL
enum EnumType { EnumeratorList };
```

The *EnumType* is the name of the newly defined enum. The *EnumeratorList* is a list of one or more identifiers that represent the possible values of the enumeration. For example, the following enum declares three identifiers, YELLOW, ORANGE, and RED:

```
//IDL
enum WarmColor { YELLOW, ORANGE, RED };
```

An enum can also be used as a type specifier, in which case the terminating semicolon is omitted. For example, an enum can be given an alias using a typedef expression, as follows:

```
//IDL
typedef enum Fruit { APPLE, PEAR } FruitAlias;
```

IDL Constant Declaration

Enumerated constants can be defined, as follows:

```
//IDL
const EnumType EnumConst = ScopedIdentifier;
const EnumType EnumConst = OtherEnumConst;
```

A new enumerated constant, *EnumConst*, can be defined either in terms of an enumerator of *EnumType* type, *ScopedIdentifier*, or in terms of an existing constant, *OtherEnumConst*. No infix or unary operators can be used in IDL enum constant declarations.

CDR Encoding

An enum is encoded as a long integer (32 bits)—see the section "long Type."

IDL Example

The following IDL example illustrates the syntax for declaring enumerations and enumeration constants:

```
//IDL
module MyModule {
    interface MyInterface {
        enum Veg { CARROT, POTATO, SPINACH, BEETROOT };

        const Veg INTERFACE_VEG = SPINACH;

        Veg useEnum(
                    in    Veg v_in,
```

```
                    inout Veg v_inout,
                    out   Veg v_out
                );
    };
    const MyInterface::Veg MODULE_VEG = MyInterface::POTATO;
};
const MyModule::MyInterface::Veg GLOBAL_VEG = MyModule::MODULE_VEG;
```

C++ Mapping

The Veg enumeration defined in the preceding "IDL Example" maps to C++ as follows:

```
//C++
namespace MyModule {
    class MyInterface : public virtual CORBA::Object {
        enum Veg
        {
            CARROT,
            POTATO,
            SPINACH,
            BEETROOT
            // Implementation-dependent extra value.
        };

        // Implementation dependent definitions generated for:
        // ===>    Veg_out
        // ===>    _tc_Veg

        static const MyModule::MyInterface::Veg INTERFACE_VEG;

        virtual Veg useEnum(
            Veg      v_in,
            Veg&     v_inout,
            Veg_out  v_out
        ) = 0;
    };

    const MyModule::MyInterface::Veg MODULE_VEG =MyModule::MyInterface::POTATO;
};
const MyModule::MyInterface::Veg GLOBAL_VEG = MyModule::MyInterface::POTATO;
...
// Initialisation of 'INTERFACE_VEG'
const MyModule::MyInterface::Veg MyModule::MyInterface::INTERFACE_VEG
    = MyModule::MyInterface::SPINACH;
...
```

C++ Usage

The following C++ code shows how to invoke the `useEnum()` operation defined in the preceding "IDL Example" section:

```
//C++
//Assume 'obj' is an object reference of MyModule::MyInterface type.
MyModule::MyInterface::Veg InVal    = MyModule::MyInterface::BEETROOT;
MyModule::MyInterface::Veg InoutVal = MyModule::MyInterface::CARROT;
MyModule::MyInterface::Veg OutVal;

MyModule::MyInterface::Veg RecvVal = obj->useEnum(InVal, InoutVal, OutVal);

printVeg(RecvVal);
printVeg(InoutVal);
printVeg(OutVal);
...
```

The `printVeg()` function can be implemented, as follows:

```
//C++
void printVeg(MyModule::MyInterface::Veg v)
{
    switch (v)
    {
        case MyModule::MyInterface::CARROT :
            cout << "carrot" << endl;
            break;
        case MyModule::MyInterface::POTATO :
            cout << "potato" << endl;
            break;
        case MyModule::MyInterface::SPINACH :
            cout << "spinach" << endl;
            break;
        case MyModule::MyInterface::BEETROOT :
            cout << "beetroot" << endl;
            break;
    }
}
```

Java Mapping

An IDL enumerated type, *<enum_name>*, maps to a Java class, *<java_enum_name>*, because there is no native enumerated type available in Java. Holder and helper classes, *<java_enum_name>*`Holder` and *<java_enum_name>*`Helper`, are generated according to the standard template described in the section “Java `Helper` and `Holder` Types” later in this chapter.

For example, the `MyModule.MyInterface.Veg` enumerated type maps to Java as shown in Table 15.5.

Table 15.5 Java Mapping of the `TicTacToe` *Array Type*

IDL Type	Java Mapped Types
MyModule.MyInterface.Veg	MyModule.MyInterfacePackage.Veg
	MyModule.MyInterfacePackage.VegHolder
	MyModule.MyInterfacePackage.VegHelper

The `MyModule.MyInterfacePackage.Veg` Java class is defined as follows:

```
//Java
package MyModule.MyInterfacePackage;

public class Veg
    implements org.omg.CORBA.portable.IDLEntity
{
    public static final int _CARROT = 0;
    public static final Veg CARROT = new Veg(0);
    public static final int _POTATO = 1;
    public static final Veg POTATO = new Veg(1);
    public static final int _SPINACH = 2;
    public static final Veg SPINACH = new Veg(2);
    public static final int _BEETROOT = 3;
    public static final Veg BEETROOT = new Veg(3);

    public static Veg from_int(int value) { ... }

    public int value() { ... }
}
```

Java Usage

The following Java code shows how to invoke the `useEnum()` operation defined in the preceding "IDL Example" section:

```
//Java
//Assume 'obj' is an object reference of MyModule::MyInterface type.
MyModule.MyInterfacePackage.Veg InVal
    = MyModule.MyInterfacePackage.Veg.BEETROOT;
MyModule.MyInterfacePackage.VegHolder InoutValH
    = new MyModule.MyInterfacePackage.VegHolder(
            MyModule.MyInterfacePackage.Veg.CARROT
      );
MyModule.MyInterfacePackage.VegHolder OutValH
    = new MyModule.MyInterfacePackage.VegHolder();

MyModule.MyInterfacePackage.Veg RecvVal
    = obj.useEnum(InVal, InoutValH, OutValH);
```

```
printVeg(RecvVal);
printVeg(InoutValH.value);
printVeg(OutValH.value);
...
```

The `printVeg()` method can be implemented, as follows:

```
//Java
public class MyModule.MyInterfaceImpl implements MyModule.MyInterfacePOATie
{
    public static void printVeg(MyModule.MyInterfacePackage.Veg v)
    {
        switch (v.value() )
        {
            case MyModule.MyInterfacePackage.Veg._CARROT :
                System.out.println("carrot");
                break;
            case MyModule.MyInterfacePackage.Veg._POTATO :
                System.out.println("potato");
                break;
            case MyModule.MyInterfacePackage.Veg._SPINACH :
                System.out.println("spinach");
                break;
            case MyModule.MyInterfacePackage.Veg._BEETROOT :
                System.out.println("beetroot");
                break;
        }
    }
}
```

`exception` Type

This section describes the IDL syntax and CDR encoding of an IDL user exception type. The mapping of an IDL `exception` to C++ and to Java is also described and illustrated by example.

IDL Syntax

An `exception` stands on its own as a type declaration and is terminated by a semicolon:

```
//IDL
exception ExcType { MemberList };
```

The *`ExcType`* is the name of the newly defined `exception`. There must be at least one member in *`MemberList`* and each member consists of a type specifier followed by a comma-separated declarator list. For example, the following `OutOfRange` exception declares three members, `minValue`, `maxValue`, and `errorDetails`:

```
//IDL
exception OutOfRange {
    long long  minValue, maxValue;
```

```
    string     errorDetails;
};
```

An exception cannot be used as a type specifier. Once an exception type has been declared, it can only be used in the raises clause of an operation declaration.

The members of an exception can, in principle, be declared using arbitrary type specifiers. From CORBA 2.4 onward, however, using anonymous type specifiers in the member list is deprecated. The following example shows the approved way to declare an exception, which avoids the use of anonymous type specifiers in the member list:

```
//IDL
typedef string<100> String100;
typedef sequence<octet> OctetSeq;
struct IncidentTime { short hours, minutes, seconds; };

exception ApprovedException {
    String100    shortDescription;
    OctetSeq     raw_data;
    IncidentTime when_happened;
};
```

Contrast this with the deprecated style of exception declaration in the following example, in which anonymous type specifiers are used directly to declare exception members:

```
//IDL
exception DeprecatedException {
    string<100>      shortDescription;  // Deprecated
    sequence<octet> raw_data;           // Deprecated
    struct IncidentTime {
        short hours, minutes, seconds;
    } when_happened;                    // Poor style, but not deprecated.
};
```

CDR Encoding

A user exception type is marshaled into an octet stream by marshaling the exception's repository ID as a string, followed by each of the exception members in the same order as they appear in the IDL definition.

IDL Example

The following IDL example illustrates the syntax for declaring a user exception type:

```
//IDL
module MyModule {
    exception OutOfRange {
        long long minValue, maxValue;
        string    errorDetails;
    };
```

```
    interface MyInterface {
        void useException(long long val) raises (OutOfRange);
    };
};
```

C++ Mapping

The `OutOfRange` user exception defined in the preceding "IDL Example" maps to C++ as follows:

```
//C++
namespace MyModule {
    class OutOfRange: public CORBA::UserException
    {
    public:
        OutOfRange();
        OutOfRange(
            CORBA::LongLong _itfld_minValue,
            CORBA::LongLong _itfld_maxValue,
            const char*     _itfld_errorDetails
        );
        void operator=(const OutOfRange&);

        CORBA::LongLong minValue;
        CORBA::LongLong maxValue;
        <impl_dependent_string_manager_type> errorDetails;

        // MEMORY MANAGEMENT: _downcast() returns a pointer to the original
        //   OutOfRange exception - that is, the exception is not duplicated.
        static OutOfRange*       _downcast(CORBA::Exception* exc);
        static const OutOfRange* _downcast(const CORBA::Exception* exc);

        // DEPRECATED: _narrow() is deprecated for exceptions
        //              - use _downcast() instead.
        static OutOfRange*       _narrow(CORBA::Exception* exc);
        static const OutOfRange* _narrow(const CORBA::Exception* exc);

        virtual void _raise() const;

        // Additional implementation-dependent functions
        ... // (not shown)
    };
};
...
```

C++ Usage

The `MyModule::OutOfRange` exception can be raised by the `useException()` operation implementation, as follows:

```
//C++
...
// Assume that 'MyModule_MyInterfaceImpl' implements 'MyModule::MyInterface'.
void
MyModule_MyInterfaceImpl::useException(const CORBA::LongLong val)
     throws (CORBA::SystemException, MyModule::OutOfRange)
{
    static CORBA::LongLong min = -15;
    static CORBA::LongLong max = 15;
    if (val < min) {
        throw MyModule::OutOfRange(min, max, "too small");
    }
    if (val > max) {
        throw MyModule::OutOfRange(min, max, "too large");
    }
    // Do something useful with the 'val' parameter...
    ...
}
```

The `MyModule::OutOfRange` exception can be caught on the client side, as follows:

```
//C++
//Assume 'obj' is an object reference of MyModule::MyInterface type.
{
    try {
        obj->useException(100);
    }
    catch (MyModule::OutOfRange& oor) {
        cout << "error: "        << oor.errorDetails << endl;
        cout << "\tMin value = " << oor.minValue << endl;
        cout << "\tMax value = " << oor.maxValue << endl;
    }
}
...
```

Java Mapping

An IDL user exception type, *<exc_name>*, maps to a Java class, *<java_exc_name>*. Holder and helper classes, *<java_exc_name>*`Holder` and *<java_exc_name>*`Helper`, are generated according to the standard template described in the section "Java `Helper` and `Holder` Types" later in this chapter.

For example, the `MyModule.OutOfRange` user exception type maps to Java as shown in Table 15.6.

Table 15.6 Java Mapping of the `OutOfRange` User Exception Type

IDL Type	Java Mapped Types
`MyModule.OutOfRange`	`MyModule.OutOfRange`
	`MyModule.OutOfRangeHolder`
	`MyModule.OutOfRangeHelper`

Each member variable declared in IDL maps to a corresponding public member of the Java `MyModule.OutOfRange` class. The `MyModule.OutOfRange` Java class is therefore defined as follows:

```
//Java
package MyModule;

public final class OutOfRange
    extends org.omg.CORBA.UserException
{
    public long minValue;
    public long maxValue;
    public java.lang.String errorDetails;

    public OutOfRange() { ... }
    public OutOfRange(
        long minValue,
        long maxValue,
        java.lang.String errorDetails
    ) { ... }
}
...
```

Java Usage

The `MyModule::OutOfRange` exception can be raised by the `useException()` operation implementation, as follows:

```
//C++
...
// Class 'MyModule.MyInterfaceImpl' implements 'MyModule::MyInterface'.
class MyModule.MyInterfaceImpl implements MyModule.MyInterfacePOATie {
    ...
    public void useException(long val)
         throw MyModule.OutOfRange
    {
        if (val < m_min) {
            throw new MyModule.OutOfRange(min, max, "too small");
        }
        if (val > m_max) {
            throw new MyModule.OutOfRange(min, max, "too large");
        }
        // Do something useful with the 'val' parameter...
        ...
    }
    private long m_min, m_max;
    ...
}
```

The MyModule::OutOfRange exception can be caught on the client side, as follows:

```
//C++
//Assume 'obj' is an object reference of MyModule::MyInterface type.
{
    try {
        obj.useException(100);
    }
    catch (MyModule.OutOfRange oor) {
        System.out.println("error: " + oor.errorDetails);
        System.out.println("\tMin value = " + oor.minValue);
        System.out.println("\tMax value = " + oor.maxValue);
    }
}
...
```

fixed Type

This section describes the IDL syntax, IDL constant syntax and CDR encoding of an IDL fixed-point type. The mapping of an IDL fixed to C++ and to Java is also described and illustrated by example.

IDL Syntax

A fixed data type has the syntax of a type specifier and it is declared as follows:

```
//IDL
fixed<Digits, Scale>
```

The *Digits* specifies the total number of significant digits, expressed as a constant integer expression that evaluates to a positive integer less than or equal to 31. The *Scale* specifies the number of digits following the decimal point, expressed as a constant integer expression that evaluates to a non-negative integer.

From CORBA 2.4 onward, the only context in which a fixed type specifier should appear is as part of a typedef expression. For example, a fixed data type can be given an alias using a typedef expression, as follows:

```
//IDL
typedef fixed<17,2> MonetaryAmount;
```

IDL Constant Declaration

Fixed-point constants can be defined, as follows:

```
//IDL
const fixed FixedConst = FixedPointExpression;
```

A new fixed constant, *FixedConst*, is defined in terms of a fixed-point expression, *FixedPointExpression*, which is composed of fixed-point literals, other fixed-point constants, arithmetical operators, and other fixed-point expressions enclosed in parentheses ( ).

The +, -, *, /, infix and +, -, unary operators are allowed in IDL `fixed` constant declarations.

Literals are specified in fixed-point literal format, for example `54.321d`, as described in Chapter 16.

CDR Encoding

A `fixed` type is marshaled to an octet stream using a form of binary coded decimal, where each digit of the `fixed` type occupies a half-octet and the last half-octet encodes the sign (`0xD` for negative, `0xC` for non-negative). It follows that a fixed type with `N` significant digits occupies `(N+1)/2` octets in the octet stream.

Alignment is on a one-byte boundary. The order in which the octets are marshaled is *independent* of the current byte-ordering—that is, the big-endian and little-endian representations of a `fixed` value are the same.

IDL Example

The following IDL example illustrates the syntax for declaring `fixed<>` types and `fixed` constants:

```
//IDL
const fixed GLOBAL_FIXED = 765.4321d;

module MyModule {
    const fixed MODULE_FIXED = GLOBAL_FIXED*100d;

    interface MyInterface {
        const fixed INTERFACE_FIXED = 0.003d;

        typedef fixed<31,2> BigMoney;

        BigMoney useFixed(
                    in    BigMoney lm_in,
                    inout BigMoney lm_inout,
                    out   BigMoney lm_out
                 );
    };
};
```

C++ Mapping

The preceding "IDL Example" maps to C++ as follows:

```
//C++
const CORBA::Fixed GLOBAL_FIXED("765.4321");

namespace MyModule {
    static const CORBA::Fixed MODULE_FIXED;
```

```
    // Implementation dependent definitions generated for:
    // ===>    BigMoney
    // ===>    BigMoney_var
    // ===>    BigMoney_out
    // ===>    _tc_BigMoney

    class MyInterface : public virtual CORBA::Object {
        static const CORBA::Fixed INTERFACE_FIXED;

        virtual BigMoney useFixed(
            const BigMoney &  lm_in,
            BigMoney &        lm_inout,
            BigMoney_out      lm_out
        ) = 0;
    };
};

...
// Initialisation of 'MODULE_FIXED' and 'INTERFACE_FIXED'
namespace MyModule
{
    const CORBA::Fixed MODULE_FIXED("76543.2100");
};
const CORBA::Fixed MyModule::MyInterface::INTERFACE_FIXED("0.003");
...
```

Fixed point values in C++ are represented using the standard class `CORBA::Fixed`, which is declared as follows:

```
//C++
namespace CORBA {
    class Fixed
    {
    public:
        // Constructors
        Fixed(int val = 0);
        Fixed(unsigned val);
        Fixed(Long val);
        Fixed(ULong val);
        Fixed(LongLong val);
        Fixed(ULongLong val);
        Fixed(Double val);
        Fixed(LongDouble val);
        Fixed(const Fixed& val);
        Fixed(const char*);
        ~Fixed();

        // Conversions
        operator LongLong() const;
```

```
        operator LongDouble() const;
        Fixed round(UShort scale) const;
        Fixed truncate(UShort scale) const;

        // Operators
        Fixed& operator=(const Fixed& val);
        Fixed& operator+=(const Fixed& val);
        Fixed& operator-=(const Fixed& val);
        Fixed& operator*=(const Fixed& val);
        Fixed& operator/=(const Fixed& val);
        Fixed& operator++();
        Fixed operator++(int);
        Fixed& operator--();
        Fixed operator--(int);
        Fixed operator+() const;
        Fixed operator-() const;
        Boolean operator!() const;

        // Other member functions
        UShort fixed_digits() const;
        UShort fixed_scale() const;
    };

    istream& operator>>(istream& is, Fixed& val);
    ostream& operator<<(ostream& os, const Fixed& val);

    Fixed operator + (const Fixed& val1, const Fixed& val2);
    Fixed operator - (const Fixed& val1, const Fixed& val2);
    Fixed operator * (const Fixed& val1, const Fixed& val2);
    Fixed operator / (const Fixed& val1, const Fixed& val2);
    Boolean operator > (const Fixed& val1, const Fixed& val2);
    Boolean operator < (const Fixed& val1, const Fixed& val2);
    Boolean operator >= (const Fixed& val1, const Fixed& val2);
    Boolean operator <= (const Fixed& val1, const Fixed& val2);
    Boolean operator == (const Fixed& val1, const Fixed& val2);
    Boolean operator != (const Fixed& val1, const Fixed& val2);
};
```

C++ Usage

The following C++ code shows how to invoke the `useFixed()` operation defined in the preceding "IDL Example" section:

```
//C++
//Assume 'obj' is an object reference of MyModule::MyInterface type.
MyModule::BigMoney InVal    = "12345.67d";
MyModule::BigMoney InoutVal = "12.34d";
MyModule::BigMoney OutVal;

MyModule::BigMoney RecvVal = obj->useFixed(InVal, InoutVal, OutVal);
```

```
cout << "RecvVal = "  << RecvVal << endl;
cout << "InoutVal = " << InoutVal << endl;
cout << "OutVal = "   << OutVal << endl;
...
```

Java Mapping

The `fixed` IDL type maps to Java as shown in Table 15.7.

Table 15.7 Java Mapping of the `fixed` Type

IDL Type	Java Mapped Types
`fixed`	`java.math.BigDecimal`
	`org.omg.CORBA.FixedHolder`
	`org.omg.CORBA.FixedHelper`

```
//Java
// File containing global constants:
public interface GLOBAL_FIXED
{
    public static final java.math.BigDecimal value
            = new java.math.BigDecimal("765.4321");
}
...

// File containing module and interface constants:
package MyModule;

public interface MODULE_FIXED
{
    public static final java.math.BigDecimal value
            = new java.math.BigDecimal("76543.21");
}

public interface MyInterfaceOperations
{
    public static final java.math.BigDecimal INTERFACE_FIXED
            = new java.math.BigDecimal("0.003");

    java.math.BigDecimal useFixed(
        java.math.BigDecimal         lm_in,
        org.omg.CORBA.FixedHolder lm_inout,
        org.omg.CORBA.FixedHolder lm_out
    );
};

public interface MyInterface
    extends MyInterfaceOperations,
```

```
    org.omg.CORBA.Object,
    org.omg.CORBA.portable.IDLEntity  { }
...
```

Java Usage

The following Java code shows how to invoke the `useFixed()` operation defined in the preceding "IDL Example" section:

```
//Java
//Assume 'obj' is an object reference of MyModule::MyInterface type.
java.math.BigDecimal    InVal     = new java.math.BigDecimal("12345.67");
org.omg.CORBA.FixedHolder InoutValH = new org.omg.CORBA.FixedHolder(
                                          new java.math.BigDecimal("12.34")
                                    );
org.omg.CORBA.FixedHolder OutValH   = new org.omg.CORBA.FixedHolder();

java.math.BigDecimal RecvVal = obj.useFixed(InVal, InoutValH, OutValH);

System.out.println("RecvVal = "  + RecvVal);
System.out.println("InoutVal = " + InoutValH.value);
System.out.println("OutVal = "   + OutValH.value);
...
```

`float` Type

This section describes the IDL constant syntax and CDR encoding of an IDL `float` type. The mapping of an IDL `float` to C++ and to Java is also described and illustrated by example.

IDL Constant Declaration

```
//IDL
const float FloatConst = FloatingPointExpression;
```

A new `float` constant, *`FloatConst`*, is defined in terms of a floating-point expression, *`FloatingPointExpression`*, which is composed of floating-point literals, other floating-point constants, arithmetical operators, and other floating-point expressions enclosed in parentheses `( )`.

The `+`, `-`, `*`, `/` infix and `+`, `-` unary operators are allowed in IDL `float` constant declarations.

Literals are specified in floating-point literal format, for example `1.6e-19`, as described in Chapter 16.

CDR Encoding

When a `float` is appended to an octet stream, it is marshaled as four octets (32 bits) and aligned on a four-byte boundary. The order in which the octets are marshaled depends on the current byte-ordering of the octet stream (big-endian or little-endian).

The encoding of the `float` follows the IEEE standard for a single-precision floating point number.

IDL Example

The following IDL example illustrates the syntax for declaring `float` constants:

```
//IDL
const float GLOBAL_FLOAT = 2E30;

module MyModule {
    const float MODULE_FLOAT = 3.14;

    interface MyInterface {
        const float INTERFACE_FLOAT = 6.0 * MODULE_FLOAT;

        float useFloat(
                  in    float f_in,
                  inout float f_inout,
                  out   float f_out
              );
    };
};
```

C++ Mapping

The preceding "IDL Example" maps to C++ as follows:

```
//C++
const CORBA::Float GLOBAL_FLOAT = 2.0e30F;

namespace MyModule {
    const CORBA::Float MODULE_FLOAT = 3.14F;

    class MyInterface : public virtual CORBA::Object {
        static const CORBA::Float INTERFACE_FLOAT;

        virtual CORBA::Float useFloat(
                   CORBA::Float     f_in,
                   CORBA::Float&    f_inout,
                   CORBA::Float_out f_out
                ) =0;
    };
};
...
// Initialisation of 'INTERFACE_FLOAT'
const CORBA::Float MyModule::MyInterface::INTERFACE_FLOAT = 18.84F;
...
```

C++ Usage

The following C++ code shows how to invoke the `useFloat()` operation defined in the preceding "IDL Example" section:

```
//C++
//Assume 'obj' is an object reference of MyModule::MyInterface type.
CORBA::Float InoutVal = 1.23456f;
CORBA::Float OutVal;

CORBA::Float RecvVal = obj->useFloat(1.0e10f, InoutVal, OutVal);

cout << "Returned value = " << RecvVal << endl;
cout << "Inout value    = " << InoutVal << endl;
cout << "Out value      = " << OutVal << endl;
...
```

Java Mapping

The preceding "IDL Example" maps to Java as follows:

```
//Java
// File containing global constants:
public interface GLOBAL_FLOAT {
    public static final float value = (float) 2.0e30;
};
...

// File containing module and interface constants:
package MyModule;

public interface MODULE_FLOAT {
    public static final float value = (float) 3.14;
};

public interface MyInterfaceOperations
{
    public static final float INTERFACE_FLOAT = (float) 18.84;

    float useFloat(
              float                          f_in,
              org.omg.CORBA.FloatHolder f_inout,
              org.omg.CORBA.FloatHolder f_out
          );
};

public interface MyInterface
    extends MyInterfaceOperations,
    org.omg.CORBA.Object,
    org.omg.CORBA.portable.IDLEntity  { }
...
```

Java Usage

The following Java code shows how to invoke the `useFloat()` operation defined in the preceding "IDL Example" section:

```
//Java
//Assume 'obj' is an object reference of MyModule::MyInterface type.
float InVal = 1.0e10f;
org.omg.CORBA.FloatHolder InoutValH = new org.omg.CORBA.FloatHolder(1.23456f);
org.omg.CORBA.FloatHolder OutValH = new org.omg.CORBA.FloatHolder();

float RecvVal = obj.useFloat(InVal, InoutValH, OutValH);

System.out.println("Returned value = " + RecvVal);
System.out.println("Inout value    = " + InoutValH.value);
System.out.println("Out value      = " + OutValH.value);
...
```

long Type

This section describes the IDL constant syntax and CDR encoding of an IDL `long` type. The mapping of an IDL `long` to C++ and to Java is also described and illustrated by example.

IDL Constant Declaration

```
//IDL
const long LongConst = IntegerExpression;
```

A new `long` constant, *`LongConst`*, is defined in terms of an integer expression, *`IntegerExpression`*, which is composed of integer literals, other integer constants, arithmetical operators, and other integer expressions enclosed in parentheses `( )`.

The +, -, *, /, %, <<, >>, &, |, ^ infix and +, -, ~ unary operators are allowed in IDL `long` constant declarations.

Literals are specified in integer literal format, for example `0x2F2E`, as described in Chapter 16.

CDR Encoding

When a `long` integer is appended to an octet stream, it is marshaled as four octets (32 bits) and aligned on a four-byte boundary. The order in which the octets are marshaled depends on the current byte-ordering of the octet stream (big-endian or little-endian).

IDL Example

The following IDL example illustrates the syntax for declaring `long` constants:

```
//IDL
const long GLOBAL_LONG = 365;
```

```
module MyModule {
    const long MODULE_LONG = GLOBAL_LONG & 0x00FF;

    interface MyInterface {
        const long INTERFACE_LONG = 07777;

        long useLong(
                 in    long l_in,
                 inout long l_inout,
                 out   long l_out
             );
    };
};
```

C++ Mapping

The preceding "IDL Example" maps to C++ as follows:

```
//C++
const CORBA::Long GLOBAL_LONG = 365;

namespace MyModule {
    const CORBA::Long MODULE_LONG = 109;

    class MyInterface : public virtual CORBA::Object {
        static const CORBA::Long INTERFACE_LONG;

        virtual CORBA::Long useLong(
                    CORBA::Long     l_in,
                    CORBA::Long&    l_inout,
                    CORBA::Long_out l_out
               ) =0;
    };
};
...
// Initialisation of 'INTERFACE_LONG'
const CORBA::Long MyModule::MyInterface::INTERFACE_LONG = 4095;
...
```

C++ Usage

The following C++ code shows how to invoke the useLong() operation defined in the preceding "IDL Example" section:

```
//C++
//Assume 'obj' is an object reference of MyModule::MyInterface type.
CORBA::Long InoutVal = -123;
CORBA::Long OutVal;

CORBA::Long RecvVal = obj->useLong(-321, InoutVal, OutVal);
```

```
cout << "Returned value = " << RecvVal << endl;
cout << "Inout value    = " << InoutVal << endl;
cout << "Out value      = " << OutVal << endl;
...
```

Java Mapping

The preceding "IDL Example" maps to Java as follows:

```
//Java
// File containing global constants:
public interface GLOBAL_LONG {
    public static final int value = (int) 365;
};
...

// File containing module and interface constants:
package MyModule;

public interface MODULE_LONG {
    public static final int value = (int) 109;
};

public interface MyInterfaceOperations
{
    public static final int INTERFACE_LONG = (int) 4095;

    int useLong(
            int                       l_in,
            org.omg.CORBA.IntHolder l_inout,
            org.omg.CORBA.IntHolder l_out
        );
};

public interface MyInterface
    extends MyInterfaceOperations,
    org.omg.CORBA.Object,
    org.omg.CORBA.portable.IDLEntity  { }
...
```

Java Usage

The following Java code shows how to invoke the `useLong()` operation defined in the preceding "IDL Example" section:

```
//Java
//Assume 'obj' is an object reference of MyModule::MyInterface type.
int InVal = -321;
```

```
org.omg.CORBA.IntHolder InoutValH = new org.omg.CORBA.IntHolder(-123);
org.omg.CORBA.IntHolder OutValH = new org.omg.CORBA.IntHolder();

int RecvVal = obj.useLong(InVal, InoutValH, OutValH);

System.out.println("Returned value = " + RecvVal);
System.out.println("Inout value    = " + InoutValH.value);
System.out.println("Out value      = " + OutValH.value);
...
```

long double Type

This section describes the IDL constant syntax and CDR encoding of an IDL `long double` type. The mapping of an IDL `long double` to C++ is also described and illustrated by example.

NOTE

There is no Java mapping for the IDL `long double` type because there is currently no support for the `long double` type in the Java language.

IDL Constant Declaration

```
//IDL
const long double LongDoubleConst = FloatingPointExpression;
```

A new `long double` constant, *`LongDoubleConst`*, is defined in terms of a floating-point expression, *`FloatingPointExpression`*, which is composed of floating-point literals, other floating-point constants, and arithmetical operators.

The +, -, *, / infix and +, - unary operators are allowed in IDL `long double` constant declarations.

Literals are specified in floating point format, for example `1.6e-19`, as described in Chapter 16.

CDR Encoding

When a `long double` is appended to an octet stream, it is marshaled as 16 octets (128 bits) and aligned on an eight-byte boundary. The order in which the octets are marshaled depends on the current byte-ordering of the octet stream (big-endian or little-endian).

The encoding of the `long double` follows the IEEE standard for a double-extended floating point number.

IDL Example

The following IDL example illustrates the syntax for declaring `long double` constants:

```
//IDL
const long double GLOBAL_LONGDOUBLE = 2E30;
```

```
module MyModule {
    const long double MODULE_LONGDOUBLE = 3.14;

    interface MyInterface {
        const long double INTERFACE_LONGDOUBLE = 6.0 * MODULE_LONGDOUBLE;

        long double useLongDouble(
                    in    long double ld_in,
                    inout long double ld_inout,
                    out   long double ld_out
                );
    };
};
```

C++ Mapping

The preceding "IDL Example" maps to C++ as follows:

```
//C++
const CORBA::LongDouble GLOBAL_LONGDOUBLE = 2.0e30;

namespace MyModule {
    const CORBA::LongDouble MODULE_LONGDOUBLE = 3.14;

    class MyInterface : public virtual CORBA::Object {
        static const CORBA::LongDouble INTERFACE_LONGDOUBLE;

        virtual CORBA::LongDouble useLongDouble(
                    CORBA::LongDouble     ld_in,
                    CORBA::LongDouble&    ld_inout,
                    CORBA::LongDouble_out ld_out
                ) =0;
    };
};
...
// Initialisation of 'INTERFACE_LONGDOUBLE'
const CORBA::LongDouble MyModule::MyInterface::INTERFACE_LONGDOUBLE = 18.84;
...
```

C++ Usage

The following C++ code shows how to invoke the `useLongDouble()` operation defined in the preceding "IDL Example" section:

```
//C++
//Assume 'obj' is an object reference of MyModule::MyInterface type.
CORBA::LongDouble InoutVal = 1.23456;
CORBA::LongDouble OutVal;

CORBA::LongDouble RecvVal = obj->useLongDouble(1.0e10, InoutVal, OutVal);
```

```
cout << "Returned value = " << RecvVal << endl;
cout << "Inout value    = " << InoutVal << endl;
cout << "Out value      = " << OutVal << endl;
...
```

long long Type

This section describes the IDL constant syntax and CDR encoding of an IDL `long long` type. The mapping of an IDL `long long` to C++ and to Java is also described and illustrated by example.

IDL Constant Declaration

```
//IDL
const long long LongLongConst = IntegerExpression;
```

A new `long long` constant, *`LongLongConst`*, is defined in terms of an integer expression, *`IntegerExpression`*, which is composed of integer literals, other integer constants, arithmetical operators, and other integer expressions enclosed in parentheses `( )`.

The `+`, `-`, `*`, `/`, `%`, `<<`, `>>`, `&`, `|`, `^` infix and `+`, `-`, `~` unary operators are allowed in IDL `long long` constant declarations.

Literals are specified in integer literal format, for example `0x2F2E`, as described in Chapter 16.

CDR Encoding

When a `long long` integer is appended to an octet stream, it is marshaled as eight octets (64 bits) and aligned on an eight-byte boundary. The order in which the octets are marshaled depends on the current byte-ordering of the octet stream (big-endian or little-endian).

IDL Example

The following IDL example illustrates the syntax for declaring `long long` constants:

```
//IDL
const long long GLOBAL_LONGLONG = 365;

module MyModule {
    const long long MODULE_LONGLONG = GLOBAL_LONGLONG & 0x00FF;

    interface MyInterface {
        const long long INTERFACE_LONGLONG = 07777;

        long long useLongLong(
                  in    long long ll_in,
                  inout long long ll_inout,
                  out   long long ll_out
```

```
            );
    };
};
```

C++ Mapping

The preceding "IDL Example" maps to C++ as follows:

```
//C++
const CORBA::LongLong GLOBAL_LONGLONG = 365;

namespace MyModule {
    const CORBA::LongLong MODULE_LONGLONG = 109;

    class MyInterface : public virtual CORBA::Object {
        static const CORBA::LongLong INTERFACE_LONGLONG;

        virtual CORBA::LongLong useLongLong(
                    CORBA::LongLong     ll_in,
                    CORBA::LongLong&    ll_inout,
                    CORBA::LongLong_out ll_out
                ) =0;
    };
};
...
// Initialisation of 'INTERFACE_LONGLONG'
const CORBA::LongLong MyModule::MyInterface::INTERFACE_LONGLONG = 4095;
...
```

C++ Usage

The following C++ code shows how to invoke the `useLongLong()` operation defined in the preceding "IDL Example" section:

```
//C++
//Assume 'obj' is an object reference of MyModule::MyInterface type.
CORBA::LongLong InoutVal = -123;
CORBA::LongLong OutVal;

CORBA::LongLong RecvVal = obj->useLongLong(-321, InoutVal, OutVal);

cout << "Returned value = " << RecvVal << endl;
cout << "Inout value    = " << InoutVal << endl;
cout << "Out value      = " << OutVal << endl;
...
```

Java Mapping

The preceding "IDL Example" maps to Java as follows:

```
//Java
// File containing global constants:
public interface GLOBAL_LONGLONG {
```

```
    public static final long value = (long) 365;
};
...

// File containing module and interface constants:
package MyModule;

public interface MODULE_LONGLONG {
    public static final long value = (long) 109;
};

public interface MyInterfaceOperations
{
    public static final long INTERFACE_LONGLONG = (long) 4095;

    long useLongLong(
            long                     ll_in,
            org.omg.CORBA.LongHolder ll_inout,
            org.omg.CORBA.LongHolder ll_out
        );
};

public interface MyInterface
    extends MyInterfaceOperations,
    org.omg.CORBA.Object,
    org.omg.CORBA.portable.IDLEntity  { }
...
```

Java Usage

The following Java code shows how to invoke the `useLongLong()` operation defined in the preceding "IDL Example" section:

```
//Java
//Assume 'obj' is an object reference of MyModule::MyInterface type.
long InVal = -321;
org.omg.CORBA.LongHolder InoutValH = new org.omg.CORBA.LongHolder(-123);
org.omg.CORBA.LongHolder OutValH = new org.omg.CORBA.LongHolder();

long RecvVal = obj.useLongLong(InVal, InoutValH, OutValH);

System.out.println("Returned value = " + RecvVal);
System.out.println("Inout value    = " + InoutValH.value);
System.out.println("Out value      = " + OutValH.value);
...
```

`native` Type

The `native` keyword is used to define types that require a special representation in a mapped programming language. It is intended for use only by the OMG when defining special CORBA features.

A native declaration has the following syntax:

```
//IDL
native NativeType;
```

The *NativeType* declared using this syntax might appear in the same sort of contexts as a built-in type but its use is typically subject to certain restrictions imposed by the target language mapping.

Object Type

The Object type is a special built-in IDL type that is the base type of all interfaces. When Object is declared to be the return type or parameter type of an operation, it is then legal to pass an object reference of arbitrary type as the return value or parameter value, respectively.

The Object type is subject to the same syntax rules as a built-in basic type (for example, short or boolean).

For details of the C++ and Java mapping of the Object type, see the section "CORBA::Object Interface" later in this chapter.

octet Type

This section describes the IDL constant syntax and CDR encoding of an IDL octet type. The mapping of an IDL octet to C++ and to Java is also described and illustrated by example.

IDL Constant Declaration

```
//IDL
const octet OctetConst = IntegerExpression;
```

A new octet constant, *OctetConst*, is defined in terms of an integer expression, *IntegerExpression*, which is composed of integer literals, other integer constants, arithmetical operators, and other integer expressions enclosed in parentheses ( ).

The +, -, *, /, %, <<, >>, &, |, ^ infix and +, -, ~ unary operators are allowed in IDL octet constant declarations.

Literals are specified in integer literal format, as described in Chapter 16.

CDR Encoding

An octet (eight bits) is marshaled by putting it into the next available position in an octet stream (alignment on a one-byte boundary). The value of an octet is guaranteed not to undergo any kind of conversion when it is transmitted.

IDL Example

The following IDL example illustrates the syntax for declaring octet constants:

```
//IDL
const octet GLOBAL_OCTET = 0xF0;
```

```
module MyModule {
    const octet MODULE_OCTET = GLOBAL_OCTET | 0x0F;

    interface MyInterface {
        const octet INTERFACE_OCTET = 255;

        octet useOctet(
                    in    octet o_in,
                    inout octet o_inout,
                    out   octet o_out
                );
    };
};
```

C++ Mapping

The preceding "IDL Example" maps to C++ as follows:

```
//C++
const CORBA::Octet GLOBAL_OCTET = 240;

namespace MyModule {
    const CORBA::Octet MODULE_OCTET = 255;

    class MyInterface : public virtual CORBA::Object {
        static const CORBA::Octet INTERFACE_OCTET;

        virtual CORBA::Octet useOctet(
                    CORBA::Octet     o_in,
                    CORBA::Octet&    o_inout,
                    CORBA::Octet_out o_out
                ) =0;
    };
};
...
// Initialisation of 'INTERFACE_OCTET'
const CORBA::Octet MyModule::MyInterface::INTERFACE_OCTET = 255;
...
```

C++ Usage

The following C++ code shows how to invoke the `useOctet()` operation defined in the preceding "IDL Example" section:

```
//C++
//Assume 'obj' is an object reference of MyModule::MyInterface type.
CORBA::Octet InoutVal = 0xAD;
CORBA::Octet OutVal;

CORBA::Octet RecvVal = obj->useOctet(0xBC, InoutVal, OutVal);
```

```
cout << "Returned value = " << (int) RecvVal << endl;
cout << "Inout value    = " << (int) InoutVal << endl;
cout << "Out value      = " << (int) OutVal << endl;
...
```

Java Mapping

The preceding "IDL Example" maps to Java as follows:

```
//Java
// File containing global constants:
public interface GLOBAL_OCTET {
    public static final byte value = (byte) 240;
};
...

// File containing module and interface constants:
package MyModule;

public interface MODULE_OCTET {
    public static final byte value = (byte) 255;
};

public interface MyInterfaceOperations
{
    public static final byte INTERFACE_OCTET = (byte) 255;

    byte useOctet(
             byte                      o_in,
             org.omg.CORBA.ByteHolder o_inout,
             org.omg.CORBA.ByteHolder o_out
         );
};

public interface MyInterface
    extends MyInterfaceOperations,
    org.omg.CORBA.Object,
    org.omg.CORBA.portable.IDLEntity  { }
...
```

Java Usage

The following Java code shows how to invoke the `useOctet()` operation defined in the preceding "IDL Example" section:

```
//Java
//Assume 'obj' is an object reference of MyModule::MyInterface type.
byte InVal = (byte) 0xBC;
org.omg.CORBA.ByteHolder InoutValH = new org.omg.CORBA.ByteHolder((byte)0xAD);
org.omg.CORBA.ByteHolder OutValH = new org.omg.CORBA.ByteHolder();
```

```
byte RecvVal = obj.useOctet(InVal, InoutValH, OutValH);

System.out.println("Returned value = " + RecvVal);
System.out.println("Inout value    = " + InoutValH.value);
System.out.println("Out value      = " + OutValH.value);
...
```

sequence Type

This section describes the IDL syntax and CDR encoding of an IDL `sequence` type. The mapping of an IDL `sequence` to C++ and to Java is also described and illustrated by example.

IDL Syntax

A `sequence` has the syntax of a type specifier. There are two forms of `sequence` syntax, *unbounded* and *bounded*, which are defined as follows:

```
//IDL
// Unbounded sequence type specifier:
sequence<ElementTypeSpec>

// Bounded sequence type specifier:
sequence<ElementTypeSpec, Bound>
```

The *`ElementTypeSpec`* gives the type of the `sequence` elements and *`Bound`* is an constant integer expression that evaluates to a positive value. From CORBA 2.4 onward, the only context in which a `sequence` type specifier should appear is as part of a `typedef` expression. For example, a `sequence` can be given an alias using a `typedef` expression, as follows:

```
//IDL
typedef sequence<long> LongSeq;
```

The element type of a `sequence` can, in principle, be declared using an arbitrary type specifier. From CORBA 2.4 onward, however, using anonymous type specifiers for the element type is deprecated. The following example shows the approved way to declare a `sequence`, which avoids using an anonymous type specifier for the element type:

```
//IDL
typedef sequence<long> LongSeq;
typedef sequence<LongSeq> LongSeqSeq;
```

Contrast this with the deprecated style of `sequence` declaration in the following example, in which an anonymous type specifier is used directly to declare the element type:

```
//IDL
typedef sequence<sequence<long> > LongSeqSeq;    // Deprecated
```

CDR Encoding

A sequence is marshaled as an `unsigned long`, specifying the number of transmitted elements, followed by the sequence elements.

IDL Example

The following IDL example illustrates the syntax for declaring `sequence` types:

```
//IDL
module MyModule {
    typedef sequence<string, 2> String2Seq;
    typedef sequence<String2Seq> String2SeqSeq;

    typedef sequence<octet> OctetSeq;

    interface MyInterface {
        String2SeqSeq useString2SeqSeq(
                    in    String2SeqSeq s2_in,
                    inout String2SeqSeq s2_inout,
                    out   String2SeqSeq s2_out
                 );
        OctetSeq useOctetSeq(
                    in    OctetSeq os_in,
                    inout OctetSeq os_inout,
                    out   OctetSeq os_out
                 );
    };
};
```

C++ Mapping

The bounded sequence, `String2Seq`, and the unbounded sequence, `String2SeqSeq`, defined in the preceding "IDL Example" map to C++ as follows:

```
//C++
namespace MyModule {
    //-----------------------------------------------------
    // BOUNDED Sequence - String2Seq

    // Implementation dependent definitions generated for:
    // ===>    String2Seq_var
    // ===>    String2Seq_out
    // ===>    _tc_String2Seq

    class String2Seq
    {
      public:
        String2Seq();
        String2Seq(
            CORBA::ULong length,
```

```
        char** buf,
        CORBA::Boolean release = 0
    );
    String2Seq(const String2Seq& seq);

    CORBA::ULong  maximum() const;
    void          length(CORBA::ULong);
    CORBA::ULong  length() const;

    char *&operator[](CORBA::ULong index);
    const char *&operator[](CORBA::ULong index) const;

    // MEMORY MANAGEMENT - When the release flag is TRUE, which is
    //                     the usual case, the sequence has responsibility
    //                     for deleting the sequence elements.
    CORBA::Boolean release() const;

    void replace(
        CORBA::ULong length,
        char **data,
        CORBA::Boolean release = FALSE
    );

    // MEMORY MANAGEMENT   - Accessing the sequence buffer:
    //     orphan = FALSE  - The return value provides read-write access.
    //                       The sequence retains ownership of the buffer.
    //     orphan = TRUE   - The return value provides read-write access.
    //                       The sequence yields ownership of the buffer.
    char **       get_buffer(CORBA::Boolean orphan = FALSE);

    // MEMORY MANAGEMENT - The return value provides read-only access
    //                     to the sequence buffer.
    const char ** get_buffer() const;

    // MEMORY MANAGEMENT - Allocate a one-dimensional array of char*
    //                     elements. Each char* (string) element is
    //                     allocated and initialized with default data.
    //                     The number of elements in the allocated buffer
    //                     is equal to maximum().
    static char **allocbuf();  // Bounded form.

    // MEMORY MANAGEMENT - Free a one-dimensional array of char*
    //                     elements.
    static void   freebuf(char **);
};

//-----------------------------------------------
// UNBOUNDED Sequence - String2SeqSeq
```

```
// Implementation dependent definitions generated for:
// ===>    String2SeqSeq_var
// ===>    String2SeqSeq_out
// ===>    _tc_String2SeqSeq

class String2SeqSeq
{
  public:
    String2SeqSeq();
    String2SeqSeq(CORBA::ULong max);
    String2SeqSeq(
        CORBA::ULong max,
        CORBA::ULong length,
        String2Seq* buf,
        CORBA::Boolean release = 0
    );
    String2SeqSeq(const String2SeqSeq& seq);
    String2SeqSeq&  operator=(const String2SeqSeq& seq);

    CORBA::ULong maximum() const;
    void         length(CORBA::ULong);
    CORBA::ULong length() const;

    String2Seq &operator[](CORBA::ULong index);
    const String2Seq &operator[](CORBA::ULong index) const;

    // MEMORY MANAGEMENT - When the release flag is TRUE, which is
    //                     the usual case, the sequence has responsibility
    //                     for deleting the sequence elements.
    CORBA::Boolean release() const;

    void replace(
        CORBA::ULong max,
        CORBA::ULong length,
        String2Seq *data,
        CORBA::Boolean release = FALSE
    );

    // MEMORY MANAGEMENT   - Accessing the sequence buffer:
    //     orphan = FALSE  - The return value provides read-write access.
    //                       The sequence retains ownership of the buffer.
    //     orphan = TRUE   - The return value provides read-write access.
    //                       The sequence yields ownership of the buffer.
    String2Seq*       get_buffer(CORBA::Boolean orphan = FALSE);

    // MEMORY MANAGEMENT - The return value provides read-only access
    //                     to the sequence buffer.
    const String2Seq* get_buffer() const;
```

```
        // MEMORY MANAGEMENT - Allocate a one-dimensional array of String2Seq
        //                     elements. Each String2Seq element is allocated
        //                     and initialized with default data.
        static String2Seq* allocbuf(CORBA::ULong nelems);  // Unbounded form.

        // MEMORY MANAGEMENT - Free a one-dimensional array of String2Seq
        //                     elements.
        static void        freebuf(String2Seq*);
    };
};
...
```

C++ Usage

The following C++ code shows how to invoke the `useString2SeqSeq()` operation defined in the preceding "IDL Example" section:

```
//C++
//Assume 'obj' is an object reference of MyModule::MyInterface type.
{
MyModule::String2SeqSeq InVal(1);  // maximum = 1, length = 0
InVal.length(1);                   // length = 1
InVal[0].length(2);  // sub-sequence: maximum = 2, length = 2
InVal[0][0] = CORBA::string_dup("Rodge");
InVal[0][1] = CORBA::string_dup("Podge");

MyModule::String2SeqSeq InoutVal(1);  // maximum = 1, length = 0
InoutVal.length(1);                   // length = 1
InoutVal[0].length(2);  // sub-sequence: maximum = 2, length = 2
InoutVal[0][0] = CORBA::string_dup("Zig");
InoutVal[0][1] = CORBA::string_dup("Zag");

MyModule::String2SeqSeq_var OutValV;

MyModule::String2SeqSeq_var RecvValV
        = obj->useString2SeqSeq(InVal, InoutVal, OutValV);

...  // Do something with *RecvValV, InoutVal, and *OutValV
}
```

The following C++ code shows how to invoke the `useOctetSeq()` operation defined in the preceding "IDL Example" section:

```
// Invoke the useOctetSeq() operation
{
// Given 'buf', which points to binary data

MyModule::OctetSeq InVal(
    1000,      // maximum
    1000,      // length
```

```
    buf,        // buffer pointer 'CORBA::Octet*'
    0           // release flag = FALSE
);
MyModule::OctetSeq InoutVal(
    1000,       // maximum
    1000,       // length
    buf,        // buffer pointer 'CORBA::Octet*'
    0           // release flag = FALSE
);
MyModule::OctetSeq_var OutValV;

MyModule::OctetSeq_var RecvValV = obj->useOctetSeq(InVal, InoutVal, OutValV);

CORBA::Octet * recvBuf = RecvValV->get_buffer();
CORBA::Octet * inoutBuf = InoutVal.get_buffer();
CORBA::Octet * outBuf   = OutValV->get_buffer();

delete[] buf;
}
...
```

The parameterless `get_buffer()` function provides read-only access to the sequence's internal buffer.

Java Mapping

An IDL sequence, *<seq_name>*, with *<element_type>* elements maps to a Java array *<java_element_type>*`[`*dim*`]` of *dim* dimension with *<java_element_type>* elements. The Java array dimension, *dim*, is related to the IDL sequence bound and length as follows:

- The array dimension, *dim*, must be less than or equal to the declared bound of the sequence (if the sequence is bounded).
- The array dimension, *dim*, is taken to be the length of the sequence. Consequently, all of the elements in the Java array are transmitted when passed as a parameter or return value.

Holder and helper classes, *<java_seq_name>*`Holder` and *<java_seq_name>*`Helper`, are generated according to the standard template described in the section "Java `Helper` and `Holder` Types" later in this chapter.

For example, the `MyModule.String2SeqSeq` IDL sequence maps to Java as shown in Table 15.8.

Table 15.8 Java Mapping of the `String2SeqSeq` Sequence Type

IDL Type	Java Mapped Types
`MyModule.String2SeqSeq`	`String[`*dim*`][`*bounded_dim*`]`
	`MyModule.String2SeqSeqHolder`
	`MyModule.String2SeqSeqHelper`

In Table 15.8 the *dim* array dimension, which limits the sequence<String2Seq> unbounded sequence index, can be an arbitrary non-negative integer. The *bounded_dim* array dimension, which defines the sequence<string, 2> bounded sequence index, can be 0, 1, or 2.

Java Usage

The following Java code shows how to invoke the useString2SeqSeq() operation defined in the preceding "IDL Example" section:

```
//Java
// Assume 'obj' is an object reference of MyModule::MyInterface type.
// Invoke the useString2SeqSeq() operation
{
// Declare a sequence of 'MyModule::String2SeqSeq' type.
String InVal[][] = new String[1][2];
InVal[0][0] = "Rodge";
InVal[0][1] = "Podge";

String SampleVal[][] = new String[1][2];
SampleVal[0][0] = "Zig";
SampleVal[0][1] = "Zag";

MyModule.String2SeqSeqHolder InoutValH
    = new MyModule.String2SeqSeqHolder(SampleVal);
MyModule.String2SeqSeqHolder OutValH = new MyModule.String2SeqSeqHolder();

String RecvVal[][] = obj.useString2SeqSeq(InVal, InoutValH, OutValH);

...  // Do something with RecvVal, InoutValH.value, and OutValH.value
}
```

The following Java code shows how to invoke the useOctetSeq() operation defined in the preceding "IDL Example" section:

```
// Invoke the useOctetSeq() operation
{
// Initialize 'buf'with binary data (of byte[] type)
byte[] buf = (new String("Sample Buffer")).getBytes();

byte[] InVal    = buf;
MyModule.OctetSeqHolder InoutValH = new MyModule.OctetSeqHolder(buf);
MyModule.OctetSeqHolder OutValH   = new MyModule.OctetSeqHolder();

byte[] RecvVal = obj.useOctetSeq(InVal, InoutValH, OutValH);

...  // Do something with RecvVal, InoutValH.value, and OutValH.value
}
...
```

short Type

This section describes the IDL constant syntax and CDR encoding of an IDL short type. The mapping of an IDL short to C++ and to Java is also described and illustrated by example.

IDL Constant Declaration

```
//IDL
const short ShortConst = IntegerExpression;
```

A new short constant, *ShortConst*, is defined in terms of an integer expression, *IntegerExpression*, which is composed of integer literals, other integer constants, arithmetical operators, and other integer expressions enclosed in parentheses ( ).

The +, -, *, /, %, <<, >>, &, |, ^ infix and +, -, ~ unary operators are allowed in IDL short constant declarations.

Literals are specified in integer literal format, for example 0x2F2E, as described in Chapter 16.

CDR Encoding

When a short integer is appended to an octet stream, it is marshaled as two octets (16 bits) and aligned on a two-byte boundary. The order in which the octets are marshaled depends on the current byte-ordering of the octet stream (big-endian or little-endian).

IDL Example

The following IDL example illustrates the syntax for declaring short constants:

```
//IDL
const short GLOBAL_SHORT = 365;

module MyModule {
    const short MODULE_SHORT = GLOBAL_SHORT & 0x00FF;

    interface MyInterface {
        const short INTERFACE_SHORT = 07777;

        short useShort(
                  in    short s_in,
                  inout short s_inout,
                  out   short s_out
              );
    };
};
```

C++ Mapping

The preceding "IDL Example" maps to C++ as follows:

```
//C++
const CORBA::Short GLOBAL_SHORT = 365;

namespace MyModule {
    const CORBA::Short MODULE_SHORT = 109;

    class MyInterface : public virtual CORBA::Object {
        static const CORBA::Short INTERFACE_SHORT;

        virtual CORBA::Short useShort(
                    CORBA::Short     s_in,
                    CORBA::Short&    s_inout,
                    CORBA::Short_out s_out
                ) =0;
    };
};
...
// Initialisation of 'INTERFACE_SHORT'
const CORBA::Short MyModule::MyInterface::INTERFACE_SHORT = 4095;
...
```

C++ Usage

The following C++ code shows how to invoke the `useShort()` operation defined in the preceding "IDL Example" section:

```
//C++
//Assume 'obj' is an object reference of MyModule::MyInterface type.
CORBA::Short InoutVal = -123;
CORBA::Short OutVal;

CORBA::Short RecvVal = obj->useShort(-321, InoutVal, OutVal);

cout << "Returned value = " << RecvVal << endl;
cout << "Inout value    = " << InoutVal << endl;
cout << "Out value      = " << OutVal << endl;
...
```

Java Mapping

The preceding "IDL Example" maps to Java as follows:

```
//Java
// File containing global constants:
public interface GLOBAL_SHORT {
    public static final short value = (short) 365;
};
...

// File containing module and interface constants:
package MyModule;
```

```
public interface MODULE_SHORT {
    public static final short value = (short) 109;
};

public interface MyInterfaceOperations
{
    public static final short INTERFACE_SHORT = (short) 4095;

    short useShort(
            short                       s_in,
            org.omg.CORBA.ShortHolder s_inout,
            org.omg.CORBA.ShortHolder s_out
        );
};

public interface MyInterface
    extends MyInterfaceOperations,
    org.omg.CORBA.Object,
    org.omg.CORBA.portable.IDLEntity  { }
...
```

Java Usage

The following Java code shows how to invoke the `useShort()` operation defined in the preceding "IDL Example" section:

```
//Java
//Assume 'obj' is an object reference of MyModule::MyInterface type.
short InVal = -321;
org.omg.CORBA.ShortHolder InoutValH = new org.omg.CORBA.ShortHolder((short)-
➥123);
org.omg.CORBA.ShortHolder OutValH = new org.omg.CORBA.ShortHolder();

short RecvVal = obj.useShort(InVal, InoutValH, OutValH);

System.out.println("Returned value = " + RecvVal);
System.out.println("Inout value    = " + InoutValH.value);
System.out.println("Out value      = " + OutValH.value);
...
```

`string` Type

This section describes the IDL syntax, IDL constant syntax, and CDR encoding of an IDL `string` type. The mapping of an IDL `string` to C++ and to Java is also described and illustrated by example.

IDL Syntax

A `string` has the syntax of a type specifier. There are two forms of `string` syntax, *unbounded* and *bounded*, which are defined as follows:

```
//IDL
// Unbounded string type specifier:
string

// Bounded string type specifier:
string<Bound>
```

The *Bound* specifies the maximum length of the string. The *Bound* is a constant integer expression that evaluates to a positive value.

An unbounded `string` type specifier can appear in any context where a type specifier is expected. From CORBA 2.4 onward, the only context in which a bounded `string<>` type specifier should appear is as part of a `typedef` expression. For example, a bounded `string<>` can be given an alias using a `typedef` expression, as follows:

```
//IDL
typedef string<128> String128;
```

IDL Constant Declaration

```
//IDL
const string StringConst = StringLiteral;
const string StringConst = OtherStringConst;
```

A new `string` constant, *`StringConst`*, can be defined either in terms of a string literal, *`StringLiteral`*, or in terms of an existing string constant, *`OtherStringConst`*. No infix or unary operators can be used in IDL `string` constant declarations.

String literal format, for example `"This is a string"`, is described in Chapter 16.

CDR Encoding

A `string` is marshaled as an `unsigned long`, specifying the length of the `string` including the terminating null character, followed by the characters themselves (including the terminating null).

IDL Example

The following IDL example illustrates the syntax for declaring `string` constants:

```
//IDL
const string GLOBAL_STRING = "String " "with " "many " "parts." "\n";

module MyModule {
    const string MODULE_STRING = GLOBAL_STRING;

    interface MyInterface {
        const string INTERFACE_STRING = "Ahoy!";

        string useString(
                    in    string s_in,
                    inout string s_inout,
```

```
                    out   string s_out
                );
    };
};
```

C++ Mapping

The preceding "IDL Example" maps to C++ as follows:

```
//C++
const char * const GLOBAL_STRING = "String with many parts.\n";

namespace MyModule {
    const char*  MODULE_STRING = "String with many parts.\n";

    class MyInterface : public virtual CORBA::Object {
        static const char * const INTERFACE_STRING;

        virtual char * useString(
                    const char *      s_in,
                    char *&           s_inout,
                    CORBA::String_out s_out
                ) =0;
    };
};
...
// Initialisation of 'INTERFACE_STRING'
const char*  MyModule::MyInterface::INTERFACE_STRING = "Ahoy!";
...
```

Some standard types and static functions are provided to help with the memory management of strings. They are defined as follows:

```
//C++
namespace CORBA {
    // Standard definitions for:
    // ===>    String_var
    // ===>    String_out
    // ===>    _tc_String

    // String memory management functions:
    char *string_alloc(CORBA::ULong len);
    char *string_dup(const char*);
    void string_free(char *);
};
```

For explanations and examples of how to use these memory management functions, see Chapter 4.

C++ Usage

The following C++ code shows how to invoke the `useString()` operation defined in the preceding "IDL Example" section:

```
//C++
//Assume 'obj' is an object reference of MyModule::MyInterface type.
CORBA::String_var InoutVal = CORBA::string_dup("EFGH");
CORBA::String_var OutVal;

CORBA::String_var RecvVal = obj->useString("ABCD", InoutVal, OutVal);

cout << "Returned value = " << RecvVal << endl;
cout << "Inout value    = " << InoutVal << endl;
cout << "Out value      = " << OutVal << endl;
...
```

Java Mapping

The preceding "IDL Example" maps to Java as follows:

```
//Java
// File containing global constants:
public interface GLOBAL_STRING {
    public static final String value = "String with many parts.\n";
};
...

// File containing module and interface constants:
package MyModule;

public interface MODULE_STRING {
    public static final String value = "String with many parts.\n";
};

public interface MyInterfaceOperations
{
    public static final String INTERFACE_STRING = "Ahoy!";

    String useString(
             String                      s_in,
             org.omg.CORBA.StringHolder s_inout,
             org.omg.CORBA.StringHolder s_out
         );
};

public interface MyInterface
    extends MyInterfaceOperations,
    org.omg.CORBA.Object,
    org.omg.CORBA.portable.IDLEntity  { }
...
```

Java Usage

The following Java code shows how to invoke the `useString()` operation defined in the preceding "IDL Example" section:

```
//Java
//Assume 'obj' is an object reference of MyModule::MyInterface type.
String InVal = "ABCD";
org.omg.CORBA.StringHolder InoutValH = new org.omg.CORBA.StringHolder("EFGH");
org.omg.CORBA.StringHolder OutValH = new org.omg.CORBA.StringHolder();

String RecvVal = obj.useString(InVal, InoutValH, OutValH);

System.out.println("Returned value = " + RecvVal);
System.out.println("Inout value    = " + InoutValH.value);
System.out.println("Out value      = " + OutValH.value);
...
```

struct Type

This section describes the IDL syntax and CDR encoding of an IDL `struct` type. The mapping of an IDL `struct` to C++ and to Java is also described and illustrated by example.

IDL Syntax

A `struct` can stand on its own as a type declaration, in which case it is terminated by a semicolon:

```
//IDL
struct StructType { MemberList };
```

The *`StructType`* is the name of the newly defined `struct`. There must be at least one member in *`MemberList`* and each member consists of a type specifier followed by a comma-separated declarator list. For example, the following struct declares six members, `s1`, `s2`, `s3`, `d1`, `d2`, and `d3`:

```
//IDL
struct SimpleStruct {
    short s1, s2, s3;
    double d1, d2, d3;
};
```

A `struct` can also be used as a type specifier, in which case the terminating semicolon is omitted. For example, a struct can be given an alias using a `typedef` expression, as follows:

```
//IDL
typedef struct VSimpleStruct { short s; } VSimpleStructAlias;
```

The members of a struct can, in principle, be declared using arbitrary type specifiers.

From CORBA 2.4 onward, however, using anonymous type specifiers in the member list is deprecated. The following example shows the approved way to declare a `struct`, which avoids the use of anonymous type specifiers in the member list:

```
//IDL
typedef wstring<100> WString100;
typedef sequence<octet> OctetSeq;
struct NameStruct { string firstName, secondName; };

struct ApprovedStruct {
    WString100 w1, w2, w3;
    OctetSeq raw_data;
    NameStruct name1, name2;
};
```

Contrast this with the deprecated style of `struct` declaration in the following example, in which anonymous type specifiers are used directly to declare `struct` members:

```
//IDL
struct DeprecatedStruct {
    wstring<100> w1, w2, w3;      // Deprecated
    sequence<octet> raw_data;     // Deprecated
    struct NameStruct {
        string firstName, secondName;
    } name1, name2;               // Poor style, but not deprecated.
};
```

A forward declaration of a `struct`, which precedes the full `struct` declaration, can be made as follows:

```
//IDL
struct StructType;
```

This construction is provided specifically to facilitate the definition of recursive `structs`. For example, a recursive `struct` can be defined as follows:

```
//IDL
struct RecurStruct;

typedef sequence<RecurStruct> RecurStructSeq;

struct RecurStruct {
    string nodeName;
    RecurStructSeq recurList;
};
```

Older (pre-CORBA 2.4) IDL compilers that do not support forward declaration of `structs` can accept the following (deprecated) syntax instead:

```
//IDL
struct RecurStruct {
```

```
    string nodeName;
    sequence<RecurStruct> recurList;  // Deprecated since CORBA 2.4.
};
```

CDR Encoding

A `struct` is marshaled into an octet stream by marshaling each of the struct members in the same order as they appear in the IDL definition.

IDL Example

The following IDL example illustrates the syntax for declaring `struct` types:

```
//IDL
module MyModule {
    struct Node;
    typedef sequence<Node> NodeSeq;

    // Variable length struct.
    struct Node {
        string nodeName;
        NodeSeq recurList;
    };

    // Fixed length struct.
    struct FixLen { long min, max; };

    interface MyInterface {
        Node useNode(
                    in    Node nd_in,
                    inout Node nd_inout,
                    out   Node nd_out
                );
        FixLen useFixLen(
                    in    FixLen fx_in,
                    inout FixLen fx_inout,
                    out   FixLen fx_out
                );
    };
};
```

C++ Mapping

The variable-length struct, `Node`, and the fixed-length struct, `FixLen`, defined in the preceding "IDL Example" map to C++ as follows:

```
//C++
namespace MyModule {
    // Implementation dependent definitions generated for:
    // ===>    Node_var
```

```
    // ===>    Node_out
    // ===>    _tc_Node

    struct Node;

    // Definition generated for:
    // ===>    NodeSeq sequence type
    ...  // (not shown)

    struct Node
    {
        <impl_dependent_string_manager_type>  nodeName;
        NodeSeq recurList;
    };

    // Implementation dependent definitions generated for:
    // ===>    FixLen_var
    // ===>    FixLen_out
    // ===>    _tc_FixLen

    struct FixLen
    {
        CORBA::Long min;
        CORBA::Long max;
    };
};
```

C++ Usage

The following C++ code shows how to invoke the useNode() operation defined in the preceding "IDL Example" section:

```
//C++
// Assume 'obj' is an object reference of MyModule::MyInterface type.
// Invoke the useNode() operation
{
// Using a variable length struct
MyModule::Node SampleVal;
SampleVal.nodeName = CORBA::string_dup("Foo");
SampleVal.recurList.length(2);
SampleVal.recurList[0].nodeName = CORBA::string_dup("Zig");
SampleVal.recurList[1].nodeName = CORBA::string_dup("Zag");

MyModule::Node     InVal    = SampleVal;
MyModule::Node     InoutVal = SampleVal;
// Variable length => No memory allocation for 'out' parameter.
MyModule::Node_var OutValV;

MyModule::Node_var RecvValV = obj->useNode(InVal, InoutVal, OutValV);
```

```
...  // Do something with *RecvValV, InoutVal, and *OutValV
}
```

The following C++ code shows how to invoke the `useFixLen()` operation defined in the preceding "IDL Example" section:

```
// Invoke the useFixLen() operation
{
// Using a fixed length struct
MyModule::FixLen SampleVal;
SampleVal.min = -10;
SampleVal.max = 10;

// For fixed length, declare all parameters on the stack.
MyModule::FixLen InVal    = SampleVal;
MyModule::FixLen InoutVal = SampleVal;
// Fixed length => Allocate memory for 'out' parameter.
MyModule::FixLen OutVal;

MyModule::FixLen RecvVal = obj->useFixLen(InVal, InoutVal, OutVal);

cout << "RecvVal.min = " << RecvVal.min << endl;
cout << "RecvVal.max = " << RecvVal.max << endl;}
...
```

Java Mapping

An IDL struct type, *<struct_name>*, maps to a Java class, *<java_struct_name>*. Holder and helper classes, *<java_struct_name>*`Holder` and *<java_struct_name>*`Helper`, are generated according to the standard template described in the section "Java `Helper` and `Holder` Types" later in this chapter.

For example, the `MyModule.Node` struct type maps to Java as shown in Table 15.9.

Table 15.9 Java Mapping of the `Node` Struct Type

IDL Type	Java Mapped Types

`MyModule.Node`	`MyModule.Node`
	`MyModule.NodeHolder`
	`MyModule.NodeHelper`

Each member variable declared in IDL maps to a corresponding public member of the mapped Java class. The `MyModule.Node` and `MyModule.FixLen` Java classes are therefore defined as follows:

```
//Java
package MyModule;

public final class Node
    implements org.omg.CORBA.portable.IDLEntity
{
```

```
    public java.lang.String     nodeName;
    public MyModule.Node[] recurList;

    public Node() {}
    public Node(
        java.lang.String nodeName,
        MyModule.Node[] recurList
    ) { ... }
}


public final class FixLen
    implements org.omg.CORBA.portable.IDLEntity
{
    public int min;
    public int max;

    public FixLen() {}
    public FixLen(int min, int max) { ... }
}
...
```

Java Usage

The following Java code shows how to invoke the useNode() operation defined in the preceding "IDL Example" section:

```
//Java
// Assume 'obj' is an object reference of MyModule::MyInterface type.
// Invoke the useNode() operation
{
MyModule.Node InVal = new MyModule.Node();
InVal.nodeName = "Foo";
InVal.recurList = new MyModule.Node[2];
InVal.recurList[0] = new MyModule.Node("Zig", new MyModule.Node[0]);
InVal.recurList[1] = new MyModule.Node("Zag", new MyModule.Node[0]);

MyModule.NodeHolder InoutValH = new MyModule.NodeHolder();
InoutValH.value = new MyModule.Node("Bar", new MyModule.Node[0]);
MyModule.NodeHolder OutValH   = new MyModule.NodeHolder();

MyModule.Node RecvVal = obj.useNode(InVal, InoutValH, OutValH);

...  // Do something with RecvVal, InoutValH.value, and OutValH.value
}
```

The following Java code shows how to invoke the useFixLen() operation defined in the preceding "IDL Example" section:

```
// Invoke the useFixLen() operation
{
// Using a fixed length struct
MyModule.FixLen       InVal     = new MyModule.FixLen(-10,10);
MyModule.FixLenHolder InoutValH = new MyModule.FixLenHolder(
                                      new MyModule.FixLen(-10,10)
                                 );
MyModule.FixLenHolder OutValH = new MyModule.FixLenHolder();

MyModule.FixLen RecvVal = obj.useFixLen(InVal, InoutValH, OutValH);

...  // Do something with RecvVal, InoutValH.value, and OutValH.value
}
...
```

union Type

This section describes the IDL syntax and CDR encoding of an IDL `union` type. The mapping of an IDL `union` to C++ and to Java is also described and illustrated by example.

IDL Syntax

A discriminated `union` can stand on its own as a type declaration, in which case it is terminated by a semicolon:

```
//IDL
union UnionType switch(SwitchTypeSpec) { CaseList };
```

The *`UnionType`* is the name of the newly defined `union` type. The *`SwitchTypeSpec`* specifies the discriminant type and it is restricted to be one of the following: `integer`, `char`, `boolean`, or enumerated type.

There must be at least one case in *`CaseList`* and each case has one of the following forms:

```
//IDL
case ConstExpr : [case ConstExpr : ...] TypeSpec Declarator;
default : TypeSpec Declarator;
```

The first form consists of one or more case labels followed by the declaration of a single union member, *`TypeSpec Declarator`*. The *`ConstExpr`* appearing in the case labels is a constant expression of the same type as the union discriminant. The member is selected if the *`ConstExpr`* value of one of the associated case labels is equal to the discriminant value.

The second form consists of a single `default` label followed by the declaration of a `union` member, *`TypeSpec Declarator`*. There can be at most one `default` label in a case list. The default member is selected if the discriminant value does not match any other case label.

For example, the following discriminated union declares six members, `us`, `s`, `ul`, `l`, `ull`, and `ll`:

```
//IDL
union FlexibleInt switch(short) {
    case 0 : unsigned short us;
    case 1 : short s;
    case 2 : unsigned long ul;
    case 3 : long l;
    case 4 : unsigned long long ull;
    default : long long ll;
};
```

A `union` can also be used as a type specifier, in which case the terminating semicolon is omitted. For example, a `union` can be given an alias using a `typedef` expression, as follows:

```
//IDL
typedef union VSimpleUnion switch(boolean) {
            case TRUE: string val;
        } VSimpleUnionAlias;
```

The members of a `union` can, in principle, be declared using arbitrary type specifiers. From CORBA 2.4 onward, however, using anonymous type specifiers within the case list is deprecated. The following example shows the approved way to declare a `union`, which avoids the use of anonymous type specifiers within the case list:

```
//IDL
typedef wstring<100> WString100;
typedef sequence<octet> OctetSeq;
struct NameStruct { string firstName, secondName; };
enum NameFormat { INTERNATIONAL, RAW_BINARY, STRUCTURED };

union ApprovedUnion switch(NameFormat) {
    case INTERNATIONAL:  WString100 wsName;
    case RAW_BINARY:     OctetSeq   binName;
    case STRUCTURED:     NameStruct name;
};
```

Contrast this with the deprecated style of `union` declaration in the following example, in which anonymous type specifiers are used directly to declare `union` members:

```
//IDL
enum NameFormat { INTERNATIONAL, RAW_BINARY, STRUCTURED };

union DeprecatedUnion switch(NameFormat) {
    case INTERNATIONAL:  wstring<100>    wsName;    // Deprecated
    case RAW_BINARY:     sequence<octet> binName;   // Deprecated
    case STRUCTURED:     struct NameStruct {
```

```
                              string firstName, secondName;
                         } name;    // Poor style, but not deprecated.
};
```

A forward declaration of a union, which precedes the full union declaration, can be made as follows:

```
//IDL
union UnionType;
```

This construction is provided specifically to facilitate the definition of recursive unions. For example, a recursive union can be defined as follows:

```
//IDL
union RecurUnion;

typedef sequence<RecurUnion> RecurUnionSeq;
enum Selector { SELECT_STRING, SELECT_RECURSE };

union RecurUnion switch(Selector) {
    case SELECT_STRING:  string value;
    case SELECT_RECURSE: RecurUnionSeq recurList;
};
```

Older (pre-CORBA 2.4) IDL compilers that do not support forward declaration of unions can accept the following (deprecated) syntax instead:

```
//IDL
enum Selector { SELECT_STRING, SELECT_RECURSE };

union RecurUnion switch(Selector) {
    case SELECT_STRING:  string value;
    case SELECT_RECURSE: sequence<RecurUnion> recurList;   // Deprecated
};
```

CDR Encoding

A union is marshaled into an octet stream by marshaling the following values:

- Discriminant value—Encoded according to the rules for the selected switch type.
- Member value (if any)—If a member exists for the current discriminant value, it is marshaled according to the rules for that type.

It can happen, therefore, that a union encoding consists solely of a discriminant value.

IDL Example

The following IDL example illustrates the syntax for declaring union types:

```
//IDL
module MyModule {
```

```
    union UNode;
    typedef sequence<UNode> UNodeSeq;
    enum SecurityRole { USER, GROUP, OTHER, MULTIPLE };

    // Variable length union.
    union UNode switch(SecurityRole) {
        case USER:
        case GROUP:    long    ID;
        default :      wstring name;
        case MULTIPLE: UNodeSeq recurList;
    };

    union USimple switch(boolean) { case TRUE: string val; };

    interface MyInterface {
        UNode useUNode(
                    in    UNode und_in,
                    inout UNode und_inout,
                    out   UNode und_out
                );
        USimple useUSimple(
                    in    USimple ufx_in,
                    inout USimple ufx_inout,
                    out   USimple ufx_out
                );
    };
};
```

C++ Mapping

The UNode and USimple unions defined in the preceding "IDL Example" map to C++ as follows:

```
//C++
namespace MyModule {
    enum SecurityRole
    {
        USER, GROUP, OTHER, MULTIPLE
        // Implementation-dependent extra value.
    };

    // Implementation dependent definitions generated for:
    // ===>    SecurityRole_out
    // ===>    _tc_SecurityRole

    class UNode;

    // Definition generated for:
    // ===>    UNodeSeq sequence type
    ...  // (not shown)
```

```
// Implementation-dependent definitions generated for:
// ===>    UNode_var
// ===>    UNode_out
// ===>    _tc_UNode

class UNode
{
public:
    UNode();
    UNode(const UNode&);
    ~UNode();
    UNode& operator=(const UNode&);

    void _d(SecurityRole);
    SecurityRole _d() const;

    CORBA::Long ID() const;
    void ID(CORBA::Long);


    // MEMORY MANAGEMENT: union assumes ownership
    //   of argument's memory and frees old value.
    void name(CORBA::WChar*);

    // MEMORY MANAGEMENT: union deep copies argument
    //   and frees old value.
    void name(const CORBA::WChar*);
    void name(const CORBA::WString_var &);

    // MEMORY MANAGEMENT: read-only access to return value.
    const CORBA::WChar * name() const;


    // MEMORY MANAGEMENT: union deep copies argument
    //   and frees old value.
    void recurList(const  UNodeSeq&);

    // MEMORY MANAGEMENT: read-only access to return value.
    const  UNodeSeq & recurList() const;

    // MEMORY MANAGEMENT: read-write access to return value.
    UNodeSeq & recurList();

    // Additional implementation-dependent details
    ...
};

class USimple;
```

```
    // Implementation-dependent definitions generated for:
    // ===>    USimple_var
    // ===>    USimple_out
    // ===>    _tc_USimple

    class USimple
    {
      public:
        USimple();
        USimple(const USimple&);
        ~USimple();
        USimple& operator=(const USimple&);

        void _d(CORBA::Boolean);
        CORBA::Boolean _d() const;

        // MEMORY MANAGEMENT: union assumes ownership
        //   of argument's memory and frees old value.
        void val(char*);

        // MEMORY MANAGEMENT: union deep copies argument
        //   and frees old value.
        void val(const char*);
        void val(const CORBA::String_var &);

        // MEMORY MANAGEMENT: read-only access to return value.
        const char * val() const;

        // _default() function - Generated only for unions that do NOT have
        //                       a 'default' case in IDL.
        void _default();
    };
};
```

C++ Usage

The following C++ code shows how to invoke the `useUNode()` operation defined in the preceding "IDL Example" section:

```
//C++
// Assume 'obj' is an object reference of MyModule::MyInterface type.
// Invoke the useUNode() operation
{
// Using a variable length union
MyModule::UNodeSeq roleList;
roleList.length(2);
roleList[0].ID(54321);             // discriminant = ??? (USER or GROUP)
roleList[0]._d(MyModule::USER);    // discriminant = USER
roleList[1].ID(12345);             // discriminant = ??? (USER or GROUP)
roleList[1]._d(MyModule::GROUP);   // discriminant = GROUP
```

```
MyModule::UNode SampleVal;
SampleVal.recurList(roleList);    // deep copy
                                  // discriminant = MULTIPLE

MyModule::UNode     InVal    = SampleVal;  // deep copy
MyModule::UNode     InoutVal = SampleVal;  // deep copy
// Variable length union ==> do NOT allocate memory for out parameter.
MyModule::UNode_var OutValV;

MyModule::UNode_var RecvValV = obj->useUNode(InVal, InoutVal, OutValV);

printUNode(*RecvValV);
printUNode(InoutVal);
printUNode(*OutValV);
}
```

The following C++ code shows how to invoke the `useUSimple()` operation defined in the preceding "IDL Example" section:

```
// Invoke the useUSimple() operation
{
// Using a variable length union
MyModule::USimple InVal;
InVal.val("This string is deep copied."); // discriminant = TRUE
MyModule::USimple InoutVal;
InoutVal._default();                      // discriminant = FALSE
// Variable length union ==> do NOT allocate memory for out parameter.
MyModule::USimple_var OutValV;

MyModule::USimple_var RecvValV = obj->useUSimple(InVal, InoutVal, OutValV);

cout << "RecvVal = { d=" << RecvValV->_d();
if (RecvValV->_d()) { cout << ", val=" << RecvValV->val(); }
cout << " }" << endl;
cout << "InoutVal = { d=" << InoutVal._d();
if (InoutVal._d()) { cout << ", val=" << InoutVal.val(); }
cout << " }" << endl;
cout << "OutVal = { d=" << OutValV->_d();
if (OutValV->_d()) { cout << ", val=" << OutValV->val(); }
cout << " }" << endl;
}
...
```

The `printUNode()` function prints the value of the `UNode` union, as follows:

```
//C++
void printUNode(const MyModule::UNode& node, int recurseLevel=0)
{
    CORBA::ULong len, j;
```

```
    switch (node._d() )
    {
        case MyModule::USER :
            cout << "UserID = " << node.ID();
            break;
        case MyModule::GROUP :
            cout << "GroupID = " << node.ID();
            break;
        case MyModule::MULTIPLE :
            cout << "{ ";
            len = node.recurList().length();
            for (j=0; j+1 < len; j++)  //Careful! Unsigned arithmetic.
            {
                printUNode(node.recurList()[j], recurseLevel+1);
                cout << ", ";
            }
            if (len > 0) {
                printUNode(node.recurList()[len-1], recurseLevel+1);
            }
            cout << " }";
            break;
        default :
            cout << "Other = ";
            printWideString(node.name());
            break;
    }
    if (recurseLevel==0) { cout << '\n'; }
}
```

Java Mapping

An IDL union type, *<union_name>*, maps to a Java class, *<java_union_name>*. Holder and helper classes, *<java_union_name>*`Holder` and *<java_union_name>*`Helper`, are generated according to the standard template described in the section "Java `Helper` and `Holder` Types" later in this chapter.

For example, the `MyModule.UNode` union type maps to Java as shown in Table 15.10.

Table 15.10 Java Mapping of the `UNode` Union Type

IDL Type	Java Mapped Types
`MyModule::UNode`	`MyModule.UNode`
	`MyModule.UNodeHolder`
	`MyModule.UNodeHelper`

Each union member declared in IDL maps to an accessor method and a modifier method of the mapped Java class. Additionally, union members with multiple case labels generate an extra modifier method in Java that lets you set both the discriminator and the member value. The `MyModule.UNode` and `MyModule.USimple` Java classes are therefore defined as follows:

```
//Java
package MyModule;

public final class UNode
    implements org.omg.CORBA.portable.IDLEntity
{
    public MyModule.SecurityRole  discriminator() { ... }

    public UNode(){}

    public boolean is_ID() { ... }
    public int ID() throws org.omg.CORBA.BAD_OPERATION { ... }
    public void ID(int value) { ... }
    public void ID(MyModule.SecurityRole discriminator, int value) { }

    public boolean is_name() { ... }
    public java.lang.String name() throws org.omg.CORBA.BAD_OPERATION { ... }
    public void name(java.lang.String value) { ... }
    public void name(
        MyModule.SecurityRole discriminator,
        java.lang.String value
    ) { ... }

    public boolean is_recurList() { ... }
    public MyModule.UNode[] recurList()
        throws org.omg.CORBA.BAD_OPERATION { ... }
    public void recurList(MyModule.UNode[] value) { ... }
    public void recurList(
        MyModule.SecurityRole discriminator,
        MyModule.UNode[] value
    )  { ... }
}


public final class USimple
    implements org.omg.CORBA.portable.IDLEntity
{
    public boolean discriminator() { ... }

    public USimple(){}

    public boolean is_val() { ... }
    public java.lang.String val() throws org.omg.CORBA.BAD_OPERATION { ... }
    public void val(java.lang.String value) { ... }
    public void val(boolean discriminator, java.lang.String value) { ... }

    // __default() functions - Generated only for unions that do NOT have
    //                         a 'default' case in IDL.
    public void __default() { ... }
```

```
    public void __default(boolean discrim) { ... }
}
...
```

Java Usage

The following Java code shows how to invoke the `useUNode()` operation defined in the preceding "IDL Example" section:

```
//Java
// Assume 'obj' is an object reference of MyModule::MyInterface type.
// Invoke the useUNode() operation
{
// Using a variable length union
MyModule.UNode roleList[] = new MyModule.UNode[2];
roleList[0] = new MyModule.UNode();
roleList[0].ID(MyModule.SecurityRole.USER, 54321);
roleList[1] = new MyModule.UNode();
roleList[1].ID(MyModule.SecurityRole.GROUP, 12345);
MyModule.UNode SampleVal = new MyModule.UNode();
SampleVal.recurList(roleList);   // discriminant = MULTIPLE

MyModule.UNode InVal = new MyModule.UNode();
InVal.recurList(roleList);
MyModule.UNodeHolder InoutValH = new MyModule.UNodeHolder(SampleVal);
MyModule.UNodeHolder OutValH   = new MyModule.UNodeHolder();

MyModule.UNode RecvVal = obj.useUNode(InVal, InoutValH, OutValH);

printUNode(RecvVal, 0);
printUNode(InoutValH.value, 0);
printUNode(OutValH.value, 0);
}
```

The following Java code shows how to invoke the `useUSimple()` operation defined in the preceding "IDL Example" section:

```
// Invoke the useUSimple() operation
{
MyModule.USimple       InVal     = new MyModule.USimple();
InVal.val("String value of union");   // discriminant = TRUE
MyModule.USimpleHolder InoutValH = new MyModule.USimpleHolder(
                                        new MyModule.USimple()
                                    );
InoutValH.value.__default();          // discriminant = FALSE
MyModule.USimpleHolder OutValH = new MyModule.USimpleHolder();

MyModule.USimple RecvVal = obj.useUSimple(InVal, InoutValH, OutValH);
```

```
...  // Do something with RecvVal, InoutValH.value, and OutValH.value
}
...
```

The following implementation of the `printUNode()` method illustrates how to access the value of the `UNode` union:

```
//Java
public static void printUNode(MyModule.UNode node, int recurseLevel)
{
    switch (node.discriminator().value() )
    {
        case MyModule.SecurityRole._USER :
            System.out.print("UserID = " + node.ID() );
            break;
        case MyModule.SecurityRole._GROUP :
            System.out.print("GroupID = " + node.ID() );
            break;
        case MyModule.SecurityRole._MULTIPLE :
            System.out.print("{ ");
            int len = node.recurList().length;
            for (int j=0; j < len-1; j++)
            {
                printUNode(node.recurList()[j], recurseLevel+1);
                System.out.print(", ");
            }
            if (len > 0) {
                printUNode(node.recurList()[len-1], recurseLevel+1);
            }
            System.out.print(" }");
            break;
        default :
            System.out.print("Other = <cannot print wide string>");
            break;
    }
    if (recurseLevel==0) { System.out.print("\n"); }
}
```

`unsigned long` Type

This section describes the IDL constant syntax and CDR encoding of an IDL `unsigned long` type. The mapping of an IDL `unsigned long` to C++ and to Java is also described and illustrated by example.

IDL Constant Declaration

```
//IDL
const unsigned long ULongConst = IntegerExpression;
```

A new `unsigned long` constant, *ULongConst*, is defined in terms of an integer expression, *IntegerExpression*, which is composed of integer literals, other integer constants, arithmetical operators, and other integer expressions enclosed in parentheses ( ).

The +, -, *, /, %, <<, >>, &, |, ^ infix and +, -, ~ unary operators are allowed in IDL `unsigned long` constant declarations.

Literals are specified in integer literal format, for example `0x2F2E`, as described in Chapter 16.

CDR Encoding

When an `unsigned long` integer is appended to an octet stream, it is marshaled as four octets (32 bits) and aligned on a four-byte boundary. The order in which the octets are marshaled depends on the current byte-ordering of the octet stream (big-endian or little-endian).

IDL Example

The following IDL example illustrates the syntax for declaring `unsigned long` constants:

```
//IDL
const unsigned long GLOBAL_ULONG = 365;

module MyModule {
    const unsigned long MODULE_ULONG = GLOBAL_ULONG & 0x00FF;

    interface MyInterface {
        const unsigned long INTERFACE_ULONG = 07777;

        unsigned long useULong(
                 in    unsigned long ul_in,
                 inout unsigned long ul_inout,
                 out   unsigned long ul_out
             );
    };
};
```

C++ Mapping

The preceding "IDL Example" maps to C++ as follows:

```
//C++
const CORBA::ULong GLOBAL_ULONG = 365;

namespace MyModule {
    const CORBA::ULong MODULE_ULONG = 109;
```

```
    class MyInterface : public virtual CORBA::Object {
        static const CORBA::ULong INTERFACE_ULONG;

        virtual CORBA::ULong useULong(
                    CORBA::ULong     ul_in,
                    CORBA::ULong&    ul_inout,
                    CORBA::ULong_out ul_out
                ) =0;
    };
};
...
// Initialisation of 'INTERFACE_ULONG'
const CORBA::ULong MyModule::MyInterface::INTERFACE_ULONG = 4095;
...
```

C++ Usage

The following C++ code shows how to invoke the `useULong()` operation defined in the preceding "IDL Example" section:

```
//C++
//Assume 'obj' is an object reference of MyModule::MyInterface type.
CORBA::ULong InoutVal = +123;
CORBA::ULong OutVal;

CORBA::ULong RecvVal = obj->useULong(+321, InoutVal, OutVal);

cout << "Returned value = " << RecvVal << endl;
cout << "Inout value    = " << InoutVal << endl;
cout << "Out value      = " << OutVal << endl;
...
```

Java Mapping

The preceding "IDL Example" maps to Java as follows:

```
//Java
// File containing global constants:
public interface GLOBAL_ULONG {
    public static final int value = (int) 0x16D;
};
...

// File containing module and interface constants:
package MyModule;

public interface MODULE_ULONG {
    public static final int value = (int) 0x6D;
};
```

```
public interface MyInterfaceOperations
{
    public static final int INTERFACE_ULONG = (int) 0xFFF;

    int useULong(
            int                      ul_in,
            org.omg.CORBA.IntHolder ul_inout,
            org.omg.CORBA.IntHolder ul_out
        );
};

public interface MyInterface
    extends MyInterfaceOperations,
    org.omg.CORBA.Object,
    org.omg.CORBA.portable.IDLEntity  { }
...
```

Java Usage

The following Java code shows how to invoke the `useULong()` operation defined in the preceding "IDL Example" section:

```
//Java
//Assume 'obj' is an object reference of MyModule::MyInterface type.
int InVal = +321;
org.omg.CORBA.IntHolder InoutValH = new org.omg.CORBA.IntHolder(+123);
org.omg.CORBA.IntHolder OutValH = new org.omg.CORBA.IntHolder();

int RecvVal = obj.useULong(InVal, InoutValH, OutValH);

System.out.println("Returned value = " + RecvVal);
System.out.println("Inout value    = " + InoutValH.value);
System.out.println("Out value      = " + OutValH.value);
...
```

`unsigned long long` Type

This section describes the IDL constant syntax and CDR encoding of an IDL `unsigned long long` type. The mapping of an IDL `unsigned long long` to C++ and to Java is also described and illustrated by example.

IDL Constant Declaration

```
//IDL
const unsigned long long ULongLongConst = IntegerExpression;
```

A new `unsigned long long` constant, *`ULongLongConst`*, is defined in terms of an integer expression, *`IntegerExpression`*, which is composed of integer literals, other integer constants, arithmetical operators, and other integer expressions enclosed in parentheses `( )`.

The +, -, *, /, %, <<, >>, &, |, ^ infix and +, -, ~ unary operators are allowed in IDL `unsigned long long` constant declarations.

Literals are specified in integer literal format, for example `0x2F2E`, as described in Chapter 16.

CDR Encoding

When an `unsigned long long` integer is appended to an octet stream, it is marshaled as eight octets (64 bits) and aligned on an eight-byte boundary. The order in which the octets are marshaled depends on the current byte-ordering of the octet stream (big-endian or little-endian).

IDL Example

The following IDL example illustrates the syntax for declaring `unsigned long long` constants:

```
//IDL
const unsigned long long GLOBAL_ULONGLONG = 365;

module MyModule {
    const unsigned long long MODULE_ULONGLONG = GLOBAL_ULONGLONG & 0x00FF;

    interface MyInterface {
        const unsigned long long INTERFACE_ULONGLONG = 07777;

        unsigned long long useULongLong(
                 in    unsigned long long ull_in,
                 inout unsigned long long ull_inout,
                 out   unsigned long long ull_out
             );
    };
};
```

C++ Mapping

The preceding "IDL Example" maps to C++ as follows:

```
//C++
const CORBA::ULongLong GLOBAL_ULONGLONG = 365;

namespace MyModule {
    const CORBA::ULongLong MODULE_ULONGLONG = 109;

    class MyInterface : public virtual CORBA::Object {
        static const CORBA::ULongLong INTERFACE_ULONGLONG;

        virtual CORBA::ULongLong useULongLong(
                    CORBA::ULongLong     ull_in,
                    CORBA::ULongLong&    ull_inout,
```

```
                        CORBA::ULongLong_out ull_out
                ) =0;
    };
};
...
// Initialisation of 'INTERFACE_ULONGLONG'
const CORBA::ULongLong MyModule::MyInterface::INTERFACE_ULONGLONG = 4095;
...
```

C++ Usage

The following C++ code shows how to invoke the `useULongLong()` operation defined in the preceding "IDL Example" section:

```
//C++
//Assume 'obj' is an object reference of MyModule::MyInterface type.
CORBA::ULongLong InoutVal = +123;
CORBA::ULongLong OutVal;

CORBA::ULongLong RecvVal = obj->useULongLong(+321, InoutVal, OutVal);

cout << "Returned value = " << RecvVal << endl;
cout << "Inout value    = " << InoutVal << endl;
cout << "Out value      = " << OutVal << endl;
...
```

Java Mapping

The preceding "IDL Example" maps to Java as follows:

```
//Java
// File containing global constants:
public interface GLOBAL_ULONGLONG {
    public static final long value = (long) 0x16D;
};
...

// File containing module and interface constants:
package MyModule;

public interface MODULE_ULONGLONG {
    public static final long value = (long) 0x6D;
};

public interface MyInterfaceOperations
{
    public static final long INTERFACE_ULONGLONG = (long) 0xFFF;

    long useULongLong(
            long                     ull_in,
            org.omg.CORBA.LongHolder ull_inout,
```

```
            org.omg.CORBA.LongHolder ull_out
        );
};

public interface MyInterface
    extends MyInterfaceOperations,
    org.omg.CORBA.Object,
    org.omg.CORBA.portable.IDLEntity  { }
...
```

Java Usage

The following Java code shows how to invoke the useULongLong() operation defined in the preceding "IDL Example" section:

```
//Java
//Assume 'obj' is an object reference of MyModule::MyInterface type.
long InVal = +321;
org.omg.CORBA.LongHolder InoutValH = new org.omg.CORBA.LongHolder(+123);
org.omg.CORBA.LongHolder OutValH = new org.omg.CORBA.LongHolder();

long RecvVal = obj.useULongLong(InVal, InoutValH, OutValH);

System.out.println("Returned value = " + RecvVal);
System.out.println("Inout value    = " + InoutValH.value);
System.out.println("Out value      = " + OutValH.value);
...
```

unsigned short Type

This section describes the IDL constant syntax and CDR encoding of an IDL unsigned short type. The mapping of an IDL unsigned short to C++ and to Java is also described and illustrated by example.

IDL Constant Declaration

```
//IDL
const unsigned short UShortConst = IntegerExpression;
```

A new unsigned short constant, *UShortConst*, is defined in terms of an integer expression, *IntegerExpression*, which is composed of integer literals, other integer constants, arithmetical operators, and other integer expressions enclosed in parentheses ( ).

The +, -, *, /, %, <<, >>, &, |, ^ infix and +, -, ~ unary operators are allowed in IDL unsigned short constant declarations.

Literals are specified in integer literal format, for example 0x2F2E, as described in Chapter 16.

CDR Encoding

When an unsigned short integer is appended to an octet stream, it is marshaled as two octets (16 bits) and aligned on a two-byte boundary. The order in which the octets are marshaled depends on the current byte-ordering of the octet stream (big-endian or little-endian).

IDL Example

The following IDL example illustrates the syntax for declaring unsigned short constants:

```
//IDL
const unsigned short GLOBAL_USHORT = 365;

module MyModule {
    const unsigned short MODULE_USHORT = GLOBAL_USHORT & 0x00FF;

    interface MyInterface {
        const unsigned short INTERFACE_USHORT = 07777;

        unsigned short useUShort(
                 in    unsigned short us_in,
                 inout unsigned short us_inout,
                 out   unsigned short us_out
             );
    };
};
```

C++ Mapping

The preceding "IDL Example" maps to C++ as follows:

```
//C++
const CORBA::UShort GLOBAL_USHORT = 365;

namespace MyModule {
    const CORBA::UShort MODULE_USHORT = 109;

    class MyInterface : public virtual CORBA::Object {
        static const CORBA::UShort INTERFACE_USHORT;

        virtual CORBA::UShort useUShort(
                    CORBA::UShort     us_in,
                    CORBA::UShort&    us_inout,
                    CORBA::UShort_out us_out
                ) =0;
    };
};
...
```

```
// Initialisation of 'INTERFACE_USHORT'
const CORBA::UShort MyModule::MyInterface::INTERFACE_USHORT = 4095;
...
```

C++ Usage

The following C++ code shows how to invoke the useUShort() operation defined in the preceding "IDL Example" section:

```
//C++
//Assume 'obj' is an object reference of MyModule::MyInterface type.
CORBA::UShort InoutVal = +123;
CORBA::UShort OutVal;

CORBA::UShort RecvVal = obj->useUShort(+321, InoutVal, OutVal);

cout << "Returned value = " << RecvVal << endl;
cout << "Inout value    = " << InoutVal << endl;
cout << "Out value      = " << OutVal << endl;
...
```

Java Mapping

The preceding "IDL Example" maps to Java as follows:

```
//Java
// File containing global constants:
public interface GLOBAL_USHORT {
    public static final short value = (short) 0x16D;
};
...

// File containing module and interface constants:
package MyModule;

public interface MODULE_USHORT {
    public static final short value = (short) 0x6D;
};

public interface MyInterfaceOperations
{
    public static final short INTERFACE_USHORT = (short) 0xFFF;

    short useUShort(
            short                          us_in,
            org.omg.CORBA.ShortHolder us_inout,
            org.omg.CORBA.ShortHolder us_out
        );
};
```

```
public interface MyInterface
    extends MyInterfaceOperations,
    org.omg.CORBA.Object,
    org.omg.CORBA.portable.IDLEntity  { }
...
```

Java Usage

The following Java code shows how to invoke the `useUShort()` operation defined in the preceding "IDL Example" section:

```
//Java
//Assume 'obj' is an object reference of MyModule::MyInterface type.
short InVal = +321;
org.omg.CORBA.ShortHolder InoutValH = new
org.omg.CORBA.ShortHolder((short)123);
org.omg.CORBA.ShortHolder OutValH = new org.omg.CORBA.ShortHolder();

short RecvVal = obj.useUShort(InVal, InoutValH, OutValH);

System.out.println("Returned value = " + RecvVal);
System.out.println("Inout value    = " + InoutValH.value);
System.out.println("Out value      = " + OutValH.value);
...
```

wchar Type

This section describes the IDL constant syntax and CDR encoding of an IDL `wchar` type. The mapping of an IDL `wchar` to C++ and to Java is also described and illustrated by example.

IDL Constant Declaration

```
//IDL
const wchar WCharConst = WCharLiteral;
const wchar WCharConst = OtherWCharConst;
```

A new `wchar` constant, *`WCharConst`*, can be defined either in terms of a wide character literal, *`WCharLiteral`*, or in terms of an existing wide character constant, *`OtherWCharConst`*. No infix or unary operators can be used in IDL `wchar` constant declarations.

The *`WCharLiteral`* consists of an uppercase `L` followed by a character enclosed in single quotes—for example, `L'a'`—or an escape sequence enclosed in single quotes—for example, `L'\n'`. See Chapter 16 "IDL Grammar" for the list of wide character escape sequences.

CDR Encoding

The CDR encoding of a `wchar` is complex and depends on the codeset being used by a particular connection. The codeset conversion framework specifies that *codeset negotiation* occurs whenever a connection is opened. The result of the codeset negotiation is an agreed set of codes for narrow characters, char, and wide characters, wchar, understood by both sender and receiver. The agreed set of codes are used for all subsequent character transmissions along the connection.

The number of octets occupied by a wchar varies, depending on the negotiated codeset. Under GIOP version 1.2, a single wchar could occupy anything up to a theoretical maximum of 256 octets. The alignment of a wchar, which also depends on the negotiated codeset, could be on a one-, two-, or four-byte boundary.

IDL Example

The following IDL example illustrates the syntax for declaring wchar constants:

```
//IDL
const wchar GLOBAL_WCHAR = L'a';

module MyModule {
    const wchar MODULE_WCHAR = L'\n';

    interface MyInterface {
        const wchar INTERFACE_WCHAR = L'\x2E';

        wchar useWChar(
                    in    wchar wc_in,
                    inout wchar wc_inout,
                    out   wchar wc_out
                );
    };
};
```

C++ Mapping

The preceding “IDL Example” maps to C++ as follows:

```
//C++
const CORBA::WChar GLOBAL_WCHAR = L'a';

namespace MyModule {
    const CORBA::WChar MODULE_WCHAR = L'\n';

    class MyInterface : public virtual CORBA::Object {
        static const CORBA::WChar INTERFACE_WCHAR;

        virtual CORBA::WChar useWChar(
                    CORBA::WChar     wc_in,
                    CORBA::WChar&    wc_inout,
                    CORBA::WChar_out wc_out
                ) =0;
    };
};
...
```

```
// Initialisation of 'INTERFACE_WCHAR'
const CORBA::WChar MyModule::MyInterface::INTERFACE_WCHAR = L'\x2E';
...
```

C++ Usage

The following C++ code shows how to invoke the useWChar() operation defined in the preceding "IDL Example" section:

```
//C++
//Assume 'obj' is an object reference of MyModule::MyInterface type.
CORBA::WChar InoutVal = L'y';
CORBA::WChar OutVal;

CORBA::WChar RecvVal = obj->useWChar(L'x', InoutVal, OutVal);

... // Do something with RecvVal, InoutVal, and OutVal.
...
```

Java Mapping

The preceding "IDL Example" maps to Java as follows:

```
//Java
// File containing global constants:
public interface GLOBAL_WCHAR {
    public static final char value = 'a';
};
...

// File containing module and interface constants:
package MyModule;

public interface MODULE_WCHAR {
    public static final char value = '\n';
};

public interface MyInterfaceOperations
{
    public static char INTERFACE_WCHAR = '\u2E';

    char useWChar(
             char                        wc_in,
             org.omg.CORBA.CharHolder wc_inout,
             org.omg.CORBA.CharHolder wc_out
         );
};

public interface MyInterface
    extends MyInterfaceOperations,
```

```
    org.omg.CORBA.Object,
    org.omg.CORBA.portable.IDLEntity  { }
...
```

Java Usage

The following Java code shows how to invoke the `useWChar()` operation defined in the preceding "IDL Example" section:

```
//Java
//Assume 'obj' is an object reference of MyModule::MyInterface type.
char InVal = 'x';
org.omg.CORBA.CharHolder InoutValH = new org.omg.CORBA.CharHolder('y');
org.omg.CORBA.CharHolder OutValH = new org.omg.CORBA.CharHolder();

char RecvVal = obj.useWChar(InVal, InoutValH, OutValH);

System.out.println("Returned value = " + RecvVal);
System.out.println("Inout value    = " + InoutValH.value);
System.out.println("Out value      = " + OutValH.value);
...
```

`wstring` Type

This section describes the IDL syntax, IDL constant syntax, and CDR encoding of an IDL `wstring` type. The mapping of an IDL `wstring` to C++ and to Java is also described and illustrated by example.

IDL Syntax

A `wstring` has the syntax of a type specifier. There are two forms of `wstring` syntax, *unbounded* and *bounded*, which are defined as follows:

```
//IDL
// Unbounded wstring type specifier:
wstring

// Bounded wstring type specifier:
wstring<Bound>
```

The *`Bound`* specifies the maximum length of the wide string. The *`Bound`* is a constant integer expression that evaluates to a positive value.

An unbounded `wstring` type specifier can appear in any context where a type specifier is expected. From CORBA 2.4 onward, the only context in which a bounded `wstring<>` type specifier should appear is as part of a `typedef` expression. For example, a bounded `wstring<>` can be given an alias using a `typedef` expression, as follows:

```
//IDL
typedef wstring<128> WString128;
```

IDL Constant Declaration

```
//IDL
const wstring WStringConst = WStringLiteral;
const wstring WStringConst = OtherWStringConst;
```

A new `wstring` constant, *`WStringConst`*, can be defined either in terms of a wide string literal, *`WStringLiteral`*, or in terms of an existing wide string constant, *`OtherWStringConst`*. No infix or unary operators can be used in IDL `wstring` constant declarations.

Wide string literal format, for example `L"This is a wide string"`, is described in Chapter 16.

CDR Encoding

A `wstring` is marshaled as an `unsigned long`, specifying the length of the `wstring` including the terminating null character, followed by the wide characters themselves (including the terminating null).

The details of the `wstring` encoding can vary depending on the particular GIOP version and wide character encoding that is used. Consult the OMG codeset conversion framework for more details.

IDL Example

The following IDL example illustrates the syntax for declaring `wstring` constants:

```
//IDL
const wstring GLOBAL_WSTRING = L"WString " L"with " L"many " L"parts." L"\n";

module MyModule {
    const wstring MODULE_WSTRING = GLOBAL_WSTRING;

    interface MyInterface {
        const wstring INTERFACE_WSTRING = L"Ahoy!";

        wstring useWString(
                    in    wstring ws_in,
                    inout wstring ws_inout,
                    out   wstring ws_out
                );
    };
};
```

C++ Mapping

The preceding "IDL Example" maps to C++ as follows:

```
//C++
const CORBA::WChar* GLOBAL_WSTRING = L"WString with many parts.\n";
```

```
namespace MyModule {
    const CORBA::WChar* MODULE_WSTRING = L"WString with many parts.\n";

    class MyInterface : public virtual CORBA::Object {
        static const CORBA::WChar * const INTERFACE_WSTRING;

        virtual CORBA::WChar * useWString(
                    const CORBA::WChar *  ws_in,
                    CORBA::WChar *&       ws_inout,
                    CORBA::WString_out    ws_out
                ) =0;
    };
};
...
// Initialisation of 'INTERFACE_WSTRING'
const CORBA::WChar* MyModule::MyInterface::INTERFACE_WSTRING = L"Ahoy!";
...
```

Some standard types and static functions are provided to help with the memory management of wide strings. They are defined as follows:

```
//C++
namespace CORBA {
    // Standard definitions for:
    // ===>    WString_var
    // ===>    WString_out
    // ===>    _tc_WString

    // String memory management functions:
    WChar *wstring_alloc(CORBA::ULong len);
    WChar *wstring_dup(const WChar* ws);
    void wstring_free(WChar*);
};
```

For explanations and examples of using these wide string memory management functions, see Chapter 4.

C++ Usage

The following C++ code shows how to invoke the `useWString()` operation defined in the preceding "IDL Example" section:

```
//C++
//Assume 'obj' is an object reference of MyModule::MyInterface type.
CORBA::WString_var InoutValV = CORBA::wstring_dup(L"EFGH");
CORBA::WString_var OutValV;

CORBA::WString_var RecvValV = obj->useWString(L"ABCD", InoutValV, OutValV);

// Do something with *RecvValV, *InoutValV, and *OutValV.
...
```

Java Mapping

The preceding "IDL Example" maps to Java as follows:

```
//Java
// File containing global constants:
public interface GLOBAL_WSTRING {
    public static final String value = "WString with many parts.\n";
};
...

// File containing module and interface constants:
package MyModule;

public interface MODULE_WSTRING {
    public static final String value = "WString with many parts.\n";
};

public interface MyInterfaceOperations
{
    public static final String INTERFACE_WSTRING = "Ahoy!";

    String useWString(
             String                        ws_in,
             org.omg.CORBA.StringHolder ws_inout,
             org.omg.CORBA.StringHolder ws_out
         );
};

public interface MyInterface
    extends MyInterfaceOperations,
    org.omg.CORBA.Object,
    org.omg.CORBA.portable.IDLEntity  { }
...
```

Java Usage

The following Java code shows how to invoke the useWString() operation defined in the preceding "IDL Example" section:

```
//Java
//Assume 'obj' is an object reference of MyModule::MyInterface type.
String InVal = "ABCD";
org.omg.CORBA.StringHolder InoutValH = new org.omg.CORBA.StringHolder("EFGH");
org.omg.CORBA.StringHolder OutValH = new org.omg.CORBA.StringHolder();

String RecvVal = obj.useWString(InVal, InoutValH, OutValH);
```

```
System.out.println("Returned value = " + RecvVal);
System.out.println("Inout value    = " + InoutValH.value);
System.out.println("Out value      = " + OutValH.value);
...
```

Pseudo-IDL from the CORBA Module

This section provides the C++ and Java mapping definitions of the core CORBA object types, most of which are defined in pseudo-IDL (see Chapter 5 for a discussion of pseudo-IDL).

CORBA::Context Interface

This section describes how the `CORBA::Context` pseudo-interface maps to C++ and to Java.

Pseudo-IDL

The following pseudo-IDL code defines the `CORBA::Context` pseudo-interface:

```
// PIDL
module CORBA {
    ...
    pseudo interface Context {
        readonly attribute Identifier context_name;
        readonly attribute Context parent;

        // C++ mapping version
        void create_child(in Identifier child_ctx_name, out Context child_ctx);
        // Java mapping version
        Context create_child(in Identifier child_ctx_name);

        void set_one_value(in Identifier propname, in any propvalue);
        void set_values(in NVList values);
        void delete_values(in Identifier propname);

        // C++ mapping version
        void get_values(
            in Identifier start_scope,
            in Flags op_flags,
            in Identifier pattern,
            out NVList values
        );
        // Java mapping version
        NVList get_values(
                   in Identifier start_scope,
                   in Flags op_flags,
                   in Identifier pattern
               );
    };
    ...
};
```

C++ Mapping

The `CORBA::Context` pseudo-interface maps to C++ as follows:

```
// C++
namespace CORBA {
    ...
    class Context
    {
    public:
        // MEMORY MANAGEMENT: Context object retains ownership
        //                    of return value's memory.
        const char *context_name() const;

        // MEMORY MANAGEMENT: Context object retains ownership
        //                    of return value's memory.
        Context_ptr parent() const;

        void create_child(const char *, Context_out);
        void set_one_value(const char *, const Any &);
        void set_values(NVList_ptr);
        void delete_values(const char *);
        void get_values(
            const char*,
            Flags,
            const char*,
            NVList_out
        );
    };
    ...
};
```

Java Mapping

The `CORBA::Context` pseudo-interface maps to Java as follows:

```
// Java
package org.omg.CORBA;

public abstract class Context {
    public abstract String context_name();
    public abstract Context parent();
    public abstract Context create_child(String child_ctx_name);
    public abstract void set_one_value(String propname, Any propvalue);
    public abstract void set_values(NVList values);
    public abstract void delete_values(String propname);
    public abstract NVList get_values(
                                String start_scope,
                                int op_flags,
                                String pattern
                            );
}
```

CORBA::ContextList Interface

This section describes how the CORBA::ContextList pseudo-interface maps to C++ and to Java.

Pseudo-IDL

The following pseudo-IDL code defines the CORBA::ContextList pseudo-interface:

```
// PIDL
module CORBA {
    ...
    pseudo interface ContextList {
        readonly attribute unsigned long count;
        void add(in string ctx);
        string item(in unsigned long index) raises (CORBA::Bounds);
        void remove(in unsigned long index) raises (CORBA::Bounds);
    };
    ...
};
```

C++ Mapping

The CORBA::ContextList pseudo-interface maps to C++ as follows:

```
// C++
namespace CORBA {
    ...
    class ContextList
    {
    public:
        ULong count();
        void add(const char* ctxt);

        // MEMORY MANAGEMENT: ContextList object assumes ownership
        //                    of ctxt argument's memory.
        void add_consume(char* ctxt);

        // MEMORY MANAGEMENT: ContextList object retains ownership
        //                    of returned value's memory.
        const char* item(ULong index);

        void remove(ULong index);
    };
    ...
};
```

Java Mapping

The CORBA::ContextList pseudo-interface maps to Java as follows:

```
// Java
package org.omg.CORBA;

public abstract class ContextList {
    public abstract int count();
    public abstract void add(String ctx);
    public abstract String item(int index) throws org.omg.CORBA.Bounds;
    public abstract void remove(int index) throws org.omg.CORBA.Bounds;
}
```

CORBA::Environment Interface

This section describes how the CORBA::Environment pseudo-interface maps to C++ and to Java.

Pseudo-IDL

The following pseudo-IDL code defines the CORBA::Environment pseudo-interface:

```
// PIDL
module CORBA {
    ...
    pseudo interface Environment
    {
        attribute exception exception;
        void clear();
    };
    ...
};
```

C++ Mapping

The CORBA::Environment pseudo-interface maps to C++ as follows:

```
// C++
namespace CORBA {
    ...
    class Environment
    {
    public:
        // MEMORY MANAGEMENT: Environment object assumes ownership
        //                    of Exception* argument's memory.
        void exception(Exception*);

        // MEMORY MANAGEMENT: Environment object retains ownership
        //                    of returned value's memory.
        Exception *exception() const;

        void clear();
    };
    ...
};
```

Java Mapping

The `CORBA::Environment` pseudo-interface maps to Java as follows:

```
// Java
package org.omg.CORBA;

public abstract class Environment {
    public abstract void exception(java.lang.Exception except);
    public abstract java.lang.Exception exception();
    public abstract void clear();
}
```

CORBA::ExceptionList Interface

This section describes how the `CORBA::ExceptionList` pseudo-interface maps to C++ and to Java.

Pseudo-IDL

The following pseudo-IDL code defines the `CORBA::ExceptionList` pseudo-interface:

```
// PIDL
module CORBA {
    ...
    pseudo interface ExceptionList {
        readonly attribute unsigned long count;
        void add(in TypeCode exc);
        TypeCode item (in unsigned long index) raises (CORBA::Bounds);
        void remove (in unsigned long index) raises (CORBA::Bounds);
    };
    ...
};
```

C++ Mapping

The `CORBA::ExceptionList` pseudo-interface maps to C++ as follows:

```
// C++
namespace CORBA {
    ...
    class ExceptionList
    {
    public:
        ULong count();
        void add(const TypeCode_ptr tc);

        // MEMORY MANAGEMENT: ExceptionList object assumes ownership
        //                    of tc argument's memory.
        void add_consume(TypeCode_ptr tc);
```

```
        // MEMORY MANAGEMENT: ExceptionList object retains ownership
        //                    of returned value's memory.
        TypeCode_ptr item(ULong index);

        void remove(ULong index);
    };
    ...
};
```

Java Mapping

The `CORBA::ExceptionList` pseudo-interface maps to Java as follows:

```
// Java
package org.omg.CORBA;

public abstract class ExceptionList {
    public abstract int count();
    public abstract void add(TypeCode exc);
    public abstract TypeCode item(int index) throws org.omg.CORBA.Bounds;
    public abstract void remove(int index) throws org.omg.CORBA.Bounds;
}
```

`CORBA::NamedValue` Interface

This section describes how the `CORBA::NamedValue` pseudo-interface maps to C++ and to Java.

Pseudo-IDL

The following pseudo-IDL code defines the `CORBA::NamedValue` pseudo-interface:

```
// PIDL
module CORBA {
    ...
    typedef unsigned long Flags;
    typedef string Identifier;
    const Flags ARG_IN = 1;
    const Flags ARG_OUT = 2;
    const Flags ARG_INOUT = 3;
    const Flags CTX_RESTRICT_SCOPE = 15;

    pseudo interface NamedValue {
        readonly attribute Identifier name;
        readonly attribute any value;
        readonly attribute Flags flags;
    };
    ...
};
```

C++ Mapping

The `CORBA::NamedValue` pseudo-interface maps to C++ as follows:

```
// C++
namespace CORBA {
    ...
    class NamedValue
    {
    public:
        // MEMORY MANAGEMENT: NamedValue object retains ownership
        //                    of returned value's memory.
        const char *name() const;

        // MEMORY MANAGEMENT: NamedValue object retains ownership
        //                    of returned value's memory.
        Any *value() const;

        Flags flags() const;
    };
    ...
};
```

Java Mapping

The `CORBA::NamedValue` pseudo-interface maps to Java as follows:

```
// Java
package org.omg.CORBA;

public interface ARG_IN {
    public static final int value = 1;
}

public interface ARG_OUT {
    public static final int value = 2;
}

public interface ARG_INOUT {
    public static final int value = 3;
}

public interface CTX_RESTRICT_SCOPE {
    public static final int value = 15;
}

public abstract class NamedValue {
    public abstract String name();
    public abstract Any value();
    public abstract int flags();
}
```

CORBA::NVList Interface

This section describes how the CORBA::NVList pseudo-interface maps to C++ and to Java.

Pseudo-IDL

The following pseudo-IDL code defines the CORBA::NVList pseudo-interface:

```
// PIDL
module CORBA {
    ...
    pseudo interface NVList {
        readonly attribute unsigned long count;
        NamedValue add(in Flags flags);
        NamedValue add_item(in Identifier item_name, in Flags flags);
        NamedValue add_value(
            in Identifier item_name,
            in any val,
            in Flags flags
        );
        NamedValue item(in unsigned long index) raises (CORBA::Bounds);
        void remove(in unsigned long index) raises (CORBA::Bounds);
    };
    ...
};
```

C++ Mapping

The CORBA::NVList pseudo-interface maps to C++ as follows:

```
// C++
namespace CORBA {
    ...
    class NVList
    {
    public:
        ULong count() const;

        // MEMORY MANAGEMENT: NVList object retains ownership
        //                    of returned value's memory.
        NamedValue_ptr add(Flags);

        // MEMORY MANAGEMENT: NVList object retains ownership
        //                    of returned value's memory.
        NamedValue_ptr add_item(const char*, Flags);

        // MEMORY MANAGEMENT: NVList object retains ownership
        //                    of returned value's memory.
        NamedValue_ptr add_value(const char*, const Any&, Flags);
```

```
        // MEMORY MANAGEMENT: NVList object retains ownership
        // of returned value's memory and assumes ownership of
        // the char* argument's memory.
        NamedValue_ptr add_item_consume(char*, Flags);

        // MEMORY MANAGEMENT: NVList object retains ownership
        // of returned value's memory and assumes ownership of
        // the char* and the Any* arguments' memory.
        NamedValue_ptr add_value_consume(char*, Any *, Flags);

        // MEMORY MANAGEMENT: NVList object retains ownership
        //                    of returned value's memory.
        NamedValue_ptr item(ULong);

        // MEMORY MANAGEMENT: NVList calls CORBA::release() on the
        //                    indexed NamedValue object.
        void remove(ULong);
    };
    ...
};
```

Java Mapping

The `CORBA::NVList` pseudo-interface maps to Java as follows:

```
// Java
package org.omg.CORBA;

public abstract class NVList {
    public abstract int count();
    public abstract NamedValue add(int flags);
    public abstract NamedValue add_item(String item_name, int flags);
    public abstract NamedValue add_value(
        String item_name,
        Any val,
        int flags
    );
    public abstract NamedValue item(int index) throws org.omg.CORBA.Bounds;
    public abstract void remove(int index) throws org.omg.CORBA.Bounds;
}
```

`CORBA::Object` Interface

Technically, the `CORBA::Object` interface is not a pseudo-interface. In common with other pseudo-interfaces, however, it exhibits a highly irregular mapping from IDL to C++ and Java.

NOTE

You cannot use the `CORBA::Object` type in your IDL because this type is not directly available in ordinary IDL. Use the special IDL `Object` keyword instead, which is a built-in IDL type specifier.

IDL

The following IDL code defines the `Object` interface:

```
//IDL
module CORBA {

    interface Object {
        void release();
        boolean is_nil();
        Object duplicate();

        ImplementationDef get_implementation();
        InterfaceDef get_interface();

        boolean is_a(in string logical_type_id);
        boolean non_existent();
        boolean is_equivalent(in Object other_object);
        unsigned long hash(in unsigned long maximum);

        void create_request(
            in Context ctx,
            in Identifier operation,
            in NVList arg_list,
            in NamedValue result,
            out Request request,
            in Flags req_flags
        );
        void create_request2(
            in Context ctx,
            in Identifier operation,
            in NVList arg_list,
            in NamedValue result,
            in ExceptionList exclist,
            in ContextList ctxtlist,
            out Request request,
            in Flags req_flags
        );

        Policy_ptr get_policy(in PolicyType policy_type);
        DomainManagerList get_domain_managers();
        Object set_policy_overrides(
            in PolicyList policies,
```

```
            in SetOverrideType set_or_add
        );
    };
};
```

C++ Mapping

The `Object` interface maps to C++ as follows:

```
// C++
namespace CORBA {
    void    release(Object_ptr obj);
    Boolean is_nil(Object_ptr obj);

    class Object
    {
    public:
        static Object_ptr _duplicate(Object_ptr obj);
        static Object_ptr _nil();

        ImplementationDef_ptr _get_implementation();
        InterfaceDef_ptr _get_interface();

        Boolean _is_a(const char* logical_type_id);
        Boolean _non_existent();
        Boolean _is_equivalent(Object_ptr other_object);
        ULong _hash(ULong maximum);

        void _create_request(
            Context_ptr ctx,
            const char *operation,
            NVList_ptr arg_list,
            NamedValue_ptr result,
            Request_out request,
            Flags req_flags
        );
        void _create_request(
            Context_ptr ctx,
            const char *operation,
            NVList_ptr arg_list,
            NamedValue_ptr result,
            ExceptionList_ptr,
            ContextList_ptr,
            Request_out request,
            Flags req_flags
        );
        Request_ptr _request(const char* operation);

        Policy_ptr _get_policy(PolicyType policy_type);
        DomainManagerList* _get_domain_managers();
```

```
        Object_ptr _set_policy_overrides(
            const PolicyList& policies,
            SetOverrideType set_or_add
        );
    };
};
```

Java Mapping

The `Object` interface maps to Java as follows:

```
// Java
package org.omg.CORBA;

public interface Object {
    void _release();
    org.omg.CORBA.Object _duplicate();

    boolean _is_a(String Identifier);
    boolean _non_existent();
    boolean _is_equivalent(Object that);
    int _hash(int maximum);

    // Deprecated by CORBA 2.3.
    InterfaceDef _get_interface();

    org.omg.CORBA.Object _get_interface_def();

    Request _create_request(
        Context ctx,
        String operation,
        NVList arg_list,
        NamedValue result
    );
    Request _create_request(
        Context ctx,
        String operation,
        NVList arg_list,
        NamedValue result,
        ExceptionList exclist,
        ContextList ctxlist
    );
    Request _request(String s);

    Policy _get_policy(int policy_type);
    DomainManager[] _get_domain_managers();
    org.omg.CORBA.Object _set_policy_override(
        Policy[] policies,
        SetOverrideType set_or_add
```

```
    );
}

abstract public class ObjectHelper {
    // A standard Helper class is generated for Object.
    ...  // (not shown)
}
```

CORBA::ORB Interface

This section describes how the CORBA::ORB pseudo-interface maps to C++ and to Java.

Pseudo-IDL

The following pseudo-IDL code defines the CORBA::ORB pseudo-interface:

```
// PIDL
module CORBA {
    ...
    interface NVList;                // forward declaration
    interface OperationDef;          // forward declaration
    interface TypeCode;              // forward declaration
    typedef short PolicyErrorCode;
    typedef unsigned long PolicyType;
    interface Request;               // forward declaration
    typedef sequence <Request> RequestSeq;
    native AbstractBase;
    exception PolicyError { PolicyErrorCode reason; };

    typedef string RepositoryId;
    typedef string Identifier;

    struct StructMember {
        Identifier name;
        TypeCode type;
        IDLType type_def;
    };
    typedef sequence <StructMember> StructMemberSeq;

    struct UnionMember {
        Identifier name;
        any label;
        TypeCode type;
        IDLType type_def;
    };
    typedef sequence <UnionMember> UnionMemberSeq;

    typedef sequence <Identifier> EnumMemberSeq;

    typedef unsigned short ServiceType;
    typedef unsigned long ServiceOption;
```

```
typedef unsigned long ServiceDetailType;
const ServiceType Security = 1;

struct ServiceDetail {
    ServiceDetailType service_detail_type;
    sequence <octet> service_detail;
};

struct ServiceInformation {
    sequence <ServiceOption> service_options;
    sequence <ServiceDetail> service_details;
};

native ValueFactory;

pseudo interface ORB { // PIDL
    string object_to_string (in Object obj);
    Object string_to_object (in string str);

    // Dynamic Invocation related operations
    void create_list (in long count, out NVList new_list);
    void create_operation_list (in OperationDef oper, out NVList new_list);

    // C++ mapping only.
    void create_named_value(out NamedValue nv);

    // C++ mapping version.
    void create_exception_list(out ExceptionList ex_list);
    // Java mapping version.
    ExceptionList create_exception_list();

    // C++ mapping version.
    void create_context_list(out ContextList ctxt_list);
    // Java mapping version.
    ContextList create_context_list();

    // C++ mapping version.
    void create_environment(out Environment env);
    // Java mapping version.
    Environment create_environment();

    void get_default_context (out Context ctx);
    void send_multiple_requests_oneway(in RequestSeq req);
    void send_multiple_requests_deferred(in RequestSeq req);
    boolean poll_next_response();
    void get_next_response(out Request req);
```

```
typedef string ObjectId;
typedef sequence <ObjectId> ObjectIdList;
exception InvalidName {};

// Initial reference operation
ObjectIdList list_initial_services ();
Object resolve_initial_references (
    in ObjectId identifier
) raises (InvalidName);

// Thread related operations
boolean work_pending();
void perform_work();
void run();
void shutdown(in boolean wait_for_completion);
void destroy();

// Service information operations
boolean get_service_information (
    in ServiceType service_type,
    out ServiceInformation service_information
);

// Policy related operations
Policy create_policy(
    in PolicyType type,
    in any val
) raises (PolicyError);

// Value factory operations
ValueFactory register_value_factory(
    in RepositoryId id,
    in ValueFactory factory
);
void unregister_value_factory(in RepositoryId id);
ValueFactory lookup_value_factory(in RepositoryId id);

// Type code creation operations
TypeCode create_struct_tc (
    in RepositoryId id,
    in Identifier name,
    in StructMemberSeq members
);
TypeCode create_union_tc (
    in RepositoryId id,
    in Identifier name,
    in TypeCode discriminator_type,
    in UnionMemberSeq members
);
```

```
    TypeCode create_enum_tc (
        in RepositoryId id,
        in Identifier name,
        in EnumMemberSeq members
    );
    TypeCode create_alias_tc (
        in RepositoryId id,
        in Identifier name,
        in TypeCode original_type
    );
    TypeCode create_exception_tc (
        in RepositoryId id,
        in Identifier name,
        in StructMemberSeq members
    );
    TypeCode create_interface_tc (
        in RepositoryId id,
        in Identifier name
    );
    TypeCode create_string_tc (
        in unsigned long bound
    );
    TypeCode create_wstring_tc (
        in unsigned long bound
    );
    TypeCode create_fixed_tc (
        in unsigned short digits,
        in short scale
    );
    TypeCode create_sequence_tc (
        in unsigned long bound,
        in TypeCode element type
    );
    TypeCode create_recursive_sequence_tc ( // deprecated
        in unsigned long bound,
        in unsigned long offset
    );
    TypeCode create_array_tc (
        in unsigned long length,
        in TypeCode element_type
    );
    TypeCode create_value_tc (
        in RepositoryId id,
        in Identifier name,
        in ValueModifier type_modifier,
        in TypeCode concrete_base,
        in ValueMemberSeq members
    );
    TypeCode create_value_box_tc (
```

```
            in RepositoryId id,
            in Identifier name,
            in TypeCode boxed_type
        );
        TypeCode create_native_tc (
            in RepositoryId id,
            in Identifier name
        );
        TypeCode create_recursive_tc (
            in RepositoryId id
        );
        TypeCode create_abstract_interface_tc (
            in RepositoryId id,
            in Identifier name
        );
        TypeCode create_local_interface_tc(
            in RepositoryId id,
            in Identifier name
        );

        //-----------------------------------------
        // Java mapping version only.
        //-----------------------------------------
        TypeCode get_primitive_tc(in TCKind tcKind);
        Current get_current();
        Any create_any();
        OutputStream create_output_stream();
        void connect(Object obj);
        void disconnect(Object obj);
        Object get_value_def(in String repid);
        void set_delegate(Object wrapper);
    };
    ...
};
```

C++ Mapping

The CORBA::ORB pseudo-interface maps to C++ as follows:

```
// C++
namespace CORBA {
    ...
    class ORB
    {
    public:
        char *object_to_string(Object_ptr);
        Object_ptr string_to_object(const char*);

        //--------------------------------------
        // Dynamic Invocation related operations
        //--------------------------------------
```

```
void create_list(Long, NVList_out);
void create_operation_list(OperationDef_ptr, NVList_out);
void create_named_value(NamedValue_out);
void create_exception_list(ExceptionList_out);
void create_context_list(ContextList_out);
void create_environment(Environment_out);
void get_default_context(Context_out);

void send_multiple_requests_oneway(
    const RequestSeq&
);
void send_multiple_requests_deferred(
    const RequestSeq&
);
Boolean poll_next_response();
void get_next_response(Request_out);

//----------------------------------------
// Obtaining initial object references
//----------------------------------------
typedef char* ObjectId;
class ObjectIdList {...};
class InvalidName : public UserException {...};
ObjectIdList *list_initial_services();
Object_ptr resolve_initial_references(
    const char *identifier
);

//----------------------------------------
// Thread-related operations.
//----------------------------------------
Boolean work_pending();
void perform_work();
void shutdown(Boolean wait_for_completion);
void run();


//----------------------------------------
// Service information operations
//----------------------------------------
Boolean get_service_information(
    ServiceType svc_type,
    ServiceInformation_out svc_info
);

// Policy related operations
Policy_ptr create_policy(PolicyType type, const Any& val);

// Value factory operations
CORBA::ValueFactory register_value_factory(
```

```
            const char*  id,
            CORBA::ValueFactory fact
        );
        void unregister_value_factory(const char*  id);
        CORBA::ValueFactory lookup_value_factory(const char*  id);


        static ORB_ptr _duplicate(ORB_ptr orb);
        static ORB_ptr _nil();

        // Type code creation operations
        // (map according to the standard IDL-C++ mapping rules)
        ...  // (not shown)
    };
    ...
};
```

Java Mapping

The `CORBA::ORB` pseudo-interface maps to two distinct Java scopes:

- `org.omg.CORBA.ORB` defines the bulk of the ORB methods.
- `org.omg.CORBA_2_3.ORB`, which inherits from `org.omg.CORBA.ORB`, defines additional ORB methods that support the use of value types.

The `org.omg.CORBA.ORB` Java class is defined as follows:

```
// Java
package org.omg.CORBA;

public abstract class ORB {
    public abstract org.omg.CORBA.Object string_to_object(String str);
    public abstract String object_to_string(org.omg.CORBA.Object obj);

    //----------------------------------------
    // Dynamic Invocation related operations
    //----------------------------------------
    public abstract NVList create_list(int count);

    // Deprecated by CORBA 2.3.
    public abstract NVList create_operation_list(OperationDef oper);

    // The oper argument must be an OperationDef
    public NVList create_operation_list(org.omg.CORBA.Object oper);

    public abstract NamedValue create_named_value(
        String name, Any value, int flags
    );
    public abstract ExceptionList create_exception_list();
    public abstract ContextList create_context_list();
```

```
public abstract Environment create_environment();
public abstract Context get_default_context();

public abstract void send_multiple_requests_oneway(
    Request[] req);
public abstract void send_multiple_requests_deferred(
    Request[] req);
public abstract boolean poll_next_response();
public abstract Request get_next_response() throws
    org.omg.CORBA.WrongTransaction;

//---------------------------------------
// Obtaining initial object references
//---------------------------------------
public abstract String[] list_initial_services();
public abstract org.omg.CORBA.Object
    resolve_initial_references(
    String object_name)
    throws org.omg.CORBA.ORBPackage.InvalidName;

//---------------------------------------
// Service information operations
//---------------------------------------
public boolean get_service_information(
    short service_type,
    ServiceInformationHolder service_info
) { ... }

//---------------------------------------
// Thread related operations
//---------------------------------------
public boolean work_pending() { ... }
public void perform_work() { ... }
public void run() { ... }
public void shutdown(boolean wait_for_completion) { ... }
public void destroy() { ... }

// Policy related operations
public Policy create_policy(short policy_type, Any val)
    throws org.omg.CORBA.PolicyError  { ... }

//---------------------------------------
// Type code creation
//---------------------------------------
public abstract TypeCode create_struct_tc(
    String id,
    String name,
    StructMember[] members);
public abstract TypeCode create_union_tc(
```

```
        String id,
        String name,
        TypeCode discriminator_type,
        UnionMember[] members);
    public abstract TypeCode create_enum_tc(
        String id,
        String name,
        String[] members);
    public abstract TypeCode create_alias_tc(
        String id,
        String name,
        TypeCode original_type);
    public abstract TypeCode create_exception_tc(
        String id,
        String name,
        StructMember[] members);
    public abstract TypeCode create_interface_tc(
        String id,
        String name);
    public abstract TypeCode create_string_tc(int bound);
    public abstract TypeCode create_wstring_tc(int bound);
    public TypeCode create_fixed_tc(
        short digits,
        short scale) { ... }
    public abstract TypeCode create_sequence_tc(
        int bound,
        TypeCode element_type);

    // Deprecated by CORBA 2.3.
    public abstract TypeCode create_recursive_sequence_tc(
        int bound,
        int offset);

    public abstract TypeCode create_array_tc(
        int length,
        TypeCode element_type);
    public TypeCode create_value_tc(
        String id,
        String name,
        short type_modifier,
        TypeCode concrete_base,
        ValueMember[] members) { ... }
    public TypeCode create_value_box_tc(
        String id,
        String name,
        TypeCode boxed_type) { ... }
    public TypeCode create_native_tc(
        String id,
        String name) { ... }
```

```
    public TypeCode create_recursive_tc(
        String id) { ... }
    public TypeCode create_abstract_interface_tc(
        String id,
        String name) { ... }

    // Deprecated by CORBA 2.2.
    public Current get_current() { ... }

    // Deprecated by Portable Object Adapter,
    public void connect( org.omg.CORBA.Object obj) { ... }

    // Deprecated by Portable Object Adapter,
    public void disconnect( org.omg.CORBA.Object obj) { ... }

    //----------------------------------------
    // Additional methods for the IDL to Java mapping
    //----------------------------------------
    public abstract TypeCode get_primitive_tc(TCKind tcKind);
    public abstract Any create_any();
    public abstract org.omg.CORBA.portable.OutputStream
        create_output_stream();

    //----------------------------------------
    // Additional static methods for ORB initialization
    //----------------------------------------
    public static ORB init(Strings[] args, Properties props);
    public static ORB init(Applet app, Properties props);
    public static ORB init();
    abstract protected void set_parameters(
        String[] args,
        java.util.Properties props);
    abstract protected void set_parameters(
        java.applet.Applet app,
        java.util.Properties props);
}
```

The `org.omg.CORBA_2_3.ORB` Java class is defined as follows:

```
//Java
package org.omg.CORBA_2_3;

public abstract class ORB    extends org.omg.CORBA.ORB {
    // The return type is a ValueDef
    public org.omg.CORBA.Object get_value_def(String repid)
        throws org.omg.CORBA.BAD_PARAM { ... }

    //----------------------------------------
    // Value factory operations
    //----------------------------------------
```

```
    public org.omg.CORBA.portable.ValueFactory register_value_factory(
        String id,
        org.omg.CORBA.portable.ValueFactory factory) { ... }
    public void unregister_value_factory(String id) { ... }
    public org.omg.CORBA.portable.ValueFactory
        lookup_value_factory(String id) { ... }

    public void set_delegate(java.lang.Object wrapper) { ... }
}
```

CORBA::Request Interface

This section describes how the CORBA::Request pseudo-interface maps to C++ and to Java.

Pseudo-IDL

The following pseudo-IDL code defines the CORBA::Request pseudo-interface:

```
// PIDL
module CORBA {
    ...
    pseudo interface Request {
        readonly attribute Object target;
        readonly attribute Identifier operation;
        readonly attribute NVList arguments;
        readonly attribute NamedValue result;
        readonly attribute Environment env;
        readonly attribute ExceptionList exceptions;
        readonly attribute ContextList contexts;

        attribute Context ctx;

        any add_in_arg();

        // C++ mapping version.
        // any add_in_arg(in string name);
        // Java mapping version.
        any add_named_in_arg(in string name);

        any add_inout_arg();

        // C++ mapping version.
        // any add_inout_arg(in string name);
        // Java mapping version.
        any add_named_inout_arg(in string name);

        any add_out_arg();

        // C++ mapping version.
        // any add_out_arg(in string name);
```

```
        // Java mapping version.
        any add_named_out_arg(in string name);

        void set_return_type(in TypeCode tc);
        any return_value();

        void invoke();
        void send_oneway();
        void send_deferred();
        void get_response();
        boolean poll_response();
    };
    ...
};
```

C++ Mapping

The `CORBA::Request` pseudo-interface maps to C++ as follows:

```
// C++
namespace CORBA {
    ...
    class Request
    {
    public:
        // MEMORY MANAGEMENT: Request object retains ownership
        //                    of returned value's memory.
        Object_ptr target() const;

        // MEMORY MANAGEMENT: Request object retains ownership
        //                    of returned value's memory.
        const char *operation() const;

        // MEMORY MANAGEMENT: Request object retains ownership
        //                    of returned value's memory.
        NVList_ptr arguments();

        // MEMORY MANAGEMENT: Request object retains ownership
        //                    of returned value's memory.
        NamedValue_ptr result();

        // MEMORY MANAGEMENT: Request object retains ownership
        //                    of returned value's memory.
        Environment_ptr env();

        // MEMORY MANAGEMENT: Request object retains ownership
        //                    of returned value's memory.
        ExceptionList_ptr exceptions();
```

```
        // MEMORY MANAGEMENT: Request object retains ownership
        //                    of returned value's memory.
        ContextList_ptr contexts();

        // MEMORY MANAGEMENT: Request object retains ownership
        //                    of returned value's memory.
        Context_ptr ctx() const;

        void ctx(Context_ptr);

        // argument manipulation helper functions
        Any &add_in_arg();
        Any &add_in_arg(const char* name);
        Any &add_inout_arg();
        Any &add_inout_arg(const char* name);
        Any &add_out_arg();
        Any &add_out_arg(const char* name);
        void set_return_type(TypeCode_ptr tc);
        Any &return_value();
        void invoke();
        void send_oneway();
        void send_deferred();
        void get_response();
        Boolean poll_response();
    };
    ...
};
```

Java Mapping

The CORBA::Request pseudo-interface maps to Java as follows:

```
// Java
package org.omg.CORBA;

public abstract class Request {
    public abstract Object target();
    public abstract String operation();
    public abstract NVList arguments();
    public abstract NamedValue result();
    public abstract Environment env();
    public abstract ExceptionList exceptions();
    public abstract ContextList contexts();

    public abstract Context ctx();
    public abstract void ctx(Context c);

    public abstract Any add_in_arg();
    public abstract Any add_named_in_arg(String name);
    public abstract Any add_inout_arg();
```

```
    public abstract Any add_named_inout_arg(String name);
    public abstract Any add_out_arg();
    public abstract Any add_named_out_arg(String name);

    public abstract void set_return_type(TypeCode tc);
    public abstract Any return_value();

    public abstract void invoke();
    public abstract void send_oneway();
    public abstract void send_deferred();
    public abstract void get_response()
        throws org.omg.CORBA.WrongTransaction;
    public abstract boolean poll_response();
}
```

CORBA::ServerRequest Interface

This section describes how the `CORBA::ServerRequest` pseudo-interface maps to C++ and to Java.

Pseudo-IDL

The following pseudo-IDL code defines the `CORBA::ServerRequest` pseudo-interface:

```
// PIDL
module CORBA {
    ...
    interface ServerRequest { // PIDL
        readonly attribute Identifier operation;
        void arguments(inout NVList nv);
        Context ctx();
        void set_result(in Any val);
        void set_exception(in Any val);
    };
    ...
};
```

C++ Mapping

The `CORBA::ServerRequest` pseudo-interface maps to C++ as follows:

```
// C++
namespace CORBA {
    ...
    class ServerRequest
    {
    public:
        // MEMORY MANAGEMENT: ServerRequest object retains ownership
        //                    of returned value's memory.
        const char* operation() const;
```

```
        // MEMORY MANAGEMENT: ServerRequest object assumes ownership
        //                    of the NVList argument's memory.
        // (see Chapter 18 for details of C++ memory management)
        void arguments(NVList_ptr& parameters);

        // MEMORY MANAGEMENT: ServerRequest object retains ownership
        //                    of returned value's memory.
        Context_ptr ctx();

        void set_result(const Any& value);
        void set_exception(const Any& value);
    };
    ...
};
```

For more details of the special C++ memory management rules that apply to `CORBA::ServerRequest` objects, see Chapter 19, "Dynamic Skeleton Interface."

Java Mapping

The `CORBA::ServerRequest` pseudo-interface maps to Java as follows:

```
// Java
package org.omg.CORBA;

public abstract class ServerRequest {
    public String operation() { ... }
    public abstract Context ctx();
    public void arguments(NVList nv) { ... }
    public void set_result(Any val) { ... }
    public void set_exception(Any val) { ... }
}
```

CORBA::TypeCode Interface

This section describes how the `CORBA::TypeCode` pseudo-interface maps to C++ and to Java.

Pseudo-IDL

The following pseudo-IDL code defines the `CORBA::TypeCode` pseudo-interface:

```
// PIDL
module CORBA {
    ...
    enum TCKind {
        tk_null, tk_void,
        tk_short, tk_long, tk_ushort, tk_ulong,
        tk_float, tk_double, tk_boolean, tk_char,
        tk_octet, tk_any, tk_TypeCode, tk_Principal, tk_objref,
        tk_struct, tk_union, tk_enum, tk_string,
        tk_sequence, tk_array, tk_alias, tk_except,
```

```
        tk_longlong, tk_ulonglong, tk_longdouble,
        tk_wchar, tk_wstring, tk_fixed,
        tk_value, tk_value_box,
        tk_native,
        tk_abstract_interface,
        tk_local_interface
    };

    typedef short ValueModifier;
    const ValueModifier VM_NONE = 0;
    const ValueModifier VM_CUSTOM = 1;
    const ValueModifier VM_ABSTRACT = 2;
    const ValueModifier VM_TRUNCATABLE = 3;

    typedef short Visibility;
    const Visibility PRIVATE_MEMBER = 0;
    const Visibility PUBLIC_MEMBER = 1;

    interface TypeCode {
        exception Bounds {};
        exception BadKind {};

        // for all TypeCode kinds
        boolean equal (in TypeCode tc);
        boolean equivalent(in TypeCode tc);
        TypeCode get_compact_typecode();
        TCKind kind ();

        // for tk_objref, tk_struct, tk_union, tk_enum, tk_alias,
        // tk_value, tk_value_box, tk_native, tk_abstract_interface
        // tk_local_interface and tk_except
        RepositoryId id () raises (BadKind);

        // for tk_objref, tk_struct, tk_union, tk_enum, tk_alias,
        // tk_value, tk_value_box, tk_native, tk_abstract_interface
        // tk_local_interface and tk_except
        Identifier name () raises (BadKind);

        // for tk_struct, tk_union, tk_enum, tk_value,
        // and tk_except
        unsigned long member_count () raises (BadKind);
        Identifier member_name (in unsigned long index)
            raises(BadKind, Bounds);

        // for tk_struct, tk_union, tk_value,
        // and tk_except
        TypeCode member_type (in unsigned long index)
            raises (BadKind, Bounds);
```

```
        // for tk_union
        any member_label (in unsigned long index)
            raises(BadKind, Bounds);
        TypeCode discriminator_type () raises (BadKind);
        long default_index () raises (BadKind);

        // for tk_string, tk_sequence, and tk_array
        unsigned long length () raises (BadKind);

        // for tk_sequence, tk_array, tk_value_box and tk_alias
        TypeCode content_type () raises (BadKind);

        // for tk_fixed
        unsigned short fixed_digits() raises(BadKind);
        short fixed_scale() raises(BadKind);

        // for tk_value
        Visibility member_visibility(in unsigned long index)
            raises(BadKind, Bounds);
        ValueModifier type_modifier() raises(BadKind);
        TypeCode concrete_base_type() raises(BadKind);
    };
    ...
};
```

C++ Mapping

The CORBA::TypeCode pseudo-interface maps to C++ as follows:

```
// C++
namespace CORBA {
    ...
    class TypeCode
    {
    public:
        class Bounds : public UserException { ... };
        class BadKind : public UserException { ... };

        Boolean equal(TypeCode_ptr) const;
        Boolean equivalent(TypeCode_ptr) const;
        TCKind kind() const;
        TypeCode_ptr get_compact_typecode() const;

        // MEMORY MANAGEMENT: TypeCode object retains ownership
        //                    of returned value's memory.
        const char* id() const;
```

```
        // MEMORY MANAGEMENT: TypeCode object retains ownership
        //                    of returned value's memory.
        const char* name() const;

        ULong member_count() const;

        // MEMORY MANAGEMENT: TypeCode object retains ownership
        //                    of returned value's memory.
        const char* member_name(ULong index) const;

        TypeCode_ptr member_type(ULong index) const;

        Any *member_label(ULong index) const;
        TypeCode_ptr discriminator_type() const;
        Long default_index() const;

        ULong length() const;

        TypeCode_ptr content_type() const;

        UShort fixed_digits() const;
        Short fixed_scale() const;

        Visibility member_visibility(ULong index) const;
        ValueModifier type_modifier() const;
        TypeCode_ptr concrete_base_type() const;
    };
    ...
};
```

Java Mapping

The CORBA::TypeCode pseudo-interface maps to Java as follows:

```
// Java
package org.omg.CORBA;

final public class TypeCodeHolder
    implements org.omg.CORBA.portable.Streamable
{
    public Typecode value;
    public TypeCodeHolder() {}
    public TypeCodeHolder(Typecode initial) {...}
    public void _read(
    org.omg.CORBA.portable.InputStream is)
    {...}
    public void _write(
        org.omg.CORBA.portable.OutputStream os)
    {...}
```

```
    public org.omg.CORBA.TypeCode _type() {...}
}

public abstract class TypeCode extends
    org.omg.CORBA.portable.IDLEntity
{
    // for all TypeCode kinds
    public abstract boolean equal(TypeCode tc);
    public abstract boolean equivalent(TypeCode tc);
    public abstract TypeCode get_compact_typecode();
    public abstract TCKind kind();

    // for objref, struct, union, enum, alias,
    // value, value_box, native,
    // abstract_interface, and except
    public abstract String id() throws TypeCodePackage.BadKind;
    public abstract String name() throws TypeCodePackage.BadKind;

    // for struct, union, enum, value, and except
    public abstract int member_count() throws TypeCodePackage.BadKind;
    public abstract String member_name(int index)
        throws TypeCodePackage.BadKind, TypeCodePackage.Bounds;

    // for struct, union, value, and except
    public abstract TypeCode member_type(int index)
        throws TypeCodePackage.BadKind, TypeCodePackage.Bounds;

    // for union
    public abstract Any member_label(int index)
        throws TypeCodePackage.BadKind, TypeCodePackage.Bounds;
    public abstract TypeCode discriminator_type()
        throws TypeCodePackage.BadKind;
    public abstract int default_index() throws TypeCodePackage.BadKind;

    // for string, sequence, and array
    public abstract int length() throws TypeCodePackage.BadKind;

    // for sequence, array, value, value_box and alias
    public abstract TypeCode content_type() throws TypeCodePackage.BadKind;

    // for fixed
    public abstract short fixed_digits() throws TypeCodePackage.BadKind;
    public abstract short fixed_Scale() throws TypeCodePackage.BadKind;

    // for value
    public abstract short member_visibility(long index)
        throws TypeCodePackage.BadKind, TypeCodePackage.Bounds;
    public abstract short type_modifer() throws TypeCodePackage.BadKind;
```

```
    public abstract TypeCode concrete_base_type()
        throws TypeCodePackage.BadKind;
}
```

CORBA::ValueBase Interface

The CORBA::ValueBase interface is a pseudo-interface that acts as the base type for all value types.

NOTE

You cannot use the CORBA::ValueBase type in your IDL because this type is not directly available in ordinary IDL. Use the special IDL ValueBase keyword instead, which is a built-in IDL type specifier.

IDL

The following IDL code defines the ValueBase pseudo interface:

```
//IDL
module CORBA {
    ...
    valuetype ValueBase{
        ValueDef get_value_def();
    };
};
```

C++ Mapping

The ValueBase pseudo interface maps to C++ as follows:

```
// C++
namespace CORBA {
    void add_ref(ValueBase* vb) { ... }
    void remove_ref(ValueBase* vb) { ... }

    class ValueBase {
      public:
        virtual ValueBase* _add_ref() = 0;
        virtual void       _remove_ref() = 0;
        virtual ValueBase* _copy_value() = 0;
        virtual ULong      _refcount_value() = 0;
        static ValueBase*  _downcast(ValueBase*);

      protected:
        ValueBase();
        ValueBase(const ValueBase&);
        virtual ~ValueBase();

      private:
        void operator=(const ValueBase&);
```

```
    };
};
```

Java Mapping

In Java, the `ValueBase` pseudo interface maps directly to the `java.io.Serializable` class.

Exception Types

Both the C++ and Java mapping specifications define a number of exception classes that serve as the base classes for CORBA system and user exceptions. The following exception classes are described here:

- `CORBA::Exception`
- `CORBA::SystemException`
- `CORBA::UnknownUserException`
- `CORBA::UserException`

The `Exception` Class

This section describes how the `CORBA::Exception` pseudo-interface maps to C++ and to Java.

C++ `CORBA::Exception` Class

The `CORBA::Exception` class is defined as follows:

```
// C++
namespace CORBA {
    ...
    class Exception
    {
    public:
        virtual ~Exception();
        virtual void _raise() const = 0;
        virtual const char * _name() const;
        virtual const char * _rep_id() const;
    };
    ...
};
```

Java `java.lang.Exception` Class

The `CORBA::Exception` pseudo interface maps directly to the built-in `java.lang.Exception` class in Java. The `java.lang.Exception` class is the base class for all CORBA exceptions in Java.

The `SystemException` Classes

This section describes how the `CORBA::SystemException` pseudo-interface maps to C++ and to Java.

C++ CORBA::SystemException Class

The CORBA::SystemException class is defined as follows:

```
// C++
namespace CORBA {
    ...
    enum CompletionStatus {
        COMPLETED_YES,
        COMPLETED_NO,
        COMPLETED_MAYBE
    };

    class SystemException : public Exception
    {
    public:
        SystemException();
        SystemException(const SystemException &);
        SystemException(ULong minor, CompletionStatus status);
        ~SystemException();
        SystemException &operator=(const SystemException &);
        ULong minor() const;
        void minor(ULong);
        CompletionStatus completed() const;
        void completed(CompletionStatus);

        // MEMORY MANAGEMENT: Neither version of the _downcast() function
        //                    duplicates the Exception argument.
        static SystemException *_downcast(Exception *);
        static const SystemException *_downcast(const Exception *);

        virtual void _raise() const = 0;

    };
    ...
};
```

Java org.omg.CORBA.SystemException Class

The org.omg.CORBA.SystemException class is defined as follows:

```
// Java
package org.omg.CORBA;

abstract public class SystemException
    extends java.lang.RuntimeException
{
    public int minor;
    public CompletionStatus completed;
    ...
}
```

The UnknownUserException Classes

The UnknownUserException type is not defined as a pseudo-interface but it is, nevertheless, provided both by the C++ mapping (as CORBA::UnknownUserException) and by the Java mapping (as org.omg.CORBA.UnknownUserException).

For a description of how the UnknownUserException type is used, see Chapter 18, "Dynamic Invocation Interface."

C++ UnknownUserException Class

The CORBA::UnknownUserException class is defined as follows:

```
// C++
namespace CORBA {
    ...
    class UnknownUserException : public UserException
    {
    public:
        Any &exception();

        // MEMORY MANAGEMENT: Neither version of the _downcast() function
        //                    duplicates the Exception argument.
        static UnknownUserException* _downcast(Exception*);
        static const UnknownUserException* _downcast(const Exception*);

        virtual void raise();
    };
    ...
};
```

Java org.omg.CORBA.UnknownUserException Class

The org.omg.CORBA.UnknownUserException class is defined as follows:

```
// Java
package org.omg.CORBA;

final public class UnknownUserException
    extends org.omg.CORBA.UserException
{
    public Any except;
    public UnknownUserException() { ... }
    public UnknownUserException(Any a) { ... }
}

final public class UnknownUserExceptionHolder {
    // Follows the usual pattern for a Holder class.
}
```

The UserException Classes

The UserException type is not defined as a pseudo-interface but it is, nevertheless, provided both by the C++ mapping (as CORBA::UserException) and by the Java mapping (as org.omg.CORBA.UserException).

C++ CORBA::UserException Class

The CORBA::UserException class is defined as follows:

```
// C++
namespace CORBA {
    ...
    class UserException : public Exception
    {
    public:
        UserException();
        UserException(const UserException &);
        ~UserException();
        UserException &operator=(const UserException &);

        // MEMORY MANAGEMENT: Neither version of the _downcast() function
        //                    duplicates the Exception argument.
        static UserException* _downcast(Exception*);
        static const UserException* _downcast(const Exception*);

        virtual void _raise() const = 0;
    };
    ...
};
```

Java org.omg.CORBA.UserException Class

The org.omg.CORBA.UserException class is defined as follows:

```
// Java
package org.omg.CORBA;

abstract public class UserException
    extends java.lang.Exception
    implements org.omg.CORBA.portable.IDLEntity
{
    public UserException() { ... }
    public UserException(java.lang.String value) { ... }
}
```

The PortableServer Module

Most of the PortableServer module maps from IDL to C++ and to Java according to the standard mapping rules. The mappings for the few exceptional types are given here.

C++ `PortableServer` Functions

The C++ functions for converting an object ID to and from a string (or wide string) are defined in the `PortableServer` scope as follows:

```
// C++
namespace PortableServer
{
    char*      ObjectId_to_string(const ObjectId&);
    WChar*     ObjectId_to_wstring(const ObjectId&);
    ObjectId*  string_to_ObjectId(const char*);
    ObjectId*  wstring_to_ObjectId(const WChar*);
};
```

The `PortableServer` Dynamic Implementation Classes

The `DynamicImplementation` type is not defined as a pseudo-interface but it is, nevertheless, provided both by the C++ mapping (as `PortableServer::DynamicImplementation`) and by the Java mapping (as `org.omg.PortableServer.DynamicImplementation`).

The `DynamicImplementation` type is used by the DSI to process invocations dynamically. See Chapter 19, "Dynamic Skeleton Interface."

C++ Mapping

The `PortableServer` dynamic implementation class maps to C++ as follows:

```
// C++
namespace PortableServer {
    class DynamicImplementation : public virtual ServantBase
    {
    public:
        Object_ptr _this();
        virtual void invoke(ServerRequest_ptr request) = 0;
        virtual RepositoryId _primary_interface(
            const ObjectId& oid,
            POA_ptr poa
        ) = 0;
    };
};
```

Java Mapping

The `PortableServer` dynamic implementation class maps to Java as follows:

```
// Java
package org.omg.PortableServer;
```

```
abstract public class DynamicImplementation extends Servant
{
    abstract public void invoke( org.omg.CORBA.ServerRequest request);
}
```

PortableServer::Servant Native Type

The Servant type is defined as a native type in IDL because its definition is highly dependent on the individual language mapping.

C++ Mapping

The PortableServer::Servant native type maps to C++ as follows:

```
// C++
namespace PortableServer
{
    class ServantBase
    {
    public:
        virtual ~ServantBase();
        virtual POA_ptr _default_POA();
        virtual InterfaceDef_ptr _get_interface() throw(SystemException);
        virtual Boolean _is_a(const char* logical_type_id)
            throw(SystemException);
        virtual Boolean _non_existent() throw(SystemException);
        virtual void _add_ref();
        virtual void _remove_ref();
        ...
    };
    typedef ServantBase* Servant;

    class RefCountServantBase : public virtual ServantBase
    {
    public:
        ~RefCountServantBase();
        virtual void _add_ref();
        virtual void _remove_ref();
        ...
    };

    class ServantBase_var
    {
        // Implementation-dependent definition.
    };
    ...
};
```

Java Mapping

The PortableServer::Servant native type maps to Java as follows:

```
// Java
package org.omg.PortableServer;

import org.omg.CORBA.ORB;
import org.omg.PortableServer.POA;

abstract public class Servant {
    final public org.omg.CORBA.Object _this_object() { ... }
    final public org.omg.CORBA.Object _this_object(ORB orb) { ... }
    final public ORB _orb() { ... }
    final public POA _poa() { ... }
    final public byte[] _object_id() { ... }

    // Methods that can be overridden.
    public POA _default_POA() { ... }
    public boolean _is_a(String repository_id) { ... }
    public boolean _non_existent() { ... }
    public org.omg.CORBA.InterfaceDef _get_interface() { ... }

    abstract public String[] _all_interfaces(POA poa, byte[] objectId);

    final public Delegate _get_delegate() { ... }
    final public void _set_delegate(Delegate delegate) { ... }
}
```

Java Helper and Holder Types

This section describes the templates that are used by an IDL to Java compiler to generate Java Helper and Holder types from a given user-defined IDL type.

Helper Types

Helper types are provided only for user-defined types. The purpose of a Helper class is to provide miscellaneous, typed Java methods that support the use of the user-defined type.

For each user-defined type, *<user_type>*, a Helper class, *<user_type>*Helper, is generated in accordance with the following template:

```
//Java
// Helper class for non-boxed value types.

abstract public class <user_type>Helper {
    public static void insert(org.omg.CORBA.Any a, <user_type> t) {...}
    public static <user_type> extract(Any a) {...}
    public static org.omg.CORBA.TypeCode type() {...}
    public static String id() {...}
```

```
    public static <user_type> read(org.omg.CORBA.portable.InputStream is) {...}
    public static void write(
        org.omg.CORBA.portable.OutputStream os, <user_type> val
    ) {...}

    // Only in Helpers for an abstract interface.
    public static <user_type> narrow(java.lang.Object obj) {...}

    // Only in Helpers for a non-abstract interface with at
    // least one abstract base interface.
    public static <user_type> narrow(org.omg.CORBA.Object obj) {...}
    public static <user_type> narrow(java.lang.Object obj) {...}

    // Only in Helpers for a non-abstract interface with
    // no abstract base interface.
    public static <user_type> narrow(org.omg.CORBA.Object obj) {...}

    // For each factory declaration in a non-abstract value type.
    public static <user_type> <factory_name> (
        org.omg.CORBA.ORB orb
        [ " ," <factory_arguments>]
    ) {...}
}
```

Holder Types

Holder types are provided for every built-in type and user-defined type to facilitate passing data as out and inout parameters in an operation invocation.

For each user-defined type, *<user_type>*, a Holder class, *<user_type>*Holder, is generated in accordance with the following template:

```
//Java
final public class <user_type>Holder
  implements org.omg.CORBA.portable.Streamable {
    public <user_type> value;

    public <user_type>Holder() {}
    public <user_type>Holder(<user_type> initial) {...}

    public void _read(org.omg.CORBA.portable.InputStream is) {...}
    public void _write(org.omg.CORBA.portable.OutputStream os) {...}

    public org.omg.CORBA.TypeCode _type() {...}
}
```

CHAPTER 16

IDL Grammar

This chapter describes the fundamentals of IDL grammar: the syntax of literals, the syntax of expressions, and a formal definition of IDL grammar in Extended Backus-Naur Format (EBNF).

Literals

This section describes the following IDL literals: integer, floating point, fixed point, character, and string.

Integer Literals

There are three forms of integer literal in IDL, as follows:

- **Decimal (base 10)**—A sequence of digits, *not* beginning with `0`. For example, `14460`.
- **Octal (base 8)**—A sequence of digits, beginning with `0`. Because the literal is base 8, the digits `8` and `9` are excluded. For example, `0771`.
- **Hexadecimal (base 16)**—A sequence of digits, from the range `0–9`, and characters, from the range `a–f` or `A–F`, prefixed by either `0x` or `0X`. For example, `0x9f2E`.

A signed integer, for example `+12` or `-12`, is technically an integer expression, with a unary `+` or `-` operator attached to the literal.

Floating-Point Literals

There are two forms of floating-point literal in IDL, as follows:

- **Without exponent**—A sequence of decimal digits including exactly one occurrence of a decimal point. For example, `40.0123`, `9933.`, and `.001` are examples of correctly formed literals.

- **With exponent**—An exponent can be included in a floating-point literal by appending `e` or `E`, followed optionally by `+` or `-`, followed by a decimal integer. The decimal point in the mantissa can be omitted when an exponent is present. For example, `6.001e-30`, `54321.e+1`, and `22E0` are examples of correctly formed floating-point literals.

Fixed-Point Literals

A fixed-point literal is a sequence of decimal digits including zero or one occurrences of a decimal point followed by `d` or `D`. For example, `40.0123D`, `9933d`, and `.001D` are examples of correctly formed fixed-point literals.

Character Literals

Both narrow (`char`) and wide (`wchar`) character literals are taken from the ISO Latin-1 (8859.1) character set. Graphic characters are represented as follows:

- **Narrow character**—a single character enclosed in single quotes. For example, `'a'`, and `'z'`.
- **Wide character**—the letter `L` followed by a single character enclosed in single quotes. For example, `L'a'`, and `L'z'`.

Non-graphic character literals are represented by escape sequences, as shown in Table 16.1.

Table 16.1 Narrow and Wide Character Escape Sequences

Description	Narrow Character Literal	Wide Character Literal
null	`'\0'`	`L'\0'`
newline	`'\n'`	`L'\n'`
horizontal tab	`'\t'`	`L'\t'`
vertical tab	`'\v'`	`L'\v'`
backspace	`'\b'`	`L'\b'`
carriage return	`'\r'`	`L'\r'`
form feed	`'\f'`	`L'\f'`
alert	`'\a'`	`L'\a'`
backslash	`'\\'`	`L'\\'`
question mark	`'\?'`	`L'\?'`
single quote	`'\''`	`L'\''`
double quote	`'\"'`	`L'\"'`
octal number	`'\`*ddd*`'`	`L'\`*ddd*`'`
hexadecimal number	`'\x`*hh*`'`	`L'\x`*hh*`'`
Unicode character	*Not available*	`L'\u`*hhhh*`'`

The octal number escape sequence consists of a backslash (`\`) followed by a sequence of one, two, or three digits from the range `0`–`7`. For example, `\144` is the octal representation of decimal 100. The allowed range of octal number values is `\000` to `\377` (an initial `0` is not required for octal numbers in the context of an escape sequence).

The hexadecimal number escape sequence consists of `\x` followed by a sequence of one or two hexadecimal digits. The allowed range of hexadecimal number values is `\x00` to `\xFF`.

The Unicode escape sequence consists of `\u` followed by a sequence of one, two, three, or four hexadecimal digits. The allowed range of Unicode values is `\u0000` to `\uFFFF`.

String Literals

A narrow string literal (`string`) is a sequence of graphic characters and character escape sequences enclosed in double quotes, excluding the null `\0` and Unicode `\u`*hhhh* escape sequences. For example, `"This is a string.\n"`. An octal or hexadecimal escape sequence is terminated by the first non-octal or non-hexadecimal digit respectively. For example, the string `"\x20Beware!"` would not be accepted by an IDL compiler because it is interpreted as `'\x20Be'` (invalid character escape!), `'w'`, `'a'`, `'r'`, `'e'`, `'!'`.

A wide string literal (`wstring`) is a sequence of graphic characters and character escape sequences enclosed in double quotes, excluding the null `\0` escape sequence. An octal or hexadecimal escape sequence is terminated by the first non-octal or non-hexadecimal digit respectively. For example, `L"This is a wide string.\n"` and `L"\u20Beware!"`. The latter string is interpreted as `L'\u20Be'`, `L'w'`, `L'a'`, `L'r'`, `L'e'`, `L'!'`.

A string literal can also consist of a sequence of adjacent substrings which are subsequently concatenated by the IDL compiler. The following narrow string literal expresses the string `"Like a 1-D jigsaw puzzle."` as a sequence of substrings:

```
//IDL
const string CONCAT_STRING = "Like " "a " "1-D " "jigsaw " "puzzle.";
```

This way of expressing strings is occasionally useful for strings that cannot be written any other way. For example, the sequence of characters `'\xB'` followed by `'B'` can be expressed as the string `"\xB" "B"` but not as the string `"\xBB"`.

The following wide string literal expresses the string `L"Like a 1-D jigsaw puzzle."` as a sequence of substrings:

```
//IDL
const wstring CONCAT_WSTRING = L"Like " L"a " L"1-D " L"jigsaw " L"puzzle.";
```

Expressions

This section describes the syntax and semantics for the following forms of IDL constant expression: integer, floating-point, and fixed-point.

Integer Expressions

An integer expression consists of a combination of the following elements:

- Integer literals.
- Integer constants.
- The +, -, ~ unary operators.
- The +, -, *, /, %, <<, >>, &, |, ^ binary operators.
- Integer sub-expressions.

The format of an integer literal is defined in the section "Integer Literals," earlier in this chapter, and the syntax of integer constants is described in Chapter 15, "IDL Data Types" (under the various subheadings for `short` type, `unsigned short` type, `long` type, `unsigned long` type, `long long` type, and `unsigned long long` type).

The ~ unary operator generates the bitwise complement of the expression that follows it. For example, in the context of an octet expression `~0xF0` is transformed to `0x0F`, and `~0` is transformed to `255`.

The binary operators that can be applied to integer expressions are described in Table 16.2.

Table 16.2 Binary Operators Used in Integer Expressions

Binary Operator	Description
+	Yields the arithmetical sum of its operands.
-	Yields the arithmetical difference of its operands.
*	Yields the arithmetical product of its operands.
/	Yields the integer quotient of its operands. For example, `5/2` yields `2`.
%	The expression `x%y` yields the remainder left from dividing `x` by `y`. For example, `5%2` yields `1`.
<<	The expression `x<<n` shifts the bits in `x` by `n` places to the left, using `0` to fill the empty bits. For example, `0xFFFF<<4` yields `0xFFF0`.
>>	The expression `x>>n` shifts the bits in `x` by `n` places to the right, using `0` to fill the empty bits. For example, `0xFFFF>>4` yields `0x0FFF`.
&	Yields the logical, bitwise AND of its operands.
|	Yields the logical, bitwise OR of its operands.
^	Yields the logical, bitwise exclusive-OR of its operands.

An integer sub-expression consists of an integer expression enclosed in parentheses, (*IntegerExpression*). For example, the following integer constant is set equal to the product of two sub-expressions:

```
//IDL
const long SAMPLE_INT = (123+456)*(12-123);
```

Floating-Point Expressions

A floating-point expression consists of a combination of the following elements:

- Floating-point literals.
- Floating-point constants.
- The +, - unary operators.
- The +, -, *, / binary operators.
- Floating-point sub-expressions.

The format of a floating-point literal is defined in the section "Floating-Point Literals" earlier in this chapter and the syntax of floating-point constants is described in Chapter 15 (under the various sub-headings for `float` type, `double` type, and `long double` type).

The binary operators that can be applied to floating-point expressions—+, -, *, /—act as normal floating-point arithmetical operators. The following binary operators *cannot* be used in floating-point expressions: %, <<, >>, &, |, ^.

A floating-point sub-expression consists of a floating-point expression enclosed in parentheses, (*FloatingPointExpression*). For example, the following floating-point constant is set equal to the quotient of two sub-expressions:

```
//IDL
const float SAMPLE_FLOAT = (1.0e6 + 2.345e6)/(1.5e8 - 5.67e9);
```

Fixed-Point Expressions

A fixed-point expression consists of a combination of the following elements:

- Fixed-point literals.
- Fixed-point constants.
- The +, - unary operators.
- The +, -, *, / binary operators.
- Fixed-point sub-expressions.

The format of a fixed-point literal is defined in the section "Fixed-Point Literals" earlier in this chapter and the syntax of fixed-point constants is described in Chapter 15.

Fixed point arithmetic expressions—involving the binary operators +, -, *, /—are evaluated using double-precision arithmetic (62 digits) for all intermediate expressions. If the result, in the format `fixed<D,S>`, has more than 31-digit precision, a 31-digit result is retained by transforming the result to the format `fixed<31,S-(D-31)>` and discarding the excess digits.

A fixed-point sub-expression consists of a fixed-point expression enclosed in parentheses, (*FixedPointExpression*). For example, the following fixed-point constant is set equal to the quotient of two sub-expressions:

```
//IDL
const Fixed SAMPLE_FIXED = (1.23D + 2.345D)/(6879D - 0.876D);
```

OMG IDL Grammar in EBNF Notation

The formal definition of the IDL grammar presented in this section is based on the CORBA 2.4.2 specification. You should bear in mind that the formal definition expressed in EBNF is not a complete description of IDL grammar—the semantics described in this and other chapters implicitly put further constraints on IDL grammar.

A brief summary of EBNF notation is provided in Table 16.3.

Table 16.3 Syntax Notation for IDL Grammar

Notation	Meaning
`"text"`	A text literal.
`<token>`	A token composed of other tokens and literals.
`::=`	The token on the left of this operator is defined by the expression on the right of it.
`|`	The expressions to the left and right of this operator are alternatives.
`{}`	The expression within braces is treated as a single syntactical unit (like a token).
`[]`	Zero or one instances of the expression within square brackets.
`*`	Zero or more instances of the preceding token.
`+`	One or more instances of the preceding token.

The formal definition of the IDL grammar, in EBNF notation, is shown in Listing 16.1.

Listing 16.1 OMG IDL Grammar in EBNF Notation

```
(1) <specification> ::= <definition>+
(2) <definition> ::= <type_dcl> ";"
                   | <const_dcl> ";"
                   | <except_dcl> ";"
                   | <interface> ";"
                   | <module> ";"
                   | <value> ";"
(3) <module> ::= "module" <identifier> "{" <definition> + "}"
(4) <interface> ::= <interface_dcl>
                  | <forward_dcl>
(5) <interface_dcl> ::= <interface_header> "{" <interface_body> "}"
(6) <forward_dcl> ::= [ "abstract" | "local" ] "interface" <identifier>
(7) <interface_header> ::= [ "abstract" | "local" ] "interface" <identifier>
                           [ <interface_inheritance_spec> ]
(8) <interface_body> ::= <export>*
(9) <export> ::= <type_dcl> ";"
               | <const_dcl> ";"
               | <except_dcl> ";"
               | <attr_dcl> ";"
               | <op_dcl> ";"
```

Listing 16.1 continued

```
(10) <interface_inheritance_spec> ::= ":" <interface_name>
                                      { "," <interface_name> }*
(11) <interface_name> ::= <scoped_name>
(12) <scoped_name> ::= <identifier>
                     | "::" <identifier>
                     | <scoped_name> "::" <identifier>
(13) <value> ::= <value_dcl> | <value_abs_dcl> |
                 <value_box_dcl> | <value_forward_dcl>
(14) <value_forward_dcl> ::= [ "abstract" ] "valuetype" <identifier>
(15) <value_box_dcl> ::= "valuetype" <identifier> <type_spec>
(16) <value_abs_dcl> ::= "abstract" "valuetype" <identifier>
                         [ <value_inheritance_spec> ]
                         "{" <export>* "}"
(17) <value_dcl> ::= <value_header> "{" < value_element>* "}"
(18) <value_header> ::= ["custom" ] "valuetype" <identifier>
                        [ <value_inheritance_spec> ]
(19) <value_inheritance_spec> ::= [ ":" [ "truncatable" ] <value_name>
                                  { "," <value_name> }* ]
                                  [ "supports" <interface_name>
                                  { "," <interface_name> }* ]
(20) <value_name> ::= <scoped_name>
(21) <value_element> ::= <export> | < state_member> | <init_dcl>
(22) <state_member> ::= { "public" | "private" }
                        <type_spec> <declarators> ";"
(23) <init_dcl> ::= "factory" <identifier>
                    "(" [ <init_param_decls> ] ")" ";"
(24) <init_param_decls> ::= <init_param_decl> { "," <init_param_decl> }*
(25) <init_param_decl> ::= <init_param_attribute> <param_type_spec>
                           <simple_declarator>
(26) <init_param_attribute> ::= "in"
(27) <const_dcl> ::= "const" <const_type>
                     <identifier> "=" <const_exp>
(28) <const_type> ::= <integer_type>
                    | <char_type>
                    | <wide_char_type>
                    | <boolean_type>
                    | <floating_pt_type>
                    | <string_type>
                    | <wide_string_type>
                    | <fixed_pt_const_type>
                    | <scoped_name>
                    | <octet_type>
(29) <const_exp> ::= <or_expr>
(30) <or_expr> ::= <xor_expr>
                 | <or_expr> "|" <xor_expr>
(31) <xor_expr> ::= <and_expr>
                  | <xor_expr> "^" <and_expr>
```

Listing 16.1 continued

```
(32) <and_expr> ::= <shift_expr>
                | <and_expr> "&" <shift_expr>
(33) <shift_expr> ::= <add_expr>
                  | <shift_expr> ">>" <add_expr>
                  | <shift_expr> "<<" <add_expr>
(34) <add_expr> ::= <mult_expr>
                | <add_expr> "+" <mult_expr>
                | <add_expr> "-" <mult_expr>
(35) <mult_expr> ::= <unary_expr>
                 | <mult_expr> "*" <unary_expr>
                 | <mult_expr> "/" <unary_expr>
                 | <mult_expr> "%" <unary_expr>
(36) <unary_expr> ::= <unary_operator> <primary_expr>
                  | <primary_expr>
(37) <unary_operator> ::= "-"
                      | "+"
                      | "~"
(38) <primary_expr> ::= <scoped_name>
                    | <literal>
                    | "(" <const_exp> ")"
(39) <literal> ::= <integer_literal>
               | <string_literal>
               | <wide_string_literal>
               | <character_literal>
               | <wide_character_literal>
               | <fixed_pt_literal>
               | <floating_pt_literal>
               | <boolean_literal>
(40) <boolean_literal> ::= "TRUE"
               | "FALSE"
(41) <positive_int_const> ::= <const_exp>
(42) <type_dcl> ::= "typedef" <type_declarator>
                | <struct_type>
                | <union_type>
                | <enum_type>
                | "native" <simple_declarator>
                | <constr_forward_decl>
(43) <type_declarator> ::= <type_spec> <declarators>
(44) <type_spec> ::= <simple_type_spec>
                 | <constr_type_spec>
(45) <simple_type_spec> ::= <base_type_spec>
                        | <template_type_spec>
                        | <scoped_name>
(46) <base_type_spec> ::= <floating_pt_type>
                      | <integer_type>
                      | <char_type>
                      | <wide_char_type>
                      | <boolean_type>
                      | <octet_type>
```

Listing 16.1 continued

```
                        | <any_type>
                        | <object_type>
                        | <value_base_type>
(47) <template_type_spec> ::= <sequence_type>
                            | <string_type>
                            | <wide_string_type>
                            | <fixed_pt_type>
(48) <constr_type_spec> ::= <struct_type>
                          | <union_type>
                          | <enum_type>
(49) <declarators> ::= <declarator> { "," <declarator> } *
(50) <declarator> ::= <simple_declarator>
                    | <complex_declarator>
(51) <simple_declarator> ::= <identifier>
(52) <complex_declarator> ::= <array_declarator>
(53) <floating_pt_type> ::= "float"
                          | "double"
                          | "long" "double"
(54) <integer_type> ::= <signed_int>
                      | <unsigned_int>
(55) <signed_int> ::= <signed_short_int>
                    | <signed_long_int>
                    | <signed_longlong_int>
(56) <signed_short_int> ::= "short"
(57) <signed_long_int> ::= "long"
(58) <signed_longlong_int> ::= "long" "long"
(59) <unsigned_int> ::= <unsigned_short_int>
                      | <unsigned_long_int>
                      | <unsigned_longlong_int>
(60) <unsigned_short_int> ::= "unsigned" "short"
(61) <unsigned_long_int> ::= "unsigned" "long"
(62) <unsigned_longlong_int> ::= "unsigned" "long" "long"
(63) <char_type> ::= "char"
(64) <wide_char_type> ::= "wchar"
(65) <boolean_type> ::= "boolean"
(66) <octet_type> ::= "octet"
(67) <any_type> ::= "any"
(68) <object_type> ::= "Object"
(69) <struct_type> ::= "struct" <identifier> "{" <member_list> "}"
(70) <member_list> ::= <member>+
(71) <member> ::= <type_spec> <declarators> ";"
(72) <union_type> ::= "union" <identifier> "switch"
                    "(" <switch_type_spec> ")"
                    "{" <switch_body> "}"
(73) <switch_type_spec> ::= <integer_type>
                          | <char_type>
                          | <boolean_type>
                          | <enum_type>
```

Listing 16.1 continued

```
                          | <scoped_name>
(74) <switch_body> ::= <case>+
(75) <case> ::= <case_label>+ <element_spec> ";"
(76) <case_label> ::= "case" <const_exp> ":"
                    | "default" ":"
(77) <element_spec> ::= <type_spec> <declarator>
(78) <enum_type> ::= "enum" <identifier>
                    "{" <enumerator> { "," <enumerator> } * "}"
(79) <enumerator> ::= <identifier>
(80) <sequence_type> ::= "sequence" "<" <simple_type_spec> ","
                        <positive_int_const> ">"
                        | "sequence" "<" <simple_type_spec> ">"
(81) <string_type> ::= "string" "<" <positive_int_const> ">"
                      | "string"
(82) <wide_string_type> ::= "wstring" "<" <positive_int_const> ">"
                          | "wstring"
(83) <array_declarator> ::= <identifier> <fixed_array_size>+
(84) <fixed_array_size> ::= "[" <positive_int_const> "]"
(85) <attr_dcl> ::= [ "readonly" ] "attribute"
                   <param_type_spec> <simple_declarator>
                   { "," <simple_declarator> }*
(86) <except_dcl> ::= "exception" <identifier> "{" <member>* "}"
(87) <op_dcl> ::= [ <op_attribute> ] <op_type_spec>
                 <identifier> <parameter_dcls>
                 [ <raises_expr> ] [ <context_expr> ]
(88) <op_attribute> ::= "oneway"
(89) <op_type_spec> ::= <param_type_spec>
                       | "void"
(90) <parameter_dcls> ::= "(" <param_dcl> { "," <param_dcl> } * ")"
                         | "(" " )"
(91) <param_dcl> ::= <param_attribute> <param_type_spec>
                    <simple_declarator>
(92) <param_attribute> ::= "in"
                          | "out"
                          | "inout"
(93) <raises_expr> ::= "raises" "(" <scoped_name> { "," <scoped_name> }* ")"
(94) <context_expr> ::= "context" "(" <string_literal>
                       { "," <string_literal> } * ")"
(95) <param_type_spec> ::= <base_type_spec>
                          | <string_type>
                          | <wide_string_type>
                          | <scoped_name>
(96) <fixed_pt_type> ::= "fixed" "<" <positive_int_const> ","
                        <positive_int_const> ">"
(97) <fixed_pt_const_type> ::= "fixed"
(98) <value_base_type> ::= "ValueBase"
(99) <constr_forward_decl> ::= "struct" <identifier>
                              | "union" <identifier>
```

CHAPTER 17

DynAny Type

The any type offers great flexibility when passing parameters to and receiving return values from an IDL operation. It is particularly useful for specifying interfaces when it is not known in advance what data types will be passed as operation parameters. This flexibility is needed for general-purpose bridges and messaging services. The OMG specification of the CORBA Notification Service provides a good example of this.

However, the standard mapping of the any type (CORBA::Any in C++ and org.omg.CORBA.Any in Java) has its limitations. It relies on stub code to provide the facility to manipulate its contents. Without stub code there is no means of inserting or extracting user-defined types.

To overcome the shortcomings of the standard any type, a number of interfaces are defined that facilitate dynamic manipulation of anys. These interfaces are grouped together in the module DynamicAny, and they consist of the interface DynAny, its derived interfaces, and a DynAnyFactory interface. With the help of these interfaces it is possible to build general-purpose bridges and messaging services without compiling stub code for user-defined types.

Introduction to the DynamicAny Module

The interfaces that constitute the DynamicAny module are listed in the section "Dynamic any IDL," at the end of this chapter. There are several different types of DynAny object. Besides the DynAny interface, there are the derived interfaces DynFixed, DynEnum, DynStruct, DynUnion, DynSequence, DynArray, and DynValue. DynAnyFactory is used to create instances of DynAny. Table 17.1 lists the DynAny interfaces with the IDL types they represent.

Table 17.1 `DynAny` *Interfaces and Corresponding Types*

DynAny Interface	IDL Types Represented
`DynFixed`	`fixed`
`DynEnum`	`enum`
`DynStruct`	`struct`
	`exception`
`DynUnion`	`union`
`DynSequence`	`sequence`
`DynArray`	`array`
`DynValue`	`value`
`DynAny`	all other types

Note that `DynStruct` can be used to represent either the `struct` or `exception` type.

`DynAny` Type Is Unchangeable

Unlike the ordinary representation of `any`, a `DynAny` instance is *not* a general-purpose container. A particular `DynAny` can be used only to hold the data type for which it is created. For example, a `DynAny` instance created to hold a `boolean` value can only be initialized with `boolean` data. Attempting to insert a different data type raises a `TypeMismatch` exception. The restrictions are

- The type of data that can be held in a given `DynAny` is given by the return value of `DynamicAny::DynAny::type()`. The `DynAny`'s type can not be changed after it is created.
- Attempting to insert or extract the wrong type raises a `DynamicAny::DynAny::TypeMismatch` exception.
- Assignment of a `DynAny` to a `DynAny` is allowed only if both `DynAny`s hold data of the same type. Otherwise, a `TypeMismatch` exception is raised.

Dynamic `any` Interfaces Are Locality Constrained

The interfaces in the `DynamicAny` module are *locality-constrained interfaces*. Instances of these interfaces are always local objects. They cannot be invoked remotely, and their object references cannot be passed as arguments to remote invocations.

Dynamic Invocation and Dynamic Skeleton Interfaces

One of the main applications of dynamic `any`s is to facilitate the use of the dynamic invocation interface (DII) and dynamic skeleton interface (DSI). See Chapter 20, "Dynamic Invocation Interface," and Chapter 21, "Dynamic Skeleton Interface," for details.

When using the DII or the DSI, parameters and return values of CORBA operations are exposed to the programmer as `any`s. To send parameters, you must be able to create `any`s containing arbitrary data. To receive parameters, you must be able to analyze `any`s that contain arbitrary data. If stub code is not available, the DynAny type is needed to create and manipulate anys that contain user-defined types. The ways in which DynAny is used by the DII and DSI are outlined in the following two sections.

Sending Arbitrary Parameters

When sending parameters using the DII or DSI, the DynAny is needed to create anys containing user-defined types. The following steps describe how to create an any holding arbitrary data:

1. Create a type code to describe the data. You can either create the type code dynamically or retrieve it from the interface repository.
2. Create a DynAny object from the type code. Narrow the DynAny to the appropriate type, if necessary.
3. Initialize the value of the DynAny.
4. Convert the DynAny to an ordinary any using the to_any() method.

Examples of this procedure are given in the section "DynAny Examples," later in this chapter.

Receiving Arbitrary Parameters

When receiving parameters using the DII or DSI, the any representing the parameter must be parsed to discover its contents. The following steps describe how to analyze the contents of an any that holds arbitrary data:

1. Create a DynAny object from the given any. Narrow it to the appropriate type, if necessary.
2. Get the type code for the data held in the DynAny.
3. With the help of the TypeCode interface and the dynamic any interfaces, use recursive descent traversal to analyze the contents of the any.

Details of this procedure are beyond the scope of this book.

Dynamic Creation of Type Codes

The first step in the creation of a DynAny is to obtain a type code that describes the layout of the data held by the any. In general, if you are building a dynamic application such as a CORBA bridge, it is necessary to create type codes dynamically.

The interface for creating type codes dynamically is defined by a subset of operations in CORBA::ORB. A number of additional data types, borrowed from the interface repository IDL, are also used. Excerpts from the relevant IDL are shown in Listing 17.1.

Listing 17.1 IDL for Creating Type Codes

```
//IDL
module CORBA {
    //-----------------------------------------------------------
    // Excerpt from the Interface Repository specification
    // The following types are needed for creating type codes:
    //     'StructMemberSeq', 'UnionMemberSeq', 'EnumMemberSeq'
```

Listing 17.1 continued

```
//------------------------------------------------------------

typedef string Identifier;
typedef string RepositoryId;
interface IDLType;

struct StructMember {
    Identifier name;
    TypeCode type;
    IDLType type_def;
};
typedef sequence <StructMember> StructMemberSeq;

struct UnionMember {
    Identifier name;
    any label;
    TypeCode type;
    IDLType type_def;
};
typedef sequence <UnionMember> UnionMemberSeq;

typedef sequence <Identifier> EnumMemberSeq;

interface ORB {
    //------------------------------------------------------------
    // Excerpt from the 'ORB interface' specification
    // Type code creation operations
    //------------------------------------------------------------
    TypeCode create_struct_tc (
        in RepositoryId id,
        in Identifier name,
        in StructMemberSeq members
    );
    TypeCode create_union_tc (
        in RepositoryId id,
        in Identifier name,
        in TypeCode discriminator_type,
        in UnionMemberSeq members
    );
    TypeCode create_enum_tc (
        in RepositoryId id,
        in Identifier name,
        in EnumMemberSeq members
    );
    TypeCode create_alias_tc (
        in RepositoryId id,
        in Identifier name,
        in TypeCode original_type
```

Listing 17.1 continued

```
    );
    TypeCode create_exception_tc (
        in RepositoryId id,
        in Identifier name,
        in StructMemberSeq members
    );
    TypeCode create_interface_tc (
        in RepositoryId id,
        in Identifier name
    );
    TypeCode create_string_tc (
        in unsigned long bound
    );
    TypeCode create_wstring_tc (
        in unsigned long bound
    );
    TypeCode create_fixed_tc (
        in unsigned short digits,
        in short scale
    );
    TypeCode create_sequence_tc (
        in unsigned long bound,
        in TypeCode element type
    );
    TypeCode create_array_tc (
        in unsigned long length,
        in TypeCode element_type
    );
    TypeCode create_value_tc (
        in RepositoryId id,
        in Identifier name,
       in ValueModifier type_modifier,
        in TypeCode concrete_base,
        in ValueMembersSeq members
    );
    TypeCode create_value_box_tc (
        in RepositoryId id,
        in Identifier name,
        in TypeCode boxed_type
    );
    TypeCode create_native_tc (
        in RepositoryId id,
        in Identifier name
    );
    TypeCode create_recursive_tc(
        in RepositoryId id
    );
    TypeCode create_abstract_interface_tc(
        in RepositoryId id,
```

Listing 17.1 continued

```
            in Identifier name
        );
        ...
    };
};
```

The `CORBA::ORB` interface provides operations, such as `create_struct_tc()`, for creating every kind of complex type code. Many more operations are provided—see Chapter 17, "IDL Data Types," for a complete list.

Type codes for basic types are not provided by the `CORBA::ORB` interface. Basic type codes are provided differently in C++ and Java:

- In C++, basic type codes are provided by standard type code constants of the form `CORBA::_tc_`*`typeName`*. See Chapter 8, "The `any` Type," for details.
- In Java, basic type codes are obtained by invoking `org.omg.CORBA.ORB.get_primitive_tc()` with the appropriate `TCKind`-enumerated constant as an argument. The method `get_primitive_tc()` is specific to the Java mapping.

Examples of how to create both basic and complex type codes in C++ and Java are presented in the following subsections.

Type Code for Structs

The Listing 17.2 shows a sample struct called `VarLen` that is declared within the scope of the module `SampleTypes`.

Listing 17.2 IDL for the Struct `VarLen`

```
//IDL
#pragma prefix "pure-corba-3.com"

module SampleTypes {
    ...
    struct VarLen {
        string theString;
        long theLong;
    };
    ...
};
```

The operation `CORBA::ORB::create_struct_tc()`, in conjunction with the type `CORBA::StructMemberSeq`, is used to create a type code for a struct. Listing 17.3 and Listing 17.4 show how to create a type code for the struct `VarLen` in C++ and Java.

Listing 17.3 C++ Creating Type Code for `VarLen`

```
//C++
#include <ifr.hh>
#include <DynamicAny.hh>
```

Listing 17.3 continued

```
...
//-----------------------------------------------------------
// Assume that the following variable is already defined:
// 'orbV' - a _var reference to an ORB instance
//
CORBA::StructMemberSeq memSeq(2);  //maximum = 2
memSeq.length(2);                  //length = 2
memSeq[0].name = CORBA::string_dup("theString");
memSeq[0].type = CORBA::_tc_string;
memSeq[1].name = CORBA::string_dup("theLong");
memSeq[1].type = CORBA::_tc_long;
CORBA::TypeCode_var TCVarLenV = orbV->create_struct_tc(
        "IDL:pure-corba-3.com/SampleTypes/VarLen:1.0",  // RepositoryId
        "VarLen",    // name of 'struct'
        memSeq       // member details
      );
```

Listing 17.4 Java Creating Type Code for **`VarLen`**

```
//Java
//-----------------------------------------------------------
// Assume that the following variable is already defined:
// 'orb' - a reference to an ORB instance
//
org.omg.CORBA.TypeCode TCstring = orb.get_primitive_tc(
          org.omg.CORBA.TCKind.tk_string
        );
org.omg.CORBA.TypeCode TClong = orb.get_primitive_tc(
          org.omg.CORBA.TCKind.tk_long
        );

org.omg.CORBA.StructMember[] memSeq = new org.omg.CORBA.StructMember[2];
memSeq[0] = new org.omg.CORBA.StructMember();
memSeq[0].name = "theString";
memSeq[0].type = TCstring;
memSeq[1] = new org.omg.CORBA.StructMember();
memSeq[1].name = "theLong";
memSeq[1].type = TClong;
org.omg.CORBA.TypeCode TCVarLen = orb.create_struct_tc(
        "IDL:pure-corba-3.com/SampleTypes/VarLen:1.0",  // RepositoryId
        "VarLen",    // name of 'struct'
        memSeq       // member details
      );
```

The type `CORBA::StructMemberSeq` is filled with the descriptions of the `VarLen` struct members. The order of descriptions in the sequence must be identical to the order in which `VarLen` struct members are declared in the IDL.

Each element of `CORBA::StructMemberSeq` is set as follows:

- The `name` field gives the name of the corresponding `VarLen` struct member.
- The `type` field gives the type code for the corresponding `VarLen` struct member.
- The `type_def` field is not used (it defaults to a nil object reference).

In Java, it is necessary to obtain type codes for the basic types `string` and `long` using the method `get_primitive_tc()`.

Type Code for a Union

Listing 17.5 shows a sample union called `Poly` that is declared within the scope of the module `SampleTypes`.

Listing 17.5 The IDL for the Union `Poly`

```
//IDL
#pragma prefix "pure-corba-3.com"

module SampleTypes {
     ...
     union Poly switch(short) {
          case 1: short theShort;
          case 2: string theString;
     };
     ...
};
```

This union does not have a `default:` case label.

The operation `CORBA::ORB::create_union_tc()`, in conjunction with the type `CORBA::UnionMemberSeq`, is used to create a type code for a union. Listing 17.6 and Listing 17.7 show how to create a type code for the union `Poly` in C++ and Java.

Listing 17.6 C++ Creating Type Code for `Poly`

```
//C++
#include <ifr.hh>
#include <DynamicAny.hh>
...
//--------------------------------------------------------
// Assume that the following variable is already defined:
// 'orbV' - a _var reference to an ORB instance
//
CORBA::UnionMemberSeq memSeq(2);  //maximum = 2
memSeq.length(2);                 //length = 2
memSeq[0].label <<= (CORBA::Short) 1;
memSeq[0].type = CORBA::_tc_short;
memSeq[0].name = CORBA::string_dup("theShort");
memSeq[1].label <<= (CORBA::Short) 2;
memSeq[1].type = CORBA::_tc_string;
memSeq[1].name = CORBA::string_dup("theString");
CORBA::TypeCode_var TCPolyV = orbV->create_union_tc(
```

Listing 17.6 continued

```
        "IDL:pure-corba-3.com/SampleTypes/Poly:1.0",  // RepositoryId
        "Poly",                 // name of 'union'
        CORBA::_tc_short,       // type of union discriminator
        memSeq                  // member details
      );
```

Listing 17.7 Java Creating Type Code for `Poly`

```
//Java
//--------------------------------------------------------
// Assume that the following variable is already defined:
// 'orb' - a reference to an ORB instance
//
org.omg.CORBA.TypeCode TCstring = orb.get_primitive_tc(
          org.omg.CORBA.TCKind.tk_string
        );
org.omg.CORBA.TypeCode TCshort = orb.get_primitive_tc(
          org.omg.CORBA.TCKind.tk_short
        );

org.omg.CORBA.UnionMember[] memSeq = new org.omg.CORBA.UnionMember[2];
memSeq[0] = new org.omg.CORBA.UnionMember();
memSeq[0].label = org.omg.CORBA.ORB.init().create_any();
memSeq[0].label.insert_short((short) 1);
memSeq[0].type = TCshort;
memSeq[0].name = "theShort";
memSeq[1] = new org.omg.CORBA.UnionMember();
memSeq[1].label = org.omg.CORBA.ORB.init().create_any();
memSeq[1].label.insert_short((short) 2);
memSeq[1].type = TCstring;
memSeq[1].name = "theString";
org.omg.CORBA.TypeCode TCPoly = orb.create_union_tc(
        "IDL:pure-corba-3.com/SampleTypes/Poly:1.0",  // RepositoryId
        "Poly",       // name of 'union'
        TCshort,      // type of union discriminator
        memSeq        // member details
      );
```

The type `CORBA::UnionMemberSeq` is filled with the descriptions of the `Poly` union members. The order of descriptions in the sequence must be identical to the order in which union members are declared in IDL.

Each element of `CORBA::UnionMemberSeq` is set as follows:

- The `label` field is an any that is set to the case label of the corresponding union member.
- The `type` field gives the type code for the corresponding union member.
- The `name` field gives the name of the corresponding union member.
- The `type_def` field is not used (it defaults to a nil object reference).

Type Code for Recursive Type

The syntax of IDL allows you to create recursive types in certain special cases. Currently, you can declare only structs, unions, or values to be recursive. Listing 17.8 shows an example of a recursive struct.

Listing 17.8 IDL for a Recursive Struct

```
//IDL
#pragma prefix "pure-corba-3.com"

struct RecursiveList {
    string item;
    sequence< RecursiveList > list;
};
```

The type `RecurseList` presents a special difficulty for type code creation, because `RecurseList` is used in the declaration of the struct before its declaration is complete. The way to break out of this impasse is to use the method `CORBA::ORB::create_recursive_tc()` to create a placeholder for the incomplete type code.

The operations `create_recursive_tc()`, `create_sequence_tc()`, and `create_struct_tc()`are used together to create the type `RecursiveList`. Listing 17.9 and Listing 17.10 show how to create a type code for `RecursiveList` in C++ and Java.

Listing 17.9 C++ Creating Type Code for `RecursiveList`

```
//C++
#include <ifr.hh>
#include <DynamicAny.hh>
...
//-----------------------------------------------------
// Assume that the following variable is already defined:
// 'orbV' - a _var reference to an ORB instance
//

//Create placeholder for recursive type code
CORBA::TypeCode_var TCplaceholderV
    = orbV->create_recursive_tc("IDL:pure-corba-3.com/RecursiveList:1.0");

//Create anonymous sequence type code
CORBA::TypeCode_var TCsequenceV
    = orbV->create_sequence_tc(
            0,                      // bound (0 = unbounded)
            TCplaceholderV.in() you to create recursive // element type
        );

//Create type code for 'RecursiveList'
CORBA::StructMemberSeq memSeq(2);  //maximum = 2
memSeq.length(2);                  //length = 2
```

Listing 17.9 continued

```
memSeq[0].name = CORBA::string_dup("item");
memSeq[0].type = CORBA::_tc_string;
memSeq[1].name = CORBA::string_dup("list");
memSeq[1].type = TCsequenceV.in();
CORBA::TypeCode_var TCRecursiveListV = orbV->create_struct_tc(
        "IDL:pure-corba-3.com/RecursiveList:1.0",  // RepositoryId
        "RecursiveList",      // name of 'struct'
        memSeq                // member details
      );
```

Listing 17.10 Java Creating Type Code for `RecursiveList`

```
//Java
//-----------------------------------------------------
// Assume that the following variable is already defined:
// 'orb' - a reference to an ORB instance
//
org.omg.CORBA.TypeCode TCstring = orb.get_primitive_tc(
          org.omg.CORBA.TCKind.tk_string
        );

//Create placeholder for recursive type code
org.omg.CORBA.TypeCode TCplaceholder
    = orb.create_recursive_tc("IDL:pure-corba-3.com/RecursiveList:1.0");

//Create anonymous sequence type code
org.omg.CORBA.TypeCode TCsequence
    = orb.create_sequence_tc(
              0,                      // bound (0 = unbounded)
              TCplaceholder           // element type
            );

//Create type code for 'RecursiveList'
org.omg.CORBA.StructMember[] memSeq = new org.omg.CORBA.StructMember[2];
memSeq[0] = new org.omg.CORBA.StructMember();
memSeq[0].name = "item";
memSeq[0].type = TCstring;
memSeq[1] = new org.omg.CORBA.StructMember();
memSeq[1].name = "list";
memSeq[1].type = TCsequence;
org.omg.CORBA.TypeCode TCRecursiveList = orb.create_struct_tc(
        "IDL:pure-corba-3.com/RecursiveList:1.0",  // RepositoryId
        "RecursiveList",      // name of 'struct'
        memSeq                // member details
      );
```

The occurrence of `RecursiveList` as the element type of the sequence is represented by a recursive type code. Since the type code for `RecursiveList` is not yet defined, a placeholder must be created by calling `create_recursive_tc()`. The repository ID

IDL:pure-corba-3.com/RecursiveList:1.0 is the you to create recursive only argument passed to create_recursive_tc().

A type code for the anonymous sequence sequence<RecursiveList> is created using create_sequence_tc(). No repository ID is associated with the sequence because the sequence is anonymous. The declaration of an anonymous sequence inside a struct is a special case of IDL syntax. Normally, sequence types must be given a name using a typedef construction.

The type code for RecursiveList is created using create_struct_tc(), in a similar way to the example described in the section "Type Code for Structs."

Once the overall RecursiveList type code is constructed, the embedded recursive type code begins to function as a normal RecursiveList you to create recursive type code.

Creating and Destroying a DynAny

Instances of you to create recursive DynAny are created using the DynAnyFactory interface, which has the following IDL:

```
//IDL
module DynamicAny {
    ...
    interface DynAnyFactory
    {
        exception InconsistentTypeCode {};
        DynAny create_dyn_any(in any value)
            raises (InconsistentTypeCode);
        DynAny create_dyn_any_from_type_code(in CORBA::TypeCode type)
            raises (InconsistentTypeCode);
    };
};
```

The first step in the creation of a DynAny is to obtain a reference to a DynAnyFactory object. Use resolve_initial_references(), passing the string "DynAnyFactory" as the ObjectId. You have a choice of creating a DynAny using the create_dyn_any() or create_dyn_any_from_type_code() operation.

The destruction of a DynAny is effected using the destroy() operation of the DynAny interface, declared as follows:

```
//IDL
module DynamicAny {
    ...
    interface DynAny
    {
        ...
        void destroy();
    };
};
```

The examples in Listing 17.11 and Listing 17.12 show how to create and destroy a `DynAny` containing a `boolean`, in C++ and Java respectively.

Listing 17.11 C++ `DynAny` *Containing a* `boolean`

```
//C++
...
//-----------------------------------------------------
// Assume that the following variable is already defined:
// 'orbV' - a _var reference to an ORB instance
//-----------------------------------------------------
// Get a handle on a 'DynAnyFactory' object
CORBA::Object_var objV = orbV->resolve_initial_references("DynAnyFactory");
DynamicAny::DynAnyFactory_var dynFactoryV
    = DynamicAny::DynAnyFactory::_narrow(objV.in() );
if (CORBA::is_nil(dynFactoryV.in() ) ) {
    cerr << "error: narrow to DynAnyFactory failed." << endl;
    exit(1);
}

// Create 'DynAny' containing a 'boolean'
DynamicAny::DynAny_var dynBooleanV;
dynBooleanV = dynFactoryV->create_dyn_any_from_type_code(CORBA::_tc_boolean);
dynBooleanV->insert_boolean(1);
...
// Destroy the 'DynAny'
dynBooleanV->destroy();
```

Listing 17.12 Java `DynAny` *Containing a* `boolean`

```
//Java
...
//-----------------------------------------------------
// Assume that the following variables are already defined:
// 'orb'       - a reference to an ORB instance
// 'TCBoolean' - a 'boolean' type code
//-----------------------------------------------------
// Exception handling not shown...

// Get a handle on a 'DynAnyFactory' object
org.omg.CORBA.Object obj = orb.resolve_initial_references("DynAnyFactory");
org.omg.DynamicAny.DynAnyFactory dynFactory
    = org.omg.DynamicAny.DynAnyFactoryHelper.narrow(obj);

// Create 'DynAny' containing a 'boolean'
org.omg.DynamicAny.DynAny dynBoolean
    = dynFactory.create_dyn_any_from_type_code(TCBoolean);
dynBoolean.insert_boolean(true);
...
// Destroy the 'DynAny'
dynBoolean.destroy();
```

A DynAnyFactory object is first obtained using the initialization service. The type code passed to the create_dyn_any_from_type_code() operation determines the type of DynAny that is created—in this case boolean. The returned DynAny cannot be used to hold a type other than a boolean.

If a DynAny is created for one of the IDL types fixed, enum, struct, exception, union, sequence, array, or value, it is then also necessary to narrow it to the correct type: one of DynFixed, DynEnum, DynStruct, DynUnion, DynSequence, DynArray, or DynValue. Examples of this are given in the next section, "DynAny Examples."

The DynAny is initialized using insert_boolean().

After you are finished with the DynAny, you must call destroy(). In some ORB implementations, invocation of destroy() might not have any effect. However, doing so is required by the CORBA specification and ensures portability of your code.

DynAny Examples

Two examples are presented in this section that illustrate many of the features of the DynAny interfaces.

- Creating and initializing a DynStruct instance
- Creating and initializing a DynUnion instance

Creating a DynStruct

Consider how to create a DynAny object that represents the struct VarLen, declared in Listing 17.2.

The code in Listing 17.13 and Listing 17.14 shows how to create and initialize a DynStruct object that represents a VarLen instance.

***Listing 17.13 C++ Creating a* DynStruct *for a* VarLen**

```
//C++
#include <ifr.hh>
#include <DynamicAny.hh>
...
//-----------------------------------------------------
// Assume that the following variable is already defined:
// 'orbV'       - a _var reference to an ORB instance
// 'TCVarLenV'  - reference to type code of a 'VarLen' struct
//-----------------------------------------------------

// Get a handle on a 'DynAnyFactory' object
CORBA::Object_var objV = orbV->resolve_initial_references("DynAnyFactory");
DynamicAny::DynAnyFactory_var dynFactoryV
    = DynamicAny::DynAnyFactory::_narrow(objV.in() );
if (CORBA::is_nil(dynFactoryV.in() ) ) {
    cerr << "error: narrow to DynAnyFactory failed." << endl;
    exit(1);
}
```

Listing 17.13 continued

```
// Get an instance of a 'DynStruct' object
objV = dynFactoryV->create_dyn_any_from_type_code(TCVarLenV.in() );
DynamicAny::DynStruct_var dynStructV
    = DynamicAny::DynStruct::_narrow(objV.in() );
if (CORBA::is_nil(dynStructV.in() ) ) {
    cerr << "error: narrow to DynStruct failed." << endl;
    exit(1);
}

// Initialize each member of the 'VarLen' struct
DynamicAny::DynAny_var memberV;
memberV = dynStructV->current_component();
memberV->insert_string("Hello World!");
dynStructV->next();
memberV = dynStructV->current_component();
memberV->insert_long(1234);

//Convert 'DynAny' to an ordinary 'any'...
CORBA::Any_var anyStructV = dynStructV->to_any();
...
//Cleanup
dynStructV->destroy();
```

Listing 17.14 Java Creating a **DynStruct** *for* **VarLen**

```
//Java
...
//---------------------------------------------------------
// Assume that the following variable is already defined:
// 'orb'      - a reference to an ORB instance
// 'TCVarLen' - reference to type code of a 'VarLen' struct
//---------------------------------------------------------

// Get a handle on a 'DynAnyFactory' object
org.omg.CORBA.Object obj = orb.resolve_initial_references("DynAnyFactory");
org.omg.DynamicAny.DynAnyFactory dynFactory
    = org.omg.DynamicAny.DynAnyFactoryHelper.narrow(obj);

// Get an instance of a 'DynStruct' object
obj = dynFactory.create_dyn_any_from_type_code(TCVarLen);
org.omg.DynamicAny.DynStruct dynStruct
    = org.omg.DynamicAny.DynStructHelper.narrow(obj);

// Initialize each member of the 'VarLen' struct
org.omg.DynamicAny.DynAny member;
member = dynStruct.current_component();
member.insert_string("Hello World!");
dynStruct.next();
member = dynStruct.current_component();
```

Listing 17.13 continued

```
member.insert_long(1234);

//Convert 'DynAny' to an ordinary 'any'...
org.omg.CORBA.Any anyStruct = dynStruct.to_any();
...
//Cleanup
dynStruct.destroy();
```

Using the type code for the `VarLen` struct (created as described in the section "Type Code for Structs"), a new `DynStruct` object is created by invoking `create_dyn_any_from_type_code()` on the `DynAnyFactory`. Because the return type of this operation is only a reference to the base class `DynAny`, it is necessary to narrow it to the derived type `DynStruct` before you proceed any further.

The `DynStruct` object (`dynStructV` in C++, `dynStruct` in Java) can be initialized using one of two approaches:

- Using a generic, iterative approach to member access. Support for this approach is provided by a group of iteration operations defined in the base interface `DynAny`.
- Using a type specific approach supported by a group of operations defined in the derived interface `DynStruct`.

The approach used here is the generic, iterative approach because it turns out to be simpler and requires less coding. The relevant operations of `DynAny` are given in the following IDL extract:

```
//IDL
module DynamicAny {
    ...
    interface DynAny {
        ...
        boolean       seek(in long index);
        void          rewind();
        boolean       next();
        unsigned long component_count() raises (TypeMismatch);
        DynAny        current_component() raises (TypeMismatch);
    };
    ...
};
```

The components of the `DynAny` refer, in this case, to the members of a struct. A current position is implicitly associated with the `DynAny`, and it initially indexes the very first struct member (index `0`).

The operation `seek()` can be used to set the current position to index an arbitrary struct member (as long as the index is less than `component_count()`). It returns true if a valid index is passed and false otherwise.

The operation `next()` is used to increment the current position by one.

The operation `rewind()` is equivalent to `seek(0)`.

The special value `-1` is used to represent a current position that does not refer to any component. The current position is automatically set to `-1` if the `DynAny` does not have any components. The current position can also be set to `-1` in a `DynAny` that has components. For example, calling `seek()` with a negative argument sets the current position to `-1`. Calling `next()` when the current position is already at the final component changes the index to `-1`.

The operation `current_component()` returns a `DynAny` for the component at the current position. Because complete type code information is provided when a `DynAny` is created, the `DynAny` returned by `current_component()` is automatically set to be the correct type.

The initialization step in Listing 17.13 and Listing 17.14 shows this approach being used. The operations `current_component()` and `next()` are used together to initialize the members of the `VarLen` struct.

The dynamic any is then converted to an ordinary `any` by invoking the method `to_any()`.

Creating a `DynUnion`

The code in Listing 17.15 and Listing 17.16 shows how to create and initialize a `DynUnion` object that represents a `Poly` instance (see Listing 17.5 for the declaration of `Poly`).

Listing 17.15 C++ Creating a `DynUnion` for `Poly`

```
//C++
#include <ifr.hh>
#include <DynamicAny.hh>
...
//-----------------------------------------------------
// Assume that the following variable is already defined:
// 'orbV' - a _var reference to an ORB instance
// 'TCPolyV' - a type code for the union 'Poly'
//

// Get a handle on a 'DynAnyFactory' object
CORBA::Object_var objV = orbV->resolve_initial_references("DynAnyFactory");
DynamicAny::DynAnyFactory_var dynFactoryV
    = DynamicAny::DynAnyFactory::_narrow(objV.in() );
if (CORBA::is_nil(dynFactoryV.in() ) ) {
    cerr << "error: narrow to DynAnyFactory failed." << endl;
    exit(1);
}

// Get an instance of a 'DynUnion' object
objV = dynFactoryV->create_dyn_any_from_type_code(TCPolyV.in() );
```

Listing 17.15 continued

```
DynamicAny::DynUnion_var dynUnionV = DynamicAny::DynUnion::_narrow(objV.in() );
if (CORBA::is_nil(dynUnionV.in() ) ) {
    cerr << "error: narrow to DynUnion failed." << endl;
    exit(1);
}

//Set the discriminator to '2'
DynamicAny::DynAny_var dynDiscrimV = dynUnionV->get_discriminator();
dynDiscrimV->insert_short(2);
dynUnionV->set_discriminator(dynDiscrimV.in() );

// Initialize the union member
DynamicAny::DynAny_var memberV;
memberV = dynUnionV->member();
memberV->insert_string("The second label is selected.");

//Convert 'DynAny' to an ordinary 'any'...
CORBA::Any_var anyUnionV = dynUnionV->to_any();
...
//Cleanup
dynUnionV->destroy();
```

Listing 17.16 Java Creating a `DynUnion` *for* `Poly`

```
//Java
//--------------------------------------------------------
// Assume that the following variable is already defined:
// 'orb' - a reference to an ORB instance
// 'TCPoly' - a type code for the union 'Poly'
//

// Get a handle on a 'DynAnyFactory' object
org.omg.CORBA.Object obj = orb.resolve_initial_references("DynAnyFactory");
org.omg.DynamicAny.DynAnyFactory dynFactory
    = org.omg.DynamicAny.DynAnyFactoryHelper.narrow(obj);

// Get an instance of a 'DynUnion' object
obj = dynFactory.create_dyn_any_from_type_code(TCPoly);
org.omg.DynamicAny.DynUnion dynUnion
    = org.omg.DynamicAny.DynUnionHelper.narrow(obj);

//Set the discriminator to '2'
org.omg.DynamicAny.DynAny dynDiscrim = dynUnion.get_discriminator();
dynDiscrim.insert_short((short) 2);
dynUnion.set_discriminator(dynDiscrim);

//Initialize the union member
org.omg.DynamicAny.DynAny member;
member = dynUnion.member();
member.insert_string("The second label is selected.");
```

Listing 17.16 continued

```
//Convert 'DynAny' to an ordinary 'any'...
org.omg.CORBA.Any anyUnion = dynUnion.to_any();
...
//Cleanup
dynUnion.destroy();
```

Using the type code for the `Poly` union (created as described in the section "Type Code for a Union"), a new `DynUnion` object is created by invoking `create_dyn_any_from_type_code()` on the `DynAnyFactory`. Because the return type of this operation is only a reference to the base class `DynAny`, it is necessary to narrow it to the derived type `DynUnion` before you proceed any further.

To initialize the `DynUnion`, set the discriminator using the operation `DynUnion::set_discriminator()()`. If the discriminator is set to a value that does not correspond to a case label, this step completes the initialization of the union.

If the value of the discriminator matches one of the case labels, as in this instance, or if there is a `default` case, it is necessary to initialize the active member as well. Obtain the `DynAny` for the active member by invoking `DynUnion::member()`, and initialize it.

Once the `DynUnion` is initialized, it can be converted to an ordinary `any` by invoking the method `to_any()`.

In addition to the general-purpose operation `set_discriminator()`, the `DynUnion` interface provides convenient operations that set the discriminator to some special values.

```
//IDL
module DynamicAny {
    ...
    interface DynUnion : DynAny
    {
        ...
        void set_to_default_member() raises (TypeMismatch);
        void set_to_no_active_member() raises (TypeMismatch);
        boolean has_no_active_member() raises (InvalidValue);
        ...
    };
};
```

If the union has a default label, you can call `set_to_default_member()`. It sets the discriminator to a value different from any of the case labels. The active member must also be initialized in this case.

If the union has no default label, you can call `set_to_no_active_member()`. This sets the discriminator to a value different from any of the case labels. The union is put into a state where it has no active member. The method `has_no_active_member()` can be used to test if a union is in this state.

If the union has no default label and all legal values of the discriminator are used up by the case labels (this could happen if the discriminator was declared to be `boolean` or `enum`), then neither `set_to_default_member()` nor `set_to_no_active_member()` can legally be called.

Creating Other DynAny Types

For IDL constructed types, the most convenient way to initialize the components of a `DynAny` is to use the generic iteration approach (see the section "Creating a `DynStruct`," earlier in this chapter).

To use the iterative approach with other `DynAny` types, you need to know what the components represent in each case:

- The components of a `DynStruct` or `DynValue` represent the members of the corresponding struct, exception, or value type.
- The components of `DynSequence` or `DynArray` represent the elements of the corresponding sequence or array.
- There can be one or two valid components in a `DynUnion`. The component at the current position `0` corresponds to the union discriminator. If the union has an active member, the component at the current position `1` is also valid and corresponds to the active member of `DynUnion`.

Dynamic any IDL

Listing 17.17 shows the complete IDL for the module `DynamicAny`. Interfaces defined within this module are locality-constrained interfaces.

Listing 17.17 IDL for the `DynamicAny` *Module*

```
//IDL
#pragma prefix "omg.org"

module DynamicAny
{
    interface DynAny
    {
        exception InvalidValue {};
        exception TypeMismatch {};

        CORBA::TypeCode type();
        void    assign(in DynAny dyn_any)
            raises (TypeMismatch);
        void    from_any(in any value)
            raises (TypeMismatch, InvalidValue);
        any     to_any();
        boolean equal(in DynAny dyn_any);
        void    destroy();
        DynAny  copy();

        void insert_boolean(in boolean value)
```

Listing 17.17 continued

```
        raises (TypeMismatch, InvalidValue);
    void insert_octet(in octet value)
        raises (TypeMismatch, InvalidValue);
    void insert_char(in char value)
        raises (TypeMismatch, InvalidValue);
    void insert_short(in short value)
        raises (TypeMismatch, InvalidValue);
    void insert_ushort(in unsigned short value)
        raises (TypeMismatch, InvalidValue);
    void insert_long(in long value)
        raises (TypeMismatch, InvalidValue);
    void insert_ulong(in unsigned long value)
        raises (TypeMismatch, InvalidValue);
    void insert_float(in float value)
        raises (TypeMismatch, InvalidValue);
    void insert_double(in double value)
        raises (TypeMismatch, InvalidValue);
    void insert_string(in string value)
        raises (TypeMismatch, InvalidValue);
    void insert_reference(in Object value)
        raises (TypeMismatch, InvalidValue);
    void insert_typecode(in CORBA::TypeCode value)
        raises (TypeMismatch, InvalidValue);
    void insert_longlong(in long long value)
        raises (TypeMismatch, InvalidValue);
    void insert_ulonglong(in unsigned long long value)
        raises (TypeMismatch, InvalidValue);
    void insert_longdouble(in long double value)
        raises (TypeMismatch, InvalidValue);
    void insert_wchar(in wchar value)
        raises (TypeMismatch, InvalidValue);
    void insert_wstring(in wstring value)
        raises (TypeMismatch, InvalidValue);
    void insert_any(in any value)
        raises (TypeMismatch, InvalidValue);
    void insert_dyn_any(in DynAny value)
        raises (TypeMismatch, InvalidValue);
    void insert_val(in ValueBase value)
        raises (TypeMismatch, InvalidValue);

    boolean get_boolean()
        raises (TypeMismatch,  InvalidValue);
    octet   get_octet()
        raises (TypeMismatch, InvalidValue);
    char    get_char()
        raises (TypeMismatch, InvalidValue);
    short   get_short()
        raises (TypeMismatch, InvalidValue);
    unsigned short get_ushort()
```

Listing 17.17 continued

```
        raises (TypeMismatch, InvalidValue);
    long    get_long()
        raises (TypeMismatch, InvalidValue);
    unsigned long get_ulong()
        raises (TypeMismatch, InvalidValue);
    float   get_float()
        raises (TypeMismatch, InvalidValue);
    double  get_double()
        raises (TypeMismatch, InvalidValue);
    string  get_string()
        raises (TypeMismatch, InvalidValue);
    Object  get_reference()
        raises (TypeMismatch, InvalidValue);
    CORBA::TypeCode get_typecode()
        raises (TypeMismatch, InvalidValue);
    long long get_longlong()
        raises (TypeMismatch, InvalidValue);
    unsigned long long get_ulonglong()
        raises (TypeMismatch, InvalidValue);
    long double get_longdouble()
        raises(TypeMismatch, InvalidValue);
    wchar   get_wchar()
        raises (TypeMismatch, InvalidValue);
    wstring get_wstring()
        raises (TypeMismatch, InvalidValue);
    any     get_any()
        raises (TypeMismatch, InvalidValue);
    DynAny  get_dyn_any()
        raises (TypeMismatch, InvalidValue);
    ValueBase get_val()
        raises (TypeMismatch, InvalidValue);

    boolean seek(in long index);
    void    rewind();
    boolean next();
    unsigned long component_count() raises (TypeMismatch);
    DynAny  current_component() raises (TypeMismatch);
};

interface DynFixed : DynAny
{
    string  get_value();
    boolean set_value(in string val)
        raises (TypeMismatch, InvalidValue);
};

interface DynEnum : DynAny
{
    string  get_as_string();
```

Listing 17.17 continued

```
        void set_as_string(in string value)
            raises (InvalidValue);
        unsigned long get_as_ulong();
        void set_as_ulong(in unsigned long value)
            raises (InvalidValue);
    };

    typedef string FieldName;

    struct NameValuePair
    {
        FieldName id;
        any       value;
    };
    typedef sequence<NameValuePair> NameValuePairSeq;

    struct NameDynAnyPair
    {
        FieldName id;
        DynAny    value;
    };
    typedef sequence<NameDynAnyPair> NameDynAnyPairSeq;

    interface DynStruct : DynAny
    {
        FieldName current_member_name()
            raises (TypeMismatch);
        CORBA::TCKind current_member_kind()
            raises (TypeMismatch);
        NameValuePairSeq get_members();
        void set_members(in NameValuePairSeq value)
            raises (TypeMismatch, InvalidValue);
        NameDynAnyPairSeq get_members_as_dyn_any();
        void set_members_as_dyn_any(in NameDynAnyPairSeq value)
            raises (TypeMismatch, InvalidValue);
    };

    interface DynUnion : DynAny
    {
        DynAny get_discriminator();
        void set_discriminator(in DynAny d)
            raises (TypeMismatch);
        void set_to_default_member()
            raises (TypeMismatch);
        void set_to_no_active_member()
            raises (TypeMismatch);
        boolean has_no_active_member()
            raises (InvalidValue);
        CORBA::TCKind discriminator_kind();
```

Listing 17.17 continued

```
        DynAny member()
            raises (InvalidValue);
        FieldName member_name()
            raises (InvalidValue);
        CORBA::TCKind member_kind()
            raises (InvalidValue);
    };

    typedef sequence<any> AnySeq;
    typedef sequence<DynAny> DynAnySeq;

    interface DynSequence : DynAny
    {
        unsigned long get_length();
        void set_length(in unsigned long len)
            raises (InvalidValue);
        AnySeq get_elements();
        void set_elements(in AnySeq value)
            raises (TypeMismatch, InvalidValue);
        DynAnySeq get_elements_as_dyn_any();
        void set_elements_as_dyn_any(in DynAnySeq value)
            raises (TypeMismatch, InvalidValue);
    };

    interface DynArray : DynAny
    {
        AnySeq get_elements();
        void set_elements(in AnySeq value)
            raises (TypeMismatch, InvalidValue);
        DynAnySeq get_elements_as_dyn_any();
        void set_elements_as_dyn_any(in DynAnySeq value)
            raises (TypeMismatch, InvalidValue);
    };

    interface DynValue : DynAny
    {
        FieldName current_member_name()
            raises (TypeMismatch, InvalidValue);
        CORBA::TCKind current_member_kind()
            raises (TypeMismatch, InvalidValue);
        NameValuePairSeq get_members();
        void set_members(in NameValuePairSeq values)
            raises (TypeMismatch, InvalidValue);
        NameDynAnyPairSeq get_members_as_dyn_any();
        void set_members_as_dyn_any(in NameDynAnyPairSeq value)
            raises (TypeMismatch, InvalidValue);
    };
```

Listing 17.17 continued

```
    interface DynAnyFactory
    {
        exception InconsistentTypeCode {};

        DynAny create_dyn_any(in any value)
            raises (InconsistentTypeCode);
        DynAny create_dyn_any_from_type_code(in CORBA::TypeCode type)
            raises (InconsistentTypeCode);
    };
};
```

CHAPTER 18

Dynamic Invocation Interface

CORBA offers two different approaches to making an operation invocation. These are the Static Invocation Interface (SII) and the Dynamic Invocation Interface (DII).

When using the SII, stub code generated from IDL makes the IDL operations available to the application in a convenient language-specific syntax.

The use of stub code, however, is too restrictive for certain applications. It requires that the IDL interfaces used by an application be known in advance. This is not always possible. For some applications, notably interoperable bridges, it is necessary to use IDL interfaces that only become known at runtime. For this reason, CORBA defines the Dynamic Invocation Interface (DII), which allows invocations to be dynamically created at runtime.

Overview of the DII

A client must have knowledge of an IDL interface before it can make an invocation. There are two possible sources of this knowledge:

- Stub code. This is generated from the IDL using an IDL compiler.
- Interface repository. The IDL is typically registered with the interface repository using a command-line utility.

In real applications, use of the DII goes hand-in-hand with use of the interface repository. When a DII client needs to make an invocation at runtime, it must consult the interface repository to discover dynamically the syntax of the operation it wants to invoke.

The interface repository is a standalone CORBA server that acts a repository for all IDL declarations. It makes the declarations available in the form of a parse tree that is accessible through standard IDL interfaces. Information about IDL interfaces can be retrieved at runtime by making remote invocations on the interface repository. For details, see Chapter 20, "Interface Repository."

Use of `CORBA::DynAny` and `CORBA::TypeCode`

The absence of stub code, apart from forcing you to consult the interface repository, has other important consequences. Stub code also provides the following useful classes:

- Type codes for user-defined data types.
- Classes that represent each of the user-defined types. These classes encapsulate the memory layout of user-defined types.

In the absence of stub code, it is very difficult to manipulate user-defined types. To cope with user-defined types, you must use the dynamic features `CORBA::TypeCode` and `DynamicAny::DynAny`.

- Type codes can be created dynamically with the help of a set of operations defined in `CORBA::ORB`. Operations of the general form `CORBA::ORB::create_`*`type`*`_tc` are used to create type codes on-the-fly. See Chapter 15, "IDL Data Types," and Chapter 17, "`DynAny` Type," for details.
- Representations of arbitrary CORBA data types (built-in or user-defined) can be constructed using the `DynamicAny::DynAny` type. The `DynAny` makes it possible to parse parameter data at runtime for arbitrary user-defined types. See Chapter 17 for details.

In a typical DII application, it is necessary to consult the interface repository to discover the layout of a user-defined type before a `CORBA::TypeCode` or a `CORBA::DynAny` can be constructed.

Using `CORBA::Request` Objects

A number of pseudo-interfaces constitute the programming interface for the DII. The most important of these is the `CORBA::Request` pseudo-interface. A `CORBA::Request` is a local object used by a client to encapsulate the details of an operation invocation. A client proceeds by creating a `CORBA::Request` object, filling it with the needed information, and calling `CORBA::Request::invoke()` to perform the invocation.

The pseudo-interface `CORBA::Object` defines one operation—`CORBA::Object::create_request()`—that is used to create a `CORBA::Request` object. However, both the C++ and Java mappings take a bit of liberty with this pseudo-interface. The following methods are provided in C++ and Java:

- A `_request()` method. The C++ method is called `CORBA::Object::_request()`, and the Java method is called `org.omg.CORBA.Object._request()`.

- An overloaded `_create_request()` method. The C++ method is called `CORBA::Object::_create_request()`, and the Java method is called `org.omg.CORBA.Object._create_request()`.

The sections below discuss how to use both the `_request()` method and the `_create_request()` methods.

Sample IDL Interface

To illustrate the use of the DII, it is convenient to consider an example that exhibits most of the syntactical features of an IDL operation. Listing 18.1 introduces the operation `confirmItem()` declared in interface `Inventory`.

Listing 18.1 Sample IDL for Use with DII

```
//IDL
//File: 'dii.idl'

interface Inventory {
    exception NoSuchItem {};

    boolean confirmItem(
              in long itemId,
              inout float price,
              out long howManyInStock)
        raises  (NoSuchItem);
};
```

The operation `confirmItem()` features a return value and `in`, `inout`, and `out` parameters and raises a single user exception, `Inventory::NoSuchItem`. One syntactical feature deliberately omitted is the `context` clause. Although not officially deprecated by the OMG, contexts are almost never used in real-world applications.

Use of `_request()`

The signature for the `_request()` method is shown in Listing 18.2 and Listing 18.3:

Listing 18.2 C++ Signature for `_request()`

```
//C++
// In namespace 'CORBA'
class Object
{
public:
    ...
    Request_ptr _request(const char* operation);
    ...
};
```

Listing 18.3 Java Signature for `_request()`

```
//Java
package org.omg.CORBA;
```

Listing 18.3 continued

```
public interface Object {
    ...
    Request _request(String s);
    ...
}
```

The distinguishing feature of the `_request()` method is that the `CORBA::Request` object is created with the minimum amount of information. Initially it is associated with an object reference and an operation name. Details of the operation syntax are subsequently filled in by invoking the attributes and operations of the `CORBA::Request` object.

Steps to Make an Invocation

If you construct a request object using the `_request()` method, these are the steps you must follow to make a complete operation invocation:

1. Create a request object using `_request()`.
2. Set all parameters (`in`, `inout`, and `out`).
3. Set return type.
4. Set list of use exception type codes (optional).
5. Set list of context identifiers (optional).
6. Make the invocation.
7. Check for exceptions.
8. If no exceptions, extract return value, `inout` parameters, and `out` parameters.

The fifth step, setting the list of context identifiers, should not be necessary if you avoid the use of contexts in your IDL.

C++ Invocation on `Inventory::confirmItem()`

The C++ code in Listing 18.4 illustrates the steps to invoke the operation `confirmItem()` using the DII.

Listing 18.4 C++ Invocation Using the DII

```
//C++
#include "dii.hh"
...
//------------------------------------------------------------
// The following variables are assumed to be given:
//     objV  - An object reference of type 'CORBA::Object_var'
//             that is initialized to an 'Inventory' object reference.

// Step 1: Create the request.
CORBA::Request_var reqV;
reqV = objV->_request("confirmItem");

// Step 2: Set all parameters.
```

Listing 18.4 continued

```
CORBA::Long itemId = 1234;
reqV->add_in_arg()    <<= itemId;
CORBA::Float price = 100.0;
reqV->add_inout_arg() <<= price;
CORBA::Long  howManyInStock;
reqV->add_out_arg()   <<= howManyInStock;

//Step 3: Set return type.
reqV->set_return_type(CORBA::_tc_boolean);

//Step 4: Set exception list.
reqV->exceptions()->add(Inventory::_tc_NoSuchItem);

//Step 5: Set context list.
//(Skipped!)

//Step 6: Make the invocation.
reqV->invoke();

//Step 7: Check for exceptions.
CORBA::Exception * excP = reqV->env()->exception();
if (excP) {
    processException(excP);
}
else {
    //Step 8: If no exceptions, process return values.
    CORBA::Boolean isAvailable;
    reqV->return_value()  >>= isAvailable;
    *(reqV->arguments()->item(1)->value() ) >>= price;
    *(reqV->arguments()->item(2)->value() ) >>= howManyInStock;

    if (isAvailable) {
        cout << "Item " << itemId << " is available." << endl
             << "price = " << price << endl
             << "howManyInStock = " << howManyInStock << endl;
    }
    else {
        cout << "Item " << itemId << " is not available." << endl;
    }
}
```

In step 2, parameters are added in the same order that they appear in the signature of the `confirmItem()` operation. The return type of the `CORBA::Request` methods `add_in_arg()`, `add_inout_arg()`, and `add_out_arg()` is `CORBA::Any&`. Parameters are inserted using the standard syntax for any insertion, with the help of the <<= operator. The precise value of `out` arguments added to the request is immaterial because they are not sent to the server.

In step 3 and step 4, type codes are needed to set the return type and list of exception types. In a real application, if the type codes were for user-defined types, you would need to use dynamic type code creation. The current example cheats in step 4: The exception type code `Inventory::_tc_NoSuchItem` is defined in the stub code. A true DII application would create this type code dynamically—see Chapter 17.

In step 6, the method `invoke()` sends a request message to the CORBA object and blocks until a reply is received. If the operation were declared as `oneway`, you would use the `send_oneway()` method instead. See the section "`oneway` Invocations," later in this chapter.

In step 7, a check is made for exceptions. The processing of exceptions in the DII is discussed in the section "Processing Exceptions," later in this chapter.

In step 8, the return value, `inout`, and `out` parameters are extracted. The extraction of `inout` and `out` parameters is slightly complicated because it requires manipulation of a `CORBA::NVList` type:

- The call `reqV->arguments()` returns a list of argument items as a `CORBA::NVList`.
- The call `arguments()->item(`*`itemIndex`*`)` returns a particular argument from the list as a `CORBA::NamedValue`.
- The call `item(`*`itemIndex`*`)->value()` returns a `CORBA::Any` that holds the value of the argument given by *`itemIndex`*.

See Chapter 15 for further details of `CORBA::NVList`.

Unconventional Memory Management

Memory management for the DII pseudo-interfaces is unconventional. Consider the following line from step 8 of Listing 18.4:

```
//C++
*(reqV->arguments()->item(1)->value() ) >>= price;
```

If conventional CORBA memory management rules applied, this line would leak three objects: the `CORBA::NVList` returned by `reqV->arguments()`, the `CORBA::NamedValue` returned by `arguments()->item(1)`, and the `CORBA::Any*` returned by `item(1)->value()`.

No such memory leaks occur, however, because the pseudo-interfaces `CORBA::Request`, `CORBA::NVList`, and `CORBA::NamedValue` have unconventional memory management semantics. Methods invoked on these pseudo-interfaces retain ownership of their return values. This means that the caller is relieved of the responsibility of deallocating return values.

Java Invocation on `Inventory::confirmItem()`

The Java code in Listing 18.5 illustrates the steps needed to invoke the operation `confirmItem()` using the DII.

Listing 18.5 Java Invocation Using the DII

```
//Java
...
//------------------------------------------------------------------
// The following variables are assumed to be given:
//     obj  - An object reference of type 'CORBA::Object_var'
//            that is initialized to an 'Inventory' object reference.
//     orb  - A reference to an ORB object of type 'CORBA::ORB'.

try {
    //Step 1: Create the request
    org.omg.CORBA.Request req;
    req = obj._request("confirmItem");

    //Step 2: Set all parameters

    // Get the parameter list from the request
    org.omg.CORBA.NVList params = req.arguments();

    // Create 1st parameter
    org.omg.CORBA.Any param1Any = orb.create_any();
    int itemId = 1234;
    param1Any.insert_long(itemId);
    params.add_value(
               "itemId",  // Parameter name
               param1Any, // Value
               org.omg.CORBA.ARG_IN.value // Direction
           );

    // Create 2nd parameter
    org.omg.CORBA.Any param2Any = orb.create_any();
    param2Any.insert_float(100.0f);
    params.add_value(
               "price",   // Parameter name
               param2Any, // Value
               org.omg.CORBA.ARG_INOUT.value // Direction
           );

    // Create 3rd parameter
    org.omg.CORBA.Any param3Any = orb.create_any();
    org.omg.CORBA.TypeCode TCint = orb.get_primitive_tc(
                   org.omg.CORBA.TCKind.tk_long
                 );
    param3Any.type(TCint);
    params.add_value(
               "howManyInStock",    // Parameter name
               param3Any,           // Value
               org.omg.CORBA.ARG_OUT.value // Direction
           );
```

Listing 18.5 continued

```
    //Step 3: Set the return type
    org.omg.CORBA.TypeCode booleanTC = orb.get_primitive_tc(
                org.omg.CORBA.TCKind.tk_boolean
            );
    req.set_return_type(booleanTC);

    //Step 4: Set the exception list
    req.exceptions().add(
        InventoryPackage.NoSuchItemHelper.type()
    );

    //Step 5: Set the context list
    //(Skipped)

    //Step 6: Make the invocation
    req.invoke();

    //Step 7: Check for exceptions
    Exception exc = req.env().exception();
    if (exc != null) {
        processException(exc);
    }
    else {

        //Step 8: If no exceptions, process return values
        boolean isAvailable;
        isAvailable = req.return_value().extract_boolean();

        if (isAvailable) {
            org.omg.CORBA.Any outAny = null;

            // Extract 2nd parameter
            outAny = req.arguments().item(1).value();
            float price = outAny.extract_float();

            // Extract 3rd parameter
            outAny = req.arguments().item(2).value();
            int howManyInStock = outAny.extract_long();

            // Print out results...
            System.out.println("Item " + itemId + " is available.");
            System.out.println("price = " + price);
            System.out.println("howManyInStock = " + howManyInStock);
        }
        else {
            System.out.println("Item " + itemId + " is not available.");
```

Listing 18.5 continued

```
        }
    }
}
catch (org.omg.CORBA.SystemException sysEx) {
    System.out.println("SystemException: " + sysEx);
}
catch (org.omg.CORBA.Bounds boundsEx) {
    System.out.println("UserException:  " + boundsEx);
}
```

In step 1, a `Request` object is created for the operation `"confirmItem"`, using the `_request()` method.

In step 2, parameters are added in the same order that they appear in the signature of the `confirmItem()` operation. A reference to the list of parameters `params` is obtained by calling the `Request.arguments()` method, which returns an `NVList` object. Initially, this list is empty. It is filled using the `add_value()` method, as declared in the following code fragment:

```
//Java
package org.omg.CORBA;

NamedValue  NVList.add_value(
                    String item_name,
                    Any val,
                    int flags
            );
```

The three arguments of `add_value()` give a complete description of an operation parameter.

- `item_name` is the parameter name as declared in IDL.
- `val` is an `any` containing the value of the parameter. For `in` or `inout` parameters, `val` must be initialized with the appropriate data type. For `out` parameters, it is only necessary to set the parameter type of `val` using the `Any.type()` method.
- `flags` is set to one of `org.omg.CORBA.ARG_IN.value`, `org.omg.CORBA.ARG_INOUT.value`, or `org.omg.CORBA.ARG_OUT.value` to indicate the direction in which the parameter is passed.

In step 3, the return type of the request is set.

In step 4, the list of exception types is set. The only item in the list is `Inventory::NoSuchItem`. The current example cheats by using an exception type code that is defined in the stub code. In a real application you would need to use dynamic type code creation—see Chapter 17.

In step 6, the method invoke() sends a request to the CORBA object and blocks until a reply is received. If the operation were declared as oneway, you would use the send_oneway() method, instead. See the section "oneway Invocations," later in this chapter.

In step 7, a check is made for exceptions. The processing of exceptions in the DII is discussed in the section "Processing Exceptions," later in this chapter.

In step 8, the return value and the inout and out parameters are extracted. The extraction of inout and out parameters requires manipulation of an org.omg.CORBA.NVList type:

- The call req.arguments() returns a list of argument items as an NVList.
- The call arguments().item(*itemIndex*) returns a particular argument from the list as a org.omg.CORBA.NamedValue.
- The call item(*itemIndex*).value() returns an any that holds the value of the argument given by *itemIndex*.

See Chapter 17 for further details of CORBA::NVList.

The _request() Method and the Interface Repository

The _request() method has one potential drawback: It might automatically consult the interface repository even if you do not want it to. Whether this happens or not depends on the particular ORB implementation you are using. If stub code for an interface is not available, the CORBA specification allows _request() to consult the interface repository to set properties of the CORBA::Request object as it is being created.

If the interface repository is consulted every time _request() is called, this leads to degradation in performance because the associated remote invocations are relatively expensive. This limitation can be overcome by using the _create_request()method instead.

Processing Exceptions

The C++ demonstration code in Listing 18.6 shows the implementation of the function processException() that was used in the Listing 18.4.

Listing 18.6 C++ Processing DII Exceptions

```
//C++
static void
processException(CORBA::Exception * excP)
{
    cout << "Processing exception:" << endl;

    CORBA::SystemException * sysExcP;
    sysExcP = CORBA::SystemException::_downcast(excP);
    if (sysExcP) {
        cout << "SystemException: " << sysExcP << endl;
        return;
    }
```

Listing 18.6 continued

```
    CORBA::UnknownUserException * unkExcP;
    unkExcP = CORBA::UnknownUserException::_downcast(excP);
    if (unkExcP) {
        cout << "UnknownUserException: <no details>" << endl;
        return;
    }
}
```

The exception type extracted from the `CORBA::Request` object has the base type `CORBA::Exception`. The implementation of `processExceptions()` identifies the class of exception by attempting to cast the exception to either `CORBA::SystemException` or `CORBA::UnknownUserException`. The method used to perform the cast is of the form *`exceptionClass`*`::_downcast()`. The `_downcast()` method is similar to `_narrow()` except that the return value is not duplicated. Therefore, it is not necessary to delete the value returned from `_downcast()`. A NULL object reference is returned if an attempt is made to downcast to the wrong type.

CAUTION

> Do not use `CORBA[edit, double colon]is_nil()` to check the return value of a `_downcast()`. A `_downcast()` returns a `NULL` pointer, which is not necessarily the same thing as a `nil` pointer.

The Java code in Listing 18.7 shows the implementation of the function `processException()` used in Listing 18.5.

Listing 18.7 Java Processing DII Exceptions

```
//Java
public static void
processException( Exception exc)
{
    System.out.println("Processing exception:");

    org.omg.CORBA.SystemException sysExc = null;
    if (exc instanceof org.omg.CORBA.SystemException) {
        sysExc = (org.omg.CORBA.SystemException) exc;
        System.out.println("SystemException: " + sysExc);
        return;
    }

    org.omg.CORBA.UnknownUserException unkExc = null;
    if (exc instanceof org.omg.CORBA.UnknownUserException) {
        unkExc = (org.omg.CORBA.UnknownUserException) exc;
        System.out.println("UnknownUserException: " + unkExc);
        return;
    }
}
```

The base class for all CORBA exceptions in Java is `java.lang.Exception`. This type is passed as an argument to the function `processException()`, which uses the `instanceof` operator to determine whether this exception is of type `SystemException` or `UnknownUserException`. System exceptions are easy to handle because there are no special marshalling requirements.

All user exceptions raised through the DII are created by the ORB as `UnknownUserExceptions` (`CORBA::UnknownUserException` in C++ and `org.omg.CORBA.UnknownUserException` in Java), which is a subclass of `UserException` (`CORBA::UserException` in C++ and `org.omg.CORBA.UserException` in Java).

Details of the user exception are accessible in the form of an `any` that can be extracted using the `CORBA::UnknownUserException::exception()0` method in C++ or the `org.omg.CORBA.UnknownUserException.except()` method in Java. In the absence of stub code, the contents of the `any` can be analyzed with the help of the `CORBA::DynAny` interface, described in Chapter 19.

Use of `_create_request()`

An alternative way of creating a `CORBA::Request` object is to use one of the two `_create_request()` methods. Listing 18.8 shows the declarations for the C++ methods, and Listing 18.9 shows the declarations for the Java methods.

Listing 18.8 C++ Signatures for **`create_request()`**

```
//C++
// In namespace 'CORBA'
class Object
{
public:
    ...
    // First form of '_create_request()'
    void _create_request(
        Context_ptr ctx,
        const char *operation,
        NVList_ptr arg_list,
        NamedValue_ptr result,
        Request_out request,
        Flags req_flags
    );

    // Second form of '_create_request()'
    void _create_request(
        Context_ptr ctx,
        const char *operation,
        NVList_ptr arg_list,
        NamedValue_ptr result,
        ExceptionList_ptr,
        ContextList_ptr,
```

Listing 18.8 continued

```
        Request_out request,
        Flags req_flags
    );
    ...
};
```

Listing 18.9 Java Signatures for **`create_request()`**

```
//Java
package org.omg.CORBA;

public interface Object {
    ...
    Request _request(String s);

    // First form of '_create_request()'
    Request _create_request(
        Context ctx,
        String operation,
        NVList arg_list,
        NamedValue result);

    // Second form of '_create_request()'
    Request _create_request(
        Context ctx,
        String operation,
        NVList arg_list,
        NamedValue result,
        ExceptionList exclist,
        ContextList ctxlist);
    ...
}
```

The first form of `_create_request()` corresponds formally to the IDL declaration of `CORBA::Object::create_request()`. However, it is best to avoid using this form because the `ExceptionList` and `ContextList` arguments are missing.

The second form of `_create_request()` has a complete set of arguments. The characteristic feature of this method is that it allows you to create a `CORBA::Request` object in a single step. The arguments supplied to `_create_request()` give a complete description of an operation's syntax.

The `ctx` argument is used as the source of context information sent with the operation. The `operation` argument gives the name of the operation being invoked.

The arg_list operation is a CORBA::NVList containing all of the operation's parameters (in, inout, and out parameters). The CORBA::NVList can be created using either of the following CORBA::ORB methods:

```
//C++
void CORBA::ORB::create_list(CORBA::Long count, CORBA::NVList_out new_list);
void CORBA::ORB::create_operation_list(
                    CORBA::OperationDef_ptr oper,
                    CORBA::NVList_out       new_list
            );

//Java
package org.omg.CORBA;
NVList ORB.create_list(int count);
NVList ORB.create_operation_list(org.omg.CORBA.Object oper);
// Argument 'oper' must be of type 'org.omg.CORBA.OperationDef'
```

The operation create_list() allocates a list in which the count argument gives the initial number of list elements allocated. The operation create_operation_list() allocates and sets the type fields of a list, in which the type of each argument is automatically set by consulting the CORBA::OperationDef object in the interface repository.

The NamedValue for the result argument is created using the following create_named_value() method:

```
//C++
void CORBA::ORB::create_named_value(CORBA::NamedValue_out nv);

//Java
package org.omg.CORBA;
NamedValue ORB.create_named_value(String name, Any value, int flags);
```

The ExceptionList and ContextList are created using the following methods defined on CORBA::ORB.

```
//C++
void CORBA::ORB::create_exception_list(CORBA::ExceptionList_out exclist);
void CORBA::ORB::create_context_list(CORBA::ContextList_out ctxlist);

//Java
package org.omg.CORBA;
ExceptionList ORB.create_exception_list();
ContextList ORB.create_context_list();
```

The flags argument, which appears only in the C++ version of _create_request(), is ignored and has no effect on the returned CORBA::Request.

oneway Invocations

If you are invoking a oneway operation, you must make the invocation by calling send_oneway() in place of invoke(). It has the following syntax in C++ and Java:

```
//C++
void CORBA::Request::send_oneway();

//Java
void org.omg.CORBA.Request.send_oneway();
```

The semantics of send_oneway() depend on the particular version of GIOP used over the connection.

- **GIOP 1.0 or 1.1** A call to send_oneway() sends a request message to the server that has the response_expected flag set to false. No reply is sent back from the server, and send_oneway() returns immediately.
- **GIOP 1.2** In this case, a call to send_oneway() provides only a hint to the ORB that a reply is not needed. The ORB might ignore this hint and ask for a reply anyway. This would enable the ORB to receive LOCATION_FORWARD or system exception replies.

A peculiar feature of the DII is that the CORBA specification permits you to use send_oneway() even if an operation was not originally defined as oneway.

Asynchronous Invocations

A special feature of the DII is that it supports the use of asynchronous invocations. There are three operations—send_deferred(), get_response(), and poll_response() —defined on CORBA::Request that are associated with asynchronous invocations:

```
//C++
void CORBA::Request::send_deferred();
void CORBA::Request::get_response();
CORBA::Boolean CORBA::Request::poll_response();

//Java
package org.omg.CORBA;
void Request.send_deferred();
void Request.get_response()
            throws org.omg.CORBA.WrongTransaction;
boolean Request.poll_response();
```

The operation send_deferred() is called in place of invoke() when you want to make an asynchronous invocation. A request is sent to the server and send_deferred() returns right away.

To retrieve the reply from the server, you must call get_response() at some later time. If the matching reply message has already arrived, get_response() returns right away. Otherwise get_response() blocks until the matching reply message arrives. After get_response() returns, the CORBA::Request is in a state from which you can extract its return value and its inout and out parameters.

If you want to avoid blocking on a call to get_response(), you can check for the arrival of a reply message by calling poll_response(). It returns true if the reply has arrived and false otherwise. Calling poll_response() does not change the values in the CORBA::Request object. You must also call get_response() before extracting the return value and inout and out parameters.

When using the CORBA Transaction Service, the send_deferred() and get_response() methods both must be invoked from the same thread for a given CORBA::Request. If not, the call to get_response() will raise a WrongTransaction exception.

Another style of asynchronous invocation is supported by methods defined on the CORBA::ORB interface. The CORBA::ORB methods allow batches of requests to be sent to servers.

```
//C++
void CORBA::ORB::send_multiple_requests_oneway(const CORBA::RequestSeq&);
void CORBA::ORB::send_multiple_requests_deferred(const CORBA::RequestSeq&);
CORBA::Boolean CORBA::ORB::poll_next_response();
void CORBA::ORB::get_next_response(CORBA::Request_out);

//Java
package org.omg.CORBA;
void ORB.send_multiple_requests_oneway(Request[] req);
void ORB.send_multiple_requests_deferred(Request[] req);
boolean ORB.poll_next_response();
Request ORB.get_next_response();
```

The CORBA::RequestSeq is defined in IDL to be a typedef of sequence<Request>; it is used to hold a batch of requests for processing. These methods work in a fashion analogous to the methods defined in CORBA::Request.

Retrieving responses works slightly differently in batch mode. Because replies arrive in random order, get_next_response() returns whatever response is next available. poll_next_response() returns true if one or more responses have arrived at the client.

Pseudo-Interfaces

A relatively large number of pseudo-interfaces are used with the DII. Details of the pseudo-interfaces are given in Chapter 15. The main ones are

```
CORBA::Request
CORBA::ORB
CORBA::Object
CORBA::Environment
CORBA::Exception
CORBA::SystemException
```

```
CORBA::UnknownUserException
CORBA::NamedValue
CORBA::NVList
CORBA::ExceptionList
CORBA:: ContextList
```

CHAPTER 19

Dynamic Skeleton Interface

A CORBA server needs detailed knowledge of an interface, including its operation names, parameters, return value, and exception declarations, in order to complete the dispatch of an incoming request to a particular function or method. This knowledge is encapsulated in the server's *skeleton code*.

Usually, the skeleton code is generated from the IDL by the IDL compiler, and then it is compiled and linked against the server application. This is known as *static skeleton code* and is used in most CORBA servers. It suffers from one serious drawback, however: The interfaces supported by the server application must be known in advance, at the time the server is built.

There are many applications that cannot operate with this restriction, such as debugging tools, bridges, and adapters. These general-purpose applications should be able to support arbitrary IDL interfaces without needing to be rebuilt. For these kinds of applications, CORBA provides the dynamic skeleton interface (DSI). The DSI provides a framework for retrieving type information at runtime and dynamically interpreting the contents of operation parameters.

This chapter provides an overview of the DSI, outlining how it could be used to build an adapter, followed by an outline of how to implement the DSI in C++ and in Java.

Overview of the DSI

This section gives an overview of the DSI by examining the architecture of a typical DSI application: a protocol adapter.

Consider a scenario in which a company has already implemented an infrastructure for making remote method calls. The old protocol is called LEGACY protocol, and legacy servers that use the LEGACY protocol are widely deployed within the company's intranet. The company would now like to build a CORBA subsystem that can talk to the old legacy servers.

Evidently, it would be far too difficult and costly to re-engineer all legacy servers to communicate directly with CORBA clients using IIOP. The most effective solution is to build a LEGACY adapter that dynamically translates CORBA invocations to LEGACY invocations. The architecture for such an adapter is shown in Figure 19.1.

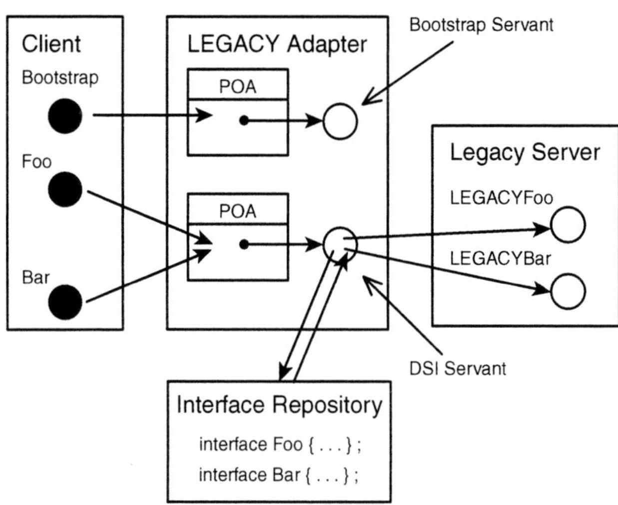

Figure 19.1

Sample application: a LEGACY adapter.

In this example, you have a CORBA client that needs to access two objects in a legacy server, `LEGACYFoo` and `LEGACYBar`. Because the client speaks only IIOP and the server understands only LEGACY protocol, it is necessary to insert a LEGACY adapter to translate IIOP requests into LEGACY requests.

The DSI servant does most of the work of the adapter. It receives the CORBA invocation that originates from the CORBA client, dynamically translates it to a LEGACY invocation request, and forwards the LEGACY invocation to the appropriate legacy server. In order to perform the translation, the DSI servant uses the following dynamic features of CORBA:

- **Dynamic anys** The `DynamicAny` module is needed to dynamically interpret and generate parameters and return values. See Chapter 17, "`DynAny` Type."
- **CORBA Interface Repository** The interface repository is used to store type information and descriptions of IDL operation signatures. See Chapter 20, "Interface Repository."

The DSI servant retrieves type information from the interface repository, as necessary, to interpret the invocations it receives from CORBA clients.

Like normal servants, the DSI servant receives invocation requests via a POA object (refer to the section "Default Servant POA" in Chapter 7, "The Portable Object Adapter"). However, the implementation of a DSI servant is very different from that of an ordinary servant.

Figure 19.1 shows another servant in the LEGACY adapter, the `Bootstrap` servant. This is just the name given to a sample object that helps establish communication between a CORBA client and a legacy server—it is not a standard object. In any adapter architecture, you typically will require some kind of `Bootstrap` object that enables CORBA clients to find particular legacy servers (or objects in legacy servers).

POA for the DSI Servant

The POA used with the DSI servant has to be configured to use a default servant. The only policy restriction required for a DSI servant is that `RequestProcessingPolicy` must have a value of `USE_DEFAULT_SERVANT`.

For the example LEGACY adapter shown in Figure 19.1, the POA policies shown in Table 19.1 are recommended.

Table 19.1 POA Policies Recommended for the DSI Example

POA Policy Type	Policy Value
`ThreadPolicy`	`ORB_CTRL_MODEL`
	or `SINGLE_THREAD_MODEL`
`LifespanPolicy`	`TRANSIENT`
	or `PERSISTENT`
`IdAssignmentPolicy`	`USER_ID`
`ServantRetentionPolicy`	`NON_RETAIN`
`ImplicitActivationPolicy`	`NO_IMPLICIT_ACTIVATION`
`RequestProcessingPolicy`	`USE_DEFAULT_SERVANT`

It is preferable to use the `ORB_CTRL_MODEL` thread policy value if you can, to make the LEGACY adapter multithreaded. A general-purpose adapter such as this needs to be as responsive as possible.

The POA lifespan policy could be either `TRANSIENT` or `PERSISTENT`. The chosen policy does not have to reflect whether objects in the legacy servers behave as session or entity objects. However, if you want to support both types of object lifecycle, you must create two corresponding POA objects—one having the `TRANSIENT` policy and another having the `PERSISTENT` policy.

Registering the DSI Servant with a POA

A DSI servant is registered with a POA by passing it as the argument to the `POA::set_servant()` operation. See the section "Default Servant POA" in Chapter 7.

Single DSI Servant Supporting Many Interfaces

Unlike an ordinary servant, which implements the operations corresponding to a single interface type, a DSI servant typically supports a large number of interfaces. Theoretically, a given DSI servant can implement an infinite number of interfaces.

One of the first things a DSI servant has to do on receiving an invocation request is figure out what kind of interface is being invoked on. As noted in Chapter 7, the interface name is *not* sent in the invocation request. Instead, the ORB uses the following basic information to identify an object and its type:

- The POA name, or sequence of POA names if at the bottom of a POA hierarchy.
- The `ObjectId`.

If you want to derive the type of an object from this information, you typically need to ensure that type information is somehow embedded in the `ObjectId` or can be derived from it.

Mapping `ObjectIds` to Interface Types

From time to time the ORB needs to know the type of an object. Therefore, when implementing a DSI servant, you are required to implement the function shown in Listing 19.1 (C++) or Listing 19.2 (Java). These functions perform the mapping of `ObjectIds` to interface types.

Listing 19.1 C++ Determining the Interface Type

```
//C++
CORBA::RepositoryId
PortableServer::DynamicImplementation::_primary_interface(
    const PortableServer::ObjectId& oid,
    PortableServer::POA_ptr         poa
);
```

Listing 19.2 Java Determining the Interface Type

```
//Java
String[]
org.omg.PortableServer.Servant._ all_interfaces(
    POA poa,
    byte[] objectId
);
```

The C++ `_primary_interface()` function returns a single repository ID string (`char *`) that is the most derived interface type for this object. For example, it might return `IDL:Foo:1.0` or `IDL:Bar:1.0`.

The Java `_all_interfaces()` method returns a sequence of repository IDs that includes the most derived interface type and all of its base classes. The first (zero index) element of the returned array must be the most derived interface type.

To implement these functions, you could store the type of an object in its `ObjectId` either by embedding the `CORBA::RepositoryId` (see the sample `ObjectIdMapper` class in Chapter 7) or by embedding a more compact form of key. When either of these functions is called, the interface type can then be determined by examining the `ObjectId`.

A Sample `Bootstrap` Interface

The LEGACY adapter has to provide some means for CORBA clients to find the objects on legacy servers—it cannot use the CORBA Naming Service because the legacy objects are not CORBA objects. A typical solution is for the LEGACY adapter to provide some sort of `Bootstrap` interface to find legacy objects—this is *not* a standard CORBA interface. Listing 19.3 shows a sample `Bootstrap` interface.

Listing 19.3 A Sample* `Bootstrap` *Interface

```
//IDL
#include <orb.idl>

interface Bootstrap {
    typedef string LEGACYAddress;
    typedef string LEGACYObjectId;

    Object find_object(
               CORBA::RepositoryId type,
               LEGACYAddress       addr,
               LEGACYObjectId      id
           );
};
```

The `Bootstrap` interface provides a single `find_object()` operation. The `type` argument gives the type of the object as a repository ID (a `string`). The `addr` and `id` arguments are placeholders for the location and identity of the object in the legacy system. The `find_object()` operation returns a plain object reference, which must be narrowed to the appropriate type.

C++ Implementing a DSI Servant

A DSI servant is implemented by defining a new class that inherits from `PortableServer::DynamicImplementation` and overriding certain inherited member functions. The inheritance tree for a C++ DSI servant is illustrated in Figure 19.2.

In the example, a new servant class, `MyDSIServant`, is defined.

The `_this()` function defined in the `DynamicImplementation` base class returns a generic `CORBA::Object_ptr` object reference. This contrasts with a normal servant, which inherits a type-specific `_this()` function.

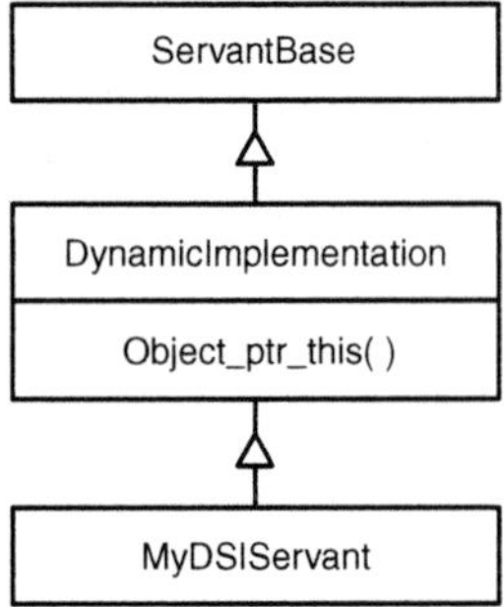

Figure 19.2

A C++ inheritance tree for a DSI servant.

C++ Overriding `DynamicImplementation` Member Functions

Listing 19.4 shows the main C++ classes that are used in the implementation of a DSI servant.

Listing 19.4 C++ Classes Used in the DSI

```
//C++
namespace CORBA
{
    class ServerRequest
    {
    public:
        const char* operation() const;
        void arguments(NVList_ptr& parameters);
        Context_ptr ctx();
        void set_result(const Any& value);
        void set_exception(const Any& value);
    };
};

namespace PortableServer
{
    class ServantBase
    {
    public:
        virtual ~ServantBase();

        virtual POA_ptr _default_POA();

        virtual CORBA::InterfaceDef_ptr
        _get_interface() throw(CORBA::SystemException);
```

Listing 19.4 continued

```
        virtual CORBA::Boolean
        _is_a(const char* logical_type_id) throw(CORBA::SystemException);

        virtual CORBA::Boolean
        _non_existent() throw(CORBA::SystemException);

        virtual void _add_ref();

        virtual void _remove_ref();

    protected:
        ServantBase();
        ServantBase(const ServantBase&);
        ServantBase& operator=(const ServantBase&);
        // ...all other constructors...
    };

    typedef ServantBase* Servant;

    class DynamicImplementation : public virtual ServantBase
    {
    public:
        CORBA::Object_ptr _this();
        virtual void invoke(
            CORBA::ServerRequest_ptr request
        ) = 0;

        virtual CORBA::RepositoryId
        _primary_interface(
            const ObjectId& oid,
            POA_ptr poa
        ) = 0;
    };
}
```

A number of `DynamicImplementation` member functions, some of them inherited from `ServantBase`, must be overridden. These are discussed in the following two subsections.

The `DynamicImplementation::invoke()` Function

The `invoke()` operation provides the logic to process DSI invocations. When the POA receives an invocation request, it passes the request, in the form of a `CORBA::ServerRequest` object, to the DSI servant by calling `invoke()`.

The following steps implement the `invoke()` operation in the LEGACY adapter example:

1. Determine the identity of the object, `ObjectId`, using the `PortableServer::Current::get_object_id()` operation. From the `ObjectId`, determine the type of object (`CORBA::RepositoryId`).
2. Call `operation()` on the `ServerRequest` object to determine the name of the invoked operation.
3. Given the type of the object and the name of the invoked operation, determine the list of parameters for the invocation.
   This step requires a named value list (`CORBA::NVList`) to be constructed that has entries for each of the IDL `in`, `inout`, and `out` parameters. The parameters in `NVList` must be in the same order as they appear in IDL.
   `NVList` can be constructed either by remotely contacting the interface repository (see Chapter 20) or by retrieving `NVList` from a cache. The use of a cache is highly recommended for reasons of efficiency.
   When constructing an operation's `NVList` for the first time, the `CORBA::ORB::create_operation_list()` operation is useful.
   Do *not* assign `NVList` to a `_var` type. Exceptional memory management semantics apply to the argument list (see Chapter 18, "Dynamic Invocation Interface").
4. Call `arguments()` on the `ServerRequest` object, passing in the `NVList` that was constructed in the previous step.
   After this call, the entries in `NVList` that correspond to `in` or `inout` parameters are initialized with the data received from the client.
   After `arguments()` has been called, `ServerRequest` assumes ownership of `NVList` (exceptional memory management). Do *not* delete `NVList` after calling `arguments()`.
5. The `in` and `inout` parameters can be parsed with the help of the `DynamicAny` module.
6. The DSI servant does some work to process the request.
   In the case of the LEGACY adapter example, the request is converted to a LEGACY request and forwarded to the appropriate Legacy server.
7. The `out` and `inout` parameters and the return value can be constructed with the help of the `DynamicAny` module.
   The `out` and `inout` parameters are updated by modifying the entries in the `NVList` that correspond to `out` or `inout` parameters.
8. Call `set_result()` on the `ServerRequest` object, passing an `any` that contains the return value of the operation. This call must be made even if the return type of the operation is `void`.
   After `set_result()` has been called, `ServerRequest` assumes ownership of the `any` (exceptional memory management). Do *not* delete the `any` after calling `set_result()`.

9. Alternatively, if you want to raise an exception, call `set_exception()` instead, passing an `any` that contains the exception.
   After `set_exception()` has been called, `ServerRequest` assumes ownership of the `any` (exceptional memory management). Do *not* delete the `any` after calling `set_exception()`.

Other `DynamicImplementation` Member Functions

The following member function must be overridden:

- `DynamicImplementation::_primary_interface()`
  This function is called by the ORB in the course of dispatching an invocation request. It performs the task of mapping an `ObjectId` and POA object reference to a `CORBA::RepositoryId` that identifies the type of the target object. See the section "Mapping `ObjectId`s to Interface Types," earlier in this chapter.
- `ServantBase::_non_existent()`
  The `_non_existent()` operation is a pseudo-operation that can be called remotely, like regular IDL operations. It tests whether or not a CORBA object exists. The CORBA object being tested can be identified using the `PortableServer::Current` interface (see Chapter 7).
  The `_non_existent()` operation returns `TRUE` if the CORBA object definitely does not exist. Otherwise, it returns `FALSE`. The default implementation of `_non_existent()` always returns `FALSE`.
  This function must be overridden by a DSI servant to return `TRUE` or `FALSE` as appropriate.

The following member functions can optionally be overridden:

- `ServantBase::_default_POA()`
  This function returns a reference to the POA associated with the servant and can be called outside the context of an invocation dispatch.
  The `_default_POA()` function is unlikely to be used by a DSI servant, but it is good practice to override this function just in case.
- `ServantBase::_is_a()`
  The `_is_a()` operation is a pseudo-operation that can be called remotely, like regular IDL operations. It tests whether a CORBA object is of a particular type. The CORBA object being tested can be identified using the `PortableServer::Current` interface. The type being tested for is passed as the `logical_type_id` argument, which is really a `CORBA::RepositoryId` although declared as a `const char *` above.
  The `_is_a()` operation returns `TRUE` if `logical_type_id` matches the type of the object exactly or if it matches any of the object's base classes. Otherwise, it returns `FALSE`.
  The default implementation of `_is_a()` identifies the fundamental type of the object using `_primary_interface()` and makes remote calls to the interface repository to identify the base classes.

It is preferable to override this function when implementing a DSI servant in the C++ mapping, because the default implementation provided is rather inefficient. You can do better by caching the list of base classes.

- `ServantBase::_get_interface()`
  This function returns a reference to a `CORBA::InterfaceDef` interface repository object for the type of CORBA object currently being invoked on. The object's type is identified using the `_primary_interface()` function. It is normally unnecessary to override this function.

The following member function cannot be overridden:

- `DynamicImplementation::_this()`
  The `_this()` function returns an object reference (of `CORBA::Object_ptr` type) for the CORBA object currently being invoked on.

Java Implementing a DSI Servant

A DSI servant is implemented by defining a new class that inherits from `PortableServer.DynamicImplementation` and overriding certain inherited methods. The inheritance tree for a Java DSI servant is illustrated in Figure 19.3.

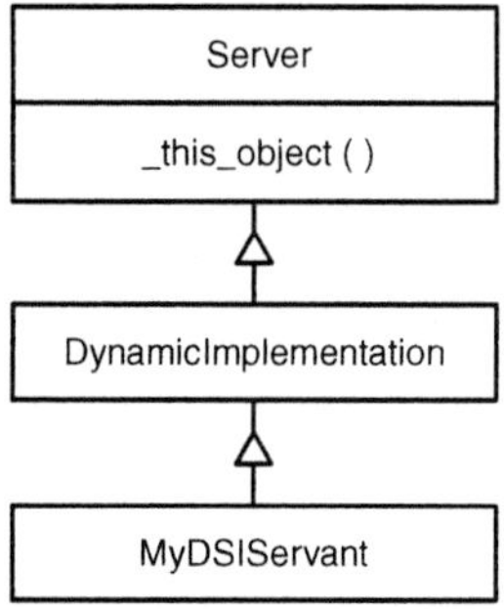

Figure 19.3

The Java inheritance tree for a DSI servant.

In this example, a new servant class, `MyDSIServant`, is defined.

The `_this_object()` function defined in the `Servant` base class returns a generic `org.omg.CORBA.Object` object reference. Unlike a normal servant, the DSI servant does not have a type-specific `_this()` function.

The next section discusses the `DynamicImplementation` member functions that can be overridden.

Java Overriding `DynamicImplementation` Methods

Listing 19.5 and Listing 19.6 show the main Java classes that are used in the implementation of a DSI servant.

Listing 19.5 Java **CORBA.ServerRequest** *Class*

```
//Java
package org.omg.CORBA;

public abstract class ServerRequest {
    public String operation() {
        throw new org.omg.CORBA.NO_IMPLEMENT();
    }
    public abstract Context ctx();
    public void arguments(NVList nv) {
        throw new org.omg.CORBA.NO_IMPLEMENT();
    }
    public void set_result(Any val) {
        throw new org.omg.CORBA.NO_IMPLEMENT();
    }
    public void set_exception(Any val) {
        throw new org.omg.CORBA.NO_IMPLEMENT();
    }
}
```

Listing 19.6 Java **PortableServer.Servant** *and* **PortableServer.DynamicImplementation** *Classes*

```
//Java
package org.omg.PortableServer;

import org.omg.CORBA.ORB;
import org.omg.PortableServer.POA;

abstract public class Servant {
    // Convenience methods for application programmer
    final public org.omg.CORBA.Object _this_object() {
        return _get_delegate().this_object(this);
    }

    final public org.omg.CORBA.Object _this_object(ORB orb) {
        try {
            ((org.omg.CORBA_2_3.ORB)orb).set_delegate(this);
        }
        catch(ClassCastException e) {
            throw new org.omg.CORBA.BAD_PARAM(
                "POA Servant requires an instance of org.omg.CORBA_2_3.ORB"
            );
        }
        return _this_object();
    }
```

Listing 19.6 contined

```
    final public ORB _orb() {
        return _get_delegate().orb(this);
    }

    final public POA _poa() {
        return _get_delegate().poa(this);
    }

    final public byte[] _object_id() {
        return _get_delegate().object_id(this);
    }

    // Methods which may be overridden by the
    // application programmer
    public POA _default_POA() {
        return _get_delegate().default_POA(this);
    }

    public boolean _is_a(String repository_id) {
        return _get_delegate().is_a(this, repository_id);
    }

    public boolean _non_existent() {
        return _get_delegate().non_existent(this);
    }

    public org.omg.CORBA.InterfaceDef _get_interface() {
        return _get_delegate().get_interface(this);
    }

    // methods for which the skeleton or application
    // programmer must provide an implementation
    abstract public String[] _all_interfaces(
        POA poa,
        byte[] objectId
    );

    // private implementation methods
    private transient Delegate _delegate = null;

    final public Delegate _get_delegate() {
        if (_delegate == null) {
            throw new org.omg.CORBA.BAD_INV_ORDER(
                "The Servant has not been associated with an ORBinstance"
            );
        }
        return _delegate;
    }
```

Listing 19.6 continued

```
    final public void _set_delegate(Delegate delegate) {
        _delegate = delegate;
    }
}


abstract public class DynamicImplementation extends Servant
{
    abstract public void invoke(
        org.omg.CORBA.ServerRequest request
    );
}
```

A number of `DynamicImplementation` member functions, some inherited from `Servant`, must be overridden. These are discussed in the following two sections.

The `DynamicImplementation.invoke()` Method

The `invoke()` operation provides the logic to process DSI invocations. When the POA receives an invocation request, it passes the request, in the form of an `org.omg.CORBA.ServerRequest` object, to the DSI servant by calling `invoke()`.

The following steps implement the `invoke()` operation in the LEGACY adapter example:

1. Determine the identity of the object, `ObjectId`, using the `Servant._object_id()` method (a convenient alternative to the `PortableServer.Current` interface). From the `ObjectId`, determine the type of object (an `org.omg.CORBA.RepositoryId`).
2. Call `operation()` on the `ServerRequest` object to determine the name of the invoked operation.
3. Given the type of the object and the name of the invoked operation, determine the list of parameters for the invocation.
   This step requires a named value list (`org.omg.CORBA.NVList`) to be constructed that has entries for each of the IDL `in`, `inout`, and `out` parameters. The parameters in the `NVList` must be in the same order as they appear in IDL. `NVList` can be constructed either by remotely contacting the interface repository (see Chapter 22) or by retrieving the `NVList` from a cache. The use of a cache is highly recommended for reasons of efficiency.
   When constructing an operation's `NVList` for the first time, the `ORB.create_operation_list()` method is useful.
4. Call `arguments()` on the `ServerRequest` object, passing in the `NVList` that was constructed in the previous step.
   After this call, the entries in the `NVList` that correspond to `in` or `inout` parameters are initialized with the data received from the client.

5. The in and inout parameters can be parsed with the help of the DynamicAny module.
6. The DSI servant does some work to process the request.
   In the case of the LEGACY adapter example, the request is converted to a LEGACY request and forwarded to the appropriate legacy server.
7. The out and inout parameters and return value can be constructed with the help of the DynamicAny module.
   The out and inout parameters are updated by modifying the entries in the NVList that correspond to out or inout parameters.
8. Call set_result() on the ServerRequest object, passing an any that contains the return value of the operation. This call must be made even if the return type of the operation is void.
9. Alternatively, if you want to raise an exception call set_exception() instead, pass an any that contains the exception.

Other DynamicImplementation Methods

The methods discussed in this section are inherited from org.omg.PortableServer.Servant.

The following methods must be overridden:

- Servant._all_interfaces()
  This method performs the task of mapping an ObjectId and POA object reference to repository IDs that identify the type of the target object. The first element (zero index) of the array must be the most derived type; the remaining elements of the array are the base types of the interface. See the section "Mapping ObjectIds to Interface Types," earlier in this chapter.
- Servant._non_existent()
  The _non_existent() operation is a pseudo-operation that can be called remotely, like regular IDL operations. It tests whether or not a CORBA object exists. The CORBA object being tested can be identified using the Servant._object_id() method.
  The _non_existent() operation returns TRUE if the CORBA object definitely does not exist. Otherwise, it returns FALSE.
  The default implementation of _non_existent() always returns FALSE.
  This function must be overridden by a DSI servant to return TRUE or FALSE as appropriate.

The following methods can optionally be overridden:

- Servant._default_POA()
  This function returns a reference to the POA associated with the servant and can be called outside the context of an invocation dispatch.
  The _default_POA() function is unlikely to be used by a DSI servant, but it is good practice to override this function just in case.

- `Servant._is_a()`
  The `_is_a()` operation is a pseudo-operation that can be called remotely, like regular IDL operations. It tests whether a CORBA object is of a particular type. The CORBA object being tested can be identified using the `Servant._object_id()` method. The type being tested for is passed as the `repository_id` argument.
  The `_is_a()` operation returns `TRUE` if `repository_id` matches the type of the object exactly or if it matches any of the object's base classes. Otherwise, it returns `FALSE`.
  The default implementation of `_is_a()` identifies the type of the object and all of its base classes using the `_all_interfaces()` method.
  It is normally unnecessary to override this method in the Java mapping.
- `Servant._get_interface()`
  This function returns a reference to a `CORBA::InterfaceDef` interface repository object for the type of CORBA object currently being invoked on. The object's type is identified by the first element of the string array returned by the `_all_interfaces()` method.
  It is normally unnecessary to override this method.

The following method cannot be overridden:

- `Servant._this_object()`
  The `_this_object()` method returns an object reference (of `org.omg.CORBA.Object` type) for the CORBA object currently being invoked on.

CHAPTER 20

Interface Repository

The interface repository is a repository of meta-data for application IDL. Once an IDL file has been put into the interface repository, a complete description of all the definitions appearing in that IDL file becomes available to CORBA applications. This is a natural complement to the dynamic features of CORBA—the dynamic invocation interface (DII) and the dynamic skeleton interface (DSI). When using either the DII or the DSI, it is necessary for an application to find descriptions of IDL interfaces at runtime. This information can be retrieved at any time from the interface repository (assuming the definitions have been entered into the repository).

The interface repository is itself a CORBA server, and interaction with the repository is performed through a set of IDL interfaces that describe the repository. This has the advantage that the interface repository can be accessed remotely, and a central interface repository can provide dynamic type information for any number of CORBA applications.

When an IDL file is put into the interface repository, it is analyzed into its component definitions and decomposed into a parse tree. Each node of the parse tree represents a particular IDL definition. For example, there are nodes to represent the definitions of an interface, an operation, each of the constructed CORBA types, and so on. This chapter describes how to traverse the parse tree and how to get at the description of various IDL definitions using the interface repository IDL.

The interface repository is most often used, in combination with the DII and DSI, to build bridges between CORBA and other distributed computing standards. A good example of this would be a bridge between CORBA and Microsoft's DCOM, for which several commercial implementations are currently available. Such a bridge can dynamically convert invocations back and forth between the CORBA and the DCOM environments, as long as the relevant IDL is stored in the interface repository.

Structure of the Interface Repository

The interface repository has an object-oriented structure and is itself described in terms of IDL. See the section "IDL for the Interface Repository," later in this chapter, for a complete IDL listing.

The interface repository IDL contains a fairly large number of interfaces. Some of these interfaces represent concrete grammatical constructs, which are the nodes of the parse tree. Other interfaces serve as base interfaces that group together different kinds of grammatical constructs.

Nodes of the Parse Tree

For each node of the parse tree within the interface repository, *NodeType*, you typically have the following corresponding entities in the interface repository IDL:

- A `CORBA::`*NodeType*`Def` interface.
  For example, the `CORBA::InterfaceDef` and `CORBA::OperationDef` interfaces represent the IDL definition of an interface and an operation, respectively.
- A `CORBA::`*NodeType*`Description` struct (not defined for all node types).
  For complicated nodes, it is more efficient to retrieve node properties all at once by retrieving a description struct. For example, a `CORBA::InterfaceDescription` and a `CORBA::OperationDescription` can be obtained to describe an interface node and an operation node, respectively.

There are a couple of special cases. Simple types, such as `int`, `long`, `octet`, and so on, do not map to a unique *NodeType*`Def` interface. They are handled generically by the `PrimitiveDef` interface instead.

CAUTION

Beware of some confusing terminology in the interface repository IDL. The grammatical construction involving the IDL `typedef` keyword is represented by the `AliasDef` interface: This is not to be confused with the `TypedefDef` interface, which is really a base interface for a variety of different node types (see the following section).

Base Interfaces

There are a number of interfaces in the interface repository that are used purely as base interfaces. These interfaces are useful for grouping similar types of objects within the interface repository. Many useful operations are also declared in these base interfaces.

Table 20.1 lists the base interfaces used in the interface repository, accompanied by a short description of each.

Table 20.1 Interface Repository—Base Interfaces

Base Interface	Description
`CORBA::IRObject`	This is the base interface for all node types in the interface repository.
`CORBA::Contained`	A base interface for nodes that can be contained within a wider scope. Nodes of `Contained` type always have a name. Unnamed types (`ArrayDef`, `FixedDef`, `PrimitiveDef`, `SequenceDef`, `StringDef`, and `WstringDef`) do not inherit from `CORBA::Contained`.
`CORBA::Container`	A base interface for nodes that can contain other nodes. The only nodes inheriting from `CORBA::Container` are `Repository`, `ModuleDef`, `InterfaceDef`, `ValueDef`, `ExceptionDef`, `StructDef`, and `UnionDef`.
`CORBA::IDLType`	A base interface for all nodes representing data types that are valid for use as operation parameters or return values. The following nodes do *not* inherit from this interface: `Repository`, `ModuleDef`, `AttributeDef`, `OperationDef`, `ConstantDef`, and `ExceptionDef`.
`CORBA::TypedefDef`	A base interface for nodes that define a new, named data type. Note that this interface does *not* represent an IDL `typedef` construction. The nodes inheriting from `CORBA::TypedefDef` are `AliasDef`, `EnumDef`, `NativeDef`, `StructDef`, `UnionDef`, and `ValueBoxDef`.

`ExceptionDef`, `StructDef`, and `UnionDef` inherit from `Container` because IDL syntax allows the following unusual type of construction:

```
//IDL
struct Foo {
    string s;
    struct Bar { long l; short s; } my_bar;
};
```

In this example, the `Bar` struct is declared within the scope of the `Foo` struct. Therefore, in terms of the interface repository parse tree, the `StructDef` representing `Foo` *contains* the `StructDef` representing `Bar`. Similar types of construction are possible using `ExceptionDef` and `UnionDef`.

Using the Interface Repository

The interface repository provides a meta-description of IDL and, of necessity, is fairly long and complex (as can be seen from Listing 20.6). This short section describes some of the basic tasks associated with using the interface repository, but it is beyond the scope of this chapter to describe the interface repository IDL in great detail. The basic tasks are as follows:

- Populating the interface repository
- Making an initial connection

- Searching the parse tree
- Iterating over the parse tree

Populating the Interface Repository

Before you can begin using the interface repository, it is necessary to populate it with some IDL definitions. If you examine Listing 20.6, later in this chapter, you can see that the `NodeTypeDef` interfaces consist of a readable part and a writeable part. The writeable part of the interface, in principle, can be used to add nodes to the parse tree, thereby populating the interface repository with definitions.

In practice, however, you almost never use the writeable interface. ORB vendors invariably provide a tool or utility to populate the interface repository. Typically, you would specify your IDL file as an argument to a command-line tool. The tool parses your IDL, checking it for grammatical correctness, and updates the interface repository while making sure that your IDL is consistent with existing definitions.

Making an Initial Connection

The interface repository is usually a standalone server that is accessed remotely by CORBA applications. There are two basic methods for getting an initial reference to the interface repository:

- Use the initialization service.
  Call `CORBA::ORB::resolve_initial_references()`, passing in the `"InterfaceRepository"` string. The object reference returned by `resolve_initial_references()` should be narrowed to the `CORBA::Repository_ptr` type (C++) or the `org.omg.CORBA.Repository` type (Java).
  This approach is illustrated in Listing 20.4 and Listing 20.5, later in this chapter.
- Use the `CORBA::Object::get_interface()` pseudo-operation.
  Given an object reference, the `get_interface()` pseudo-operation lets you find the object's `CORBA::InterfaceDef` using just a single invocation. The `get_interface()` operation maps to C++ and Java as follows:

  ```
  //C++
  CORBA::InterfaceDef_ptr CORBA::Object::_get_interface();

  //Java
  org.omg.CORBA.Object org.omg.CORBA.Object._get_interface_def();
  //The return value is actually of type 'org.omg.CORBA.InterfaceDef'
  ```

  Once a reference to a `CORBA::InterfaceDef` object has been obtained, a complete description of the object's interface can be retrieved from the interface repository.

Searching the Parse Tree

Most of the interface repository's search capability is provided by the `CORBA::Container` base interface. It defines two search operations, as shown in Listing 20.1.

Listing 20.1 Search Operations in `CORBA::Container`

```
#pragma prefix "omg.org"
module CORBA {
    typedef string Identifier;
    typedef string ScopedName;
    typedef string RepositoryId;
    //...
    enum DefinitionKind {
        dk_none, dk_all,
        dk_Attribute, dk_Constant, dk_Exception, dk_Interface,
        dk_Module, dk_Operation, dk_Typedef,
        dk_Alias, dk_Struct, dk_Union, dk_Enum,
        dk_Primitive, dk_String, dk_Sequence, dk_Array,
        dk_Repository,
        dk_Wstring, dk_Fixed,
        dk_Value, dk_ValueBox, dk_ValueMember,
        dk_Native
    };
    //...
    interface Container : IRObject {
        Contained lookup (in ScopedName search_name);

        ContainedSeq lookup_name (
            in Identifier search_name,
            in long levels_to_search,
            in DefinitionKind limit_type,
            in boolean exclude_inherited
        );
        //...
    };
};
```

The search operations work as follows:

- `CORBA::Container::lookup()`
  The `search_name` argument is the scoped name of the node you are trying to locate, relative to the container you are invoking on.
  Consider, for example, the `RecycleBroker` module of Chapter 3, "A Sample CORBA System." If you invoke `lookup()` on the `ModuleDef` that represents the `RecycleBroker` module, you can specify a `search_name` of `"Customer::get_details"` to get a reference to the `OperationDef` object for `get_details()`. Alternatively, you could specify the absolute scoped name `"::RecycleBroker::Customer::get_details"` instead.
- `CORBA::Container::lookup_name()`
  The `search_name` argument is the local (non-scoped) name of the node you are trying to locate. For example, it might be the operation name, `"get_details"`. The `levels_to_search` argument specifies how many levels of containment are descended in the course of the search. A value of `1` searches only the current object. A value of `-1` searches all levels of containment without limit.

The `limit_type` argument is used to restrict the search to certain kinds of node. Each kind of node is identified by a `CORBA::DefinitionKind` enumerated constant. For example, to restrict the search to `OperationDef` nodes, you can pass `CORBA::dk_Operation` (C++) or `org.omg.CORBA.DefinitionKind.dk_Operation` (Java). To make an unlimited search, you can pass `CORBA::dk_all`. The `exclude_inherited` flag applies only to `InterfaceDef` and `ValueDef` nodes (otherwise it is ignored). It specifies whether inherited definitions should also be searched.

There is one additional search operation provided by the `CORBA::Repository` interface, as shown in Listing 20.2.

Listing 20.2 Search Operation in `CORBA::Repository`

```
#pragma prefix "omg.org"
module CORBA {
    interface Repository : Container {
        Contained lookup_id (in RepositoryId search_id);
        //...
    };
};
```

The `lookup_id()` search operation works as follows:

- `CORBA::Repository::lookup_id()`
  The `search_id` argument is a standard repository ID. If you consider, for example, the `RecycleBroker` module from Chapter 3, the `RecycleBroker::WasteItemAdmin` interface can be found by passing the string `"IDL:RecycleBroker/WasteItemAdmin:1.0"` to `lookup_id()`.

Iterating Over the Parse Tree

Occasionally you might need to iterate over a part of the interface repository. For example, there might be some actions that you want to perform for every interface in a certain module or for every operation and attribute in a certain module. For these sorts of action, you need to be able to iterate over the complete contents of a container. Listing 20.3 shows the `Container` operations that provide this functionality.

Listing 20.3 Content Operations in `CORBA::Container`

```
#pragma prefix "omg.org"

module CORBA {
    //...
    interface Container : IRObject {
        ContainedSeq contents (
            in DefinitionKind limit_type,
            in boolean exclude_inherited
        );
```

```
        struct Description {
            Contained contained_object;
            DefinitionKind kind;
            any value;
        };
        typedef sequence<Description> DescriptionSeq;

        DescriptionSeq describe_contents (
            in DefinitionKind limit_type,
            in boolean exclude_inherited,
            in long max_returned_objs
        );
        //...
    };
};
```

Two operations are provided in the `CORBA::Container` interface to allow you to iterate over a container's contents:

- `CORBA::Container::contents()`
  The `limit_type` argument is used to restrict the list of contents to certain kinds of node. Each kind of node is identified by a `CORBA::DefinitionKind` enumerated constant, as explained in the previous section, "Searching the Parse Tree." The `CORBA::dk_all` value can be used to search without restrictions.
  The `exclude_inherited` flag applies only to `InterfaceDef` and `ValueDef` nodes (otherwise it is ignored). It specifies whether inherited definitions should also be listed.
  The return value is a sequence of `Contained` nodes that are either directly contained or inherited by this object.
- `CORBA::Container::describe_contents()`
  `describe_contents()` is provided as an optimization over the simpler `contents()` operation. It lists the contents and retrieves description structs in a single step.
  The `limit_type` and `exclude_inherited` arguments have exactly the same effect as for the `contents()` operation.
  The `max_returned_objects` argument allows you to set an upper limit to the length of the returned `DescriptionSeq` sequence. A value of `-1` allows the length to be unlimited.
  The return value is a sequence of `Description` structs that contain full details of each node that has been found. Consider, for example, a case where the returned contents are all `OperationDef` nodes. For each `Description` struct in the sequence, `Container::Description::kind` is equal to `CORBA::dk_Operation`. `Container::Description::contained_object` is a reference to an `OperationDef` object. The `Container::Description::value` is an any that contains a `CORBA::OperationDescription` struct.

An Example of Reading from the Interface Repository

This example is based on the `RecycleBroker` IDL as described in Chapter 3. It is assumed that the interface repository is already populated with the `RecycleBroker` IDL before this example is run.

The code in Listing 20.4 and Listing 20.5 shows the `CORBA::Container::lookup()` operation being used in two ways:

1. In the first part of the example, `lookup()` is used to find the `"RecycleBroker::WasteItemAdmin"` interface. This identifier is specified relative to the `Repository` scope because it is invoked on a `CORBA::Repository` object.
   The code prints out all of the operation names belonging to the `WasteItemAdmin` interface.
2. In the second part of the example, `lookup()` is used to find the `"::RecycleBroker"` module.
   All of the interfaces in the `RecycleBroker` module are enumerated using `CORBA::Container::contents()`, and the names of their operations and attributes are printed.

Listing 20.4 C++ Printing the Names of Operations and Attributes

```
//C++

#include <iostream.h>
#include <fstream.h>
#include <stdlib.h>

#include "RecycleBrokerAll.hh"


// main() -- the main client program.
//
int
main(int argc, char **argv)
{
    try
    {
        // Initialise the ORB.
        // Note: ORB_init will process any -ORB arguments
        // and remove them from argc/argv, so it should
        // be called before any other argument processing.
        //
        CORBA::ORB_var orbV = CORBA::ORB_init(argc, argv);

        CORBA::Object_var objV;
```

Listing 20.4 continued

```
// Get a reference to a 'Repository' object
objV = orbV->resolve_initial_references("InterfaceRepository");
CORBA::Repository_var intf_repV
    = CORBA::Repository::_narrow(objV.in());
if (CORBA::is_nil(intf_repV.in()) ) {
    cerr << "error: narrow to 'CORBA::Repository' failed." << endl;
    exit(1);
}

//------------------------------------------------------------
// List the Operation Names of a Specific Interface
//------------------------------------------------------------

// Find the 'RecycleBroker::WasteItemAdmin' interface
CORBA::Contained_var contV
    = intf_repV->lookup("RecycleBroker::WasteItemAdmin");

CORBA::InterfaceDef_var intf_defV
    = CORBA::InterfaceDef::_narrow(contV.in());
if (CORBA::is_nil(intf_defV.in() ))
{
    cerr << "error: narrow to 'CORBA::InterfaceDef' failed." << endl;
    exit(1);
}

CORBA::InterfaceDef::FullInterfaceDescription_var full_descV
    = intf_defV->describe_interface();

// List the names of all the operations.
for (CORBA::ULong l=0; l < full_descV->operations.length(); l++)
{
    cout << "operation: \"" << full_descV->operations[l].name
         << "\"" << endl;
}

//------------------------------------------------------------
// Operations and Attributes of all Interfaces in 'RecycleBroker'
//------------------------------------------------------------

// Get a list of all interfaces in the 'RecycleBroker' module
contV = intf_repV->lookup("::RecycleBroker");
CORBA::ModuleDef_var module_defV
    = CORBA::ModuleDef::_narrow(contV.in());
if (CORBA::is_nil(module_defV.in() ))
{
```

Listing 20.4 continued

```
            cerr << "error: narrow to 'CORBA::ModuleDef' failed." << endl;
            exit(1);
        }

        CORBA::ContainedSeq_var cont_seqV
            = module_defV->contents(
                  CORBA::dk_Interface,  // DefinitionKind
                  0                     // exclude_inherited (ignored)
              );
        for (CORBA::ULong n=0; n < cont_seqV->length(); n++)
        {
            intf_defV = CORBA::InterfaceDef::_narrow(cont_seqV[n]);
            if (CORBA::is_nil(intf_defV.in() ))
            {
                cerr << "error: narrow to 'CORBA::InterfaceDef' failed."
                     << endl;
                exit(1);
            }

            full_descV = intf_defV->describe_interface();
            cout << endl
                 << "interface: \"" << full_descV->name << "\"" << endl;

            // List the names of all the operations and attributes.
            CORBA::ULong m;
            for (m=0; m < full_descV->operations.length(); m++)
            {
                cout << "operation: \"" << full_descV->operations[m].name
                     << "\"" << endl;
            }
            for (m=0; m < full_descV->attributes.length(); m++)
            {
                cout << "attribute: \"" << full_descV->attributes[m].name
                     << "\"" << endl;
            }
        }

        // No exceptions, return gracefully.
        //
        return 0;
    }
    catch(CORBA::Exception &ex)
    {
        cerr << "Unexpected CORBA exception: " << ex << endl;
    }
```

Listing 20.4 continued

```
    // We had an exception, return a non-0 exit status.
    return 1;
}
```

Listing 20.5 Java Printing the Names of Operations and Attributes

```
//Java
package Pure.IFRDemo;

import java.io.*;
import org.omg.CORBA.*;

public class javaclient
{

  public static void main (String args[])
  {
    System.out.println("Initializing ORB");
    ORB orb = ORB.init(args, null);

    org.omg.CORBA.Object obj = null;

    try {
        // Get a reference to a 'Repository' object
        obj = orb.resolve_initial_references("InterfaceRepository");
        Repository intf_rep = RepositoryHelper.narrow(obj);

        //-------------------------------------------------------
        // List the Operation Names of a Specific Interface
        //-------------------------------------------------------
        System.out.println("About to lookup 'WasteItemAdmin' interface");
        // Find the 'RecycleBroker::WasteItemAdmin' interface
        Contained cont = intf_rep.lookup("RecycleBroker::WasteItemAdmin");

        InterfaceDef intf_def = InterfaceDefHelper.narrow(cont);

        System.out.println("About to call 'describe_interface'");
        org.omg.CORBA.InterfaceDefPackage.FullInterfaceDescription full_desc
            = intf_def.describe_interface();

        // List the names of all the operations.
        for (int l=0; l < full_desc.operations.length; l++)
        {
            System.out.println("operation: \""
                 + full_desc.operations[l].name + "\"");
        }
```

Listing 20.4 continued

```
        //-------------------------------------------------------------
        // Operations and Attributes of all Interfaces in 'RecycleBroker'
        //-------------------------------------------------------------
        // Get a list of all interfaces in the 'RecycleBroker' module
        cont = intf_rep.lookup("::RecycleBroker");
        ModuleDef module_def = ModuleDefHelper.narrow(cont);

        Contained[] cont_seq
            = module_def.contents(
                DefinitionKind.dk_Interface,  // DefinitionKind
                false                         // exclude_inherited (ignored)
              );
        for (int n=0; n < cont_seq.length; n++)
        {
            intf_def = InterfaceDefHelper.narrow(cont_seq[n]);

            full_desc = intf_def.describe_interface();
            System.out.println("\ninterface: \"" + full_desc.name + "\"");

            // List the names of all the operations and attributes.
            int m;
            for (m=0; m < full_desc.operations.length; m++)
            {
                System.out.println("operation: \""
                    + full_desc.operations[m].name + "\"");
            }
            for (m=0; m < full_desc.attributes.length; m++)
            {
                System.out.println("attribute: \""
                    + full_desc.attributes[m].name + "\"");
            }
        }
    }
    catch (org.omg.CORBA.SystemException sysEx) {
        System.out.println("SystemException: " + sysEx);
    }
    catch (Exception ex) {
        System.out.println("Exception: " + ex);
    }

    System.out.println("Done");
    orb.shutdown (true);
  }
}
```

An interesting feature of this example is that it uses `CORBA::InterfaceDef::describe_interface()` to get hold of a `FullInterfaceDescription` struct. The `FullInterfaceDescription` struct is provided in addition to the plain `InterfaceDescription` struct as a convenient optimization. The `FullInterfaceDescription` struct provides not only information about the interface but also complete details of its operations and attributes. These details are retrieved at once using a single remote invocation of `describe_interface()`.

IDL for the Interface Repository

Listing 20.6 shows the complete IDL for the interface repository.

Listing 20.6 Complete IDL for the Interface Repository

```
//IDL
#pragma prefix "omg.org"
module CORBA {
    typedef string Identifier;
    typedef string ScopedName;
    typedef string RepositoryId;

    enum DefinitionKind {
# pragma version DefinitionKind 2.3
        dk_none, dk_all,
        dk_Attribute, dk_Constant, dk_Exception, dk_Interface,
        dk_Module, dk_Operation, dk_Typedef,
        dk_Alias, dk_Struct, dk_Union, dk_Enum,
        dk_Primitive, dk_String, dk_Sequence, dk_Array,
        dk_Repository,
        dk_Wstring, dk_Fixed,
        dk_Value, dk_ValueBox, dk_ValueMember,
        dk_Native
    };

    interface IRObject {
# pragma version IRObject 2.3
        // read interface
        readonly attribute DefinitionKind def_kind;
        // write interface
        void destroy ();
    };

    typedef string VersionSpec;

    interface Contained;
    interface Repository;
    interface Container;

    interface Contained : IRObject {
# pragma version Contained 2.3
```

Listing 20.6 continued

```
        // read/write interface
        attribute RepositoryId id;
        attribute Identifier name;
        attribute VersionSpec version;
        // read interface
        readonly attribute Container defined_in;
        readonly attribute ScopedName absolute_name;
        readonly attribute Repository containing_repository;
        struct Description {
            DefinitionKind kind;
            any value;
        };
        Description describe ();
        // write interface
        void move (
            in Container new_container,
            in Identifier new_name,
            in VersionSpec new_version
        );
    };

    interface ModuleDef;
    interface ConstantDef;
    interface IDLType;
    interface StructDef;
    interface UnionDef;
    interface EnumDef;
    interface AliasDef;
    interface ExceptionDef;
    interface NativeDef;

    interface InterfaceDef;
    typedef sequence <InterfaceDef> InterfaceDefSeq;

    interface ValueDef;
    typedef sequence <ValueDef> ValueDefSeq;

    interface ValueBoxDef;

    typedef sequence <Contained> ContainedSeq;
    struct StructMember {
        Identifier name;
        TypeCode type;
        IDLType type_def;
    };
    typedef sequence <StructMember> StructMemberSeq;
```

Listing 20.6 continued

```
    struct Initializer {
# pragma version Initializer 2.3
        StructMemberSeq members;
        Identifier name;
    };
    typedef sequence <Initializer> InitializerSeq;

    struct UnionMember {
        Identifier name;
        any label;
        TypeCode type;
        IDLType type_def;
    };
    typedef sequence <UnionMember> UnionMemberSeq;

    typedef sequence <Identifier> EnumMemberSeq;

    interface Container : IRObject {
# pragma version Container 2.3
        // read interface
        Contained lookup (in ScopedName search_name);
        ContainedSeq contents (
            in DefinitionKind limit_type,
            in boolean exclude_inherited
        );
        ContainedSeq lookup_name (
            in Identifier search_name,
            in long levels_to_search,
            in DefinitionKind limit_type,
            in boolean exclude_inherited
        );

        struct Description {
            Contained contained_object;
            DefinitionKind kind;
            any value;
        };
        typedef sequence<Description> DescriptionSeq;

        DescriptionSeq describe_contents (
            in DefinitionKind limit_type,
            in boolean exclude_inherited,
            in long max_returned_objs
        );
        // write interface
        ModuleDef create_module (
            in RepositoryId id,
            in Identifier name,
```

Listing 20.6 continued

```
            in VersionSpec version
        );
        ConstantDef create_constant (
            in RepositoryId id,
            in Identifier name,
            in VersionSpec version,
            in IDLType type,
            in any value
        );
        StructDef create_struct (
            in RepositoryId id,
            in Identifier name,
            in VersionSpec version,
            in StructMemberSeq members
        );
        UnionDef create_union (
            in RepositoryId id,
            in Identifier name,
            in VersionSpec version,
            in IDLType discriminator_type,
            in UnionMemberSeq members
        );
        EnumDef create_enum (
            in RepositoryId id,
            in Identifier name,
            in VersionSpec version,
            in EnumMemberSeq members
        );
        AliasDef create_alias (
            in RepositoryId id,
            in Identifier name,
            in VersionSpec version,
            in IDLType original_type
        );
        InterfaceDef create_interface (
            in RepositoryId id,
            in Identifier name,
            in VersionSpec version,
            in InterfaceDefSeq base_interfaces,
            in boolean is_abstract
        );
        ValueDef create_value(
            in RepositoryId id,
            in Identifier name,
            in VersionSpec version,
            in boolean is_custom,
            in boolean is_abstract,
            in ValueDef base_value,
```

Listing 20.6 continued

```
            in boolean is_truncatable,
            in ValueDefSeq abstract_base_values,
            in InterfaceDefSeq supported_interfaces,
            in InitializerSeq initializers
        );
        ValueBoxDef create_value_box(
            in RepositoryId id,
            in Identifier name,
            in VersionSpec version,
            in IDLType original_type_def
        );
        ExceptionDef create_exception(
            in RepositoryId id,
            in Identifier name,
            in VersionSpec version,
            in StructMemberSeq members
        );
        NativeDef create_native(
            in RepositoryId id,
            in Identifier name,
            in VersionSpec version,
        );
    };

    interface IDLType : IRObject {
# pragma version IDLType 2.3
        readonly attribute TypeCode type;
    };

    interface PrimitiveDef;
    interface StringDef;
    interface SequenceDef;
    interface ArrayDef;
    interface WstringDef;
    interface FixedDef;

    enum PrimitiveKind {
# pragma version PrimitiveKind 2.3
        pk_null, pk_void, pk_short, pk_long, pk_ushort, pk_ulong,
        pk_float, pk_double, pk_boolean, pk_char, pk_octet,
        pk_any, pk_TypeCode, pk_Principal, pk_string, pk_objref,
        pk_longlong, pk_ulonglong, pk_longdouble,
        pk_wchar, pk_wstring, pk_value_base
    };

    interface Repository : Container {
# pragma version Repository 2.3
        // read interface
```

Listing 20.6 continued

```
        Contained lookup_id (in RepositoryId search_id);
        TypeCode get_canonical_typecode(in TypeCode tc);
        PrimitiveDef get_primitive (in PrimitiveKind kind);
        // write interface
        StringDef create_string (in unsigned long bound);
        WstringDef create_wstring (in unsigned long bound);
        SequenceDef create_sequence (
            in unsigned long bound,
            in IDLType element_type
        );
        ArrayDef create_array (
            in unsigned long length,
            in IDLType element_type
        );
        FixedDef create_fixed (
            in unsigned short digits,
            in short scale
        );
    };

    interface ModuleDef : Container, Contained {
# pragma version ModuleDef 2.3
    };

    struct ModuleDescription {
        Identifier name;
        RepositoryId id;
        RepositoryId defined_in;
        VersionSpec version;
    };

    interface ConstantDef : Contained {
# pragma version ConstantDef 2.3
        readonly attribute TypeCode type;
        attribute IDLType type_def;
        attribute any value;
    };

    struct ConstantDescription {
        Identifier name;
        RepositoryId id;
        RepositoryId defined_in;
        VersionSpec version;
        TypeCode type;
        any value;
    };
```

Listing 20.6 continued

```
    interface TypedefDef : Contained, IDLType {
# pragma version TypedefDef 2.3
    };

    struct TypeDescription {
        Identifier name;
        RepositoryId id;
        RepositoryId defined_in;
        VersionSpec version;
        TypeCode type;
    };

    interface StructDef : TypedefDef, Container {
# pragma version StructDef 2.3
        attribute StructMemberSeq members;
    };

    interface UnionDef : TypedefDef, Container {
# pragma version UnionDef 2.3
        readonly attribute TypeCode discriminator_type;
        attribute IDLType discriminator_type_def;
        attribute UnionMemberSeq members;
    };

    interface EnumDef : TypedefDef {
# pragma version EnumDef 2.3
        attribute EnumMemberSeq members;
    };

    interface AliasDef : TypedefDef {
# pragma version AliasDef 2.3
        attribute IDLType original_type_def;
    };

    interface NativeDef : TypedefDef {
# pragma version NativeDef 2.3
    };

    interface PrimitiveDef: IDLType {
# pragma version PrimitiveDef 2.3
        readonly attribute PrimitiveKind kind;
    };

    interface StringDef : IDLType {
# pragma version StringDef 2.3
        attribute unsigned long bound;
    };
```

Listing 20.6 continued

```
    interface WstringDef : IDLType {
# pragma version WstringDef 2.3
        attribute unsigned long bound;
    };

    interface FixedDef : IDLType {
# pragma version FixedDef 2.3
        attribute unsigned short digits;
        attribute short scale;
    };

    interface SequenceDef : IDLType {
# pragma version SequenceDef 2.3
        attribute unsigned long bound;
        readonly attribute TypeCode element_type;
        attribute IDLType element_type_def;
    };

    interface ArrayDef : IDLType {
# pragma version ArrayDef 2.3
        attribute unsigned long length;
        readonly attribute TypeCode element_type;
        attribute IDLType element_type_def;
    };

    interface ExceptionDef : Contained, Container {
# pragma version ExceptionDef 2.3
        readonly attribute TypeCode type;
        attribute StructMemberSeq members;
    };

    struct ExceptionDescription {
        Identifier name;
        RepositoryId id;
        RepositoryId defined_in;
        VersionSpec version;
        TypeCode type;
    };

    enum AttributeMode {ATTR_NORMAL, ATTR_READONLY};

    interface AttributeDef : Contained {
# pragma version AttributeDef 2.3
        readonly attribute TypeCode type;
        attribute IDLType type_def;
        attribute AttributeMode mode;
    };
```

Listing 20.6 continued

```
    struct AttributeDescription {
        Identifier name;
        RepositoryId id;
        RepositoryId defined_in;
        VersionSpec version;
        TypeCode type;
        AttributeMode mode;
    };

    enum OperationMode {OP_NORMAL, OP_ONEWAY};
    enum ParameterMode {PARAM_IN, PARAM_OUT, PARAM_INOUT};

    struct ParameterDescription {
        Identifier name;
        TypeCode type;
        IDLType type_def;
        ParameterMode mode;
    };

    typedef sequence <ParameterDescription> ParDescriptionSeq;
    typedef Identifier ContextIdentifier;
    typedef sequence <ContextIdentifier> ContextIdSeq;
    typedef sequence <ExceptionDef> ExceptionDefSeq;
    typedef sequence <ExceptionDescription> ExcDescriptionSeq;
    interface OperationDef : Contained {
# pragma version OperationDef 2.3
        readonly attribute TypeCode result;
        attribute IDLType result_def;
        attribute ParDescriptionSeq params;
        attribute OperationMode mode;
        attribute ContextIdSeq contexts;
        attribute ExceptionDefSeq exceptions;
    };

    struct OperationDescription {
        Identifier name;
        RepositoryId id;
        RepositoryId defined_in;
        VersionSpec version;
        TypeCode result;
        OperationMode mode;
        ContextIdSeq contexts;
        ParDescriptionSeq parameters;
        ExcDescriptionSeq exceptions;
    };

    typedef sequence <RepositoryId> RepositoryIdSeq;
    typedef sequence <OperationDescription> OpDescriptionSeq;
    typedef sequence <AttributeDescription> AttrDescriptionSeq;
```

Listing 20.6 continued

```
    interface InterfaceDef : Container, Contained, IDLType {
# pragma version InterfaceDef 2.3
        // read/write interface
        attribute InterfaceDefSeq base_interfaces;
        attribute boolean is_abstract;
        // read interface
        boolean is_a (
            in RepositoryId interface_id
        );
        struct FullInterfaceDescription {
# pragma version FullInterfaceDescription 2.3
            Identifier name;
            RepositoryId id;
            RepositoryId defined_in;
            VersionSpec version;
            OpDescriptionSeq operations;
            AttrDescriptionSeq attributes;
            RepositoryIdSeq base_interfaces;
            TypeCode type;
            boolean is_abstract;
        };
        FullInterfaceDescription describe_interface();
        // write interface
        AttributeDef create_attribute (
            in RepositoryId id,
            in Identifier name,
            in VersionSpec version,
            in IDLType type,
            in AttributeMode mode
        );
        OperationDef create_operation (
            in RepositoryId id,
            in Identifier name,
            in VersionSpec version,
            in IDLType result,
            in OperationMode mode,
            in ParDescriptionSeq params,
            in ExceptionDefSeq exceptions,
            in ContextIdSeq contexts
        );
    };

    struct InterfaceDescription {
# pragma version InterfaceDescription 2.3
        Identifier name;
        RepositoryId id;
        RepositoryId defined_in;
        VersionSpec version;
```

Listing 20.6 continued

```
        RepositoryIdSeq base_interfaces;
        boolean is_abstract;
    };

    typedef short Visibility;
    const Visibility PRIVATE_MEMBER = 0;
    const Visibility PUBLIC_MEMBER = 1;

    struct ValueMember {
# pragma version ValueMember 2.3
        Identifier name;
        RepositoryId id;
        RepositoryId defined_in;
        VersionSpec version;
        TypeCode type;
        IDLType type_def;
        Visibility access;
    };
    typedef sequence <ValueMember> ValueMemberSeq;

    interface ValueMemberDef : Contained {
# pragma version ValueMemberDef 2.3
        readonly attribute TypeCode type;
        attribute IDLType type_def;
        attribute Visibility access;
    };

    interface ValueDef : Container, Contained, IDLType {
# pragma version ValueDef 2.3
        // read/write interface
        attribute InterfaceDefSeq supported_interfaces;
        attribute InitializerSeq initializers;
        attribute ValueDef base_value;
        attribute ValueDefSeq abstract_base_values;
        attribute boolean is_abstract;
        attribute boolean is_custom;
        attribute boolean is_truncatable;
        // read interface
        boolean is_a(
            in RepositoryId id
        );
        struct FullValueDescription {
# pragma version FullValueDescription 2.3
            Identifier name;
            RepositoryId id;
            boolean is_abstract;
            boolean is_custom;
            RepositoryId defined_in;
```

Listing 20.6 continued

```
            VersionSpec version;
            OpDescriptionSeq operations;
            AttrDescriptionSeq attributes;
            ValueMemberSeq members;
            InitializerSeq initializers;
            RepositoryIdSeq supported_interfaces;
            RepositoryIdSeq abstract_base_values;
            boolean is_truncatable;
            RepositoryId base_value;
            TypeCode type;
        };
        FullValueDescription describe_value();
        ValueMemberDef create_value_member(
            in RepositoryId id,
            in Identifier name,
            in VersionSpec version,
            in IDLType type,
            in Visibility access
        );
        AttributeDef create_attribute(
            in RepositoryId id,
            in Identifier name,
            in VersionSpec version,
            in IDLType type,
            in AttributeMode mode
        );
        OperationDef create_operation (
            in RepositoryId id,
            in Identifier name,
            in VersionSpec version,
            in IDLType result,
            in OperationMode mode,
            in ParDescriptionSeq params,
            in ExceptionDefSeq exceptions,
            in ContextIdSeq contexts
        );
    };

    struct ValueDescription {
# pragma version ValueDescription 2.3
        Identifier name;
        RepositoryId id;
        boolean is_abstract;
        boolean is_custom;
        RepositoryId defined_in;
        VersionSpec version;
        RepositoryIdSeq supported_interfaces;
        RepositoryIdSeq abstract_base_values;
```

Listing 20.6 continued

```
        boolean is_truncatable;
        RepositoryId base_value;
    };

    interface ValueBoxDef : TypedefDef {
# pragma version ValueBoxDef 2.3
        attribute IDLType original_type_def;
    };

    enum TCKind { // PIDL
# pragma version TCKind 2.3
        tk_null, tk_void,
        tk_short, tk_long, tk_ushort, tk_ulong,
        tk_float, tk_double, tk_boolean, tk_char,
        tk_octet, tk_any, tk_TypeCode, tk_Principal, tk_objref,
        tk_struct, tk_union, tk_enum, tk_string,
        tk_sequence, tk_array, tk_alias, tk_except,
        tk_longlong, tk_ulonglong, tk_longdouble,
        tk_wchar, tk_wstring, tk_fixed,
        tk_value, tk_value_box,
        tk_native,
        tk_abstract_interface
    };

    typedef short ValueModifier; // PIDL
    const ValueModifier VM_NONE = 0;
    const ValueModifier VM_CUSTOM = 1;
    const ValueModifier VM_ABSTRACT = 2;
    const ValueModifier VM_TRUNCATABLE = 3;

    interface TypeCode { // PIDL
# pragma version TypeCode 2.3
        exception Bounds {};
        exception BadKind {};
        // for all TypeCode kinds
        boolean equal (in TypeCode tc);
        boolean equivalent(in TypeCode tc);
        TypeCode get_compact_typecode();
        TCKind kind ();
        // for tk_objref, tk_struct, tk_union, tk_enum, tk_alias,
        // tk_value, tk_value_box, tk_native, tk_abstract_interface
        // and tk_except
        RepositoryId id () raises (BadKind);
        // for tk_objref, tk_struct, tk_union, tk_enum, tk_alias,
        // tk_value, tk_value_box, tk_native, tk_abstract_interface
        // and tk_except
        Identifier name () raises (BadKind);
        // for tk_struct, tk_union, tk_enum, tk_value,
```

Listing 20.6 continued

```
        // and tk_except
        unsigned long member_count () raises (BadKind);
        Identifier member_name (in unsigned long index)
            raises (BadKind, Bounds);
        // for tk_struct, tk_union, tk_value, and tk_except
        TypeCode member_type (in unsigned long index)
            raises (BadKind, Bounds);
        // for tk_union
        any member_label (in unsigned long index)
            raises (BadKind, Bounds);
        TypeCode discriminator_type () raises (BadKind);
        long default_index () raises (BadKind);
        // for tk_string, tk_sequence, and tk_array
        unsigned long length () raises (BadKind);
        // for tk_sequence, tk_array, tk_value_box, and tk_alias
        TypeCode content_type () raises (BadKind);
        // for tk_fixed
        unsigned short fixed_digits() raises (BadKind);
        short fixed_scale() raises (BadKind);
        // for tk_value
        Visibility member_visibility(in unsigned long index)
            raises(BadKind, Bounds);
        ValueModifier type_modifier() raises(BadKind);
        TypeCode concrete_base_type() raises(BadKind);
    };

    // Only the TypeCode related part of interface ORB shown below.
    // For complete description of interface ORB see Chapter 4.

    interface ORB { // PIDL
# pragma version ORB 2.3
        // other operations ...
        TypeCode create_struct_tc (
            in RepositoryId id,
            in Identifier name,
            in StructMemberSeq members
        );
        TypeCode create_union_tc (
            in RepositoryId id,
            in Identifier name,
            in TypeCode discriminator_type,
            in UnionMemberSeq members
        );
        TypeCode create_enum_tc (
            in RepositoryId id,
            in Identifier name,
            in EnumMemberSeq members
        );
```

Listing 20.6 continued

```
        TypeCode create_alias_tc (
            in RepositoryId id,
            in Identifier name,
            in TypeCode original_type
        );
        TypeCode create_exception_tc (
            in RepositoryId id,
            in Identifier name,
            in StructMemberSeq members
        );
        TypeCode create_interface_tc (
            in RepositoryId id,
            in Identifier name
        );
        TypeCode create_string_tc (
            in unsigned long bound
        );
        TypeCode create_wstring_tc (
            in unsigned long bound
        );
        TypeCode create_fixed_tc (
            in unsigned short digits,
            in unsigned short scale
        );
        TypeCode create_sequence_tc (
            in unsigned long bound,
            in TypeCode element_type
        );
        TypeCode create_recursive_sequence_tc (// deprecated
            in unsigned long bound,
            in unsigned long offset
        );
        TypeCode create_array_tc (
            in unsigned long length,
            in TypeCode element_type
        );
        TypeCode create_value_tc (
            in RepositoryId id,
            in Identifier name,
            in ValueModifier type_modifier,
            in TypeCode concrete_base,
            in ValueMemberSeq members
        );
        TypeCode create_value_box_tc (
            in RepositoryId id,
            in Identifier name,
            in TypeCode boxed_type
        );
```

Listing 20.6 continued

```
        TypeCode create_native_tc (
            in RepositoryId id,
            in Identifier name
        );
        TypeCode create_recursive_tc(
            in RepositoryId id
        );
        TypeCode create_abstract_interface_tc(
            in RepositoryId id,
            in Identifier name
        );
    };
};
```

CHAPTER 21

CORBA System Exceptions

CORBA provides a set of exceptions that can be raised in the course of any operation invocation without having to be declared in IDL. These are called *system exceptions.*

The standard system exceptions are defined by a set of categories that should be understood by any CORBA-compliant ORB.

System exceptions are transmitted across the network in a format defined by the General Inter-ORB Protocol (GIOP—see Chapter 14, "Internet Inter-ORB Protocol"). The content of a system exception is defined by the struct shown in Listing 21.1.

Listing 21.1 GIOP Format of a System Exception

```
//IDL
// Valid for GIOP versions 1.0, 1.1 and 1.2
struct SystemExceptionReplyBody {
    string   exception_id;
    unsigned long minor_code_value;
    unsigned long completion_status;
};
```

The `exception_id` string identifies the major category of exception. The name of the major category is thus transmitted over the network in the form of a string, for example `OBJECT_NOT_EXIST` or `BAD_OPERATION`.

`minor_code_value` is used to identify the exception more exactly. It is subdivided into the high-order 20 bits, the *Vendor Minor Codeset ID* (VMCID), and the low-order 12 bits, the minor code. Every vendor is allowed to define its own set of minor codes to use in conjunction with its own, unique VMCID. VMCIDs are assigned by the OMG. The OMG itself has a VMCID assigned to it, called the OMGVMCID (equal to `0x4f4d0000`), that is used to define standard minor codes.

`completion_status` indicates whether or not the operation finished before the exception was raised. The possible values for `completion_status` shown in Table 21.1.

Table 21.1 Possible Values of **`completion_status`**

Value	Description
`COMPLETED_YES`	The operation definitely finished before the exception was raised.
`COMPLETED_NO`	Processing of the operation had not begun when the exception was raised.
`COMPLETED_MAYBE`	It is impossible to determine whether the operation finished or not.

Listing 21.2 shows how the standard system exceptions are represented in pseudo-IDL.

Listing 21.2 Standard System Exceptions IDL

```
//IDL
module CORBA {
    const unsigned long OMGVMCID = \x4f4d0000;

#define ex_body {unsigned long minor; completion_status completed;}
    enum completion_status { COMPLETED_YES,
                             COMPLETED_NO,
                             COMPLETED_MAYBE};

    enum exception_type { NO_EXCEPTION,
                          USER_EXCEPTION,
                          SYSTEM_EXCEPTION};

    exception UNKNOWN ex_body;        // the unknown exception
    exception BAD_PARAM ex_body;      // an invalid parameter was
                                      // passed
    exception NO_MEMORY ex_body;      // dynamic memory allocation
                                      // failure
    exception IMP_LIMIT ex_body;      // violated implementation
                                      // limit
    exception COMM_FAILURE ex_body;   // communication failure
    exception INV_OBJREF ex_body;     // invalid object reference
    exception NO_PERMISSION ex_body;  // no permission for
                                      // attempted op.
    exception INTERNAL ex_body;       // ORB internal error
    exception MARSHAL ex_body;        // error marshaling
                                      // param/result
```

Listing 21.2 continued

```
    exception INITIALIZE ex_body;     // ORB initialization failure
    exception NO_IMPLEMENT ex_body;   // operation implementation
                                      // unavailable
    exception BAD_TYPECODE ex_body;   // bad typecode
    exception BAD_OPERATION ex_body;  // invalid operation
    exception NO_RESOURCES ex_body;   // insufficient resources
                                      // for req.
    exception NO_RESPONSE ex_body;    // response to req. not yet
                                      // available
    exception PERSIST_STORE ex_body;  // persistent storage failure
    exception BAD_INV_ORDER ex_body;  // routine invocations
                                      // out of order
    exception TRANSIENT ex_body;      // transient failure - reissue
                                      // request
    exception FREE_MEM ex_body;       // cannot free memory
    exception INV_IDENT ex_body;      // invalid identifier syntax
    exception INV_FLAG ex_body;       // invalid flag was specified
    exception INTF_REPOS ex_body;     // error accessing interface
                                      // repository
    exception BAD_CONTEXT ex_body;    // error processing context
                                      // object
    exception OBJ_ADAPTER ex_body;    // failure detected by object
                                      // adapter
    exception DATA_CONVERSION  ex_body;  // data conversion error
    exception OBJECT_NOT_EXIST ex_body;  // non-existent object,
                                         // delete reference
    exception TRANSACTION_REQUIRED
                                 ex_body; // transaction required
    exception TRANSACTION_ROLLEDBACK
                                 ex_body; // transaction rolled
                                          // back
    exception INVALID_TRANSACTION
                                 ex_body; // invalid transaction
    exception INV_POLICY         ex_body; // invalid policy
    exception CODESET_INCOMPATIBLE
                                 ex_body; // incompatible code set
};
```

The major exception categories in Listing 21.2 are explained in the rest of this chapter.

`BAD_CONTEXT`	When a client invokes an operation whose declaration includes a context clause, `BAD_CONTEXT` might be raised if the invocation does not include context values required by the operation.
`BAD_INV_ORDER`	This exception might be raised if a client invokes the operations of an object, or pseudo-object, in the wrong order.

`BAD_OPERATION`	This exception is raised if a client attempts to invoke an operation that is not part of the target object's interface. This exception can occur only if the target object does exist.
`BAD_PARAM`	This exception is raised under the following circumstances: • If a parameter is of the wrong type, which can happen when using the dynamic invocation interface (DII). • If a parameter is of the correct type but has a value that is unacceptable. For example, it might be raised if a parameter is out of range.
`BAD_TYPECODE`	This exception is raised by the `CORBA::ORB` object if it encounters a malformed type code value.
`CODESET_INCOMPATIBLE`	This exception is raised when the process of codeset negotiation fails to find compatible native codesets for strings and wide strings.
`COMM_FAILURE`	This exception is raised if a communication failure occurs after the request has been sent to the server but before a reply has been received. For example, a connection that has been established using sockets over TCP/IP might give rise to a `COMM_FAILURE` if the socket is closed before the reply is received or if an attempted socket `read()` gives an error.
`DATA_CONVERSION`	This exception is raised if an ORB cannot convert marshaled data to or from its native representation. This generally indicates a feature limitation of the ORB. For example, `DATA_CONVERSION` might be raised if an ORB is unable to convert a wide string to its native format.
`FREE_MEM`	This exception is raised if the ORB attempts unsuccessfully to free dynamic memory.
`IMP_LIMIT`	The exception is raised if an implementation limit of any sort is reached by the ORB at run time.
`INITIALIZE`	This exception is raised if an ORB encounters a problem during its initialization phase. For example, it might be raised if the ORB fails to obtain the system resources that it needs.
`INTERNAL`	This exception is raised if a failure that is not connected to either application code or external resources occurs in the ORB. For example, the `INTERNAL` exception might be raised if an ORB's internal data structures were corrupted.

`INTF_REPOS`	This exception is raised if the ORB cannot contact the interface repository or if some other problem with the interface repository is detected.
`INVALID_TRANSACTION`	When using the CORBA Object Transaction Service (OTS), a client might embed a transaction context in a request message. The `INVALID_TRANSACTION` exception is raised if the transaction context is considered to be invalid by the server that receives the request.
`INV_FLAG`	This exception can be raised in the context of the dynamic invocation interface (DII) when `CORBA::ORB::create_request()` is invoked. It can also be raised in other contexts where flags are passed in ORB operations.
`INV_IDENT`	This exception is raised in the context of dynamic features of CORBA, if a syntactically incorrect IDL identifier is used. For example, `INV_IDENT` might be raised when using the DII if a specified operation name includes illegal characters.
`INV_OBJREF`	This exception is raised if an object reference is malformed in some way. For example, `INV_OBJREF` is raised by the `ORB::string_to_object()` operation if a corrupted stringified interoperable object reference (IOR) is passed as its argument.
`INV_POLICY`	This exception is raised if a `CORBA::Policy` object of the wrong type is passed to an operation or if a set of `CORBA::Policy` objects with incompatible values is passed to an operation. For example, the `INV_POLICY` exception might be raised by the `PortableServer::POA::create_POA()` operation if an incompatible set of policy values is passed to it.
`MARSHAL`	This exception is raised if a General Inter-ORB Protocol (GIOP) request or reply message is malformed in some way.
`NO_IMPLEMENT`	This exception is raised if the invoked operation exists but no implementation is provided for it. For example, a developer might choose to throw a `CORBA::NO_IMPLEMENT` system exception in the body of an operation that has not been implemented yet.
`NO_MEMORY`	This exception is raised if the ORB runtime runs out of memory.

`NO_PERMISSION`
This exception is raised if a client has insufficient privileges for an attempted operation. It usually occurs in the context of the CORBA Security Service.

`NO_RESOURCES`
This exception is raised if the ORB encounters a resource limitation of any kind.

`NO_RESPONSE`
The dynamic invocation interface (DII) provides a mechanism for making deferred synchronous calls. The `NO_RESPONSE` exception is raised if an attempt is made to retrieve the result of an invocation before the response is available. In practice, it can be raised when either `CORBA::Request::result()` or `CORBA::Request::return_value()` is invoked prematurely (in C++) or when either `Request.result()` or `Request.return_value()` is invoked prematurely (in Java).

`OBJ_ADAPTER`
This exception is raised if any kind of error occurs that is associated primarily with an object adapter. For example, the `OBJ_ADAPTER` exception may be raised if an error occurs during the configuration or initialization of an object adapter.

`OBJECT_NOT_EXIST`
This exception is raised whenever a client attempts to make an invocation on a non-existent object. It is intended as an authoritative notice that the object never existed or has been permanently deleted.
In practice, however, it is difficult to guarantee that this exception implies non-existence. For example, a buggy implementation of a servant activator might fail to activate an object that does exist, thereby mistakenly raising an `OBJECT_NOT_EXIST` exception.

`PERSIST_STORE`
This exception can be raised if any kind of error occurs that has to do with persistent storage (database errors).

`TRANSACTION_REQUIRED`
When using the CORBA Object Transaction Service, a client can embed a transaction context in a request message. The `TRANSACTION_REQUIRED` exception is raised if the server requires a transaction context for the invocation but none was present in the request message.

`TRANSACTION_ROLLEDBACK`
When using the CORBA Object Transaction Service, the `TRANSACTION_ROLLEDBACK` exception is raised within the context of a transaction to indicate that the transaction has been rolled back or marked to roll back by the server.

`TRANSIENT`	This exception is raised if an invocation request cannot be sent to the server. For example, if the request is mediated via sockets over TCP/IP, the `TRANSIENT` exception might be raised if the socket connection cannot be opened to the remote server.
`UNKNOWN`	This exception is a catch-all for unidentified exceptions. There are three main kinds of `UNKNOWN` exception: • Exceptions that do not fit into any of the existing categories of system exception. • System exceptions received from a remote server that have an unknown `exception_id`. These exceptions are converted to the `UNKNOWN` system exception on the client side before being raised to the client application code. • User exceptions not declared in the `raises` clause of the corresponding IDL operation. The client stub does not have the necessary code to process the user exception in this case and raises the `UNKNOWN` system exception instead.

INDEX

B

C

D

E

F

G

H

J

N

O

P

Q-R

S

T

U

V

W

X-Z